WHOLE MATE
The Future of Relationships

Whole Mate: The Future of Relationships

©2025 Dr. Marc Gafni and Barbara Marx Hubbard. All Rights Reserved. No part of this publication may be reproduced, stored in a retrieval system or transmitted in any form by any means electronic, mechanical, or photocopying, recording or otherwise without the permission of the author.

For more information, please contact:
World Philosophy & Religion Press
Dandy Lion Publishing Group
4401 Friedrich Lane #302
Austin, TX 78744
contact@worldphilosophyandreligion.org

Cover art by Kohlene Hendrickson (kohlene.com)

ISBN-979-8-9928719-0-6

Printed in the United States

In conjunction with

IP Integral Publishers

Marc
Dedicated to Barbara Marx Hubbard,
evolutionary partner and beloved whole mate
from the day we met
until the day she passed.

Barbara
Dedicated to Dr. Marc Gafni,
evolutionary partner and beloved whole mate.
"I asked Marc to continue the important writing
of his and our shared work together long after I have passed.
'And the Promise Will be Kept.'"

WHOLE MATE

The Future of Relationships

Dr. Marc Gafni and
Barbara Marx Hubbard

In conjunction with

IP Integral Publishers

CONTENTS

Foreword i

Notes on Process and Authorship iii

Introduction 1

    I. Relationship Crisis and Evolution of Love 1

        Entry 1. A Revolution in Relationships 1

        Entry 2. Beyond Mars and Venus 2

        Entry 3. New Roles, New Rules 4

        Entry 4. Reenvisioning the Hero 7

        Entry 5. Unanswered Questions 8

    II. A New Operating System for a New Vision of Relationship 11

        Entry 1. The Three Levels of Relationship 12

        Entry 2. Transformation of Identity 13

        Entry 3. Evolutionary Relationship 14

        Entry 4. Reality Is Relationship 15

        Entry 5. An Invitation to Evolve Love 17

Chapter 1. The Arc of Evolution 21

    Entry 1. The Mysterious Drive for Life and Love 21

    Entry 2. Survival of the Fittest Means the Fittest for Love 22

    Entry 3. Reality Is Evolution of Relationship 24

    Entry 4. Allurement toward Relationship Is the Nature of Reality 26

    Entry 5. Trajectories of Evolution 27

    Entry 6. Intimacy and Eros 29

    Entry 7. The LoveIntelligence, LoveBeauty, and LoveDesire of Reality 31

    Entry 8. Emergencies Create Emergents 33

    Entry 9. Passionate Protozoa 34

    Entry 10. Relationship Is Transformation 36

    Entry 11. Evolution Accelerates 37

    Entry 12. Conscious Evolution 39

PART ONE. THE THREE LEVELS OF RELATIONSHIP

Chapter 2. Role Mate 45

    Entry 1. Mars and Venus: The Essence of Role Mate Relationship 45

    Entry 2. Duty, Honor, and Obligation: The First Language of Heroes 46

    Entry 3. The Gifts and Shadows of Role Mate Relationships 48

    Entry 4. Falling in Love in Role Mate Relationships 53

    Entry 5. The End of Role Mates? 54

    Entry 6. Clan of the Cave Bear 56

    Entry 7. Living at the Edge: From Role Mate to Soul Mate 57

    Entry 8. Evolution Responds to Crisis 61

    Table 1. Role Mate 63

Chapter 3. Soul Mate 65

    Entry 1. Soul Mates Look Deeply into Each Other's Eyes 65
    Entry 2. Personal Fulfillment and Loneliness 67
    Entry 3. To Be Intimate Is to Be Known 68
    Entry 4. *Love Story* 71
    Entry 5. *Four Weddings and a Funeral*—from Role Mate to Soul Mate 73
    Entry 6. The Soul Mate Mantra 76
    Entry 7. Venus and Mars: New Yearnings, New Expectations 78
    Entry 8. From Commitment to Communication 83
    Entry 9. Falling in Love as Soul Mates 86

Chapter 4. Limitations of Soul Mate 89

    Entry 1. The Limitations of *I Love You* 89
    Entry 2. Passion Dies without Polarity 93
    Entry 3. No One Can Make Someone Else Happy 95
    Entry 4. The Narcissism of Two 95
    Entry 5. The Three Stations of Love 98
    Entry 6. The Idolatry of Children 100
    Entry 7. The End of Men? 103
    Entry 8. Does Soul Mate Work Without Role Mate? 107
    Entry 9. Passion in Egalitarian Marriage: Experiment One 110
        Is Equality a Panacea for Sexuality? 110
        Who Is Having Sex Tonight? 111
        Polarity, Passion, and Power 113
        Stories from the *Zeitgeist* 115
        Key Results from Experiment One 118
    Entry 10. Middle-Class Marriage: Experiment Two 119
        Can a High-Powered Woman Love a Laid-Back Guy? 119
        Why Do I Need a Man? 121
        When Marriage Disappears 123
    Entry 11. In Search of Solutions 126
        A Prince on a White Horse? 127
        Adjustment to Reality Is Not a Solution 129
        We Need a New Language of Heroes 131
    Entry 12. Deeper Yearnings 133
    Entry 13. Beyond *Romeo and Juliet* 137

Chapter 5. From Soul Mate to Whole Mate 141

    Entry 1. The Dawning of Evolutionary Consciousness 141
    Entry 2. A Calling to Serve Love 146
    Entry 3. Relationship to the Whole 148
    Entry 4. Transforming Holes into Wholeness 149
    Entry 5. Love Is the Third Side 152
    Table 2. Role Mate and Soul Mate 156

Chapter 6. Whole Mate 159

Entry 1. The Mystery of the Cosmos Is the Mystery of Relationships 159
Entry 2. The Next Step in the Evolution of Love 161
Entry 3. Whole Mate Is an Emergent 162
Entry 4. Searching for My Evolutionary Partner 165
Entry 5. Looking at a Shared Horizon 167
Entry 6. From *Love Story* to *The Matrix*—from Soul Mate to Whole Mate 169
Entry 7. The Focus of Whole Mate Relationship Is a Larger Whole 170
Entry 8. The Relationship Crisis Begins to Disappear at Level Three 173
Entry 9. Unique Gender and Unique Polarity 174
Entry 10. Making Love: Soul Mate versus Whole Mate 177
Entry 11. Dying: Whole Mate versus Soul Mate 181
Entry 12. What Is Your Context for Relating? 187
Entry 13. Up-Leveling Your Intention 190
Entry 14. The Third Side 191
Entry 15. To Be a Whole Mate Is to Be in Service to a Larger Whole 194
Entry 16. Exercise: Shared Value Discovery in Whole Mate Relationship 197
Entry 17. Whole Mates Love the World through Loving Each Other 199
Entry 18. Value in Role Mate, Soul Mate, and Whole Mate Relationships 203
Entry 19. Eros and *Ethos*: A Deeper Look for the Advanced Reader 204
Table 3. Role Mate, Soul Mate, and Whole Mate 207

PART TWO. EVOLUTION OF SELF IN RELATIONSHIP

Chapter 7. Unique Self 211

Entry 1. Four Selves 211
    Separate Self 211
    True Self 214
    Unique Self 216
Entry 2. Two Transformations of Identity: Unique Self and Unique Gender 218
Entry 3. Finding Your One True Authentic Swing 220
    Finding the Field Exercise 225
Entry 4. Unique Self Is the New Context for Relating 225
Entry 5. You Are Your Unique Self 229
    To Find Who You Are, Find Your Yearning 229
    Uniqueness Is Your Birthright 231
    Your Unique Need Is Your Transformation 232
Entry 6. Your Unique Frequency of Light 234
Entry 7. Your Unique Self Can Never Be Taken Away 236
Entry 8. Write Your Letter in the Cosmic Scroll 240
Entry 9. You Are Not a Cosmic Accident 242
Entry 10. A Memory of the Future 244
Entry 11. Confess Your Greatness 245
Entry 12. Reality Needs Your Unique Self 247
    Holon as the Basic Unit of Reality 247
    The Whole Is in the Part 248

       The Whole Needs the Part. 249

       I Love You = I Need You. 252

       Your Whole Mate Needs Your Unique Self 254

       The Radical Joy of Being Needed. 256

  Entry 13. Revelations of Uniqueness. 258

  Entry 14. The Whole Mate Returns to the Beloved the Missing Piece of Their Story 261

  Table 4. Separate Self, True Self, and Unique Self. 268

Chapter 8. Evolutionary Impulse at the Heart of Evolutionary Relationships 273

  Entry 1: Evolutionary Unique Self 273

  Entry 2. Between Being and Becoming 275

  Entry 3. The Inner Experience of Evolutionary Unique Self—
Sexuality, Innovation, Transformation. 277

       Sex Erotic: From Procreation to Co-Creation 278

       Innovation 281

       Transformation. 282

  Entry 4. The Unrelenting Positivity of *Yes!*. 283

  Entry 5. Urge to Emerge 285

  Entry 6. Democratization of Greatness 286

  Entry 7. The Evolutionary Impulse toward More Wholeness and More Love 288

  Entry 8. Evolution Awakening to Itself in Us 291

       Conscious Evolution and Evolutionary Relationships 291

       The Self-Actualizing Cosmos Driven by You. 293

       From Unconscious to Conscious Uniqueness 295

  Entry 9. Evolutionary Context for Relating 297

  Entry 10. Unique Gifts and Unique Obligations. 299

       Answering the Call 299

       To Give Your Unique Gift Is Your Unique Obligation. 299

       Living Your *Mitzvah* 302

       For the Sake of the Whole. 306

  Entry 11. Exercise: Direct Access to the Four Selves. 309

  Entry 12. The Four Big Bangs: A Meditation on the Reality of Evolution as You . . . 311

  Entry 13. Evolutionary Unique Self and Evolutionary Relationships 318

  Table 5. The Four Selves: Separate Self, True Self, Unique Self,
and Evolutionary Unique Self 320

Chapter 9. Outrageous Love. 325

  Entry 1. Yearning for the Evolution of Love 325

  Entry 2. The Only Response to Outrageous Pain Is Outrageous Love 327

  Entry 3. Evolution of Love and Intimacy 330

       From Elementary Particles to Human Beings. 331

       From Egocentric to Ethnocentric Love 332

       From Egocentric Intimacy to Ethnocentric Intimacy: Jet Li's *Hero* 334

       From Ethnocentric to Worldcentric Love: The Red Baron Story of World War I . . . 337

       From Worldcentric to Cosmocentric Love. 340

Entry 4. Love Is the Ultimate Truth at the Heart of Creation 341
Entry 5. Ordinary Love and Outrageous Love 344
    Eros and Pseudo-Eros. 345
    Eight Distinctions Between Ordinary and Outrageous Love 346
        1. Fickle versus Steady 346
        2. Scorecards versus the Secret of the Kiss 347
        3. Codependent Grasping versus Interdependent Devotion 347
        4. Comfort versus Pleasure 348
        5. Disconnect versus Melting 348
        6. Separate Self versus True Self, Unique Self, and Evolutionary Unique Self . . 348
        7. Conventional versus Surprising 349
        8. Unconditional Love versus Outrageous Love 350
    Outrageous Love Is the Strongest Force in the Cosmos 350
    Outrageous Love Is Perception and Action 351
    All Love Is Sourced in the Great Love 353
Entry 6. Taking Responsibility for Your Own Arousal 356
    Reality Practice 356
    From Power to Passion 358
    From *I Love You* to *You Love Me* 362
    From *Do You Love Me?* to *You Love Me* 364
    Awaken as Outrageous Love 366
Entry 7. The Birth of Evolutionary Intimacy 367
Entry 8. Unique Self and Outrageous Love 370
Entry 9. Love the Moment Open 374

PART THREE. EVOLUTIONARY RELATIONSHIPS AND UNIQUE SELF SYMPHONY

Chapter 10. Evolutionary Relationships: A New Vision Emerging 379

Entry 1. Evolutionary Relationships Reloaded. 379
Entry 2: Role Mate, Soul Mate, and Whole Mate in Evolutionary Context. 380
Entry 3. Confession of Greatness 387
Entry 4. Unique We 388
Entry 5. The Unique We Plugs Whole Mates into the Larger Field 391
Entry 6. Evolutionary Relationships and Outrageous Love 393
Entry 7. Falling in Love as Arousal from Above 396
Entry 8. From Sex to Supra-Sex; from Joining Genes to Joining Genius 398
Entry 9. Eros in Evolutionary Relationships 400
    Outrageous Love and Eros 400
    Eros and Pseudo-Eros 401
    Eros and Evolution of Desire 403
Entry 10. Evolution of Dependency in Relationship 404
Entry 11. Loneliness and Happiness 407
Entry 12. Evolution of Honor, Duty, and Obligation 408
Entry 13. From Choice to Choicelessness 409

Chapter 11. The Universe: A Love Story and Unique Self Symphony 413

    Entry 1. Unique Self Is a Central Star of the Universe Story. 413
    Entry 2. Reality Is an Outrageous Love Story 415
    Entry 3. The Universe Feels, and the Universe Feels Love 417
    Entry 4. Science Whispers in Your Ear: *You Are Evolution* 419
    Entry 5. Outrageous Love Is Ceaseless Creativity and Allurement 421
    Entry 6. Outrageous Love and Outrageous Obligation 422
    Entry 7. Our Ability to Feel and Our Ability to Heal 424
    Entry 8. Unique Self and Unique We in Unique Self Symphony 426
    Entry 9. Evolutionary Unique Self in the Self-Organizing Universe. 429
    Entry 10. Evolutionary We-Space 432

Chapter 12. Evolutionary Heroes 435

    Entry 1. The New Hero of Whole Mate Relationships 435
    Entry 2. A Generation in Need of Heroes 441
        The First Shock of Existence and the Emergence of Role Mate Relationships 441
        The Second Shock of Existence and the Emergence of Whole Mate, Evolutionary
        Relationships in Response to the Meta-Crisis 443
        Outrageous Acts of Love 445
    Entry 3. Whole Mates, Outrageous Love,
    and the Emergence of the Evolutionary Hero 447

Chapter 13. Joining Genius: A Case Study. 451

    Barbara's Story 451
        We Need a Story Equal to Our Power. 453
        New Meaning of Conscious Evolution 455
        Joining Genius 463
    Marc's Story 465
        Loving Your Way to Enlightenment. 465
        Unique Self Realization 467
        The Evolution of Conscious Evolution 473
        Responding to the Second Shock of Existence 477
        Joining Genius 479
        A Word on Power. 483

EPILOGUE. There Are No Externalities in the CosmoErotic Universe 485

Supplementary Essays 491

    Essay 1. Four Core Principles of Soul Mate Relationship 491
        Principle One. Soul Mates Hold Pieces of Each Other's Stories. 492
        Principle Two. Intimate Communion Requires Contact in the Present. 500
            Radical Presence 500
            Invitations of Time 502
            Collecting Your Days 503
            There Are No Extra Moments 506
            Always the Very First Time. 507

  Love Is Only in the Now 508
  The Pain Trance 510
  Staying in the Present. 513
  Staying in the Symptoms 516
  Unfinished Business 518
  Mind Trance and Mindfulness 520
 Principle Three. Labels Obstruct Contact 522
 Principle Four. The Power of Not Knowing 526

Essay 2. Wounds in Role Mate, Soul Mate, and Whole Mate Relationships . . . 530
 Principle One. Get Over It 531
 Principle Two. Honor, Engage, and Work to Transform Wounds. 531
 Principle Three. Don't Cry More Than It Hurts 532
 Principle Four. Experience Your Wounds in an Evolutionary Unique Self Context . 534
 Principle Five. Stay Open through the Pain 536
  Obsession with Personal Hurt Activates the Ritual of Rejection. 536
  Live as Outrageous Love 539
 Principle Six. Bring Your Wounds to the Mother 542
 Principle Seven. Hurt Is a State 543
  Opening as Love to the Pain: An Outrageous Love Whole Mate Practice 544
 Principle Eight. Never Bypass Authentic Wounding 545

Essay 3. Unique Gender 548
 Entry 1. Lines, Circles, and Living the Erotic Life 549
 Entry 2. Between the Literature of Difference and the Literature of Androgyny . . . 552
 Entry 3. Why We Need Mars and Venus Today 554
 Entry 4. Does the Feminine Have Shadow?
 Between Hurt and What We Do with Our Hurt 557
 Entry 5. From Transgender to Unique Gender 561

Conclusion: Birthing a New Human, by Barbara Marx Hubbard 565
 TABLES 572
  Table A: Role Mate, Soul Mate, and Whole Mate 572
  Table B: The Four Selves: Separate Self, True Self, Unique Self,
  and Evolutionary Unique Self 574

Bibliography 579
 Books and Essays 579
 Articles 586
 Bible, Talmud, Zohar, and Quran Passages .587

About the Authors 589

Index 593

FOREWORD

by Aubrey Marcus

There comes a certain point in time where ideas no longer serve the collective culture and are in desperate need of evolution and transformation. Our understanding of relationships is in that position right now. Like tectonic plates that are stuck under tension, the inspired concepts contained within this volume, *Whole Mate: The Future of Relationships*, will assuredly change your world and quite possibly the world itself in ways that are beyond our capacity to imagine. The first step of course begins with the transformation of your own most intimate relationships.

I have experienced this firsthand in the relationship with my partnership dynamic. The elucidation of the three types of relating, role mate, soul mate, and whole mate, clarified the areas of my marriage that were no longer serving us and the world at large. It pointed the way forward to a different way of loving, not because it was simply a new cultural construct, but because it contained a deeper truth about relationships that was true all the way up and down the Cosmic Order.

I have taught the models contained within this paradigm-shifting book in my community, *Fit for Service*, and seen similarly powerful effects. By placing attention on each of the three "contexts for relating," each quality of relationship had the opportunity to reach the full wonder and fruition of its unique potential.

Before answering the heavy question, "Should I stay with my partner, or should I leave?" the first step is to analyze the relationship from these different perspectives. Only from this place can the question be effectively explored.

The strength of any community is built upon the strength of each dyad. The aphorism that a chain is only as strong as its weakest link indeed contains important truth. To solidify and immeasurably deepen the strength of each individual relationship is not only the remedy for loneliness, although it is surely that. And that alone is more than enough. But it is a solution to what Dr. Gafni calls the "***global intimacy disorder.***"

The macro is a model of the micro. How you relate to a friend or a partner participates in the same pattern through which national superpowers relate to each other in this increasingly multipolar world. **It is not hyperbole to imagine that this book might not only help your marriage, but it also might save the world.**

It has been with great delight and a voracious appetite that I have consumed the teachings of Dr. Marc Gafni and colleagues, which they call the world philosophy of CosmoErotic Humanism. Gafni holds the distinguished position in my heart as my lineage master in the original Wisdom of Solomon and later in the CosmoErotic Humanism lineage.

But Gafni is also my beloved brother and inspired evolutionary partner in changing our world. A world in desperate need of what Dr. Gafni calls a "new world religion, rooted in a universal grammar of value—telling a Story of Value—as a context for our diversity."

And there is no better Story of Value than the one proposed by the Center for World Philosophy and Religion, founded by Marc Gafni in partnership with Ken Wilber, Sally Kempton, and Zachary Stein, which is where our book publishing imprint gets its moniker.

Our first title, *First Principles and First Values*, written by Gafni together with Stein and Wilber under the pseudonymous moniker of David J. Temple, is the tip of the spear in articulating the road from "Crisis to Crossing." This work is already beginning to catalyze the emergence of a New Human and New Humanity in response to the meta-crisis of our time, which threatens our very humanity.

This book, *Whole Mate: The Future of Relationships*, and its sister volume, *The Evolution of Love from Quarks to Culture: The Rise of Evolutionary Relationships in Response to the Meta-Crisis*, place attention on a crucial aspect of that new story. Keep your eye out for new titles releasing regularly from World Philosophy & Religion Press, and check out the Aubrey Marcus Podcast for more conversations surrounding this groundbreaking work.

NOTE ON PROCESS AND AUTHORSHIP

by Dr. Marc Gafni

I was greatly delighted to be the first writer of the core distinctions in this book and its companion volume. They are sourced in my own interior process, as well as in my readings of the lineage of Solomon, coupled with decades of study in the world philosophies and religions, as well as in new ways of reading the hidden implied ontologies and phenomenologies in the classical sciences, often with my dear friend Ken Wilber's Integral Theory as the invisible scaffolding, which clarifies the framework in which all insights are offered.

My co-author in this volume, and others that will follow, is Barbara Marx Hubbard, long recognized as the preeminent philosopher and passionate advocate of the new world view of *Conscious Evolution* in the latter half of the twentieth and early twenty-first century. As Barbara was formulating this world view, I was formulating, based on a very different set of sources and internal realizations, what we came to call *CosmoErotic Humanism*. CosmoErotic Humanism is a new story of value, that myself, Zak Stein, Sally Kempton, Ken Wilber, and later Barbara, have been formulating at our think tank, the Center for World Philosophy and Religion.

A word on the Center for World Philosophy and Religion,[1] the think tank where Barbara served as board chair, is perhaps in order, as it was the precious and wondrous context for our co-creation. I co-founded the think tank with Ken, Sally, and Zak. All four of us have remained active in leadership since the inception of the think tank until now. Sally, sadly, passed in the summer of 2023. Among key board chairs and leaders across the

---

1 Formerly the Center for Integral Wisdom.

years were Lori Galperin, Kate Maloney, John P. Mackey, Shareef Malnik, Gabrielle Anwar, Adam Bellow, Carrie Kish, and Daniel Schmachtenberger. The entire board community remembers poignantly the beautiful moment when John P. Mackey completed his term and passed the board leadership to Barbara. Barbara was the board chair and a key partner in the think tank for multiple years before her passing. She was not a titular chair, but she was profoundly energized and active every single day. The board chair who took the reins after Barbara is also the visionary publisher of World Philosophy & Religion Press, the inestimable Aubrey Marcus. The Center and Barbara's own think tank, the Foundation for Conscious Evolution, are now part of a larger holding organization called the Office for the Future, chaired by Stephanie Valcke, Wouter Torfs, and Mathi Gijbels, where Barbara was deeply involved as well.

The Center is the context for the emergence of what we are calling *the Great Library of CosmoErotic Humanism in response to the meta-crisis*. The emergence of the great library was one of Barbara's great dreams. The volume you hold in your hands is one part of the fulfillment of that dream. Another online expression of CosmoErotic Humanism that Barbara and I enacted together is a program entitled "The 11th hour."[2]

CosmoErotic Humanism includes Unique Self theory, the Amorous Cosmos, the Tenets of Intimacy, and multiple other vectors, including a vision of conscious evolution somewhat different than the version of conscious evolution that Barbara had been advocating. The synergy of our views in this regard was an integral part of what we might call *our whole mate process of joining genius in evolutionary love*.

In this volume, I formulated the core set of distinctions around the whole mate level of consciousness, which resonated quite beautifully with Barbara's distinctions around what we both called *evolutionary relationships*. Indeed, the original title of the book was *Evolutionary Relationships*, a volume we intended to publish in early 2016. Barbara also loved the language of supra-sexual co-creation, and the move from *joining genes* to *joining genius*. And indeed, our life destiny was to be evolutionary whole mate beloveds, joining genius for evolutionary co-creation, for the sake

---

2 See https://vanburenpublishing.com/11th-hour/.

of the whole. This story of joining genius to co-create is told in more depth in Chapter 13, the only chapter in the book written as a duet of two individual voices.

Painful life events diverted our attention from this work while at the same time deepening the felt integrity of our whole mate vision and of the urgent need for what we would come to call a New Story of Value. In the months and weeks before Barbara's passing, we returned and reviewed this manuscript and its surrounding material with new devotion and depth.

This book would have been impossible without all people who have been involved in its development. Zachary Stein has been my key interlocutor in the broader project of CosmoErotic Humanism; we have held the context of regular Holy of Holies studies since 2009. Dr. Clint Fuhs formed the raw material into a book with his trademark depth, precision, and brilliance. The baton was passed to the wonderful couple, our dear friends Paul Bennet and Carol Herndon, who took the manuscript a second key step, and to the inestimable Kerstin Zohar, editorial director of the Great Library, who took it an equally significant third step on multiple levels (including but not limited to the depth of the footnotes), and finally all of this landed with the artist intellectual Dr. Elena Maslova-Levin, who approached the book as an artistic canvas, first masterfully embracing the entire manuscript, and then significantly impacting the aesthetics of structure and argument on so many levels.

Dr. Marc Gafni
March 2019 (Portland, OR)—February 2025 (Saint Johnsbury, VT)

INTRODUCTION

I. Relationship Crisis and Evolution of Love

Entry 1. A Revolution in Relationships

A revolution in relationships is taking place across the Western world. It is just as significant—perhaps even more significant—than the sexual revolution of the 1960s. The relationship revolution will have a far more powerful effect on the quality, joy, and potency of our lives than any other single shift in our lives and our global culture. It is happening in different ways for all people in all classes of society, and it is breathing life into a new vision of relationship and self.

Self and relationship seek higher and deeper forms. Love seeks its own evolution. We want to play a larger game in our lives and our love. Not only do we want to move from surviving to thriving, but we also want to move from thriving to experiencing real purpose and meaning. We want success as much as we ever have—especially those among us who are just reaching for financial and academic success. But for many of us, success is no longer enough. We want to evolve our lives and love from success to significance.

This larger game is one we are all creating. One of the core rules of the new game is that the rules do not yet exist. Choosing the deepest expression of our wholeness is part of the new game. This is not at all like the relationships game of the sixties where, more often than we admitted, we sought to shirk responsibility under the veneer of consciousness. We want to get out of the stands and into the game, full out and full on—and we want to do so as our most authentic, whole, and therefore powerful selves. We do not want either our core identities or what it means to love to be determined by traditional societal norms. We do not want to be told that our only options are to fail or to succeed. We want to love well and love fully. More than anything else, we want to participate in the evolution of love. We want no less than a new deal in identity and relationships. We want a new vision of success. We want a new vision of what it means to be a real man and a true woman.

Entry 2. Beyond Mars and Venus

We are also not like we were in the 1960s in that we are not antitraditional. We understand and, in many ways, embrace the traditional distinctions between Mars and Venus.[1] We love relationships, we love marriage, and we love weddings. We have made *Family Circle* and bridal magazines more popular than ever before. Many of us dream of living forever with our ideal partner and the family we make together. Some of us do not. But more and more, we all want our life to be a *choice*, not a social role that we must fulfill as others instruct us to.

We may still dream of the white-picket-fence life, but we want to do so differently. We want to shape our dream as a unique expression of our deepest authenticity and wholeness, and we do not want to close ourselves off behind the fence. Rather, we want our relationships and love to be in service of something larger than ourselves. We want our lives to extend beyond ourselves and our limited circles.

We want to be responsible even as we want to be wild. We want the city and the wilderness, civilization and exploration, to live together in a more passionate and integrated embrace. We honor traditional wisdom even as we seek the next edge of emergence.

The move to efface all distinctions between Mars and Venus is not *trans*gender but *anti*gender.[2] To deny all distinctions is to dishonor what

---

[1] On the distinction between Mars and Venus, see John Gray, Men Are from Mars, Women Are from Venus: A Practical Guide for Improving Communication and Getting What You Want in Your Relationships (1992).

[2] See Supplementary Essay 3 for a deeper discussion of this issue.

poet Mary Oliver called *the soft animal* into which we are born. We honor the animal. The animal expresses itself in the wisdom of very real distinctions between men and women. To deny it is disastrous, whether encouraged by outmoded religious dogma that rejects the body or by politically correct dogma that rejects the distinctions between Mars and Venus.

We are grateful that the core distinctions between Mars and Venus have been validated by hundreds of new studies in neuroscience. It is clear to us that there are fundamental differences between the male and female—biological, neurological, and hormonal. The notion that we can deny masculine and feminine is an absurdity from any truly informed scientific perspective. And we also know that we are masculine *and* feminine. Masculine and feminine are expressions of deeper qualities of Reality present from the first nanoseconds after the Big Bang (we refer to them as *lines* and *circles*). Each of us is a unique integration of lines and circles. This is not a weak androgyny but rather a new emergent configuration of Eros and intimacy—*Unique Gender*.[3]

In other words, we now know that androgyny is not the way. But we also want to move beyond traditional, often limited conceptions of Mars and Venus, men and women. We want to move *beyond* Mars and Venus in a way that doesn't deny our animal but transcends and includes it.

Our desire to move beyond Mars and Venus includes both *a self* that is beyond Mars and Venus and *a relationship* that is beyond Mars and Venus. The former is a prerequisite for the latter, as we will see throughout this book. In this desire, we welcome the wisdom of neuroplasticity, which reveals in clear scientific terms that every human being can choose to evolve. We can all choose to evolve—our identities and our relationships—beyond Mars and Venus.

All of this is to say that we want to take the next step in the evolution of relationships, a step that will honor all that we have received from the past yet will walk us into the future. We want a new vision of what it means to be a hero. We want to articulate new insights and distinctions

---

[3] See Chapter 6, "Whole Mate" (Entry 9), Chapter 7, "Unique Self" (Entry 2), and Supplementary Essay 3 for an unpacking of this notion.

that declare the terms of a new relationship deal.

The purpose of this book is to articulate a vision of this new relationship deal. This new deal must be based upon a new model of self and a new model of relationship. If these models are to have the power to inspire and guide us, they cannot be fanciful or contrived. They must be rooted in the wisdom of the best science and spirituality available to us today. But models are not enough. We also need the practical technologies that show us how to live these models in our lives.

Entry 3. New Roles, New Rules

This (r)evolution in relationships, like all great revolutions, is catalyzed by our interior consciousness meeting exterior changes in technology and the marketplace. As always, money and economics play a big part in the story. A major premise of the old relationship deal was that mutual dependency and imposed social roles were necessary for survival. Men were breadwinners. They guided and directed. They were protectors and providers. Women were homemakers. They mused and inspired. They were nurturers and caregivers. Men operated in the public sphere; women operated in the private sphere.

Now, man as sole or even primary breadwinner is no longer a given. It is nearly impossible to overstate the significance of this momentous shift. It changes the very structure of society and is every bit as dramatic as the Industrial Revolution. Like the Industrial Revolution, this change is evoking a complete re-visioning of both identity and relationship.

Today, women are a growing majority among undergraduate and graduate degree holders across the United States. They now constitute the majority of the workforce. In only 23 percent of American homes is the man the sole breadwinner.[4] That figure has plummeted in the last

---

[4] Pew Research Center, "In a Growing Share of U.S. Marriages, Husbands and Wives Earn About the Same," April 2023: "Far fewer husbands are the sole breadwinner in their marriage these days. The share of marriages where the husband is the primary or sole breadwinner has fallen steadily in recent decades, driven mainly by the declining share of marriages where the husband is the sole provider—this was the arrangement in 49% of marriages in 1972, while today that share is 23%."

decades. Women are now co-earners or primary breadwinners in the majority of American marriages. In fact, 41 percent of mothers in the United States are now the primary breadwinners.[5] And in almost 45 percent of the households where both partners work, the woman is either the primary breadwinner or both partners earn about the same amount.[6]

It is not just economic conditions that are driving the emergence of the new relationship deal. A huge driver is that women are discovering new answers to the question of identity. They are responding very differently to the questions of *Who am I?* and *Who do I want to be and become?* than they did just a short time ago.

In the past half-century, the shift in women's consciousness has expanded their sense of choice. As women—especially women of the upper-middle and professional classes—were liberated from the role of homemaker, many discovered that they could *choose.* They can choose the beauty and grace of traditional roles, or to pursue professional and public success, or to integrate their efforts in the public and private sphere. This increase in options encourages women to wake up from socially imposed roles and choose for themselves what it means to be a woman. Put differently, women hunger for a way to access the full power of their Mars qualities without losing the depth of their Venus qualities.

Changes are equally dramatic for men. Until now, societies survived based on men's ability to play very specific roles, namely provider, protector, and leader. Playing those roles successfully meant they were *real men.* Their success earned them society's respect and women's love. Failure to play those roles meant a failed life, dishonor, and shame. Society imposed such roles in order to survive. To survive wars, revolutions, movements,

---

[5] "Breadwinning Mothers Continue to Be the U.S. Norm," Center for American Progress, 2019: "In 2017, the latest year with available data, 41 percent of mothers were the sole or primary breadwinners for their families, earning at least half of their total household income . . . this includes single working mothers and married mothers who out-earn their husbands. An additional 23.2 percent of mothers are what Boushey originally coined 'co-breadwinners,' married mothers whose wages comprise at least 25 percent of their total household earnings." Retrieved January 2024 (https://www.americanprogress.org/article/breadwinning-mothers-continue-u-s-norm/).

[6] Ibid.

and rapid change, we needed boys and men not to question their duty to give their lives for their families and their countries. We needed them to buy into the belief that being a good protector, provider, and leader would make them heroes and bring them glory, love, and respect.

As women moved into the workplace and their old networks of feminine support were consequently dismantled, they turned to the communion of the couple for intimacy and communication. Ironically, in man doing what he needed to do to be a provider and protector, he was often unavailable for intimacy. For example, success as an attorney meant learning to argue, but being intimate as a husband or dad meant *listening like the sky*. Being a great warrior meant developing a *killer reflex*, but being an available husband and dad meant developing a *love reflex*. As a result, a woman often felt that her deep need for intimacy was not being satisfied. For a long time, that did not matter; passion and intimacy were not part of the old relationship deal. As women found their voice, independence, and power, however, they also related in a whole new way to their need for intimacy and passion with their partners.

Men have generally awakened to the realization that being the sole breadwinner did not train them for intimacy. They realized that the very skills they needed for traditional success were often antithetical to intimacy, and that success training was all too often divorce training. Their jobs took them away from the home so they could support the home. The home they supported often became the home they were thrown out of, for failing to be good husbands.

While the men thought that being a good husband meant providing, newly conscious women found their voice and asked men to provide something else—a greater depth of intimacy and communication. When men could not meet women's needs, women felt unfulfilled and often left. Many men have recognized their partners' unfulfilled needs, and they are now reaching for increased depths of intimacy and communion. They are seeking to access and deploy a far greater range of their Venus qualities than ever before.

Entry 4. Reenvisioning the Hero

The need to achieve as a breadwinner hijacked men's self-chosen sense of mission and purpose. Their mission became to provide and protect. Honor, integrity, and heroism were directly related to their degree of potency in these endeavors. Today, success-as-survival consciousness focuses on how to get higher up the ladder faster, but it doesn't always understand which wall to put the ladder on. It is focused more on profit and less on people because more honor is awarded to the *successful* CEO than to the *socially conscious* CEO.

Once men had children, few dads felt they could choose whether they wanted to be a full-time dad, artist, actor, writer, or contemplator of the path to consciousness. Being a *starving artist* was acceptable for single males, but not for anyone who strived to be a *real man*, namely a hardworking dad with children. Men had to put aside their own sense of self and fulfill the mission imposed upon them by the larger society.

For contemporary men, the traditional sense of purpose and mission is less compelling. The role as the sole or primary breadwinner is disappearing, and so, too, is the hero role that came with it. As a result, men face a void of purpose.

Men need to define anew what it means to be a man. And they are asking what it means to be a hero. Some writers are saying that men must grow up to be *post-heroic*. The heroes in their books are the ones who do not need to be a hero anymore. Paradoxically, however, women do not fall in love with men who are not heroes. Lois Lane did not fall in love with her kind and sensitive colleague Clark Kent. She fell in love with Superman. Once he was Superman, she was moved to see him cry.

Fortunately, not only do women want to fall in love with heroes, but men also want to be heroes. Men want to be strong, to make a difference, and to love. Men want to engage in the transformation of identity that will allow them to integrate the full range of all their Venus qualities. To do this, men need to figure out what it means to be a hero in today's world. And women need to evolve in order to inspire and inform this new vision of the male hero. If women lock men into the old deal (you are a hero only if you are successful on one of the many forms of modern battlefields), then men, driven by what Darwin called *sexual selection*, will aspire to this old vision of hero. Women need to participate in the liberation of men from the old form of hero. Only then can the new hero inform new forms of relationships and contribute to the evolution of love.

Moreover, the very notion of *hero* is culturally and etymologically identified with men. We need to articulate a new vision of the feminine hero. We have already expanded the notion of hero to include women. But who is the *feminine* hero? What is the texture and cast of the feminine hero as distinct from the masculine hero?[7] This is a question that culture has not addressed, and it needs urgent articulation. The hero that lives in culture is ultimately an incarnation of Reality's deepest values, toward which the entire population must be allured and aspire. The answer to the question of who the hero is, not only for every little boy but also for every little girl, is the north star for the future of relationships.

Entry 5. Unanswered Questions

To evolve love, the new relationships deal needs to address a few pressing questions. Women are saying, *I want my man to meet me and partner with me in whatever I choose—work, home, or a combination of both.* And men have changed dramatically to meet women. They replied with a resounding *yes* and transformed themselves in myriad ways in order to give that *yes* an authentic potency and power. When you are attracted to someone, you naturally change yourself to meet them. This is one of the rules of Reality. When you adore someone else, you want to earn their love by supporting them. But here's the irony: the newly emerged egalitarian relationships, while big on communication and intimacy, often seem to be lacking in passion, purpose, and commitment.

She says: *Why am I not attracted to you anymore, even though*

---

[7] A good place to begin this inquiry is to turn to the feminine goddesses of the ancient pantheons, particularly the Greek and Hindu interior sciences. Jean Shinoda Bolen's work on the Greek goddesses is important here, as well as my dear friend and colleague Sally Kempton's beautiful work on the Hindu goddesses, Awakening Shakti. See Jean Shinoda Bolen, Goddesses in Everywoman: Powerful Archetypes in Women's Lives (2014) and Sally Kempton, Awakening Shakti: The Transformative Power of the Goddesses of Yoga (2013).

you do the dishes and sometimes manage to listen to me without solving my problem?

She says: *Why is your adoring and supporting me not enough?*

She says: *Why do I still need to feel your ambition and aspiration?*

She says: *I want to be adored by a man I admire.*

She says: *I cannot fully love a man who lacks drive and purpose.*

How does an egalitarian relationship maintain the polarity required to create passion? Can a relationship survive without sustained passion? What is the *beyond Venus and Mars* vision of polarity and passion in the new relationship deal? Beyond procreation and fleeting pleasure, which none of us want to underestimate, what is the purpose of passion? What is the sexual narrative that informs a *beyond Venus and Mars* relationship (what we will call a *whole mate* or *evolutionary* relationship)?

This raises questions that lurk even more deeply in the shadows: Why are we together? What are the core values of our relationship? Is our relationship built on core values that are larger than the relationship itself? Why don't good communication and loving each other work as a compelling basis for lasting passion or commitment?

In the past, partners were clear as to why they were in relationship. They needed to be married and have children. That is what good and decent people did. It was also the right thing to do. Now, neither marriage nor kids are a given for most couples. For some of them, those are not necessities. For others, they amount to an economic ball and chain.

She says: *More of us working women are saying to ourselves, our friends, and men, "We can support ourselves and do not need a man. We feel that a partner who cannot contribute to our thriving because he is less educated or less successful is the new ball and chain and not a joy."*

For others, particularly those who are both educated and in a reasonably successful marriage or committed relationship, the partnership seems to relieve their loneliness, but it also seems to lack a deeper passion and purpose. Once partners have talked about their wounds for the umpteenth time, then what?

He says: *Relationship and marriage seem to have lost their compelling foundation. My commitment flounders without foundation. Yes, I agree that it is wonderful to break out of the dynamics of dependency that defined the old relationship deal, but what comes in its place?*

When couples finally achieve some semblance of a half-working partnership, why does this seem so much less compelling than the image of love and passion that we hoped would ravish us open to life?

He says: *I want the woman who loves me to appreciate me too.*

He says: *I want an intimate partner, not just a roommate who shares the economic burden and with whom I have occasional sex.*

He says: *Why do I not feel appreciated by you and met by your radiance?*

He says: *If I am not needed, then why am I here?*

He says: *I want to be a hero, not just your loving assistant.*

He says: *I want to look into your eyes and know I am a good child of the Universe.*

Not surprisingly, as women are accessing a fuller range of their Mars qualities, they are finding it harder to find their way back to Venus. Men are now complaining that they cannot find their women's radiance or sensuality. This complaint parallels women's complaint that men are not available for intimate communication. How do men and women live together in the fullness of Venus and Mars?

We are on the verge of a pivotal transition. At this moment, the majority of households are still primarily supported by men. But in just one generation, the majority of households will likely be primarily supported by women. The terms of the new relationship deal are being enacted, and they will define the future of our relationships.

These questions, along with the stunning relational shifts that motivate them, are barely noticed in the daily media. We live such rushed and harried lives that we have become oblivious to the hints that these shifts provide about the next great stage in the evolution of relationships. In so many ways, these questions reveal the contours of our current relationship crisis. Fortunately, crisis almost always precedes transformation.

II. A New Operating System for a New Vision of Relationship

In our quest to improve our relationships, we turn to relationship books, seminars, and counselors. Yet, taking their advice is mostly like installing a new piece of software on our computer: it enhances our experience and improves functionality, but the operating system itself remains the same. What we propose in *The Future of Relationships* is an upgrade to the operating system itself.

This book does not merely offer a new piece of software. It does not present a series of life hacks and techniques to make relationships work better. Nor does it point out what is wrong with him, her, or relationships themselves. It doesn't even offer new ways of coping or better ways of communicating. Instead, *The Future of Relationships* offers a fundamental upgrade to the source code of relationships and, ultimately, to the nature of love itself.

This book invites you to play an active and conscious role in the momentous evolution of relationships and love.

The core concepts and distinctions of this book—*the three levels of relationship, Unique Self, evolutionary relationship, Reality Is Relationship,* and *Outrageous Love*—comprise a new operating system, new models of self and relationship.

Entry 1. The Three Levels of Relationship

The core distinction at the center of this book delineates three primary levels of human relationship: *role mate* (level one), *soul mate* (level two), and *whole mate* (level three). In Part One, we explore what they look like, how they feel, and how they work. At each level, partners live their relationship differently. Each level engages a different set of relationship technologies. The first two levels, role mate and soul mate, are old-deal relationships. The third, whole mate, level is a new relationship deal.

Each type of relationship gives a different answer to the basic relationship question: *What is your context for relating?*

The answer to that question establishes the nature of the relationship. Of course, there might be more than one answer, but there is always a primary center of gravity that becomes the major motif of the relationship. Every relationship has a theme. That theme is the context for relating. Everything else flows from there. A relationship *wakes up* when the context for relating goes from implicit to explicit. A relationship *evolves* when the context for relating evolves.

The context for relating in a role mate relationship is to survive and thrive. To survive and thrive in a role mate relationship, partners need to excel in their respective roles and make personal sacrifices. Traditionally, role mate roles included being either a protector and provider or a homemaker and nurturer. For role mates, fulfilling their obligations is a matter of great honor. It is a matter of duty. Being successful at fulfilling their obligations gives role mates an inner sense of pride and accomplishment and helps them feel accomplished, especially according to societal standards. Role mates feel at home in the world when they successfully align with their roles.

The context for relating in a soul mate relationship is personal fulfillment and liberation from loneliness. Personal fulfillment is about being happy. Personal fulfillment is about feeling loved. To be loved as a soul mate means to feel understood and received. While the currency of love in role mate relationships is personal sacrifice, in soul mate relationships, it is personal fulfillment and devotion to a beloved other. Communication is the holy grail Actually saying the words *I love you*, regularly and convincingly, is essential.

The context for relating in a whole mate relationship is devotion to a shared purpose that is larger than the relationship itself. People reach for whole mate relationships when personal fulfillment is no longer personally fulfilling. They evolve beyond role mate and soul mate relationship when they have the powerful realization that they are personally fulfilled only when they share values with their partners *and* fulfill upon missions and visions beyond themselves.

Whole mate, or evolutionary, relationship contains the best of everything that came before it. It includes all the goodness of the old deal relationships plus the beauty of the next stage of evolution. It includes an entirely new dimension of passion, purpose, and possibility. Once you can visualize and sense evolutionary relationships, you can begin to live them in your life. The goal of this book is to steep you in this beautiful new possibility.

Entry 2. Transformation of Identity

In Part Two of the book, we describe a new level of identity that moves us well beyond our ego-based selves. When we transform our identities, we transform our relationships. After all, who we understand ourselves to be deeply impacts all of our relationships. When we transform our relationships, we transform Reality. **To participate in the transformation of identity is to participate in the transformation of Reality.** While the precise meaning of the last sentence might elude you right now, it will become increasingly clear as we continue. For now, consider that when we transform our identities, and therefore our reality, we respond to one of the greatest crises of our time: the crisis in relationships.

Divorce, loneliness, neglect, and even starvation, injustice, and war, are just some of the myriad expressions of our current relationship crisis. There is a breakdown in our sense that we all share connection, intimacy, and purpose. At the same time, there is a breakdown in our sense that we each have something unique to contribute in response to our current global crisis. Indeed, that is why so many of us fail to act.

There is a profound truth often attributed to Albert Einstein, which will become our guiding mantra in this book: *No problem can be solved from the same level of consciousness that created it.*[8] Even if we cannot fully articulate the precise contours of our current relationship crisis, we can understand at some level that we cannot respond to it from the same level of identity that created it. We intrinsically know that we have to respond to our global crisis from a new level of identity and consciousness.

In this book, we introduce the concept of *Unique Self*, a level of identity and consciousness that exists beyond the consciousness that led to our current crisis. Unique Self offers a new way of being and acting in life and love. It is the level of identity and consciousness that allows us to move from role mate to soul mate to whole mate, and to transform our world through relationships.

Entry 3. Evolutionary Relationship

A core new emergent introduced and explored in depth in this book is *evolutionary relationship* (Chapter 7 and Part Three of the book). An evolutionary relationship is not ordinary. It is not for the weak-hearted or the lazy. An evolutionary relationship is for those of us who are committed to living an extraordinary life. For that, you need an extraordinary relationship—an *evolutionary* relationship, a whole mate relationship that exists inside the context of *evolution*. This book is as much about

---

8 Einstein didn't express this understanding in these words exactly. He said, "A new type of thinking is essential [in the atomic age] if mankind is to survive and move toward higher levels" ("Atomic Education Urged by Einstein: Scientist in Plea for $200,000 to Promote New Type of Essential Thinking," The New York Times, May 25, 1946), in the context of the new risks posed by the atomic bomb.

the evolution of the Universe as it is about love.

We will explore the emergent phenomenon of evolutionary relationships in the same way we would write a piece of progressively deepening music. We will circle the same themes, each time moving forward.

A potent image of the structure of this book is the spiral. The spiral is a form of creativity in the Universe. It shows up in mathematical sequences, biological structures, chemical arrangements, and the shapes and forms of galaxies (one of the great new insights of science is that galaxies must have spirals to generate new creativity).

In this book, where we want to birth new consciousness, we, too, will spiral. That means that we will often return to the core themes. But each time we circle around, we will also move the conversation forward. That is the nature of the spiral that births a new possibility.

Entry 4. Reality Is Relationship

One of our primary themes in this book is *Reality is Relationship*. Said differently, Reality is a Field of Relationship. Every relationship participates in this Field of Relationship, like every value participates in the Field of Value.[9]

The process of evolution itself is the evolution of relationships. Therefore, as your relationships evolve, you are catalyzing the evolutionary process. What this means, and how it plays out in life and love, will become clear as you read this book. The first chapter, "The Arc of Evolution," is dedicated to an in-depth exploration of this theme, but its essence can be summarized in a few concise statements.[10]

---

9 The term Field of Value attempts to synergize the interior science of multiple wisdom traditions with contemporary field theory and refers to Value as the very Ground of Being, the very fabric of Cosmos within which we live. Value is not a contrivance but the very air we breathe, the Field of Existence, in which we all live and participate. We live in the Field of Value, and the Field of Value lives in us. The issue is not specific values, but Value itself.

10 For an even deeper discussion of the scientific underpinnings of this framework, see the companion volume, The Evolution of Love: From Quarks to Culture—the Rise of Evolutionary Relationships in Response to the Meta-Crisis.

Reality is Relationship. Reality is evolution. Reality is the evolution of relationships. Science describes snippets of structure in our Universe's great weave of interconnectivity. For example, Earth emerges out of trillions upon trillions of living and nonliving parts, all of which self-organize to ever-higher and ever-deeper patterns of intimacy and relationship. Earth's very nature is relationships. So is the nature of the whole Universe.

The Universe has *direction*—not direction imposed from without, but direction from the inherent nature of Reality itself. From quarks to atoms to molecules to living cells, from subatomic particles to stars and galaxies, from the unicellular life procreating through division to the highest peaks of human love and communion, the core movement of all of Reality is toward greater relationship and greater love. In other words, evolution is driven by Reality's intrinsic desire for ever-deeper contact and ever-greater wholeness. In a profound sense, the Evolutionary Story of the Cosmos is the story of the evolution of relationships.

Crisis is an evolutionary driver. When life is challenged, it does not roll over and die. Life challenged by crisis seeks new life. Emergency generates emergence. Breakdown generates breakthrough. Why? Why does life seek not just to continue but to evolve? In other words, why does life seek not only to survive but to thrive? Because crisis cannot be solved by the same level of consciousness that created it.

Any crisis is a crisis of relationship, or, said differently, a crisis of intimacy. Since levels of consciousness include the quality of relationship and intimacy, a relationship crisis at one level of consciousness can be resolved only by the emergence of a higher level of relationship or intimacy.

The present crisis is the evolutionary driver for the evolution of relationships, which we might as well call the *evolution of intimacy* or *the evolution of love*.

We know from evolutionary science that to survive does not necessarily mean to engage in a competition in which only the strongest survives. Rather, to survive means to thrive through relationship. We ensure our personal and global survival through relationship. The more *life* we desire, for ourselves and our planet, the more ever-deeper and ever-wider forms of relationship we evolve. The greater our capacity to engage in deep, purposeful relationship, the greater our aliveness. Our need to survive and thrive and our desire for ever-greater connection and intimacy move us to develop ever-deeper forms of relationship.

Role mate and soul mate are two expressions of relationship along the trajectory of evolution. Each has its beauty and its limitations. The Universe, devoted to human survival, birthed role mate relationships. Driven by the challenges and conditions of role mate relationships, it birthed an upgrade in relationship—soul mate. This is clearly a beautiful and much-desired relationship transformation. Yet soul mate by itself is not enough. With all its beauty, we face the crisis and limitation of soul mate relationships. In response, evolution is birthing a new level of relationship—whole mate. It transcends and includes the best insights and strategies of role mate and soul mate relationships.

Entry 5. An Invitation to Evolve Love

Our mission in writing *The Future of Relationships* is to participate in the next great evolution of relationship and love. Our purpose as writers is not to be social commentators, sociologists, or cultural critics. The idea that love evolves is perhaps shocking to those who think of love as eternal, or at least as the one unchanging constant that has existed since the beginning of time. How can love be eternal *and* evolve?

Recently, I was watching a movie about a Chinese patriarch who shared a beautiful love with his wife. At one point in the movie, the couple's son disobeyed the father. The mother supported her son. According to the law of the time, she could have been put to death for dishonoring her husband. Instead, the patriarch slapped her three times and then hugged her. She tearfully thanked him for the depth of his love. At that moment in time, three slaps instead of death was the best love had to offer. Today, if a man slapped his wife to punish her, she might correctly call the authorities to report domestic violence. What has changed? Love has evolved. Love today cannot express itself in violence between partners. The transformation of how we express our love through time is precisely the evolution of love.

We also see love's evolution in our ever-widening circles of intimacy over the span of a lifetime. We begin life by identifying only with ourselves, but we gradually widen our sense of love to include family, clan, tribe, nation, and even the whole world. Each time our circles widen, we witness the evolution of love.

The old relationship deal was an important step in the evolution of love. It asked men and women to consider each other's perspectives. It was a momentous leap in the evolution of relationships for men and women to embrace their full equality but also to be willing to fully understand and acknowledge each other's differences.

However, Mars and Venus relationships are limited. They were perfect for their time, like all things emergent in evolution. But there is always a next step in the evolution of love. What is good, true, beautiful, and functional for one stage of evolution is not necessarily so for the next. Though we always embrace the very best of the old wisdom, we evolve relationships (often in response to changing life circumstances), and we witness new wisdom and consciousness emerge. Mars and Venus, therefore, while limited, offered crucial insights that guide us into the next stage. *Beyond-Mars-and-Venus*, evolutionary relationships are the next stage, the next evolution of love.

Men and women are hungry for the next leap in the evolution of love. We have a potent desire to play a larger game in relationships and an urgent need to do so. We can palpably sense that we have exhausted the old models of relationship. We are searching for new models of intimacy, and we are searching for an articulation of the next evolution.

The desire for a new model is strong among millennials, but no less urgent for Gen-Xers and baby boomers starting anew or seeking to reinvent their current relationships. We can hear the yearning for the new model in early-morning and late-night conversations between beloveds of all ages. We can also witness the search for its articulation in leading-edge relationship literature and seminars. But the next evolution of love remains indistinct.

This book articulates the next expression of the evolution of love. It is the manual, map, and invitation to participate in enunciating and integrating the next level of relationship. It summons you to experience and create a level of joy, fulfillment, and depth in relationship that was unimaginable at love's earlier levels of evolution. The ideas introduced and deeply explored in this book birth possibilities for love that are undeniably fresh and powerful.

CHAPTER 1

THE ARC OF EVOLUTION

Entry 1. The Mysterious Drive for Life and Love

Have you ever noticed that pop-psychology writers, often quoted in the mainstream media, sometimes dismiss the deepest human motivations for relationship and love as merely the drive for survival? As if by using the word *survival* they could hide the magic and mystery of it all.

Our desire for life is not a biological given. It is one of the great mysteries of the Universe. The desire for survival is the interior desire for life. It's the built-in, axiomatic purpose of the Universe. In a sense, *survival* is just another way of saying *life*.

Reality is organized to increase the possibility of life. All organisms are wired for, to borrow Bruce Lipton's expression, the *ferocious and inexplicable drive for life*.[11] The insatiable desire for life is programmed into our cells. No organism will readily give up its life. Try to kill a bacterium, and this most primitive of organisms makes every evasive maneuver possible to ensure that it will live. It does not say, *OK, I will wait here until you kill me*. When our lives are threatened, our fight-or-flight response typically kicks in well before our rational minds have registered the threat. This will to live and to create life is an expression of consciousness, coded into our exterior cellular structure.

As *survival* is another word for *life*, so *life* is another word for *love*, because both point to full *aliveness*. Life and love signify some level of consciousness or awareness. Life and love imply some level of *telos*—focused direction or purpose. Life and love are as much entwined with the

---

11 Chapter 1: "Our Drive to Bond," in Bruce H. Lipton, The Honeymoon Effect: The Science of Creating Heaven on Earth (2014).

will to connect as they are with the will for aliveness. That is why, when we find ourselves in love, we are fully alive and motivated to survive and thrive.

When we are in love with a beloved, the loss of him or her sometimes causes the loss of our will to live. But if we live and love more deeply, from a higher level of relationship consciousness, we know that our beloved is an expression of life itself. Madly loving our beloved is part of being in love with life. His or her uniqueness connects us to all of life. Through uniquely loving our beloved's uniqueness, we love all of life.

The desire for survival is the mysterious drive for life and love. The method for life is love, and love is relationships.

Entry 2. Survival of the Fittest Means the Fittest for Love

Relationships and survival are inextricably intertwined. The first stage in the old relationship deal, role mate relationship, was based on our will to survive. Survival and relationship were one and the same. These relationships were an expression of our will to live. They served us well. We are all children of survival.

We now know that to survive does not necessarily mean to engage in a competition where only the strongest survive. Rather, to survive means to thrive through *relationships*. Survival of the fittest includes the fittest for relationship, cooperation, and collaboration. Survival of the fittest means the fittest for love. Survival through relationships *is* the process of evolution.

To survive means to be in the relationships that best assure survival. Love and survival are bound to each other. We survive through love in the form of relationships. To be in love is to be willing to sacrifice one's own survival for the sake of the other. This is what providers and protectors, as well as homemakers and nurturers, have done throughout history. Precisely *how* these roles play out, and whose role it was to incarnate these core features of love, evolved as relationships have been evolving. **This evolution of relationships is also the evolution of love.**

In a recent book, evolutionary biologist David Sloan Wilson argued that altruism is a fundamental evolutionary driver.[12] Although Darwin's work is primarily known for the idea of survival of the fittest, he also wrote about love as a primary driver of evolution. Evolutionary theorist David Loye points out that, in Darwin's early notebooks, as well as his last great classical work *The Descent of Man*, terms referring to Eros and *ethos* appear over a hundred times as being central to the lifeworld and the human evolutionary process.[13]

This notion is echoed in the work of philosopher Charles Sanders Peirce, who describes *Evolutionary Love* as the core driver of the entire evolutionary process.[14] The core impulse of Evolutionary Love is the force that draws together, integrates, and drives the entire process of evolution toward survival—toward life and love. Evolutionary Love is the allurement that lives at every level of the Cosmos.

The first mysterious impulse of all of Reality is survival. But survival is but an exterior expression, which points to a core interior quality of life and consciousness: *self-love*. The desire to survive is sourced in the

---

12 David S. Wilson, Does Altruism Exist? Culture, Genes, and the Welfare of Others (2015). Wilson is part of a long lineage of evolutionary thinkers. This line of thought was powerfully articulated by Kropotkin in his epic work Mutual Aid: A Factor of Evolution (1902). Kropotkin was followed by many thinkers including Charles Sanders Peirce, James Mark Baldwin, and many others, who read Darwin more carefully than the neo-Darwinian reductionists (who hijacked the mainstream discourse with a dogmatic materialism, as flawed as the religious fundamentalist dogmatism against which they were properly rebelling).

13 Darwin scholar David Loye makes this point in several of his books. See for example, Darwin's Second Revolution (2010, p. 2). Loye searched for terms like love and various other terms connoting moral sensitivity. The particular phrases Eros and ethos are not Darwinian, of course. We mean these terms as two meta-topics expressed, according to Loye's research, in a variety of different terms. See also the Prologue of Rediscovering Darwin: The Rest of Darwin's Theory and Why We Need It Today, by D. Loye (2018). In his own words: "How could it go for so long unnoticed that in Origin's classic sequel on human evolution, Darwin wrote only twice of 'survival of the fittest' but 95 times about love. And this with only a single trivial entry for love in the loveless index still in use worldwide. Even more remarkable in a battered world desperately in need of moral guidance is the Darwin who wrote 92 times not of selfishness but of the Moral Sense as the ultimate over-riding prime driver of evolution."

14 See Charles S. Peirce, "Evolutionary Love," The Monist (1893), 176—200.

inherent self-loving realization of life that it has intrinsic, irreducible value that deserves to live. Relationships are the evolutionary key to survival. From the interior perspective, they are the key to ever deeper life and consciousness. The inherently creative intelligence of self-organizing Cosmos lures itself to higher and higher levels of surviving and thriving—or, said only slightly differently, of life and consciousness.

Everything—from quarks to human beings—survives, thrives, and evolves its own depth of life, uniqueness, creativity, complexity, and consciousness through relationship.

Entry 3. Reality Is Evolution of Relationship

One of the core mysteries of Reality is how a new whole emerges out of many parts. A star is fundamentally distinct from an atom, yet both are wholes that arise mysteriously from an aggregate of parts. How this happens is not merely a scientific mystery. It is not a riddle with an engineered solution. **The mystery of a new whole emerging from many parts is the very mystery of relationship itself.** An atom emerges from the relationships between the subatomic particles that constitute it. A star emerges out of a vast cloud of distinct atoms in relationship with each other. A living cell emerges when molecules discover new pathways of intimacy that connect and bond them so intensely that new life is born. The Earth system is a complex set of mysterious relationships beyond our wildest imagination.

This is the core movement of Reality toward relationship. The leading-edge emergence theory knows with great certainty that Reality has *direction*. Not direction imposed from without, but direction from the inherent Eros and *telos* of Reality itself—a direction that moves toward deepening intimacy. The meaning of this sentence is unpacked in the next sections of this chapter (and indeed, in the rest of this book).[15]

Inner reality and outer reality—interiors and exteriors—always mirror each other. As the great hermetic philosophers wrote: *As above so below*. We now know that it is not about *an above* and *a below*, a heaven

---

15 In particular, Eros and intimacy are defined in Entry 6 of this chapter.

and an earth. Rather it is about *inside* and *outside*. **Love is an *interior* quality, and it shows up in the *exterior* laws of how the scientific structure of the Universe operates.** How could interior and exterior sciences not mirror each other? They are describing the same Reality from two different perspectives, inside and outside.

Let us get radically clear about these ontological truths on the structure of Reality. Evolution moves toward ever-deepening relationships. The Universe brought forth elementary particles. In the first nanoseconds, quarks moved to create relationships, combining to form protons and neutrons. At the beginning, relationship attempts between protons and neutrons failed. The Universe was too hot, and the first relationships were torn apart by the pull of other particles. Reality could not unfold or evolve until relationship wisdom deepened. Mixing physics and psychology, we might say that a single neutron had to learn sufficient communication skills before it could interact with a proton and remain bonded in stable intimacy. The laws of relationship apply all the way up and all the way down. However, it took Reality only three minutes to cool enough for these protons and neutrons to form a new form of relationship, *heavy hydrogen nuclei*. The neutrons, in fact, desperately needed the protons in order to survive. Without forming a stable bond with a proton, a neutron disintegrates within fifteen minutes.[16]

Imagine a trajectory of cosmological evolution: the spiraling line of emergence from a subatomic particle at the moment of the Big Bang to the whole system of chemical elements in the Universe. Subatomic particles come together to form an atom; atoms come together to form a molecule; simple molecules come together to form a complex molecule; and complex molecules come together to form the structural basis for life. A staggering number of individual parts come together; they survive and thrive *through relationship*. At each step, a new whole is born.

Now imagine complex molecules transforming and evolving into single cells. Imagine single cells coming together to birth multicellular life. Imagine multicellular organisms coming together to create the wildly

---

[16] The technical name for that is decay. A neutron decays into a proton, an electron, and an electron antineutrino.

elegant and dazzling relationships that eventually manifest as fish and, much later, as amphibians and reptiles. Finally, imagine how ever-deeper relationships eventually manifest the first mammals and, over time, human beings.

The story of the entire Universe is the story of the emergence of ever more functional, complex, and beautiful forms of relationship. Surviving and thriving through relationship is the core motivating energy of the evolutionary journey. The Universe moves toward greater relationship—to greater love. In a very profound sense, **the story of the Cosmos is the story of the evolution of love**.

Entry 4. Allurement toward Relationship Is the Nature of Reality

The Universe did not have to be this way. It is theoretically possible for it to have existed as trillions of individual disconnected particles that never create bonded relationship. Yet the Universe moves toward ever-deepening relationships in all of its expressions. Relationships are at the heart of creativity at all levels of Reality. The Universe Story is the story of the emergence of ever better, truer, more functional, and beautiful forms of relationship.

Relationships are an expression of the primal force of Evolutionary Love.

Relationships emerge at every level of Reality in response to *allurement*. A few moments after the Big Bang, quarks were drawn together by the allurement of *strong nuclear attraction*. Planets and stars are drawn together by the allurement of *gravity*. People are drawn together by the allurement of *love*. All three are expressions of the same mysterious allurement toward relationship that is the very nature of Reality, and which we can also call *love*. The exterior expressions of love might be strong nuclear attraction, gravity, electromagnetic attraction, mating behavior, or pair bonding. All these terms refer to relationships. All are external expressions of an internal quality we call *love*, or *Eros*.

Allurement toward relationship is the nature of Reality. At the level of galaxies, we call it *gravity*. At the level of quarks, we call it *strong nuclear attraction*. At the level of protons and electrons, we call it *electromagnetic attraction*. These physical expressions of relationship are what cosmology calls *primordial*. In other words, they explain everything, but nothing explains them. For example, there is nothing deeper one can use to *explain* gravity. It is primordial. In that sense, gravity is revelatory of the nature of the Universe. It just *is*. All of these exterior expressions refer to the inner allurement that is the animating structure of all of Reality's being and becoming.

It makes sense, then, that the evolution of relationships is the core structure of Reality. If the attraction that generates relationships on all levels is an exterior expression of the interior quality of allurement or love, it is literally *natural*, biologically speaking, that the evolution of relationships participates in the evolution of love. From a scientific perspective, relationships are the cause *and* the method of evolution.

It is shocking when you realize how simple it is. Reality is Relationship. Every step that drives Reality forward is an evolutionary transformation in the nature of relationships.

Entry 5. Trajectories of Evolution

Exterior and interior evolution have at least five major trajectories, and we can trust each of them to occur again and again. In this sense, Reality is honorable and trustworthy.

First, **the Universe moves from simplicity to ever-greater *complexity* and *interconnectivity*.** More complexity entails more interconnectivity. For example, an amoeba is more complex and has more nodes of interconnectivity than an atom. This is self-evidently true because the amoeba includes and transcends the complexity of an atom. The amoeba contains the world of matter, in which the intimate configuration of the atom is fundamental and transcends it to add cellular life. Each level of evolution includes and transcends basic dimensions of what came before it and adds distinct new dimensions. We can trust the Universe to move to ever-increasing levels of complexity and interconnectivity.

Second, **the Universe expresses complexity through ever-greater *uniqueness*.** The more complex an organism, the more unique it is (*more* *uniqueness*, in this context, means more and deeper distinctions between individual organisms). An amoeba is more complex and therefore more unique than an atom. A human being is more complex, and therefore more unique, than an amoeba. We can trust the Universe to reach for more and more uniqueness.

Third, **the interior of interconnectivity is *intimacy*.** Evolution may be understood as the progressive deepening of intimacies. We define intimacy as shared identity in the context of (relative) otherness, coupled with mutuality of recognition, mutuality of *pathos* (= feeling), mutuality of value, and mutuality of purpose. The evolution of intimacy can also be expressed as the evolution of relationship.

Fourth, **the Universe is ceaselessly *creative* at ever-evolving levels of depth and complexity.** It always brings forth *newness*. *The creative advance into novelty*, to borrow Alfred North Whitehead's expression, is one of the core features of Reality.[17] We can trust the Universe to be ever-more creative throughout the process of evolution.

Fifth, **the Universe evolves to ever-higher levels of *consciousness*.** Different levels of evolution express different levels of consciousness. Consciousness is an interior expression of complexity and uniqueness. *More consciousness* means that every level of evolution is more *aware* of its surroundings, others, and itself. An amoeba has more consciousness than an atom. A plant has more consciousness than an amoeba. We can trust the Universe to reach for ever-greater depth of consciousness at every level of evolution.

A human being has a more evolved consciousness than that of a plant or even a dog. A human being has a deeper, wider, and more subtle relationship to self, to other, and to Reality. A human being can write

---

17 See Alfred N. Whitehead, "Process and Reality. An Essay in Cosmology. Gifford Lectures Delivered in the University of Edinburgh During the Session 1927–1928" (1929). In this essay, he mentions creative advance into novelty four times: "'Becoming' is a creative advance into novelty" (p. 28); "The aim of the philosophy of organism is to express a coherent cosmology based upon the notions of 'system,' 'process,' 'creative advance into novelty,' . . . as ultimate agents of stubborn fact" (p. 128); "The universe is thus a creative advance into novelty" (p. 222); "Both are in the grip of the ultimate metaphysical ground, the creative advance into novelty. Either of them, God and the World, is the instrument of novelty for the other" (p. 349).

poetry about her inner state. A human being can be conscious of her part in a human community, and she can feel called to steward the planet in a way that is not possible for either dogs or amoebas. Human beings have more capacity to be loving. Human beings can liberate each other from loneliness and communicate at a level of depth unavailable at earlier levels of evolution. Human beings also can evolve to include wider and wider circles of love throughout their lifetimes.

To sum up our conversation so far: the Universe is driven to ever-evolving levels of creativity, complexity, consciousness, intimacy, and uniqueness by the profoundly nonrandom processes of ever-deepening allurement and love.

Entry 6. Intimacy and Eros

Human beings have the capacity to evolve to deeper and wider forms of relationship. This is the evolution of love, which can express itself in multiple relational vectors, only two of which we will discuss here.

The first is the evolution of intimacy. We define intimacy through the following *interior science equation*:

Intimacy = shared identity in the context of (relative) otherness
x mutuality of recognition x mutuality of *pathos* (= feeling)
x mutuality of value x mutuality of purpose

Intimacy is an expression of *Eros*, the animating energy of all of Reality, which we describe by another interior science equation:

Eros = the experience of radical aliveness, seeking,
moving toward, desiring, ever-deeper contact and
ever-greater wholeness

These qualities of Eros are expressed in intimacy as shared identity and the other elements of the intimacy equation—mutualities of recognition, feeling, value, and purpose. In effect, intimacy and Eros are overlapping yet distinct dimensions of relationship. Eros is the energy of being and becoming in Cosmos that drives Reality to ever-deeper intimacies. Eros and intimacy govern all levels of evolutionary reality. **Reality is the evolution of Eros expressed as the progressive deepening of intimacies—in other words, the evolution of relationships.**

An example of the evolution of intimacy at the human level is the movement from egocentric to ethnocentric to worldcentric to cosmocentric intimacy.[18] At every step of this evolution, intimacy means a felt sense of shared identity (expressed as love, care, and concern) with those in your *circle of intimacy*, with mutualities of recognition, *pathos*, value, and purpose. But at every level, the circle of intimacy grows wider and wider:

- An egocentric circle of intimacy includes your family and/or a few close friends.

- An ethnocentric circle of intimacy includes your tribe, nation, religion, company, or team.

- A worldcentric circle of intimacy includes every human being on the face of the planet.

- Finally, a cosmocentric circle of intimacy includes not only human beings, but also animals, and eventually plants, and then the planet itself. It evolves to include other galaxies in all of their expressions. Eventually, the entire Universe is included in your circle of intimacy. You have a realization of intimacy with all things.

The same intimacy formula applies all the way down and all the way up the evolution chain. For example, it applies when subatomic particles are allured by the Eros of Cosmos to become an atom. Protons, neutrons, and electrons come together in a shared identity (being elements of the same atom), while retaining their (relative) otherness. For this to become

---

[18] See Entry 3 in Chapter 9, "Outrageous Love," for an in-depth exploration of this evolutionary trajectory.

possible, they need to recognize and feel each other (in the language of physics, this happens through the medium of *strong force* between the quarks within the protons and neutrons, the *residual strong force* between protons and neutrons, and through *electromagnetic attraction* between the nucleus and electrons). Mutuality of value, in this case, points to the informational and value structure inherent in the subatomic particles, which synergize as the informational or value structure of the atom. Finally, the subatomic particles form an atom, which allows them to function as a whole within larger wholes (molecules). This is their shared purpose: participating, as an atom, in larger wholes.

Entry 7. The LoveIntelligence, LoveBeauty, and LoveDesire of Reality

There are three core levels of relationship in the human realm: role mate, soul mate, and whole mate. It might be easy to think of the level-one role mate relationship as the *beginning* of relationship, but it is not. Reality is Relationship, and Reality existed long before human beings engaged in what we currently think of as relationships. The evolution of life and love is the ever-deepening emergence of more passionate, profound, and powerful forms of relationship. Role mate relationship marks only one of those evolutions.

About five hundred million years ago, in the early Paleozoic era, the stickleback fish represented the edge of the evolution of love. The male stickleback fish expresses his desire through his mating dance. After a successful dance, his mate deposits her eggs in his nest, and he quickly moves in to fertilize them. That was the level of intimacy available at that moment in the evolution of love.

Over a hundred million years later, reptiles have evolved from their amphibian and fish ancestors. With this physical evolution comes the evolution of intimacy. Sex organs now exist. The vagina and the phallus come into being, allowing for a direct intimacy between the masculine and the feminine that was previously impossible and unimaginable. This new level of intimacy, brought about by the inherent relationship intelligence of Reality, changed the very course of life's evolution.

This inherent relationship intelligence, this desire for ever-deepening expressions of intimacy, is not *imposed* on Reality. It is an inherent feature of the ceaseless creativity of Reality itself. Reality is creative. There are no conventional English words (yet) for the *interior* of Reality's ceaseless creativity; we refer to it as *LoveIntelligence*, *LoveBeauty*, and *LoveDesire*. This interior impulse generates ever-deeper forms of love, relationship, and intimacy. This is not random. It is the expression of nonrandom plotlines of Reality, moving from matter to life to the depth of self-reflective mind.

When evolution moved from reptiles to mammals and eventually to humans, love and intimacy again went through a momentous leap. Not only were these more evolved organisms able to be intimate by merging their bodies, but they also became so profoundly bonded that some could stay in relationship for entire lifetimes. In time, Reality evolved, and humans and other creatures enjoyed increased capacities for arousal, relationship, and even ecstasy.

The deepest levels of human intimacy and relationships are the most complex, conscious, creative, and unique. When humans and, with them, human relationships first emerged, there was a momentous leap forward in the evolution of love. But all the same principles apply at each level. Each new level of relationship *transcends and includes* what came before it. At each level there is more consciousness, more uniqueness, more capacity to love, more creativity, and more depth or complexity. All of this means that **the continued movement of evolution in human beings is the evolution to higher and deeper forms of relationship**.

The physical sciences now tell us what the interior sciences have long been saying: **human beings are personally implicated in the great Universe Story.** In the language of the interior sciences: *That which is above comes from you.* In the language of exterior sciences, the direction of the whole is directly dependent on the action of its parts, and a higher order can arise from chaos through local interactions.[19] Our relationships, and the emergence of new forms of relationship, participate in and generate the great movement of Reality.

---

[19] This is the process of self-organization, first described by the Nobel-winning chemist Ilya Prigogine.

Entry 8. Emergencies Create Emergents

In the introduction, we outlined some of the core features of today's relationship crisis that invite and demand a relationship revolution. **Evolution has only one possible response to crisis in relationships: a profound and potent evolution of consciousness, which is an evolution of relationship.** When a crisis reveals itself, a new expression of relationship seeks to emerge.

This is not a fanciful conjecture but the very nature of Reality itself. When there is a crisis, new forms of relationship rise to meet the new life conditions. There are myriad examples that illustrate this, but we will give one of the most dramatic. One of the key momentous leaps in relationship history has been described by many evolutionary theorists as *the oxygen crisis*.[20]

Three and a half billion years ago, single-celled life (prokaryotes) appeared in the Earth's seas.[21] Life became semi-immortal. Single-celled life divided in order to procreate. For vast stretches of time, the seas were filled with life, absorbing the nutrients of the Earth. Prokaryotes used hydrogen from water for an early form of photosynthesis. This process gradually produced an overabundance of oxygen in the atmosphere, which began poisoning the single-celled life that dominated the planet. Faced with this threat, life might have decided to adapt and live within its limitations. It did not.

Instead, life followed the call of its own creativity. Alfred North Whitehead called this essential property of life *the creative advance into novelty*. It is the move toward ever higher and deeper forms of intimacy.

---

[20] We discuss this event in deeper detail in the companion volume, The Evolution of Love: From Quarks to Culture—the Rise of Evolutionary Relationships in Response to the Meta-Crisis.

[21] What we conventionally refer to as life has a number of key features like sentience and reproduction that did not exist before. This is a great emergent leap from the previous level where sentience, or life as we know it, did not exist. Having said that, we know now that matter is not dead. It is driven by its own inherent self-organizing processes that move it to higher forms of complexity. The old sharp split between sentience (life) and nonlife is rapidly disappearing in evolutionary science. As one leading scientist remarked to us, "It looks more like sentience all the way up and all the way down."

The oxygen crisis became an evolutionary driver. The crisis motivated innovation and transformation, leading to a revolution in relationships.

In an extraordinarily complex process, life evolved a completely new form of relationship. For the first time, cells learned to join with each other, and the core structure of life moved from prokaryotes to eukaryotes (complex single-celled organisms), and then to the multicellular life as we know it. This took place without the aid of scientists, researchers, or computers, billions of years before anything vaguely approximating a human brain existed. This took place through the inherent self-organizing LoveIntelligence, LoveBeauty, and LoveDesire of Reality, which always move toward ever-higher forms of intimacy and relationship.

With the emergence of multicellular life, pretty much everything changed. When multicellular organisms learned to join their genes to create new life (through sexual reproduction), a radical newness and diversity was created. It was a radical leap in both exterior structure and interior consciousness. This movement of LoveIntelligence, LoveBeauty, and LoveDesire directly seeded the future emergence of plants, animals, mammals, and human beings.

The crucial point is that **crisis is an evolutionary driver that always deepens relationship.** In response to new life conditions, the current form of relationships is replaced by more capable, more complex, and more conscious forms. We are now poised to take the next momentous leap in the evolution of relationships. It is a move from *joining genes* to *joining genius*. It is the move from role mate and soul mate to whole mate—the rise of *evolutionary relationships*.

The Universe is an honorable place. The Universe can be trusted. The Universe can be trusted to manifest crisis. The Universe can be trusted to respond to crisis by evolving love into deeper forms of intimacy and relationships.

Entry 9. Passionate Protozoa

The same laws of relationship exist all the way up and all the way down the evolutionary chain. Partners who want to form a relationship must find each other first and always need a catalyst to do so.

You can observe this in a simple experiment.[22] Put a couple of old, half-rotten leaves in a glass filled with water. Put the glass under a lamp for a while. Here is what you will see:

Soon, the protozoa hanging on the leaves come to life. They procreate through asexual division. A few days later, their food supply runs low. The protozoa begin to seek the best place in the glass to survive. Some gravitate to the bottom of the glass where there are many nutrients (leaf debris and dead bacteria), but there is little light. Others gravitate to the top of the glass, nearest to the light. The environment near the top is quite different from that of the bottom of the glass. There is plenty of light, but there are hardly any nutrients. Soon, the protozoa are doing so badly that they can no longer procreate. The ones on top are missing food, and the ones at the bottom are missing light. There is a crisis.

In response to the crisis, something wondrous and beautiful happens: All of the protozoa in the glass produce attractants to which the other protozoa are irresistibly drawn. Eros is activated. Both groups of protozoa swim along the trail of scent and meet in the middle. Two protozoa, one from above and one from below, link together. Their cell membranes abut, and an opening manifests, through which the protozoa exchange cell components. In the exchange, the protozoa share some of the skills they have developed to survive at either end of the glass. Crisis catalyzes the creation of new relationship. This relationship allows the protozoa to grow strong and begin to reproduce again. Crisis leads to a transformation in identity, a transformation in relationship, and a transformation in Reality itself. Crisis gives birth to new emergents.

The wondrous exchange quickly ends. The partners split up. Each returns to its part of the glass but with new skills, more knowledge, and an expanded capacity. For many of the protozoa, the merger opens new possibilities. They are better able to thrive even with limited food and light. They once again begin to reproduce actively until they run low on nutrients or light. And then it begins again: the release of the attractant, the swim to the middle of the glass, and the erotic goings-on to survive and thrive.

---

[22] We are gratefully indebted for this example to German neurobiologist Gerald Hüther.

These are the antecedents of role mate relationships in the biological realm.

Much has changed since protozoa first covered the Earth, but some things have remained the same. Like protozoa, men and women try to survive on their own. They try to earn enough income to be independent, find enough hobbies to avoid feeling lonely, and deny their desire and need for a partner or spouse. But they always meet crisis, just like protozoa. They struggle to pay for everything they want, they find themselves lonely on a Saturday night, and they recognize that sometimes it's just nice to have a partner. For humans as well as protozoa, crisis catalyzes relationships. Humans also find their way into relationships to promote their own survival.

Entry 10. Relationship Is Transformation

Among the three levels of human relationship, the first two—role mate and soul mate—are part of the old relationship deal. The third level, whole mate, is a core component of the new deal. All three levels express different levels of consciousness. Each one has a different core motive for relationship. Each one lives relationship differently. Each one has a very different set of relationship technologies. Whole mate relationships include the best dimensions of role mate and soul mate plus entirely new dimensions, skills, and capacities. It is a new level of relational consciousness that we call *evolutionary relationships*.

The new dimensions of whole mate are not limited to new ways of coping or better ways of communicating in relationship. They involve a fundamental upgrade in the source code of relationships and, ultimately, in the nature of relationships and love itself. The new relationship deal invites you to play an active and conscious role in the momentous evolution of relationship and of love.[23]

While the old-deal relationships always involve exchange and negotiations, a balance of giving and receiving, whole mates realize that the very distinction between giving and receiving is an illusion. Whole mates know that giving and receiving are one.

---

[23] See Chapter 6, "Whole Mate."

In some sense, all relationships come with a cost. To receive the gift of a relationship, there is always a gift to be given. The First Principle and First Value of *Eros*, by its very nature, asks us to give up our ego's grasp for superficial pleasure. Through that sacrifice, depth pleasure returns to us a thousandfold. In our transformation to a higher level of relationship, we are driven to give our partner pleasure. We are amazed that in giving pleasure, we receive even greater pleasure. This transformation allows the scorecard to disappear as beautiful sex, connection, and intimacy take us into the Heart of Reality.

These laws of relationship are built into the very structure of the Cosmos. A neutron does not simply bond with a proton. For a neutron to create a stable relationship with a proton, both the neutron and the proton have to undergo transformations. What happens is almost beyond imagination in its beauty: the protons and the neutrons each give over a part of their mass, and it is transformed into an explosion of heat and light.[24] The essence of whole mate relationship is similar, mirroring the basic processes of most elemental structures.

Entry 11. Evolution Accelerates

In the past, leaps in development took billions of years. But the rate of growth and transformation is now exponential. Between our lifetimes and the lifetimes of our great-grandmothers—literally a blink on the time scale of eternity—pretty much *everything* has changed. We moved from horse-drawn buggies to cars and then to planes as modes of expedient transportation. We moved from newspapers, to radio, to television, to the internet, to Facebook as means of sharing information. We moved from handwritten letters, to telephones, to faxes, to cell phones, to texting as ways to communicate. The move from muscle to microchip, from industrial manufacturing to an information/service economy, has changed everything. Our medical technology, education, food, business, international relations, politics, and economics—everything has changed.

---

24 This mass, which by Einstein's mass-energy relation $E=mc^2$ is released as energy, is known as binding energy. The Sun and other stars use this process of nuclear fusion to generate thermal energy, which is later radiated from their surface.

This increase in the pace and depth of transformation is sometimes called *the rate of accelerating returns*. It points to the exponential nature of new growth and new possibility. Truly getting the idea of exponential growth is a hugely powerful realization. To illustrate the concept, teachers often use a classic Indian legend of chess and seeds of grain.

The legend tells of a game of chess between the local king and Lord Krishna himself. In the Hindu religion, Krishna is one of the forms in which Spirit or God appears in human guise. The king was a big chess enthusiast and had the habit of challenging wise visitors to a game of chess. One day a traveling sage—Krishna in disguise—was challenged by the king. To motivate his opponent, the king offered any reward that the sage could name. The sage modestly asked just for a few grains of rice, but he did so in the following manner: if he won the chess match, the king was to put a single grain of rice on the first chess square and double it on every following one.

Having lost the game and being a man of his word, the king ordered a bag of rice to be brought to the chess board. Then he started placing rice grains according to the arrangement: 1 grain on the first square, 2 on the second, 4 on the third, 8 on the fourth and so on. Following the exponential growth of the rice payment, the king quickly realized that he was unable to fulfill his promise because on the twentieth square the king would have had to put 524,288 grains of rice. On the fortieth square, the king would have had to put 549,755,813,888 grains of rice. And, finally on the sixty-fourth square, the king would have had to put 9,223,372,036,854,775,808 grains of rice, or about 659 billion US tons. It was at that point that Lord Krishna revealed his true identity to the king and told him that he didn't have to pay the debt immediately but could do so over time. That is why, according to legend, pilgrims in Indian temples are fed rice, called *Paal Payasam*. The king's debt is still being repaid.

In the arena of relationships, the core structure of Reality itself, evolution is accelerating exponentially, as the grains on the chess board. Everything is changing.

The snapshot of the evolution of relationships in which we are engaged in this book is but a snippet of the evolution of relationships that has been the plotline of the evolutionary story since the first nanoseconds after the Big Bang.

Role mate relationship was the primary form of relationship for two hundred thousand years.[25] The first glimmerings of soul mate relationship appeared only relatively recently in evolutionary history. It is only in the last few decades that it has become the fundamental form of relationship in the Western world. Now, within our lifetime, relationships are undergoing their next great evolution.

The inherent creativity—or LoveIntelligence, LoveBeauty, and LoveDesire—of Reality self-organizes from within to evolve and transform relationships. Each new challenge, every crisis, is an evolutionary driver that gives birth to new possibilities. New and momentous leaps emerge out of the Field of pure Potentiality. While it may have taken several million years for single-celled organisms to make the leap to multicellular organisms, everything is changing much faster now. New and never-before-dreamed-of possibilities for relationship are being born in this very time that we live.

Entry 12. Conscious Evolution

The story of evolution was not available to human understanding in previous generations. Evolution is finally awakening to itself, as a part of the emergence of *Conscious Evolution*.[26] This does *not* mean that evolution first becomes conscious in us. It *does* mean that we awaken to the realization that evolution is conscious *in us*, in at least two distinct forms:

---

25 Of course, throughout history, the roles themselves were very different than the roles in the relatively recent form of role mate relationship, which we talk about in this book.

26 See Chapter 8, "Evolutionary Impulse at the Heart of Evolutionary Relationships," Entry 8, for a more in-depth discussion of Conscious Evolution.

- We realize that the evolutionary impulse moves *in us*, *as us*, and *through us*.

- For the first time in human history, we are able to feel, sense, and know the evolutionary story from matter to life to the depth of the self-reflective human mind.

We become aware of the evolutionary story and become the storytellers, even as we realize that we are also both the authors and actors in the next chapters of the story.

All stories have plotlines, and the evolutionary story is no exception. A key plotline of this story is the evolution of relationships. Conscious Evolution in this sense means that we are finally awakening to the evolution of relationship—the animating Eros of the Universe Story itself.

To recapitulate:

- Reality is Relationship.

- Allurement is the core feature of Reality; it is its fundamental nature. It is one expression of what we usually call *love*. Love, therefore, is the force that binds atoms, molecules, cells, plants, animals, mammals, and ultimately human beings. Relationship is the exterior structural expression of the interior drive to love.

Now consider this:

- At each level of relationship and evolution, the depth of the bond, the awareness of the bond, and the pleasure and delight of the bond evolve to higher and deeper levels. Relationships seek deeper and deeper forms of intimacy and love.

- There is a crisis in human relationships, a breakdown in love's inherent drive to bond and evolve.

- Evolution, or Reality, responds by evolving relationships and therefore evolving love.

- The evolution of relationships and love catalyzes the entire evolutionary process, which resolves the current crisis.

When we use our own lives to evolve our relationships or, even more dramatically, to evolve *through* our relationships, we participate directly in the evolution of love. Isn't that amazing? All of Reality depends on the evolution of relationships.

PART ONE

—

THE THREE LEVELS OF RELATIONSHIP

—

CHAPTER 2

ROLE MATE

All three levels of relationship have *telos* and Eros. *Telos* is the purpose of the relationship, and Eros is the quality of love, aliveness, and allurement in the relationship. The *telos* of role mate relationship is to survive. Its Eros is also enmeshed with survival. Role mates find and love those who can help them survive and thrive. The *telos* of survival virtually always trumps the Eros of intimacy. Effectiveness and function, not love and connection, are the key factors in determining the goodness and success of role mate relationships.

Entry 1. Mars and Venus: The Essence of Role Mate Relationship

For thousands of years, there has been a clear division of roles between men and women, which we will refer to as *Mars* and *Venus*. Mars was protector and provider, and Venus was homemaker, child-bearer, and nurturer. There was no confusion between Mars and Venus. There was no move toward androgynous identity. There was a potent and clear, even if limited, sense of what it meant to be man or woman. In role mate relationships, knowing one's role and obligation created a sense of power and purpose.

Role mate relationships were rooted in the dynamics of dependency and obligation. For a long time and in many ways, this dynamic facilitated the achievement of a good life. Men and women could depend on each other to make money, raise healthy and happy children, and respond successfully to challenges and crises. In role mate relationships, men and women needed each other for very clear reasons. Dependency, obligation, and clarity of purpose were the impetus for staying together.

The goal of role mate relationship was the survival and thriving of the couple and the family. That meant different things for different families at different moments in history. There was a time when it meant teaching sons to hunt and daughters to sew. Later it meant sending children to college or to trade school to ensure future success.

In role mate relationships, the emphasis is not on the internal journey of the children or the parents. The general view is that surviving and thriving will take care of everything else. Moreover, the need to focus on surviving and thriving takes up virtually all the energy, with little left for more internal reflections.

In early role mate relationships, men and women played their respective roles to ensure survival, which was a very physical affair. Initially, in the early prehistoric times, it meant not getting eaten within the next fifteen minutes. As society evolved, time became more expansive. The purpose of survival expanded to a day, a week, a month, and into years and decades. By the time farming emerged, the goal became to survive for the full biological span of a lifetime. Role mate relationships supported that outcome.

For a long period of time, the dynamics of dependency facilitated much of the good that was born of both life and civilization. Men and women—Mars and Venus—have needed each other for very obvious reasons. This was the core of the old relationship deal. It lasted in various iterations throughout recorded history—that is, until this time. The old love story between men and women was designed to ensure survival. It is only very recently that the old relationship deal was upgraded and ultimately *undermined* at its very core.

Entry 2. Duty, Honor, and Obligation: The First Language of Heroes

There are two ways to describe the evolution of consciousness, which is the evolution of relationships—the evolution of love—in the movement from role mate to soul mate to whole mate. The first is in terms of the developmental trajectory of an individual human living today (*ontogeny*). The second is in terms of the level of historical evolutionary development (*phylogeny*). Scholars of phylogeny and ontogeny—for example,

Habermas—have correctly noted that there are some important parallels between these processes. The evolution of relationships, from role mate to soul mate to whole mate, takes place in both of these vectors, in our individual human evolution and in the evolution of humanity.

Let's first look briefly at phylogeny and then turn to ontogeny.

In the heyday of the role mate relationship, at the dawn of human history perhaps, the stakes were life or death. There was a felt sense of *gravitas* in one's commitments. Being a provider was a matter of duty, obligation, and honor. To fulfill one's obligation was to be a hero. Being a hero meant being a breadwinner, a protector, and a provider. Being willing to risk one's life to protect others was woven into the fabric of life.

The context of role mate relationships was present, immediate, and limited. This is a pretribal era. There is as of yet no tribe and no farming. It is before the massive bands of hunter-gatherers banded together for long seasons, as described by anthropologists David Wengrow and David Graeber.[27] This is the time of the beginning, when groups did not exceed what is called the Dunbar number—about 150 people, who all knew each other and were, for the most part, in intimate, familiar blood relationships—a kind of extended clan family.

This was the age of role mate. Partners were willing to lay down their own lives for each other's survival and the survival of their immediate family and clan, for the 150 who were in their Dunbar family. All members of the small clan were in some real sense role mates to each other.[28]

As their sense of love evolved, their sense of who was in their family widened as well. At the first level of love in role mate relationship, partners risked their lives only for their partners and children and their extended family in the Dunbar number clan. As their families expanded, their love evolved, and they expanded their sense of family to include their larger biological families or tribe. Intimacy, care, concern, and

---

[27] David Graber and David Wengrow, The Dawn of Everything: A New History of Humanity (2021).

[28] This sense of familial intimacy, of course, already shows up to some degree in the animal world, but usually for clan groups that are somewhat smaller. But there as well the mother is ready to lay down her life for her child.

willingness to sacrifice for the other moved from small band to tribe.

Role mate love in the Dunbar tribe, or small band, can be fairly understood as *egocentric love*—within an egocentric circle of intimacy—with the ego being that of the familial group who were all role mates to each other. In the larger tribe, however, love evolved from *ego*centric to *ethno*centric. There was a sense of felt care and concern, and a willingness to risk and even sacrifice for the entire tribe, even if one had no personal connection at all to a distant tribe member. Intimacy was rooted not in direct knowing, but in knowing mediated by allegiance to a shared code and a mystical participation in a common tribal bloodline.

At this point love evolved, and role mate relationships became ethnocentric in their context. Heroes became willing to risk their lives for their entire nation or religion. This expansion of their felt sense of love and caring, expressed as a willingness to sacrifice their lives for a wider circle, is a very big deal. It involved the transformation of identity *and* the evolution of love from egocentric to ethnocentric intimacy, thus extending very broadly the circle of role mates.

Identity transformed, as role mates widened their identities to include their larger circles. Love transformed, as role mates' circle of love expanded and evolved. They now loved more widely and deeply than they had before. Ultimately, however, even in all of those expressions, being a hero meant being a provider and protector who was willing to kill others and lay down his own life to provide and protect. Such was the first language of heroes in role mate relationships.

A second vector in the evolution of relationships, which evolve from role mate to soul mate, takes place in the personal life of an individual human. We trace this evolution in Chapter 3.

Entry 3. The Gifts and Shadows of Role Mate Relationships

Every level of relationship has its gifts and its shadows. In role mate relationships, mutual dependency—the sense of absolute need for one other—created a great deal of good. A sense of potent intimacy arose from depending on each other. When role mates battled for survival side-by-side, the dynamics of need often created a profound depth of closeness. This was one of the gifts of role mate relationships.

Another gift was that it helped partners satisfy some of the needs listed as critical in Maslow's hierarchy of needs. In the healthiest of role mate relationships, partners helped each other and their children meet their needs for physical survival and safety, as well as their needs for love and belonging. In role mate relationships, partners *belonged* somewhere. They had specific roles, and they knew their spouses and families needed them.

However, the gift of belonging also expresses itself as one of the shadows of role mate relationships. Belonging and being loved were not about being profoundly understood, witnessed, and held. They were about belonging and being loved and cared for on the most elemental level—survival. While having their basic survival needs met was obviously important, it was not enough for many role mates. They yearned for more.

Role mate relationships also tended, detrimentally, to ignore the individual. Role mates put the family first, striving to meet obligations and fulfill agreed-upon roles. Because role mate relationship was about supporting the unit and surviving and thriving materially, individuals often felt unmet and unseen. This was the second shadow of role mate relationships.

A third shadow was its potential for manipulation and unhealthy expressions of power. When either or both of the partners felt forced by life circumstances to stay in the relationship, it often became rife with subtle or even overt power struggles. If the power struggle was hidden, manipulation and adversarial power moves became stock in trade. Life often became tumultuous, bleak, and banal.

A dear friend of ours told us a story about his family that perfectly illustrates some of the gifts and shadows of role mate relationship. That's why we are retelling it here:

> In the fifties, when our friend was growing up, his father secretly confessed to his mother that he was having an affair. What had probably started out as a moment of passion gradually became more serious. He asked his wife for a divorce.

His mother loved his father and was deeply hurt. Instead of sharing her tender feelings by showing him how much she loved and needed him, she became strong. In the most loving way she knew, she said, "If that's what you want, then I will give you a divorce. Let's think about it for a month, and then you decide."

Fate intervened when, a week later, his mother discovered that she was pregnant with their seventh child. With this new responsibility, his father decided not to leave her and the family. His mother was very happy. Nothing more was said about his *other interests*. For several years, he continued to have affairs in other cities, but they never talked about it. Role mate triumphed over soul mate.

Though they never divorced, this was a major turning point in their relationship. They continued to love and support each other as husband and wife, but something was missing. They were great role mates in many ways. But the soul mate dimensions that had glimmered when they got married did not last. The loving romance and playfulness of love gradually but inexorably disappeared.

When our friend became an adult, he eventually heard the rumors of his dad's affairs and asked him about it. His response was: *What you don't know can't hurt you.* Even as our friend persisted in asking more questions, his father always said the same. This was the way his father had justified his affairs—he didn't want to hurt his wife and had rationalized that if he was discreet, she wouldn't be hurt.

To some extent, his dad was right. His mother seemed to be OK with his affairs and never broached the subject or asked him to stop. What neither of them knew was that without profound intimacy, they would eventually snuff out the delicate and tender feelings of affection that had attracted them to each other. Like many couples, they mistakenly assumed that it was natural to lose physical attraction and passion after years of marriage.

After his father's death, our friend and his mother came across a snapshot of him with one of his mistresses. When his mother saw it, tears came to her eyes—tears that were not shed when her husband was alive. Our friend knew why his mother was crying. He could feel her pain at seeing his father so open and free with another woman, seeing in his father's eyes the sparkle they had once shared, which had gradually disappeared from their relationship.

Our friend also felt the personal pain of never having seen his dad so happy. He had been a loving father, but often moody, angry, or depressed. In the photograph, in his secret world, he appeared charming, helpful, and happy. This was the father our friend had longed to know and emulate.

When our friend asked his mother why his father had felt the need to stray, she answered: *Your father and I loved each other very much. But as the years passed, I became a mother, and your father wanted a wife.* He was amazed by how accepting his mother was of his father's infidelity. She told him: *I admired your father for staying. It was a great sacrifice on his part. He had strong desires, but he didn't desert us.*

On that day, our friend could finally understand why his father had betrayed her: He had stopped being romantically attracted to her and didn't know what to do about it. He didn't know how to share the responsibilities of a family *and* be romantic. He did not know how to be a role mate *and* a soul mate.

Our friend also realized that his mother had done the best she could. She knew well how to be a loving mother, but she was not adept at the art of keeping romance alive. She was following in the footsteps of her mother and her mother's mother. It was, after all, a different world then, with different rules. She was too busy raising seven children to explore her feelings. Even if she had explored her feelings, she never would have considered sharing her heartaches with her husband, and she likely wouldn't have known how to unburden herself without making him feel controlled or defensive.

When his father decided not to leave, his mother was enormously relieved that the family would stay intact. She, like her female ancestors, put the good of her family ahead of her personal needs. His father also put aside his personal needs and honored his commitment to the family by staying married. That is what role mates did. But, like his male ancestors, his father continued, discreetly, to have affairs.

Despite everything, his mother assured our friend that they loved each other very much, and that they had, in many ways, grown closer through the years.

At that time, similar dynamics took place among millions of couples around the world, in part because the first fragrance of soul mate possibility was in the air. But during the Depression and World War II, role mate survival was more important than the romantic and emotional needs of soul mate. The role mate commitment was so powerful that it virtually always prevailed. That was how it had been for most of time. Being a role mate required a great sacrifice and had its own nobility. Love meant living up to the obligations of the roles and staying married, even if their relationship didn't satisfy them emotionally.

Entry 4. Falling in Love in Role Mate Relationships

What makes us fall in love? The answer is different at each of the three levels of relationship.

For role mates, falling in love involves chemistry and hormones, especially when potent sexual attraction and desire are present.[29] Role mates often meet and fall in love *biologically* (even *chemically*) and marry because society tells them to. Because the goal of role mate relationship is to ensure the continuity of life, *bio-logic* matches make evolutionary sense. However, while this purely hormonal experience is potent and beautiful, it is also, for many, a woefully insufficient basis for forming an enduring relationship.

One name for the powerful force that awakens in role mates when they fall in love is *Evolutionary Love*. It is the drive toward life built into the very structural foundations of Reality itself. Evolutionary Love is the Force of Eros that moves the entire evolutionary process. Falling in love gives a momentary glimpse of Evolutionary Love and stimulates Reality's drive to ever-more relationship and ever-more life.[30] This happens even, and especially, at the most basic level of role mate relationship.

This momentary glimpse of Evolutionary Eros happens in *your* life and in every relationship. It is essential to your survival. When you fall in love, you feel personally addressed by the Cosmos. The great Force of Life needs you. You can't quite articulate it, but you sense that you are playing your role—that finding your partner and having children fulfills something aligned with Reality itself.

Falling in love in a role mate relationship affirms the goodness of Reality in the most potent and powerful way. There are no obstacles that you cannot overcome, for you are awake, even if only for a short time, to the Eros and energy of Evolutionary Love. This energy is always coursing through us, but we are often not aware of it. The potent chemical mix of

---

29 This describes the role mate dynamics of falling in love in a relatively recent period, when arranged marriages and different forms of marrying for the sake of the tribe had already become outdated (compare Entry 6).

30 See Chapter 1, "The Arc of Evolution," especially Entries 2, 4, and 6.

hormones that initiates falling in love is the same elixir that drives all of Reality toward survival and relationship. That's why this *bio-logic* dynamic of love appears at all three levels of relationship. However, it was and is *the driving force* of love in role mate relationships.

When we fall very hard into love, we are sometimes attracted to people whom we actually do not want to share our lives with but who make good evolutionary matches.[31] A strong dynamic of role mate love is the exchange dynamic: each partner seeks someone with whom they can exchange equal value. This dynamic exists at all three levels of relationship. However, at each level, the nature of the exchange changes.

At the role mate level, the exchange revolves around role mate functions, duties, and obligations. It affects the decisions of role mates to fall in love and get married. This point is critical because, even at the role mate level, love does not just *happen*. Role mates are not simply blinded by *bio-logic* love. Their decision to love is also fueled by an image of the partner they seek. Role mates do not fall in love with individuals, per se, but with their partner's skills and capacities to help them and their future family survive and thrive.[32]

Entry 5. The End of Role Mates?

The gifts and shadows of role mate relationships show up and continue differently throughout time and across individual relationships. In some relationships, the darker aspects never emerge or express themselves. For many couples, role mate relationships are, and continue to be, a completely healthy expression.

---

31 During ovulation, for example, women are attracted to men who do not necessarily share their interests or values but who are good evolutionary survival matches.

32 In many cultures there have been times in which marriages were arranged and the partners didn't even know each other before the wedding. At some point, this practice was given up in favor of the initial spark being the attraction between the partners. But even then, people were not allowed to marry every person they felt attracted to. Role mate criteria triumphed over soul mate criteria. And once they were married, they were expected to stay together, after the attraction was gone. All of this changed only very recently.

While the role mate dynamics of dependency and obligation are still in place in many, if not most, relationships, they are not a given, for several reasons. For one, social expectations and gender roles have changed. Men and women do not *have* to marry. In the Western world at least, they can date any number of people and choose to settle down or not. Also, women are increasingly in the workforce, support themselves, and no longer have to depend on men to do so. They can choose to raise children without a father living in the home. Men, meanwhile, can pursue interests other than making a living. They, too, can raise kids, for example. They no longer have to depend on women to provide all of the nurturing in the home.

Despite these and other apparent changes in our social and gender roles, role mate relationships have not disappeared. In the developing world, where survival remains the primary challenge, the role mate relationship is alive and well. It also exists elsewhere. In many if not most families, it is far easier to survive if at least one partner dedicates his or her time to providing an income. Role mate relationships still work for couples who desire to have children and to raise them to be happy, healthy adults. To meet that goal, and to keep at least one partner in the workforce, the other partner typically must become the primary caretaker and nurturer. For most people, even if the idea of a partner as a role mate provides insufficient ground for love, the capacity to be a role mate for their partner is a highly prized and desired quality. Even if this is not the primary driver in the relationship, it remains a pivotal dimension for many.

Role mate dynamics are also revealed in the expression of early parenting roles when the infant's need for the mother strongly influences the roles played by both parents. As we will discuss later, role mate dynamics are apparent in the idea that many women still don't want to *marry down* economically. In other words, they don't want to marry a man who does not play the classic provider and protector role by making money and taking care of business. At the same time, many men still expect women to play the nurturer and caretaker role, even if the women hold full-time jobs. That is why so many working women feel overwhelmed by the double shift of working and nurturing.

While being a role mate is still attractive, required, and prevalent in many ways, it is no longer ultimately fulfilling. Many of us are pushing away role mate relationships in the name of personal satisfaction, independence, and the search for soul mate love. In much of the Western world, it has become politically incorrect and even inappropriate to emphasize the traditional elements of role mate relationships. But the role mate's gifts of mutual dependency and belonging continue to exert an inexorable and potent influence on our lives and love. Role mate relationships will therefore never completely go away. We need certain dimensions of the role mate relationships. We like them. We find them alluring—and allurement is the most fundamental quality of Reality.[33]

Entry 6. Clan of the Cave Bear

Some movies capture—often unbeknownst even to the moviemakers themselves—something of a new sensibility being born. Sometimes they give language and visual form to a deep movement happening at that moment in culture. At other times, they are several years or even decades ahead of their time.

One movie that expresses the origins of role mate relationships is *The Clan of the Cave Bear*, a 1986 film based on the excellent historical novel by Jean Auel. It vividly imagines clan life some twenty-five thousand years ago. Relationships serve the survival of the tribe. The key protagonist, Ayla, is a young Cro-Magnon girl, whose family was destroyed by an earthquake. She wanders until she is close to death, when she is found by Iza, wife of Brun, head of a Neanderthal clan. Ayla is taken in and raised as one of their own.

We learn about the clan's customs, taboos, and ways of relating through Ayla's breaking of the clan's rules. We understand that every member of the clan and all relationships within the clan must serve the survival of the clan. Love is an expression of survival. All mates in the clan are role mates. Relationships are rooted in dependency dynamics.

Even so, allurement and attraction are alive just below the surface in the clan life. However, the notion that attraction and allurement could

---

[33] See Chapter 1, "The Arc of Evolution," Entry 4.

cause a marriage that does not support the survival of the clan is an impossibility. Marriage is never just between the couple. Relationship is always between the couple and the clan itself.

The essence of these core dynamics sometimes shows up in our own lives. For example, dependency sometimes creates significant imbalances in power between men and women. Imbalance of power by itself is not necessarily problematic. But when power imbalances become the grounds for abuse, massive problems emerge.

In the film, Brun's son Broud rapes Ayla. While not approved by the clan, rape does not appear to be forbidden. Her absolute dependency on Broud and the clan, coupled with Broud's willingness to abuse that power, created a horrific act of abuse. The dynamics underlying such abuse have persisted. In the United States, for example, as long as role mate dependency was the primary component in relationship, marital rape was not illegal in many states. Shockingly, the criminalization of marital rape began only in the mid-1970s, and it wasn't until 1993 that all fifty of the United States outlawed it. Not coincidentally, it was during this same timeframe that the move from role mate relationship to soul mate relationship was in full swing.

Entry 7. Living at the Edge: From Role Mate to Soul Mate

The leading edge of one level births the beginning of the next: the leading edge of role mate births the beginning of soul mate, and the leading edge of soul mate births the beginning of whole mate. Healthy role mate relationships are not inherently abusive. They just fail to address our deeper needs.

Role mate love emerges from within the dynamics of dependency. The leading edge of role mate appears when a couple falls in love as a result of fulfilling their roles with integrity and commitment. However, the falling in love is not of the soul mate variety. It is neither the result of early hormonal attraction nor the expansive, based-on-shared-interests, totally-complete-each-other ecstasy of romantic love. It has a quieter, more reserved sense to it.

Role mate love, beyond its *bio-logic* component, is gradual. Often, it does not consciously awaken until years into the relationship. But then at some point, often in response to a crisis, something awakens, and the couple realizes that they love each other deeply. This is the edge of role mate leading into soul mate. The great relationship teachers of the role mate era pointed couples toward soul mate awakening, while encouraging them not to give up their role mate responsibilities.

We can witness the emergence of soul mate from role mate in a story about the famed teacher, Israel, who lived in Eastern Europe in the late eighteenth century. He was wise, mystically attuned, and prone to all sorts of unconventional behavior. With Master Israel, you never knew what to expect, but you also knew that his *insides were lined with love*.[34]

> One Sabbath eve, Master Israel dined with his disciples, as was his custom. He was making the blessing over wine when he suddenly burst into laughter for several minutes. The disciples looked askance, but let it pass. A few minutes later, as he was blessing the bread, he again interrupted the blessing with even more energized laughter. This was beyond strange, but again his disciples, having little other choice, let it pass. At the end of the meal, he once again, for the third time, burst into laughter as he was saying grace, this time more raucously than before. The disciples were quite horrified. After all, it was against the law to interrupt a blessing. But what to do? One dared not question the master.
>
> Saturday evening, at the conclusion of Sabbath rest, two of the master's oldest disciples could not bear it any longer: "You must tell us, Master," they implored, "why did you dishonor the blessings by laughing three times in the middle of their recital?" Master Israel smiled. "Call Alexi," he said. Alexi was the wagon driver who drove Master Israel and the disciples

---

[34] From the Song of Songs, 3:10. The Song of Solomon esoterically describes the ontology of Cosmos as Tocho Ratzuf Ahavah—"Its insides are lined with love." See also Marc Gafni, Chapter 7, in Radical Kabbalah (Vol. 1), 2012.

on their adventures. When Alexi arrived, he loaded into the wagon as many disciples as he could.

They traveled far and arrived at the outskirts of a town called Koshnitz. The horses stopped at a very modest home at the edge of town. It was late, but the master told his assistant to knock at the door. A man and his wife opened the door and were told that the famous Master Israel was there to see them. They went white, and before they could say anything, all the disciples piled into the small home along with the master.

"Tell my disciples, Shabtai [the man of the house], what happened here last night." Shabtai could not imagine how the master knew of the last night's events, but he could not refuse, so he spoke.

"Sarah and I are very poor," he said. "Our marriage was arranged by our parents, and we have done our best to make a living and take care of our children. I am the bookbinder here in Koshnitz, but business has been very bad. In the last months, worse than ever. Friday morning, we had absolutely no money for food or even candles for the Sabbath, and I had nowhere to turn. I was worried that our poverty would humiliate us in front of our community, so I made Sarah promise not to borrow money from our neighbors. Somehow, we would get through this.

"On Friday evening, I went to the synagogue early to pray the Sabbath prayers. I lingered after services, so I could walk home alone. I did not want anyone to accompany me and to see our dark and bare home on this Sabbath eve. But as I approached our house, I saw that it shone with light. As I entered, I smelled the most beautiful aroma. The table was set with a white tablecloth and laden with food.

"I was furious with Sarah. I was sure she had disobeyed me and borrowed money from friends. Before I could raise my voice—which we both did all too often in recent years—I saw to my amazement that Sarah was wearing her wedding dress. Moreover, she had laid out my special tunic that I had last worn at the wedding.

"'What is this all about?' I demanded.

"'My husband,' she said, 'when you left to pray, I had nothing to cook. I was sad, so I began to clean. I came upon the old chest that we had not opened for many years. It held my wedding dress and your tunic. Your tunic had seven gold buttons, about which we had both forgotten. I cut them off and sold them in the market. They were very valuable and brought us food and provisions for the next six months! Please husband, won't you wear your tunic as I am wearing my wedding dress?'

"Nothing remotely like this had ever happened to Sarah or me. I was confused, but I put on my tunic."

"Thank you, Shabtai," said Master Israel. He turned to Sarah. "Please continue the story."

"Well," said Sarah, "we sat to make the first blessing over wine in accordance with law. But in the middle of the blessings, Shabtai looked at me in my wedding dress and began to laugh. 'Come, let's dance,' he said. And so, we danced. And we laughed and danced. We then sat to make the second blessing over the bread. But as Shabtai said the blessing, I could not contain myself. I laughed out loud in a way I never had before, and I said to my husband, 'Come, we must dance.' And so, we danced and laughed again. Eventually, we both sat to eat our meal. We talked and talked throughout the meal in a way we never had before. We both realized, for the first time, that after all these years together, we loved each other. We were so happy to be together. We spoke of our feelings and hurts and tenderness in a way we never quite had before. When it came time to say grace after the meal, neither of us could contain ourselves! In the middle of the blessing, we once again began to dance and laugh like never before. And that," she concluded, "is what happened last night."

Master Israel then spoke. "Thank you both," he said. He then turned to his disciples. "Let me tell you, dear ones, what happened last night. When Shabtai and Sarah started dancing and laughing, the angels on high heard great joy on Earth unlike anything they had heard before. They looked down and saw that the source was this small house where Shabtai and Sarah were dancing and laughing. Their joy was so powerful that the angels stopped singing their praise and began to laugh with them. God became puzzled. Why were the angels not singing their praise? God looked down and saw that the angels were laughing with Shabtai and Sarah. God was filled with joy and laughed along with them. This happened three times over the course of their meal. So, with God and all the heavenly angels laughing, how could I, Master Israel, not laugh with them?"

So ends the story. It is a story about role mates who awaken in a moment of crisis to have a momentous breakthrough. They realize, even without the language to express it, that they were not only role mates but also soul mates.

Entry 8. Evolution Responds to Crisis

As we saw in Shabtai and Sarah's story, the leading edge of role mate birthed the beginning of soul mate. It did so in response to crisis. As we saw in Chapter 1, evolution always has one possible response to a crisis in relationship—the profound and potent evolution of love and consciousness. Soul mate relationship appears when role mate relationship faces a dire crisis.

For all its usefulness and function, the classic role mate relationship was limited, and lovers yearned for deeper intimacy, greater connection, and more personal fulfillment. They longed for a new expression of love that would respond to the crisis of their time.

What was the crisis? In classic role mate relationships, men's and women's individual needs were subservient to those of the family. Having children and a family ensured survival of the family name, family genes, and the human species, but it failed to support an individual's quest for intimacy, self-expression, and purpose. Role mates increasingly craved relationships in which profound connection and the pursuit of authentic fulfillment constituted the core of the relationship. In role mate relationships, the family's capacity to survive and thrive, especially socially and materially, took precedence. As such, role mates typically embraced *till death do us part*, even if one or both partners were deeply unhappy.

In classic role mate relationships, women were often viewed as the property of men, while men were viewed as the hero-servants to women. Children were not an option, but an obligation. Marriage was not an option, but an obligation. Much of life was lived inside a context of mutual dependency, social obligation, and material survival. Role mates were boxed into roles with few other options. While the very best expressions of dependency, obligation, and survival were and continue to be valued and useful, they often veered off into control, social incarceration, and survival at all costs.

Because of these limitations, couples throughout the world yearned for a new expression of relationship.

Evolution answered, as it always does, with a new and powerful context for relating. It shifted relationship consciousness from that of role mate to that of soul mate, dramatically altering the way we loved, made love, played together, and worked together. It required us to reenvision, at the most fundamental level, what it meant to be a partner. It shifted the cultural paradigm of relationship from role mate to soul mate.

Table 1. Role Mate

ROLE MATE

Self	• Separate self
Level of Consciousness/ Intimacy/ Identity	• Egocentric • Ethnocentric
Core Value	• Survival and thriving
Relationship to the Field of Value	• As separate self, role mate does not necessarily experience oneself as part of the Field of Value
Falling in Love	• Social, religious, cultural fit • Chemistry • Exchange of value
Quality of Love	• Ordinary love experienced as a human sentiment or a social construct, even if a beautiful and moving social construct
Characteristics	• Dependency: I need you • Protectiveness • Achievement
Shadow	• Power-plays • Manipulation • Narcissism of one
Language (Key Words)	• Protect • Honor • Sacrifice • Obligation • Duty
Goals	• Personal survival • Thriving of self and family • Fulfillment of obligations
Question	• "What is in it for me?"

CHAPTER 3

SOUL MATE

Evolution leaves nothing behind. The emergence of soul mate relationship transcends and includes the best of role mate. We easily recognize many traits of role mate in today's relationships, yet we also see that something radically different is experienced and expected in soul mate relationships—a deeper level of intimacy and communication, commitment to personal fulfillment and to holding and healing each other's wounds.

Entry 1. Soul Mates Look Deeply into Each Other's Eyes

The second level of Mars and Venus relationships is the soul mate relationship. Throughout history, such relationships have appeared in fits and spurts. As love evolved, emergent expressions pushed relationships beyond the prevailing role mate norms. Many of our parents, and virtually all of our grandparents, experienced role mate relationships. However, over the past forty to fifty years, soul mate relationships have become the norm, the birthright of present-day lovers.

At the soul mate level of consciousness, being a role mate is no longer a sufficient basis for marriage and relationship. For soul mates, the essence of the relationship is about loving each other. Survival takes a back seat and is replaced by passion, romance, and love. Soul mate relationships do not begin when someone finds a partner who would make a socially appropriate or functional role mate; they begin with allurement, attraction, and aliveness.

One aspect of soul mate allurement is rooted in the same impersonal evolutionary force that called role mates together biologically.[35] Soul

---

[35] See Chapter 2, "Role Mate," Entry 4.

mate relationship, however, is intensely personal in an entirely new way. Soul mates look deeply into each other's eyes, and this is what makes life self-evidently worthwhile.

The depth of allurement in soul mate relationship becomes so central and potent that, for many, it becomes the meaning of life. The survival quest is replaced by the journey into love. The journey of relationship itself becomes the holy grail. It would be absurd to leave a role mate, as long as survival was assured and the partners were relatively decent to each other. Not so in a soul mate relationship, which requires not only decency, but also depth of intimacy.

Lack of intimacy is grounds for ending a soul mate relationship. Intimacy means being understood, validated, and held, which has always been particularly important for Venus. Intimacy also means being appreciated, honored, and received—dimensions particularly important for Mars. Lack of true depth in these qualities becomes grounds for divorce in soul mate relationships.

How might this look in daily life?

When a man in a soul mate relationship comes to the point where he says to his pals, *Nothing I ever do for her is enough* or *Nothing I do ever makes her happy*, then the relationship is in dire need of realignment, or it will break down. The man in a soul mate relationship, just like in a role mate one, needs to be a hero. Being a hero at level one meant fulfilling your role. For the level-two man, however, that is not enough to make him feel like a hero. For the level-two man, being a hero must also include making his partner happy.

When the woman in a level-two relationship says, *I just cannot have a conversation with him* or *He just does not listen to me* or *He barely sees me*, then the level-two soul mate relationship is in dire need of realignment, or it will break down. The soul mate relationship demands communication that leads to intimacy and communion. The lack of it is considered self-evident grounds for separation in a way that would be unheard of in a role mate relationship.

Entry 2. Personal Fulfillment and Loneliness

The goal of a soul mate relationship is personal fulfillment. Values like *duty*, *honor*, and *obligation*, especially to one another, are no longer front and center. Soul mates do not focus on fulfilling the roles imposed upon them by society or their partners, and having children is no longer a given. The purpose of the relationship becomes personal satisfaction and the success of the relationship itself. If soul mates do not achieve personal fulfillment through the relationship, the chances of the relationship enduring are slim.

In soul mate relationships, personal fulfillment is achieved, at least partially, because partners seek to liberate each other from loneliness. In role mate relationships, the greatest danger is being alone; in soul mate relationships, simply not being *alone* is not enough. In soul mate relationships, the great fear is *loneliness*.

Whenever I think of loneliness, I am transported back to a Denver hotel room I once visited. The way hotel rooms are set up, at least in the United States, you will usually find a Gideon Bible in a drawer next to the bed. That night in Denver, my suitcase full of books had missed its connecting flight, so there I was, at the hotel, tired and without loved ones or books. I was bereft. A hotel room far from home can be the loneliest place in the world. I turned to the only book in the room.

I was surprised to see a detailed index of how to use the Bible. If you're depressed, it said, read Psalm 19. If you're drunk, read Psalm 38. If you're feeling lonely, read Psalm 23. I was feeling lonely, so I read Psalm 23. "The Lord is my shepherd, I shall not want," the famous psalm began. "Yea, though I walk in the shadow of the valley of death I fear no evil . . ." I read the psalm slowly and carefully, yet I have to admit that I still felt lonely upon finishing. Just as I was about to close the book, I saw a note scrawled at the bottom of the page: "If you're still lonely, call Lola."

Once I recovered from laughing, I had one of those magic moments of grace when everything falls into place. Years of study, thinking, and teaching suddenly crystallized into a few simple and authentic sentences. Those sentences are now the core of this chapter. They capture the lifeblood that courses through soul mate relationship.

I realized that what drives me—and what drives all of us, to a large extent—is **a desire to move from loneliness to connection, from loneliness to loving**. "If you're lonely, call Lola." In soul mate relationships, we are looking for Lola—not the Lola one might beckon to a lonely hotel room, but the soul mate Lola with whom we can assuage our loneliness, and whose stories, fears, hopes, dreams, joy, and pain we can receive and honor.

To be lonely as a soul mate is a completely different experience than being alone as a role mate. To be lonely is to be unable to share the essence of your story with another person. Your story includes your hopes, your fears, and your dreams. It is your silliness and your pathology, your most grandiose self and your darkest self.

Entry 3. To Be Intimate Is to Be Known

In biblical myth, the word for erotic intimacy is *knowing*. To be intimate is to be known. Let me share a story I have told at weddings for many years. I like to imagine that God told this story at the very first wedding. The myth exists in various versions throughout cultures, and it transmits an essential purpose of soul mate relationships: to surmount and transform loneliness.

> There once existed a South American tribe that received its main nourishment from milk. Yet somehow, as happens in the world, the tribe's source of milk dried up one day. The cows, struck by disease, died, one by one. The tribe was left parched with thirst, with no way to meet their need. The famine persisted for three weeks, and many meetings of the elders were held, but no one could come up with a way to restore the supply of milk.
>
> One misty morning, however, after days of intense prayer and fasting, the villagers awoke to see a huge vat of steaming hot milk in the main clearing of the village. They were overjoyed at this gift of the gods, and celebrations ensued. One morning, two mornings, three mornings, the vat kept reappearing, and with bellies full of the divine drink, the villagers continued life, contented.

One eighteen-year-old man from the village was unsatisfied simply to receive the mysterious nourishment. As much as he needed the milk, he also needed the knowledge of where the milk came from. And so, breaking with the village taboo against investigating the miracle, he got up early in the morning and waited. He was not disappointed, for within the purple mists of morning light, he saw the most beautiful maiden he'd ever beheld descend from the heavens and place the vat of milk in the middle of the village.

The young man was overcome by her beauty and smitten immediately with love. The next morning, he returned to watch her, and the third day and the fourth, and by the fifth day, he could endure it no more. He emerged from the bushes, grasped her graceful hand, and said, "I will not let you go until you agree to marry me."

Such a demanding marriage proposal seldom worked in this village or elsewhere in the world, but lo and behold, this divine creature of a woman agreed to marry the young man. She had only one condition, which she would stipulate upon her return from one last journey to her home in the heavens.

She returned from the heavens a day later with enough milk to last a lifetime. Clutched to her heart was a golden box. She agreed to marry the bedazzled young man, as long as he promised never to open the golden box that she had mysteriously brought with her. "For if you do open this," she said with a touch of sadness, "I may very well have to leave."

The man agreed, and this marriage between heaven and earth proceeded wonderfully. The young man and the maiden had children, built a home, and lived happily as the years sped by.

One afternoon, when his wife was away with the children, something snapped in her husband. Overwhelmed with an unquenchable curiosity that had been gradually building for years, he rushed to open the box. He cracked open the creaking lid, slowly, just a sliver, then a slight bit more, until it was fully open. He stared, bewildered, and slammed it shut.

The man's wife returned. (Now keep in mind that women always know what men do while they're not home.) She immediately understood that he had opened the box. She confronted him. "You opened it, didn't you? Now I may have to leave."

"What do you mean, you may have to leave?" the man cried. "Yes, I opened it—of course I opened it—but it was empty!"

"Indeed, I must now leave. I cannot stay," she responded sadly.

"But why?" he asked. "The box was empty! The box was empty!" Shaking her head, the heavenly woman declared, "Don't you see? That is precisely why I must leave. For that empty box was not empty at all. When I took my final journey to the heavens before our marriage, I gathered all the sights, sounds, and smells that were dearest and most precious to me. I gathered my hopes and my dreams, my fears and my memories, all the special moments of my life, and I placed them into that box. And you opened my box and thought that it was empty. That is why I cannot stay."

When someone else opens our box and thinks it empty, *that* is the definition of loneliness. The powerful experience of human loneliness is produced by the sense that another cannot recognize the fullness of our experience—the complexity and diversity of the stuff that fills our box and makes it uniquely ours.

In the life of a role mate, there is not much time to feel into loneliness. If you are continually afraid of not finding your next meal or failing to support your family, avoiding loneliness is not your highest priority. Survival needs trump all others. In soul mate relationships, where survival needs are almost always assuredly met, avoiding loneliness becomes central.

Consider two possible experiences. One is to be misunderstood, misrecognized, and consequently lonely. This marks a failure in soul mate relationship. The other is to be recognized, seen, and known. To move from loneliness to loving is to be received by your beloved, to communicate your essence to your beloved. To give your partner the gift of your presence and to know it has been received is the greatest gift and deepest joy of soul mate relationships. The goal of a soul mate relationship is to be seen and liberated from loneliness.

Soul mates say to each other:

Let's work with our wounds together. Let's be in true love together. Let's listen to each other. Let's really work on our sexuality together. Let's work on our pathologies together. Let's look deeply in each other's eyes and see the beauty in each other. We'll have arguments, but we will work it out together. We were called together, to complete each other. We're soul mates!

Soul mates are all about each other's fulfillment and each other's completion. Soul mates want to hold the depth of each other's wounding. Soul mates witness the depth of each other's beauty. Soul mates find themselves and each other in the eyes of their partner.

Does this sound like role mates? Not at all. This is a wholly different level of relationship.

Entry 4. *Love Story*

The twentieth-century classic film *Love Story*, based on the novel by Erich Segal, beautifully captures soul mate relationship. I remember seeing it when I was a very little boy, a few years after its release. It has been indelibly imprinted on my psyche ever since.

Oliver Barrett IV attends Harvard and is heir to his family fortune. He is emotionally wounded by his relationship with his father, who does not understand him. He meets Jenny Cavilleri, a working-class, quick-witted, and emotionally insightful Radcliffe girl. They fall madly in love.

Oliver's father does not think Jenny makes a good role mate. She comes from a different class and cannot, therefore, play the role of wife. It is the final straw in the already estranged relationship between Oliver and his father. Despite his father making good on his threat to cut him off financially, Oliver and Jenny marry into soul mate bliss. She tells him early on, "Love means never having to say you're sorry."

Tragically, Jenny eventually becomes sick and dies before they can start a family. His father comes to New York and hears that Jenny is ill. He meets his son at the hospital. Oliver says two words to his father, "Jenny's dead." His father replies, "I'm sorry." Oliver repeats Jenny's mantra, "Love means never having to say you're sorry."

Love Story heralded the move from role mate to soul mate in broader culture. It is beautiful, evocative, and filled with poetry and passion. It is not about survival; both Jenny and Oliver would have survived just fine without each other. It is about being seen and recognized. It is about liberation from loneliness.

Oliver's father and upbringing set him on the path of success. Harvard, wealth, a star role on the hockey team, and law school were all dimensions of Oliver's journey. He subscribed, at least in part, to his father's role-mate-inspired vision of success, and, for a while, he played in his father's world.

His father had a role mate relationship with Oliver's mother. But Oliver wanted something more. And that something more captured the yearning of an entire generation. Segal's novel immediately sold five million copies, not because it was a literary masterpiece, but because it gave voice to people's yearning for a new form of relationship. Once the success journey has met our needs to survive and thrive, we need a new, more potent journey. We need *the love journey*.

The love journey is the liberation from loneliness coupled with the feeling of being met, known, and blissfully lost in great love. A potent dimension of the love journey is engagement with one's depths and the sharing of that engagement with one's partner. Each partner enters his or her own depths of psyche and soul. Wounds, trauma, hurt, and fears, as well as dreams, hopes, yearnings, and aspirations, are all on the table.

Through intimate heart-sharing, soul mates engage the depths of each other's most shadowy and brilliant places. Sharing everything with complete transparency is a core dimension of the soul mate relationship. In role mate relationship, transparency and sharing were not required. In soul mate relationship, the lover and beloved share the psychological and emotional journey of self-discovery. Self-discovery becomes the great voyage of intimacy that cannot be taken alone. This quest for self-knowledge, paradoxically, is fully possible only when we are witnessed by our beloveds. This is the soul mate journey into the next level of intimacy—the evolution of love.

Entry 5. *Four Weddings and a Funeral*— from Role Mate to Soul Mate

Four Weddings and a Funeral, the famous late-twentieth-century movie starring Hugh Grant and Andie MacDowell, captures the *ethos* and Eros of soul mate relationships.[36] The entire movie consists of Hugh Grant and his group of friends showing up at each other's weddings, along with the funeral of the most beloved character in the movie, a wildly alive gay man who celebrates life and dies of a sudden heart attack. Here is the opening scene where Charles, the best man, played by Hugh Grant, offers a toast to his friend's marriage.

---

36 The movie appeared in 1994, just two years after John Gray's book Men Are from Mars, Women Are from Venus was published into the same cultural listening.

Charles: *Ladies and gentlemen, I'm sorry to drag you from your delicious desserts. There are just one or two little things I feel I should say as best man. This is only the second time I've ever been a best man. I hope I did the job all right that time. The couple in question are at least still talking to me.*

Unfortunately, they're not actually talking to each other. The divorce came through a couple of months ago.

But I'm assured it had absolutely nothing to do with me. Apparently, Paula knew that Piers had slept with her younger sister before I mentioned it in the speech.

The fact that he slept with her mother came as a surprise, but I think was incidental to the nightmare of recrimination and violence that became their two-day marriage. Anyway, enough of that. My job today is to talk about Angus, and there are no skeletons in his cupboard. Or so I thought.

I'll come onto that in a minute. I would just like to say this. I am, as ever, in bewildered awe of anyone who makes this kind of commitment that Angus and Laura have made today. I know I couldn't do it, and I think it's wonderful they can. So anyway, back to Angus and those sheep.

So, ladies and gentlemen, if you'd raise your glasses. The adorable couple.

Charles's toast is to the *adorable couple*, which pretty well captures the movie and level-two relationships in most of their expressions. The couple is in love. They are adorable. They are not quite sure why they are together. There is still a lot of role mate mixed in with soul mate.

The ideas that you marry and have a partner, that the man is still the primary breadwinner, and that the woman is holding the feminine pole are all very much in place in the movie. It is crystal clear that none of the weddings are, in any sense, evolutionary relationships. The relationships do not have a shared horizon that attracts both partners. There is no sense of shared vision or core values that transcends the adorable couples themselves.

The movie is rife with a sense of the inevitable, unconscious, and sometimes even banal nature of so many level-two relationships. As such, the only redemptive move the movie can make revolves around seeking ever-more dramatic forms of soul mate relationship. This is accomplished by Charles and Carrie falling in love at first sight but being unable to admit it to each other. She continues her natural life trajectory and marries a man who is a natural role mate for her. She divorces soon after she realizes the relationship does not fill her true yearning for soul mate love.

Carrie does not tell Charles of her divorce—they have, after all, never even fully admitted their love for each other to themselves. Moreover, he is a less appropriate role mate than the man she married. He is less successful and less powerful and, in that sense, is less of a protector and provider. The movie implicitly suggests that giving up a more powerful role mate for a somewhat less powerful role mate was about as far as she could go. The idea of marrying someone who is only a soul mate and not a role mate does not even arise as a possibility.

Carrie shows up shortly after her divorce at his wedding to a natural role mate partner. He is about to announce his love in vows at the altar, almost out of cultural habit. Literally right before the wedding begins, she tells him she is divorced and therefore free. He is thrown into a vortex of confusion and, while standing at the altar, he declares—in a delightful mix of comedy and *pathos*—that he loves another. His bride promptly decks him.

By the end of the day, there is a happy end. Charles and Carrie have declared their love and joined their souls in humorous but till-death-do-us-part commitment. The primary message in the movie is that the most compelling relationship narrative is being so totally in love that you are willing to stand down from the wrong wedding—a habitually imposed role mate wedding—and stand up for your soul mate, even if it means public humiliation and a black eye from the jilted bride.

Entry 6. The Soul Mate Mantra

The mantra of level-two relationships is most certainly *I love you*. In the mid-1960s, the famous play *Fiddler on the Roof* premiered on Broadway. Perhaps its most popular and poignant song was *"Do You Love Me?"*—a conversation between Tevye and his wife, Golde. Role mate relationship was all they knew. But within their role mate relationship, a new kind of love grew. The song debuted precisely as the transition from role mate to soul mate began to go viral in the heart of Western culture. The song begins when Tevye tells Golde that he has given permission for their daughter to marry a man who is obviously not an appropriate role mate.

> *Tevye*: *I have decided to give Perchik permission to become engaged to our daughter Hodel.*
>
> *Golde*: *What??? He's poor! He has nothing, absolutely nothing!*
>
> *Tevye*: *He's a good man, Golde. I like him. And what's more important, Hodel likes him. Hodel loves him. So what can we do? It's a new world . . . a new world. Love. Golde . . . do you love me?*
>
> *Golde*: *Do I what?*

Golde does not understand the question. What is he asking? This is not a language he has ever used. This is not part of the role mate conversation. The question is so foreign to her, she thinks he must have indigestion. She tells him to go and lie down.

> *Tevye*: *Do you love me?*
>
> *Golde*: *Do I love you? With our daughters getting married . . . and this trouble in the town. You're upset, you're worn out. Go inside, go lie down! Maybe it's indigestion.*
>
> *Tevye*: *Golde, I'm asking you a question. Do you love me?*

Golde: *You're a fool.*

Tevye: *I know, but do you love me?*

Golde still does not understand Tevye's question. Why talk about love now? Why introduce a soul mate relationship? *I have fulfilled all the roles that a wife fulfills in every way that I could. Why are you asking me about love in this new way, in a way that I do not understand?* And out of this conversation, they go to a territory that they have never visited before. They go to a territory of vulnerability.

Golde: *Do I love you? For twenty-five years, I've washed your clothes. Cooked your meals, cleaned your house, given you children, milked the cow. After twenty-five years, why talk about love right now?*

Tevye: *Golde, the first time I met you . . . was on our wedding day. I was scared.*

Golde: *I was shy.*

Tevye: *I was nervous.*

Golde: *So was I.*

Tevye says his parents told him that even if he and Golde did not know each other or love each other when they met, over the years love would grow. But now Tevye is seeking a different quality of love, something cut from a different cloth than perhaps even his parents knew. In some sense, they are having the conversation about love languages. She says, *I have done acts of service for you constantly over twenty-five years.* He says, *I know. But I would like to hear your words of affirmation. I would like to hear you say, I love you.*

In a soul mate relationship, saying it *matters* and saying it in the right love language matters a lot. Of course, Tevye and Golde are not quite in a level-two soul mate relationship. They are role mates who gradually fell in love without ever quite realizing it. The catalyst for their love was their lived life together. And one day, twenty-five years later, they realized, we love each other—not just in the old role mate sense, but in a new way. That is what Tevye means when he says at the outset of the dialogue, "It's a new world, Golde. Love. A new world."

> *Tevye*: But my father and my mother said we'd learn to love each other, and now I'm asking, Golde, do you love me?
>
> *Golde*: I'm your wife.
>
> *Tevye*: I know. But do you love me?
>
> *Golde*: Do I love him? For twenty-five years, I've lived with him, fought with him, starved with him. Twenty-five years my bed is his. If that's not love, what is?
>
> *Tevye*: Then you love me?
>
> *Golde*: I suppose I do.
>
> *Tevye*: And I suppose I love you too.
>
> *Both*: It doesn't change a thing. But even so, after twenty-five years, it's nice to know.

Entry 7. Venus and Mars: New Yearnings, New Expectations

Since the late 1960s, a huge social shift has been taking place. Large swaths of society have moved *en masse* from level-one role mate relationships to level-two soul mate relationships. They are not yet part of the new deal; they are not yet beyond Mars and Venus.

Relationships built exclusively on level-one consciousness were fundamentally challenged starting in the mid-to-late 1960s. New desires and demands were made of relationships even as the old deal remained in place. Well into the '90s and beyond, even as the old deal was beginning to show cracks, its essential qualities were much in force. This is something Barbara felt deeply in her own life:

> I was married in 1951, straight out of Bryn Mawr College, and began to have babies. The cultural mandate for educated women at that time was basically, get married, have as many babies as possible, and take good care of your husband and house.
>
> My marriage was a combination of role mate and soul mate bordering on a partial whole mate relationship. I served my husband as role mate, fully being his wife and mother of five. He was the master of the house, and a Victorian! For example, when I hired a cleaning woman early in our marriage, he said imperiously, "I don't want cleaning women in my house!" I fired her and did the cleaning myself.
>
> I loved him and fully accepted the cultural dictate of the '50s. The fact that neither motherhood nor housecleaning were my natural impulse or vocation did not matter. At that time there was little emphasis on finding life purpose. Even at a good college, there was no emphasis on what we are really born to do, only what degree we want, or what job we would like.
>
> I wrote constantly in my journals, to see if I could find deeper meaning in my life. Though I had an abiding love for my children, as well as my husband, the fact was that being wife and mother was not my vocation. It was not until depression set in that I had to take new action . . . but at that time, I did not know even what I was looking for.

Meanwhile, in the soul mate component of the relationship, I was his soul mate, but he was not mine. I was his muse, taping his dialogues, editing his books, serving him wonderful French cooked dinners. I believed fully in his effort to find the new Story and never imagined that I would be equally involved. The whole mate component was one-sided, to say the least. I was the editor and producer of his books and the promoter of his work. He made me promise never to publish my journals because they had quotes from him in them that he needed to get first credit for.

One day while he was giving a talk, I was standing behind a tree crying.

"What's the matter?" he asked, concerned.

"I want to speak too; I have something to say," I cried, sobbing as though it was a terrible insult to him.

He was crestfallen and said: "I'm the genius; you're the editor. I can't make you happy."

"That's true," I said miserably. "No one can make another person happy."

It felt to both of us like some serious failure had happened. And that was true.

It was the beginning of the end of my twenty-year marriage as role mate and partial soul mate. My desire to speak and be heard could not be suppressed. I began to feel that my mission was calling to me. But I had no soul mate or whole mate, so I set forward in the 1970s, taking my five children to Washington, DC, to form *The Committee for the Future*.

This brilliant work partner became jealous, fearful that I would leave him for another. It was a disaster to the relationship. His jealousy grew into an obsession and destroyed what was so good in our relationship.

When I asked Gay Hendricks many years later, "What happens to men when women are vocationally aroused?" he said, "It is very difficult for men; they don't like it."

This has been true for all the men who loved me . . . until I encountered a whole mate. For as we shall see, a whole mate loves your purpose and finds that it reinforces and expands his own.

It turned out in my own journey of so many years that the key next step after the depression in my marriage and divorce was to find vocation, life purpose, Unique Self Expression. Until that occurred, I would not be ready for the whole mate relationship. As a teacher of Conscious Evolution in spiritual and social expression, I have found that many women, especially those over fifty with a high degree of life purpose, do not quite dare to express their full vocational arousal for fear of wounding and alienating the men they love. Because it so often does really hurt the relationship.

John Gray's book *Men Are from Mars, Women Are from Venus* was intended to give the old deal the best upgrade possible. When it was published in 1992, the old deal was not yet off, but new dynamics and expectations in relationship had come into play. The new expectations were for deeper intimacy, better communication, sexier passion, and mutual understanding. As is always the case in the evolution of consciousness, interior and exterior factors came together to produce transformation. The first cracks in the dependency relationship of role mates started appearing. With the proliferation of the birth control pill, sex and procreation split. Women demanded a bigger and more intense experience of life. The stifling of creativity and expression in the postwar 1950s exploded in the feminine desire for expression, Eros, autonomy, and creativity. The desire for love and depth flooded through the heart of the American sixties, whether on liberal college campuses or in the heartland.

By the time *Men Are from Mars, Women Are from Venus* was published, women had begun to work actively outside the home helping to support their families. Women were powerfully accessing a new sense of autonomy and power. Women now wanted from their partners a completely different level of intimacy and communication than had been typical in earlier generations. But of course, it was not just women. Men craved greater depth and greater intimacy too.

Men felt boxed in by their roles just as women did. In the '60s, men were seeking to redefine masculinity. Men wanted, as they have from time immemorial, to meet women in their deepest desire.[37] Women were demanding that relationships evolve from role mate to soul mate. Men were driven not only to meet women, but also to meet their own yearning for something more than the painful constriction of their old roles. Men did not want to stop being protector and provider, but they also wanted something more. The image of the protector hero also took a significant hit in the 1960s. In the United States, a key catalyst was the Vietnam War, which did not have the clarity of World War II, when soldiers were heroes in popular culture. While that was also true for some soldiers of the Vietnam War, many were labeled as war criminals, while draft-dodgers were considered heroes. By the 1990s, men felt an inchoate sense of joy after being freed from their constricted roles. Most men were excited to meet their lovers and partners in deeper intimacy. They, too, craved deeper love.

Books like *The Liberated Man* and *Why Men Are the Way They Are*, by Warren Farrell, gave expression to the larger, inarticulate yearning in men for this new level of relationship. Like women, they craved the move from role mate to soul mate.

---

37 We have already mentioned Darwin's insight that the desire of men to meet women's yearnings is one of the core drivers of the evolutionary process. Together with Alfred Wallace, he called it sexual selection (see Chapter 1, "The Arc of Evolution," Entry 2).

Entry 8. From Commitment to Communication

Communication is the key to radical transparency and deep sharing in soul mate relationship. In the role mate world, good communication skills were not part of a partner's job description. A woman felt honored not because her man validated her, but because he went out and risked his life in the hunt to bring back food. As providers, men naturally felt loved and appreciated by women. Women were proud of men's sacrifice. Meanwhile, men revered women as life-givers and homemakers. What we now call great communication skills were not on the list for a desirable mate.

For most soul mates, fulfillment, intimacy, and lasting passion are the highest priority. The assumption here is that none of these will be achieved without strong communication. The soul mate, therefore, strives to improve communication skills in order to meet these other needs.

Today, marriage is not a requirement for survival. Rather, it is a freely chosen enterprise, built on the desire for personal fulfillment. In role mate relationships, men and women lived in separate spheres and naturally completed each other. Their communication consciousness was appropriate for the role mate level. In soul mate relationships, communication consciousness is very different. Communication is connected to subtle and nuanced emotional needs.

Three essential books powerfully addressed the new, level-two yearning for communication. They were, in the order of publication, *Getting the Love You Want*, by our friend and colleague Harville Hendrix (1988); *The Five Love Languages: How to Express Heartfelt Commitment to Your Mate*, by Gary Chapman (1992); and *Men Are from Mars, Women Are from Venus: A Practical Guide for Improving Communication and Getting What You Want in Your Relationships*, by John Gray (1992). Each of these books expressed and guided the culture's desire to move from role mate to soul mate relationships.

Even the titles of these books teach us a lot about what it means to be a soul mate. The first book, *Getting the Love You Want*, indicates clearly that you can be in a functional relationship that enables you to survive and thrive but still not *get the love you want*. The book focuses its most popular section on ten powerful communication exercises that couples can do together.

Chapman's book on love languages is about communication as well. Language is our core tool of communication. As soul mates, we not only need the material currency of love, but we also need the *languages of love*. The title also points to the kind of commitment level-two relationships command: *heart commitment*. The commitment of level one is not enough. But even *heart* commitment is not enough. To engage in soul mate relationships, we need to *feel* the commitment. Our commitment must be, as the title says, *heartfelt*. Moreover, we must be able to *express* heartfelt commitment.

The book made the simple but powerful point that people have different love languages and that, in order to feel seen, recognized, and met by our partners—the essence of soul mate relationship—we must speak the language of love in a way our partner understands.

The five love languages are:

- **Words of Affirmation:** For example, "Thanks for putting the kids to bed."

- **Gifts:** For example, flowers, gifts at special events, tickets to a concert, buying dinner.

- **Acts of Service:** For example, doing the dishes, taking care of the baby in the middle of the night, or getting done items on the family to-do list.

- **Quality time:** Time for presence without distraction, like taking a walk, or watching a movie, or vacationing together.

- **Physical touch:** Sexual or nonsexual, including hugging, holding hands, massage, back scratching, and all forms of kissing and sex and more.

If one partner's love language is gifts and the second one's love languages is words of praise, then they will not understand each other. Both will feel *unseen* and hence, at level two, *unloved*. Neither will get the love they want. At level two, not getting the love you want is a reason to leave. Love language—knowing it and deploying it—is not a role mate function, but a new level of intimacy that, while present in some role mate relationships, was not seen as a requirement. When it existed, it was wonderful, but it was not the bedrock of the relationship.

This is no longer the case at the soul mate level of relationship. Identifying your partner's love language and practicing it is presented in the book as essential to the existence of the relationship itself.

The third major book was the number one best-selling self-help book of all time: *Men Are from Mars, Women Are from Venus: A Practical Guide for Improving Communication and Getting What You Want in Your Relationships*, written by our dear friend John Gray. Again, note the title. It is a practical guide for improving communication. Without communication, we cannot get what we want in relationships.

For the fifty million people who bought the Mars and Venus book, this upgrade was essential to their operating system for relationships. It showed that men and women not only communicate differently, but also think, feel, perceive, react, respond, love, need, and appreciate differently. The image of Venus and Mars helped people get this in a deep way by suggesting that men and women almost seem to be from different planets. In so many ways, they speak different languages and need different nourishment. This expanded understanding of our differences has helped resolve much of the frustration in dealing with and trying to understand the opposite sex.

Misunderstanding could be quickly dissipated, easily resolved, or altogether avoided by embracing Mars and Venus principles. When you remember that your partner is as different from you as a person from another planet, then you can relax and love the differences instead of making them wrong. Once you stop feeling offended, disrespected, not appreciated, or invalidated in a relationship, the space for love expands. The book pointed out the differences in key technologies of loving and relating. For many readers, it created love and relationships that were deeper than they ever thought possible. It helped people understand each other and move from role mate to soul mate relationship.

If we had to sum up *Men Are from Mars, Women Are from Venus*, we would say that it was about disentangling *intent* and *impact*. The two phenomena are often conflated. What that means is very simple. If you say something or fail to say something in a way that seems hurtful, invalidating, or even insulting, I assume that this *impact* was your *intention*. That is, I believe that you intended to hurt me, invalidate me, or insult me. The Mars and Venus book taught people how to disentangle intent and impact.

In the traditional image of Mars and Venus, when a man comes home after work, he is often filled with stress. He needs transition time. For transition time he often goes into his cave. That may have a negative impact on this wife. She feels unseen, fears of abandonment might be triggered, or she might just feel ignored and dishonored. She automatically conflates intent and impact. She thinks, *Since this impacted me in a certain way, this must have been his intention.* The conflation of intent and impact creates a downward spiral of UnLove, which all too often does not end well.

Entry 9. Falling in Love as Soul Mates

There are two major drivers at play when soul mates fall in love. The first driver is dominant in role mate relationship and secondary in soul mate relationship. The second driver is barely existent in role mate relationships and dominant in soul mate relationships.

The first driver, as we saw earlier, is *biologic* in origin and often referred to as *chemistry*.[38] The chemistry between role mates can be truly powerful. The beloveds are flooded by a cascade of hormones that all say the same thing: this is a good evolutionary match for surviving and producing children. She is a good child-bearer and homemaker, and he is a good provider and protector. This quality of love animates role mate *and* soul mate relationships.

The second driver has a very different quality and animates soul mate relationships. It is often described as the desire to complete unfinished business with early caretakers. People are attracted to others who match a combined image of their early caretakers. That combined image, often

---

38 See Chapter 2, "Role Mate," Entry 4.

referred to as *imago*, may be strongly colored by mother, father, or both. It might also be colored to various degrees by other prominent early caretakers.

Our friends and colleagues, Harville Hendrix and his wife, Helen LaKelly Hunt, call this dynamic *the Imago Theory of relationships*. It derives from an understanding of the reptilian brain, which is sourced deep in evolutionary history and holds a precise recording of every encounter you've ever had. These recordings become the composite imago picture of your interactions with mother, father, and other primary caretakers who played prominent and powerful roles. Specifically, you hold a precisely imprinted etching of all their negative and positive traits. These imprints drive you to seek a partner who provides a complementary match.

The people with whom we fall in love might have our mother's negative traits, or they might have the opposite of our mother's negative traits. This is why we often notice our partners doing things *just like my dad* or *just like my mom*. Or we might notice that they do things exactly the opposite of Mom or Dad.

When a person falls in love with someone who either resembles or is the opposite of their imago, they are often driven to close the gap between themselves and the early caretaker, or to rebel against and gain distance from the early caretaker. In both instances, falling in love is a reaction to mother and father, a reaction that leads us to seek greater intimacy or greater distance. In either case, the person is driven by an unconscious reaction to their imago. This unconscious pull toward another is one of the key ingredients that causes soul mates to fall in love. This is the natural quality of falling in love that animates soul mates. While it is also present in role mate relationships, it is not primary nor obvious nor explored. In soul mate relationships, it is front and center.

What all of this illustrates is that the nature of falling in love at the soul mate level, much like at the role mate level, is largely unconscious and reactive. This might be surprising because we generally think of role mate relationships as the ones in which we have little personal choice, while soul mate relationships give us more space for conscious choice. To the extent that our pressing survival challenges are resolved, there is much truth in that. However, choice is also somewhat limited in soul mate relationships. For soul mates, the unconscious drivers toward love are connected to personal fulfillment, and we use our relationships to complete unfinished business in our close family circles. Hence, we find our *imago* in our soul mate partner.

Let's describe these dynamics a bit more precisely. There is a certain quality that exists in the relationship that we had with our parents and therefore evokes a sense of familiarity. Naturally, we look for that quality when we seek our partners. Whether we are drawn toward or pushed away from that quality, we are almost always unconsciously reacting to it. What Harville and Helen discovered in their early studies is that the reason we are attracted to that quality is not just because of familiarity. Rather, it is because we want to heal our early wounds. This type of explanation strikes a resonant chord with soul mate consciousness, which views intimate relationships as a crucible for healing early wounds.

In soul mate relationships, we fall in love with our partners because we feel like we have known them forever. They feel familiar and intimate to us. This is because they *are* familiar to us. We grew up with them. We might also feel safe with them because they do not embody the traumatic characteristics of our early caretakers. However, the Imago Theory, taken alone, is not enough to explain the selectivity we demonstrate in falling in love. To really get the precision and selectivity of falling in love, we need to add something more, an entirely fresh and more powerful perspective. That is what we will share when we get to the level-three evolutionary whole mate relationship.[39] This beyond-Mars-and-Venus level of relating includes the best elements of the old deal and births something undeniably new and emergent. To go beyond Mars and Venus, you must become even more of what you already are, plus something greater!

Before we explore that momentous transition to whole mate, we must delve more deeply into the nature of soul mate relationship and the crisis that soul mate relationship is not able to overcome—triggering the emergence of whole mate.[40]

---

39 See Chapter 10, "Evolutionary Relationships: A New Vision Emerging," Entry 7.

40 Supplementary Essay 1 offers a deeper conversation on how soul mate relationships thrive.

CHAPTER 4

LIMITATIONS OF SOUL MATE

As relationships evolve, every next level aims to fulfill a new set of expectations. In many ways, these are formed in response to the limitations of the previous level of relationship. Consider the shift from role mate to soul mate. Over the last several decades, in response to the painful constriction of their old roles, women demanded a bigger and more intense experience of life, and men yearned to meet women in their deepest desire. Men craved a redefining of masculinity, and women asked for the same regarding femininity. The new expectations for deeper intimacy and better communication illuminated the limitations of role mate relationships and came to define the soul mate experience. Yet, despite all its beauty, the soul mate experience is not without its shortcomings. Soul mates' drive for intimacy and communication is often hampered by a handful of important limitations.

Entry 1. The Limitations of *I Love You*

The felt sense of being in love has become the hallmark of the soul mate relationship. It is central to our sense of having a successful life. However, despite its immense beauty, soul mate relationship is no longer enough to get the depth of love we truly want. It's fair to say that in our generation, we have embraced Aphrodite, the goddess of love, patron of the soul mate relationship. Virtually all of our sacred creeds and dated dogmas are long forgotten, except one: *I love you*.[41] Submersed in that felt

---

41 The story we live in is the inescapable framework of our lives. The old story of premodernity was a religious story in which every religion was in a win/lose metric with every other religion, each one claiming to have the only divinely revealed rule

sense of love is the one place where most of us still feel a primal sense of larger meaning and even transcendence. For example, as the horrors of September 11 unfolded, people facing death found time for one phone call. They all uttered virtually the same sacred credo: *I love you*. What we really value and hold precious always reveals itself in the shadow of the valley of death.

But here is the truth that people are afraid to speak: for many of us, this sacred creed has lost its luminosity as an organizing principle in our lives. Soul mate love, the love we have spent the last several decades idolizing, seems to have diminished in its power to guide us to the fulfillment we yearn for. Saying *I love you* has become banal and desiccated. The words have become tepid and worn, their power made flaccid by tedium. The once-nurturing balm of *I love you* has lost much of its healing power. When our sacred words lose their power, the center does not hold. **We need a new and more potent vision of what it means to say *I love you*.**

The feeling of love has ceased to be a home in which we can fully and predictably rest. One day we feel love; the next day we do not. We are struck by Cupid's arrow, and we fall in love, and then, some years later, our partner is struck by Cupid's arrow, and he or she falls in love with someone else. Love seems so terribly unreliable. We are struck by love, blindsided by love, bowled over by love, and slain by love. Love is always something that happens *to* us. We seem to have no part in its activation, and we easily fall victim to its fickleness. At any moment, our partners can tell us, *I am sorry, but I am just not feeling it anymore*, and the relationship is over. The court of love, governed by the laws of soul mate relationship, gives us no recourse or avenue of appeal.

When soul mate relationship first exploded in our hearts and culture,

---

book for salvation. Modernity rejected that story and instead spoke in terms of universals—an approach that united all people, but its mainstream thinkers also deconstructed value and spirit as being mere human contrivances. The new story replacing the religious story was the success story: rivalrous conflict governed by win/lose metrics where the goal was to be successful, which means not merely accomplishment in economic, intellectual, artistic, athletic, or even spiritual forms, to name but a few, but cashing in on accomplishment through public recognition, status, and material gain. This version of the success story was, however, felt to be insufficient, so it was complemented by culture with the romantic story.

hearing the words *I love you* was the yearned-for destination. There was no goal more worth attaining. *I love you* was the end of the line. The classic romantic movie always ended with some version of *I love you*—a kiss, the hero or heroine riding off into the sunset, the lover expressing regret for leaving. *I love you*, expressed in the context of a soul mate relationship, became the very meaning of life. It was not an extra, as it was for Tevye and Golde.[42] It was the essence of everything, the elixir of existence. Without Jenny, Oliver's life was barely worth living.[43] If you had achieved what appeared to be true love, then you had come home. Your life made sense, and the world was good.

Instead of the soul mate relationship being the best context for living one's life and discovering its meaning, it became the meaning of life itself. **When we make the soul mate relationship the meaning of life, it collapses under a weight it cannot bear.** Soul mate relationship is beautiful and good. It is also, however, incapable on its own of satisfying our deepest desire for creativity, knowledge, meaning, and living a purpose-driven life.

The painful truth is that we no longer know what we mean when we say *I love you*. It used to mean: *I am committed to you! I will live with you forever.* Or: *You are the most important person in my life.* And for a while, that was enough. But for many of us, it is no longer enough.

We are looking for a larger meaning in our lives. We are seeking significance to our lives, and we want our partnerships to aid that search. We want our partnership to serve our larger purpose—to provide great meaning in our lives and to make our lives rich. But being in love, by itself, potent and poignant as it may be, does not answer our deepest yearning for purpose.

Even if we put the issue of purpose aside, the words themselves no longer express the commitment we once thought they did. When we were role mates, we understood the compelling context of our commitment. Our union was dedicated to surviving and thriving as a couple and as family. That was a compelling context.

---

42 See Chapter 3, "Soul Mate," Entry 6.

43 See Chapter 3, "Soul Mate," Entry 4.

But when we lack shared purpose and shared vision, what does *I love you* really mean? It certainly no longer means that we are committed to each other forever. Indeed, many of us say *I love you* without committing to lifelong partnership. So what does it mean? We are not quite sure.

The ancient Greek historian, Thucydides, wrote in his great work *The Peloponnesian War* something to the effect that *when words lose their meaning, culture collapses.* When we no longer understand our own deepest declarations of love, we are lost. Our very foundation of meaning, the words in which we have rested, are undermined.

We have lost our way in love. We have become alienated from soul mate relationships, in which we try so valiantly to find our home. The natural result of our loss is always the same: despair, addiction, and numbness are now our constant companions. We desperately need a deeper context for our relationships.

To sum up:

- Role mate relationships served a larger cause. The cause was to survive and thrive as a couple and family. Surviving and thriving meant different things at different times, but the shared goal made the partnership compelling. The shadow of role mate relationships is that you get lost in the role. Both you and your partner are so intent on fulfilling your roles that you forget about yourselves. The relationship becomes a means to a greater end instead of being the end in itself.

- In soul mate relationships, the relationship is not the means but the end in itself. The measure of successful relationship is the phrase we have all heard: *Is the relationship meeting my needs?* The questions that the relationship must affirmatively answer if is to be considered successful are, *Am I being met? Do I feel loved, validated, understood, and adored?* The obvious shadow of level-two relationships is that it becomes all about *you.* That is both their strength and their limitation.

You might ask: Why is it a limitation? Because here is the wonderful paradox of *you*. You, in the sense of *just* you, your skin-encapsulated ego, as beautiful as you are, are too small a context for your own larger yearning. You in and of yourself, just you, are not big enough to satisfy YOU! Soul mate relationship, as beautiful as it is, just cannot satisfy your yearning to play a larger game.

Entry 2. Passion Dies without Polarity

In level-one role mate relationships, men are men, and women are women. Both have separate, differentiated roles. There is a genuine sexual polarity and attraction between the sexes. They naturally polarize and attract each other because of these very different roles.

Sustained passion must be fed by *polarity*, along with poignancy and presence. In historical role mate relationships, there was often a failure of presence and poignancy in sexuality. There is far more poignancy and presence during relationships at level two, but both Mars and Venus begin to develop their *opposing* polarities. Men begin to develop their feminine essence through listening and emotional literacy. Women begin to develop their masculine qualities in terms of entering the workforce and asserting their autonomy and independence. However, these relationships often have a roommate quality because they lack polarity. **Passion dies without polarity, just as it dies without presence and poignancy.**

We hoped that, with the move from role mate to soul mate, passion and sexuality would come back online. The reasoning made sense. In the founding period of many of the great wisdom traditions, women were known to be powerfully sexual and imbued with desire. Desire itself was seen as holy. At some point, however, desire started getting a bad name. It started under the influence of Plato's otherworldly mysticism and the anticarnal dogmas of the church. In a further antisensual development, a new dogma found its way deep into our cultural psyche. This dogma asserted as fact that men were motivated by sexuality and desire, while women were motivated by tenderness, intimacy, and a desire for children. This assumed asymmetry between men and women did not do much to stimulate sexual satisfaction in role mate relationships. The result of this belief was that for much of the nineteenth and twentieth centuries, role mate sexuality was less than satisfying.

The move from role mate to soul mate relationships was supposed to be the great panacea for sexuality in relationships. As the transition from role mate to soul mate took place, women's sexual desire was recognized and affirmed. Indeed, this reclaiming of feminine desire stimulated, in part, the emergence of soul mate relationship. Another premise of the emergence was that if men could be more sensitive, more present, and more intimate, the rote sexuality of level-one role relationships could elevate and transform.

The assumption of therapists and couples alike was that more communication equals more sexual communion. For a while, this was true. Women claimed the power of orgasm, self-pleasuring, and desire. Men accessed a fuller range of their own sexual natures and learned about delayed gratification, foreplay, and cuddling—or at least staying awake after orgasm. Men began to take pride in fulfilling their woman sexually, and women started asking men to satisfy them. Women's satisfaction became part of the covenant of the soul mate hero.

Many imagined that liberating soul mate intimacy from role mate obligation would be a key to increasing passion and fulfillment in couples. The assumption was that less role mate dependency plus more intimacy and communication would equal more passion in relationship. The model of this triumph of passion in relationships would be the egalitarian couple—or so everyone thought.

In egalitarian couples, neither partner necessarily needs the other to survive or thrive, and both partners have learned the arts of communication and intimacy. Passion, we thought, would thrive when power and its distortions were removed from the relationship. Seeing the other in the full vulnerability of their naked soul would create the passion that all generations had waited for. For some, this worked. For most, it did not.[44]

---

44 In a sense, modern egalitarian couples have been Reality's way to conduct an experiment on the evolution of love, to see how the soul mate relationship would fare without the role mate polarity. We describe it in more detail in Entry 10.

Entry 3. No One Can Make Someone Else Happy

The soul mate relationship is going bankrupt for yet another reason: the metrics by which it is measured. The primary soul mate metric is happiness. *Do I make my partner happy? Does my partner make me happy?* The soul mate relationship has become about balancing that scale. But here is the problem: while you can make a person miserable, you cannot make them happy or even satisfied.

In role mate relationships, partners are content if they fulfill the duties of their role. The husband supports his wife, assures her survival, and provides an appropriate level of comfort and dignity. The wife keeps the home, raises good kids, and partners in whatever ways ensure survival and thriving. Throw in a bit of occasional sex, and satisfaction follows. The success of a role mate relationship is relatively easy to evaluate: houses, cars, clothes, children, regularity of sex, each of which is readily measurable. Measuring our progress toward making someone happy is a far more elusive goal.

The problem runs deeper, however. Making someone happy is not only an elusive goal; it is an impossible one. No one can make someone else happy. You can, of course, *contribute* to someone's happiness, but ultimately, happiness comes from an internal source. True and lasting happiness can never be sourced outside the self. The fatal flaw in the viability of soul mate relationships is that they are based on providing partners with a gift that is impossible to give. That has not augured well for success.

Entry 4. The Narcissism of Two

Soul mate relationship has been such a holy grail that we didn't want to shatter its noble halo of goodness. However, if we truly seek to transform and find joy, we must become iconoclasts and smash our idols. While role mate relationships speak of duty and honor, soul mate relationships speak of personal fulfillment. Often, there is no larger context; the relationship becomes its own purpose, unguided and uninspired by a larger orientation. The core values of the relationship orient around the perpetuation of the relationship itself.

The problem with this is that soul mate relationship devolves very quickly into a sophisticated and stealthy form of narcissism. The hidden agreement is that we are willing to expand our own narcissism to include our partners. We agree that:

> *I want to be happy, and you want to be happy, so we are going to make ourselves happy together. We will watch the right movies. We will figure out what food we like. We will go dancing together. We will take great vacations. We will work on our issues. We will read Rumi together. We will totally commit to each other's happiness and fulfillment.*

Our agreement is fantastic. It is beautiful. It is definitely an important step from role mate to soul mate—but it is terribly stuck in itself.

Sometimes soul mate relationships get confused with therapy. Who feels hurt and who is working through what issues become the central preoccupations of the relationship. The couple circles around the same issues without moving forward. They wallow together in the stories of wounding and victimhood, and they retreat into the very small circle of their relationship. Soul mate relationship becomes a sneaky strategy for avoiding full engagement with the larger invitations of life and love.

For many people, soul mate relationship no longer has sufficient power to generate lasting commitment. It does not speak to their deepest yearning to play a larger game in the world. It does not invite them into significance. Instead, the relationship itself becomes the significance. Relationships and love can either open us to the world or close us to the world. This limitation of soul mate relationships tends to lead toward contraction rather than expansion.

Soul mate relationship marked a crucial movement beyond role mate relationship, but its capacity to create sustained joy, lasting love, and significant shared meaning is limited. Together, we must step into relationships that become a portal to the larger meaning and bigger joy of shared evolutionary purpose. We must move beyond Mars and Venus to what we are calling *whole mate* or *evolutionary relationships*.

Barbara's story continues:

I remember, after my fifth child, loving each of them as a full-time mom, loving my husband, helping him write books, caring for the house, cooking great meals, training the dog, planting a vegetable garden. Yet I got depressed. I felt guilty. Here I was, cared for, loved, loving . . . and depressed. How dare I? *Life, Liberty and the Pursuit of Happiness* is our national mantra, but who was happy in Lakeville, Connecticut? I decided to find out. I went to my friends and asked them if they were happy. The answer was, *Well, sort of, not quite* . . . They were comfortable, bored, having lots of children, and planting huge gardens.

It wasn't until I read psychiatrist Abraham Maslow's seminal book, *Toward a Psychology of Being*,[45] focusing on the characteristics of people who were well (rather than those who were sick), what he called *self-actualizing* people, that I found the answer. He said all self-actualizing people had one trait in common: *a chosen vocation they found intrinsically self-rewarding and of service to at least one other.*

Ah, there was the problem! My friends and I did not have genuine vocation, a unique calling that motivated us to do our best and live fully. I was determined to find my vocation. It was not easy. The signal of vocation comes spontaneously when you discover what you are *born to do*, what your innate quality of being is designed to appreciate. As Marc has pointed out, the intrinsic nature of evolution is Evolutionary Love propelled forward by the longing for more pleasure, allurement, contact, and intimacy.

I have found that the *compass of joy* is a good signal, once you have found your calling. If you feel joy, keep going. If you feel great stress, fear of failure, or inertia, stop. Check it out. It

---

[45] Abraham H. Maslow, Toward a Psychology of Being (1962).

is not always easy, but if it is true vocation, it gives you new energy, vitality, and life, no matter how challenging it is.

We are designed by human nature itself to give our gifts fully and to feel we are of service to others in order to be fulfilled ourselves. This is one of the powerful attractions toward whole mate relationship—shared purpose.

Shared purpose calls forth the intimate, intrinsic essence of each partner's unique being. It activates the impulse of evolution, the force of creation that lives uniquely in each of us, yearning to be joined. Whole mate relationship is a further expression of the evolution of the Universe itself, which has been tending toward greater consciousness, intimacy, freedom, connectivity, and creativity for billions of years.

Entry 5. The Three Stations of Love

Let's go back to *Love Story*.[46] Jenny and Oliver are madly in love. The state of being madly in love is the first of the three *stations* of love, a concept rooted in *The Zohar, The Book of Illumination*.[47] Knowing the three stations of love and how they show up in your life is a key to the evolution of love.

- The first station is called *submission*. You are submitted to love. Love conquers all. You are madly in love and a servant to its expression.

- The second station is called *separation*. You do not feel the same automatic oneness with your partner that you did at station one. You sense separation again. The first flush of falling in love has quieted or even disappeared. Old boundaries spring back into place. A power struggle begins. This is where, in a good

---

46 See Chapter 3, "Soul Mate," Entry 4.

47 See, for example, Daniel Matt et al., editor and translator, The Zohar: Pritzker Edition (12 vols.), 2004–2017.

relationship, you commit to learning the art of loving. In the wrong relationship, or in one where you or your partner are not ready to commit, you leave and seek another relationship.

- The third station is called *sweetness*. You recover the original experience of station one, the sweetness and ecstasy of being madly in love with your committed partner. Station three looks like station one but has an entirely new quality of depth and devotion. Its bliss emerges after you have done the work of learning the art of love, or healing, but not before.

In *Love Story*, the experience of falling in love is powerful enough that its intensity and delight temporarily suspends the pain of Oliver's emotional alienation from his father. It is a beautiful station of love, but it is only one part of its full story. It is only at this first station that the mantra for love could be the *Love Story* quote, "Love means never having to say you're sorry." Anyone who has advanced beyond the first station of love knows that this is simply a crock. The only way for Jenny and Oliver's love story to retain its station-one purity was for Jenny to die. The writer has Jenny die, so the reader and viewer can stay in the experience of station-one delight and ecstasy.

Soul mate relationships all too often do not have sufficient depth to make it past the first station of falling in love. When they arrive at station two—the station of doing the work—the initial bliss has worn off, and the relationship frequently dissolves.

While great communication helps, especially the kind taught in *Men Are from Mars, Women Are from Venus* and its sequels,[48] it is not enough. In soul mate relationships, the problem runs deeper than communication. The larger problem of soul mate relationships is that the narrative of

---

[48] After the enormous success of Men Are from Mars, Women Are from Venus, John Gray wrote many sequels to the book, applying the general principles of Mars and Venus to different situations in relationships. See, for example, Mars Venus on a Date: A Guide to Navigating the 5 Stages of Dating to Create a Loving and Lasting Relationship, and Mars and Venus in the Bedroom: A Guide to Lasting Romance and Passion. See also, Mars and Venus Starting Over: A Practical Guide for Finding Love Again after a Painful Breakup, Divorce, or the Loss of a Loved One.

personal fulfillment is not compelling enough to sustain a passionate and potent relationship.

Entry 6. The Idolatry of Children

If you have kids, chances are you love them madly. In role mate relationships, kids were a social requirement and simply an evolutionary necessity for survival. At the soul mate level, kids cease to be an absolute necessity, but remain a big part of the meaning of life.

The soul mate level often lacks a larger context of values that demand loyalty beyond the couple itself. But it is actually hard to live without loyalty to higher values. So, in soul mate relationships, the kids often become the higher value to which the couple is loyal. After all, for most soul mate couples, the kids are the fruits of their shared love. In the case of blended families, taking care of a soul mate's kids is one of the greatest ways to receive or make that partner happy. And receiving your partner and making him or her happy is the Holy Grail of soul mate relationships. Once again, Barbara says it best:

> As wife and mother of five, I began to realize that both my role mate and soul mate relationship was causing deep depression. I finally found the reason: even though I loved my children and husband, I lacked vocation. Yet I could not even search for that greater purpose, because my husband interpreted my need as not loving him. I felt guilty because I wanted to express myself, as well as supporting him in expressing himself. When he said to me: "Barbara, you are the editor; I am the genius!" I finally realized my mission was my own responsibility. At first it felt like a deep failure, but actually it was the next stage of my own evolution. However, it led to divorce. I realized that I was facing a deep life choice: to give my energy to my sense of mission and vocation—not that I had found it—or continue to care for my marriage in my exclusive role of wife and mother. I told my children that I had to go to Washington, and that I wanted to take them with me.

The children were not pleased! Yet when I told my nine-year-old son, Wade, that his mother was a pioneer, that I had to go to Washington and wanted him to go with me, he put his little arms around me and said: "Mom, I know you love me. This is what mothers are for . . . it's to make a better future for their children."

Even though it was difficult, in the long run the result was that each of my five children and eight grandchildren has a vocation and a life purpose. My granddaughter Renee said to me, "Granny, would you like to know what you have given us? It's two things: a trajectory and a family clan."

Every child has a life purpose, each different, and every one is seeking to help the other. The family clan meetings have grown from small yearly family reunions, including my sisters and their husbands and children. Now the result is that my eldest daughter, Suzanne, is hosting a genuine family clan of forty people, many of whom hardly even know each other, yet all are motivated by passionate vocation. It seems to be a family trait.

Yet the truth was, in my dedication to the work and to greater meaning in my own life, I lost my loving husband. I was lonely. I did find a deep relationship for twenty-five years with a brilliant man, but he could not realize his own vocation and so became jealous of whatever I did. Since my marriage, I went more than fifty years without finding a really meaningful relationship with a whole mate!

What very few people are willing to say out loud is that the emperor has no clothes. Children, as beautiful and awesome as they are, provide an insufficiently compelling narrative for a potent and passionate relationship. Being in love with our children gives us great joy. But it does not in and of itself fulfill our lives and relationships. It is not just that the myriad details of children's lives sap the energy we once reserved for our beloveds. It is simply that having our gene pool survive does not engender a passionate or potent relationship between parents.

In fact, all too often, we hide behind the children to avoid the emptiness of the relationship. This sense of using the children as a fig leaf to avoid the invitation of larger purpose and personal destiny was a major theme of one great wisdom master known as Levi Isaac of Berdichev:

> It is said that Levi Isaac used to walk in the marketplace every day. One day a man was hurriedly sprinting down the small street on which Levi Isaac was walking and barreled into him, literally bowling him over. The man recognized the master and was very apologetic. Levi Isaac was unperturbed but curious. He got up and asked the man, "Why are you running so fast?"
>
> The man thinks for a moment and said, "To make a living."
>
> "Well," said Levi Isaac, gently pressing his inquiry, "why are you working so hard to make a living?"
>
> No one had ever asked the man that. He paused for several minutes to consider the question until a light bulb seemed to go off in his mind. A broad smile crossed his face. "Master, I work so hard to make a living for my children."
>
> "Ahhh," said Levi Isaac. "Thank you and have a good day."
>
> Some twenty years later, Levi Isaac was again walking through the marketplace as he was known to do. Once again, a man was hurriedly sprinting down the small street on which Levi Isaac was walking and barreled into him, literally bowling him over. The man recognized the master and was very apologetic. Levi Isaac was unperturbed but curious.

He got up, this time more slowly than twenty years earlier, and asked the man, "Why are you running so fast?"

The man thought for a moment and said, "To make a living."

"Well," said Levi Isaac, gently pressing his inquiry, "why are you working so hard to make a living?"

No one had ever asked the man that. He paused for several minutes to consider the question until a light bulb seemed to go off in his mind. A broad smile crossed his face. "Master, I work so hard to make a living for my children."

Levi Isaac looked closely at the face of the young man and realized he was the child of the man he had met twenty years ago. "Ahhh," said Levi Isaac. "Thank you and have a good day."

When the man had gone on his way, Levi Isaac lifted his eyes heavenward and exclaimed in frustrated irony, "When will I finally meet the one child for which all the generations have labored so mightily?"

All too often, in both role mate and soul mate relationships, children become a place to hide to avoid the fullest calling of our lives.

Entry 7. The End of Men?

The old model of relationship was based on a few foundational premises. One of these was the man in the role of primary protector and provider. Economic power in this model was on the male side of the equation. In 1963, close to the end of the era where the role mate model was a given, Sylvia Plath published her only novel, *The Bell Jar*. The soul mate model was just finding its way from an inchoate longing into words and reality. Plath writes with disdain of the women "hanging around New York waiting to get married to some career man or another." She says quite bluntly, "Girls like that make me sick."

This has all changed. Hanna Rosin, leading chronicler of the fall of the primary male provider, suggests that because many women do not need a man to be a provider, "they can find one they really want to be with instead. And isn't that a purer form of love, anyway?" Not accidentally Rosin's last line ends it with a question mark—meaning that it should be that way, shouldn't it? After all, once we move from role mate provider to soul mate, shouldn't love get purer and more beautiful? The truth is, however, that it does not. In fact, the most powerful evidence that it does not is from Hanna Rosin herself.

Rosin's book, *The End of Men: And the Rise of Women*,[49] is a great book in many ways, raising a number of key questions. The book cover is yellow with the words *The End of Men* in lavender taking up three quarters of the cover. There is more than just a fragrance of triumphalism in both the title and the content of the book. Although it does not clearly articulate it, the book discusses the distinction between role mate and soul mate. It considers what happens when soul mate is separated from role mate. Does the relationship work?

Let's ask ourselves a very simple question: What would the response be if a man wrote a book with the title (in huge lavender caps on a yellow background, of course) *The End of Women: And the Rise of Men*? Imagine also that the cause of the *End of Women*, as is the case in the book *The End of Men*, is not laziness but rather the shift from an industrial to an informational era, coupled with the massive loss of industrial jobs—nearly 7.5 million in the US alone.

Imagine the truth that this loss was creating massive transitional pain and trauma for men in the United States and across the developed world. At stake are men's dignity, happiness, and productivity. None of this is taking place because of some male malaise that deserves to be

---

[49] Rosin's view of men, and particularly their future role in society, is aptly characterized in the title of her book, The End of Men: And the Rise of Women. In Rosin's epilogue, she tells her final story about the male character Calvin, a man who had lost his manufacturing job and through that lost his family. Desperate, that man then begins training as a nurse. Rosin both compliments him and implicitly expresses her primal recoil (as a woman) from such a man. Rosin evinces the same recoil when describing the stay-at-home father that she meets in her child's schoolyard.

subtly gloated over or even celebrated. And yet, according to Rosin, no one has raised an eyebrow at her title, except for Jacob, Rosin's son. She mentions this in the acknowledgments at the end of the book: "My son Jacob asks me every day why I would write a book with such a mean title." Jacob has a point.

But even more telling is the implicit message: when men can no longer fulfill their role as providers and breadwinners, we have reached the *End of Men*. That is about as clear an indictment as you can get of the efficacy of the level-two soul mate model when it is divorced from the level-one role mate model. In Rosin's book, which is quite nuanced and insightful on many issues, there is one particularly startling passage, which conveys the energy of Rosin's and society's visceral sense of soul mates without role mates:

> *In the fifteen years I've been married, I've started to encounter more families where the wife is, at least for some period, the main breadwinner . . . One woman at our pre-school can't stop bragging about her stay-at-home husband—although, I can't help it, I am still startled by the sight of him hanging around the school making handprint T-shirts for the teachers.*

The story appears at a prominent place in the pivot of Rosin's narrative on what we are calling the possibility of soul mate to be successful without a provider role mate. She returns to this story of being startled and emphasizes there the deliberateness of her choice of the word *startled*. She acknowledges that her being startled essentially prevents men from inhabiting the role of soul mate without role mate. She ends her revisiting of this startling incident with the question, "Why should I be anything but delighted?" Meaning, "Why should I not be delighted by a soul mate partner who is not a role mate partner?" She does not answer the question, but it is clear that while intellectually this possibility makes sense to her, viscerally she remains startled and unable to access her delight. It is not a great recipe for passion or any other dimension of a successful relationship. Certainly, it is not something that will convey to a man the sense of being appreciated or honored.

It is instructive to check the dictionary to confirm our sense of Rosin's careful choice of the word. *Startle* means sudden shock or alarm, as in *a sudden sound in the doorway startled her*. Synonyms for *startle* are *surprise, frighten, scare, alarm, shock, fright,* or *jolt*. Rosin is alarmed, frightened, scared, or shocked by the specter of soul mate relationship independent of role mate dynamics. But this is exactly the social and intellectual dynamic that her book and others of its ilk are promoting. This is not a particularly ringing endorsement of this relationship possibility.[50] Indeed, soul mate without role mate of some form, or the future possibility of whole mate, simply does not work.

Liza Mundy, writing at around the same time as Rosin, is a second chronicler of the fall of the primary male provider. Her book is called *The Richer Sex: How the New Majority of Female Breadwinners Is Transforming Sex, Love, and Family*. "Both sexes," writes Mundy, "will be freer to make purely romantic choices—choices that have nothing to do with marriage as an economic partnership."[51] Her book also has its title in lavender

---

50 In the same chapter, "Seesaw Marriage," Rosin goes to great pains to tell the reader that, based on an informal survey she did through Slate, the online platform where she and her husband have worked, it seems that 8 percent of couples where the woman is the primary breadwinner are happy. Rosin clearly wants to endorse this possibility. But her more visceral sense of discomfort and her startled energy at this possibility perfumes her narrative. In a book filled with well-told and evocative anecdotes, there was not one inspiring anecdote about a couple in which the woman was the primary breadwinner. There was no anecdote describing this kind of relationship where the reader was even vaguely moved to echo the woman sitting next to Sally in the famous orgasm scene in the movie When Harry Met Sally. (After Sally quite convincingly simulates an orgasm, the woman sitting next to her says, "I'll have what she had.") The failure to portray a couple where the woman is the primary breadwinner speaks volumes. In her conclusion Rosin almost gets there with the letter she received from Robert, one of the respondents to her Slate survey. But Robert is not inspiring. He simply does not have the negatives she ascribes to Calvin (see p. 260ff). She describes Robert as being "considerably further along" than Calvin. But he does not embody an inspired vision of men. If we cannot find a genuine possibility for passionate marriage or articulate a relationship model where this possibility is indeed hot, love will not evolve. This is precisely the intention of the beyond-Venus-and-Mars relationship model, evolutionary relationships.

51 Liza Mundy, The Richer Sex: How the New Majority of Female Breadwinners Is Transforming Sex, Love, and Family (2012), 16.

taking up most of the book cover. The fragrance of triumphalism is also equally pronounced in both Mundy's title and her content. The clear direction of the evidence she marshals is that most women do not want to marry a man who is predominantly a soul mate. When the relationship cocktail includes a male partner who is both a soul mate and a role mate and who is at least an equal provider, it can work. When the relationship includes a male partner who is only a soul mate or a male role mate who earns much less than the woman, its chances of working go down exponentially, at least according to Mundy's data.

Now, just to reemphasize the crucial point we made earlier, neither Rosin nor Mundy, nor virtually any other observer of the scene, disagrees with the idea that soul mate relationship is an important relationship upgrade. They do not want to make a regressive move in relationship. But soul mate without role mate is equally problematic and no less unappealing.

Entry 8. Does Soul Mate Work without Role Mate?

Earlier, we talked about the greatest shift in relationships since the beginning of the farming era. In growing sectors of the population, men are no longer playing the role of sole or primary breadwinner. In the moderately educated working class and the highly educated class, the role mate relationship deal is off.

In the moderately educated class, where usually only one partner has a degree beyond high school, the classic male jobs are disappearing quickly. By dint of economic necessity, the woman is almost always a partner in breadwinning in some significant way. In more and more families, she is the primary breadwinner.

In the more highly educated socioeconomic strata, where both partners have college degrees, along with jobs that could support them independently, the role mate relationship deal, based in absolute economic need, is also coming apart. The classic relationship in which the male was the protector and provider is no longer firmly in place. It is disappearing before our eyes. Early feminism thought that the influx of women into the marketplace would free men of the huge social, financial, and psychological burden of being the protector-provider. In many ways, that vision of early feminism is now being fulfilled. As we pointed out in the introduction, the expectation is that women and not men will be the top earners in most households within one generation.

This might very well look like any of the following scenarios:

- Amy is making $75,000 a year, and Tim is making $50,000 a year. He is a significant participant in creating their home and raising their child. The combination of their efforts, financial and otherwise, creates a viable life for them.

- Elizabeth makes $100,000 a year, and Jack does not have paying work. He is really excited about personal growth and development. At this point in his life, he wants to focus deeply on his own growth. He participates in creating a home. They have no children.

- Betsy is a doctor. She earns $175,000 a year. Mark is a writer who earns $50,000 a year. They are raising one child together.

- Meredith makes $95,000 a year as a pharmacist. Joe was a welder who was recently laid off. He is collecting unemployment now. He is looking for odd jobs, which might bring in $30,000 a year. Meredith's earnings are likely to increase steadily; Joe's may not.

Virtually all of the literature and advice written and spoken into our current relationship reality is based on trying to make the old Mars and Venus model work. But the old Mars and Venus relationship deal, and even the old conceptualization of Mars and Venus *gender*, are no longer a given. We need the *beyond-Venus-and-Mars* model, including a new level of relationship and new idea of gender,[52] to learn how to love fully alive and awake at this important juncture of history.

Without the beyond-Venus-and-Mars evolution of relationships,

---

52 See Chapter 6, "Whole Mate," Entry 9, and Supplementary Essay 3.

too many people find that love just does not work. You will notice a kind of grasping and flailing around in the case studies and experts that we reference.[53] There is a yearning to return to an old world that does not exist.

In each of the four scenarios, the role mate relationship, in which the male is the protector and provider, and the woman is the nurturer and homemaker, is either partially or fully undermined. However, in all of the scenarios, the soul mate relationship is potentially fully available, at least in theory. Indeed, Tim, Jack, Mark, and Joe all have, to varying degrees, *more* time to invest in loving, listening to, and supporting Amy, Elizabeth, Betsy, and Meredith. We can safely say that each of them has, in effect, more time to invest in being a better soul mate.

There is a clear trend in the varied experiences of women and men in these scenarios, which are commonplace across America and elsewhere. Relationships are very far from ideal. In many instances, it is not going well at all. The reason is clear: for many women and men, soul mate is an insufficient basis for relationship. Both men and women simply feel better in relationships where each partner plays both soul mate and role mate roles. Women and men feel considerably less alive and in love in situations where either partner is playing only one role, even if it's the role of soul mate.

They feel much less alive and in love in a situation where either partner plays a major soul mate role without playing an equally (or close to equally) powerful role mate role. The more a man or woman is successfully filling a role mate position, the more easily love flourishes at the level of soul mate. The less a partner fills a role mate position, the more complex and painful the soul mate relationship becomes.

The soul mate relationship does not work easily or flourish by itself. So Tim, who is making $50,000 a year relative to his wife's $75,000, is doing OK. He is making a real living, and the $25,000 gap in their salaries, although not inconsequential, can be balanced through other exchanges in their relationship. But in the other three scenarios, where there is a much larger gap between the protector-provider role that has been assumed

---

53 See Entries 9–10.

by the woman, and the much smaller financial protector-provider role assumed by the man, these couples are not having an easy time at all. That is true even though all three men have more time and energy to devote to being attentive and emotionally sensitive soul mates.

There are two different great life experiments happening now in culture. The key to these experiments is to see how level-two soul mate relationship fares when it is separated from the classic role mate structure of the male being the primary provider and protector and the woman being the primary homemaker and nurturer.

In Entries 9 and 10, we will consider two compelling sets of images from the real lives of real people. Both point to the weakness of the soul mate model when it tries to stand on its own. Each comes from a different reality experiment that is orchestrating the emergence of new life conditions. An experiment works by trying to isolate a variable in order to be able to see more clearly how it behaves under different conditions. In the case of our relationship experiments, the variable we are trying to isolate is soul mate relationship. We want to see how it shows up in life when they are isolated from the role mate relationship.

In both experiments, we will look at scenes where men are not playing their classic roles as protector-provider.

Entry 9. Passion in Egalitarian Marriage: Experiment One

Is Equality a Panacea for Sexuality?

The first experiment is playing out in couples where both parties are college graduates and have good jobs. **Key to the experiment is that neither side needs the other in order to survive or to meet imposed social expectations.** Each party can earn enough to support themselves. If the relationship does not work, divorce is a viable option with no social stigma attached. These couples also have the viable option of not getting married at all. If they do get married, it is fully up to them whether or not to have kids, and if they do, when and how many to have. No generation in history has ever had more choice, more options, more possibility, and such a small degree of social pressure, stigma, or censure. For all of these reasons, the men and women in these relationships cannot be said to be role mates in the sense of needing each other to survive and thrive.

At the same time, this social group, which comprises about 30 percent of the US population, is in love with love and in love with marriage. Freed from the burden of the old *choose-a-partner-to-survive* relational structure, they are now free to choose the man or woman of their wildest dreams. Egalitarian marriage is a common term for this type of partnership. Egalitarian marriage is a way of taking a *soul mate without role mate relationship* for a test drive. The question is, Does it work?

As we discussed in Entry 3, the move from role mate to soul mate relationships was supposed to be the great panacea for sexuality in relationships. The assumption was that less role mate dependency to survive and thrive plus more intimacy and communication would equal more passion in relationships. The model of this triumph of passion in relationships would be the egalitarian couple. In egalitarian couples, neither partner necessarily needs the other to survive or thrive, and both partners have learned the arts of communication and intimacy. Passion, we thought, would thrive when power and its distortions were removed from the relationship. Seeing the other in the full vulnerability of their naked soul would create the passion that all generations had waited for. For some, this worked. For most, it did not.

Who Is Having Sex Tonight?

Egalitarian soul mate relationship works for some people. For most others, however, it does not work at all. Imagine the scene portrayed in a 2014 *The New York Times Magazine* article.[54] Several couples are at a dinner party. All are in their forties and married or in committed relationships. The author of the article describes the scene. "The mood was jovial until, after dessert, one guest made an offhand joke about Internet porn." It did not go over well with his wife. All of the guests, the author wrote, could sense that an argument was inevitable and that the

---

54 Lori Gottlieb, "Does a More Equal Marriage Mean Less Sex?," The New York Times Magazine, February 2014.

guests would "learn way too much about their personal lives."

Another guest steps in and deftly moves the conversation in a different direction. A collective sigh of relief goes through the room. Lori Gottlieb, a guest and the author of the article, then writes: "In the car, I turned to my boyfriend and said, 'I bet there won't be any sex happening in *their* bedroom tonight.'" He smiled and shook his head in disagreement. He predicted that another couple, the hosts, would actually be the least likely to have sex that night. Lori thought he was kidding. The host couple were "my model marrieds," she said:

> *True equals who share the housework and child care, communicate openly and prioritize each other's careers. The best friends of happy-couple cliché. Earlier in the evening, I watched them work together in the kitchen, cheerfully cooking and cleaning: She bringing out hors d'oeuvres, and he chopping and dicing. When their 6-year old woke up with a nightmare, they wordlessly agreed that he would be the one to soothe her. It was the kind of marriage many people wish for.*

"Exactly," her boyfriend had said. "Least likely."

And the data backs up Lori's boyfriend's prediction. For couples in purely egalitarian relationships, with no distinction between the roles of the man and women, passion fizzles and often disappears entirely. A study from the American Sociological Association, "Egalitarianism, Housework, and Sexual Frequency in Marriage"[55] pretty much gives it all away in the title. If men did the more masculine chores like trash, the lawn, and fixing the car instead of folding laundry, cooking, and vacuuming, then passion increased, along with her reported sexual satisfaction. If they did the same chores, passion decreased, as did her reported sexual satisfaction. The less differentiated their roles, the more sameness, the less passion—even when there is a very high dose of level-two soul mate intimacy. Some dimension of role differentiation appears to be quite good for passion.

---

55 Sabino Kornrich et al., "Egalitarianism, Housework, and Sexual Frequency in Marriage," in American Sociological Review 78 no. 1: 26–50.

Another piece of scintillating data is from the National Bureau of Economic Research. The more there is a substantive gap in an egalitarian marriage between the man and woman's income, with the gap favoring the woman, the less happy the marriage and the greater the possibility of divorce. But shouldn't egalitarian soul mate relationship carry the day? The answer is that it does not. Gottlieb reports that the less differentiation between the couple's roles, the less passion there is on both the man's and the woman's side of the bed.

Gottlieb describes marriages in which the attraction to relationship is a partner similar in intellect, background, and interests. It is what Betsey Stevenson, a well-known economist who studies relationships, calls emotional *kindred spirits*. It is what we have called level-two soul mate relationship. The problem is that being emotional kindred spirits or soul mates, without a profound differential in *roles*, kills passion.

Polarity, Passion, and Power

Stephanie Coontz, the famed historian of love and marriage, noted that the old idea seemingly still holds sway: If "you're only half a person," she writes, then "you can't be complete" until you find your other half.[56] Passion dies unless we feel that our partner completes us, not just emotionally but also for some larger purpose. If there is not some essential way in which the couple needs each other, the polarity needed for passion disappears.

One thing we did not realize was critical until we lost it was the polarity inherent in role mate relationships.[57] In role mate relationships, there was a sense of difference between partners, and men and women operated in different realms of power and potency. Therefore, there was a sense of needing and even completing each other. What was often missing in historical role mate relationships, however, was the presence and poignancy that comes from shared intimacy, shared feelings, and intensely transformative communication.

When we up-leveled to soul mate relationships, we developed our

---

56 Gottlieb, "Does a More Equal Marriage Mean Less Sex?"

57 See Entry 2.

poignancy and presence, but we lost our connection with the best of level one—the polarity birthed from distinct realms of power and purpose. Clearly, nobody wants to revert to the pre-soul-mate period. Soul mate relationship is a momentous leap forward; we all agree with that. It is just insufficient for passion, as this first experiment reveals. This first great experiment points in two important directions.

First, passion and potency may require a shared sense of purpose and not just poignancy. Role mate relationships had purpose but often lacked presence and poignancy. Soul mate relationships often have presence and poignancy, but lack purpose. Potency and passion seem to require all of these ingredients together plus one more crucial quality: power.

Second, without a sense of a partner's power, passion dies. By *power* we do not mean coercion or power in any of its negative senses. We mean power in the sense of the quality of aliveness and Eros that the great religions always associate with the Divine. We are attracted to power—the attractive power of beauty, or the alluring power of drive, talent, art, or impact. The president, the model, the queen, the rock star, the sports star, the female country singer all arouse passion—each in their own way. What they share in common is the potency of power. Egalitarian soul mates, however, often level power or view it as negative. In their view, power must be split precisely fifty-fifty at all times.

In role mate relationships, men and women incarnated different spheres of power. There was an *otherness* to their power spheres that aroused polarity. What was missing in role mate relationship was not power but *presence*. Women yearned for their man to be present. In soul mate relationships, particularly of the egalitarian kind, the play of power disappears. And along with the play of power, the polarity required for the potency of passion has often disappeared. Classic intimacy breeds sameness and familiarity between separate selves. But it does not necessarily arouse passion or sensuality. In the literature on this current relationship crisis, the authors offer no compelling image of polarity in the egalitarian dynamics of today's soul mate relationships.

Stories from the *Zeitgeist*

Let us look at two stories:

> A couple, Ryan and Kate, are at the end of marriage therapy. They have been married for five years and came to therapy to work out issues around balancing their jobs, incomes, and household responsibilities, as Kate put it, in an equal way.
>
> The therapy was successful, and over the course of time, the couple reported less conflict and increased harmony. That is good news, right? But toward the end of therapy, as things seemed to be concluding well, Ryan brought up a new issue. Now that everything seemed to be working out, his wife seemed to have become less passionate with him. He wondered if she was less attracted to him, which seemed strange to him since their relationship, after successful therapy, was now much more aligned with her egalitarian vision. "I'm very attracted to you," she insisted. "You know I am really hot for you when you're just back from the gym all sweaty and you take off your clothes and get in the shower."
>
> Her husband was not convinced. He said that this very situation had just happened, and her response to him, when he tossed his clothes on the floor, was, "Why are you so sloppy?" This led to the real issue, which was, Why had he not vacuumed the night before when it had been his turn? As he recounted it, he had worked late, which accounted for the messy room. But she hated to wake up to a messy room, and it was his turn to vacuum. "Right," she agreed. "I wasn't focused on sex because I wanted you to get out the vacuum. It was your turn." "So, if I got out the vacuum, you would be turned on?" Ryan countered. "Actually, probably not," Kate replied slowly. "The vacuuming would have killed the weight-lifting vibe."

A second couple, Mellissa and Kurt, had been going out for two years. She was an entrepreneur, who had exited four of her companies. He was an artist. He understood her better than anyone she had ever met. He had the kind of integrity she loved. She could relax in his arms in a way she never quite had with a man. He loved her capacity and her power to manifest. But most of all, he wanted to take care of the girl beneath the woman, who seemed to have gotten lost a long time ago. She wanted to marry him but could not quite commit. They were not role mates, in the sense that both were completely able to make a good living independently of each other. They had each been successful in significant ways before they met. She, however, could not quite commit to someone who did not have financial power equal to hers. This impacted the level of desire for him that she was able to arouse. When asked if there was ever a time that she felt totally aroused by him, she thought for a moment, and it dawned on her. For a moment, the politics of passion were replaced by the poetics of passion. "Yes", she said, "right after I heard him give a talk about his art. I saw the crowd entranced, and I could feel him channeling spirit. He felt like a god to me then. Powerful, potent, and pure."

As we noted earlier, Lois Lane famously falls in love with Superman and not with Clark Kent. In *The Proposal*, a workplace romance movie starring Sandra Bullock and Ryan Reynolds, she is the crazy tough boss, and he is the assistant. Through a series of events, they wind up falling in love in a beautiful soul mate kind of way. But their relationship becomes credible only when she visits his family and discovers that he is from a wealthy family and has significant sources of power independent of her.

What all these stories point to is that, in spite of what many of us would love to believe, pure love by itself is insufficient. Soul mate without some dimension of role mate or other forms of potency and power is insufficient to create sustained passion and relationship.

The vast amount of words spilled in articles, books, and studies do not give us an answer to this key question: *How do we restore passion in egalitarian relationships?* Unlike in role mate relationships, passion is often considered a prized requirement for marriage, but for many soul mates, passion fizzles as relationships progress.

Yet in a large sector of society, egalitarian relationships are the new norm and, for many, the aspiration. If soul mate relationships are not passionate, if they are simply not sustainably sexy, there is a core crisis in the evolution of love.

It is not a disaster, however; it is an *evolutionary crisis*. Remember, crisis is the core driver of evolution. Or, said differently, key crises are evolutionary drivers. Crisis births transformation. Crisis in relationship births new and deeper forms of relationship. Crisis in relationship births the next stage in the evolution of relationship. So, this loss of passion in soul mate relationships invites a restoration of passion at a higher level of consciousness.

We return again and again to our mantra. You cannot solve a problem on the level of consciousness that created it. New consciousness births new structures, which create new possibilities in our lives. This happens when crisis births transformation. The transformation can only come from an evolution of consciousness. The evolution of consciousness is the evolution of love. The new consciousness must birth, express, articulate, and catalyze a new vision of polarity and attraction. A new vision of polarity births a new dance of Reality.

Polarity is the balance between attraction and independence that creates passion in life, love, and of course the natural expression of life and love—relationships. It is time for a new vision of wholeness, which emerges from a new dance of polarity between the core principles of Mars and Venus. This new vision is the next evolutionary dance. It is the new way for Mars and Venus, what we call *lines* and *circles* in level-three relationships, to be in relationship with full passion, integrity, and integration. The restoration of passion is the evolution of passion, which is the evolution of relationship. This is the matrix for birthing beyond-Mars-and-Venus, evolutionary relationships into Reality.

Key Results from Experiment One

We can fairly summarize several simple but crucial conclusions from this first reality experiment. Egalitarian relationships are soul mate relationships. In these relationships, passion is typically lost; the less differentiation in roles, the less passion. Our conclusion is that passion must be poetically correct and not just politically correct. Poignancy and presence, the two hallmark characteristics of egalitarian, soul mate marriage, do not create passion. To create passion, one needs poignancy and presence *plus* potency and purpose. Add to the mix one more ingredient, power, and we've got the energy and Eros of level-three whole mate relationship.

What kind of relationship combines these treasured ingredients in the right configuration? Only a relationship that brings together the best energy of role mate relationship and the best energy of soul mate relationship. This mixture of key role mate and soul mate ingredients creates the polarity that births passion. This perfect equation produces what science calls a *synergistic emergence*, which is a new level of relationship. This is the move from role mate to soul mate to whole mate. It is the emergence of level-three, beyond-Mars-and-Venus, evolutionary relationship.

A key component of beyond-Mars-and-Venus relationships is the wholeness that emerges out of claiming and living your Unique Gender. It fosters unique polarity, which is at the core of every successful evolutionary relationship. As we will see, the evolutionary dimension of whole mate relationship restores purpose, polarity, and ultimately, passion.

The Unique Gender distinction restores the full power of the masculine and feminine expressed fully in the wholeness of both partners living their fullness and accessing the full range of their Unique Gender. Together with the presence and poignancy of soul mate relationships, which are fully integrated into whole mate relationships, a recipe is born for an entirely new relationship consciousness and the Unique Gender of level-three evolutionary relationships.

Entry 10. Middle-Class Marriage: Experiment Two

We now turn to the second great experiment of soul mate without role mate that humanity has been conducting. This is critical because, as we have pointed out, when we watched *Love Story* in 1979 and fell in love with soul mate relationships, we didn't quite notice that **in most cases soul mate had not *displaced* role mate but was living side-by-side with it**. Moreover, at the time when all the pivotal soul mate relationship books were written, the old deal was still very much in place. In the overwhelming majority of American homes, men were either the sole or the primary breadwinners. When level-two soul mate relationships appeared, everything changed—and nothing changed.

Our first experiment covered the 30 percent of Americans who are college educated and have well-paying jobs. Our second experiment considers the reality of the other 70 percent of Americans: **the moderately educated working class, which has long been the heart and soul of America**. We will focus on the relationships in which both parties have a high school degree, or in which one party (the woman in increasing numbers) has more advanced training or a college diploma. In these situations, the woman has left her old role as keeper of the hearth. For many reasons, the man cannot find his place in the old role of provider and primary breadwinner.

Can a High-Powered Woman Love a Laid-Back Guy?

Liza Mundy tells the story of Jessica Gasca, a resident of South Texas who works as a paralegal, supporting a husband and three children. Jessica likes working. She much prefers it to staying home. "Our kids see me as the father," she says.[58] Jessica has several sisters who have also emerged as the primary earners in their families. This is fairly typical in many parts of the Hispanic community, where marriage is becoming rarer, and woman as primary breadwinner is becoming commonplace. For many women and men, this creates "profound discomfort." Jessica displaces her own discomfort to her mother's voice, where it is easier

---

58 Mundy, The Richer Sex, chapter 1, "The New Providers."

to hold internally. "My mom always says: 'All my daughters—I've never taught you to be that way. I can't believe it.' She says that we're providing for the man when it should be the other way around."

Mundy also speaks of "Alicia Simpson, a psychiatrist, and her sister, Tracy Parker, a banker."[59] They are both alumnae of "Howard University, an elite, historically black university in Washington, DC." Today, "nearly 70 percent of the student body is female." Both Alicia and Tracy grew up in families where the man was the primary breadwinner. They had no intention of overturning that applecart. They expected, in their lives, a relationship that was closer to a partnership—emotionally *and* economically.

For both sisters, the fact that the man was not carrying his economic weight undermined their marriages. Alicia divorced her husband; she said he was not ambitious enough. "I had to push him out of the nest: it was like, either you're going to fly or you're going to perish." He could not fly as high as Alicia would have liked, so the marriage perished. Tracy, in Mundy's words, "worked through her resentment and struggled to accept her new role." "My husband's a great dad and I need him there," Tracy said. "So it was a mind-set that I had to develop." For both these women, the full presence of the husband, accommodation, struggle, divorce, and settling for the sake of the kids, are a far cry from embracing the soul mate relationship on its own merits.

Another woman, a consultant from Atlanta, Georgia, is one of four women Mundy writes about who make between $65,000 and $90,000 a year.[60] She was recently promoted and received a raise that was even higher than she expected. Her boyfriend loves her deeply. He took a job as manager at a Waffle House because it was the only job that he could find that was near her. She loves her job; he hates his. He is supportive and happy for her, and yet she does not know how to handle it. She keeps imagining people thinking, "What's she doing with that guy?"

Mundy's question is whether a high-powered woman can love a laid-back guy who idles at a lower speed than she does, and, in her own

---

59 Ibid.

60 Ibid.

words, "much of the evidence says no."[61]

Why Do I Need a Man?

Soul mate without role mate is not working out well. Consider Betsy, a senior at Florida International University in Miami.[62] At twenty, Betsy is making $70,000 a year directing the social networking program at the university. Mundy explains that Betsy didn't have a boyfriend yet wanted one, but stopped every now and then to ask why she did.

> "I almost feel like guys aren't necessary anymore, and it's kind of a terrible thing," she reflected. "I'm not sure what to do. I guess you keep hoping to meet this guy who is Prince Charming—who has as great a job as you do, and is I guess as aspiring as you are. But it almost seems impossible."

Betsy is clear that a guy who has soul mate qualities but not role mate qualities does not cut it. She rejects soul mate by itself as a primary relationship model.

Mundy speaks of the relationship crisis from a woman's perspective and summarizes it in this way:

> Now that I am self-sufficient, what do I need a man for? Remind me: Why would I want to get married? And within marriage, how would our lives unfold? And assuming I would like a man to go out with, where would I find him?

A huge sector of the American female population is choosing to remain single rather than partner with or marry a man who earns significantly less than they do. Particularly, according to Mundy's data, women are choosing not to *marry down*. Throughout history, until relatively recently, men have always *married down*. As famed biological anthropologist Helen Fisher argues, according to Mundy, "this is hard for men

---

61 Ibid.

62 Mundy, The Richer Sex, chapter 4, "The New Rules of Mating."

and women alike." Mundy quotes Fisher: "We've got 10,000 years of a belief system to shed. Nobody knows how to do it."[63]

Hanna Rosin tells the story of Rob and Connie from Alexander City, Alabama.[64] Until recently, that city's major employer was an athletic wear manufacturer, the Russell Corporation. In a town with about fifteen thousand citizens, the company employed nearly eight thousand people. Nearly all were laid off due to cutbacks in the manufacturing sector. There and across the United States, the manufacturing sector supported the entire middle-class infrastructure. The direct result of changes in the manufacturing sector was a rapid increase in divorce as men lost their jobs, a sharp decline in marriage, and a steady surge of single motherhood. The rules for sex, marriage, and love changed as the economy changed. Virtually all of the jobs lost were men's jobs. Dyeing, finishing, and other textile jobs created steady middle-class lives, paid mortgages, and sent kids to college. In Alabama and elsewhere, the women's jobs are growing to the precise extent that the men's jobs are disappearing.

Education, health, information, service industries, and nine out of ten of the other growing job markets are being flooded with capable and powerful women. Men are having a hard time shifting out of their traditional roles into fields like nursing, teaching, and administration. These roles are not addressing the sense of masculinity that men require in order to get excited about work.

Precisely how to engage this challenge is something we address in the beyond-Mars-and-Venus model of relationships—evolutionary, whole mate relationship. The old role mate deal is falling apart. Women are not willing to be defined exclusively by their old roles as homemaker and nurturer. In this sector of society, men are losing access to their classic provider-protector roles. They are finding it profoundly painful and sometimes almost impossible to find their way in the new postmanufacturing world. Being a soul mate without being a role mate is not working well.

Now let's get back to Connie and Rob in Alexander City, Alabama. Rob learned he was going to lose his job a couple of months after he and

---

63 Ibid.

64 See chapter 3, "The New American Matriarchy" in The End of Men.

Connie started dating. The result was that he could not bring himself to ask her to marry him. Connie was a teacher making a steady salary. Rob had tried everything with no success. Now he is struggling week-to-week to start a network consulting business. "He is absolutely the guy who says, 'I provide for the family. I'm the man of the house,'" said Connie to Hanna Rosin in an interview for her book, *The End of Men*. "You're saying that as if I'm the dictator," says Rob. "But the way I was brought up, it's a man's responsibility to take care of his family." He turns to Hanna Rosin and says, "I don't want to make the queen analogy, but my job is to make her the queen." "Honey, you know I would teach anyway," says Connie reassuringly. "But the point is you shouldn't have to," replies Rob. "It bothers him a lot," Connie says to Rosin. Rob replies, "I pretty much internalize it. It's like, if I can't take care of her, then I'm not a man."[65]

Connie is rare in that she is committed to Rob even if he cannot provide. In general, however, many women are reluctant to take on the role of sole or even primary provider. They can imagine earning a little bit more than their man, but they do not aspire to switch financial roles with men.

"We are all so incredibly independent that we know we're always going to take care of ourselves," said Meredith Hopps, an Atlanta engineer speaking for herself and her circle of friends. But financially, "we don't want to have to take care of anybody else."[66]

When Marriage Disappears

According to Rosin, the African American and Hispanic communities are at the leading edge of this trend. But white, moderately educated women appear to be closing the gap very quickly.[67] Ralph Richard Bank wrote a 2011 classic called *Is Marriage for White People?*[68] Black women

---

65 Ibid., 84.

66 Mundy, The Richer Sex, "The New Rules of Mating."

67 Ibid. According to Mundy, "All women could follow the example of African American women, who—not necessarily of their own volition—are increasingly estranged from the married state."

68 Ralph R. Banks, Is Marriage for White People? How the African American Marriage Decline Affects Everyone (2011). See footnote in The End of Men, 284.

have historically been more likely than white women to earn more than their male partners. They are historically much more likely to be better educated than their partners. Black women have not had the luxury of staying at home since the end of slavery. One of the bitter fruits of slavery was that black men rarely earned wages that allowed them to be the sole breadwinners.[69] Over 70 percent of black children are born to single mothers.

This is not good news for Mom, Dad, or child. The black man was fully available, at least potentially, to be a great soul mate. But the soul mate model without the dignity of the role mate position did not work. All across middle-class America, the model of African American and Hispanic communities is being adopted by default. Divorce is high, marriage is disappearing, and single-parent families abound. The "first generation college-educated white women," who are living in a world where the old relationship deal is off, may well "join their black [and Hispanic] counterparts in a new kind of middle class, where marriage is increasingly rare."[70] Virtually no one wants this to be true. The price in loneliness, depression, acting out, children without fathers, and loss of love is too enormous to contemplate. Reality cannot succeed if relationship fails. But if we are to avoid this, then we have to—in response to this crisis—evolve to the next level of relationships.

A groundbreaking report by Brad Wilcox refers to this great cultural experiment. The report questions whether the soul mate relationship works without the role mate component. It is called "When Marriage Disappears: The Retreat from Marriage in Middle America."[71] The study focuses on the 58 percent of Americans who are high school graduates but without a college degree. The basic point is that soul mate without

---

69 See Donna Franklin quoted in Mundy, The Richer Sex, "The New Rules of Mating," 76.

70 Rosin, The End of Men, "The New American Matriarchy," 94.

71 W. Bradford Wilcox, ed., "When Marriage Disappears: The Retreat from Marriage in Middle America," The National Marriage Project at the University of Virginia, December 2010, (https://archive.org/details/whenmarriagedisa0000unse/page/n1/mode/2up).

role mate does not work. If the man does not have the ability to claim at least somewhat of a role mate position, the woman is not interested.

We know from evolutionary history that women drive sexual selection: the female mate-choice determines the nature of relationships, and men change themselves to be great mate choices. When women say that soul mate without some real role mate component is not working for them, and men actually feel the same way about themselves, we have a massive relationship crisis on our hands.

Again, none of the writers we quoted thinks that we should stop aspiring to be in soul mate relationships. No one wants to go back to the pre-soul-mate period. Sociologist Kathryn Edin and her cowriter Maria Kefalas, speaking of the crisis, write that neither men nor women have given up the white-picket-fence vision, at the center of which is a "big wedding, a soul mate, a best friend."[72] Or, as Rosin writes, "The middle class still aspires to a happy soul-mate marriage"; but increasingly, it is just not working.[73]

Rosin and Edin use the terms *soul mate* and *soul-mate marriage* without being aware of the three levels of relationship discussed here. They are simply reporting the aspirations and dreams of men and women, together with the facts on the ground as they met them in scores of interviews.

The facts are not pretty. Rosin speaks of Darren Henderson from Kansas City.[74] Darren "was making $33 an hour laying sheet metal until the real-estate crisis hit and he lost his job." He has always been very responsible throughout his life. He had saved enough to buy a great duplex and a car, and he never missed a child-support payment for his beloved daughter. He lost his duplex, what he called, his "little piece of the American dream," and then his car. Not long afterward, he fell behind on his child-support payments. He did everything he could to find a new source of steady and sufficient income. When interviewed by Rosin, he threw his recently acquired commercial driving and bartending

---

[72] Kathryn Edin and Maria Kefalas, Promises I Can Keep: Why Poor Women Put Motherhood Before Marriage (2005).

[73] Rosin, The End of Men, "The New American Matriarchy," 95.

[74] Ibid., 89.

licenses "down on the ground like jokers for all the use they'd been." They were useless. His daughter's mother has a $50,000-per-year job and was getting her master's in social work. Darren had just signed up for food stamps. In contrast with a multitude of social welfare programs that are wonderfully available to women, food stamps are virtually the only benefit available to men.

Rosin also speaks of Mustafaa El-Scari, a teacher and a social worker who leads groups for men who are in positions similar to Darren's.[75] Virtually all of the men want to work. Virtually all of them *want to be a man* in the best way they understand it. This is what he says to a group of thirty or so men, ages ranging from twenty to forty. "What's our role?" he asks them. "Everyone's telling us we are supposed to be head of a nuclear family, so you feel like you got robbed. It's toxic, and poisonous, and it's setting us up for failure." As he speaks, they put down their sodas and sit up. He has their attention. "When she is making twice or four times as much as you, who's the damn man? Who's the man now?" He totally has their attention. A murmur rises. "That's right, she's the man."

Clearly, a new vision of what it means to be a man and a woman, and a new vision of relationships are in order. What we are seeing in these anecdotes is that the vaunted level-two soul mate relationship does not work, for either men or women, without something of the Eros and energy that men used to get almost exclusively from being protectors and providers—the old standard vision of role mate.

Entry 11. In Search of Solutions

Many women want in their partners a certain quality that we used to associate with the classic protector-provider, role mate husband. But we can never regress to an earlier period of time. The only way through the crisis is forward. As we will see, this will take us to level-three relationship: whole mate, which will transcend and include the best of role mate and soul mate. Fortunately, Reality is leaving trails of clues about how we will move forward.

---

75 Rosin, The End of Men, "The New American Matriarchy," 89.

There is an old story of a man lost in the forest. He wanders by himself for weeks until he meets another man, right as he is about to give up hope. He cries out in relief, "Ah, thank God! Please help me! Tell me what path to take out of the forest." The second man responds, "I do not know what path will take you beyond the forest, but I will help you." "What help could you possibly be?" retorts the lost man, not without a hint of despair. To which the second man answers, "I, too, have been lost for many years. I have tried many paths. I can tell you of all the ones that do not work, and that will help us find our way."

Hanna Rosin's book *The End of Men: And the Rise of Women* shows us a path that doesn't work, but it will help us catch a glimmer of a path that does.[76] She tells the story of Bethenny and Calvin, a couple who almost made it but didn't quite pull through. Their story opens and closes Rosin's book. They are the implicit thread of the book. Rosin's clearly intentional choice of using their story in such a way is instructive and revealing, almost more so than the story itself.

A Prince on a White Horse?

Rosin meets Bethenny in a supermarket in 2009 in a beach town in Virginia. The once prosperous middle-class town used to be fueled by the construction business, but it has dried up. Rosin is describing her visit to the depressed town. She opens with, "I almost never saw any men."[77] The book begins with the disappearing of men. "I recalled in earlier years seeing groups of men riding in pickup trucks down the main streets."[78] But now the men are gone. The book chronicles the disappearing of men, and in Rosin's telling, they never quite reappear.

---

76 To be clear, we learned a lot from Rosin's research and think that in many ways her book is important. We join with Rosin in her celebration of women. However, we think Rosin fails to understand men, to celebrate men, or to offer a vision to men and women of what is possible in relationship. In order for a relationship to flourish, it must be alluring to both parties. Rosin's vision of men is not alluring to men, and as Rosin herself makes implicitly and sometimes explicitly clear at numerous junctures in the book, neither is it alluring to women, nor even to Rosin herself.

77 Rosin, The End of Men, "Introduction," 1.

78 Ibid.

Implicitly, however, she is speaking not only of the disappearing of men, but the disappearing of a *relationship dynamic* of passionate love, honor, and commitment between men and women. In Rosin's telling, there is no potent vision on the horizon to replace the disappearing one. When she runs into Bethenny at the supermarket, Bethenny is twenty-nine and runs a daycare center out of her home. She is also studying to get a nursing degree and is raising her ten-year-old daughter.

"Are you married?" Rosin asks this forthcoming and friendly stranger in the supermarket. "No," says Bethenny. "Do you want to be?" continues Rosin. "Kind of," Bethenny says and spins "a semi-ironic fantasy of a Ryan Reynolds look-alike swooping in on a white horse or maybe a white Chevy."[79] What is clear at the outset is that Bethenny still believes in love and still holds a vision of a man on a white horse. In other words, she still holds on to a memory of the old role mate relationship combined with the best of soul mate but has no idea how this might show up in her reality.

That vision, however, seems to have become unattainable. "Is there any mortal male who might qualify for the role?" Rosin asks her. "Well, there's Calvin." Calvin is her daughter's father. She looks over at her daughter and tosses her a granola bar, and they both laugh. "But Calvin would mean one less granola bar for the two of us."[80] It is a potent story of male impotency, and a fitting way to begin a book about *the end of men*.

Rosin likes Bethenny, and we like her through Rosin's eyes. "There was genuine pleasure in that laugh, a hint of happy collusion in hoarding those granola bars for herself and her daughter," writes Rosin.[81] The story is also a little bit shocking. On the one hand, Calvin is the name that Bethenny comes up with as the only man she can think of who might be her man. At the same time, Bethenny understands with her daughter that by "keeping Calvin at arm's length, Bethenny could remain queen of her castle, and with one less mouth to feed, they might both be better off."[82]

---

79 Rosin, The End of Men, "The New American Matriarchy," 2.

80 Ibid.

81 Ibid.

82 Ibid.

Not exactly a celebration of Calvin, of manhood, or most importantly, of the possibility of love and relationship. What is telling is that, even as we get to know Calvin and Bethenny better (Calvin evolves by the end of the book), we never get to a place where we can hope for a great relationship model that can hold Calvin and Bethenny's obvious love. At the end of the book, Rosin will arrive at the end of her exploration—at a limp compromise that contains no scent of passionate possibility or genuine Eros.

Adjustment to Reality Is Not a Solution

At Rosin's request, Bethenny connects her to Calvin. They have many conversations. They are trying to figure out together how Calvin has become so invisible. The theme of disappearing men appears again. Her description of him is telling. "A gentle, earnest type and hard not to like."[83] Calvin is not passionate. He is not fierce. He is not potent. He is not powerful. He is not a hero. Rosin, like other writers in the same genre, keeps Calvin in his postheroic position, even as they report that neither they nor other women are allured by the possibility of being in relationship with Calvin.

Bethenny hopes to stay in touch with Calvin long enough for him to start earning money to pick up the grocery bill again so that he might find his way home. That is, until she realizes that for both Calvin and Bethenny, that old home no longer exists. For both men and women, the economy and the culture have shifted in ways that would require an adjustment to an "entirely new way of working and living and even falling in love."[84]

Rosin seeks an *adjustment to reality* as the solution of Bethenny and Calvin's love. Like them, however, she is unable to articulate a vision of relationship that would hold their love. They never get together. We would suggest, tenderly and fiercely, that an adjustment to reality is *not* what is needed here. Rather, when there is a crisis in relationship, then reality seeks an evolutionary transformation. Crisis opens the portals

---

83 Ibid.

84 Ibid., 3.

of transformation. In *this* book, we want to move past adjustments to a new vision.

We agree with Rosin that "Calvin was not going to drive up in a Chevy and take his rightful place at the head of the table."[85] That would entail a regressive move to the old role mate relationship. That is clearly the wrong direction—not only because it is not possible, but also, more significantly, because it is not desirable. Evolution meanders; it often does not move in a straight line. But it does not go backward. One of the reasons that Calvin cannot take his *rightful place* is because it is no longer his rightful place.

The old role mate relationship model in which the male breadwinner is automatically head of the house is over. Rosin continues:

> *Bethenny was already occupying that place, not to mention making the monthly payments on the mortgage, the kitchen renovations, and her own used car. Bethenny was doing too much, but she was making it work, and she had her freedom. Why would she want to give all that up?*[86]

Bethenny is accessing her Mars qualities, which include her potency, her self-responsibility, her breaking of dependency, and her freedom. These are critical steps on the path to a beyond-Mars-and-Venus relationship. Rosin is absolutely right; she should not give all that up. We celebrate and delight in Bethenny's emergence. But we do not yet have a new vision of identity, love, or gender that works for either Bethenny or Calvin. No less crucial, we also need a new vision of relationship that creates the possibility for Bethenny and Calvin's potent, productive, and passionate relationship.

The old relationship deal is off. We must imagine the new deal. We need to feel the poetic possibility before we can feel the practical or political possibility. We need the poetics of relationship, before we can work out the politics of relationship. That is what *The Future of Relationships* seeks, and

---

85 Ibid.

86 Ibid.

this is where nonvisions like portending the fall of men fail us. Let's celebrate the rise of the New Woman together with the rise of the New Man.

We Need a New Language of Heroes

We are focusing on Bethenny and Calvin because Rosin makes them symbolically prominent in her book. Only when ideas become incarnate in the stories of our lives can we begin to understand their peril or their promise. Rosin contacts Calvin again at the end of her research for her book. She writes that as always, "he had plenty of time to talk, although not as much as he'd had when we first met."[87] Having plenty of time to talk is a slight jab. Calvin's having somewhat less time to talk is meant to indicate that some progress has been made, although clearly no transformation.

Rosin reports that Calvin is now seeing his daughter more regularly. She adds that she has a daughter the same age, "so we relate on that front," a not-so-oblique reminder that they do not relate on other fronts. The big news is that Calvin had decided to check out the nursing program. "Even though the classes looked like 'all skirts' to him, he'd decided to give it a try."[88]

One of the key themes in Rosin's and others' books on the topic is that men are failing to make the necessary adjustments to fill the jobs available in a postmanufacturing world. Women are showing up dramatically in nine out of ten categories of the growing job markets, while men are not. Prominent among those growing job sectors is nursing, a category where men have not had an easy time finding their way.

When Calvin decides to become a nurse, Rosin is delighted. "If he had started out as my muse for the 'end of men,' Calvin is now showing that end' might not be a permanent state of existence. I could almost see it," she writes, "Calvin was big but pretty gentle and not all that intrusive, qualities that might be soothing in a nurse." Rosin continues: "I could imagine patients feeling safe in his presence, particularly since 'safe' in a

---

87 Rosin, The End of Men, "Conclusion," 261.

88 Ibid.

hospital context does not entail long-term commitment."[89]

The crisis of imagination, which demands a new vision of relationships, is not met by Rosin's imagining of Calvin as a nurse. She ends the book by saying she can "almost see it"—not exactly a ringing endorsement of the possibility of restored manhood and passionate relationship. Rosin confers on Calvin a somewhat sad and more than a little bit condescending set of compliments laced with *semi-ironic* barbs. He is "not all that intrusive." He "might be soothing." He is "pretty gentle." She can "almost see it." She can imagine being safe in his presence in a short-term hospital setting but clearly not in a context that entails "long-term commitment."

She tells him that she is delighted but feels obliged to tell us, the reader, the only time she does this in the entire book, that she is telling the truth when she says she is delighted. Apparently, she feels that we might have reason to doubt her. Indeed, her mix of praise and jabs indicates that, for her, Calvin is not yet an attractive model of a man. This was apparently true for Bethenny as well. "Bethenny had laughed when Calvin told her he was considering following in her footsteps. But when he asked, 'You got any other ideas?' she admitted that she didn't."[90]

When Bethenny responds to Calvin's initiative with laughter, it does not bode well. One of the great relationship and passion killers is a woman laughing at her beloved's direction. When the masculine asks, "You got any better ideas?" and the feminine *admits* that she doesn't, we are not left with a sense of possibility for the future of love. Bethenny and Calvin never get back together as far as we know. Apparently, Calvin's move to nursing was not quite enough to attract Bethenny. Rosin struggles to find the necessary adjustments to make something work. But it is not enough for Bethenny. You cannot solve a problem on the level of consciousness that created it. Bethenny and Calvin must up-level their game into a new vision of relationship. The evolution of relationship into a new passionate possibility can happen only in the hearts, minds, and bodies of Bethenny and Calvin.

Together with Bethenny and Calvin, we need to reimagine

---

89 Rosin, The End of Men, "Conclusion," 262.

90 Ibid., 263.

relationship. The old deal is off. We need to articulate the new deal. The new deal must be sexy, compelling, and heroic for both Bethenny and Calvin. That is the possibility of a level-three whole mate relationship.

For this to become possible, Calvin must delight and honor Bethenny's newfound power. Calvin must celebrate her qualities of King and Queen. She must be whole in herself even as she reaches for Calvin. At the same time, Bethenny must invite Calvin back into the language of heroes. This is where Rosin fails us.

Level-three whole mate relationship must invite the possibility of passionate relationship filled with potency, power, and purpose on the one hand (role mates), and poignancy and presence (soul mates) on the other. Both Bethenny and Calvin need to be in their full power. But they need a shared vision to bring them together. If Bethenny and Calvin can articulate and embody the possibility of a level-three relationship, they can find each other as home again.

Entry 12. Deeper Yearnings

By reading Rosin carefully, we know what will *not* get us home. But every once in a while, when we read the literature about the crisis of the old relationship deal, a sentence jumps out that points toward something new. Neither the book authors, nor those they speak with, can quite articulate what the new emergent is. That is always the case with a new evolutionary emergent. It is pregnant and in the wings, tangible but invisible, until it can be seen. We will mention each hint briefly. They are not full ideas or fully articulated insights. They are just as we are calling them—*hints*.

Virtually all social commentators looking at the relationship scene observe that women will not *marry down*. They don't want partners who make significantly less income than they do. There is some truth in this. This creates a pretty bleak outlook for the future. If within one generation the majority of households will have a woman as the primary breadwinner, then we may be at the end of the era of relationships as we know it. Women's apparent refusal to marry down is seen as a confirmation of the old cliché that women view men as success objects, while men view women as sex objects. There is some truth in it. After all, a cliché can become a cliché only if it is true to at least some significant degree.

This is, of course, not just a women's problem. Men do not experience themselves as heroes when they are not accessing some of the energy and Eros that used to be available through their old roles. But what if men could access a genuine sense of being a hero through a different portal than the old primary breadwinner role? Wouldn't that shift the self-experience of men, and then naturally shift how men are experienced by women? Of course, it would! Moreover, a careful listening suggests that women have a deeper yearning, beneath the success-object desire, just as men have a deeper yearning beneath the sex-object desire. This is all very good news.

There is a yearning on the part of men and women even deeper than the important social and economic shifts at play here. Glimmerings of this deeper yearning can be heard in the conversations that are taking place about the crisis. Let's listen in on some of them.

Hint One: Famed relationships researcher Helen Fisher says that men and women are required to make an adjustment of the kind that has not been made for ten thousand years. She is referring to the end of the old relationship deal. "This generation is going to have to rise to the occasion," she says. "All these women are not going to be able to find a really high-powered man. For millions of years, women have wanted a partner who helps provide. We're a pair-bonding animal. We raise our children as a team. However, there are many ways a man can provide without having a lot of money . . . as women's roles expand men's roles get to expand, too."[91]

Fisher's insight, with which we heartily agree, is that men need a new job description. There are many new ways for a man to be a hero. There are many ways that men need women and that women need men that are not connected to money. A wider vision of man as provider is essential, and we will return to that vision in the following chapters.[92]

---

91 Mundy, The Richer Sex, "The New Rules of Mating," 73–74.

92 This idea of the man as provider in a wider sense than finances has been a major theme in John Gray and Warren Farrell's work. See W. Farrell, The Myth of Male Power: Why Men Are the Disposable Sex (2001); W. Farrell, Why Men Earn More: The Startling Truth behind the Pay Gap and What Women Can Do about It (2005);

What is equally important is that Fisher herself buys into the fallacy that she is trying to help people move beyond. She writes that "women are not going to be able to find a really high-powered man," but they can find a man who provides in ways other than money. Why can't women find a high-powered man? Fisher assumes that *high-powered* refers to finances or some other form of the usual definitions of material success. What if being a high-powered man were sourced in something much deeper and more essential? What if men and women have gifts to offer each other that would empower them in a way previously unimagined? What if men and women have access to deeper and more potent forms of power than money and shallow success? What if each stops seeking merely what the other can provide in a kind of exchange theory negotiation? What if, instead, an entirely new form of power emerges from the space between them? What is the true source of power in a human being? This is a question that points us to the right direction.

Here are some more hints, easily missed, from the literature on the relationship crisis:

Hint Two: While women often speak about wanting a man with a higher or at least equal income, even more often they speak about qualities like intellect and drive. They speak about needing their men to be college-educated, but they use *college-educated* as a symbol for their men being motivated and interesting. "They want a man who is not boring; a man they do not have to explain things to; a man who has similar aspirations and interests . . . high-achieving women live in a culture of achievement and want men who inhabit the same reality."[93] "They don't have to be equally educated," said one successful woman explicitly, "but [they have to be] . . . intelligent. And have a desire to succeed."[94] Intellect, motivation, aspiration are all sexy. All of these hints point in the right direction.

---

and W. Farrell and J. Gray, The Boy Crisis: Why Our Boys Are Struggling and What We Can Do about It (2018). Also relevant here is: M. Gafni, Your Unique Self: The Radical Path to Personal Enlightenment (2012).

93 Mundy, The Richer Sex, chapter 4, "The New Rules of Mating," 72.

94 Ibid.

Hint Three: Mundy writes, describing her interviewees: "Drive is also crucial." Another woman spoke about *transformation.* "It's about always trying to be a better version of yourself. I find somebody's lack of desire—their contentment to stay where they are and not move forward—it's not attractive . . . I want to make sure a guy is driven. There's always something you can be striving for."[95] Drive is sexy: again, a hint pointing in the right direction.

Hint Four: "The person I marry I have to admire. Not because I'll have a better life or economic status. But because I have to admire that person."[96] What makes a partner admirable in a way that is deeper than economics? Another hint pointing in the right direction.

Hint Five: Churches in the black community "urge women to treat men as the household leader, as a way of binding men to family life and giving them 'identity and purpose.'"[97] Whether this is a futile effort, as we believe it is, is beside the point. The core recognition is crucial. Men's bonds to their partners and kids are not merely about income. It is about identity and purpose. The crucial implication that this policy hints at is that identity and purpose can be achieved regardless of whether the man is the primary breadwinner. We believe the effort is futile because a man must claim identity and purpose internally, through his very essence. It cannot be contrived through a social ruse. If women treat their men with appreciation and honor, it ought to be for three reasons. First, they feel appreciative and honoring. Second, they have learned how to look at their man outside of a purely financial lens. Third, their men have *earned* respect and honor. Clearly this is not yet a full vision of the new level of relationship, but it is also a hint pointing in the right direction.

Hint Six: Liza Mundy suggests in a passing reference that partnerships work best when a couple finds a common endeavor outside of work and school. This is a promising direction. Unfortunately, Mundy means something insufficient by *common ground.* She talks about "common ground in leisure and hobbies," or as "shared memories," as in "they went

---

95 Ibid., 73.

96 Ibid.

97 Ibid., 76.

to high school together." Or "they have "a shared group of friends," or "they both value children and stable home life." In yet another passage, she talks about creating a common ground through talking together in "a seminar on death and dying."[98] None of these are particularly compelling as the common ground that might infuse a relationship with potency and passion. But the fleeting intuition of common ground nonetheless holds the seeds of promise. Common ground might begin to seed passion, but not if the common ground is hobbies. Although a bit misleading, we have another hint with some degree of promise.

Hint Seven: An example of a recurring theme is "Lori, an attorney who makes half a million a year." She was "tired of dating men who considered her professional competition, and whose 'entire mood depended on whether they'd inched one step closer that day to being CEO.' So, she married a train conductor she met on Match.com. 'I wanted a man who didn't talk about his work all day, who would rather go for a bike ride on the beach.'" All of this is not yet inspiring. The next sentence, however, holds the seeds of promise even if the vision is still not yet articulated. "My husband knows who he is. He's just comfortable in his own skin."[99] Of course this is not yet the new vision, but again it is a seed that is connected not to economic realities but to something deeper and wider—a man who is comfortable in his own skin and knows who he is. This image begins to seed passion and potency—an important hint.

All of these hints point in the same direction. There is a new vision of relationships being born, but there is yet no language to describe it. There is a yearning for something more, something waiting to be named. Our recurrent motif guides us again: *you cannot solve a problem on the level of consciousness that created it.*

Entry 13. Beyond *Romeo and Juliet*

Neither soul mate nor role mate relationships work very well by themselves. This is a new piece of information that Reality is downloading

---

98 All of these quotes are from Mundy, The Richer Sex, "The New Rules of Mating," 78.

99 Rosin, The End of Men, 52.

into our consciousness.

To really get a sense of the refusal of both men and women to embrace soul mate relationship by itself, let's go back and revisit Connie in Alexander City.[100] She teaches junior high English. Teaching Shakespeare's great soul mate story of Romeo and Juliet used to be one of her great pleasures. The kids loved it. They were moved, inspired, and absorbed by this great soul mate drama. Romeo and Juliet did not make good role mates, not for economic but for social and political reasons. Their families hated each other in a world in which there was no identity outside of family. Yet the purity of their soul mate love moves them to abandon the limitations of appropriate roles and go for broke.

The story was so potent for the kids that Connie needed to put in a strong warning about teen suicide, lest some heart-struck teen foolishly tried to imitate the path of Shakespeare's doomed soul mates. Not anymore. As the old models of relationship fell apart around them, her students changed dramatically in their relationship to relationship. Her students are now not only unmoved by the story; they are disgusted. "He's just a little sissy boy and he's not normal," one student says. "Any other guy would just go get him another girl. What's the big deal? *Find another one.*"

"Well, does anyone think its romantic?" asks Connie. The response is a chorus of *nos*!

"He's just lame," one student says. "Yeah, and crazy." Most of Connie's students have witnessed up close, in the relationships of their parents, the transition from the old world of role mates/soul mates to the new world in which their parents valiantly tried to remain soul mates even when the old roles fell apart. For too many of them, the failed vision of soul mate relationship in their parents' lives shifted their view of relationship and of themselves. To what did it shift, however? It did not shift away from relationship and marriage.

At the end of her last Romeo and Juliet class, Connie asked her students how many of them wanted to get married. Most of them raised their hands. And even the ones that didn't, we suspect, would have if they could have conceived of a new model of committed relationship

---

100 See Entry 10. The story is told in Rosin, The End of Men, 99ff.

that inspired delight, respect, and abiding love between the partners. When there is a crisis of imagination—when you cannot imagine what a great relationship might look like—you keep your hand down, both in class and in life.

As the old role mate model falls apart, the soul mate model is not stepping up to the plate. There is a palpable yearning for a new vision. People are desperate. They do not know where to turn.

Remember the mantra that guides our exploration: you cannot solve a problem on the same level of consciousness that created it. We need a new model of relationship. That can emerge only from an evolution of consciousness, which is an evolution of love. It is clear that neither the soul mate nor role mate models work by themselves. However, both the role mate model and the soul mate model have unique and beautiful dimensions. What is needed is a higher integration of the best of level-one and level-two relationships into something undeniably new and better than both.

We need a new synergy. In response to new life conditions, the creative intelligence of Reality takes two parts, each one a whole unto itself, and *synergizes* them into a larger whole. Synergy creates a whole that is greater than the sum of the parts.

In the classical triad of *thesis*, *antithesis*, and *synthesis*, *thesis* is typically the given reality that has been around for a long time. In this case, that would be the level-one role mate relationship model. The second part is called the *antithesis*. The antithesis always arises as a rejection of or in response to the thesis. In this case, that would be the soul mate relationship model. The third level is the higher integration of both of them into a new evolutionary emergent. The new evolutionary relationship will manifest a new model for relationships and a new way of being in love. This new level will create infinitely greater depth, joy, passion, and goodness than either of the two previous models. It will be provoked or evoked by existence itself. New life conditions will produce a crisis in relationships that will demand a new emergence.

This new emergence is precisely the beyond-Venus-and-Mars model that we are unfolding in this book. Its first key dimension is level-three relationship, whole mate, which we explore in great depth Chapter 6 and in Part Two of the book.

CHAPTER 5

FROM SOUL MATE TO WHOLE MATE

The leading-edge expression of one level of relationship already holds in it the beginning of the next level. We saw earlier that the leading-edge expression of role mate relationship holds the beginnings of soul mate relationship. In the very same way, the leading edge of soul mate relationship holds the beginnings of whole mate relationship.

Entry 1. The Dawning of Evolutionary Consciousness

When the soul mate relationship emerged into the mainstream, it was successful for two reasons. The obvious reason was all the great gains in personal fulfillment that came from a deeper sense of intimacy and communication. The hidden reason was that even as people evolved into the soul mate model, they remained, for the most part, role mates as well, for both economic and social reasons. Men were still the overwhelming majority of primary breadwinners, and marriage and kids were still taken as a given by most people. The role mate imperative gave the relationship purpose and power. The soul mate relationship gave the relationship poignancy and presence. This was a potent combination that birthed the potential for passionate marriage. But once the role mate dimension of the relationship fell away, the soul mate vessel proved insufficient as a container to hold the next evolution of love and relationship.

The role mate relationship is disappearing as women are becoming the majority of primary breadwinners. It is disappearing because egalitarian couples no longer need each other to survive and thrive. It is disappearing because social pressure for marriage and children is all but gone. The role mate relationship is anachronistic because sex and children and marriage are no longer inexorably related.

We yearn for the honor, the duty, and the gravitas of the shared purpose that defined the role mate relationship. Even more, we yearn for the polarity of attraction that is born when two people *complete* each other. We yearn for the polarity of passion that is born from two people who are at once both radically similar and profoundly different. *Radically similar* means they share both vision and competencies. *Profoundly different* means they may choose different roles in different spheres with different gifts and then come together as a larger whole.

We may not want to do it the way we used to as role mates, but we seek a way to take the most potent energy and Eros of role mates into the future with us. At the same time, we rightly love and swear by our desire for a soul mate, a best friend, a partner.

You cannot solve a problem on the level of consciousness that created it. A new level of consciousness must be born. This requires an evolution of consciousness, which is the evolution of love and the evolution of relationship. Again, Barbara said it well:

> Now eighty-eight years old (or new!) I have personally shifted from role mate as wife, supporter, and mother of five for ten years, into many years alone doing my work, then into a soul mate relationship for twenty-five years, where my partner was brilliant and sexy, but not able to fulfill his own vocation through joining with me, or anyone else.
>
> Finally, I was blessed to discover a whole mate relationship, joining creativity in love and high purpose. The result, at the age of eighty-eight, is the feeling of getting newer every day. When our cells receive the signal that there is more for us to do, they try to do it! Aging feels as though it slows down. Since the impulse of evolution itself is for more creativity and love, it is as though evolution itself is yearning for us to say a big YES to life extension. As we know through epigenetics, consciousness affects DNA. Our cells are responsive to

request, up to a point. If and when radical life extension takes hold, as is predicted, and if we do indeed live ever-longer lives by choice, the yearning to be whole mates will intensify. Its pleasure will increase. Just as sexual fulfillment is an art form, so fulfilling life purpose is even a more challenging and yet fulfilling artform. It takes time to produce significant work for the world, just as it does to raise a child to adulthood.

It seems to me that life extension and joining genius to co-create is the direction of evolution itself. We tend to become *telerotic* naturally, when we say YES to vocation and YES to joining genius with our whole mate. We enter the lifelong process of co-conceiving new memes, new solutions, new innovations for life ever-evolving!

This may well be the direction of evolution itself as we gain the opportunity for life extension as members of the new species: *Homo amor*. It takes a while to learn everything we need to take our next steps in evolution! Life extension and whole mating for shared life purpose may be the naturally emerging relationship in the story of evolution. When I think of the Universe with its billions of galaxies and trillions of planets, the short life span of *Homo sapiens* seems almost outmoded!

What is the new level of consciousness that must be born? It is the dawning of evolutionary consciousness. It is an intimate, intrinsic sense of emergence within yourself, toward something more, something new, something vital, and as yet unexpressed. You are longing to give your unique expression of the mighty 13.7-billion-year impulse of evolution incarnating as YOU!

You feel, as Marc puts it, that Reality needs YOU! That you are intended, that you are *Homo imaginus*. You become an expression of Evolutionary Love, which has no age, which gets better all the time, and which creates radical newness in evolution in YOU and as YOU. You become newer the more you say YES to the impulse of evolution within you, because that evolutionary impulse creates newness all the time. That is what evolution does!

One of the great attractors for whole mate relationship is that, when you are in the presence of a person who is personally attracted to that, you, too, are encouraged to feel more of your own unique creativity coming forward. You realize you are needed for what you most long to give, that you are fully seen by another, so that you can embody that which is driving you forward, often without name, label, job, or description. Your evolutionary potential is new. It has no good job description or label. It's hard to recognize real newness alone. Your whole mate sees your newness and loves it, often even before you do.

In this sense, a whole mate relationship calls forth your still-amorphous impulse of evolution and makes it more real and vital to you. This is a great gift of whole mate loving. If the match between whole mates is mutual—that is, drawing forth more creativity from both, simultaneously, through joining genius—then you get the juicy, powerful attractor that evolves the evolutionary impulse inside of you! This is why whole mates are appearing at the edge of soul mate relationship at this precise moment in evolution.

The very first evolutionary person I ever met was Dr. Jonas Salk, in 1964, when I was still depressed, feeling unexpressed and lost. I told Jonas everything that was "wrong with me—my love of the future and my desire to connect with everything." He smiled and said, "Barbara, this is not what's wrong about you; these are not faults. These are exactly the characteristics needed by evolution. You are a mutant!" He introduced me to several others, who shared this inner impulse of creativity and emergence.

Suddenly the strange and somewhat lost person I had been grew into a highly motivated futurist and social innovator.

At that time, I had never met another person with this deep impulse of evolution activating within them consciously. Now there are countless ones of us. This type of human, sensitive to what is emerging, is everywhere. We are called forth by the evolutionary crisis on Earth right now. Evolutionary relationships of all kinds are vital. When they mature into whole mate with whole mate, evolution itself is moving forward through each of us.

When a whole and healthy new level of consciousness is born, it transcends and includes the previous level. Level-three whole mate relationship, therefore, must transcend and include the best of role mate and soul mate. It must also add more beautiful, truer, better, and more passionate new dynamics. The basic formula is therefore simple: *The best of role mate dynamics (honor, duty, obligation, larger commitment) + the best of soul mate (radical intimacy and depth) + emergent dimensions = evolutionary relationship.*

The bleak and fearful conclusion that our new economic and social world will bring the end of relationship fundamentally misunderstands the nature of evolution. Evolution can always be trusted to birth new transformation through crisis.

From the Big Bang, Reality evolves by evolving new levels and forms of relationships. We are at a new moment in evolution, which holds the promise of love, passion, and depth undreamed of by any previous generation. We are not only *birthing* the new emergent of evolutionary relationships, but we are also *democratizing* this new emergent. It is about to become a genuine option for every human being who is ready to wake up.

Entry 2. A Calling to Serve Love

The soul mate relationship is about personal love, personal transformation, personal fulfillment. The goal of the relationship is the success of the relationship itself. But as soul mate intimacy deepens and evolves, something more poignant and powerful begins to reveal itself. **In its highest expression, soul mate relationship is not just for the sake of the couple's love and transformation, but for the sake of love and transformation itself.** The beloveds begin to love and do the work of transformation for the sake of the larger Whole.

There is a deeper Field of Interconnectivity and Intimacy. Quantum physicists refer to its physical expression as *the zero-point field*. It reveals the presence of the larger Field of LoveIntelligence, LoveBeauty, and LoveDesire, the Source of the inherent, ceaseless creativity of Cosmos. This is the animating energy that drives the entire process of life.[101]

When soul mates deepen their erotic intensities—emotionally, psychologically, spiritually, and physically—they feel their significance in this larger Field. They realize that the integrity of their love matters not only for themselves, but for the larger Whole. This is the first glimmer of whole mate consciousness. When soul mates enter fully into the intoxication of love, it has the capacity to lift them to a higher level of consciousness.

In this transition from level two to level three, the lovers realize that love does not only serve them. Love is for its own sake. They realize that their own growth and transformation is not merely about themselves. It participates in, and is for the sake of, the growth and transformation of the Whole. They realize that their love energizes the innermost process at the very Heart of Reality itself.

Love itself becomes *the third side* of the relationship. When lovers begin to serve not only each other but Love itself, the relationship undergoes a momentous leap in consciousness. The difference is subtle (they serve Love by loving each other), but also crucial. When they begin to serve Love itself through each other, they break out of the lurking narcissism of two that so often hinders level-two relationships. The Persian poet Hafiz referred to this devotion to love itself when he wrote:

---

[101] See Chapter 1, "The Arc of Evolution," Entries 6 and 7.

You are a Divine elephant with amnesia

Trying to live in an ant hole.

I love you.

This is our oath of allegiance to a higher order of Being.

This shift in intention, which takes place at the highest end of level-two relationships, opens the space for level three. Whole mate relationship is literally, as Hafiz wrote, a higher order of being.

Soul mate relationship, in most of its early and middle stages, is a partnership. Each partner seeks fulfillment through the other. There is a sense of negotiation and dealmaking that takes place as part of an egalitarian relationship. All too often, however, it feels like the commodity being traded is love itself. But at the higher levels of soul mate relationship, the partners surrender into the third side, Love itself. Love is no longer traded. Love is served for its own sake. Lebanese poet Khalil Gibran said the following about the realization of love being for its own sake:

Love gives naught but itself and takes naught but from itself.

Love possesses not nor would it be possessed; For love is sufficient unto love.

When you love you should not say, God is in my heart, but rather, I am in the heart of God.

And think not you can direct the course of love, for love, if it finds you worthy, directs your course.

Love has no other desire but to fulfill itself.

But if you love and must needs have desires, let these be your desires:

To melt and be like a running brook that sings its melody to the night.

To know the pain of too much tenderness.

To be wounded by your own understanding of love;

And to bleed willingly and joyfully.

To wake at dawn with a winged heart and give thanks for another day of loving.

Entry 3. Relationship to the Whole

Soul mate relationships are very focused on the untransformed wounds of the past. Bearing witness to those wounds, holding them, and ultimately transforming them together is an essential part of the lover's journey at the soul mate level of relationship.[102]

In the shift from level two to level three, something happens. You begin to transform your story not only for yourself, but as part of the larger story of transformation. You begin to realize that evolution is not a process outside of you but is actually awake within you. You not only live in the Universe; the Universe lives in you. Every expression of the evolutionary process literally lives in the human body. Everything from the hydrogen atoms released at the Big Bang to the proteins required for food digestion—all of this is alive and active within your being, and all of it depends on earlier evolutionary emergents.

One of the things we know from systems theory is that there are small fluctuations that can jump an entire system in chaos to a higher order. Those small fluctuations are known as *islands of coherence*. To be an awake human being is to be an island of coherence. It is to know that your transformation is the small fluctuation that can jump the entire

---

[102] See Supplementary Essay 2, "Wounds in Role Mate, Soul Mate, and Whole Mate Relationships."

system to what Hafiz called *a higher order of being*. Your transformation is not only *part* of the transformation of the Whole, but also a crucial *catalyst* in the transformation of the Whole. As you begin to reflect on these scientific principles, you begin to move from level-two soul mate to level-three whole mate relationship. You are beginning to live in relationship to the Whole.

Entry 4. Transforming Holes into Wholeness

Sans was a small town in Eastern Europe. Its master was a particularly powerful master of stunning brilliance and radiant love. When people pressed him to explain the source of his exceptional luminosity, he would always refer to the story of his parents' relationship. He believed it was the relationship between his parents that formed him and invested him with all his gifts. He told one story about his parents that said everything:

> My father was studying one night very late in the study hall. It must have been near to 3:00 a.m. He was sitting behind his table, deeply inside the texts. Into the study hall walks a man, my mother's father. My mother was a strong and powerful woman. She refused all of the arranged matches that her father had offered her. Each one felt wrong. But he had heard that there was a great teacher in Sans who was unwed. For some reason, this match pleased his daughter, my mother.
>
> The great teacher was my father. So, my mother's father traveled a great distance and arrived in the middle of the night. Determined to make the match, he did not even wait till morning. He had heard of my father's late-night study and thought he might find him in the study hall. My father was forty at the time, and my mother was twenty. Both had refused many offers of marriage. Both were considered very unconventional in this regard. Both seemed to be waiting for someone. From what I have been told, when the two men met late that night, they spoke only for a few short minutes. My

father did not even get up from his seat. But they agreed that the engagement would precede the wedding by some months.

It was some months later that my father and his entourage arrived at the town of my mother. My mother, however, was in a strange mood. She insisted on seeing my father before the wedding. This was strictly against the custom. Her father was aghast at the request. But she insisted, saying she would not attend the wedding otherwise. She was told that my father went early every morning to the bathhouse to bathe before the morning prayers.

She hid herself behind the bathhouse in order to see him when he emerged. When she saw him, she let out a shriek. He looked up. Their eyes met and she ran. What she saw is that my father was wounded on the left side of his body. He dragged his wounded left leg. She had not been told about these wounds. She told her father that she would not marry him. There was great sadness and confusion during those days.

My father, after waiting quietly for several days, made an equally unusual request. He asked to meet her in a room by themselves for only ten minutes. He promised not to try and persuade her to marry him. My mother agreed to the meeting. This was also against the custom, but there seemed little else to do. Even more strangely, my father requested that a great mirror be brought to the room.

They met in the room. She looked at him, tears running down her face. She said: "When my father spoke of you, I thought you were the one, but when I saw your infirmity, God have mercy—I could not bear it. I know it is petty and small, but I just cannot do it. I am sorry."

"I understand," my father replied. "I have only one request to make of you."

"What is it? If I can fulfill it, I will," she responded.

"Please just look at yourself in the full-length mirror against the wall and walk a few steps," he requested. She did as he asked and let out a shriek twice as loud as when she saw him for the first time leaving the bathhouse. When she looked in the mirror and walked, the wounded left leg did not show up on him. It showed up on her. Her left side was wounded, and when she walked, she dragged a wounded left leg. "Let me tell you what happened," he said.

"When I was very young," he explained, "I prayed to know my soul mate's name. The angels on high refused to tell me. This is not how things were done. But I insisted and eventually they relented. Once I knew your name, however, I could not stop. I felt—I did not even know why—like I had to see you. The angels were furious and absolutely refused my request. I would not relent. I fasted, meditated, and prayed forty days and forty nights until finally they gave in. You were not even born yet."

He continued: "They showed me a picture of you in your twentieth year, when we would marry. I cried out in pain. For the entire left side of your body was wounded. I could not bear it. I cried and cried and begged the angels to let me take your wounding on myself. They would not hear of it. But I insisted, praying and fasting for another forty days and forty nights. In the end, they relented, and at age twenty, I fell sick and received all of your wounds onto me.

"In us coming together," he explained, "know we will both be made whole again, and we will offer that wholeness up for the sake of the Wholeness of All-That-Is. For you are not only my *Basherte*, or soul mate, but you are my *Hashlamah*, or that which makes me whole. May it be thy will that through our love, we contribute to the Wholeness of everything."

"That," concluded the master, "is the special quality of relationship that birthed me into the world. All my wisdom, and all my power, is from that quality."

This is a story about working with wounds. Soul mate beloveds, in a profound and poignant sense, take on each other's wounds. But it is not merely working with wounds for the sake of personal healing. In this evolutionary story, the personal and the Cosmic are one. Healing the hole in my beloved makes us both whole. But it is not just *our* wholeness that is at stake. By transforming our holes into wholeness, we reweave the very fabric of the Whole. Our transformation is offered up in service of the Whole.

In a whole mate relationship, we act for the sake of a third side, and we do this in three ways. We begin to act for the sake of love, for the sake of transformation, and for the sake of the Whole.

Entry 5. Love Is the Third Side

Being in relationship to and in service of the third side is part of the new relationship deal. In whole mate, evolutionary relationships, we join with our partners in service of something entirely beyond ourselves.

When you have a profound sense of your relationship being for the sake of love, then you begin to view conflict in your relationship in a whole different way. One couple, our close friends, let's call them Jack and Lily, have really committed their relationship to the move from level two to level three. They consider their relationship to be in service to what they call *true love*. This naturally moved them to reframe conflicts:

A lot of times you see conflict as you *versus* the other person's perspective, so there's going to be a winner and there's going to be a loser. It's like a duel. I've got to make my points, get my jabs in, and you've got to make yours. Someone's going to win, and someone's going to lose.

Now we do think that conflict is a battle, but it is a battle where you and your partner are in tandem, united against a common enemy. That enemy is the misunderstanding. The misunderstanding stands against love. And we as a couple are identified with love. The misunderstanding stands against our love. But not just *our* love. It stands against *Love*, so we stand on the side of Love against the misunderstanding.

This is a compelling glimpse of what we have called *a third side*. The transition from level two to level three starts to happen the second you realize that your love is not only about your personal fulfillment. When you begin to act for the sake of love, the shift begins to unfold. Love becomes the third side that you serve, and misunderstanding becomes the third side that you oppose, together.

When we step into a whole mate relationship, we begin to realize that our love story is an irreducibly unique part of a much larger love story, without which the larger Love Story of the Universe would be missing something essential. We realize that there is a particular and unique dimension of the larger story that is UnLove. That unique dimension of UnLove can be made whole only through our unique love story. The implications of realizing that the Universe is a Love Story are stunning. To be in service of love is not some hyperromantic or spiritual posture. Understanding that your love relationship is not merely about you, but is in service of love, is simply to be aligned with Reality. It is both scientifically correct and, no less importantly, poetically correct.

You may not do anything differently, but your intention changes—and that changes everything. Your wider circle of love and your larger context for relationship shifts something essential in the very core quality of your life. Everything becomes more alive, brighter, more colorful, and more meaningful.

In the following passage from Khalil Gibran, you can sense the transition from soul mate to whole mate. It is only in this evolution of relationship, which is an evolution of love, that you can begin to bear the wounds of love. You begin to understand that you cannot *seek love's pleasure* only for yourself. You come to recognize that love wounds you to transform you so that "you may know the secrets of your heart, and in that knowledge become a fragment of Life's Heart."

Then said Almitra, Speak to us of Love.

And he raised his head and looked upon the people, and there fell a stillness upon them.

And with a great voice he said:

When love beckons to you, follow him,

Though his ways are hard and steep.

And when his wings enfold you, yield to him,

Though the sword hidden among his pinions may wound you.

And when he speaks to you, believe in him,

Though his voice may shatter your dreams as the north wind lays waste the garden.

For even as love crowns you so shall he crucify you.

Even as he is for your growth, so is he for your pruning.

Even as he ascends to your height and caresses your tenderest branches that quiver in the sun, so shall he descend to your roots and shake them in their clinging to the earth. Like sheaves of corn he gathers you unto himself.

He threshes you to make you naked.

He sifts you to free you from your husks.

He grinds you to whiteness.

He kneads you until you are pliant;

And then he assigns you to his sacred fire, that you may become sacred bread for God's sacred feast.

All these things shall love do unto you that you may know the secrets of your heart, and in that knowledge become a fragment of Life's Heart.

But if in your fear you would seek only love's peace and love's pleasure,

Then it is better for you that you cover your nakedness and pass out of love's threshing-floor,

Into the seasonless world where you shall laugh, but not all of your laughter, and weep, but not all of your tears.

Whole mate does not leave soul mate behind. Once you realize that your heart is a fragment of Life's Heart, you enter the bliss of soul mate love from a portal of potency of an entirely different order of being. Gibran concludes with precisely this vision:

To rest at the noon hour and meditate love's ecstasy;

To return home at eventide with gratitude;

And then to sleep with a prayer for the beloved in your heart and a song of praise upon your lips.

Table 2. Role Mate and Soul Mate

	ROLE MATE	SOUL MATE
Self	Separate self	Separate self
Level of Consciousness/ Intimacy/ Identity	Egocentric Ethnocentric	Ethnocentric Worldcentric
Core Value	Survival and thriving	Personal fulfillment
Relationship to the Field of Value	As separate self, role mate does not necessarily experience oneself as part of the Field of Value	As separate self, soul mate does not necessarily experience oneself as part of the Field of Value
Falling in Love	Social, religious, cultural fit Exchange of value	*Chemistry* between the beloveds Imago theory Looking deeply into each other's eyes
Quality of Love	Ordinary love experienced as a human sentiment or a social construct even if a beautiful and moving social construct	Ordinary love experienced as a human sentiment or a social construct even if a beautiful and moving social construct
Characteristics	Dependency: I need you Protectiveness Achievement	Independence: I choose you Intimacy/ Communication Presence
Shadow	Power plays Manipulation Narcissism of one	Leveling of differences Loss of passion Narcissism of two

	ROLE MATE	**SOUL MATE**
Core Concepts	Protection Sacrifice Duty Honor Obligation	Poignancy Presence Communication Transcending loneliness Healing of wounds
Goals	Personal survival Thriving of self & family Fulfill obligations	A good relationship (A good life has a good relationship in it.)—Liberation from loneliness Heal wounding Love each other
Question	"What is in it for me?"	"What am I getting in exchange for what I have given?"

CHAPTER 6

WHOLE MATE

The leading edge of soul mate relationship leads us to the beginnings of whole mate love. We want to participate in the evolution of love. We want to be Superman and Superwoman. We want to feel that our lives matter and that our lives transform something in Reality. We want to look at a shared horizon with our partners, including a shared horizon of *value*. We want to look at a shared vision of what we want to do in this unique *We* that is our relationship. We want to stand for something larger than ourselves.

This happens into three distinct but often interincluded steps. First, we simply feel *the Whole*. We feel our selves in relationship to the Whole even as we feel the Whole that lives in us, as us, and through us. Second, we simply declare that our relationship itself is participating in a larger transformation. Third, we act together for the sake of the Whole.

Entry 1. The Mystery of the Cosmos Is the Mystery of Relationships

Reality is Relationship. Virtually every branch of science agrees that relationship is the core structure of Reality. From the first quarks that came together to create stable relationships nanoseconds after the Big Bang, to the most evolved level of human relationships, relationship is the essence of Reality.[103] But that is not the end of the story.

The impulse for relationship lives in the Eternity *before*[104] the Big Bang and beyond even the most evolved human being. According to the

---

103 See Chapter 1, "The Arc of Evolution."

104 The word before should perhaps be put in quotation marks here, as time came into existence with the Big Bang. Eternity is not infinite time; it is beyond time.

interior sciences, Reality itself is born from the will to engage in relationship. In the 1940s, this insight found physical expression when science discovered the quantum vacuum from which everything is born. It is a physical expression of *the primordial Ground of Being* that the interior sciences have perceived over millennia. This Ground of Being, the realm of pure potentiality, is always beyond measurement. It manifested Reality. We call this moment of manifestation *the Big Bang*, but some leading-edge cosmologists refer to it more eloquently as *the Great Flaring Forth*.[105]

Wherever science goes with its methodologies, the poets have so often gone before. The great romantic poet William Blake wrote, "Eternity is in love with the productions of time."[106] Reality is all about being in love. Reality is all about relationship.

Reality is relationship.

Reality is evolution.

Reality is the evolution of relationships.

Being in connection makes us alive. Relationship is not extra, but essential to our very existence. From subatomic particles, to trees, to human beings, we arrive at new levels of existence when we are witnessed by another in relationship. If I am not witnessed, some essential dimension of my aliveness dies. *If a tree falls in a forest and there is no one there to hear it, does it make a sound? If my voice is not witnessed and received, does it make a sound?*

But it is not enough to be witnessed. We need to be *potently* witnessed for our most powerful and highest selves to be called into being. This, as we will see, is at the heart of whole mate relationship.

---

[105] See, for example, B. Swimme and T. Berry, The Universe Story: From the Primordial Flaring Forth to the Ecozoic Era–A Celebration of the Unfolding of the Cosmos (1992).

[106] William Blake, "Proverbs of Hell," in The Marriage of Heaven and Hell, 1790–1793.

Entry 2. The Next Step in the Evolution of Love

As we have seen, role mate and soul mate relationships each have their own beauty and limitations. Soul mate relationships marked a massive leap in the evolution of love. The LoveIntelligence, LoveBeauty, and LoveDesire of Reality, driven by the challenges and conditions of role mate, birthed an upgrade in relationship. Soul mate was clearly a beautiful and much-desired transformation of relationship. And yet, as we have seen in Chapter 4, soul mate by itself is not enough.

The next level of relationship is whole mate relationship. It is a beyond-Mars-and-Venus relationship that marks the starting point of the new relationship deal. For all their depth and beauty, role mate and soul mate relationships cease to meet our deepest yearnings. Practically no one wants to revert to role mate relationships where the sole commitment was to survival and material success for the couple and immediate family. At the same time, soul mate relationships, while infinitely more satisfying than role mate relationships, no longer satisfy us in and of themselves. We need a new vision of the hero and a new invitation to the deepening of the feminine.

Egalitarian couples suffer from a profound loss of passion.[107] Even in the depths of their poignancy and presence, soul mate relationships lack compelling narratives to keep couples in love. They lack the spark that creates potency and passion. Each partner in egalitarian couples can *make it by themselves*. Survival no longer drives the relationship. **Soul mates are searching for new passion, new power, and new contexts for relating.** They're ready for the next step.

Many soul mate couples relied upon the Mars-and-Venus communication techniques we briefly discussed earlier.[108] These techniques helped them avoid pitfalls that may have ended their relationships. They also helped them increase emotional intimacy and connection. However, they did not lead to enduring passion. Nor did they provide a sufficient basis, in and of themselves, for a long-term, satisfying relationship. Soul mates are looking for a new purpose and the enduring potency and passion

---

107 See Chapter 4, "Limitations of Soul Mate."

108 See Chapter 3, "Soul Mate," Entry 8.

that emerge with whole mate relationships.

As we have seen, women are not clear about what they want. On the surface, there seems to be a demand for economic partnership, but the deeper desire is more profound. The desire of the feminine, not yet clearly articulated, is for a masculine with a potent sense of himself and drive. In other words, women want a man with a purpose. The purposeful man is the powerful man. The powerful man is passionate and filled with potential. And there is no passion or potency without purpose.

The LoveIntelligence, LoveBeauty, and LoveDesire of Reality, provoked by new life conditions, is now seeking another momentous leap in relationship. Crisis created on one level of consciousness can be solved only by evolving to a higher level of consciousness. This is the move made in whole mate relationships.

They will transcend and include the best insights and strategies of role mate and soul mate relationships, yet birth something undeniably new. This is a moment of crisis that precedes transformation. New potency, new depth of intimacy, new passion, and new power in relationships are becoming possible. This is being birthed in the next stage in the evolution of love.

The purpose and potency of role mate relationships are coming together with the poignancy and presence of soul mate relationships to birth an entirely new possibility for passion and power in whole mate relationships. We are now poised to take the next momentous leap in the evolution of relationships. It is a move from *joining genes* to *joining genius*. It is the move from role mate and soul mate to whole mate. It is the rise of evolutionary relationships.

Entry 3. Whole Mate Is an Emergent

Whole mate relationship is an evolutionary emergent. As an illustration of this concept, consider a baby. At first, the baby has virtually no capacity for mobility. Except for waving her arms and legs, she is locked into a stationary position. At a certain point, however, early motor ability develops, and she turns over. Eventually, she develops even further and begins to crawl. Development continues along this path and, eventually, she stands up. Finally, in a tour de force of individual emergence, she walks. Once the baby has been walking for a while, you barely remember a time when she could not walk. To get this even more dramatically, apply this sequence of emergence to yourself. Try to remember back to a time when you did not know how to walk. It is probably impossible to access the felt sense of not being able to do that in your body. Once an emergent makes its appearance, its existence becomes entirely self-evident.

New emergents are not born out of nowhere. They are always synergistic—they always take the best dimensions of what came before and integrate them into a larger whole. The new whole is always greater than the sum of its parts. When learning to walk, for example, a baby needs all the milestones that came before. The incremental development of muscles and balance for turning over, crawling, and standing are all transcended and included in the dramatic emergent of walking. There are also entirely new cellular relationships between motor neurons, muscle cells, and other biological components that must emerge for the baby to shift from lying to crawling to walking.

Emergents exist in every dimension of Reality. For example, there are cultural emergents. One great example is democracy. The idea that we vote for our elected officials seems obvious to all of us. Yet a thousand years ago, the idea of democracy was not part of our collective consciousness. The idea that every single adult citizen would participate in the political process was absurd. Not only was it absurd, but it was also dangerous. Expressing such a progressive idea could get you killed. Today, it is a given. Democracy and all its attendant human rights are cultural emergents.

In the realm of relationships, whole mate is the new cultural emergent. Like democracy, whole mate relationships have emerged as evolution's loving response to crisis. The limitations of soul mate relationships, along with the challenge of soul mate relationships without role mate dynamics, have paved the way for this new emergent. The leading edge of soul mate has delivered us into whole mate.

To make the power of this emergence strikingly clear, let's consider the metamorphosis of a caterpillar into a butterfly. Within the caterpillar's cocoon, there are *imaginal discs*, which contain the blueprint of the butterfly yet to come. Although the discs are a natural part of the caterpillar's evolution, the caterpillar's immune system recognizes them as foreign and tries to destroy them. As the imaginal discs begin to link, the caterpillar's immune system breaks down, and the caterpillar's body begins to disintegrate. As this happens, the discs mature and become *imaginal cells*. Those cells establish a new pattern, and the disintegrating body of the caterpillar transforms into a butterfly. The breakdown of the caterpillar's old system is essential for the breakthrough of the new butterfly. Yet, in actuality, the caterpillar has neither died nor disintegrated. It has simply emerged as something new.

The caterpillar was coded with hidden possibility from the beginning. Its innate destiny was to transform and to be reborn as the butterfly. As Ferris Jabr wrote in *Scientific American*: "Before hatching, when a caterpillar is still developing inside its egg, it grows an imaginal disc for each of the adult body parts it will need as a mature butterfly or moth—discs for its eyes, for its wings, its legs and so on. In some species, these imaginal discs remain dormant throughout the caterpillar's life . . . once a caterpillar has disintegrated all of its tissues except for the imaginal discs, those discs use the protein-rich soup all around them to fuel the rapid cell division required to form the wings, antennae, legs, eyes, genitals and all the other features of an adult butterfly or moth."[109]

This is precisely what happens in the evolution of relationships. Humans have always held in their hearts new possibilities for love. They've always known, at some level, that the leading edge of one type of relationship held the blueprint for the next. The imaginal cells of soul mate love once commanded the disintegration of role mate relationship. Soul mate emerged as the beautiful new butterfly. The new butterfly transcended and included—indeed *emerged from*—role mate's gorgeous and protective cocoon. Now, the same thing is happening as the disintegration of soul mate calls forth the emergence of whole mate.

Of course, role mate and soul mate relationships are precious to us all. We would never want them to disappear completely. But something

---

[109] Ferris Jabr, "How Does a Caterpillar Turn into a Butterfly?," Scientific American, August 10, 2012, retrieved January 2024, https://www.scientificamerican.com/article/caterpillar-butterfly-metamorphosis-explainer/.

much greater, something that transcends both role mate and soul mate relationships while including their essential features, wants to emerge. We are its catalysts, its imaginal cells.

Entry 4. Searching for My Evolutionary Partner

I remember quite specifically hungering for the emergence of something new. In early 1990s Jerusalem, there was a venerable wisdom teacher revered for his piety and audacious insight. He accepted very few private meetings, which were always held in the early hours before dawn. I had been waiting for weeks for an appointment. One day, at 4:00 a.m., I was awakened by the phone ringing. It was the assistant of this most respected teacher.

Meetings with him were very short. Within thirty minutes of waking, I was in a cab, where I rehearsed how I would share my dilemma. Should I ask Naomi to marry me? Was she the one? Our relationship was different from any I had known before. It did not fit into any model that I knew.

This beloved teacher was known to receive a question and then enter a mystical reverie, apparently drawing guidance from deep wells of inspired wisdom. I rather haltingly tried to explain the situation. I didn't think that I had conveyed it all that clearly, but he put his hand up to signal that I should stop talking. He went deep into his trance, and when he came out, he said: "To marry, you need the right physical attraction; you need to each fulfill your duties, and you need to care about and support each other's wounded places. Without that, it cannot work; with that, you have my blessing."

Unwittingly, he was referring to role mate and soul mate relationships. In the ultrareligious world in which he operated, to mention role mates was predictable. But to bring soul mates into the equation in such a central way, by referring to the healing of each other's wounds, was radical in and of itself.

The appropriate response on my part would have been to thank him for his guidance and to take my leave. But I could not. "You do not understand," I said more impatiently than was appropriate. "There is something new happening here." I did not know quite how to explain it. "She is my visionary partner. She is my partner in purpose." I searched for any phrase I could find to describe this new basis for relationship. I blurted out, "She is my *Chevruta*." *Chevruta* is the Aramaic word for one's study partner.

He looked at me, taken aback and somewhat shocked, but interested. He put his head down and entered his mystical reverie once again. When he raised his head, he said, "We have no tradition on this." He paused for what seemed like forever. And then he said, "But there is always new revelation." His assistant ushered me out.

Naomi and I did not get married. We followed Orthodox law in our relationship, so we never had physical contact. I always dreamed of our making love from that place of *Chevruta*. I knew it would be of a higher order of Reality than anything I had ever known. I knew that if we could make it, our relationship would be the place where bliss and blessings met.

We did not make it. Fierce parental and social opposition to our partnership trumped our love. I still miss her. As I searched for my wife, my primary desire had always been to find my *Chevruta*, or what I would now call my *evolutionary partner* or *whole mate*.

The master, revered and holy as he was, lived deeply in his lineage tradition, and he had never heard of a whole mate relationship. He could not find it in the past. He called it a new revelation. We call it an emergent. Whole mate relationship is truly an emergent. We sense its necessity and yearn for its appearance even as we cannot quite articulate its contours.

Because of the difficulty of articulating the contours of something new, people on the leading edge of emergence often question themselves. They wonder, *Why am I not satisfied with the status quo? Why am I looking for something more? I have everything I need; shouldn't I be happy?* Gradually, they come to realize that their deepest yearnings are valid and even sacred. They realize that they are reaching toward a higher level of consciousness that has not yet taken shape, and therefore has not yet been adequately described. They realize that they are the imaginal cells transcending the immune system's attack to give birth to the butterfly. Their success, indeed all of our success, evolves the very source code of relationship.

The yearning for beyond-Mars-and-Venus relationship—for whole mate relationship—is undeniable. The imaginal cells are waking up. Like-minded and like-hearted people throughout the world are transcending the old distinctions of race, religion, and politics. They are articulating a new level of love and relationship. People are saying directly and simply: *We want to play a larger game. We want a new context for relationship. We want to participate in the evolution of love.*[110] People are calling off the old relationship deal. Their search for the new deal is on.

Entry 5. Looking at a Shared Horizon

The ultimate experience in a soul mate relationship is looking deeply into each other's eyes. After all, the eyes are said to be the windows to the soul, so what could be more appropriate for soul mates than to locate themselves in the deep wells of being found in the eyes of the other? Each feels held, received, and witnessed. Soul mate is one of the most beautiful and potent expressions of the old relationship deal.

Soul mate works particularly well in its first station of love, which we often call *falling in love* or *infatuation*.[111] I remember a particular moment of infatuation when I was going out with my girlfriend Erica. We had left the car on the Upper West Side of Manhattan in what seemed like a perfectly legal spot. When we returned at 1:00 a.m., the car had been towed. After making the appropriate calls, we realized that we would have to go down to the pier on Eleventh Avenue to pick up the car. We were ecstatic. It would take us two more hours to get the car. That would mean two more hours of being together. Two more hours of being able to bask in each other's eyes.

Soul mate relationships do not end when the first joy of falling in love gives way. But at some point, when your primary focus is looking deeply into each other's eyes, your eyes start to blur. At some point, the joy of

---

110 See, for example, T. R. Rochon, Culture Moves: Ideas, Activism, and Changing Values (2018).

111 See Chapter 4, "Limitations of Soul Mate," Entry 5.

simply being with one another becomes insufficient, and you search for a deeper, clearer vision of why you are together.

Evolutionary relationships are whole mate relationships. Whole mate is whole in several distinct ways. We will point to them as they come up naturally in the course of conversation. But for now, one orienting sentence will be helpful. Whole mate relationship is characterized by two distinct yet deep interrelated forms of wholeness: both parties come to the relationship with their own *prior sense of wholeness*, and both parties in the relationship relate not only to each other, but—individually and together—to *the larger Whole*.

In an evolutionary relationship, you engage not just by looking deeply into each other's eyes, but by looking *at a shared horizon*. An evolutionary relationship is sourced in a shared vision. There is a dream of fulfillment you both can see. You look deeply at a shared horizon, and from that place, you turn to look deeply into each other's eyes.

I recently read an interview with Rolling Stones' lead singer Mick Jagger. The Stones have made it as a band for a startlingly long period of time; at the time of the interview, the relationship between the core members had lasted fifty years. They had survived the many relationship challenges that usually lead bands to break up. When the interviewer asked Jagger how they did it, he said something like *The Stones were always larger than us. Holding the vision of the Stones kept us together*. His words point to the essence of whole mate relationships.

Every level of relationship has its own core value. The core value of role mate is survival and material thriving. The core value of soul mate is personal fulfillment and the success of the relationship itself. Whole mate relationship includes the best of role mate and soul mate, but its core value and essence go one momentous step further, *beyond* the relationship itself. The relationship serves core values and the fulfillment of something outside of itself.

At level two, we generally understand having a good relationship as the sign of a good life, and the goal of the good life is the good relationship. At level three, in evolutionary relationships, we reverse the equation: the goal of the good relationship is the good life. The relationship becomes the vehicle that serves the larger goal of living a good life.

Entry 6. From *Love Story* to *The Matrix*— from Soul Mate to Whole Mate

Soul mate relationships have been depicted in the movie that we already explored in Chapter 3, the ever-poignant *Love Story*. From the perspective of level-three evolutionary relationships, it is crucial to notice that Jenny and Oliver do not have a shared horizon. There is nothing that draws them forward or unites them beyond the horizon of their own love and relationship. Their love does not have a larger context beyond themselves. As such, there is something immature in their love. As moved as we are, there remains something almost infantilizing about it. This childlike sense is captured in the movie's mantra, "Love means never having to say you're sorry." This is a looking-deeply-into-each-other's-eyes kind of love, but it has little to do with the depth of a shared horizon, which attracts and commits both partners to a shared purpose larger than themselves. As beautiful as their love is, Jenny has to die in order for the love to sustain itself in a way a popular audience could consume.

The popular movie trilogy *The Matrix*, on the other hand, beautifully illustrates several important aspects of whole mate relationship. Created beginning in 1999, the trilogy of *The Matrix* movies was, and continues to be, ahead of its time. It offers glimmers of new possibilities for relationships. Some of these possibilities were explicit in the mind of the moviemakers, and some were not. The magic of the foreshadowing that happens in movies like *The Matrix* is that it intuits rather than insists, invites rather than demands, and hints rather than preaches.

The Matrix was made by a friend and colleague, Lana Wachowski. I spent one long evening talking to Lana and her wonderful partner, Karen, about its meaning. For Lana, the "matrix" represents the hidden, dehumanizing automatic scripts of culture which deaden our Eros and *ethos*, in which we do something that we call living. To wake up and step out of the matrix is to move out of dark and deadening unconscious narratives and into the Eros of radical aliveness, *ethos*, and new possibilities. In the context of *beyond Mars and Venus*, to wake up and step out of the matrix is to step out of role mate and soul mate relationship, and into the new possibility of whole mate relationship. Of course, nowhere in the film is the idea of whole mate relationship explicitly spelled out, but it is phenomenologically demonstrated and poetically evoked.

Entry 7. The Focus of Whole Mate Relationship Is a Larger Whole

The story of *The Matrix* unfolds between its primary characters, Neo and Trinity. They move through three classic scenes that parallel *Love Story*: a first-meeting scene, a lovemaking scene, and a death scene.

Despite this parallel, the scenes themselves are completely different. Most of the scenes in *The Matrix* would actually not make sense within the context of soul mate relationship. That is the power of whole mate relationship: it offers a completely new context for relating. To get a deeper sense of this, consider the first meeting between Neo and Trinity:

Trinity: Hello, Neo.

Neo: How do you know my name?

Trinity: I know a lot about you.

Neo: Who are you?

Trinity: My name is Trinity.

Neo: The Trinity that cracked the IRS d-base?

Trinity: That was a long time ago.

Neo: Jesus.

Trinity: What?

Neo: I just thought you were a guy.

Trinity: Most guys do.

Neo: *That was you on my computer. How did you do that?*

Trinity: *Right now, all I can tell you is that you're in danger. I brought you here to warn you.*

Neo: *What?*

Trinity: *They're watching you, Neo.*

Neo: *Who is?*

Trinity: *Please just listen. I know why you're here, Neo. I know what you've been doing. I know why you hardly sleep, why you live alone, and why, night after night, you sit at your computer. You're looking for him. I know because I was once looking for the same thing. And when he found me, he told me I wasn't really looking for him. I was looking for an answer. It's the question that drives us, Neo. It's the question that brought you here. You know the question, just as I did.*

Neo: *What is the matrix?*

Trinity: *The answer is out there, Neo. It's looking for you. And it will find you, if you want it to.*

When they met, Neo and Trinity were not looking deeply into each other's eyes. They were looking for the answer to the same question: "What is the matrix?" They were looking in the same direction. They had a shared horizon.

In a whole mate relationship, it is *after* partners have looked in the same direction that they turn to look deeply into each other's eyes. Trinity is moved by Neo's mission to wake up by understanding the matrix. Neo is moved by Trinity's mission to do the same. Even though the precise contour and details of their missions are not clear at this early meeting point, they understand that they are looking at a shared horizon—that they are looking for the same thing. They know they have a job to do together. That job is their third side.

Trinity and Neo are committed to waking up. Neo and Trinity want to step out of the automatic narratives of their lives and find a deeper purpose and passion to their existence. That is what it means to unplug from the matrix. They are drawn to each other by this shared purpose, and they pursue this purpose in order to awaken others. They do this as a service to a larger context, one that extends well beyond themselves and their partnership. This is the very essence of whole mate relationship. Neo and Trinity are together in partnership, while being keenly aware that they are part of a larger Whole and are acting in service to that Whole.

What is so remarkable about this first meeting scene is that, while it is not obviously romantic, it is nevertheless dripping with Eros. There is a difference in quality between this meeting and the first meeting between Oliver and Jenny in *Love Story*. In comparison, there is something almost trite about Oliver and Jenny's meeting, which is very consistent with traditional soul mate meetings. It lacks the gravitas, the ecstatic urgency, and the sense of possibility that suffuse the meeting between Trinity and Neo.

Jenny and Oliver meet when Oliver goes to the Radcliffe library at Harvard to get a book that he needs for an exam the next day. She jousts him verbally, saying she is smart and poor, while he is rich and stupid. Stupid, that is, for not asking her out for coffee. Exasperated by the teasing, he says, "Why did you force me to buy you coffee?" She responds deftly, "Because I like your body." There is no context for their first meeting other than themselves. There is no fragrance of any larger context, and certainly no shared vision that draws them together.

Love Story is poignant, funny, wildly evocative—and all about Jenny and Oliver. We never get beyond them to a larger vision within which they live or to which they are committed. All of their integrity and purpose is invested in their own emotional life. There is no awareness that they are a part of a larger Whole. The focus of their relationship is on the relationship itself. The notion of some larger context that brings couples together is not even a remote possibility. Indeed, if the filmmakers tried to insert a shared vision, it would not be believable.

One of the shadows of role mate relationship is that the relationship itself is never the topic of conversation. One of the shadows of soul mate relationship is that the relationship itself is the *constant* topic of conversation. Whole mate relationship embraces the intensity of the relationship, but this intense and radically personal embrace is infused by the shared vision of the beloveds. Whole mate relationship is erotically intense because it is permeated by a larger intensity. The relationship is laden with meaning because the partners are drawn by meanings that are larger than themselves.

Entry 8. The Relationship Crisis Begins to Disappear at Level Three

As we feel into the very different qualities of relationship at the soul mate and whole mate levels, another distinction between these movies feels important to touch on. In *Love Story*, Jenny and Oliver are both soul mates and role mates. Oliver is clearly the primary breadwinner, which is established early on in the movie. Oliver makes the money, while Jenny pursues her passion for music and literature. In *The Matrix*, the framework of primary breadwinner and homemaker doesn't even show up.

In *The Matrix* and other films of the trilogy, Neo and Trinity's whole mate relationship articulates a new vision of provider and protector, and a new vision of hero. Neo is a hero not because he is the primary breadwinner, but because he is the One. Trinity's attraction to Neo is stimulated by his commitment to their shared vision. Neo is a hero because, in partnership with Trinity, he is fulfilling a shared destiny that they both recognize and are both committed to. Trinity is also a hero. She has seen through the illusion of the matrix. She is a computer genius and legendary coder as well as being a martial arts master and dazzling woman filled with integrity, guts, and sleek, erotic beauty. Moreover, she is a woman who has the capacity to love Neo, to see and hold a shared vision with him. It is only through her unwavering confidence that they are able to take crucial steps toward the fulfillment of their shared purpose for the sake of the Whole.

At a key point in the film, Neo questions if he is indeed the One, but

Trinity never does. Her unwavering belief in their joint mission, and in Neo as her partner, keeps them on track and largely enables their shared journey. Together, our whole mate heroes experience a degree of passion so large and so infused with Eros that the old relationship deal's issues of roles and attraction simply do not apply. A new level of consciousness effortlessly dissolves the problems created by the previous one. As we unfold the core structure of whole mate relationship, we will see that, at the level of consciousness that drives evolutionary relationships, the great relationship crisis in our culture is solved naturally.

That is what it means for a crisis in relationship to birth a new and higher level of relationship. From a role mate and soul mate perspective, there is a crisis. But from a whole mate perspective, not only is there no crisis, but there is an entirely new promise of passion, power, and possibility.

Entry 9. Unique Gender and Unique Polarity

The first meeting scene between Trinity and Neo also illustrates another core dimension of level-three consciousness: *Unique Gender*.

Unique Gender is not simply a balance between your masculine and feminine qualities. In soul mate relationships, there is already a sense that each sex has access to both their masculine and feminine energies. Unique Gender is something beyond balance. It is something much newer and much more potent. Like evolutionary relationships, it is a new emergent. It is the emergence of a new wholeness.

Before and beyond the masculine and feminine, there are two essential sets of qualities: *line* qualities and *circle* qualities (terms borrowed from the Renaissance-era interior scientist Isaac Luria).[112] These qualities are essences that are present in both Mars and Venus. However, at

---

112 On lines and circles, see, for example, Isaac Luria, Sod Iggulim Ve-yosher (1964). For a discussion of this Lurianic distinction, see Chapter 8: "Circle and Line: The Dance of Male and Female," in M. Gafni, The Mystery of Love (2003). For classical Kabbalistic texts expressing the masculine-feminine polarity in the Name of God, see R. Moshe Cordovero, Pardes Rimonim (Orchard of Pomegranates), and R. Yosef Gikatilla, Sha'are Orah (Gates of Light). See also S. Schneider, Kabbalistic Writings on the Nature of the Masculine and Feminine, a carefully annotated translation and rudimentary analysis of a classic set of mystical Hebrew texts related to this trope.

particular times in history, line qualities have been largely, sometimes exclusively, associated with the masculine. Circle qualities have been largely associated with the feminine. With the emergence of whole mate relationship, a unique expression of line and circle qualities comes online for every human being, regardless of their sex.

The configuration of line and circle qualities for every human being emerges from the hardwiring of the brain, body structure, including, of course, lactation, breasts, genitalia, and upper body strength, as well as cellular structure, hormones, and culture. Many men begin their journeys rooted in qualities of line essence. Many women begin their journeys rooted in qualities of circle essence. However, there are many men born with distinct circle qualities, and many women born with distinct line qualities.

As men and women grow, they change. Their interior qualities change as do their exterior qualities. On the interior side, values and beliefs change. Men can choose to develop their circle qualities, and women can choose to evolve their line qualities. On the exterior side, there is a change in anatomy as men and women develop an *intersex brain*, which is comprised of a unique integration of line and circle qualities.[113]

Trinity perfectly illustrates such a unique integration. In the first meeting scene, once Neo learns who Trinity is, he replies, "Jesus . . . I just thought you were a guy." He was shocked because he attributed her reputation as an accomplished hacker to line qualities, which he rigidly associated with men. While such skills may be traditionally associated with men, they are more appropriately understood as associated with line qualities, meaning that they can be developed equally by women. "Most guys do," she replies, alluding to her Unique Gender.

Since Neo and Trinity share a whole mate relationship, they naturally model Unique Gender. Trinity is tough, aggressive, and commanding. These are classic line qualities. At the same time, her love sustains Neo's drive to pursue their joint mission, even when his confidence wavers. This demonstrates classic circle qualities. Her physical appearance also portrays classic line qualities. She is taut and angular. Her tight, black

---

113 On the intersex brain, see, for example, D. Joel, "Male or Female? Brains Are Intersex," Frontiers in Integrative Neuroscience 5 (2011): 57.

leather outfit, dark glasses, strong body, and physical ability to run, fight, and jump are all line qualities. These line qualities are essential to the fulfillment of their shared mission. At the same time, she is nurturing and caring throughout the movie. Her circle radiance emerges at the end of the first movie, just after Neo dies. First, she whispers, "You can't be dead because I love you." Then she kisses him, restarting his heart and saving his life. Crucially, these circle qualities also inspire their shared mission.

Trinity incarnates all of the paradoxes and power of her Unique Gender. To be in whole mate relationship, we all need to incarnate a new type of wholeness. This wholeness includes full access to our unique combinations of line and circle qualities. This unique combination is critical for our shared missions, and it emerges through Unique Self Realization, which we will discuss in the next chapter.

Your Unique Gender births your **unique polarity**. Polarity is usually thought of as the charge between differences that creates attraction. Classically, we think of polarity as having a masculine and feminine charge. That is the model often present in the old relationships deal. In the new deal, however, we move from *binary* polarity to *unique* polarity.

Unique polarity is an expression of Unique Gender. Your Unique Gender is the unique combination of your line and circle qualities and the unique texture of the new wholeness that they incarnate. The whole is greater than the sum of the parts, so what is produced in every person is an undeniably new emergent that we call their *Unique Gender*. Two beings with Unique Genders, like Trinity and Neo, may be attracted to each other, but they are not merely attracted to each other because one has more line essence and the other has more circle essence. It is not merely their differences that attract.

Because each being has a Unique Gender, they will be similar in some qualities and different in other qualities. Their Unique Gender creates a unique and potent charge. That unique charge creates a unique attraction. Neo and Trinity are two Unique Genders with unique polarity between them that creates their unique attraction or allurement. They complete each other, but not in the old role mate sense; it has nothing to do with a balance between masculinity and femininity.

The Unique Gender of Trinity, a uniquely textured integration of lines and circles, is attracted to and by Neo, himself a uniquely textured integration of lines and circles. In some ways, Trinity and Neo are the same. In other ways, they are different. Each of them is a completely unique whole. Those wholes merge into a larger whole mate relationship that is greater than the sum of its parts. When each person in a couple incarnates their Unique Gender, they are called *whole mates*—wholes who become mates.

Neo and Trinity are superhot together not because she is more circle and he is more line, but because their Unique Genders polarize each other. The magnetic attraction between them is created by the unique combinations of their sameness and differences.

Unique polarity is a subset of unique attraction. In physics, attraction is rooted not only in difference but also in sameness. Electromagnetic charge is rooted in positive and negative poles, a charge created by difference. There is, for example, an electromagnetic attraction between a positively charged proton and a negatively charged electron. On the other hand, gravitational attraction exists between bodies that have the *same* quality, mass. In whole mate relationship, both sameness and difference generate attraction.

Entry 10. Making Love: Soul Mate versus Whole Mate

Armed with insights into Unique Gender and unique polarity, let's look at the lovemaking scenes in the movies we've discussed so far. What characterizes the lovemaking scene in *The Matrix*, simply said, is that it is wildly hot. It embodies unique polarity in all of its erotic arousal. It is hot in a way that the lovemaking scene in *Love Story* simply is not.

In *Love Story*, the lovemaking scene occurs at a moment when wounds and fears are put aside, and the lovers become open and vulnerable. This is par for the course in soul mate relationship. Just before they make love, Oliver says to Jenny: "I think you're scared. You put up a big glass wall to keep from getting hurt. But it also keeps you from getting touched. It's a risk, isn't it, Jenny? At least I had the courage to admit I cared. Some day you will have to come up with the courage to admit you care." Jenny replies, "I care." The movie cuts to the lovemaking scene, and the viewer witnesses the significance of their having moved through their fears.

Soul mates are caught up in witnessing each other's wounds.[114] That is, in many ways, a great advance. Role mates denied, ignored, or just failed to acknowledge each other's wounds and vulnerability. Their primary intention to survive and thrive left little room to grapple with the tenderness of wounding. By contrast, soul mates tend to focus overly on wounds. While that is beautiful, it also has its limits. Soul mates are whole when together but broken when apart. The brokenness is never fully healed, and once the relationship has ended, both partners are once again relegated to confronting their wounds alone.

Whole mate relationships are not sourced in brokenness or wounding. They emerge from each partner's individual wholeness, and they reach for a wholeness that is beyond the relationship itself. Neo and Trinity are called by a larger wholeness beyond themselves or even their relationship. This is a quality of consciousness that includes but transcends soul mates. The romantic poets, very much mired in soul mate love, wrote of broken hearts. *Romeo and Juliet* is a heartbreaking story. Romantic poets never wrote about a great evolutionary partnership between the lover and the beloved.

Whole mates may very well work with brokenness and wounding, but they do so for the sake of the third side of the relationship. Unlike soul mates, whole mates do not make their wounding a primary component of their relationships. Neo and Trinity do not spend the movie salving their wounds.

In soul mate relationship, making love is a beautiful moment where wounds are set aside, and a goodness and depth appear that get to a place beneath the wounding. It does not matter if the sex is marked by quivering tenderness or raw passion. Making love in soul mate relationship is always marked by two qualities. First, the sex is always intimate and personal between the couple. The goal of soul mate relationships is

---

114 See Supplementary Essay 2, "Wounds in Role Mate, Soul Mate, and Whole Mate Relationships."

personal fulfillment, and making love in that context is the apex of that fulfillment. Secondly, sex allows access to the beauty and depth that lie beneath wounding. Soul mate relationships are about communication and intimacy. Most soul mate relationship therapists teach that the deepening of communication and intimacy are the portal to more sexual passion. Naturally then, the lovemaking scene in *Love Story* is preceded by a dialogue filled with poignancy and presence. That is because, at the level-two consciousness of soul mates, we feel that poignancy and presence lead to potency and passion.

The lovemaking scene between Neo and Trinity has an entirely different texture and quality than the scene involving Jenny and Oliver. This shows up in three distinct ways.

First, while there is a sense of poignancy between Neo and Trinity throughout *The Matrix*, their poignancy does not wallow in wounds. Getting stuck in *woundology* would mean getting stuck in the matrix of yesterday.

The wounds inflicted on Oliver by his alienation from his archetypal patriarchal father are at the core of *Love Story*. At the end of the movie, after Jenny's death, he meets his father. When his father says *I'm sorry*, Oliver responds by channeling Jenny: "Love means never having to say you're sorry." Jenny becomes the vehicle for healing his father wound.

Soul mates' singular focus on wounding has no place at the level of whole mate. We never meet Neo's or Trinity's parents or other people responsible for their wounds. That would make no sense in *The Matrix*. In a whole mate relationship, the healing of wounds ceases to be the core of the lovers' identities. Whole mate relationships are present today, attracted by tomorrow, and not lost in yesterday.

Second, no words are spoken in the Neo-Trinity love scene or leading up to it. While whole mate relationship includes communication, it is not obsessed with communication. There is power in Neo and Trinity's silence. It is a *silence of presence*, not a *silence of absence*. Silence of absence occurs when communication is necessary but does not take place. In a silence of absence, partners often fumble, awkwardly and painfully, for the right words. Silence of presence, however, is of an entirely different quality. It is a silence beyond words. It is not preverbal, it is transverbal; it is beyond words. It is the ecstatic silence of a space in which words are too limiting. Whole mate relationship invites us into silence of presence.

Third, the Neo-Trinity scene takes place in what can only be described as an evolutionary dance rave. The rave has the flavor of a sacred temple celebration and is filled with beauty, raw sensuality, and pulsating music. The dancers, overtaken with an undulating, evolutionary passion, are filled with promise and hope for what is possible, despite looming danger. It is against this backdrop, in one of the private caverns above the large celebratory hall, that Neo and Trinity make love. The focus of the camera is on their faces, which is where their ecstasy is revealed. Throughout the scene, the camera cuts between them and the sacred revelry unfolding in the larger hall below.

The scene is wildly erotic and utterly tasteful—PG-13 all the way. But there is another dimension as well. While Neo and Trinity make love, there is something almost public in their lovemaking. Their lovemaking is not merely a private affair taking place between two lovers; it is a movement in a larger symphony. Their passion partakes of a wider and deeper intimacy. Their lovemaking participates in the lovemaking that is the core pulsation of the cosmos itself.

Because of the whole mate context, the scene manages to be wildly erotic and arousing without being gratuitous. This whole mate passion comes from a deeper well than soul mate sexuality. Paradoxically, the wider context of passion creates a level of arousal that cannot be easily rivaled by level-two sexuality.

At the level of role mate, passion is born of power, potency, and purpose, yet poignancy and presence, the key characteristics of soul mate relationships, are often absent. Whole mate relationship transcends and includes level two. Neo and Trinity are in evolutionary or whole mate relationship—and they are soul mates as well. Their lovemaking artfully weaves purpose with poignancy and presence, which come together to create the almost unimaginable potency of whole mate sexing.

The creative tension between the dimensions of soul mate and whole mate is not simple. There are three *Matrix* movies. Neo and Trinity fall in love at the end of the first movie. She coaxes Neo back to life by telling him that she loves him. In the second movie, Neo has to choose between his mission to save Zion and saving Trinity. In that moment, he abandons the mission and saves Trinity. By the third movie, they have integrated level-two and level-three relationship. They have arrived at a beyond-Mars-and-Venus consciousness, which fully incorporates the beauty of Mars and Venus. Poignancy and presence seamlessly merge with potency and purpose, birthing new possibilities for passion and power. At this point, the distinction between looking at a shared horizon and looking deeply into each other's eyes disappears. When they look into each other's eyes, they see the whole world. They see together. They share a vision.

Entry 11. Dying: Whole Mate versus Soul Mate

For whole mates, the commitment to serve the larger Whole doesn't waver, even in the face of death. In both *Love Story* and *The Matrix*, the woman dies in the arms of her beloved. Both scenes are heart-wrenching. But this is where the similarity ends.

To understand the difference between the death scenes in the two movies, it is essential to remember that whole mates have a shared purpose, while soul mates do not. In an earlier action sequence, Neo and Trinity take on Agent Smith in the matrix. They walk into Smith's headquarters looking totally hot and powerful. They are not *face-to-face*, as soul mates often are. They are *shoulder-to-shoulder*, and they fight *side-by-side*, with seamless grace and power. There is a symmetry in their movement. It is like watching an incredibly romantic dance, in which they make love by fighting their common adversary. The Eros of their partnership is palpable. This potency and passion are birthed by the unity of their purpose. Unsurprisingly, *Love Story* does not have a similar scene, simply because soul mates are not on a shared mission.

Steeped in the context of whole mate relationship, we can now take a look at the death scene in *The Matrix*. Toward the end of the third movie, Neo and Trinity embark on what turns out to be the final leg of their shared evolutionary mission to save Zion, the only remaining human city. It's an underground city populated by people who, like Neo and Trinity, are unplugged from the matrix. Zion is under mortal threat from the machines, who use the matrix to placate the rest of the human race, who are being used as batteries to generate power.

In other words, in the key gnosticlike world structure described in *The Matrix*, human beings are asleep, with their life power being drained to support the artificial-intelligence-driven digital world, while they are experiencing the illusion of being awake and living normal lives.

Neo and Trinity must succeed in their mission to end the war between the humans and machines. They are headed to the machine city. As they proceed, they come under attack from legions of the machines' defenses. Neo instructs Trinity, who is piloting their craft, to fly over a machine onslaught to avoid destruction. She steers their craft upward, piercing a thick layer of clouds and catching a glimpse of the Sun—for the first time in her life. She simply says: "Beautiful." Neo is not able to see it since he was blinded in an earlier fight. Even though his outer vision has been compromised, his inner vision has become more acute. He fully understands her utterance because they share a vision, whether or not Neo can physically see. As they reenter the atmosphere, their craft loses power. They crash on the outskirts of the machine city. Trinity is mortally wounded:

Neo: Trin . . . ? Trinity? Trinity?!?

Trinity: *I'm here.*

Neo: Where?

Trinity: *Here!*

Neo: We made it!

Trinity: *You said we would.*

Neo: *It's unbelievable, Trin. Light everywhere! Like the whole thing was built of light. I wish you could see what I see.*

Trinity: *You've already shown me so much.*

Here we encounter their shared vision once again. Above the clouds, it was Trinity who saw and shared with Neo. They shared a vision of beauty, even though Neo was blind. Now, as Trinity lies dying, Neo is the one who sees for both of them.

Neo and Trinity live in a whole mate relationship; its essence is a shared horizon devoted to the Whole. In their final encounter, the distinction between looking at a shared horizon and looking deeply into each other's eyes has disappeared. When they look into each other's eyes, they see the whole world. They see, together. They share vision. The scene continues:

Neo: *What is it, Trinity? What's wrong?*

Trinity: *I can't go with you, Neo. I've gone as far as I can.*

Even though their relationship is rooted in their shared evolutionary journey, *where* they are going is just as important as *who* they are going with. By honoring their respective roles and being connected, loving, and intimate with one another, Neo and Trinity have integrated the very best qualities of role mate and soul mate into their whole mate relationship. They serve a larger mission—to save humanity from the oppression of the machines. It is on the eve of this mission being fulfilled that Neo and Trinity part:

Neo: *What?* [He feels her injuries] *Oh, no! Oh, no, no, no!*

Trinity: *It's all right. It's time. I've done all that I can do. Now, you have to do the rest. You have to finish it. You have to save Zion.*

Neo: *I can't . . . not without you!*

Trinity: *Yes, you can. You will. I believe it. I always have.*

Neo: Trinity! Trinity, you can't die. You can't . . . you can't!

Trinity: Yes, I can. You brought me back once, but not this time. Do you remember . . . on that roof, after you caught me, the last thing I said to you?

Neo: You said, "I'm sorry."

Trinity: I wish I hadn't. That was my last thought. I wished I had one more chance to say what really mattered—to say how much I loved you, how grateful I was for every moment I was with you. But, by the time I knew how to say what I wanted to . . . it was too late. But you brought me back. You gave me my wish—one more chance to say what I really wanted to say. Kiss me . . . once more . . . kiss me.

Trinity's first words to Neo, ending with *You have to save Zion*, are said whole-mate-to-whole-mate. She is Neo's evolutionary partner. Despite being unable to continue at his side, she implores him to complete their mission. But her very last words to Neo are spoken as his soul mate. Neo and Trinity are in evolutionary relationship, and, as whole mates, they have integrated and operationalized every level of relationship that came before.

This illustrates a critical point. Whole mate relationship transcends and includes Mars-and-Venus relationships. An important aspect of the beyond-Mars-and-Venus relationship, the whole mate relationship, is that it has full and functional access to soul mate relationship. To be a *whole* mate is to have full access to the *whole* thing—all three levels of relationship.

The death scene at the end of *Love Story* has an entirely different quality. Jenny spars with Oliver on her deathbed, just as she did the day they first met. As they playfully spar over music, funerals, and the painful event in front of them, her death, it is clear that the scene is completely between them:

Jenny: It doesn't hurt Ollie, really, it doesn't. It's like falling off a cliff in slow motion, you know? Only after a while, you wish you'd hit the ground already, you know?

Oliver: Yeah.

Jenny: Bullshit, you never fell off a cliff in your whole life.

Oliver: Yes, I did, when I met you.

Jenny: Yeah. What a falling off was there? Who said that?

Oliver: I don't know, Shakespeare?

Jenny: Yeah, but who? I mean what play? I went to Radcliffe, I'm supposed to remember those things. I once knew all the Mozart Köchel listings.

Oliver: Big deal.

Jenny: You bet it was. What number is the A major concerto?

Oliver: I don't know. I'll look it up.

Jenny: No, but I used to know all those things, I really did, I used to know all those things.

Oliver: You want to talk music?

Jenny: What do you want to talk, funerals?

Oliver: No . . . I . . . I [shakes head].

Jenny: Ollie, I told Phil you could have a Catholic service and you'd say OK. OK? I mean it'll really help him a lot, you know?

Oliver: OK.

Jenny: Now you've gotta stop being sick.

Oliver: Me?

Jenny: That guilty look on your face, it's sick. Would you stop blaming yourself, you goddam stupid preppie? It's nobody's fault. It's not your fault. That's the only thing I'm going to ask you, otherwise I know you are gonna be OK.

Oliver: [nods]

Jenny: Screw Paris.

Oliver: What?

Jenny: Screw Paris and music and all that stuff you thought you stole from me. I don't care. Don't you believe that?

Oliver: [shakes head]

Jenny: Then get the hell out of here. I don't want you at my goddam deathbed.

Oliver: I believe you. I really do.

Jenny: That's better. Would you please do something for me, Ollie? Would you please hold me? I mean really hold me, next to me?

This scene clearly shows that Jenny and Oliver are not on a mission. They do not share a vision beyond their own relationship. Their soul mate moment is about poignancy, pain, and presence. "Would you hold me?" she asks of her soul mate as she passes. "I mean, really hold me . . ." In both movies, we cry. But these death scenes speak in different voices. Each has a distinct feeling, tone, and quality. *Love Story* speaks the language of soul mate; *The Matrix* speaks the language of whole mate.

Entry 12. What Is Your Context for Relating?

The major distinction between the different levels of relationship lies in the *context* for relating.

The context for relating in a level-one role mate relationship is first to survive and then to succeed and thrive. To succeed and thrive in a role mate relationship, we need to excel in our roles. Being successful at fulfilling your role, however, is not just an external accomplishment. It gives you an inner sense of being at home in the world, because you are aligned with the larger obligation of your social role.

Feeling loved is a function of how we fulfilled our role mate obligations. The way to say *I love you* is to be a great provider, homemaker, or parent. The way to say *I love you* is to raise our children together. That is why, in the hit Broadway play *Fiddler on the Roof*, Golde does not quite understand what Tevye means when he asks, "Do you love me?" She answers as a role mate would, "For twenty-five years I've washed your clothes, cooked your meals . . ." and she goes on to list all of her *roles*. What she is expressing is the core consciousness of role mate relationships. You feel loved when your partner fulfills their roles. Those are the basics. Everything else is extra. Feeling lonely was painful but certainly not sufficient basis to leave a marriage. As we saw in Chapter 3 (Entry 7), Tevye is inviting Golde to explore with him a new level of consciousness, level-two soul mate relationship. In the old role mate relationship, the currency of love was personal sacrifice.

The context for relating in a soul mate relationship is personal fulfillment. Placing that front and center is a major goal of this level of relationship. It is about being happy and feeling loved. To be loved at level two means feeling understood and received. The currency of love is personal fulfillment. Communication is the holy grail. Action is insufficient. Saying the words *I love you*, regularly and convincingly, is essential.

The personal fulfillment of soul mate relationship is closely tied to moving beyond personal loneliness. The context for relating is liberation from loneliness. Your sense of being at home in the world is simply being with your beloved. My ex-partner liked to say, "I just want to sit and watch whales with you. That is enough for me." That is level-two relationship.

I grew up in an excruciatingly painful family context. My first great love was a girl named Betty, whom I met when I was fifteen years old. The context in which I grew up was a rigid orthodox fundamentalism, in which any physical contact before marriage was, as my teacher drove home time and time again, "biblically prohibited on multiple grounds." All through high school, I tried valiantly to keep the law. So, Betty and I never kissed. We never even held hands.

There were only a few times that we actually spent several hours together, but I can remember each one of them clearly. Just being with her in the same room, feeling the grace of her presence, the inherent tenderness of her heart, stopped me in my tracks. We took several walks by the Hudson River. As I write these words decades later, the presence and poignancy of those moments are fully alive for me.[115]

It was in those moments that I felt at home in the world for the first time. They taught me it was *possible* to feel at home in the world. The wounds of my childhood were, if not healed, at least softened and suspended by those moments. I felt seen by Betty. I was alive in her gaze. In her presence, I felt like a good child of the Universe. I was received, and I was wildly honored to receive her. Nothing was left out. No words were left unspoken. For those short times, the searing pain of my youth, the ruptures in my spiritual lineage that occurred in the Holocaust, and the enormity of suffering that haunted my young mind, were at peace. Betty was not to be my wife; indeed, we rarely communicated after those years. But our moments together were soul mate moments. In all of my

---

115 I have not seen her or talked to Betty for thirty-five years. As I wrote these lines, I was moved to look her up online. I just saw a picture of her at her dad's funeral. She looked exactly the same. She is married with kids. She married a fantastic man, who is a great teacher and community activist. It is unlikely that we will talk again in this lifetime. We live in different worlds today. But the beauty and goodness of those moments stay with me.

subsequent relationships, I looked to recreate something of the soul mate magic I had learned was possible.

In level-two relationship, you feel at home in the Universe through the depth of your contact with your beloved. Part of why we look for our soul mate is because we are looking for our deep sense of home.

The context for relating at level three, whole mate, is a shared purpose larger than the relationship itself. A relationship always has core values. At the leading edge of business today, companies that want to become conscious engage in processes designed to explicate their core values. We do the same in level-three whole mate relationships.

The core values of role mate relationships are to fulfill your roles. In a soul mate relationship, they are the relationship itself. The core value of level three is the shared vision that holds the relationship. The shared vision is not the fulfillment of the relationship. Rather, the purpose of the relationship is to fulfill the vision.

We reach for level-three relationships when personal fulfillment is no longer personally fulfilling. We reach for level three, when we awaken to the powerful realization that we are personally fulfilled when we embrace shared values and embark upon a mission that lies beyond ourselves and our relationships. We are together—omniconsiderate for the sake of the Whole.

When I was in my twenties, I met a missionary couple. They married with the intention to start a mission for their religion in some remote outpost in the world. Through them, I met their broader network of some thirty-five hundred couples, who had each planted their mission's flag across the globe. As I got to know them, I was always blown away by the depth of their love and relationship. This surprised me. For the most part, they did not do any couples' therapy. They were not part of the human potential movement that involved conscious work on healing and transformation in relationships. They were not big consumers of relationship literature. So, what did they have or know that gave them such fantastic relationships?

Both curious and inspired, I began to informally interview the young couples that I met. Over the years, their answer was virtually always the same. It was always some version of what one of the wives said to me:

"We are passionate about our relationships because we have shared passions." This is akin to saying: *We have a shared mission. We are spreading the good word. We are sharing values with the world that we know to be transformative. We are starting soup kitchens and nursery schools. It is our shared work that binds us, that attracts us to each other, and that animates our love and Eros.* By the way, another one of the wives shared in a rare direct moment, "Our sexual passion is sustained over the years. It lasts way beyond the early period of infatuation."

Entry 13. Up-Leveling Your Intention

Not every whole mate couple must start a nursery school or a soup kitchen together. While that is an awesome vision, it might not be possible or appropriate for most. But whole mate relationship does mean, at a minimum, that we must shift the very orientation of our relationship. We must up-level the *intention* of our relationship.

For example, one of the core engagements of level-two relationship is to work with the untransformed wounds of each of the partners. Susan Sontag captured the level-two relationship sensibility when she wrote, "I am only interested in people engaged in a project of self-transformation."[116] Rather than the old role mate relationships, in which the value of love rises as the value of self dwindles, in level two, the project of love is the project of self.

Level-three relationship does not abandon the project of self. Sometimes it looks on the outside exactly the same as a level-two relationship. The actions and lifestyle might indeed be exactly the same. But there is a profound shift in intention that changes the whole relationship.

The move from soul mate to whole mate begins with an evolution of intention. The beloveds are able to say to each other and to themselves:

---

116 Susan Sontag, As Consciousness Is Harnessed to Flesh: Journals and Notebooks, 1964-1980 (2012).

We are doing our work of transformation, of holding each other, not just for each other, but for the sake of the larger Whole. We are loving each other not just for each other, but for the sake of the larger context. We're offering up the work we're doing for the sake of the evolution of love. We're offering up our transformation for the sake of the transformation of all of Reality. As we look deeply into each other's eyes, we begin to widen our vision to see a much larger Field.

In one mystical tradition,[117] every single personal act between lover and beloved was done with what is called the intention of *LeShem Yichud*, or *for the sake of unifying*, the masculine and feminine in all of Reality. This tradition anticipated modern physics and systems theory discoveries: the individual is not in any ultimate sense separate from the larger Field. Because of this, the personal is the political, and the personal is the global. As we shall see, the personal is also the cosmic.

In level three, we realize the truth of what meteorology calls *the butterfly effect*. A butterfly flapping its wings in Tokyo affects weather patterns in the Gulf of Mexico. Yet the butterflies don't flap their wings to change the weather; they do so in the name of a larger intention and purpose: migration. The first step toward living in an evolutionary relationship is not to take any particular action, but to transform your intention. That is the way to start playing a larger game. The work you do to develop and deepen your love is no longer merely for your own fulfillment, but for the sake of the larger context: the evolution of love.

Entry 14. The Third Side

In a level-three relationship, there is what our colleague Bill Ury calls *a third side*.[118] Ury is talking about negotiating a conflict. If the conflict is

---

117 This tradition birthed the troubadours in medieval Europe and was the matrix for the popular The Da Vinci Code novel at the beginning of this century.

118 See W. L. Ury, The Third Side: Why We Fight and How We Can Stop (2000).

a battle between two sides, it is very hard to resolve.[119] For many, if not most, people relationships are a level-two proposition with the goal of personal fulfillment. For that precise reason, soon after the first stage of falling in love ends, the power-struggle stage of relationship begins. It often lasts through most, if not all, of the relationship. The power struggle usually ends when the relationship ends or when hope for the relationship dies. The hidden desire of each side is to have it all their way.

Much relationship advice is about the art of negotiation and dealmaking. How can I make a deal to get as much as I can and to be as happy in my relationship as I can? Since people are basically good, they want the deal to be fair. Since people are basically kind, they want their partner to feel good. Since people are fundamentally loving, they enjoy giving to their partner. Nonetheless, the power struggle continues.

In an argument, each side says: *I want it my way.* The other side says in response: *No, I want it my way.* One side says: *My preference is better.* The other side says: *My preference is better.* The relationship becomes a courtroom with each partner acting as a lawyer opposing the other, and adducing evidence for the superiority of its client's preference.

It doesn't matter what the issue is. It can be taking out the trash, doing the dishes, spending and earning money, living here or there, having a baby or not. The same dynamic applies to both major and minor issues—to sexuality, lifestyle choices, and all of the everyday, totally mundane, but life-making stuff. Each side fights for personal fulfillment and satisfaction.

The level-two challenge is this: *How do I get what I want without him or her being resentful?* After all, if one partner is resentful, the outcome will not work for either. First, it won't work because each loves the other and does not want to feel bad for him or her. Second, one will feel bad for making the other resentful. Third, one doesn't want the other to treat him or her less kindly out of resentment. Thus, the soul mate dyad comprises a triple threat of loss for personal fulfillment. Most relationship seminars and books offer a set of tools to resolve this impossible paradox of relationships. Dealmaking between two separate entities remains

---

119 See Chapter 5, "From Soul Mate to Whole Mate," Entry 5.

the core staple of most level-two relationships. Dealmaking is about compromise. Willingness to compromise is commonly understood as the most important virtue to look for in a level-two partner.

But remember our guiding mantra: *we cannot solve a problem at the level of consciousness that created it.* To transcend the power struggle that is the bane of every relationship, we have to evolve our relationship from level two to level three. At level three, we transcend the conflict because it ceases to be about the two sides. As we described in the story of Lily and Jack in Chapter 5 (Entry 5), a third side is introduced. This third side is the larger context and purpose of the relationship that both sides share. Both parties commit to the third side as much as, or even more than they do to each other. The third side forms a triangle. We move from a dyad to a triad. Triangles are exceptionally stable. Instead of there being a constant win-or-lose dynamic based on compromise, there is something much more potent: both sides check in with how their positions align with the third side.

The third side is the attractor that draws the couple into the future. It has a pull dimension rather than a push dimension. Usually, soul mate relationships are pushed from behind by all of the yesterdays, including personal histories and the wounds of each party as well as the couple itself. All too often, this factor pushes the relationship off a cliff. Evolutionary relationships, by contrast, are pulled forward by the creation of a future rather than being weighed down by memories of the past.

The third side of a whole mate relationship is not about mere preferences, like eating Italian food. That is fabulous if you both like Italian food. But it is more of a shared lifestyle passion. It is a shared interest. These are at the heart of a soul mate or even a role mate relationship. But a shared interest is not a third side. Shared *purpose* is a third side that transcends personal taste.

Jack and Lily, the couple we met in Chapter 5, shared with us that they move from the soul mate power struggle to whole mate stability and passion by standing together, side-by-side, against relational conflict. Standing side-by-side against conflict is a whole mate ninja move. Looking deeply into your partner's eyes is a soul mate ninja move. It is lovely, but doing so is particularly unpleasant when you or your partner are constantly triggered by each other. In a whole mate relationship, however, this is the precise moment when partners can move to the same side. From that place, they can stand together against the conflict. The commitment to stand together against conflict manifests as harmony. Harmony becomes the third side.

The third side can be created by shared values, such as harmony in the relationship. But to really establish a third side in a whole mate relationship, harmony *solely in your own relationship* is insufficient. You might begin with harmony in your own relationship, but it must evolve to include the Value of Harmony itself. You might begin with the value of love in your own relationship, but you must up-level to include the Value of Love itself. Creating success in your own relationship then becomes not only about personal fulfillment, but also about evolving what it means to be in relationship itself.

Entry 15. To Be a Whole Mate Is to Be in Service to a Larger Whole

Whole mates must devote their relationships to something beyond themselves. As we said in Entry 13, whole mates must say to each other,

> *We are doing our work of healing and holding each other, not just for each other, but for the sake of the larger Whole. We are loving each other, not just for each other, but for the sake of the larger context. We are offering up our work, both in our relationship and in the world, for the sake of the transformation of our families, communities, and society.*

Ultimately, whole mates must say,

> *We are offering up our relationship for the sake of the evolution of relationship itself.*

Within this context, creating love, passion, and success becomes not only about personal fulfillment, but also about acting in service and devotion to love, passion, and success for the Whole.

We used to teach that the moment you act in service and devotion to a value beyond your relationship, you transition from soul mate to whole mate. In the fullness of time, we realized that the evolution starts even earlier. The emergence of evolutionary whole mate relationship begins with a shift of intention. You begin to live in an evolutionary context, in relation to the Whole. This evolution changes everything. To engage actively in whole mate relationship is to participate in the larger evolution of consciousness. This is what it means to participate in the evolution of love through your love and devotion.

Said another way, the evolution of love and consciousness *for everyone* is pushed just a little bit forward when you and your whole mate evolve your own love and consciousness in the lives of actual relationships.

It might seem wild that two individuals and their interpersonal relationship can impact the evolution of love for everyone. But every action you and your partner take creates a unique pattern of intimacy. This unique configuration of intimacy opens up new possibilities, whose purpose is to potentiate ever-deeper intimacies. Your unique pattern ripples through the Universe and makes it just a bit more likely that other couples will repeat the pattern. Over time, the more a pattern is enacted, the more that pattern becomes a common and everyday expression of future couples.

For example, imagine that you and your partner have come up with a new way to have an argument. Instead of arguing for your point of view, both of you vehemently argue for the position that you think best integrates your point of view with your partner's. Let's say that you have been doing this for years, and it really works to help you both get past what would otherwise be intractable arguments. These actions ripple throughout the Universe, influencing the actions of couples everywhere. To be clear, we are not suggesting that couples will behave in the exact same way as you. Rather, we are suggesting that because of your actions, the probability that couples will seek out more evolved ways of arguing will increase.

Level-two relationships have two sides with a primary goal that the relationship be balanced or fair. However, relationships are never exactly fair; that is just not how it works. You will never balance the equation, and you will die trying. At different times, different sides need to do more or be more than the other. It may balance out over the course of a lifetime, or it may not. But if your goal is fairness, you are setting yourself up for failure.

This is where the third side in whole mate relationships becomes so crucial. The goal of a relationship at level three is not fairness but greatness. A relationship is great when it fulfills a shared vision and purpose beyond the relationship itself. Reality is relationship, and relationships are in service to Reality. At level three, service to a third side replaces compromise. The third side becomes the decision maker. Compromise, contrary to popular wisdom, does not enliven the relationship, but rather deadens it. The constant demand for minicompromises actually drains life energy. In an unconscious defense, you bring less and less of yourself to the relationship to avoid constant compromise. After all, in each compromise you give up something essential to yourself.

In level-two relationship, beautiful as it may be, there are two pulls, and the one who pulls harder wins. Pulling harder might mean persuading better, being more convincing, being more persistent, or being a better dealmaker. But the person who feels pulled by an energy that opposes their own energy is never happy. In a level-three relationship, each side is pulled by the same energy. That energy is what we refer to as *the third side*. It is the apex of the triangle that calls both partners to a space beyond themselves and beyond their relationship. What naturally happens in that space is that both parties bring more and more of themselves to the relationship.

When the third-side value is a commitment to living *an extraordinary life*,[120] the question ceases to be who is right or what is fair. The question becomes: *Which decision is consistent with living an extraordinary life?*

To be in a whole mate relationship is to admit something very big: that there is something in life that is larger than you, your partner, and even your relationship. When you admit that, everything else opens up.

---

[120] We thank Tony Robbins for the phrase an extraordinary life.

That is the beginning of being truly alive. We truly live and love when we identify and align with a value that is larger than ourselves and calls our relationship to evolve.

Entry 16. Exercise: Shared Value Discovery in Whole Mate Relationship

The following exercise will help you to discover the third side in your relationship. Sit with your partner and write a list of what you most cherish or find most important, which exists beyond your relationship itself. If you are currently single, sit and write a list of values that you would be willing to devote yourself and that you would like to pursue with a future partner. Discuss or journal about these values.

What is most important and why?

What do you most want for the world and what does that look like?

How do you rely upon each other to serve these values?

Once you are clear on at least a handful of compelling values, imagine a time and place where you are fulfilling these values in a direct and complete way. Then transform this probable future into the present by writing these values on note cards in the form of affirmations.

For example, if your value is *to serve the growth and transformation of everyone you work with*, your affirmation might be:

Our relationship is deep, stable, and powerful. We serve the transformation of others with clarity and compassion.

Place these affirmation cards wherever you spend time reflecting, either alone or with your partner. Where you meditate or like to read are ideal places. Then, whenever you encounter them, read them to yourself or to each other and feel deeply the truths that they are calling into existence.

Making a list of your most closely held values and discussing them with your partner is one of the most powerful conversations you can have. This is because *together* you unearth a shared reality—a third side to your relationship. You answer the question,

Why are we in a relationship? Is it for love? Is it for joy? Is it for growth? Why are we doing this?

When you agree on what your third side is, you have discovered why you are in relationship. You take your relationship off the automatic setting, and you create a deliberate reason to be together.

If you are currently single, don't think for a second that this discussion doesn't also apply to you. While you can't identify a third side outside the context of a relationship, you can identify a purpose that is beyond yourself. When you do, you create the single most powerful context for finding a partner with whom you'd be able to share this purpose as a third side. In a sense, this purpose can act as an attractor for an ideal partner. And in the meantime, you'll be serving a larger vision and supporting the evolution of the Whole.

In level-two relationships, the goal of life is a good relationship. A good life has a good relationship in it. In level-three consciousness, the relationship serves the shared vision of a good life. At level three, relationship is not the life goal, but the most potent vehicle for serving life's goals. A relationship that does not contribute significantly to the realization of life's goals beyond the relationship eventually stagnates and dissolves, even if the couple stays together. But an evolutionary relationship allows us to pursue the goals that give meaning to our lives.

Shared life vision beyond personal fulfillment is the elixir of level-three relationship. A wise man once said, "If you don't know where you are going, you might wind up someplace else."[121] A relationship without purpose beyond the relationship itself almost invariably winds

---

[121] A famous quote by baseball legend Yogi Berra, considered by many to be the greatest catcher in history.

up someplace unintended—usually woefully so. A relationship cannot survive as a mutual admiration society. That is true on every level of relationship. At the same time, every relationship must be rooted in a mutual admiration society. And then it must be more. Again, Barbara said it well:

> In our experience, that shared purpose for a goal far greater than could be accomplished alone, or even with a soul mate, is intensely pleasurable. It leads to deep personal fulfillment. The separation between personal, social, and evolutionary fades into a new shared impulse infused with Eros. I came up with a definition of this whole mate experience as **the Three E's**.
>
> The first E is *Emergence*: Something new is coming forth from you as you join your genius with your whole mate. You are becoming newer, more attractive, more alive.
>
> The second E is *Embodiment*: You begin to embody the shared purpose as a passionate living impulse that wakes you up in the morning and puts you to sleep every night. This impulse courses through your body-mind animating you, healing you, inspiring you.
>
> The third E is *Eros*: You become *telerotic*, animated by *telos*—high purpose, and Eros—passionate Evolutionary Love, the Love that creates new life, new consciousness, new freedom and order. You become an Evolutionary Lover filled with joy and gratitude.

Entry 17. Whole Mates Love the World through Loving Each Other

At level three, we take a momentous leap beyond the mutual admiration society. We realize that we do not exist behind the wall of our relationship. Rather, we and our relationship are an inextricable part of the larger Whole.

In that precise sense, we are whole mates, not just with each other but with the Whole. From that place of connection to the larger Whole, we offer up our own transformation for the sake of the transformation of the Whole. We commit to our love not only to fulfill ourselves, but to strengthen love for the Whole. We participate in our own evolution for the sake of the evolution of love. It is through this larger shared intention and commitment that we begin to step out of our fragmented selves and relationships. We begin to feel and taste a connection to the larger Wholeness, in which we are full participants. In this, we become whole mates, partners in evolutionary relationship.

When you choose an evolutionary partner, or when you choose to evolve with your current partner into an evolutionary relationship, there is a thrill and sensual attraction that runs much hotter than hormones and infatuation. You are allured to your evolutionary partner because you fulfill your most precious life dreams and purpose with them and through them in a way that you could not by yourself. More than that, your evolutionary partner shares your dreams and purpose and stands for them. What you are saying to your level-three partner is, "I can be *me* better than I could ever be through us being a *we*."

That is the kind of shared horizon that births evolutionary partnership. In an evolutionary relationship, you want not only to love and appreciate each other's good qualities or cuddly bodies, but also to share an aesthetic of the Good, the True, and the Beautiful that creates shared purpose. Infused by a devotion to the Good, the True, and the Beautiful, that is the third side to which both sides are committed. To quote Barbara again:

> I have also the intensely personal experience that each of us is becoming better, truer, and more beautifully Our Self. In some sense the *out there* and *in here* blend into a form of wholeness in the Field of Love of whole mates. Whole mates feel themselves to be part of a larger Field of Wholeness. We are calling that new Field a new species: *Homo amor*. It is the Field of the species-wide integration into a new whole system far greater than the sum of our parts.
>
> *Homo sapiens* co-created a new whole system, a new culture,

and consciousness in the Neanderthal world. So now, members of the new species we are calling *Homo amor* are co-creating a reality that transcends and includes the growing edge of all our capacities—personal, psychological, spiritual, vocational, social, innovative, and high-tech, evolving at an exponential rate of growth, to make radical newness—as new as *Homo sapiens* once was new.

A growing, astonishing inner newness, combined with the pain of the world, is part of the extraordinary experience of whole mate. The experience that I can compare with it is being pregnant and giving birth to the unknown child who had grown within me all on its own! The immediate outpouring of astonishment and love both parents feel for that really difficult little creature is comparable to the awesome joy whole mates feel as they are giving birth to new memes as part of a new world.

I remember with one of my birth moments, when I was being wheeled into the delivery room, I had my big black journal on my tummy. It was bouncing up and down with the kicking of the unknown child within me. The labor pains had begun. It was really painful. I remember saying to the nurse, "If I did not know I was giving birth, I would think I was dying!" The same is true for us as humanity now. Some of our problems are excruciating. The pain and suffering are terrible. There is no guarantee that we will make it, just as with the emerging child. No one knows for sure how it will turn out. But it makes a huge difference to know that our crisis is a birth, on the evolutionary scale. With the baby, we know what to expect, but not fully. With ourselves as an evolving humanity under the threat of devolution and self-destruction, we don't know fully. Yet, if we tune in to our inner sense of Reality, to the impulse of creativity and faith within each of us uniquely, if we can remember that, as Marc describes it, the Universe is a Love Story, with purpose and direction (witness the 13.7 billion years of supramental genius that created us out of nothing at all), we can feel an immense anticipation and intuition. We can sense that we are giving birth to a species of divine capacities in a Universe undoubtedly filled with life.

As *Homo imaginus*, we can imagine what we are becoming as a universal species. We can remind ourselves that imagination creates; it's the only thing that does! We can activate that awareness and inspire our unique yearning to contribute to the Planetary Awakening in Love through Unique Self Symphonies, in which every one of our voices is heard.

A shared purpose leads us as partners to evolve and grow together, rather than to devolve and grow apart. One might say that whole mate relationship is emerging wherever Eros or passion is sourced by shared *telos* or purpose. Shared purpose plus passion equals whole mate relationship. Whole mates *live* in a potency of purpose and passion that can last a lifetime. Together, *telos* and Eros create what we have called *Teleros*. Whole mate relationships are therefore *telerotic* partnerships: *partnerships rooted in passion and purpose*.

Whole mates love the world through loving each other.

In a soul mate relationship, the beloveds look at each other, and the world—the Whole—*disappears*. The soul mates experience themselves as the whole. And they are right—in part.

In a whole mate relationship, the beloveds look at each other, and the world *appears*. And they are right—in part.

But whole mate includes and transcends soul mate. The beloveds look at each other. They experience soul mate magic, and the world disappears. Whole mates gaze at each other even more deeply, and the whole world reappears in ever-more depth, color, and bold relief. Whole mates look into the eyes of their beloved and see their beloved, and in their beloved's eyes, they see the whole world.

Entry 18. Value in Role Mate, Soul Mate, and Whole Mate Relationships

In role mate relationships, the centrality of shared value has always been taken as a given. To function, role mates need to share both an implicit theoretical *vision* of value and a pragmatic *practice* of value. This is self-evidently true for beloveds who are parents. It is almost impossible to raise children without a shared Ground of Value. But parenting needs to be the model and not the exception. In our own lives, we can somehow manage to ignore the fact that we are living in relation to Value, and that the nature of *that* relationship shapes every single dimension of our lives.

The proscription against racial or tribal intermarriage, whether of soft social nature or of more serious legal/tribal nature, generally had something to do with the community's desire to perpetuate both its particular vision of Value and its accurate view of Value as the foundation stone of relationship. Granted, of course, that some of these proscriptions in society were also related to an ethnocentric sense of racial superiority, and that a dimension of these proscriptions needs to be roundly rejected, as it has been by liberal societies world over. But that rejection should not blind us to the essential wisdom of the great traditions: relationship is bound up with Value.

In the emergence of soul mate relationships, the classic proscription against relationships with shared communities of ethnicity and value was swept away. Indeed, such proscriptions were regarded as regressive. But beyond the rejection of ethnocentric proscriptions, the level of soul mate consciousness is making a more essential proclamation: Love is said to conquer all, *including* Value. Therefore, for soul mates, Value was simply not part of the relationship's conversation. Many times, I have met with couples in counseling and asked what drew them together. Italian food and dancing and their equivalents came up far more often than a shared framework of Value.

It is not, however, that the soul mate level of consciousness *necessarily* opposes Value. In some cases, soul mate relationship assumed value in the sense of what we have identified as the *common-sense sacred axioms of value*.[122] This strain in modernity borrowed the *reality* of Value from

---

[122] See David J. Temple, First Principles and First Values: Forty-Two Propositions on CosmoErotic Humanism, the Meta-Crisis, and the World to Come (2024).

premodernity, even as it rejected premodern *sources* of Value. *Value just is, and you don't need to think about it a lot; it is a self-evident given, and get on with your life.* The underlying cultural assumption of this strain of thought is that we don't know its source, and we don't really care.

However, other strains of soul mate consciousness are more caught up in various forms of existentialism, or early postmodernism, which followed the primary thread of modernity that deconstructed Value altogether.

Either way, Value was written out of the essential terms of the soul mate equation. This became one of the primary reasons that soul mate relationships failed. Once the experience of looking deeply into the eyes of the beloved is no longer sufficiently compelling, the beloveds need to turn to a shared ground and vision of Value. When that is no longer available, the relationship loses its allure. Part of the ground of allurement between beloveds is Value itself.

At the level of whole mate relationship, Value comes back online. As at the role mate level, it is utterly central to the relationship. When we say that whole mates need to look at a shared horizon and only then turn and look deeply into each other's eyes, we are talking in large part about a shared horizon of Value. The allurement of Value is central in the play of Eros, intimacy, and joy that binds the whole mates.

Of course, the nature of value often changes from role mate to whole mate. For role mate the context is often local, whether *local* means cultural, economic, political, or religious. For whole mates, value is always the intrinsic Value of the Whole as it applies to their lives and their intentions for the sake of the Whole.

Entry 19. Eros and *Ethos*: A Deeper Look for the Advanced Reader

It is not that Value was entirely rejected in soul mate relationship. Rather, love (or what we have referred to as *Eros*) was taken to be the primary value, at whose altar all other values were required to kneel.

One of the qualities of Value is that Value arouses will. The word *will* in the original Hebrew (*ratzon*) is an Eros word, drawn from, among other sources, the *Song of Songs*, otherwise known as the *Song of Solomon*.

The *Song of Songs* is an erotic expression of Reality, which declares that its insides are lined with love.[123] In other words, Reality itself is Eros. Akiba, the central figure in the transition from the Jerusalem Temple to the oral law, understood the *Song of Songs* as participating in the ontology of the Holy of Holies of the Jerusalem Temple. In another text, he talks about it as a sufficient basis to guide the moral world, even if the *Torah* had never been given.

At the outset of the *Song of Songs*, the lover says to her beloved: *Draw me after you, and I will run toward you.*[124] The term *run toward you* (in Hebrew *rutza*) shares its etymological root and meaning with the Hebrew word *ratzon*, which translates as *will*. In other words, *draw me after you* means: *I will surrender my lower will to you and allow myself to be taken over by the deeper Will of Reality, of Eros moving through me, that arouses me to you and overwhelms all separation and boundary.*

In the deeper presentations of soul mate relationship, this Eros was understood, intuitively if not explicitly, to be the Ground of Value itself, hence the appropriate devotion at its altar. For soul mates, however, this centrality of Eros as Value sweeps away all other values.

By contrast, at the level of whole mate consciousness, there is a deeper clarification at work. It understands that Eros as Value does not sweep away the Field of Value but is the *Ground* of Value. At this clarified level of consciousness, Eros does not *oppose* ethics; a clarified Eros becomes the source and ground of all ethics.

In this sense, we often talk of Eros and ethics in terms of three levels. **Level one** is the level of Eros that precedes the depth of work in *ethos* and discernment: Eros prior to *ethos*. This is followed by **level two**, which *is* the great work of *ethos* and distinction. This is then theoretically followed by **level three**: Eros that includes and transcends *ethos*, even as it is both the ground of *ethos* and shaped by it. Indeed, in the *Song of Songs*, as it is read by the interior sciences of Hebrew wisdom, Eros is understood as Value itself. In other words, Eros is ontologically understood to be *identical* with *ethos*. There is no ultimate split between Value and Eros at all.

---

123 Song of Songs, 3:10.

124 Song of Songs, 1:4.

This is part of the general sense of the interior sciences of Hebrew wisdom that, from an ultimate perspective, Will and Eros are identical. Will is the interiority of Cosmos that desires Value. Or, said differently, Will is the appetite of Cosmos itself for Value. This is captured in the root word *ratzon* that stands for *will*, which includes both moral will and Eros, or erotic will.

Rooted in these considerations, Value—either its fulfillment or its violation—quite literally arouses our will. When we see Value violated, we are aroused to action—just as our desire to fulfill Value arouses us to action. When we experience ourselves as having stepped out of the Field of Value, which in the East is sometimes referred to as *the Tao*, our will to action goes limp, whether it concerns politics, morality or economy. We become impotent.

This relationship of Value to will is intimately linked to the vision of a shared *Ground of Value*, a Field of Value that lies beneath polarizing clashes around specific dogmatic applications of specific values. Reality itself is Eros, which means that Reality is Value. That is the essential realization of the Solomon lineage, exemplified in many texts including the *Song of Songs*.

In this sense as well, whole mate consciousness includes and transcends soul mate consciousness. Whole mate recognizes, as does soul mate, the utter centrality of Eros. But for soul mate, Eros becomes the only value. Sometimes that means that soul mate consciousness replaces the Field of Value with the romantic story. But in other writings and expressions, it is because soul mate consciousness may have killed all the other goddesses but still offers devotion to Aphrodite, the Value of Eros. In other words, the Field of Value has been deconstructed, and only the Value of Eros still allures us.

But soul mate relationship breaks down because it makes a false division between the Value of Eros and the Eros of Value. The Value of Eros is embraced while the Eros of Value is rejected.

Table 3. Role Mate, Soul Mate, and Whole Mate

	ROLE MATE	SOUL MATE	WHOLE MATE
Self	Separate self	Separate self	True Self, Unique Self, Evolutionary Unique Self, and participation in the Unique Self Symphony
Level of Consciousness/ Intimacy/ Identity	Egocentric Ethnocentric	Ethnocentric Worldcentric	Worldcentric Cosmocentric
Core Value	Survival and thriving	Personal fulfillment	Service to the Whole
Relationship to the Field of Value	As separate self, role mate does not necessarily experience oneself as part of the Field of Value	As separate self, soul mate does not necessarily experience oneself as part of the Field of Value	Experiences oneself as inside and participatory in the Field of Value
Falling in Love	Social, religious, cultural fit Exchange of value	*Chemistry* between the beloveds Imago theory Looking deeply into each other's eyes	Third side Looking at a shared horizon
Shadow	Power plays Manipulation Narcissism of one	Leveling of differences Loss of passion Narcissism of two	Individual self and personal intimacy are lost in the desire to liberate or heal the Whole

	ROLE MATE	**SOUL MATE**	**WHOLE MATE**
Quality of Love	Ordinary love experienced as a human sentiment or a social construct even if a beautiful and moving social construct	Ordinary love experienced as a human sentiment or a social construct even if a beautiful and moving social construct	Outrageous Love, Evolutionary Love, or the Eros of Cosmos as the intrinsic Reality of the Cosmos, not mere human sentiment but the Heart of Existence itself
Characteristics	Dependency: I need you Protectiveness Achievement	Independence: I choose you Intimacy/ Communication Presence	Interdependency: I choose to need you Evolutionary partnership Guided by larger narrative/ Telerotic
Core Concepts	Protection Sacrifice Duty Honor Obligation	Poignancy Presence Communication Transcending Loneliness Healing of wounds	Shared Horizon Transformation Evolution Purpose Vision
Goals	Personal survival Thriving of self & family Fulfill obligations	A good relationship (A good life has a good relationship in it.)—Liberation from loneliness Heal wounding Love each other	A good life (The relationship serves the shared vision of a good life—for the Whole of Life.) Transform the Whole Be lived as Love
Question	"What is in it for me?"	"What am I getting in exchange for what I have given?"	"What am I willing to give up in mad love and devotion to the larger Whole?"

PART TWO

—

EVOLUTION OF SELF IN RELATIONSHIP

—

CHAPTER 7

UNIQUE SELF

The first step in the transformation from soul mate to whole mate is to up-level identity itself. As beautiful and important as the consciousness of role mate and soul mate relationships and their correlated levels of identity have been, they are no longer at the leading edge. They are no longer a sufficient basis for relationships that seek to participate in the evolution of love. To up-level identity and therefore up-level relationship, we need to move beyond the ego. We need to cultivate an entirely new identity as the basis for the next level of relationship. The new form of identity that lies at the core of whole mate relationship is what we call *Unique Self*.

Entry 1. Four Selves

What we typically understand as *self* is made up of four distinct selves: separate self, True Self, Unique Self, and Evolutionary Unique Self. In this chapter, we offer you a simple way to experience the **first three selves**. Then, in the next chapter, we'll introduce the **fourth**. When you know them, you can recognize and embody each of them when needed. Knowing the four selves is an essential part of beyond-Mars-and-Venus consciousness. It is also absolutely essential in up-leveling your identity and bringing your Unique Self online.

Separate Self

The first self is *separate self*. Upon entrance into the world, there is no clear boundary between the infant and his environment. Over time, the infant *individuates* by differentiating self from environment. Separate self is a massive developmental milestone. According to developmental psychologist Margaret Mahler, this is the true moment of birth.[125] As growth continues, the separate self gains strength by making further differentiations: body from mind, self from others, and so on, and by creating and reinforcing these new boundaries.

We can understand the four selves through the metaphor of a puzzle: A self is an individual piece of a larger puzzle. The experience of separate self is that of the first puzzle piece. It has its own boundaries and shape, and it knows the integrity and importance of those boundaries. The puzzle piece also wants to fit in. It feels that in finding the larger puzzle, it might be able to make a unique contribution that will somehow make the world more complete. The puzzle piece seeks the larger puzzle. If society tells the puzzle piece that there is no larger puzzle, the puzzle piece becomes depressed. It hobbles along—puzzle pieces do not fare well alone. It always feels that it should be connected to the larger puzzle.

The puzzle piece yearns for something more. It cannot believe that this is all there is. It is pathologized by society for not fitting in and for not being happy.

As a person's separate self grows, she begins to get over the fantasy of her idealized life. She recognizes the story of her life for what it truly is. She embraces her life in all of its complexity, ecstasy, and pain. She bears it all, and she delights in it all, because it is her life. In claiming her life as it is, she starts to feel something deeply right about it and herself.

Yet even in what feels like progression, the separate self is limited. If the separate self focuses too closely on her experience of separateness, she winds up alienated or disassociated from the larger Whole. This is the source of much personal and collective suffering. Moreover, the separate self is a shaky foundation for relationship at any of the three levels. Because she is not able to step out of herself to feel the pain and passion of her beloved, she finds true understanding of her partner to be difficult if not impossible. The relationship between two separate selves

---

125 See, for example, M. Mahler, Psychological Birth of the Human Infant. Symbiosis and Individuation (2000); M. S. Mahler, "On Human Symbiosis and the Vicissitudes of Individuation," In J Am Psychoanal Assoc. (October 1967); M. S. Mahler, "On Child Psychosis and Schizophrenia: Autistic and Symbiotic Infantile Psychoses," The Psychoanalytic Study of the Child 7 (1952): 286–305.

often falls into crisis.

Separate self consciousness is what is considered *normal*. In reality, it is insane. Sanity is to know your true identity. If I claim to be Prince William and insist on that claim, and you realize that I am not merely joking, then you have incontrovertible evidence that I am insane. But the claim to be merely a separate self, a skin-encapsulated ego disassociated from the whole, is far more insane. It violates the leading-edge realization of all of the interior and exterior sciences. It is simply not true. That is what Albert Einstein meant when he referred to the claim to be a separate self as *an optical delusion of consciousness*.[126]

To get a deeper sense of the insanity of separate self consciousness, consider this: 200 million human beings were killed during the twentieth century by war and oppression. Approximately 3.1 million children died from undernutrition in 2018,[127] in a world where there is enough food to feed every child, four times over. That is more than eight thousand children who die every day because of issues related to starvation or malnutrition, even though a thousand times the amount of food needed to feed them is thrown out every day. This is the product of separate self consciousness, which believes that everyone is separate from everyone else. The separate self is the source of the grasping, the fear, and the drive for power that lie at the heart of every conflict. The belief that we are each separate is what fuels the political and social consciousness that thinks that eight thousand starving children is somehow normal or in any way unpreventable. Is this not insane?

The experience of separateness is an illusion of our consciousness. This delusion is a kind of prism, locking us into the prison of our personal

---

126 Einstein in a letter in 1950 to Robert S. Marcus. In Einstein's own translation: "A human being is a part of the whole, called by us 'Universe,' a part limited in time and space. He experiences himself, his thoughts and feelings as something separated from the rest—a kind of optical delusion of his consciousness. The striving to free oneself from this delusion is the one issue of true religion. Not to nourish the delusion but to try to overcome it is the way to reach the attainable measure of peace of mind." Retrieved January 2024 from https://www.thymindoman.com/einsteins-misquote-on-the-illusion-of-feeling-separate-fromthe-whole/.

127 See "World Child Hunger Facts," Hunger Notes, retrieved January 2024, https://ww.worldhunger.org/worldchild-hunger-facts/.

desires and a conditional affection for a small circle of people. We must free ourselves from this prison. By widening our circles of compassion to embrace all living beings and the whole of nature, we can find a way out.

When we move beyond the *normal* consciousness, we restore ourselves to sanity. To be sane is to be aligned with the deeper truth of Reality. To be aligned with Reality is simply to know that there are no externalities. Nothing is outside, disconnected, or alone. We are all part of the same fabric of life. Every decision we make affects all of us. To wake up is to know that you are not separate. This is the first step in the evolution of your identity: the transformation from separate self to *True Self*.

True Self

True Self is the second expression of Self. The move from separate self to True Self is often called *evolution beyond ego* (*ego* is another word for separate self). But that is not quite accurate. We should never fully evolve beyond ego or separate self. Rather, to realize our true nature, we need to evolve beyond our *exclusive* identification with our ego. The interior scientists might say: *Separate self is a reality in the mind of God*. Or more directly: *A healthy sense of our separate individuated self is a crucial part of our wholeness*. But it is very far from the whole thing. To be sane, to be aligned with our own true nature, we need to evolve beyond our exclusive identification with our ego.

This is why, at some point, we all yearn to evolve beyond our separate selves, particularly when we are no longer able to identify wholeheartedly with a self that is so painfully limited. We may then awaken to a larger identity by recognizing that we live as part of the larger Reality. We may realize that the space beyond our personal story, the awareness beyond our separate self, has become foreground instead of background. We may come to see that our true nature is not that of an isolated and individuated person, but rather an essential part of the larger context of life. Sometimes this dissolution occurs spontaneously. Sometimes it occurs through overwhelming pain or extreme fatigue. At other times, it emerges as the fruition of years of dedicated study or meditation.

The experience of True Self is not that of being a puzzle piece, per se, but rather of being the puzzle itself. Your sense of being separate is blurred. You lose yourself in experiences of dance, music, sexuality, and sports. That is the good news.

The danger is that the classical teachings of enlightenment tell you that the puzzle pieces are just an illusion, that the only True Reality is the larger puzzle, and that only your experience of the Whole is Real. Intuitively, this does not seem right. You clearly see the outlines of the distinct puzzle pieces, but you're told they are illusions. You are encouraged to move beyond your story and to evolve beyond your ego. You are told not to just to evolve beyond *exclusive* identification with your ego, but simply to evolve beyond your ego entirely. This leads you to feel just as torn and, strangely, just as fragmented as you did when your separate self was told there was no larger puzzle.

A great illustration of waking up to True Self is the famous red pill or blue pill scene in *The Matrix*. Morpheus is speaking with Neo about the matrix:

Morpheus: *Do you want to know what it is?*

[Neo nods]

Morpheus: *The matrix is everywhere. It is all around us, even now in this very room. You can see it when you look out your window or when you turn on your television. You can feel it when you go to work, when you go to church, when you pay your taxes. It is the world that has been pulled over your eyes to blind you from the truth.*

Neo: *What truth?*

Morpheus: *That you are a slave, Neo. Like everyone else you were born into bondage, born into a prison that you cannot smell or taste or touch, a prison for your mind. Unfortunately, no one can be told what the matrix is. You have to see it for yourself. This is your last chance. After this there is no turning back. You take* *the blue pill: the story ends, you wake up in your bed and believe whatever you want to believe. You take the red pill: you stay in Wonderland and I show you how deep the rabbit hole goes.*

[Neo reaches for the red pill, pauses]

Morpheus: *Remember, all I'm offering is the truth, nothing more.*

[Neo takes the red pill and swallows it]

Morpheus: *Follow me.*

In the movie, human beings who are plugged into the matrix are slaves. They are used to power the world of the machines while believing they are living normal lives, which are, in fact, generated by the matrix. The matrix is the world of illusion. If you take the red pill, you become unplugged. You wake up from this illusion, and you step out of the prison into the larger truth of who you truly are.

Normal consciousness is the illusory belief that you are a separate self, disconnected from the Whole. Normal consciousness is insane. The deeper truth, revealed by both systems science and interior sciences, is that *Reality is Relationship*. No person is truly separate; nobody is an extra on the set of life. This realization is part of what has been called *enlightenment*. But at its core, enlightenment is simply sanity.

Unique Self

The third experience of Self is *Unique Self*.[128] Your sense of personal distinction, the hallmark of separate self, comes back online at a higher

---

[128] The notions of Unique Self and Unique Self Symphony emerged at the interface of religious scholarship, psychological meta-theory, and evolutionary meta-theory—expressed collaboratively in different forms by Gafni, Stein, and Hubbard. This work naturally integrates with Hubbard's seminal work expressing and exploring Conscious Evolution: Awakening the Power of Our Social Potential, by B. Marx Hubbard (2015). For a detailed look at the genesis of Unique Self Theory itself, see the special scholarly issue of the Journal of Integral Theory and Practice, 6, no. 1, which is dedicated to Unique Self Theory. The volume was edited and largely

level of consciousness. You realize that you are not merely an indistinct part of a larger Whole, as you were as True Self. Now you recognize that you are indeed a self that is an essential part of the Whole, but that you are a part which expresses itself *uniquely*.

Your Unique Self, which begins to reveal itself at the level of personality, fully flourishes after freeing itself from the grasping of separate self. Unique Self makes parallel appearances with True Self during peak experiences. An example of this can be a moment of *flow*, sometimes called *being in the zone*, when ego temporarily drops, and a felt, or even lived, experience of Unique Self becomes available.

As a True Self, we move from an experience of ourselves as separate, as a mere *part*, to an experience of ourselves as inseparable from a larger Oneness or Wholeness, where our sense of distinction is overcome, even if momentarily. As a Unique Self, we experience an even deeper realization. We experience ourselves as a part once again, but from the place of vast awareness, where we realize that our unique part-ness is not separate from the Whole. As Unique Selves, we transcend the limitations of separate self while affirming the autonomy, value, and infinite dignity of our uniqueness. We realize that our unique shapes and perspectives complete a part of the larger puzzle as no other piece can.

Despite the roles we play in this larger Whole, we often experience ourselves as separate. The distinction between *unique* and *separate* is essential. Uniqueness is the currency of connection. Separation is the coin of alienation. Separation creates loneliness and disassociation. Uniqueness, on the other hand, is the key that opens the lock. It's the way that the puzzle piece fits into the puzzle. It's the way that an instrument brings the symphony to life. The very contour of uniqueness creates integration, connection, and wholeness.

As you begin to develop a relationship to this larger Whole, you move to complete an important prerequisite for becoming a whole mate. When

---

penned by M. Gafni, with the lead article, "The Evolutionary Emergent of Unique Self: A New Chapter in Integral Theory," JITP 6, no. 1 (2011): 1–36. See also M. Gafni's works Your Unique Self: The Radical Path to Personal Enlightenment (2012) and Self in Integral Evolutionary Mysticism: Two Models and Why They Matter (2014) on the core articulation of Unique Self Theory.

you move past the grasping of your separate-self ego, you realize your nature as indivisible from the larger Field of Reality. You recognize and value both your distinctness and the wholeness. From there, you can move to fully access your Unique Self and to engage in a whole mate relationship.

Entry 2. Two Transformations of Identity: Unique Self and Unique Gender

It is impossible to talk about relationship independently of the identities of the lover and beloved. The relationship is an expression of the identity of each of the parties. When we come to a point where level-two relationships cease to work, it is because the old identities cease to work. Remember our guiding mantra: *you cannot solve a problem at the level of consciousness that created it.* If we want to up-level relationship, we must up-level identity. Said simply, the transformation of relationships is directly based on the transformation of identity. The evolution to whole mate relationship requires the transformation to Unique Self Identity.

The old identity of role mate and soul mate consciousness has two important components, one based on gender, and one based on individual needs. Both components are transformed as identity is up-leveled.

The first transformation required to up-level identity is straightforward. At the role mate and soul mate levels, both men and women see themselves as individual *separate selves* who want to love and be loved. Role mates earn love by responsibly fulfilling their individual obligations with honor and dignity. Soul mates earn love by being empathetic, validating, and communicative partners who liberate their beloveds from loneliness. More recently, individuals earn love through an integration of both role mate and soul mate qualities.

A separate self is not an essential part of any larger whole. It is not rooted in any larger field of belonging. It has no essential calling or vocation besides the apparent coincidence of talent and interest. When the goal of life is to be a happy and successful individual, the basis of relationship is weak. As a separate self, being needed and valued in relationship becomes a desperate attempt to cover up the essential fear of not being needed or valued by Reality.

The first transformation of identity, then, is the move from separate self to Unique Self. As Unique Selves, our experience of what it means to be loved evolves radically, along with the needs that we are each able to address uniquely. We recognize that we are loved and needed by all of Reality. We no longer experience ourselves as being loved only by our separate-self partners. Rather, we realize that Reality itself is loving us open in every moment.

As Unique Selves, we are no longer separate selves addressing the local needs of other separate selves. Instead, when we are addressing the needs of others, we are addressing the needs of Reality itself. When we love our partners, for example, we are not just loving the separate selves that give us egocentric security. Rather, we are loving them as unique expressions of All-That-Is. The people we are loving are indivisible from the larger Whole and can be loved only in our unique fashion.

The second transformation is also straightforward. Men were from Mars, and women were from Venus. That remains true, but there is a higher level of wholeness that wants to emerge. **In that higher level of wholeness, which is fundamental to becoming a whole mate, a new identity rooted in Unique Gender is emerging.** As we have seen when talking about Neo and Trinity, Unique Gender is a unique combination of the line and circle qualities.[129] This unique combination is greater than the sum of its parts.

Let's say your name is Tami. You are not merely Tami who has access to both line and circle qualities. Your unique integration of line and circle qualities creates a unique emergent called *Tami-ness*.

In popular culture, line qualities used to be exclusively associated with masculine and men. Circle qualities used to be exclusively associated with feminine and women. Now we realize that these two qualities of Reality show up fully in both men and women. Many men are rooted primarily in line qualities, while many women are rooted primarily in circle qualities. But there are also many men who do not identify readily with line qualities, and many women who do not identify readily with

---

[129] Lines and circles are qualities of Reality traditionally identified as masculine and feminine (see Chapter 6, "Whole Mate," Entry 9).

circle qualities. Moreover, the key is that every human being has a deeper identity than their gender. **Unique Gender is part of the unique erotic quality of one's Unique Self.**

We can trust evolution to create crisis and then respond by opening the door for transformation.[130] The crisis at this moment is not merely a crisis in relationship. It is also *a crisis in identity*. There can be only one response to such a crisis: an evolution of identity. Identity means one thing. It's how you answer the question of *Who am I?* Once your answer becomes *a Unique Self*, a transformation of gender and needs unfolds, up-leveling your identity in the process.

Entry 3. Finding Your One True Authentic Swing

The movie *The Legend of Bagger Vance* tells the story of a relationship lost and rekindled. It takes place in Savannah, Georgia, in 1931. Rannulph Junuh[131] (Matt Damon) is the favorite son of Savannah and a promising golfer. Adele Invergordon (Charlize Theron) was his girlfriend before he went to war and is a wealthy member of the community.

> While serving as a captain in the army, R. Junuh was traumatized when his entire company died in battle. Although he earned a Medal of Honor, he returns to the US sad and depressed. He lives life in a drunken cloud. His love for golf, a sport in which he once connected with his Unique Self, becomes a distant memory. R. Junuh and Adele, once in love, cannot reconnect because R. Junuh refuses to talk to her. R. Junuh, after all, has lost his game. As a result, he has also lost any hope for a reunion with Adele.
>
> Years after R. Junuh returns to Savannah, Adele holds a golf tournament to recover a portion of her family's lost fortune.

---

[130] See Chapter 1, "The Arc of Evolution," Entry 8.

[131] The names are obvious plays with names from the Bhagavad-Gita: R. Junuh is Arjunah, and Bagger Vance is Bhagavan, which is another name for Krishna.

She arranges a grand prize of $10,000 and secures the participation of Bobby Jones and Walter Hagen, the two best golfers of the era. She needs a local participant to generate local interest, so she asks her estranged love to play. R. Junuh still can't find his game, but he ultimately says yes.

At his point of greatest need, help appears. R. Junuh is approached by an unfamiliar and somewhat mysterious traveler while hitting golf balls at night. The man identifies himself as Bagger Vance (played by Will Smith) and says he will be R. Junuh's caddy. R. Junuh accepts.

When the tournament starts, Jones and Hagen play well, and R. Junuh falls far behind by the end of the first round. While Bagger Vance caddies for R. Junuh, he gives him advice that R. Junuh mostly ignores. R. Junuh clearly suffers through much of the tournament.

Then, Bagger Vance speaks, and R. Junuh finally starts to listen: "Junuh, I think it's time."

"Time for what?" R. Junuh asks.

"Time for you to see the Field."

We can understand the *Field* that Bagger Vance refers to as the LoveIntelligence, LoveBeauty, and LoveDesire that connects everything with everything else; it is a radical wholeness of interconnection. Because R. Junuh is lost in the pain of his past and the wound of his ego, he cannot see the Field. The weight of his history has closed his eyes and limited his perception.

"The Field?" says R. Junuh, in the irritated voice of one who's blinded. "I see the field; it's 445 yards long, it's got a little black flag at the end of it, and it's twelve strokes ahead of me.

The field? Come on."

"That ain't it," replies Bagger Vance, "because if you'd seen the Field, you wouldn't be hacking at that ball like you was chopping at weeds out from under your front porch."

R. Junuh ignores Bagger Vance, just as we as human beings often ignore the evolutionary voice calling us to Unique Self. As he is about to hit the ball, he realizes he can't do it. He can't find his swing. At that moment, R. Junuh faces all his pain and desperation. The pain of his unlived life overwhelms the pride of his posturing. He turns to Bagger Vance and says, "All right, what's the Field?"

This question marks the turning point in R. Junuh's life. He has finally reached out for help. He wants to know the Field. This is akin to the moment when we step out of the narrowness of our separate-self-identity and seek to know our connection to the larger Whole. It is the pivotal point of transformation.

Bagger Vance responds: "Here. Fix your eyes on Bobby Jones." Jones is in his game. His game is sourced in his Unique Self. One of the best ways to access Unique Self Consciousness is for someone to model it for us. R. Junuh fixes his eyes on Jones.

In the movie, the camera pans to Jones as Bagger Vance talks. He describes Jones's actions as he finds his way into the Field. The Field is the space in which everything, including you, is alive, in the right place, and connected to everything else. When you realize that you are inseparable from the larger Field, you access True Self. True Self *is* the Field. True Self is not Unique Self; it is the Ground out of which Unique Self emerges.

Suppose you are solving a difficult problem, or you need to make a challenging personal decision, and you are not sure what direction is right. You might take a walk to clear your head. Or maybe you go for a run, take a shower, or sleep on it. As you are walking, letting your thoughts freely wander, something happens. Your thoughts suddenly organize themselves. New connections become apparent. A new possibility presents itself. That is an experience of accessing the Field. The Field is the True Self from which all creativity emerges. The Field sources all energy, direction, and creativity.

> Bagger Vance guides R. Junuh's eyes toward Jones. "Look at his practice swing. Almost like he's searching for something, then he finds it. Watch how he settles himself right into the middle of it. Feel that focus. He's got a lot of shots he can choose from, duffs, and tops, and skulls. But there's only one shot that's in perfect harmony with the Field. One shot that's his authentic shot. And that shot's going to choose him."

You are not alone in looking for your Unique Self. Your Unique Self is also looking for you. To be unique is to be chosen. All of Reality has chosen you to express a dimension of being and becoming that can be expressed only through you and as you. The idea that the Field of LoveIntelligence, LoveBeauty, and LoveDesire wove Reality to manifest *you* is mind-bending. You are chosen, and you are needed. Reality requests your service. That is the core of Unique Self Realization.

> Bagger Vance continues as R. Junuh watches Jones awaiting the arrival of his swing. "There's a perfect shot out there. There's a perfect shot out there trying to find each and every one of us. All we gotta do is get ourselves out of its way. Let it choose us."

To get out of the way, you have to move beyond the limiting belief that you are a separate self. You have to find your way into the Field. The field is the seamless coat of the Universe—seamless but not featureless. You are a unique feature. Recognizing this is the realization of Unique Self. When you are in harmony with the Field, *the shot*, or your Unique Self, has the opportunity to choose you.

Bagger Vance elaborates, "You gotta look with soft eyes. See the place where the tides and the seasons and the turning of the Earth all come together, where everything that is becomes One. You gotta seek that place with your soul, Junuh. Seek it with your hands. Don't think about it; feel it. Your hands is wiser than your head is ever gonna be. I can't take you there, Junuh. Just hope I can help you find a way. It's just you, that ball, that flag, and all you are. Seek it with your hands. It's the home of your authentic swing."

The camera pans to R. Junuh. It is his turn to swing. We watch R. Junuh with the same intensity that he watched Jones. The frame goes silent. The music is perfect. He finds the Field, and he swings. The ball sails with power and grace down the field. The shot is precise and potent. R. Junuh has accessed the Field. He has found his swing.

R. Junuh pulls back to a tie with Jones and Hagen. He has a chance to win on the final hole but calls a penalty on himself when his ball moves as he is removing an obstacle. R. Junuh has transformed. He is not home yet, but he is on the road to Unique Self Realization. Bagger Vance leaves as mysteriously as he appears, with the eighteenth hole unfinished. Even though he lost the chance to win because of the penalty, R. Junuh sinks an improbable putt, ending the match in a three-way tie. The three golfers shake hands with all of Savannah cheering.

R. Junuh has found his game, and unsurprisingly his relationship with Adele is reignited.

This is a Unique Self story that rekindles the passion of relationship. It is the beginning of an evolutionary relationship because R. Junuh and Adele have found each other in common cause—to save her father's legacy by successfully staging the golf tournament and inspiring local support by helping R. Junuh, the local hero, to recover his game.

A transformation in relationship is always sourced by a transformation of identity. The transformation of identity required to move us fully into whole mate relationship starts with recognizing our Unique Selves.

Finding the Field Exercise

To *find the Field*, you have to escape the narrow contraction and grasping of your egoic mind. In its own insidious way, this is always comparing you to everyone else.

Find your own inner rhythm and get quiet. Find the Field. You might find it by watching the ocean. You might find it through music or dance. You might find it by walking. You might find it simply by sitting quietly. When you find the Field and let yourself sit in it, resisting the compulsive need to fill it up with busyness or thinking, you feel the quality of your Unique Self arising in you. First, you access the Field—the True Self. Then, from the Ground of True Self, your Unique Self arises.

> **Finding the Field Exercise:** Get quiet. Follow your breath. Listen to a beautiful piece of music. Look at pictures of nature. Focus on a phrase that compels you and repeat it in your mind. Do whatever works for you to quiet your mind and enter the Field. Just be in the Field. All of Reality conspires to support you in awakening to your Unique Self. When you genuinely commit to the search, when you genuinely commit to being in harmony with the Field, the Field turns to find you.

Entry 4. Unique Self Is the New Context for Relating

As we have seen in Part I of this book, every level of relationship has its own context for relating. Evolutionary, whole mate relationships are based on an entirely new context for relating, a context created by the higher vision and purpose of the whole mate relationship.

Evolutionary relationships are rooted in the larger Universe Story. We call this new Story *CosmoErotic Humanism*. That Story is revealed in leading-edge scientific information about the nature of Reality and our place in it, which discloses three key realizations:[132]

Reality is evolution.

Reality is Relationship.

Reality is the evolution of relationship.

This new information does not cancel out the old wisdom of the great traditions. Quite the opposite. In important ways, it confirms the deepest intuitions shared by the world's great traditions.

CosmoErotic Humanism asks three core questions.

1. The first is: *Who Are You?* This question is about the narrative of identity. How I understand my identity changes everything.

2. But the first question cannot be answered without the second: *Where are you?* This is the question about the very nature of the Cosmos. What is the Universe Story[133] in which we live? Is the Universe dead or alive? Is Reality purely exterior and mechanistic or is the Universe filled with interiors? Does the Universe *feel*, and does it feel *love*?

3. And finally, there is the question of *What.* (*What* depends on the *Who* and the *Where.*) The *What* question is: *What do I really want? What ought I do? What is my true desire? What is my*

---

132 See Chapter 1, "The Arc of Evolution," and the companion volume, The Evolution of Love, for an in-depth exploration of this theme.

133 Of course, by story or narrative we don't mean the subjective story that catches our superficial fancy. Rather we mean the leading-edge set of validated insights from premodern (traditional), modern, and postmodern wisdom streams, woven together and synergized into a new Story of Value, greater than the sum of all the previous parts.

deepest heart's desire?[134]

At this juncture, we have been focusing on the *Who* question. A bit later we will naturally focus more specifically on the *Where* question and the *What* question. For now, the following is sufficient in terms of the *Where* and *What* questions:

Reality is not merely a fact.

Reality is a story.

Reality is not an ordinary story.

Reality is a love story.

Reality is not an ordinary love story.

Reality is an Evolutionary Love story.

And your story, your love story, is chapter and verse in the Universe: a Love Story.

Waking up to evolutionary relationships means realizing that your love story is part of the larger Love Story of Reality. Your relationship is an expression of the impulse toward intimacy, which is the very impulse of Cosmos itself, waking up as you. New forms of relationship drive life forward to new levels of love. New forms of relationship drive the process of emergence. The trajectory of evolution is the evolution of relationships, which is the evolution of love.

Unique Self relationships emerge as evolutionary relationships. You

---

[134] It is worth pointing out here, that the Why question is, paradoxically, off the table. The Why question almost always gets mired down in dogma and abstract philosophy and theo-logic, none of which is grounded in any direct sense of knowing. If we engage the Where, Who, and What questions, the Why resolves itself in a self-evident way.

can choose to ignore the context of Reality that science has revealed. But Reality keeps being true, even if you do not believe in it. To be sane and whole is to be aligned with Reality. To be insane is to deny Reality. Sanity means knowing one's Unique Self. Unique Self is one of the core structures of Reality. Not to know your Unique Self doesn't mean that you miss some abstract or elite form of spiritual or psychological intuition. **Not to know your Unique Self is simply to be insane.**

Evolutionary relationship is rooted in evolutionary partnership. Two parts come together to fulfill a shared purpose larger than themselves. You may have noticed that this sounds somewhat like the level-one role mate relationship. Indeed, at level three, some of the core features of level one come back online but at a different level of consciousness.

The values of purpose, duty, honor, heroism, dependency, and obligation are all on the table once again. But at level one, the purpose, obligation, or duty are external to the beloveds. They are imposed upon them by the stories prescribed by society. They need to fulfill their purpose, pay their dues, do their duty, meet their obligation. The purpose must be pursued even if it goes against their own inner truths, desires, or sensibilities. At level three, the purpose is not external but internal. It is freely chosen with delight. Responsibility becomes not a burden, but a joy. Purpose is sourced by a higher passion.

Unique Self is the new context for relating. Unique Self realization sources the purpose and potency for each of the partners and for the relationship itself. Your Unique Self story plays out in the larger evolutionary context and forms the parameters of your purpose. These are the sources of sustained power and passion, suffused with the poignancy and presence of your evolutionary relationship. In a word, the sacred autobiography of each of the partners, each Unique Self, becomes the new context for relating.

Your Unique Self is your contribution to a whole mate relationship. It is powerful, potent, and alluring. A man or woman living their Unique Self exudes a quiet confidence that attracts people more than anything else.

Over many years, we have asked thousands of men and women the following question: *What is the single most powerful attractor between beloveds?* The most common answer has always been *confidence*. We are not referring to bravado or the posturing of an unsure ego. Self-involvement, arrogance, and narcissism cover up a lack of authentic confidence. To meet a person who exudes the potent confidence of being fully in his or her Unique Self is to fall madly in love. That kind of authentic confidence births passion, creativity, kindness, and courage. It births people who are heroes of their own lives. The only way to be the hero of your own life is to live from your Unique Self. Unique Self is the language of heroes.

Over the last four decades, we have encountered countless couples who were separating. Often, the problem was rooted in a complaint about their partner. "I could not make her happy" and "I felt like he never really saw me," were the two most common complaints. The path to healing these sad and desperate dynamics emerges directly from the beyond-Mars-and-Venus vision of whole mate relationship.

This new vision engenders a relationship comprised of Unique Selves. In such relationships, both partners are filled with joy. Both feel radically appreciated and seen. These are the natural features of a whole mate relationship.

Entry 5. You Are Your Unique Self

To Find Who You Are, Find Your Yearning

Unique Self Realization is the best response we have available at this juncture to answer the great question: *Who am I?* This is the question of our lives. We ignore it by being busy, successful, or asleep. But it always comes back, knocking at our door.

Every single decision and action in your life ultimately traces back to how you answer this question. And you cannot be in a whole mate relationship without answering it. When you are truly honest with yourself, when you get beneath your personality and all the demands of your life, who *are* you?

To find your way into the answer, you must start by finding your yearning. Not your surface desperations, not the grasping of your separate self, but the truest and deepest longing that lives inside of you. Your yearning is your deepest heart's desire, which is the Desire of Reality itself uniquely incarnate in you. Your most authentic longing is the truest indication of your identity. Your longing points you in the right direction.

Let us try to articulate the dimension of your yearning that we all share. This is, paradoxically, our desire for our uniqueness, the desire to live our unique stories. Read the following paragraphs with an open heart, to hear what expression of yearning resonates with you.

> I want to be more. I want my life to be infused with vitality, purpose, and meaning. I want to be delighted to get out of bed in the morning.

> I want my life to be a love letter to Reality, to all the people in my life, and to myself. Right now, I am stuck in commitments I need to fulfill, but which do not enliven me. I have bursts of energy at peak moments in my life. At those times, I get a glimpse of what might be possible, but much of my life is dull, heavy, and painful. The old wounds I thought I'd worked out long ago resurface constantly. I am, more often than I care to admit, angry, petty, or jealous. I am ashamed at how regularly I am caught in the clutches of anger and jealousy. Even when I am not caught in their clench, I feel somewhat limited and lackluster. I find myself acting from the shadow version of my light. I want so desperately to be seen. And that does not feel right to me. My life feels ordinary, and I know that my life should be epic and extraordinary. I feel small, but I want to be large. I want my life to be responsible, but also alive and ecstatic. I want to live outrageously! I want to play a larger game!

In its pathological form, our dissatisfaction creates disease. But in its potent form, dissatisfaction is the source of our authentic yearning and, therefore, of our authentic power. Our yearning is not mere grandiosity, as some psychologists may have us believe. Rather, our yearning is the truest indicator of our essential nature. Just as a fish does not yearn for dry land, we do not long for that which is not ourselves.

We feel that there is something larger than life that lives in us. We yearn for a passion larger than any we have ever felt. We want to create life and to make a contribution. We want our lives to matter in the grand scheme of things. We yearn for potency and purpose. We may hide our yearning, deny our yearning, or medicate our yearning, but it won't go away.

We often lose ourselves in our external obligations, to dull the pain of an unfulfilled dream of living a larger life. We sacrifice ourselves on makeshift altars to false gods. If we cannot find a true altar at which to prostrate ourselves, then we choose an alternative path of deadening ourselves to the pain of the smallness of our lives. We *lose* ourselves in television, novels, social media, or work, when what we really want is to *find* ourselves. We want to find that drive, that power we've felt in the peak moments of our lives. The drive to sacrifice ourselves is universal, existing in every culture, and at every time. Makeshift altars and false gods mislead us. But in the act of sacrifice on a true altar, we transcend our small selves, even if just for a moment. We ask ourselves: *What would it mean to live that way every day? To live from whatever that source is?*

Uniqueness Is Your Birthright

The source from which you desire to live is your Unique Self. Your Unique Self is the answer to the great question, *Who am I?* You are an irreducibly unique expression of the LoveIntelligence, LoveBeauty, and LoveDesire of All-That-Is. The LoveIntelligence, LoveBeauty, and LoveDesire that drives all of Reality lives in you, as you, and through you. There is no one like you who ever was, is, or will be. *You are a Unique Self.*

It took Reality 13.7 billion years of complex and dazzlingly precise synchronicities to produce you. Your cellular signature is the unique dance of trillions of unique cells, distinct from any others that ever were, are, or will be, in unique symphonic relationship.

Imagine that you could see your immune system, in all its complexity, intricacy, and beauty. On the one hand, all human immune systems would appear to share the same core features and structures (and indeed, they do). On the other hand, and herein lies the magic, each of our immune systems is wildly and gorgeously unique. The radical uniqueness of each of our immune systems would render each a magnificent piece of art, unrivaled by the greatest artists of all time.

Uniqueness is an objective structure that expresses itself physically. It is also an interior quality, the unique essence of each of us. Each of us has unique perspectives, tastes, and qualities of intimacy that are expressions of our unique interior qualities. Our unique interiors are our inheritances, our birthrights. They have evolved through the mythic tales of our sacred autobiographies. Every single person in the world has the birthright of uniqueness.

Your Unique Self is your unique perspective. Your unique perspective births your unique insight. Your unique insight is actually *Reality's* unique insight *through* you. Your unique insight births your unique gift. Your unique gift to Reality is your unique capacity to live life as only you can.

Reality needs your unique gifts. Your unique gifts create your unique capacity to respond to a unique need in your circle of intimacy and influence. You are Reality's eyes, hands, legs, and love. You are a unique expression of evolution. Evolution is love in action. Evolution awakens *as you*, in person. You have unique gifts to give and a unique life to live, one that is utterly and essentially needed by the Whole. You are in relationship to all of Reality. Reality needs your service. There is a corner of the world that will remain unloved unless you stand on the abyss of that particular darkness and say, *Let there be light!*

Your Unique Need Is Your Transformation

Who are you? You are a Unique Self. What does that mean?

It means that you are an irreducibly unique expression of the LoveIntelligence, LoveDesire, and LoveBeauty that is the animating energy and aliveness of All-That-Is. This unique expression lives in you, as you, and through you. It never was, is, or ever will be again—other than through you. You are here to be the poem that only you can be. You are here to sing the song that only you can sing. You are here to be the unique presence of being and becoming in the world that no one else but you can be.

Through your unique gift, you are uniquely empowered to address a unique need in your unique circle of intimacy and influence, that can be addressed by you and you alone—in the particularized special way that you are able to address it.

To address that unique need is your unique calling and your unique, inherent obligation. This obligation is not imposed from without but is the unique expression of your unique configuration of LoveIntelligence, LoveDesire, and LoveBeauty. You recognize the unique need that is yours to address because it arouses your deepest heart's desire. Giving your unique gift to address that unique need is the unique joy and unique responsibility of your unique life.

Even more: Giving your unique gift, which addresses a unique need in your unique circle of intimacy and influence, is *your own* deepest need. Your own deepest need is your deepest heart's desire. In giving your unique gift, you awaken as the leading edge of evolution and incarnate a unique quality of Evolutionary Love. You become the personal face of Conscious Evolution.

Your Unique Self is your unique configuration of *being* and *becoming*.

Your unique configuration of *being* includes the full spectrum of your qualities of presence and interiority.

Your unique configuration of *becoming* includes your unique transformation, which is evolution itself continuing its own process of transformation in you, as you, and through you. In the depth of your Unique Self Realization, it becomes clear that **your unique need is your transformation**, which is the transformation of the Whole that can be uniquely accomplished only by you.

Your Unique Self means:

There is a song that is yours to sing, a poem that is yours to write,

a way of being, loving, laughing, living, suffering, gifting, and transforming,

which is yours and yours alone to experience.

And through that experience you are more.

Reality is more.

God, the Infinite Intimate, is more.

She, God/Goddess, the Infinite Intimate, experiences a shocking self-recognition that could be evoked only by you.

Entry 6. Your Unique Frequency of Light

One way to think of your Unique Self is as the unique frequency of light that emanates from you.

This is not a metaphor; it is hard science. In the 1970s, while investigating a possible cure for cancer, German physicist Fritz-Albert Popp discovered that all living things, from single-celled plants to human beings, emit a tiny current of light.[135] He called it *biophoton emission*. This emission is an expression of the unique frequency of light embodied in every human being. Popp understood that it is through this light that organisms communicate with their different parts and the outside world. Popp and about forty other scientists around the world have carried out several decades of research on biophoton emissions. They suggest that it is these unique frequencies of light that conduct the unique cellular processes within the human body.[136]

Biophotons live within the DNA, setting of certain frequencies of light within the molecules of individual cells. They are a method of communication within the living organism a well as *between* organisms.[137] Popp adds that it is the *coherence* of the biophotons, emerging from *an almost fully coherent field*[138] that allows for communication. As the DNA

---

[135] L. McTaggard, The Intention Experiment: Using Your Thoughts to Change Your Life and the World (2008), 27. See also J. J. Chang, Communication between Dinoflagellates by Means of Photon Emission (1995), 317–330.

[136] See Biophotons, ed. by J. J.Chang et al. (1998).

[137] This is, of course, one more piece of scientific evidence in support to a core insight of this book: Reality is Relationship.

[138] See Fritz-Albert Popp, "About the Coherence of Biophotons," in: Macroscopic Quantum Coherence, Proceedings of an International Conference on the Boston University, edited by E. Sassaroli et al. (1999).

from which the coherent field of biophotons emerges is unique for each living being, the communication from this field is unique. Both within the human organism and between the human being and the world, we communicate and create relationships through our uniqueness.

Love is a meeting between Unique Selves. Unique Self is the property of uniqueness that exists all the way up and all the way down the evolutionary chain—and awakens *as you*. Not only are we unique, but we are also *aware* of our uniqueness. We fall in love with the uniqueness of our beloved. Love, at all levels of Reality, is a series of relationships between unique expressions, from electrons to human beings. In this precise sense, the Universe is a Love Story. The coherent frequencies of biophotons are but one external expression of your Unique Self.

Every human being is a particular frequency of light, which is to say, of the LoveIntelligence of Reality. A meeting of beloveds is a meeting of lights. When lights unite, new intensities are formed. That is the nature of synergy, one of the key concepts of systems science: whenever two parts join in authentic relationship, the whole is greater than the sum of its parts.

The mystical master Israel Baal Shem Tov disclosed, through the methods of the interior sciences, the great realization that Reality is the Infinity of Intimacy (the Infinity of Relationship), which the more classical exterior sciences later corroborated with their methods. He said:

> *From every human being, there rises a light that reaches straight to heaven. And when two souls that are destined to be together find each other, their streams of light flow together, and a single bright light goes forth from their united being.*[139]

In Unique Self relationships, each person gives their unique gifts and lives their unique life in a way that would not be possible outside of the relationship. Through the union, a unique *We* is formed that is greater than the two Unique Selves and has its own unique gifts to give and life to live.

---

139 Meyer Levin, The Golden Mountain, retrieved January 2024, https://sacred-texts.com/jud/gm/gm10.htm.

Entry 7: Your Unique Self Can Never Be Taken Away

Herman Hesse did not know about the biology or the physics of Unique Self. However, he saw something akin to Unique Self at play in the deep structures of the web of relationships that come together to create our sacred autobiographies. He once wrote:[140]

> Every man is more than just himself; he also represents the unique, the very special and always significant and remarkable point at which the world's phenomena intersect, only once in this way, and never again.

The nature of your Unique Self is that it can never be taken from you. It is not dependent on anything external. Clearly, exterior circumstances support your giving of certain gifts, but the profound essence of your Unique Self lives in you and can be shared with others in virtually any and every circumstance. Your Unique Self is the source of your dignity, confidence, and joy. Your sacred autobiography—your Unique Self story—always invites you to live your uniqueness and give your unique gift.

This realization was driven home to me years ago in a pivotal moment.

> It was a sweltering Thursday morning in Salt Lake City. Three weeks earlier, my life had come to a careening crash. This was caused by a combination of circumstances that included my personal misjudgments and ordinary mistakes, and other

---

[140] This is a quote in the translation it is commonly quoted online (translator unknown) from Hermann Hesse, Demian. The Story of a Youth. Originally published by Harper & Row/NY in 1925. New translation by Damion Searls: Hermann Hesse: Demian: The Story of Emil Sinclair's Youth. Penguin Publishing Group; New Translation edition (2013), p. 1: "But every person is more than himself: he is also the unique, entirely particular, and in every case meaningful and remarkable point of intersection where the phenomena of the world overlap, only once and never again in just this way." Original German edition: Hermann Hesse, Demian. Die Geschichte von Emil Sinclairs Jugend.

people's misjudgments and ordinary mistakes. False complaints had been made about me, and adversaries, playing on the hysteria and fear that envelop these kinds of events, had made sure that there would be no forum to allow for any kind of due process, or even to consider both sides of the issue.

Close colleagues and others in my circle, to whom I had given my heart and life energy for many years, had turned away from me. Most were driven by fear, confusion, or self-protection, while others were motivated by the darker drives of power, jealousy, and legacy. As far as I knew at the time, I might never teach, write, or even see my friends again.

I was not at all sure that my body would survive the trauma. The brokenheartedness I felt was so fresh that I could barely function. The phrase *broken heart* is no mere metaphor. I felt the brokenness jutting out of my chest, feeling that at any moment I would explode into death from the raw pain of it all. Love and loyalty, the deep, abiding commitment to the best and most beautiful in another through whatever life throws at us, is what I stake my life on every day. The experience of love's betrayal was so intense for me that it literally took my breath away. My vocation as a teacher and fierce lover who tried to receive and honor the Unique Self of everyone who came my way seemed dead, trampled in the mud of false complaints and malice-driven rumors. I felt there was no way back to my path.

That morning, I was scheduled to meet with a law firm in downtown Salt Lake City that would help me determine my actions in response to the challenge I faced at that moment. I was staying with a dear friend, the skier and teacher Kristen Ulmer, some distance from downtown, and I had no car or any sense of direction in the city. I thought I would take a bus from the mountains to downtown.

Having cried most of the night, I pulled myself together and left the house around nine in the morning for my meeting at ten. But when I got to the bus station, it turned out that the next bus wouldn't come for two hours. I had no cell phone, not much cash, and no American credit card. As I stood there, feeling totally lost, realizing that I wasn't going to make it to the meeting, a car slowed down by the bus stop, and the driver motioned for me to get in. I was confused. Why is this car stopping, and who is this woman motioning for me to get into her car? As I approached the car, a slightly plump, fiftyish woman, with very lovely yet ordinary features and thick, graying hair, leaned out and said to me, "I woke up this morning knowing that I had to leave for work early. I knew there was something I had to do, but I did not know what. Now I know. I need to take you wherever you need to go. Don't worry—I have plenty of time. Hop in."

I was more than amazed at this small act of kindness from a random stranger. I rejected the dark thought that perhaps she was a serial murderer, thanked her, and stepped into her car. We began driving toward downtown, quite a distance from where she had picked me up. I asked her name, which she reluctantly gave me, and then, my heart's curiosity naturally aroused, I started to ask her about herself. Slowly, bit by bit, she began to tell me her story.

Before I knew it, we were both lost inside the lining of her story. What a story it was! It was about a husband who had left her, and her having to raise three kids by herself. It featured her private, but epic and tragic struggles with her boys. It was a story of love and betrayal, a story of love won and love lost, a story of profound pain and courage. It was a story that would have opened the most contracted heart. For the rest of the car ride, I forgot about my own pain, and lived and breathed inside her Unique Self story.

About forty-five minutes later, we arrived at the law offices. As she pulled over to the curb, still finishing her story, we were lost and found together on the inside. My heart was blown wide open by her goodness, her depth, and her heroic beauty in the face of so much suffering. My heart told me at this moment that there was only one real set of questions I needed to answer every day of my life: "Are you in love? Are you in love with the unspeakable beauty that lives in every person? Can you receive that beauty and give it back to every person you meet?"

As she pulled to the curb, she was crying profusely. I, too, had more than one tear rolling down my cheek. She was a Mormon woman raised on the tradition of the tabernacle, high priest, and temple, and her next words came out of the context of her tradition. She looked at me and said softly, "Who are you? Are you the high priest in the temple? No one has ever listened to me like that and made me feel so beautiful."

Now, we were both crying, for different reasons. As I thanked her and stepped out of her car, I realized that everything was going to be OK, even if it did not turn out well. I knew that while my ego could be crushed and my dignity debased, my Unique Self could never be taken from me. I could, wherever I was, hear and receive people's stories and remind them of their wonder and beauty. Nothing could ever stop that from happening. My Unique Self was inviolate. Everything else would find its way.

In the end, I did find my way back to my vocation—teaching, loving, and writing in the ways that have always delighted my soul. But on that day, I realized that the expression of Unique Self is not confined to what happened externally or in public. It is not dependent on optimal life circumstances. Ego depends on these things, but Unique Self always finds a way to flourish. It is, of course, wonderful when life conditions meet you and support your most glorious manifestation. But you never know when the mystery of fragility will again intrude on your life. You do know, however, that the apparent unfairness of the world can never take your Unique Self away from you.

Entry 8. Write Your Letter in the Cosmic Scroll

There is a tale that educators love about the girl who paints a purple tree. The teacher, who has drawn a tree on the board and asked the children to copy it, says disapprovingly, "You didn't copy my tree."

"I know," says the girl. "I drew my tree."

"But I've never seen a purple tree," replies the teacher.

"Isn't that a shame?" says the girl.

Sometimes our educators, our leaders, and our parents haven't the eyes to read our insides. And so we write our own stories in a way that fits their skewed sight, even if it means a betrayal of our own tales. Children are all unique until they *try* to be unique. They try to be unique in order to get us to notice them. And yet we weren't paying attention when they were painting purple trees. The job of an educator is to impart basic skills to the student and to honor their purple trees. The purple tree is rooted in the part of us that we cannot narrow to fit others' expectations.

Ultimately, every person is completely free and has their own special salvation. No form of instruction exists, no savior exists to open up the road. No road exists to be opened. The road is you.

Reality has placed a pen in our hands, inviting us, some might even say *needing* us, to become both the authors and the heroes of our own tale. Every incident, relationship, residence, and experience is part of the plot. As Dickens wrote in *David Copperfield*, "Whether I shall turn out to be the hero of my own life, or whether that station will be held by anybody else, these pages must show."[141]

One of the great Unique Self mystics, Isaac Luria, taught that every person has an obligation to write their own letter in the Cosmic Scroll. This means that the ultimate purpose of your life is to bring forth and live the unique expression of the LoveIntelligence and lifeforce that can be manifested only by you. In other words, it means to incarnate your Unique Self. Nothing from our unique sacred autobiography is lost in the Cosmic Scroll. Our unique passion, our unique dreams, our unique anguish, and our unique loss are woven into the fabric of the Universe itself.

In the mythic teaching of ancient Hebrew mysticism, the calligraphy of your unique letter in the Cosmic Scroll is determined by the particular angle at which you were situated in relationship to the revelation at Mount Sinai. In the Hebrew myth, Sinai is the portal through which the Infinite discloses itself in love through the medium of a sacred text. Based on one's distinct angle in relationship to the mountain, perceptions of the revelation vary. Your perspective forms the unique calligraphy of your letter in the Torah, the Cosmic Scroll. This is an ancient version of the new scientific understanding of True Self and unique perspective—the Unique Self by another name.

> Reb Zushya of Anipol, mystical master, was found crying on his deathbed.
>
> "Why are you crying?" his students asked. "You who were so pious—what do you have to regret or fear?"
>
> Reb Zushya of Anipol responded, "If they ask me at the bar of judgment why I was not a teacher like Moses, I will have an answer. If they ask me why I was not devout like Elijah, I will have an answer. But if they ask me why I was not Zushya, to this I will have no answer."

This is the great teaching of Unique Self. There is only one you, and

---

141 C. Dickens, Chapter 1, David Copperfield (1850).

you are it. There is only one Zushya, and YOU ARE IT. To live is to know that "the powerful play goes on and you may contribute a verse."[142] Your purple tree is your verse.

Entry 9. You Are Not a Cosmic Accident

Once you understand, at the cellular level of your being, that your uniqueness is not a historical accident but an intentional expression of Essence, you realize that you have superpowers. Greatness is a genuine option for every human being, including you! The living Universe took 13.7 billion years of intentional evolution to manifest the new and original evolutionary potential of your Unique Self. When you realize this and remember that your Unique Self is Reality having a *You* experience, everything in your essential experience of life changes.

Once you understand that your uniqueness is not the haphazard result of your cultural, social, or psychological conditioning, your essential experience of life transforms. You move from having a desperate need to escape your life to radically embracing your life. When this happens, fate transforms to destiny. Every detour becomes a destination. Desperation becomes celebration. Grasping becomes purposeful action, and resignation becomes activism. The contracted smallness of your frightened, suffering self becomes the expanded, joyful realization of your Unique Self.

At such times, you know that the irreducible uniqueness of every awakened human being is a sign that Reality actually invites, and even lovingly demands, *your* showing up. Reality yearns for a full and authentic expression of your uniqueness, for you to live in the world as God's verb. **Unique essence, living in you, as you and through you, is the essence of being alive.**

It is from this place that you answer the call of Unique Self. It is from this place that you give the world your desperately needed unique gifts, those charismatic endowments that arise from your Unique Self. This is what it means to answer the call of your life.

There is a wonderful movie, *The Truman Show*, in which the main

---

142 Walt Whitman, "O Me, O Life!," in Leaves of Grass (1892).

character thinks he is living an ordinary life, but in reality, he and all the people in his life are actors in a globally televised show. The subtext of the film plays with the themes of enlightenment, the shocking process of waking up to the true nature of your reality.

The movie almost got it. However, it suffered from the same mistake as early Christianity. There was only one Truman in the film, just as there is only one Christ in early Christianity. When we are truly awake, we realize that the world is really something like eight billion interlocking Truman Shows. Each of us is the absolute unique star of our own show. But at the same time, we are all costars, supporting actors, minor characters, and extras in one another's shows. Your Truman Show is nothing less than your own—globally broadcast and cosmically significant—unique life story.

A few years ago, we saw a wonderfully long, obscure film from 1974 by Claude Lelouch: *Toute Une Vie* (*And Now My Love*). Though never explicitly mentioned, it was very much about falling in love. The film followed three generations in just three hours, so we were not quite sure where we were being led. All of those strange and random scenes, however, built to the very last moment of the story, when a young man and woman meet *by accident* on a plane. We realize that what appears to be a chance encounter has in fact been planned by the Universe for three generations. A seemingly meaningless story has suddenly flourished forth with stunning significance. Everyone in the movie was present, from one perspective, in order to create the conditions necessary for the dramatic moment of their *chance* encounter. Myriad allurements between different characters over generations were necessary to generate this chance encounter.

The hidden language of the intentional Cosmos is allurements that set into motion ever-more allurements. All of them—when allurement is clarified as your deepest heart's desire—intend toward love, toward goodness, truth, and beauty. The significance and intentionality invested by the Universe in your unique story is life-affirming beyond imagination.

Entry 10. A Memory of the Future

Allow us to tell you a story. It is a story that we really love, and it was also reputed to be the writer Franz Kafka's favorite story.

> It is a story about a king. The king has an advisor. There is a famine in the land and yet there is enough grain to feed people. The problem is: if you eat the grain, you go insane. That is your choice. Eat the grain and stay alive but go insane or remain sane but starve. We consume because we think it keeps us alive, but we actually go insane. To be sane is to know Reality. To be insane is to lose connection, to lose alignment with Reality.
>
> Everyone in the kingdom keeps eating the grain. They come to a point where they feel like they are about to starve, so they eat the grain. Finally, the only people who haven't eaten the grain are the king and his advisor. Everyone else in the kingdom is insane. The king asks his advisor, "What should I do? On the one hand, I'm the king, so I have to be sane. On the other hand, my people are insane, and how can a sane king rule insane people? That would alienate me from my people, and a king can never be alienated from his people and remain king."
>
> Here is what the advisor suggests: "We'll both eat the grain. But before we eat the grain, we're going to make a mark on our forehead. We will become insane like everyone else, but when we look at each other, we will notice the mark on each other's forehead. We will ask each other, 'What is the mark on your forehead?' And then we will begin to remember."

If you want to find your Unique Self, you must recover a memory. But not just a memory of your past. Soul mate relationships are very tied in to therapy, working with old trauma, wounds, and the recovery of past memories. That is all important work. But to enter an evolutionary relationship, you must first find your Unique Self. Your Unique Self is not just the memory of your past. It is the memory of your future.

As Hafiz said:[143] *You are a divine elephant with amnesia.* There is a mark on your forehead, but you've forgotten. You've gone insane. You are an elephant *trying to live in an ant hole.*

Do you know how that feels like? You do, because every time you're a little depressed, you wonder: *Is this all there is?* Every once in a while, in an unguarded moment, you glimpse again the dreams you had when you were seventeen, but you quickly banish them from your mind. The gap between the dream and your reality is too great to bear. You are an elephant trying to live in an anthill.

Entry 11. Confess Your Greatness

Your Unique Self is the authentic source of your greatness. Stop for a moment and prepare to truly confess. The aim here is not to confess your shortcomings. That is easy for many of us. We are all imperfect vessels for the light. We all recognize our own brokenness. For many of us, confession of our failures is routine and has little impact. Try instead to confess your greatness.

> **Confessing Your Greatness Exercise:** Access a moment of your greatness. Think of one moment where you were yourself. You ran faster than you could run. You were more comfortable in your skin than you ever were before. You formulated your words somehow better than you ever did. You felt most at home in your body, in your expression, in your action, in your laughter, in your tears. Find any moment when you were in your Unique Self, a moment of greatness, public or private. Now, confess your greatness to yourself. Tell yourself the story of your greatness. Write the story. Write your confession of greatness as a mythic story where you are the hero.

---

143 More accurately, this is the fragrance and general sense of Hafiz restated or formulated by Daniel Ladinsky in his multiple collections.

Confessing your greatness is a much more important and challenging practice than confessing your smallness. **Confessing that *you are something* is far more central to your transformation than confessing that *you are nothing*.** If you are just a skin-encapsulated ego, a bundle of nerves, a heap of determined responses, a set of preprogrammed actions and reactions—if you are just a side effect in your own life— then there is nothing Reality can expect from you.

Find a moment of breakthrough in your life. In that moment, you saw yourself clearly. In that moment, you made a decision out of deep integrity, against social pressure and expectation. In that moment, you acted, loved, and showed up in your greatness. That is a moment of breakthrough when your Unique Self showed up.

It is only your confession of your own greatness, of your Unique Self, that invites you to the full potency and passion of your life. Because the only thing in the world that obligates you, the only call you have to answer, the only judgment you'll ever be judged for is this:

Did you live your story?

Did you write your unique song?

Did you respond to the call of your Unique Self?

Did you give the unique gift that was yours to give?

Did you live the unique life that was yours to live?

Those are the significant questions in your life. That is the reason you were born. That *is* the purpose-driven life. Live the unique expression of you. Then, give the gift, the wisdom, the being, and the becoming that comes from that unique expression. Everything else flows from it.

Entry 12. Reality Needs Your Unique Self

Holon as the Basic Unit of Reality

The democratization of greatness is not a choice or a preference.[144] It is not something nice that we thought we would say to make you feel included. Instead, it is an expression of the very structure of Reality. To get a deeper sense of this, we will have to speak briefly about this structure and why it results in a Cosmos where every being, every potential Unique Self, is radically needed by Reality itself.

The basic units of Reality are not quarks, or atoms, or whatever other smaller subunits you might dream up. The basic unit of Reality, in the words of Hungarian philosopher Arthur Koestler, is a *holon*[145]—that is, a whole that is also a part, a whole-part. Reality is made of holons, all the way up and all the way down the evolutionary chain. This is another way of saying *Reality is Relationship*.[146] Whenever parts come together in relationship, a new whole is created. That new whole then enters relationship with other wholes. Together, these wholes become the parts of even larger wholes. This evolution of relationships is the mechanism of the mystery that is life.

Atoms are wholes, which contain elementary particles. Atoms can also be parts of larger wholes, called *molecules*. Molecules are wholes but can also be parts of cells. Everything is a whole-part, all the way up the evolutionary chain. Humans are also holons. We are comprised of many parts, some of which emerged earlier in the evolutionary process. At the same time, we are enmeshed in a web of profound interconnectivity where nothing gets lost, and everything affects everything else.

There are two types of holons: individual and social. Individual holons are what we have been talking about here: atoms, molecules, and organisms. Social holons are the groups or collectives that these individual holons come together to create. Early on in evolution, atoms

---

144 See Entry 6 of Chapter 8, "Evolutionary Impulse at the Heart of Evolutionary Relationships," for a deeper conversation on the democratization of greatness.

145 The term holon was coined by Arthur Koestler in The Ghost in the Machine (1967).

146 See Chapter 1, "The Arc of Evolution."

came together to form galaxies. Molecules came together to form planets. Fast-forward to the emergence of complex life, and we see that early humans came together to form tribes. Present-day humans bring together social holons like the United Nations.

As evolution moves from one level to the next, from one whole to the next larger whole, more and more choice becomes possible. This increased choice is born out of an increased possibility for creativity. Sometimes, however, this gets us into trouble. When a part pretends to be a whole, things can get more than a bit messy.

Increased potency of choice in a part alienated from the whole always generates increased pathology. Indeed, the part disassociating from the whole can be said to be the primary cause of evil and suffering in the world. Imagine what would happen if one organ acted out of accord with the whole system, or if the leader of an organization acted like he controlled the group, or if one nation went against the United Nations in an attempt to subvert or dominate other countries. When a part acts out of accord with the whole, loneliness and dysfunction are the result. A cell, an idea, a sentence, a person, or even a musical note which is not in right relationship with other parts is fundamentally lonely and dysfunctional.

Cancer cells have two profound qualities: they violate the Unique Self signature of the unique body, and they disassociate from the larger cellular and biological whole. Only right relationship between parts and wholes produces balance and harmony. Whole-part harmony is essential for uncovering significance and meaning in life.

The Whole Is in the Part

Here is the core truth of the new sciences: Infinity incarnates from the void of pure potentiality as the initiating and sustaining energy of the evolutionary process of All-That-Is. Infinite Reality manifests the mystery of a world driven toward ever-deeper intimacies. Another name for *Infinite Reality*, therefore, might be *the Infinity of Intimacy*. This Face of Infinity lives and courses through you when you realize your Unique Self. Your Unique Self is Reality's Intimacy expressing itself uniquely as you.

You are a unique intimacy of evolution. Of course, merely a part of Infinity cannot exist in you. According to physicist David Bohm,

Reality—All-That-Is—is holographic.[147]

In mathematical terms, all of Reality is composed of fractals. Simply put, that means that in every part is the Whole. The Whole lives in all of its parts and in all of its particularized expressions. The mystery is that the more the part emphasizes its *part* nature, the more highly particularized the part is in its authenticity, the more freely the Whole can express itself in the part.

The more you live your Unique Self as part of the Whole, the more your essence and power come online. The more you move beyond your ego (the part of you that forgets that you are part of a larger Whole), the more your full, personal, particular gorgeousness can emerge as your Unique Self. Your uniqueness does not *separate* you from the Whole. It *connects* you to the Whole. Uniqueness is the currency of connection. It allows you to be a whole mate to your partner and, with your partner, to be a whole mate to all of Reality.

The Whole Needs the Part

Reality's need is your deed. Without your deeds—your gifts—part of Reality dies. This is a core realization of complexity and systems science. Without your gift, something essential dies in the world. The following story, often told in our family, is a wonderful expression of this living tradition.

---

147 D. Bohm, Wholeness and the Implicate Order (2002). The book contains many references to the holographic nature of the Universe. See, for example, p. 186: "So we may say that in current research in physics, an instrument tends to be relevant to a whole structure, in a way rather similar to what happens with a hologram." See also p. 240: "Indeed, as has already been pointed out earlier in this chapter, the electromagnetic field, which is the ground of the holographic image, obeys the laws of the quantum theory, and when these are properly applied to the field it is found that this, too, is actually a multidimensional reality which can only under certain conditions be simplified as a three-dimensional reality. Quite generally, then, the implicate order has to be extended into a multidimensional reality. In principle this reality is one unbroken whole, including the entire universe with all its 'fields' and 'particles.' Thus we have to say that the holomovement enfolds and unfolds in a multidimensional order, the dimensionality of which is effectively infinite. However, as we have already seen, relatively independent sub-totalities can generally be abstracted, which may be approximated as autonomous. Thus the principle of relative autonomy of sub-totalities which we introduced earlier as basic to the holomovement is now seen to extend to the multidimensional order of reality."

It is the turn of the last century on the lower east side of Manhattan. A family of four live in a single-room flat on Ludlow Street. All day and into the night, mother and father work hard in a sweatshop. Every Friday, however, their table is set for a Sabbath meal. Their daughter Sarah and their son go to services with their father, and every Sabbath, Papa brings home a guest to share in the Sabbath meal.

Now, Sarah knows that they do not have much to eat, and that the presence of the guest means less food for everyone. "Why, Papa?" she asks.

"It is written: *Charity saves from death*," her father answers. One day, Papa comes back from the sweatshop alone. "Mama is sick," he says. For several long days, Papa goes every night to the two flats that serve as the makeshift hospital for the families of Ludlow Street. When Sabbath Eve comes, Sarah takes her brother to services. She doesn't know it, but at dusk, her mother breathes her last breath.

Sarah dutifully brings home a guest for the Sabbath meal she has prepared. Long after the guest has left, and after Sarah and her brother have gone to sleep, Sarah awakens to see her father sitting in a corner of the room, weeping. She comes and sits on his lap. "Don't worry, Papa," she says. "Mama will get better."

He stares at her blankly. "What do you mean?"

"Mama will get well," Sarah says. "I went to services, Papa, and I brought home a guest for the Sabbath meal, and you always told me *charity saves from death*."

Papa smiles sadly. "My little one, you misunderstood. Charity does not save Mama from death. Charity saves God from death."

What does this mean, *charity saves from death*? It is not merely a phrase from a story; it is sourced from a sacred text by the third-century wisdom masters. But what could it possibly mean? There is an evolutionary mystical and an evolutionary scientific explanation of the phrase. In the ethical tradition out of which this story emerges, giving is not charity. It is an obligation.

The original Hebrew word used in the epigram is *tzedakah*. Often mistranslated as *charity*, it really means *justice*. The difference between the two words is everything. Charity means that the money is mine, and if I feel magnanimous, then I can give some to you. Justice, on the other hand, is understood by the masters to mean that your money is not owned by you at all. In Hebrew law, a portion of your money is in reality *owned* by the poor in the community. According to one legal school, the only right you have to the money is to determine which poor person will receive it.

Wow! What this law reminds us of is the great truth of evolutionary science—all of Reality is Relationship. The Universe is a Love Story. Systems science reminds us that you are not separate from everyone else. And as part of the Whole, you have a unique gift that can be given by Reality only through you. The accumulation of property and possessions in this lifetime is overwhelmingly due to sets of circumstances entirely beyond your control. You may have worked hard, but there are a million people who have worked just as hard, and the Universe did not allow them to accumulate your level of wealth. Those possessions are not essentially yours. A portion of your possessions belongs to those less fortunate than you, not because the government legislated taxes, but because nonseparateness is the essential evolutionary truth of Reality.

Not to experience the interconnectivity of all Reality is to live a nonerotic, dead existence. Not to experience the *unique fixing*, which is yours to do, your unique stitch in the tapestry of Wholeness, is to wither and die. *Charity saves from death.*

A piece of Reality dies in the coiled contraction of the separate self. To be awake means only one thing: to know that Reality is one fabric of interdependent essences, and that we are born in the space in between. We are born in relationship.

Reality needs your service. This means that Reality, in an act of radical love, also *receives* your service. Reality makes the evolution of love dependent on us.

How does Reality need us? Evolutionary science tells us we are entering a new era. The previous era was called the *Holocene* period. The era we are now entering is called the *Anthropocene*. The word derives from *anthropocentric*, which means *human-centered*. For the first time in history, physical and social reality will be shaped most prominently by human systems instead of natural systems. Reality needs us to advance evolution. The greatest gift you can give to Reality is to acknowledge its need for your unique offerings. Reality is turning to you and saying: "*You*, in all your uniqueness, are needed." Reality's gift back to you is unconditional receptivity.

I Love You = I Need You

The call of relationship at every level of Reality is to say, *I love you, I need you*, and to know that there is no split between the two. There is no Ultimate Love that does not address need and no Ultimate Need that does not require love to address it. This does not mean you are codependent, which would imply that you are not a whole unto yourself. But you are not entirely independent either. That would imply that you are a whole unto yourself. Saying *I need you* unifies that contradiction. You are both a whole and a part: a whole-part, or holon. You are interdependent because *Reality is Relationship*.

As much as we are sometimes afraid to need each other, deep inside of us we know that the people who know their needs and are willing to be filled with gratitude when they are met are more developed, more perfect, and more powerful. The moment in a relationship when one is willing to say *I need you* is always the moment of transformation.

Allow us to enlist the aid of *Rocky*, Sylvester Stallone's iconic, late-twentieth-century movie about an underdog boxer. It is a Unique Self story.

> Rocky is living the opposite of the Unique Self life. He does collection for a loan shark, and fights in sleazy clubs. His true gifts are hidden. He is mocked and jeered by crowds. At the

same time, he begins successfully courting Adrian, the love of his life. Clearly, Adrian sees him and loves him.

Apollo Creed is supposed to have a fight in Philadelphia, Rocky's hometown. His opponent is injured. Seeking to create buzz, Creed challenges local fighter Rocky to a title bout, believing it will be an easy win. Rocky is not a better boxer than Apollo Creed, but he has two qualities: grace and grit. The most famous scene in the movie is when Rocky finds his stride during training. He breaks through old limitations and, as part of a training run, bounds up the stairs of the Philadelphia Art Museum with the famous theme music accompanying him.

However, it is the scene before, overlooked by many critics, that is the catalyst for the famous running scene. That previous scene is a poignant relationship moment between Adrian and Rocky. Rocky's training is not finding its groove. Adrian doesn't want him to do the fight, believing it is too dangerous. Rocky will not step out of the fight. She loves Rocky, but decides to leave him, and Rocky falls, weak and exhausted, into a hospital bed.

At the movie's great turning point, Rocky awakens from his sick bed and cries out from the depths of his being, "Aaaadddrrriiiaann! I need you!" His training takes off as Rocky finds his stride. The Rocky theme starts playing. Once Rocky is able to say *I need you*, the relationship becomes possible. From the place of relationship, he locates his Unique Self mojo and finds his way. We see him running, boxing, training, all with a completely different energy and radiance. He is in his Unique Self. He has acknowledged need, and he has become more whole.

The Rocky story is about a particular form of whole mate relationship. In the sense of level-two soul-mate dynamics, Rocky and Adrian were doing fine. The question is, Could Rocky realize that he could not achieve his goal without Adrian's partnership? Was his partner willing to fully support the emergence of his Unique Self, even if it was not her vision of his life? It turns out that only Rocky's owning his need for Adrian allowed her to support him radically. An evolutionary relationship does not always mean that the couple acts in partnership in the world. It may also mean that the beloveds get underneath each other and become a trampoline for each other's dreams.

Your Whole Mate Needs Your Unique Self

To be in relationship is to know that we need each other. At all three levels of relationship—role mate, soul mate, and whole mate—we need each other. However, the nature of our need transforms and evolves across each level, just as our consciousness does.

In role mate relationship, *I need you* often means *I need you as a protector and provider* or *I need you as a nurturer and homemaker*. The needs are for surviving and thriving. They are self-evident and clear.

In soul mate relationship, needs are not necessarily about physical surviving and thriving. In soul mate relationship *I need you* often means *I need you to stand by my side as I go through this difficult or profound moment. I need you to hold my woundedness and to bear witness to the unique contours of my trauma.*

For us as role mates and soul mates, to confess *I need you* is to be vulnerable. To be vulnerable means to confess that we are impacted by others. It requires us to open ourselves and to receive our beloved in potent, profound, and poignant ways.

In whole mate relationship, *I need you* means, *I need your Unique Self.* To say to our partners, *I need your Unique Self* is to give our partners the greatest of gifts. It means, *I need you because only together can we form our Unique We.* It means, *I need you because I cannot give my unique gift alone.*

Deeper still, there is an even more shocking ontology of need at play: I need *thee* in order to be *me*. This dynamic is in play in evolving forms all the way down and all the way up the evolutionary chain. In the very first minutes after the Big Bang, there is a way in which a neutron cannot retain its identity as a neutron without being in relationship to a proton. This principle shows up in myriad ways all the way up the evolutionary chain. In a profound way, I am not *I* without the context of our *We*. You evoke in me something without which I cannot be my full self. That is the precise and potent nature of whole mate relationship.

To confess that *I need you* is to be vulnerable. The nature of the vulnerability is more intense, but also requires more depth of discernment at every next level of relationship. The vulnerability at the role mate level is obvious because we are talking about survival needs. To be vulnerable at the level of soul mate means that you have an impact on me. It requires me to open myself and to receive you in potent, profound, and poignant ways. To say to your partner, *I need your Unique Self* is to give your partner a great gift.

> Once, I stumbled across the most passionate and stunning acts of Unique Self giving and receiving I have ever seen. It took place on a darkened side street in Jerusalem. A man and woman were walking arm in arm. They did not see me, but I saw them. I should not have looked, but I did. They were very old. I caught this all in a fleeting moment, but apparently her shoe came untied.
>
> Seeing this, he stopped. They made eye contact for the briefest of seconds, and then he bent down, very slowly. Gently, and somewhat painfully with his arthritic hands, he tied her shoe. It must have taken a full five minutes. All the while I watched, paralyzed by awe, in the shadows.
>
> Her acceptance of that act of loving was an ultimate erotic expression. She was being received by him, and his offering was fully accepted by her. In this one act, the Unique Selves of a lifetime came together. Infinite moments of joy, laughter, poignancy, and partnership, and almost certainly, heartbreak and tears, all merged together in that eternity of a moment.

To be at the whole mate level is the most vulnerable of all. It means *I cannot be me without thee*. At the level of whole mate, the split between self-love and the love of the beloved disappears. I love you, and in loving you I give you the power to evoke a crucial dimension of me, the best of me, that could not exist or emerge without thee.

We have already invoked two key declarations from the lineages of the interior sciences of Hebrew wisdom. The first is *Charity saves from death*, and the second is *God needs our service*.

Charity saves from death means that charity not only saves human beings from death, but—in the deeper reading of the hidden lineage sources—*Charity saves God from death*. In other words, there is a way in which human love enlivens the lifeforce of the Divine.

God needs our service means that God, the Infinite Intimate, very much like our beloveds, loves us so insanely much that She allows Herself to need us. She accepts the gift of our Unique Self Service in fulfillment of Her needs. In needing and then receiving our gifts, She is affirming our human adequacy, worth, and dignity. But it is even more than that.

Both *charity saves from death* and *God needs our service* mean that the Divine, the Infinity of Intimacy, needs us to be intimate as Her, for Her sake. In the moment when the evolutionary process commences, She makes Herself dependent on us. *Reality needs our service* means that Reality needs the gift of your Unique Self.

The Radical Joy of Being Needed

Your experience of yourself has a massive effect on your health. This truth was told to us by our grandmothers and confirmed by the relatively new field of psychoneuroimmunology. It suggests that being needed is absolutely essential to your basic sense of feeling good about your life. When one partner in a couple dies, studies show that the other partner is much more likely to die soon after, especially if he or she is not truly needed in some other domain of life. Need is not only the spice of life. It is also the joy and literally the *life* of life. It is a direct function of Unique Self. The more you live from your Unique Self and give your unique gift, the more you experience the need for your gift, and the more joy you experience.

Let's do a simple reality consideration together. It is a form of meditation, and it will help you get a sense of the joy that comes from being needed.

Imagine your phone ringing. It is the president. Your favorite president. Or your prime minister. Or the leader in the world whom you most honor and respect.

Somehow, you are able to verify that it is not a prank. It is indeed the president calling. He says, "[Your name], it is great to meet you." Shocked, you stumble out the words, "Great to meet you as well, Mr. President." He tells you that he and his staff have been tracking you for some time now. In fact, he says, prior presidents have tracked you as well. He received your file when he was elected. He tells you all sorts of facts about yourself, and you are astounded by what he knows.

He then goes on to share, with great depth and insight, his sense of your unique gifts. He mentions capacities that even your beloved has rarely encountered. He sees you as your largest and most extraordinary version of yourself. You are beside yourself with radical amazement and joy. You thought that this version of yourself was known only to you, in your most private moments of grandiose fantasy. He then says, "The world needs you, [Your name]. There is something crucial that needs to be done that can only be done by you. Are you up for it?"

You virtually scream, "Yes!" Your voice echoes the primordial *Yes* of the Big Bang itself. For what is the Big Bang if not Reality shouting the unrelenting positivity of *Yes*! *Yes* to life. *Yes* to existence. *Yes* to evolution. *Yes* to all of it! As you shout your *Yes*, you feel his smile. You agree to talk next week to work out the details. You hang up the phone.

How do you feel? Are you depressed? Are you filled with dread, questioning the very meaning of life? We don't think so. You feel just like we would. You are ecstatic; filled with joy and delight! You cannot wait to tell everyone, especially your beloved. All of a sudden, your entire life makes sense in a way that was unimaginable only an hour earlier. The intensity of the joy is beyond anything you could have dreamed possible. This is precisely the experience of Unique Self Realization.

> Let's add one crucial dimension. Imagine that the president said something slightly different to you. Imagine that the president said that he needs not just *you,* but you *and* your partner. The two of you together, supporting each other's gifts, can do something that no other partnership that ever was, is, or will be could do. Neither of you can give these desperately needed gifts without the support of the other. These are the gifts that can be given only by your Unique We.

You get off the phone. You turn to your partner. Has your love ever been stronger? Has your passion ever been more potent? Suddenly, you realize that you are together not only for each other, but for a rendezvous with destiny.

The gifts of your Unique Selves and your Unique We are desperately needed by Reality. This is the power, potency, and passion of whole mate relationship. This potency emerges from the realization of Unique Self and the coming together as a Unique We.

Entry 13. Revelations of Uniqueness

Science studies the observable aspects of Reality. It uses the Eye of the Senses and the Eye of the Mind. It speaks of exterior processes, fields of attraction, and interrelationship at all levels of physical reality. However, science also alludes to interiors. We know that now in a way that we could not just several hundred years ago.

Newton and Galileo assumed an eternal Earth. They had no idea that stars are born from elementary particles or that operas are born from molten rock. In a world where consciousness emerges from matter, where Mozart arises from stardust, we understand the essential unity of Reality in an entirely new way. Science is not *the basis* of spirit, but it confirms the leading edges of spirit just as spirit confirms the leading edges of science. The historic battle between science and spirit is fought between the old dogmatic religion and the old dogmatic science. That battle is over. The conclusions of science and spirit reinforce each other. Each field uses a different faculty of perception.

Science uses the Eye of the Senses and the Eye of the Mind. Spirit deploys the Eye of Consciousness, which has four key expressions: the Eye of Value, the Eye of the Heart, the Eye of Contemplation, and the Eye of the Spirit. The Eyes of Consciousness have their own experimental methods, those of the interior sciences, which they deploy in plumbing the inner realms. Each realm has its own experts, its own validity tests, and its own language. Just as the Eye of the Senses points to exteriors, the Eye of the Heart and the Eye of Value point to interiors.

Emergent from these experiments, the interior sciences were able to declare, *You truly are a son or daughter of God.* In Christian language, you realize that you are Christ as you live your Unique Self. In the Hebrew mystical language, one might say, *You are a truly substantial part of God.* Hindu interior scientist Muktananda used to teach that *God lives in you, as you.*

If we shift to Buddhist language, what we are describing as the movement toward Unique Self awakening has two distinct steps. The first is the liberation into spaciousness that results from evolution beyond your exclusive identification with your separate-self ego. This is called *resting in the Ground of Being* and is sometimes called the *realization of your Buddha Nature*. This is what we have called *True Self*. This is the true nature of your identity beneath the illusion of separation. The second step[148] is the emergence of your unique Bodhicitta quality, the aspect of

---

148 This footnote is for interior science initiates only, particularly those engaged in Buddhist study or practice. To be accurate, this second step is absent in most Buddhist texts. But a more careful reading finds the fragrance of Unique Self, so central in a careful reading of Hebrew and Sufi interior sciences, peeking out of Buddhist texts as well. It is that reading of Buddhist texts, originally read in this

your Buddha Nature that might be understood as your Unique Self. This refers to the expression of your Buddha Nature, where according to one Buddhist text, *the unique texture and pattern of the grain of wood which is you* becomes readily apparent and beautiful.

In the interior science of Hebrew wisdom, which had a deeper grasp of uniqueness than most eastern interior sciences, this might be referred to as the *ani-Ayin-ani*. *Ani* literally means *I* in Hebrew. *Ayin* refers to the Ground of Being out of which Reality is birthed. *Ayin* is True Self. In the context of parts and wholes, the true relationship between *ani* and *Ayin* becomes clear.

The first stage, or *ani*, is what we call *separate self*. This part thinks itself a whole, while forgetting the larger context, the larger Whole. This is the puzzle piece stumbling along, who has forgotten that there is a puzzle.

The second stage, *Ayin*, True Self, is the spaciousness of liberation achieved when the illusion of separation is recognized for what it is. It is here that the human being tastes the sweetness of evolution beyond exclusive ego-identification. The part realizes that it is not separate but part of a larger whole.

The second *ani* (beyond *Ayin*) is the larger *I*, the Unique Self that emerges directly from the Ground of the *Ayin* realization. At this stage, the distinct nature of the part within the Whole is realized and celebrated. So, there is a level-one *ani* and a level-three *ani*. The former is the *I* of the separate self. The latter is the *I* of Unique Self. The difference between them is *Ayin*, True Self, contact with the spacious, the Whole Ground of All Being of which you are a part. *Ayin* is recognized as your True Nature through the overthrowing of the separate-self illusion. This is accomplished through different forms of awareness and contemplative practice.

The softening of ego, or the egoic illusion of separate self, takes place through direct contact with the Whole or at least awareness of the Whole. This is whole mate consciousness. This helps you move past the

---

fashion in dialogues between Marc Gafni, Ken Wilber, and Genpo Roshi in 2005, that we are suggesting here as the second step. Particularly (and this sentence is meant only for those familiar with these things) what is called the tenth ox herding picture in Buddhism, may be well read as an allusion to something phenomenologically similar to what we are calling Unique Self.

elements of personal pettiness, false self, and the neurotic personality. When that starts to happen, your gorgeous personal qualities of Essence begin to emerge as Unique Self.

Entry 14. The Whole Mate Returns to the Beloved the Missing Piece of Their Story[149]

There is nothing that arouses our love more than witnessing a person living the fullness of their story. You fall in love with such people. This is the interface of Eros and Unique Self. During such an experience, you explode into the larger Field of Eros, and life becomes larger than life. Meaning melts into mystery.

To get a sense of the erotic nature of your story, you must first touch deeply the essential meaning and quality of Eros in your own life. You must move toward a higher intimacy and union with the purpose of your own existence.

We conclude this chapter with a mythical story of Eros about my friend the Dalai Lama. But before I share this story, allow me to share a relevant personal account about how we met. It is relevant because it begins as a profoundly nonerotic story which in the end was transformed into a whole mate Eros story.

We met in 2004 at a conference called *Synthesis Dialogues III*. Thirty-five spiritual leaders from around the globe were invited for a week to hang with the Dalai Lama in Castel Gandolfo, the Pope's summer residence. Now to be clear, spending the week with thirty-five spiritual leaders is both wonderful and a bit overwhelming. Everyone is being just a bit too profound a bit too much of the time.

I was living in Israel at the time, and Israel was the subject of much controversy (read animus) among the participants. On a personal level I was having a wonderful time with everyone. And yet I was Israeli—and Jewish, and there was an uncomfortable anti-Israel sentiment with

---

149 This process of returning a piece of the lost story begins already at the level of soul mate relationship. We discuss this in Supplementary Essay 1, "Four Core Principles of Soul Mate Relationship," especially in "Principle One: Soul Mates Hold Pieces of Each Other's Stories."

vaguely anti-Semitic undertones. At one point, a man who was to become my dear friend, Michael Beckwith, turns to the group and says, "Marc is Jewish and Marc is showing us that Jewish means *Joyish*." As in *Joy*. Everybody laughed.

A bit later in this complex week of love and relationship and real anti-Israel bias, the Dalai Lama, in front of the group, turned to me and said, "Israelis very hard. Marc very nice." I was furious with him for this insensitive remark. In psychological terminology, I was somewhat triggered. The entire room of teachers knew barely one true fact about Israel. Without even vaguely understanding even the simple facts, platitudes, mixed with analogies between Israel and apartheid in South Africa, abounded in the conversation. And the blurring between Israel and Jewish was always vaguely present in the conversations.

So I got up—unthinking—crossed the room, looked the Dalai Lama in the eye, gave him my yarmulke, the ritual skull cap worn at all times by Orthodox Jews, and said to him, "If you think it is so easy, you wear it."

No one moved. The room went thickly silent for a very long time.

We looked at each other.

He took my yarmulke and said, laughing, "Buddhist monk no hair. Yarmulke very hard."

He called his attendant to bring his sun visor. He then used the sun visor to hold the yarmulke in place and wore it the entire day. At the end of the day, he was sitting five places from me and still wearing my yarmulke. He looked at me, looked at the yarmulke, put it in his pocket, and walked out. He then sent his close associate, the head of the Tibetan Library, Achok Rinpoche, to invite me to Dharamshala to get my yarmulke back.

The end of the story is that we became good friends. I went to Dharamshala to get the yarmulke back, which I did. We spent some truly beautiful time together and did a public dialogue, what we called a dialogue between Tibet and Jerusalem. In the dialogue we fell in love. We were role mates, soul mates, and whole mates.

- We were role mates in that each of us had a precise role to play. He represented Tibet as a monk, and I represented Jerusalem as a rabbi.

- We were soul mates because we shared stories of wounding, suffering, and personal joy and looked into each other's eyes.

- We were whole mates, because we met in a vision of the larger Whole to which we were both clearly in service. We found a shared horizon, even as we witnessed each other's delight, depth, and beauty.

I had brought him a gift, which I shared with him at the end of our time. It was a ceremonial Tibetan religious garment to which I attached the ritual fringes of the Hebrew wisdom traditions: a synergy of Tibet and Jerusalem, in which neither lost its Unique Self, yet the synergy of Unique Self Symphony[150] began to play. Whole mates playing our instruments together for the sake of the Whole, a Unique We greater than sum of the parts, in which the part do not disappear.

All of which brings us to the point of this entry, a story of whole mate relationship—not of the romantic variety, but of a great love between evolutionary partners, who met for only a very short time. Whole mate partnerships exist across the spectrum of love. They appear when two Unique Selves meet and recognize that their stories are connected. They recognize that each one of them has a piece of the other's story, or that both are unique expressions of the same larger narrative. The relationship in this story unfolds through the eyes of the Dalai Lama when he was a boy:

> Reports reached the fourteenth Dalai Lama, Tenzin Gyatso, that a certain Master of Kung Fu was roaming the countryside, converting young men to the study of violence. Against all Buddhist laws, there had been unnecessary slaughter of yaks in order to provide the many husky monks, who had abandoned their lamaseries and robes, with black-leather outfits like the one the Master of Kung Fu wore from neck to ankle. His huge muscles made the costume tight as his own flesh.

---

[150] See Chapter 11, "The Universe: A Love Story and Unique Self Symphony" (especially Entry 8) for a deeper discussion of this concept.

These leather-sheathed disciples followed their master everywhere, challenging each other to duels, many of which ended in death or crippling. The regent and other advisors to the Dalai Lama were concerned, especially after blasphemous rumors began circulating that the Master of Kung Fu was an incarnation of Shiva Nataraj, Hindu god of destruction.

The Dalai Lama decided to invite the master for a visit. Pleased with the invitation, the Master of Kung Fu strode into the Dalai Lama's ceremonial hall. The Master of Kung Fu was indeed a handsome, dashing fellow, with thick blue-black hair falling down over the shoulders of his leather suit. He assured the Dalai Lama that he wanted to do no harm.

"Well, when you do want to harm," asked the Dalai Lama, "what kind of harm can you do?"

The Master of Kung Fu explained that he was a lover of beauty, and that his only enemy was ugliness. He offered to demonstrate. "Royal Highness, the best way to show you would be for you to stand here in front of me while I do a little dance that took me fifteen years to perfect. Though I can kill a dozen men instantly with this dance, have no fear. This will only be a demonstration of ugliness-destruction."

The Dalai Lama stood up, and immediately felt as if a wind had blown flower petals across his body. He looked down but saw nothing. "You may proceed," he told the Master of Kung Fu.

"Proceed?" said the Master of Kung Fu, grinning jovially. "I've already finished. What you felt were my hands flicking across your body. If it pleases Your Highness, this was a demonstration in slow motion, extremely slow motion, of the way I could have destroyed the organs of your body one-by-one."

"Impressive, but I know a master greater than you," said the Dalai Lama.

"Without wishing to offend Your Highness, I doubt that very much," the Master of Kung Fu said.

"Yes, I have a champion who can best you," insisted the Dalai Lama.

"Let him challenge me then, and if he bests me, I shall leave Tibet forever."

"If he bests you, you shall have no need to leave Tibet."

The Dalai Lama asked for tea to be served and told the regent to summon the Dancing Master. Soon the regent returned with the Dancing Master, a small, wiry fellow who seemed to be well past his prime. His legs were entwined with varicose veins, and he was swollen at the elbows from arthritis. Nevertheless, his eyes were glittering merrily, and he seemed eager for the challenge.

The Master of Kung Fu did not mock his opponent. "My own guru," he said, "was even smaller and older than you, yet I was unable to best him until last year."

The two opponents faced off. The Master of Kung Fu was taking a jaunty, indifferent stance, tempting the other to attack. The old Dancing Master began to swirl very slowly, his robes wafting around his body. His arms stretched out, and his hands fluttered like butterflies toward the eyes of his opponent. His fingers settled gently for a moment upon bushy eyebrows.

The Master of Kung Fu drew back in astonishment. He looked around the great hall. Everything was suddenly vibrant with rich hues of singing color. The faces of the monks were radiantly beautiful. It was as if his eyes had been washed clean for the first time.

The fingers of the Dancing Master stroked the nose of the Master of Kung Fu, who suddenly could smell the pungent barley from a granary in the city far below. He could smell butter melting in the most fragrant of teas, as the Dalai Lama, incomparably beautiful, watched him calmly.

The Dancing Master flicked a foot at the Kung Fu Master's genitals, and he began throbbing with desire. The sound of a woman's voice in the distance filled him with yearning. The Dancing Master was now assaulting him with joy at every touch, and he found himself removing his leather garments. His whole body began to hum like a finely tuned instrument. He seemed to have many arms and legs, all of them wishing only to nurture the blossoming of life.

The Master of Kung Fu began the most beautiful dance that had ever been seen in the great ceremonial hall of the grand Potala Palace. It lasted for three days and nights, during which time everyone in Tibet feasted, and visitors crowded the doorways and galleries to watch.

Only when the Kung Fu warrior finally collapsed at the throne of the Dalai Lama did he realize that another body was lying beside him. The old Dancing Master had died of exertion while performing his final and most marvelous dance. But he had died happily, for he had found his successor. The new Dancing Master of Tibet took the frail body of the old master in his arms and, weeping with love, drew the last of his energy into his body. Never had he felt so strong.

The Dalai Lama's tale is one of Unique Self and whole mate relationship. The darts and lunges of emptiness and violence become the erotic soaring of fullness and Evolutionary Love. Initially, the Kung Fu Master is estranged from his own Unique Self. Those who remind him how far he has strayed, he moves to destroy. The Dancing Master, fully immersed in his own story, in the depth of his own Unique Self, calls the dark lord of Kung Fu back home. Back home to his story. To the depth of his Unique Self.

When you are in the depth of your story, it is so filled with erotic allurement that you have the capacity to call the beloved back to the depth of his or her own story. From the depth of our own love story, a love story with our own life, we have the capacity to return to the beloved the lost plotline of their story.

They fall in love, the Kung Fu Master who has lost himself and the old Dancing Master. An evolutionary or whole mate partnership is born. In their meeting, both of their unique stories are fulfilled. It is only the Unique Self of the Dancing Master that can call the Kung Fu Master back to himself. When you encounter someone fully living their Unique Self, all that is false in you melts away, and you are called back to your own Unique Self. Whole mate partnership can then be formed. It is only the Kung Fu Master who can complete the last chapter in the Dancing Master's story, by becoming his successor. Their meeting is a Unique Self encounter that creates a whole mate relationship.

Table 4. Separate Self, True Self, and Unique Self

	SEPARATE SELF	TRUE SELF	UNIQUE SELF
Emergence	Emerges from the pre-personal, around the age of three Persists throughout life	Begins with awakening to a larger context, to the larger Field of Wholeness Often results from an awakening experience, a crisis, or pivotal life events	Includes and transcends True Self Includes a fundamental location in and as the Field of Wholeness Begins with awakening to the notion that one is both a unique part of and indivisible from the larger Whole—a unique incarnation of the Whole
Identity	Ego-based Identity revolves around survival needs	Transcends the exclusive identification with the ego Individual self-sense still operates but is known as part of larger Field of Wholeness	Self-sense is that of a unique expression of the Whole with a unique perspective, unique gifts, and unique obligations Unique obligation is a natural expression of the unique configuration of Eros and intimacy that is the Unique Self fostering unique gifts that are needed by the Whole Ego points toward Unique Self, but Unique Self is, at least in part, liberated from the perpetual grasping of the ego

	SEPARATE SELF	TRUE SELF	UNIQUE SELF
Importance of Individual	The individual is important as an individual. Its perspective is limited to that directly around him or her.	The individual is important because he or she is also the Whole. There is no distinction between the individual and the Whole. Its perspective is limited to the Whole because it is no longer important as an individual.	The individual is important as an individual because he or she offers a completely unique perspective and expression to the Whole. The Whole needs the uniqueness of the individual.
Goals	Develop personality and capacities Seek personal healing Move from victim to self-responsibility	Move beyond the personal story Transcend personality to identity with one's essence Generate appreciation for personality and use it as an ally	To confess one's greatness To live one's greatness To live into the future and not from the past To give one's unique gifts and fulfill one's unique obligations
Place in the Puzzle	Individual puzzle piece with distinct boundaries Embraces puzzle piece-ness Longs to know the whole puzzle Told the puzzle does not exist	Not a puzzle piece but the puzzle itself (the Wholeness itself) Separation and distinction disappear into the Whole	The individual is a distinct puzzle piece Its unique shape and perspective completes a part of the larger puzzle that no other piece can

	SEPARATE SELF	TRUE SELF	UNIQUE SELF
Levels of Relationship	Role mate: role is the primary source of self Soul mate: identifies as part of a couple Whole mate: entices separate self into True Self and Unique Self	Entices role mate into soul and whole mate Gateway to Unique Self once whole mate emerges	May characterize the leading edge of soul mate relationships (often unconscious) Is the basis of whole mate relationships
Shadow	Isolation, lonely, limited identity Appears to be the whole picture Does not experience self as inside or participatory in the Field of Value Can only access ordinary love, not Outrageous Love Alienated from the Whole—both from interior wholeness and from the larger exterior context of the Whole	Beauty of the individual is lost or disregarded Sense of uniqueness, importance, and relevance often disappears into the Whole	Unique Shadow—not discussed in this book On Unique Shadow, see Gafni, Marc. *Your Unique Self: The Radical Path to Personal Enlightenment*, with Introduction and Afterword by Ken Wilber, Integral Publishers, 2012, Chapter 4, Station 6, and Chapters 17-19.
Gifts	Healthy separate self facilitates development, healing, and growth Sets up the individual to recognize True and Unique Self	All beings included in one's circle of compassion and concern Intimately aware of the connection with the larger Whole	Knows that Unique Self is valued and needed by Reality Contributes uniqueness to the Whole Has unique gifts and makes unique contributions to relationship

	SEPARATE SELF	TRUE SELF	UNIQUE SELF
Questions	1. How can I make myself a better person? 2. What actions can I take to bring more happiness into my life? 3. What actions can I take to bring my body, mind, and soul into better health? 4. What actions can I take to make my life more stable and secure? 5. What actions can I take to heal my personal wounds? 6. What can I do to make my life more beautiful, happy, and fulfilling? 7. How can I improve my romantic, platonic, and familial relationships and make them happier, healthier, and more fulfilling?	1. What do I need to liberate myself from to realize my True Nature? 2. What attracts my attention that I need to let go of in order to focus my attention on the nature of Self? 3. In what ways do I most want to serve my communities and the world? 4. Who is suffering and how can I help? 5. How can I get out of my own way to help the Whole? 6. What parts of my personality seem to keep me from connecting with others or contributing to my communities?	1. What do I most love about myself and my unique personhood? 2. What do I most love to do? 3. What are my unique gifts that the world needs? 4. What personal growth and development can I engage in to become more self-expressed as a distinct expression of the Whole? 5. What do I seem to be most allured to in this world? 6. What kind things do other people say about me that feel most right and true? 7. What is my unique essence? Or what makes me who I am? 8. Who do I say I am for myself, my communities, and the world?

CHAPTER 8

EVOLUTIONARY IMPULSE AT THE HEART OF EVOLUTIONARY RELATIONSHIPS

The transformation of identity generates a transformation of relationships. Evolutionary relationships, which we also call *whole mate relationships*, emerge when whole mates choose to live and relate from their Unique Selves in an evolutionary context. *Evolutionary Unique Self* is the deepest context for relating that we know at this moment in history.

Entry 1: Evolutionary Unique Self

The final and most crucial step in the up-leveling of identity is the move from Unique Self to Evolutionary Unique Self. In our puzzle metaphor, it is the piece that not only completes the puzzle, but also *evolves* the puzzle.

Let's recall the stages leading to this point.

First, you awaken from separate self to True Self, and then, you awaken to your Unique Self. When you awaken to your True Self, you realize that you are part of the larger Field of Existence. It is what Bagger Vance was pointing to when he told R. Junuh, "It's time for you to see the Field." It's what happens to Neo when he takes the red pill and realizes he has been in the matrix.

Quantum physicists refer to the Field, through its exterior manifestation, as *the zero-point field* or *the quantum field*. The wisdom traditions call its deeper interior essence *Ayin, Sunyata, Maat, Geist, Atman is Brahman,* or *the Ground of Being*. In none of these traditions is the Field believed to be empty. Rather, it is understood as radically full, alive, and erotic. The Field is superexponential Eros—*Eros on steroids*.

During the first stage of transformation, when you awaken from separate self to True Self, you are blown away by the realization that you are not separate from the larger Field. As systems science tells us, you are literally inseparable from the seamless coat of the Universe. Sometimes, however, in True Self's radical emphasis on the One Field of Consciousness, you start to lose yourself. As the next stage of the transformation unfolds, your Reality consideration deepens, and you awaken to your Unique Self. You realize you are an irreducibly unique expression of the Field of Eros and Consciousness. You are an irreducibly unique configuration of Eros and intimacy.

Junuh and Neo, in their mythic film stories, do not disappear when they awaken to the Field. On the contrary, they draw energy from the Field and become vastly more potent and powerful. It infuses their relationships with an entirely new quality of life and passion. Your Unique Self is the aliveness of the Field awakening uniquely in you, as you, and through you. Your Unique Self fosters your unique gift, the unique expression of the LoveIntelligence, LoveBeauty, and LoveDesire sourced in your connection to the larger Field.

Now let's return to the final transformation of identity, Evolutionary Unique Self.

To awaken as Evolutionary Unique Self is to really *know* that your Unique Self is an expression of the larger Field. You begin to live in an evolutionary context. Not only are you a unique piece of the puzzle—your unique puzzle piece *is* the creative impulse that evolves the entire puzzle. You begin to feel, alive in you, the evolutionary impulse that moves quarks to become atoms, atoms to become molecules, and molecules to become cells. The entire process of unfolding is driven by the inherent ceaseless Creativity of Reality, which is pulsing through you, uniquely, right now. You begin to align not with the narrow interests of your separate self, but with the evolutionary impulse that moves in you. The evolutionary impulse is the LoveIntelligence, LoveBeauty, and

LoveDesire that drives all of Reality to more life, more goodness, more truth, and more beauty.

Entry 2. Between Being and Becoming

Science gives us new information on the nature and quality of the Field, from which the consciousness of Evolutionary Unique Self is born. It turns out that the Ground of Being is not only a Field of pure, formless *Being*, but also a Field of *Becoming*. In fact, science now realizes that being and becoming are the two main features of Reality.

This might sound a bit abstract, and we want to make this very clear. Getting what this means, and what it has to do with you, is key to your next transformation of identity. It opens the door to the passion, power, and potency of evolutionary relationships.

When you imagine the Field of Being, what comes to mind? You might imagine spaciousness, infinite expanse, radical embrace, or bliss. You might think of qualities like *rest* and *peace*. Perhaps you even sense qualities like eternity, continuity, or essence. To get another sense of the Field of Being, imagine cuddling after having great sex with a person you madly love. There is nothing you want to do. There is no place you want to go. There is nothing that needs to be changed or fixed. You want the moment to last forever. The Field of Being is the experience of sitting by the vast expanse of a tranquil ocean; it is the quality of sound in your favorite genre of music; it is the feeling of satiation after devouring an insanely delicious gourmet meal. These are all qualities of the Field of Being.

When you imagine the Field of Becoming, what comes to mind? Perhaps the very opposite of restful. The Field of Becoming is not quiet. It is not spacious bliss. It is constant motion, change, and transformation. It is dynamic and sometimes turbulent. It is not calm, but ecstatic. It is not stillness, but urgency. A beautiful description of the Field of Becoming might be *ecstatic urgency*.[151] Ecstatic urgency is the quality

---

[151] We are indebted to our friend and colleague Andrew Cohen for the expression ecstatic urgency.

of the evolutionary impulse. It is not the quality of cuddling, but the intensity of desire, attraction, and need. It is the artist desperate to birth new beauty, the scientist yearning to reveal new truth, and the activist fighting for radical social transformation. The Field of Becoming is the raging ocean in the midst of a storm.

The Field of Being is marked by presence, satisfaction, and stillness; it is the eternal Ground of Existence that lives beneath the flux and turbulence of Reality. The Field of Becoming is marked by sexuality, innovation, and transformation; it is the ever-changing expression of Reality emerging. Being lies in the silent depths of the ocean floor. Becoming roils in the surging waves of the ocean surface. Being is peaceful knowing and subtle continuity. Becoming is creative tension and constant transformation.

It is important to recognize that becoming is not divorced from being. Becoming emerges through and out of being. Think of Eric Liddell, the famous British runner, whose story is captured in the classic movie *Chariots of Fire*. In the major race scene, Liddell breaks through the narrow limitations of his body and becomes the wind. He becomes the evolutionary impulse itself. You can see the quality of ecstatic urgency in the pure joy on his face. You can even hear the quality of ecstatic urgency in the musical score by Greek composer Vangelis. The evolutionary impulse of *Chariots of Fire* becomes audible through music.

All too often, however, the idea that being allows for becoming is taken too far, and being is privileged over becoming. This is especially true in the spiritual world, where words like *spacious*, *bliss*, and *equanimity* have come to signify the goal of personal enlightenment. In the very same circles, urgency is often portrayed as a grasping quality of the unenlightened ego. This exclusive emphasis on being over becoming is a partial view. There is indeed a spacious, restful, and blissful dimension of being that lies beneath our busyness. However, there is also a dynamic, transformative, and creative dimension of becoming that resides beneath our busyness, as well. *Ecstatic urgency* captures this dimension of becoming.

Urgency and *busyness* are completely distinct. We often keep ourselves busy with pseudo-urgency and never have the true delight of accessing ecstatic urgency. The difference between pseudo-urgency (busyness) and ecstatic urgency (evolutionary impulse) is simple. When you are busy, you take actions that are either not necessary or should be completed by someone else. Busyness is pseudo-becoming. It is a quality of the separate-self ego trying its best but never finding the wings to soar. When you act from ecstatic urgency, however, you are pulled to do something that absolutely needs to be done and can be done only by you.

Ecstatic urgency is the wildly potent and irreducibly unique expression of the evolutionary impulse that pulls you into the future. Ecstatic urgency is a distinct quality of the Field of Becoming.

In summary, there are two faces of the Field, two qualities in Reality: being and becoming. These two dimensions of the Field live in and as you. You can access their feeling and taste the difference between them in your body. The evolutionary impulse is the ecstatic urgency of becoming, drawing its power from the very depth of the Ground of Being. You can feel them coming together in your body as you run, create, or make love. To live in an evolutionary context, you must plug into the Field of Being and Becoming. As you experience the spaciousness of being living in you and the aliveness of becoming pulsing as you, you experience the evolutionary impulse awakening through you.

Entry 3. The Inner Experience of Evolutionary Unique Self— Sexuality, Innovation, Transformation

To really understand the quality of evolutionary relationships, we need to understand the transformation of identity from Unique Self to Evolutionary Unique Self. The evolution of relationships is dependent on the evolution of identity. Let us dive into the deep feeling of the Evolutionary Unique Self. This will lead us directly from soul mate to whole mate. It will reveal some of the qualities that, at their highest level, might animate evolutionary relationships.

One word of caution is in order before we dive into the interior experience of evolutionary relationship. Just as soul mates do not live in the middle of a searing, poignant love poem every second of their lives, whole mates do not live in the midst of ecstatic urgency and evolutionary ecstasy every second of their lives. Soul mate and whole mate are visions of the best that we can be. They are our north stars. They are the frameworks of our aspirations and the languages of our yearnings.

The evolution from soul mate to whole mate is supersignificant because it expands and evolves our very aspiration. We can never become anything more than our highest dreams for ourselves. We are tugged by the cords of our highest yearning.

So let us now unpack the interior experience of the Evolutionary Unique Self who partners in evolutionary relationship. This experience manifests in *sexuality*, *innovation*, and *transformation*. These are expressions of evolution's movement toward more becoming. In this sense, they are manifestations of the evolutionary impulse awakening in us, as us, and through us. Poets have long captured this core insight of evolutionary science. According to Dylan Thomas, the evolutionary impulse is . . .

> The force that through the green fuse drives the flower
> Drives my green age;
> . . .
> The force that drives the water through the rocks
> Drives my red blood.[152]

Sex Erotic: From Procreation to Co-Creation

Becoming is the core movement of evolution. Reality is always becoming more. In Chapter 1 ("The Arc of Evolution"), we saw that evolution is not idle. Evolution has direction. Reality is always moving toward greater wholeness. This is one of the greatest revelations of evolutionary science. Greater wholeness functions as an attractor, always pulling evolution forward. This wholeness has many expressions.

Reality becomes ever-more loving and caring.

Reality moves toward ever-more contact and connectivity.

---

[152] Dylan Thomas, "The force that through the green fuse drives the flower" (see, for example, The Poems of Dylan Thomas, 2017).

Reality becomes more creative, more conscious, and more complex.

Sexuality is a dimension of the evolutionary impulse. Next time you feel a sexual impulse, pay attention not to the person to whom it is directed, but to the impulse itself. The quality of the impulse is often lost to us because of our rapt focus on the person to whom we are attracted. The impulse, like love itself, lives beyond any particular person. It is evolutionary Eros arising in us. It produces an overwhelming desire to make contact, and it stimulates a sense of inexorable necessity. This is the evolutionary impulse clothed in the sexual. Naturally, the evolutionary impulse expressed as the sexual can be a source of great power in our lives.

The sexual expression of the evolutionary impulse has long been demonized, neutralized, limited, or reduced. All of this has led us to misunderstand, ignore, and even deny the power of this face of the evolutionary impulse.

There are four basic views of the sexual in the world today: *sex negative*, *sex neutral*, *sex positive*, and *sex sacred*. Each holds a partial truth, but none actually captures the deeper reality of the evolutionary impulse expressing itself through our sexual experiences.

Sex negative is well known and rooted in the Neo-Platonic strain of religion. In this view, sex is dangerous and causes us to make bad decisions, abandon cherished commitments, and lose sight of the full humanity alive in others. But dangerous as sexing may be, it is self-evident to us that sex is more than just dangerous in a negative sort of way.

Sex neutral is a common context within the social and physical sciences. Scientific researchers, for example, often write about sex in a neutral way. It's neither good nor bad, simply a natural behavior. In the sex-neutral view, sex is just like any other physical process and needs to be understood and treated as such. Sex is more of a biological function than anything else. Procreation happens, and it's required to sustain life. Important as it is to locate sex in the larger biological context, it is self-evident to almost all of us that having sex is not the same as having lunch.

Sex positive sees sex as a wonderful, positive, relational experience that brings human beings into closer intimacy. It recognizes sex as a biological process, but places emphasis on the emotional and relational dimensions. This view suggests that we should treat sex with honor and delight. But as lovely as it seems to be, sex is more than simply lovely. The sex-positive view is too bland and Pollyannaish to capture accurately our radical experience of the sexual.

The core expression of **sex-sacred** view is that sex is sacred because it creates the miracle of life through a process that is itself the height of intimacy and personal connection. Sex sacred is that which allows us to create children, strengthen our lineage, and experience the deepest of intimate communions with our beloveds. Sex sacred is beautiful, but the overwhelming majority of our sexing is not in the context of procreation. And since we live in a moment of radical population threats, procreation itself needs to be engaged with fresh eyes.

None of these sexual narratives even begins to be equal to our sexual experience. We need to articulate a new story of sexing. We call this new sexual narrative *Sex Erotic*. It is a fifth understanding of sex that honors the truth and beauty of the previous four views but moves beyond them. When sex is understood as an incarnation of the Eros of Reality itself,[153] the evolutionary impulse, it becomes Sex Erotic.

The evolutionary impulse expressed in the sexual in its highest form is ecstatic urgency. The sexual becomes the erotic drive, not only for the *joining of genes* but also for the *joining of genius*, in which body, heart, and mind fuse in devotion to a larger vision. This is not only the process of *procreation* or *recreation*, which are, in different ways, served by the first four views. The new sexual narrative is rooted in the erotic ground of *co-creation*.

As the new narrative of Sex Erotic emerges, we understand for the first time that the sexual is an expression of the essential evolutionary Eros of Reality. Reality moves to more and more contact, to more and more relationship, to the progressive deepening of intimacy. In effect, it is the evolution of deeper and deeper levels of Eros. In Sex Erotic—the direct expression of the evolutionary impulse of love awake and alive personally

---

[153] See Chapter 1, "The Arc of Evolution," Entry 6.

in us—we realize that the sexual is an expression of the larger force of Eros.

Sex Erotic can heal shame, because only Sex Erotic has the narrative power to explain the mysterious drive for radical aliveness, deeper contact, and greater wholeness that moves in us in every moment. In Sex Erotic, the sexual becomes a vessel that holds the full power of the evolutionary impulse. The evolutionary impulse awakens in the potency of your yearning for, and sexing with, your evolutionary whole mate.

Sex Erotic does not exclude what came before it. It transcends and includes the best qualities of all the previous levels of sexing. Sex Erotic invites all of the qualities of sex negative, sex neutral, sex positive, and sex sacred into an evolutionary context. When you make love to your whole mate in the context of Sex Erotic, you heal the wounding of sex negative, celebrate the miracle of sex neutral, submerge in the joy of sex positive, and delight in the possibility of sex sacred. You do so in ecstatic service to each other and to the Whole.

Innovation

Innovation is also an expression of the evolutionary impulse. Reality and relationships are constantly compelled by the delight of innovation, which drives them toward more complex and effective forms. That is how we got from dirt to seafaring to Shakespeare; from colonization to democracy to civil rights; from role mate to soul mate to whole mate.

How does the evolutionary impulse feel when expressed as innovation? Think about the times in your life when you were fully engaged in creative innovation. You might have been involved in the arts, the sciences, or a project at home or at work. You might have been engaged in intellectual conversation, dancing to your favorite music, or solving a complex problem. In those moments, you were likely fully alive, fully engaged, and fully willing to work beyond normal limits. How did those moments feel, whether they were short or extended? That is the felt sense of the evolutionary impulse expressing itself as innovation through you.

That very same impulse is what moved the Universe to burst forth with an ecstatic *Yes!* almost fourteen billion years ago. It is the same *yes* of unrelenting positivity that drives us to connection, intimacy, and new levels of aliveness and awareness. When you plug into the innovative energy of the evolutionary impulse, you access a portal of passion and purpose that far exceeds anything available to the separate self.

The possibility and fulfillment that derive from living in alignment with the innovative impulse of evolution last beyond our typical experiences of success or accomplishment. When you live from and as this impulse, the old split between means and ends falls away. The path and the destination become one.

Transformation

The final expression of the evolutionary impulse is transformation. Transformation is distinct from innovation, because it includes not just the evolutionary drive toward greater effectiveness, but also the drive to *become better*. *Better* means more conscious, more aware, and more capable of choice. It means kinder and more loving. It means more beautiful and more pleasurable. The evolutionary impulse's drive to transformation is the drive toward better expressions of identity and relationship. It is also the drive toward new evolutionary emergence.

The drive to be better—to transform—is what moves us to seek higher truths. It is what pulls us to transcend our own limitations. The evolutionary impulse's drive to transformation is why we strive to become better. It's why we choose to align with an impulse that we often cannot easily identify. This transformational impulse that lives in us is the very evolutionary impulse that drives our personal story—and, indeed, the Whole Story. Being connected to the transformational expression of the evolutionary impulse shifts the most fundamental aspects of our lives.

Sexuality, innovation, and transformation are three dimensions where we can feel the evolutionary impulse pulsing our hearts. They are the three faces of becoming.[154] They are the three dimensions of life where we make direct contact with the evolutionary impulse alive as us.

You awaken to your Evolutionary Unique Self when you recognize that you live in an evolutionary context. When you interface directly with

---

[154] Different variations of this idea are clear in many thinkers over the last 150 years. I love the modern synthesis of this structure by my colleague and friend Andrew Cohen. See Chapter 5 of Evolutionary Enlightenment: A New Path to Spiritual Awakening (2011).

the evolutionary manifestations of sexuality, innovation, and transformation, your experience of Evolutionary Unique Self deepens, and your capacity to take part in an evolutionary relationship becomes a natural expression of who you truly are.

Entry 4. The Unrelenting Positivity of *Yes!*

One way to get access to the evolutionary impulse in the most direct fashion is to ask a question. The question might be: *Why did something come from nothing?* We do not mean this as a philosophical question. Neither abstract philosophy nor sciences have the tools to address it. Evolutionary science traces the magnificence and complexity of the urge to evolve. But *why?*

The only thing we know is that the impulse for Reality to emerge through Evolutionary Unique Self is fundamentally positive. The great flaring forth of something from nothing does not derive from a *No!* The Big Bang was a dramatic *Yes!* The LoveIntelligence, LoveBeauty, and LoveDesire of Reality said *Yes!* to everything. *Yes* to creation! *Yes* to innovation! *Yes* to transformation! *Yes* to Reality moving to ever-higher and ever-deeper forms of love, life, and relationship! *Yes* to expressing itself through you.

To feel into the unrelenting positivity of *Yes!* is to feel into the evolutionary impulse and to live as Evolutionary Unique Self. When you wake up to the realization that evolution is not separate from you, but alive *in you* and *as you*, you experience this radical *Yes!* You realize that your life does not merely comprise several decades of existence and a small circle of loved ones. Your life, in all of its moments and expressions of intimacy and influence, *emerges* from all of life and *impacts* all of life. What happens in your lifetime in your circle of intimacy and influence is driven by the same evolutionary impulse that drives all of life. You can feel into the core goodness of the Whole Story and, at the same time, feel everything evolving and self-organizing to become better, deeper, and higher.

Once you understand that Reality has direction, and that it is not the product of a capricious God but rather the inherent direction of the self-organizing Universe, you begin to realize the essential goodness of the Story. The direction of Reality is toward ever-higher levels of the Good, the True, and the Beautiful. That does not mean that we are ignoring suffering, pain, and evil. Quite the opposite. Our affirmation of the essential goodness of Reality—our great *yes*—moves us to heal suffering, comfort pain, and fight against evil. We do so, however, not merely as separate and disconnected selves, but as unique expressions of the evolutionary impulse itself coming alive in us.

Your *Yes!* to the impulse to evolve is a *yes* to your life and to all of life. Repeated daily, it suffuses you with a positivity that is profound, potent, and poignant. It is the same *yes* as the original impulse that *yes*-ed Reality into existence.

In some true sense, you have been here since the beginning. Where else could you have been? We now understand Reality to have been birthed by what is called a *singularity*. Everything, including you and including me, emerged from a single point. There was no place else we could have been except for there. This is a deep realization. When you access the part of you that is beyond time and space, the part of you that is consciousness—inseparable from the larger Field of Consciousness—you realize that it must have been present from the very beginning. Where else could it have been?

You were literally present in the infinite density that emerged from absolute nothingness. You were part of the first relationships between quarks, and between protons and neutrons. You were here when those subatomic particles achieved new levels of intimacy and atoms came together in relationship some 380,000 years after the first flaring forth. You were here when those atoms formed deeper intimacies of relationship in the form of gas clouds, which came together in the unique patterns of relational intimacy called *galaxies*. You have been here when the force of self-organization produced the first single-celled organism.

This tendency toward self-organization is the expression of the evolutionary impulse—the driving force of Reality all the way up to and through you. The evolutionary impulse in you is your own urge to emerge and evolve. The very energy and intelligence that drove the Big Bang moves you to continue the evolutionary process through your own transformation and through the giving of your unique gifts in service to the transformation of All-That-Is. To the precise degree that you evolve personally, *all of Reality* evolves. To the precise degree that you give your unique gifts to Reality, *you* have evolved.

You are creating the future through your evolution. This is one of the differences between a soul mate and a whole mate. While soul mates are delighted by being present, being fulfilled, and deriving personal satisfaction, whole mates move a step beyond. Whole mates are on the court, in the game, creating the future. The whole mate delights in the ecstatic urgency of the impulse that always invites her to be more and better. Whole mates look together at the exciting horizon of the future and are always creating tomorrow. There is no looking back and no getting stuck. There is only creating the future.

Whole mates are not about being. Whole mates incarnate becoming.

Entry 5. Urge to Emerge

In their highest expression, whole mates are Evolutionary Unique Selves joined together in a Unique We. Evolutionary Unique Self is the evolutionary impulse becoming awake and conscious of itself in you. You are the personal creative expression of the evolutionary impulse.

Being is often pulled by the urge to merge. *Becoming* is characterized by the urge to *emerge*. The urge to emerge is always sourced in uniqueness.

We talked about the three faces of becoming—the three places where you can feel the evolutionary impulse pulsing your heart: sexuality, innovation, and transformation. Sexuality is the experience of *desire*. Desire asks us to go somewhere, to do something, to create something new. Desire is creative. Creativity manifests new emergence. Said simply, creation makes something new. Emergence is the evolutionary quality of something new being born.

The evolutionary impulse gives birth to new emergents at every level. When parts come together new realities are born, each greater than the sum of its parts. Each new emergent takes in all of the structures of life that preceded it and synthesizes all of them into something undeniably new. A new level of order, complexity, depth, and creativity manifests.

Evolution births new emergents. This is precisely the case when it comes to being a Unique Self, which is itself an emergent, with a unique quality of intimacy and a unique perspective, which manifest unique gifts that address a unique need in your unique circle of intimacy and influence. Living in an evolutionary context, with an evolutionary relationship to life, the Evolutionary Unique Self swings her perfect swing, which is needed by All-That-Is. That is what Bagger Vance was trying to tell R. Junuh:

> "There is a perfect shot out there, trying to find each and every one of us. All we gotta do is get ourselves outta its way, and let it choose us."

Entry 6. Democratization of Greatness

In Evolutionary Unique Self, evolution and Unique Self synthesize into a higher order of being and becoming. Evolution is the vast process taking place over billions of years as reality moves from subatomic particles to Mozart's symphonies, from molten rock to moral heroism. Unique Self means that the individual is not lost in the vastness of space or time.

As we were writing this book, we went to see a wonderful movie called *The Martian*, starring Matt Damon. In the movie, an astronaut is left behind for dead on Mars during a storm. With tears, laughter, and *pathos*, the story chronicles his heroic struggle to survive. The realization of Evolutionary Unique Self is coded into the drive for survival illustrated throughout the movie. The drive to survive is the evolutionary impulse saying through you: *your unique life matters!* Why does it matter? Not because you will live in this body forever; you will not. But because you have a unique gift to give, a poem to write, a song to sing, a life to live that can happen only through you. And all of that is infinitely valued, honored, and needed by All-That-Is.

The drive to survive is the coding of the Unique Self in the body. There is something for you to do while you are here. *You* are needed to do it. That is ecstatic, and that is urgent. That is the feeling tone of the evolutionary impulse.

That is the experience the viewer has when watching Matt Damon in

The Martian. One man is trapped in space. Even before NASA discovers he is there, the viewer is watching him. We realize that although he may be trapped in space he is not *lost* in the vastness of space. As we watch him growing potatoes, eating, and recording both serious and funny entries in his video journal, we understand that he matters. The viewer is watching with the eye of eternity, the omniscient *I*.

The viewer knows with utter certainty that he *matters*. His mood matters. His survival matters. His life matters. He is irreducibly unique. He is special. That means that his love and loving him matters. That means that his loyalty and loyalty to him matters. That means that his integrity and being in integrity with him matters. That means that his laughter and laughing with him matters. That means that his tears and crying with him matters.

When NASA finds out that he is alive, some fantastic scientific creativity allows them to open a channel of communication with Mars. The whole world then watches him. The whole world is riveted by his story. Political divisions built on the deluded insanity of separate selves are broken down. The Chinese space program partners with NASA. Everyone comes together to launch a risky rescue mission. His former crew decides to head back to Mars, doubling their time in space. Everyone understands that in a single man's life is *all of life*. Everyone remembers in the texts of their hearts the words of the ancient scribe: *anyone who saves one life has saved the entire world.*[155]

That is what it means to be an Evolutionary Unique Self. That is what it means to be the One. We are past the moment in time where one man or one woman is *the One*. In the ancient world, the king or queen was the One. Without using these exact words, anthropologists point out that the king and queen were the first expressions of Evolutionary Unique Self. They were the One. Their story mattered. Their journey was the hero's journey. What the king or queen does matters enormously. It affects not only their destiny but all of Reality. When the queen is sad, the crops wilt. When she experiences joy, the meadows dance. Greatness and uniqueness and the infinite value and dignity of the individual were

---

155 Talmud, Sanhedrin 37a. The same principle is also mentioned in Quran, 5:32.

initially incarnated in the persons of kings and queens.

The new information of the interior and exterior sciences has revealed an evolution of consciousness. Core to that evolution is what we call *the democratization of greatness*: the uniquely great potency and power of every distinct person is recognized and honored. Every human being is an Evolutionary Unique Self. Every human being matters infinitely and can change the destiny of nations.

Entry 7. The Evolutionary Impulse toward More Wholeness and More Love

Beginning to live in a larger evolutionary context simply means plugging into the Field of Becoming. Both science and the wisdom traditions used to think that Reality was a fact. Now we realize that it is not a fact, but a process. It is a Story. All of Reality *is becoming*. It is evolving. Like a story, Reality has a beginning, and it has direction—a plot. Things change and transform along the way.

Reality is not static; it is a Story. It is one interconnected energy field pulsing with life (being) and direction (becoming). Reality is throbbing with Eros (aliveness) and *telos* (purpose and direction). Purpose and direction are qualities of a story. The *telos* of the Universe is to move toward more life, more connection, and more and deeper relationships. As leading-edge theorists have shown, evolution self-organizes to higher and higher levels of the Good, the True, and the Beautiful. This process of life's deeper and higher emergence continues within the human realm. Evolution continues to drive toward higher levels of the Good, the True, and the Beautiful. In that sense, we live in what physicist Bernard Haisch called a *purpose-guided Universe*.[156]

Consider one simple example: The evolutionary process evolved microbiologists from microbes. It is clear that no amount of natural selection and accidental mutation could take us from microbes to microbiologists without an inherent direction toward greater emergence,

---

156 Bernard Haisch, The Purpose-Guided Universe: Believing in Einstein, Darwin and God (2012).

greater synergy, greater life, and greater wholeness. Moved by its own inherent creativity, the Universe has brilliantly self-organized the life process from elementary particles to human beings.

What drives the Universe toward its purpose? Physicist Stuart Kauffman talks about the inherent *ceaseless creativity* of Cosmos.[157] This inherent ceaseless creativity is always driving the Universe forward. This quality of ceaseless creativity is, like all creative processes, ecstatically urgent and delightful. It is known by many names. The great Indian philosopher Aurobindo called it the *evolutionary imperative*. Process philosopher Alfred North Whitehead, perhaps the greatest philosopher of science who ever lived, called it *the creative advance into novelty*. Our colleague and friend, leading evolutionary theorist Ervin Laszlo, coined another name for this core process of Reality. In a highly sophisticated scientific analysis of evolutionary science, physics, and biology, Ervin called this process *the self-actualizing Cosmos*.[158] The name we give to it is *the evolutionary impulse of the CosmoErotic Universe*.

Reality's Story has a plotline—an evolutionary narrative that science has been revealing for decades. The driver of the plot is the evolutionary impulse. In Chapter 1, "The Arc of Evolution", we explored five major trajectories, or plotlines, of the Universe Story:

---

[157] In Reinventing the Sacred: A New View of Science, Reason, and Religion, Kauffman mentions ceaseless creativity twenty-eight times, for example: "This web of life, the most complex system we know of in the universe, breaks no law of physics, yet is partially lawless, ceaselessly creative. So, too, are human history and human lives. This creativity is stunning, awesome, and worthy of reverence. One view of God is that God is our chosen name for the ceaseless creativity in the natural universe, biosphere, and human cultures." From S. A. Kauffman, "Preface," in Reinventing the Sacred: A New View of Science, Reason, and Religion (2010).

[158] E. Laszlo, The Self-Actualizing Cosmos: The Akasha Revolution in Science and Human Consciousness (2014).

1. The Universe moves from simplicity to ever-greater **complexity** and **interconnectivity.**

2. The Universe expresses complexity through ever-greater **uniqueness**.

3. The interior of interconnectivity is **intimacy**. Evolution may be understood as the progressive deepening of intimacies.

4. The Universe is ever-more **creative** at new levels of depth and complexity. It always brings forth *newness*.

5. The Universe evolves to ever-higher levels of **consciousness**. *More consciousness* means that every level of evolution is more *aware* of its surroundings, others, and itself. It also means more freedom and choice. One expression of the evolution of consciousness is *Conscious Evolution*.

All these plotlines of evolution contribute to the progressive **deepening of *wholeness***. Reality (human beings most certainly included) yearns for ever-greater wholeness. Wholeness is a property of both intimacy and Eros. It is the very aspiration of Eros (which moves toward greater wholeness) and intimacy (which moves toward ever wider and deeper shared identities). In this sense, the drive for intimacy, Eros, or wholeness—all virtual synonyms but not ultimately isomorphic—can be understood as the most fundamental of the plotlines of Cosmos.

Evolution is not a dogma of science, but one of the central strategic processes of the manifest world. Some may think it is guided by God. Others may think it is guided by its own inherent creativity. Others (like us) may think those are the same thing. The key is to understand that evolution is not a process happening *out there*. We are part of the evolutionary process. The fact that we are aware of that truth is unique. It means that evolution is becoming conscious in us and as us.

Reality is the story of evolution. Evolution means higher and higher levels of complexity, consciousness, creativity, relationship, uniqueness, and complexity. Evolution also means the movement to higher and higher levels of love. The arrow of evolution points toward more love. Evolution is love in action. The plotline of the evolutionary Story is no less than the plotline of the evolution of love.

Entry 8. Evolution Awakening to Itself in Us

Conscious Evolution and Evolutionary Relationships

At this moment in history, something new is happening in the process of evolution itself, unprecedented in human history. You might say that **evolution is evolving.** *The force that drives the flower*[159] does not (as far as we know) allow the flower to reflect on itself or to record its unique experience of the evolutionary impulse, yet that same force has driven human beings to become increasingly self-reflective.

Until the last several hundred years, human beings have not experienced themselves as participating in the process of evolution.[160] We had no idea, until very recently, that evolution was taking place at every level of being. Even Einstein thought the cosmos was eternal. We did not know that there was a narrative arc to evolution that moves from matter to life to mind. Simply put, we did not realize that Reality was a Story. The realization that Reality is not a fact, but an evolutionary Story, that evolution itself is evolving, was shocking and radically transforming. And we are part of that evolutionary process. We are personally implicated in the evolutionary Story because your story is chapter and verse in the Universe: A Love Story. Awakening to that realization is what it means to awaken to Conscious Evolution.

We are evolution in person. Evolution is awakening to itself through us. We are evolution becoming self-conscious. We know, for the first time in history, that all the previous levels of evolution live in us. From the

---

159 Dylan Thomas, "The force that through the green fuse drives the flower."

160 One important exception to this generalization would be certain key strains in the interior sciences of Hebrew wisdom, for example Lurianic Kabbalah. I have labeled these strains evolutionary Kabbalah. See www.MarcGafni.com on evolutionary Kabbalah.

elementary particles of the Big Bang and the elements in stardust released from supernovae to the complex processes for respiration, digestion, and cellular reproduction—*all of it literally lives in us.* Each layer of biological evolution is recorded in our DNA. Each layer of evolution functions in our physical, biological, and mental structures. Evolution lives as us. This has always been true, but we humans were never aware of it before! For the first time in history, we know this. **This realization is evolution awakening to itself.** Evolution is awakening as us in person. For the first time, we are becoming aware that we are living in an evolutionary context. We are developing an evolutionary relationship to life. We realize that our creativity, our gifts, our innovation, and our care are the engines of evolution. The life process is not outside of us. *It is living as us.* The evolutionary impulse awakens in us and pulses our heart. That does not mean that the evolutionary process is an impersonal process, which demands that we move beyond our story. Rather it demands that we know that our story, particularly the vector of evolution in our most personal story, participates in the evolutionary Story. That is precisely the realization of Conscious Evolution.

Now we know that the world is interconnected in a larger Field, in which every part affects every other part. The life process, the self-actualizing cosmos, is aware of itself through us and as us. We are now awakening to the realization that not only are we *part* of the Field of Evolution, but we are also *influential actors* in the Field. Our newly found power for creation and destruction makes us the most potent force on planet Earth.

We are moving from unconscious evolution to Conscious Evolution. We are *aware* of the evolutionary process. Evolution is awakening in us and as us. We are aware that we are part of the process. Therefore, we can consciously choose not only to fulfill our narrow personal goals, but to serve the goals of evolution—more life, more love, more creativity, more consciousness, more uniqueness, more goodness, more truth, and more beauty.

An evolutionary relationship occurs when the relationship becomes the vehicle for Conscious Evolution. In their highest form, evolutionary relationships are the expression of Conscious Evolution in the realm of relationships. They enact Conscious Evolution through the Unique We of the beloveds.

Evolutionary relationships are made up of people who have awakened to their Unique Selves and who live in an evolutionary context. To live in an evolutionary context simply means to be aware of what you just read, and to let that awareness foster in you an evolutionary relationship to life. Fostering an evolutionary relationship to life simply means that you make choices not just for the sake of your separate self, but for the sake of the larger Whole. People who share an evolutionary relationship to life create the most potent, passionate, and powerful form of evolutionary relationship.

From that place you develop Evolutionary Integrity. That means that you consider your relationship decisions, and all decisions, not only from the perspective of your immediate circle, but from the perspective of its larger impact over generations.

The Self-Actualizing Cosmos Driven by You

Science reveals that we live in a self-organizing Universe. For example, imagine an anthill. An anthill is organized to a magnificent degree. Every ant knows precisely what to do. Each ant functions as part of the larger social holon of the anthill. For example, the garbage dump in an anthill is geometrically the farthest possible distance from the cemetery. Who organized the anthill that way? The answer is: *no one*. There is an inherent intelligence in nature that self-organizes the anthill.

How does each ant know what to do? One scientific possibility is that each ant receives intelligently encoded secretions of the pheromones from other ants as they cross paths. These pheromones contain the information that tells ants what is needed and what they should do. This process, repeated exponentially, self-organizes the anthill.

The process of self-organization always uses a variety of means to communicate information. For example, each of the thirty trillion cells in your body knows precisely what to do. Each cell acts in fine-tuned and precise harmony with all the other cells. Who tells them what to do? The self-organizing intelligence of the body communicates through at least a dozen different chemical, cellular, atomic, and energy systems.

Self-organization is the natural property of Reality, all the way up and all the way down the evolutionary chain.

The human world also self-organizes. That is the nature of Reality! What guides self-organization at the human level? Unlike ants, the key actions we take in our constructed world are not necessarily guided by pheromones. Instead, they are guided by Unique Self. **At the human level, Unique Self is the attractor calling evolution forward.** We act out of the evolutionary creativity of our Unique Selves. Evolution awakens in human beings through Unique Self. Each human being is guided by their unique capacities to contribute, support, or directly catalyze the deepening of life and the creation of society.

Human beings enjoy the unique opportunity to *choose* to live from Unique Self consciousness and to give their unique gifts. That is a conscious human choice that needs to be made again and again, in every decisive moment, by every human being. That is precisely what we mean by Conscious Evolution. Conscious Evolution is the choice made by every human being to live not just as a Unique Self, but also as an Evolutionary Unique Self. **Conscious Evolution is the realization that our choices change Reality.**

It is the realization that, in a vastly interconnected world, every individual choice ultimately matters. Complexity science and systems theory teach us clearly that every choice we make can set off a ripple that can dramatically change the course of history. Acting powerfully and audaciously from this knowing is what it means to live within an evolutionary context, and to have an evolutionary relationship to life.

Evolutionary Unique Selves realize that their gifts, their very next decisions, and their choices in love, relationship, and every other area are literally evolution taking its next steps through them—*through us*.

One evolutionary master, Isaac Luria, who wrote before science caught up with mysticism, taught that in the consciousness of Evolutionary Unique Self every action that a person takes must be with the explicit consciousness and intention of *Tikkun*. *Tikkun* is a Hebrew word that is best translated as *fixing*. You realize that there is a unique fixing to be done in the world that can happen only through you. The fixing always takes place within your unique circle of intimacy and influence. Every action is invested with evolutionary intention. In the language of this teacher, every action must be *LeShem Yichud*. This means it must bring together lines and circles in a way that serves the evolutionary healing and transformation of all of Reality.

From Unconscious to Conscious Uniqueness

Evolution moves not only toward more uniqueness, but also toward more *consciousness* of uniqueness. It is fair to say that part of the evolutionary journey is the move from unconscious to conscious uniqueness. In other words, we are increasingly conscious of our uniqueness.

The human being is not only more unique than an amoeba or even a dog, but the human being is also more *conscious* of her uniqueness than an amoeba or a dog. Not only is the capacity to experience uniqueness present only at the human level; it also evolves over the course of a person's life. Here is where the distinction between separate self and Unique Self is so helpful. When a person evolves from separate self to Unique Self, his or her experience of uniqueness fundamentally transforms.

At the level of separate self, we feel like our uniqueness is *ours*. We own our uniqueness. It is a commodity over which we have authority and ownership. We can deploy it or not at will. We protect it at all costs, from any and all enemies. At this level, we live from deficiency or lack. We feel the constant need to defend ourselves and to delineate an arena of safety and security. We define ourselves over and against others. At this level of self, we have a zero-sum-game attitude toward life, even if we do so unconsciously. Within this context, we deploy our uniqueness as a commodity or a weapon.

At the level of ego, your uniqueness is comparative. You are unique, but always in comparison to someone else. If you win, someone else must lose. If you are good, someone else must be bad. If you are more, someone else is less. Because it is rooted in the consciousness of being separate, egoic uniqueness is always measuring itself, always shoring up its shortfalls.

Uniqueness **at the level of Unique Self** overflows from your fullness. It is intrinsic and noncomparative. It wells up from your deepest interiors and can never be taken away.

Uniqueness at the ego level is almost always defined not only in relation to others but by the standards of external societal values. Since money and what it can buy lie at the core of so much of our society, uniqueness at the ego level is defined in the same terms.

Uniqueness at the level of separate self is generally not clarified. There is an overall sense of the centrality of *me* but, paradoxically, there is rarely a nuanced or discerning sense of the true, unique quality of one's own self. Unique Self approaches the self from a much deeper level. At this level, your sense of your own uniqueness is far more clarified and distinguished. It is often surprisingly different than it seems in public.

At the ego level, you are not in service of your uniqueness. You are claiming your uniqueness to buttress the grasping ego, which is desperately trying to claim your own goodness. At the level of Unique Self, you are in service to your uniqueness. You realize that you are the steward of your unique gifts, which are needed and honored by All-That-Is. At the level of Unique Self, you do not claim your uniqueness; it claims you. It wells up from your deepest depths and wants to be known and gifted through you.

Rosa Luxemburg, one of the great social activists of the early twentieth century, describes her experience of this rising of Unique Self in a letter to her boyfriend, Leo Jogiches:

> *In my "soul," a totally new, original form is ripening that ignores all rules and conventions. It breaks them by the power of ideas and strong conviction. I want to affect people like a clap of thunder, to inflame their minds, not by speechifying but with the breadth of my vision, the strength of my conviction, and the power of my expression.*[161]

To love yourself is to be in service to your Unique Self. Self-love is the realization that your Unique Self, along with the wondrously unique quality of intimacy and gifts that are emergent from you alone, is necessary, indeed indispensable to Reality's Desire to love. To love another

---

161 The Rosa Luxemburg Reader, ed. by P. Hudis and K. B. Anderson (2004), 382.

is to be in service to their uniqueness. Love is not merely an emotion, but a unique perception.

Humans are also uniquely capable of *transmitting* uniqueness. The emergence of human culture, especially language, allows human experience to be passed down through the generations. Language allows the experience of any single human being to become part of the enduring legacy of humanity. Language and transmission at the level of separate self often take place through the more narcissistic dimensions of contemporary social media and its seemingly obsessive sharing of every detail of life. But underneath that apparent narcissism, there is actually a healthy impulse. The impulse says: *My life matters! The details of my life matter! They deserve to be recorded and shared.* That apparent narcissism is not merely a self-absorbed ego but potentially, if nurtured by a new Story of Value, the first flickering of a Unique Self Realization.

Evolutionary Unique Self takes Unique Self one step further and reminds us that our uniqueness offers unique gifts, not just for the sake of self-expression or the delight of our soul mates, but for the entire evolutionary process waking up uniquely through us. Far from uniqueness being merely a function of the ego or separate self, as many enlightenment traditions taught us, we now realize, through evolutionary science, that uniqueness is the Desire of the Universe. **Uniqueness itself evolves as you awaken from being a skin-encapsulated ego, essentially separate and apart from everything and everyone else, to being a unique expression of the evolutionary impulse awakening as you in person.**

Entry 9. Evolutionary Context for Relating

To awaken to your Unique Self is to realize that you live in relationship to the larger Whole. To awaken to your Evolutionary Unique Self is to live in an evolutionary context. The Evolutionary Unique Self naturally acts with the "healing and flourishing of the whole in mind."[162] While both whole mates and soul mates are natural activists for the good of the beloved, a whole mate acts together with her beloved for the Good

---

162 A. Cohen, Autobiography of an Awakening.

of the Whole. The larger Whole is organically included in her circle of love. It is crucial to remember the scientific truth, rooted in the exterior and interior sciences, that the Universe is a communion of subjects and not a collection of objects. Anything or anyone that is only objectified is left out of the Whole. Anything that is external to my circle of caring is an object. To be a whole mate is to always expand your circle of caring to include more and more of the Whole. That is the context for whole mate relationship.

To awaken to your Evolutionary Unique Self is to see with evolutionary eyes. It is to shift your perspective from your limited view to evolution's view. You shift your alignment. You begin to align with the evolutionary impulse awakening as your Unique Self. The evolutionary impulse living in you is the creative Force of the Cosmos, which moves All-That-Is toward healing and transformation. When you make a decision as an Evolutionary Unique Self, your primary question is no longer *What do I want?* or even *What does my family or beloved want or need?* The question becomes: *What does Reality, what does evolution, need from me at this moment?* You may not always know the answer, but once you start asking that question, everything changes. You have the capacity to incarnate the evolutionary impulse toward healing and transformation that initiates, animates, and guides Reality. You have the capacity to incarnate it consciously and in a way that no one else can. No one else in the world can respond as you can to the unique need of All-That-Is, a need that is yours and only yours to address. Responding to that need is the place of your full liberation and power.

From within the evolutionary context, the whole mate relationship asks a different question than does a level-one role mate or a level-two soul mate relationship. The evolutionary whole mate relationship asks: *How can we give our deepest and most beautiful unique gifts for the sake of all of Reality?* Those gifts might be public, or they might be private. They might involve personal healing, raising children, or making some other form of contribution. But they are always for the sake of the larger context. It is this intention that begins to transform soul mates into whole mates. Choosing to give your unique gifts for the sake of All-That-Is is what it means to awaken as Conscious Evolution.

Experiencing your relationship as a vehicle through which to give those unique gifts is what it means to be in an evolutionary relationship—a whole mate relationship. In this context, all of the personal work you do—the businesses you are building, the children you are raising, the personal growth and development you are enjoying—ceases to be merely for your own sake. You are now living in a larger context.

Entry 10. Unique Gifts and Unique Obligations

Answering the Call

The evolutionary impulse expresses itself through the unique gifts of Unique Selves. When evolution expresses itself as your unique gift, it is literally taking its next steps *through you*. Your unique gift is the contribution that only you can make to the world. Giving your unique gift is the way you answer the call of Reality to you. Your capacity and the overwhelming desire to give your unique gift is a direct and spontaneous expression of the evolutionary impulse arising through your Unique Self.

Your Unique Self and its unique gift are *being* and *becoming*. They arise in each moment. It is possible for you to live in the presence of your Unique Self and share its unique gift, by choice, in every moment of every day.

Unique gifts come in many expressions. Each expression is particular to each Unique Self. Unique gifts might be private or public, small or large, subtle or obvious. They may be joyfully public-facing or, just as often, they may be utterly private-facing. A hermit may live from his Unique Self and give his unique gifts to no lesser of a degree than the leader of a country or a corporation. Unique Selves and unique gifts, regardless of how they are expressed, are evolutionary gifts to all of Reality. Your unique gift is the unique face of evolution alive and awake in you, as you, and through you.

To Give Your Unique Gift Is Your Unique Obligation

In the Buddhist tradition, the *bodhisattva* is one who seeks Buddhahood through practicing noble action. In one Buddhist vision, the bodhisattva vow is to postpone his or her complete awakening until all other beings are awakened and fulfilled. In the interior sciences of Hebrew wisdom, this same archetype is called the *Tzadik*. The determining factor in the bodhisattva's or Tzadik's actions is Eros, which is deployed through insight and wisdom.

In a similar fashion, we could say that the Evolutionary Unique Self vow is the commitment to fulfill one's evolutionary obligation. Many of us recoil when we hear the word *obligation*. We identify obligation as an arbitrarily imposed expectation set by the church, family, or state. Such expectations suffocate the naturally free human being. We also commonly understand obligation to be the opposite of love. In role mate relationships, for example, staying with someone out of obligation, rather than love, was an all-too-common route to relational pain and suffering.

Obligation takes on a new meaning at a higher level of consciousness. In Hebrew, love and obligation derive from the same root words—*chiba* and *choba*. The deeper truth of obligation is that to act in obligation is to act in love. Or said slightly differently: Obligation is the radical obligation that emerges from the personal address of love. In this sense, obligation is the ultimate liberation. Obligation frees us from ambivalence and confusion and allows us to commit one thousand percent to Unique Self's invitation. Obligation at the level of Evolutionary Unique Self is an expression of the evolutionary impulse. It is created by the direct and clear recognition of the Universe's authentic need that you, and you alone, can uniquely address.

An illustration:

> Let's say you are stuck on a gorgeous tropical island with another person. Let's assume for the sake of this illustration that you know with absolute certainty that you will never be rescued. Your companion, however, drives you virtually insane. She is rude, triggering and altogether morose, melancholy, and full of rage, to the point of some relatively mild degree of emotional pain. There is abundant food on the island. The problem is that due to a physical ailment, your companion is unable to feed herself. **Are you obligated to feed her?**

Virtually every single human being of a certain generation would readily agree that in this situation, you have an absolute obligation to feed her. But if you ask the young people the same question—as I have done at leading educational institutions around the western world—in the overwhelming majority of cases, they say that while they may well decide to feed her, it is not an obligation. You could make the decision not to feed her and not be morally culpable in any objective or ultimate fashion. The reason they draw this conclusion is that their teachers have told them, much as a key figure in Harvard Divinity School told me, that we no longer have the capacity to formulate objective, real obligation. This is because we have rejected the very realization that Value is Real, and that we participate in the Field of Value, and that Value fosters obligation and that obligation itself is a Real Value.

In response to this collapse of value we have articulated the *Fivefold Principles of Authentic Obligation*:

First, there is a need.

Second, it is a genuine need, not contrived.

Third, you can clearly recognize the need.

Fourth, you are capable of fulfilling the need.

Fifth, you are not only capable, but *uniquely* capable: the need can be addressed by you and you alone.

The combination of these five factors comprises your unique obligation to give the unique gift that only you can give in this moment. It is the LoveIntelligence, LoveBeauty, and LoveDesire of Reality, acting uniquely through you and offering itself to the world. The unique expression of the LoveIntelligence living in *you*, as *you*, and through *you* creates your unique obligation to give your unique gifts.

While most of our gifts address needs that are more subtle than those related to food, there is no person who does not possess unique gifts that respond to unique needs. To live your Unique Self and to offer your unique gifts is to align yourself with the evolutionary impulse. There is no more powerful and joyous realization available to a human being. It is the matrix of meaning that fills your life and is the core of your awakening as Evolutionary Unique Self. It is also the highest context for relating in evolutionary relationships.

Living Your *Mitzvah*

Here is a story that begins to get the flavor of unique obligation and unique gift.

> There was a great master in Eastern Europe who was born to what appeared to be a very simple father. The father, Sendor, was a very poor man. Sendor heard that a man had gone bankrupt and was selling one of his properties for the very low price of ten thousand rubles. This was an enormous bargain. Sendor, who was known as an honest man, went to ten merchants in town and borrowed a thousand rubles from each. He then went to buy the property. On his way, he saw a terrible scene. A landowner was driving to the market with a boy and girl chained to either side of his wagon. The children were obviously terrified, crying silent tears, afraid to make a sound.
>
> Sendor, without thinking, shouted to the landowner, "What's going on? What have they done?" The landowner responded, "Their father has not paid the rent in three years. He owes me ten thousand rubles, so I am taking his children to sell them as slaves." Without a moment's hesitation, Sendor said audaciously, "May I buy them?" "Do you have ten thousand rubles?" the landowner asked incredulously. That was, after all, a very, very large sum of money. Sendor responded, "I

do!" and produced the money. "Well, if you have the money, they are yours," said the landowner, pleased to have settled his ordeal. He unchained the children and handed them over to Sendor.

Sendor immediately assured the children that he would help them find their way home. He did just that promptly after buying them a sumptuous meal at the local tavern. After he had left the boy and girl with their overjoyed father, Sendor became incredibly scared. He did not know what to do or where to go. He would never make enough money in his entire life to repay the ten thousand rubles. What had he done? Had he just exchanged his position with that of the destitute father? He would surely be ruined. Moreover, he would wind up in debtor's prison. How could he face his wife?

Sendor went to the local tavern and sat. He drank a glass of schnapps [whiskey], paralyzed by fear. At some point, a well-dressed man—clearly not from those parts—came in and sat next to him. He, too, drank a glass of schnapps. Then he turned to Sendor and said, "You seem troubled, dear sir. Perhaps you would like to talk about it?" "No, no," said Sendor, "I am fine." The man drank another glass of schnapps and turned to him again. "You really do seem troubled, new friend! Perhaps I might help." Sendor, having no one else to confess to, spilled the entire story to the sympathetic stranger. "Well, I understand," said the stranger, "but that is no problem. I can help you out." "How?" asked Sendor. "How can you possibly help me?" "Well," said the stranger, "simply sell me the merit of half of your *mitzvah* (good deed), and I will give you ten thousand rubles. You will have the money you require to repay your debt and still own half of the merit of your good deed." "Why, I can't do that," said Sendor. "That was my special *mitzvah*!" "Well then, sell me a quarter of your merit," the man said. "No, no—I can't do that," replied Sendor.

They haggled and haggled until the stranger said, "Listen—just sell me 1 percent of your *mitzvah*, and I will give you ten thousand rubles, and you will keep 99 percent of your *mitzvah*." "You just don't understand," said Sendor. "I can't do that. I can't sell my *mitzvah*."

The stranger got up to leave and said, "Know, Sendor, that you have done a very great thing. When you stopped the landowner and liberated the children with your ten thousand rubles, the power of your *mitzvah* rippled through the heavens. The heavens were in a joyful uproar. But there were cynical angels who said you were a fraud. They said that surely you would sell your *mitzvah* for the right price. So, they sent me to try to buy at least a part of it from you. Your refusal to sell any part of your *mitzvah* shook the heavens even more than the *mitzvah* itself. Your reward will be a great son who will be a light unto the generation." And so it was. This simple man was given a son who became one of the *greatest masters of his generation*.

Mitzvah is an ancient Hebrew word that literally means *commandment*. It is what one is commanded to do. It has a second meaning, however, that is more like *alignment* or *intimacy*. Every human being has a personal *mitzvah*. It is not legislated in any external code. Rather, it is written on the hearts of men and women. It is the expression of the Intimate Universe speaking through us when we align with the evolutionary impulse. *Mitzvah* speaks through us. To live your *mitzvah* is to respond to the intimate command of the evolutionary impulse. It is to listen to the evolutionary impulse as it speaks a private and intimate language that only you can understand. To live your *mitzvah* is to give your unique gift. The giving of your unique gift fills your life with delight, direction, and meaning. Sendor's action is the evolutionary impulse awake uniquely as Sendor. In that moment, Sendor is perfectly aligned with Reality. Sendor is intimate with Reality.

Knowing how to listen for and then respond to that private and intimate language is what it means to live in Evolutionary Intimacy with Reality itself. Your Evolutionary Unique Self is intimate with the larger Whole, and it is intuitively aligned with the evolutionary impulse awake as you. The thirteenth-century Persian poet Rumi spoke of this unique sense of Evolutionary Intimacy in his great verse, "The One Thing You Must Do":

> There is one thing in this world you must never forget to do. If you forget everything else and not this, there's nothing to worry about, but if you remember everything else and forget this, then you will have done nothing in your life.
>
> It's as if a king has sent you to some country to do a task, and you perform a hundred other services, but not the one he sent you to do. So human beings come to this world to do particular work. That work is the purpose, and each is specific to the person. If you don't do it, it's as though a priceless Indian sword were used to slice rotten meat. It's a golden bowl being used to cook turnips, when one filing from the bowl could buy a hundred suitable pots. It's like a knife of the finest tempering nailed into a wall to hang things on.
>
> You say, "But look, I'm using the dagger. It's not lying idle." Do you hear how ludicrous that sounds? For a penny an iron nail could be bought to serve for that. You say, "But I spend my energies on lofty enterprises. I study jurisprudence and philosophy and logic and astronomy and medicine and the rest." But consider why you do those things. They are all branches of yourself.
>
> Remember the deep root of your being . . . give yourself to the one who already owns your breath and your moments. If you don't, you will be like the man who takes a precious dagger and hammers it into his kitchen wall for a peg to hold his dipper gourd. You'll be wasting valuable keenness and forgetting your dignity and purpose.[163]

---

163 The Soul of Rumi: A New Collection of Ecstatic Poems (2010), 191–192.

For the Sake of the Whole

Evolutionary Unique Self demands that you see your entire life—everything that you live, breathe, feel, think, or desire on all levels of your being—within the larger framework of your direct participation in the evolution of Reality. It is this larger context that unlocks your liberation. Unique Self masters have taught for over a thousand years that every human action should be preceded by an affirmative statement of meaning: It is called, in the lineages of the interior sciences,[164] *LeShem Yichud*, literally meaning *for the sake of intimate union*. The nature of the intention is the declaration that *I do this act for the sake of unifying and evolving the infinitely valuable Divine Whole of Reality*. When every action you take is for the sake of the Whole and infused with a profound awareness of an evolutionary context, you stop reacting from ego and begin acting from powerful Evolutionary Integrity. That is what we refer to as *whole mate* or *evolutionary consciousness*.

The Renaissance Kabbalist Isaac Luria developed a highly elaborate series of *kavanot*, or intentions. Each was a formal affirmation, said at different moments during the day, to awaken and align the intention of the individual with the evolutionary Divine Context, in which they lived and breathed. For Luria, arguably the most significant Kabbalist of the last thousand years, the ecstatic human obligation to awaken to Unique Self is the primary source of joy. It is the giving of your unique gift that fills your life with direction, meaning, and delight.

Every action that you take in the world can be invested with evolutionary intention once you awaken to an evolutionary context. Awakening not just to your Unique Self but to your Evolutionary Unique Self is a shift in your alignment. But you have to *allow yourself* to awaken to the evolutionary context that your Unique Self lives in and recognize that your Unique Self is not merely a Unique Self, it's an Evolutionary Unique Self. You shift your perspective to align with the evolutionary imperative, the evolutionary impulse, which expresses itself as your Evolutionary Unique Self.

---

164 Isaac Luria, sixteenth century. See L. Fine, Physician of the Soul, Healer of the Cosmos: Isaac Luria and His Kabbalistic Fellowship (2003).

You shift your perspective the way the Kabbalists did it, the way the evolutionary mystics did it in every tradition. You shift your perspective from your will—your narrow, contracted, constricted, egoic will—from what is considered *your* side to *God's* side.[165] You move from finite to infinite games.

The split between the personal and the impersonal disappears as you awaken to your unique *tikkun* (fixing) in the larger context of the Field of all Life that ever was, is, and will be. For this reason, there is little talk in the *Kabbalah* about individual enlightenment. The danger of excessive emphasis on the individual is that you become a spiritual narcissist, totally focused on your experience of freedom and spaciousness. You then confuse that with liberation, which it is not. Enlightenment is an embodied activist relation to Reality, infused with Evolutionary Integrity, which is far beyond the awakening of True Self.

In the kabbalistic teaching, everything takes place in the larger context of community and for the sake of the larger Whole. And yet the Whole is never quite reduced to a process. Somehow, in both the liberation teachings and the life in communities of the Kabbalists, the sacred and paradoxical tension between the individual and the process was held in fine attunement.

Liberation always requires that you make yourself transparent to Self. But it also demands that you realize your place in the larger historical evolutionary context. These are two distinct forms of awakening. Your life is never limited by your go-around in this incarnation, at this particular time and place, with these particular people. That realization allows you to relax the usual obsessions with all the relational details of your life. And yet you must never so identify with the process that you lose your felt sense of the infinite value, dignity, and adequacy of yourself as individual—and of every single individual that you encounter in your life. You must engage people personally and not merely hold them as cogs in the cosmic process of evolution. The dialectical dance of the personal and impersonal must never stop.

---

165 Whenever encountering the word God, we must always remember, the god you don't believe in does not exist. We all have a version of the god we don't believe in, which is virtually always a caricature of the Divine.

When you fail to hold the personal, you may begin to engage in manipulation or possibly even psychological abuse. When you begin to see yourself as aligned with the process, which was the great teaching of Hegel, you may inadvertently give birth to the worst evils of Fascism, Communism, and Nazism, all of which were very heavily influenced by Hegel's teaching that demanded that the individual must awaken and identify with the great evolutionary process of Divine Unfolding in absolute Spirit. In Hegel's powerful clarion call to align with the ecstatic impulse of the historically unfolding evolutionary God, the holiness of the individual was somehow crushed in all the grand rhetoric, with devastating results for God and humans. The process must always remain personal.

The Hasidic master Levi Isaac of Berdichev radically reminded me of the primacy of the personal even when in the throes of evolutionary ecstasy.

> He was once leading the prayers at the close of *Yom Kippur* services. *Yom Kippur* is a fast day and the holiest day in the Hebrew calendar. According to the evolutionary mystics of Kabbalah, the twilight hours at the end of the fast are filled with potency. During that time, the enlightened prayer leader may potentially enter the virtual source code of Reality and effect a *tikkun*; that is, effect a momentous leap in the evolution of consciousness for the sake of all sentient beings in all generations.
>
> This is precisely what the greatest of all enlightened evolutionary prayer leaders Levi Isaac was doing on that *Yom Kippur*. Night had already fallen. The fast was officially over, but the ecstasy of Levi Isaac was rippling through all the upper worlds. All beings held their breath in awe of the evolutionary power of Levi Isaac's consciousness. All of Reality was pulsating with him toward an ecstatic, evolutionary crescendo. And just as the great breakthrough was about to happen, Levi Isaac spotted out of the corner of his eye an old man who was thirsty. The

fast had been very long, and the old man needed to drink. And so, in the midst of his ecstasy, Levi Isaac brought the whole evolutionary process to a halt. He immediately ended the fast and personally brought the old man a drink of water.

Entry 11. Exercise: Direct Access to the Four Selves

Next, we invite you to deepen what you are learning about the evolutionary impulse and Evolutionary Unique Self. We want to give you a direct sense of the four selves.

Start by finding a pen and a piece of paper. Below, you'll find a series of sentence stems. Your task is to complete each sentence. We'll start with the separate self. Be honest. Be real. We all have separate selves; we all have ego selves. We are all fear driven. We have a lot going on and, in so many ways, we are all just trying to survive. Give yourself space to feel into all of that and to engage your separate self. Let every other self recede into the background for a moment:

As separate self, what motivates me is
_____

As separate self, what frightens me is
_____

As separate self, what excites me is
_____

As separate self, the purpose of my life is
_____

Now step into True Self. You are indivisible from the seamless coat of the Universe. You realize that your deepest truth is not your separate self. You step into your True Self, the singular that has no plural. You realize that the total number of True Selves is One.

As True Self, what motivates me is
_____

As True Self, what frightens me is
_____

As True Self, what excites me is
_____

As True Self, the purpose of my life is
_____

Next, you will step into your Unique Self and answer another set of questions. Remember, as Unique Self, you recognize that you are an essential part of the Whole and that you are a part that expresses itself uniquely. As your Unique Self, you have a unique capacity to love, and that love is needed by Reality. You have unique gifts, which are a function of your unique perspective and your unique quality of intimacy. Your Unique Self is an irreducibly unique expression of the LoveIntelligence, LoveBeauty, and LoveDesire of all that is acting in you, as you, and through you. Give yourself space to express the unique gorgeousness that only you can. Once you have touched in with that, complete the following sentence stems:

As Unique Self, what motivates me is
_____

As Unique Self, what frightens me is
_____

As Unique Self, what excites me is
_____

As Unique Self, the purpose of my life is
_____

Next, we'll invite you to step into your Evolutionary Unique Self and complete a final set of sentences. Remember, when a Unique Self begins to live in a larger evolutionary context, Evolutionary Unique Self emerges. As an Evolutionary Unique Self, you recognize that your gifts, creativity, and love are the engines of evolution. You feel the evolutionary impulse awakening in your own heart. Through that awakening, you come to realize that not only are you a part of the Field of Evolution, you are also an influential actor in the Field. Give yourself space to stay in touch with this recognition. Rest in your Evolutionary Unique Self as you complete the following sentence stems:

As Evolutionary Unique Self, what motivates me is
_____

As Evolutionary Unique Self, what frightens me is
_____

As Evolutionary Unique Self, what excites me is
_____

As Evolutionary Unique Self, the purpose of my life is
_____

That practice gives us direct access to at least a glimmering of the realization of all four selves. Now, in our next entry, let's deepen our access to Evolutionary Unique Self, which is the very core of whole mate, evolutionary relationships.

Entry 12. The Four Big Bangs: A Meditation on the Reality of Evolution as You

Reality begins with what cosmologists have called *the Big Bang* or, perhaps more accurately, the *great flaring forth*. We are going to go on a meditative journey to actually feel this great flaring forth. There was not, however, merely one Big Bang or flaring forth. There were four.

What happens when you realize that the next step of evolutionary creativity depends on you?

What happens when you realize that your next set of actions can affect all of Reality, because lines of connection, visible and invisible, fully connect All-That-Is? What happens when you realize that we are in a system in which nothing is separate from anything else? What happens when you realize that the *butterfly effect* is true on all levels of Reality?

When you shift something in your consciousness, when you awaken to your Evolutionary Unique Self, something shifts in the entire system, and you actually become responsible for everything.

Because, dear friend who is reading, who was it who began the Whole Story?

Where were you at the Big Bang? Could you have been anywhere else? In that moment of singularity, when it all happened, where could you possibly have been? Remember that great event, my friend, that great event when you breathed out and created this entire Cosmos.

Remember this great emptying, when you threw yourself out as the entire world wanting the evolution of the Good, the True, and the Beautiful. Remember the forms and the forces through which you have traveled thus far. You emerged as helium and oxygen and carbon, and you became galaxies, you became verdant planets filled with vegetation, reaching upward to the Sun through the miracle of photosynthesis. Then, you became animals, stalking day and night, often exhausted with your weary search. Then, you became the primates of millions of years ago yearning for the light. Then, you became the primal men and women, laying the groundwork for early culture. Finally, you became the very person you are now, reading in this very moment. Remember who and what you have been, what you have done, what you have seen, what you actually are in all of those guises. You are the masks of God and Goddess, the masks of your own original face, expressed irreducibly and simply as your Evolutionary Unique Self.

Feel into it, my friend. Feel into what we know in this generation that we've never known in any previous generation. We are the first generation to actually learn the comprehensive scientific dimensions of the Universe Story. We know that the Universe is, in fact, a Story. It has a beginning, and it has a middle. We know, for the first time, that the Universe has purpose. It has direction. It emerged 13.7 billion years ago. We live on a planet orbiting our Sun. The Sun is one of the trillions of stars in one of the billions of galaxies in an unfolding Universe that's profoundly creative and interconnected.

Feel into it, friend. Feel the single immense energy of the event that began in that tiny speck. You were there. You breathed out, and it unfolded into galaxies and stars, palms and pelicans, the music of Bach, and every one of us alive today. It took 13.7 billion years of evolution to produce the unique singularity that is the irreducible you. All of Reality waited for your birth. You're not extra; there is no one like you that ever was, is, or will be. That, my friend, is the first great discovery of contemporary science. All of evolution leads to you. The second discovery: The Universe isn't simply a place; it's a Story. It's a Story in which we are immersed, to which we belong, and out of which we emerge. Just as the Milky Way is the Universe in the form of a galaxy, you are the Universe in the form of a Unique Self.

You see through your unique set of eyes, through your unique perspective. The Universe sees through your unique way of looking, engaging, living, and breathing in the world. When you reflect on the world in your unique way, when you give your gift into the awesome, grander beauty and complexity of the Universe, the Universe is awakening to itself, through your Unique Self. Feel that. Feel that alive and awake in you, in this moment, right here, right now.

Let's go back together to the very beginning. How did it all start? There was a beginning, a great flaring forth of light and luminous matter that would eventually become stars and galaxies. As well as dark matter that no one's ever seen. All of space and time, in mass and energy, began as a single point that was trillions of degrees hot, and instantly rushed apart.

Feel it! The Universe isn't simply a vast space in which things exist, large things like stars and small things like atoms. That's what we used to think. Scientists knew that matter changed form in the Universe, but they assumed that the Universe as a Whole wasn't changing. That was wrong.

The Universe itself is unfolding, the Universe itself is a Story, and you are a unique letter, a unique chapter in that Story. In the beginning, the

Universe brings forth quarks and leptons, the quanta collide, and a gluey form of plasma emerges. Then, these elementary particles begin forming stable relationships. And those stable relationships, that initial bonding, begins the entire process of evolutionary emergence and unfolding.

Feel into it, my friend: 13.7 billion years ago we were a singularity, a single point. We were smaller than the head of a pin. Nothing—*no thing*—and in that nothing was literally everything.

We were there. You were there. We were all there. Where else could we have been? Emergence scientists now know that everything that was coming into existence was encoded in the initial moment of the Big Bang. All information—all possibility and the possibility of possibility—was all encoded in that moment.

The very impulse to evolve is a part of that encoding. The impulse begins from inside that point. The great Universe Story begins to unfold. The evolutionary impulse begins to activate Reality. Cosmic firestorms, chaotic burning, wildness slowly forces a bonding that drives the Universe closer and closer together. Burning balls of hydrogen gas, intensity, supernovae exploding, immensities of all forms, ultimately give birth to the higher elements. Carbon and oxygen scatter across the Universe. Ultimately, they organize into galaxies and then into planets, including Earth. That, my friend, is the first Big Bang. That's the evolution of the Cosmos.

Understand this because it's a bigger deal than you can possibly imagine. A hundred years ago, we didn't know that the essence of Reality was that everything was evolving in every moment. Einstein thought that everything was happening in an eternal Universe. We now know that it's all evolving. It is all driven by the evolutionary impulse. **It originates with the first Big Bang, in which nothing gives birth to something.**

Then, it happens again. The second Big Bang. The inert and inanimate Cosmos, which is nonetheless self-organizing and ceaselessly creative, awakens in this huge leap of emergence unexplainable by any force. And **life is born—the second Big Bang**.

You unleash creative, dynamic life. Biological evolution comes into being. The movement that bonded quarks in relationships now moves toward higher and higher levels of mutuality, recognition, union, and embrace. That relationship, that attraction, that currency of connection drove those quarks to become atoms and those atoms to become molecules. Those molecules then become complex molecules. Then at some moment, against any possibility of chance, those molecules awaken, guided by what some call *ceaseless creativity*, guided by an internal Eros.

An internal Eros is not intelligent design. It is not merely an external god saying *let there be*, and it is. Rather, it is a ceaseless creativity—the evolutionary impulse moving the Cosmos itself, intelligent, awake. The Cosmos is intelligent. The Cosmos is Infinite Being and Infinite Intelligence, encoded information that guides the evolutionary impulse. **The first Big Bang takes billions of years. The second Big Bang takes hundreds of millions of years.**

Then it happens again for the third time. And, once again, you are there. This is all happening with you, in you. **The third Big Bang is the third great movement of evolution, the emergence of human culture—the evolution of humanity. It is only some fifty thousand years ago that this begins.** As time begins to contract, things begin to move in real time.

The creative evolutionary impulse leads to a Big Bang involving the human heart and mind. Culture is born. There is artwork on cave walls, and there is burial. There is celebration of the cycles of Moon and Sun. Musical instruments are created and used to honor the cycles of life and death. Each new emergent is undetermined by that which comes before it. Each one is drawn forward by the very Eros of the Cosmos. And it goes through stages. We go from early stages of hunter-gatherer to horticultural to early agriculture and then to more sophisticated forms of agriculture. We then move to more dramatic and advanced, techno-economic structures, until we finally arrive at the Industrial Revolution. This is followed by the information revolution some forty or fifty years ago. **These are stages of cultural evolution.** Evolution always moves through stages, from hunter-gatherer to horticultural to agrarian to industrial to informational. This is the trajectory of one line of evolution.

We move from cave paintings to pyramids and then from pyramids to Lao Tzu. From Lao Tzu, we move to Shakespeare. The family unit moves from a two-, three-, four-person unit to a clan, a tribe, a city, a state, a nation, and finally to a global village. We move from preverbal to symbols to concepts to advanced forms for written and spoken expression. We move from papyrus, to printing press, to phone, to fax, and then to the internet. **This gives you a sense of the first three Big Bangs, cosmological, biological, and cultural. Then, a couple of hundred years ago, it happens once more.**

With the fourth Big Bang, evolution is awakening to itself. We have become aware of evolution. Evolution is beginning to recognize all of its previous cycles and stages. We are able to look back at the Story. We are able to tell a story of the Story. We are beginning to realize that there is a purpose and there is a direction. We recognize that we are going someplace. Evolution is moving to higher and higher levels of love—to higher and higher levels of recognition, mutuality, union, and embrace.

The human being embodies the evolution of love at the heart of cultural evolution. We begin with egocentric love. I love only those people who are connected to me and to my family. Then I awaken from egocentric to ethnocentric love. My felt sense of caring, concern, and love extends beyond myself to those people who are in my group. I am willing to sacrifice for my people. I'll live and die for those people who share my race, creed, or tribal identity.

Then it bursts forth again, this force of Evolutionary Love. I begin to actually love not only my people, not only my ethnocentric tribe, but I move from ethnocentric love to worldcentric love. I begin to experience myself as a global citizen, and I recognize that everyone is part of this Whole Story. I realize that I am related to all humans regardless of group distinctions. Although I may locate myself in a particular place, and I honor my ethnocentricity, I am not limited by it. My egocentric sensibilities don't disappear, either. I still care for myself and my family in a particular way. I transcend and include everything that has come before, but the furthest reaches of my caring and concern now extend to all of humanity.

The awakening deepens. My love shifts from worldcentric to cosmocentric. I awaken as Unique Self, and I recognize that I am a unique expression of the larger Field. Then, I awaken as Evolutionary Unique Self. When evolution awakens to itself, we realize that we are at the center of the evolutionary process. We come to see that our creativity, our consciousness, our expanding circles of love, our depth, our creativity, our Eros, and our evolving conscious uniqueness are actually the eyes, feet, and hands of the Universe.

Evolution awakens uniquely through you once the evolutionary impulse has awakened as your Evolutionary Unique Self. So, in this moment, you are actually experiencing yourself, or you are reexperiencing yourself, as you are right now. You are not just a limited separate self, living your life. Your limited life as a skin-encapsulated ego would be a terribly lonely and alienated way to live.

When you realize, in this moment, that the evolutionary impulse is awakening through you, you'll see that God is having a *you* experience. God is having a Terry experience. God is having a Mary experience. God is having a Tonya experience. God is having a Christina experience, and a Tim experience, and a Zach experience.

The entire process of evolution is, in this moment, awakening to itself, realizing itself as Steve, as Brett, as Ken. *Oh my God* takes on a new application, a new meaning. It becomes a proclamation—God is awakening in you, as you, and through you. When you feel the fourth Big Bang awakening through your realization, you come to see that, wow, we are part of the whole thing, and the whole thing is part of us.

As an Evolutionary Unique Self, you realize that the next minute depends on you. The next unfolding of goodness, of truth, of beauty, depends on your ability to wake up and give the unique gift that emerges from the expression of your unique creativity that no one in the world has but you. If you want to find and access your deepest sense of meaning, if you want to access joy, if you want to access a sense of being ultimately needed by All-That-Is, then access and awaken to your Evolutionary Unique Self.

That is the experience of Evolutionary Unique Self. It is the ability to awaken and experience Reality as your Evolutionary Unique Self, as God living in you, as you, and through you as a unique expression of the LoveIntelligence, Love Beauty, and LoveDesire that initiated Reality itself.

When you awaken in that way, you experience *Outrageous Love*.[166] Do you think that the movement from the unmanifest to the manifest, from nothing to something, was anything less than Outrageous Love? Is there

---

166 See Chapter 9, "Outrageous Love."

anything less than outrageous in Infinity being willing to contract itself into a point and to begin the entire Story of Evolution again? This Outrageous Love moves through the four Big Bangs—through cosmological, biological, and cultural evolution before awakening as you in this very moment.

Entry 13. Evolutionary Unique Self and Evolutionary Relationships

As we come to the end of this chapter, let's briefly recapitulate some of the essential points as they relate to level-three whole mate relationships.

What do Evolutionary Unique Self and the evolutionary impulse have to do with relationships? The answer is *everything*. **The transformation of identity generates a transformation of relationships.** Each transformation of identity creates a deeper and wider context for relating. Evolutionary Unique Self is the deepest context for relating that we know at this moment in history. When beloveds live from their Evolutionary Unique Selves, they source the most passionate and potent form of relationship, which we have called *whole mate* or *evolutionary relationship*. Evolutionary relationships emerge when whole mates choose to live from their Unique Selves in an evolutionary context.

To do so simply means to be aware that you are a Unique Self who plays a central role in the evolutionary process. As you let that awareness percolate through you, an evolutionary relationship to life begins to emerge. A whole mate, evolutionary relationship to life simply means that you make choices not just for the sake of your separate self, but for the sake of the larger Whole. Just that, and nothing more. People who come together and share an evolutionary context for life create the most potent, passionate, and powerful form of relationship there is—a whole mate, *evolutionary relationship.*

To engage in evolutionary relationships, whole mates simply shift their alignment. When they shift their alignment, they no longer align with their individual will, their partner's will, or even the will of the relationship. Instead, they align with the Will of the Cosmos. The Will and Purpose of the Cosmos expresses itself through the evolutionary impulse that awakens in each *unique* person and couple.

In a whole mate, evolutionary relationship, there are two core expressions. In one, each partner radically witnesses the other's Unique Self. As whole mates, they call and support each other to align ever-more deeply with the evolutionary impulse. In the second expression, whole mates join genius to co-create a Unique We. As such, whole mates consciously give the unique gift that is an expression of their unique union. In their highest expression, whole mates are Evolutionary Unique Selves joined together in a *Unique We.*

When you experience your Evolutionary Unique Self and your *Unique We* as vehicles through which you give your unique gifts, you participate in evolutionary relationship. In this context, all of the personal growth that you do, all of the businesses that you build, all of the children that you raise, all of the adventures that you take, and all of the conversations that you have cease to be merely for your own sake. Instead, they are done for the sake of the larger Whole, for the sake of evolution.

As you align your intentions with the intention of the Whole, you awaken to Conscious Evolution. Your own actions help to create the future of the Whole. This is precisely what whole mates do in evolutionary relationships. Whole mates ask two primary questions:

What does Reality need from us at this moment?

and

How can we give our unique gifts to the world for the sake of evolution?

Whole mates look together at a shared horizon, and they are passionately moved to create a better tomorrow.

Table 5. The Four Selves: Separate Self, True Self, Unique Self, and Evolutionary Unique Self

	SEPARATE SELF	TRUE SELF	UNIQUE SELF	EVOLUTIONARY UNIQUE SELF
Emergence	Emerges from the prepersonal, around the age of three Persists throughout life	Begins with awakening to a larger context, to the larger Field of Wholeness Often results from an awakening experience, a crisis, or pivotal life events	Includes and transcends True Self Includes a fundamental location in and as the Field of Wholeness Begins with awakening to the notion that one is both a unique part and indivisible from the larger Whole—a unique incarnation of the Whole	Includes and transcends Unique Self and True Self Emerges when one awakens to the evolutionary impulse living uniquely in and through one's own Self
Identity	Ego-based Identity revolves around survival needs	Transcends the exclusive identification with the ego Individual self-sense still operates but is known as part of larger Field of Wholeness	Self-sense is that of a unique expression of the Whole with a unique perspective, unique gifts, and unique obligations Unique obligation is a natural expression of the unique configuration of Eros and intimacy that is the Unique Self fostering unique gifts that are needed by the Whole Ego points toward Unique Self, but Unique Self is, at least in part, liberated from the perpetual grasping of the ego	Identity is the Unique Self living fully and freely in an evolutionary context Unique obligation is not only to foster the unique gifts that are needed by the Whole, but also the unique gifts that are needed for the evolution of the Whole. Another unique obligation of Evolutionary Unique Selves is to come together as Unique Wes and give the unique gifts that emerge from these Wes.

	SEPARATE SELF	TRUE SELF	UNIQUE SELF	EVOLUTIONARY UNIQUE SELF
Importance of Individual	The individual is important as an individual. Its perspective is limited to that directly around him or her.	The individual is important because he or she is also the Whole. There is no distinction between the individual and the Whole. Its perspective is limited to the Whole because it is no longer important as an individual.	The individual is important as an individual because he or she offers a completely unique perspective and expression to the Whole. The Whole needs the uniqueness of the individual.	The individual is a unique expression needed by the Whole. The individual devotes his or her uniqueness not only to the Whole, but to the evolution of the Whole.
Goals	Develop personality and capacities Seek personal healing Move from victim to self-responsibility	Move beyond the personal story Transcend personality to identity with one's essence Generate appreciation for personality and use it as an ally	To confess one's greatness To live one's greatness To live into the future and not from the past To give one's unique gifts and fulfill one's unique obligations	To consciously participate in the process of evolution To devote relationships to the transformation of the Whole To express goodness, truth, and beauty in feelings and behavior

	SEPARATE SELF	TRUE SELF	UNIQUE SELF	EVOLUTIONARY UNIQUE SELF
Place in the Puzzle	Individual puzzle piece with distinct boundaries Embraces puzzle piece-ness Longs to know the whole puzzle Told the puzzle does not exist	Not a puzzle piece but the puzzle itself (the Wholeness itself) Separation and distinction disappear into the Whole	The individual is a distinct puzzle piece Its unique shape and perspective complete a part of the larger puzzle that no other piece can	The individual is a distinct puzzle piece Its unique shape and perspective not only complete but evolve a part of the larger puzzle that no other piece can
Levels of Relationship	Role mate: Role is the primary source of self Soul mate: Identifies as part of a couple Whole mate: Entices separate self into True Self and Unique Self	Entices role mate into soul and whole mate Gateway to Unique Self once whole mate emerges	May characterize the leading edge of soul mate relationships (often unconscious) Is the basis of whole mate relationships	Primary sense of Self in evolutionary relationships Recognized by some but not all whole mates Unique Self Symphony

	SEPARATE SELF	TRUE SELF	UNIQUE SELF	EVOLUTIONARY UNIQUE SELF
Shadow	Isolation, lonely, limited identity Appears to be the whole picture Does not experience self as inside or participatory in the Field of Value Can only access ordinary love, not Outrageous Love Alienated from the Whole—both from interior wholeness and from the larger exterior context of the Whole	Beauty of the individual is lost or disregarded Sense of uniqueness, importance, and relevance often disappears into the Whole	Unique Shadow—not discussed in this book On Unique Shadow, see Gafni, Marc. *Your Unique Self: The Radical Path to Personal Enlightenment*, with Introduction and Afterword by Ken Wilber, Integral Publishers, 2012, Chapter 4, Station 6, and Chapters 17-19.	Unique Shadow—not discussed in this book On Unique Shadow, see Gafni, Marc. *Your Unique Self: The Radical Path to Personal Enlightenment*, with Introduction and Afterword by Ken Wilber, Integral Publishers, 2012, Chapter 4, Station 6, and Chapters 17-19. Shadow of impersonal identification with the evolutionary impulse in which the individual is lost [often comes to the fore in Marxist or Fascist forms as well as in various forms of evolutionary humanism]
Gifts	Healthy separate self facilitates development, healing, and growth Sets up the individual to recognize True and Unique Self	All beings included in one's circle of compassion and concern Intimately aware of the connection with the larger Whole	Knows that Unique Self is valued and needed by Reality Contributes uniqueness to the Whole Has unique gifts and makes unique contributions to relationship	Contributes uniqueness to the evolution of the Whole Experiences joy of being an expression of evolution in action Recognizes and accepts that Evolutionary Unique Self is needed to evolve consciousness and complexity

	SEPARATE SELF	TRUE SELF	UNIQUE SELF	EVOLUTIONARY UNIQUE SELF
Questions	1. How can I make myself a better person? 2. What actions can I take to bring more happiness into my life? 3. What actions can I take to bring my body, mind, and soul into better health? 4. What actions can I take to make my life more stable and secure? 5. What actions can I take to heal my personal wounds? 6. What can I do to make my life more beautiful, happy, and fulfilling? 7. How can I improve my romantic, platonic, and familial relationships and make them happier, healthier, and more fulfilling?	1. What do I need to liberate myself from to realize my True Nature? 2. What attracts my attention that I need to let go of in order to focus my attention on the nature of Self? 3. In what ways do I most want to serve my communities and the world? 4. Who is suffering and how can I help? 5. How can I get out of my own way to help the Whole? 6. What parts of my personality seem to keep me from connecting with others or contributing to my communities?	1. What do I most love about myself and my unique personhood? 2. What do I most love to do? 3. What are my unique gifts that the world needs? 4. What personal growth and development can I engage in to become more self-expressed as a distinct expression of the Whole? 5. What do I seem to be most allured to in this world? 6. What kind things do other people say about me that feel most right and true? 7. What is my unique essence? Or what makes me who I am? 8. Who do I say I am for myself, my communities, and the world?	1. How does my unique essence distinctly evolve to the Whole? 2. What actions can I take personally, professionally, or as a part of my communities that would evolve the Whole? 3. What actions of mine and my relationships can I devote to the evolution of the Whole?

CHAPTER 9

OUTRAGEOUS LOVE

Evolutionary, whole mate relationships are both sourced in and cause for the evolution of love, which we desperately need. The next step of the evolution of love is *Outrageous Love*—a core quality of evolutionary relationships. It is quite distinct from what is usually called *love—ordinary love*. In this chapter, we explain the concept of Outrageous Love and its key distinctions from ordinary love.

Entry 1. Yearning for the Evolution of Love

For generations, mystics, religious leaders, and self-help gurus have told us that *love is the answer*. They told us we can find meaning in love—in the love of the beloved, the love of family, and the love of community. We have been told we can find meaning in the love of work, in the love of country, in the love of God, and in the love of humanity. But if we are really honest with ourselves, we must admit that it doesn't seem to be working. Our big experiences of love are often short-lived romantic highs or simple moments of bonding. These moments don't last, and even when they do, they don't seem to be enough.

In fact, many of us don't even seem to believe in love anymore. Neuroscience reduces love to brain chemicals like oxytocin and dopamine. Psychology tells us that it's all about early conditioning. Some religions tell us that the only *real* love is the love of God. And it is hard to distinguish our own feelings of love from feelings of egocentric security or comfort. The people we think we love are often simply people who make us feel secure.

Half a century ago, John Lennon sang in "Mind Games,"

Love is the answer
And you know that for sure

For most people, however, love has not been the answer. Yet, despite all of this, the most potent remaining shared value in the world is love. Music is the universal language of love. Our deepest yearning, our implicit values, and our most naked desire all appear in our songs. It is surely significant, then, that the majority of songs in the history of modern music are love songs. This is true in virtually every language and every culture.

These songs usually speak of the amorous love between human beloveds. But they might also speak of love of country, nature, God, or family. They might be about love desired, love fulfilled, or love lost. But they are virtually always about love. The Beatles sang to us, "*All you need is love.*" But if love is our final frontier, we have crossed it and been left wanting. We have competed in the great race of love, crossed the finish line, and found ourselves frustrated, hurt, or bitter. But even more significant, we have found ourselves empty, lost, lonely, and deadened, even if our love relationships have gone relatively well.

Even those of us who sense we have found love have found it to be lacking. Love does not seem to deliver on its promises. Yes, there is a short period of time when we feel deeply and truly in love, but this time of bliss is often short-lived. We rarely know how to find our way back to this fleeting paradise of yesterday.

In those rare moments when we find ourselves in the throes of true love, we have a dramatically heightened sense of being alive. We experience personal power, relatedness, and creativity. More than that, we feel that our life has radical meaning. In such moments, the meaning of our life is self-evident. We feel personally addressed by the Cosmos.

The fleeting nature of experiences like this leads us to ponder many questions about love:

What is it?
How do I get it?
How do I give it?
What does love mean in my life?
Why do I get so hurt by love?
Why do I feel I'm not loved or that I don't love enough?

Even as we ask these questions, we continue to look to love for the deepest meaning in our lives. We want and expect to experience the fullness and aliveness that only love can bring. We want and expect to experience love in our relationships, friendships, and even our workplaces. But much of the time we are disappointed. The relationships on which we stake our investment in love feel stale. Our partners do not seem to fully understand us. When we communicate, it seems like we are often talking past each other. We never quite feel heard. Our fundamental experience is usually of UnLove.

Our professional relationships don't fare much better. There seems to be little place for workplaces based on love. We see ample evidence of a politics of fear, but few glimmerings of a politics of love. And paradoxically, we feel quite alive in the midst of conflict, which is one of the reasons that we unconsciously seek it out. Yet, even when we seem to be upset at someone else, it is actually a lack of personal aliveness that is the core of our pain. This is the true angst of our contemporary situation.

Despite all of this, we have an inherent sense of love's invitation. We have an intimation that the evolution of love holds a far greater possibility. We have an intuition, a vague memory, of what a love-drenched life would feel like. We hold a memory of the future, in which we are fully alive and fully experiencing love. This memory indicts the dreariness of our current realities. We recollect something in our unconscious of the possible allure of a life well-loved. We sense the motivation and energy that is potentially there. We sense the coming evolution of love.

Entry 2. The Only Response to Outrageous Pain Is Outrageous Love

The coming evolution of love can be summarized in two central verses of CosmoErotic Humanism:

We live in a world of outrageous pain.

The only response to outrageous pain is Outrageous Love.

We have shared these lines with audiences from all around the world. People from different cultural and socioeconomic backgrounds have a similar response. These lines move something deep within them, awakening them to a new possibility—a possibility that they might awaken as an Outrageous Lover. To be an Outrageous Lover is to be in evolutionary relationship. To be an Outrageous Lover is to love yourself and others from the deepest expression of your Evolutionary Unique Self. To be an Outrageous Lover is to love at the very edge of love's own evolution.[167]

The source of outrageous pain is often relationships. It is also sourced outside of our immediate personal lives. Eight thousand children die of starvation or starvation-related diseases every day. Every night a billion people on the planet go to sleep hungry. Yet there is enough food to feed everyone three times over. There are over six hundred million people in the world today who lack access to safe water.[168] Yet we have the technology and know-how to provide that access.

Many of us grew up with the impression that slavery had ended many years ago. Yet despite the efforts of Abraham Lincoln and William Wilberforce, slavery still exists. According to some reports, upwards of forty-nine million people are subjected to sexual and labor slavery in today's world.[169] That is four times as many slaves as there were shipped from Africa across the Atlantic over a span of four hundred years[170] until the time when most industrializing countries abolished the practice. Add to that the horrors of rape, the brutality of war, and the evils of corruption

---

[167] Early versions of two Outrageous Love books, The Outrageous Love Manifesto and The Radical Path of the Outrageous Lover: The Path and Practice of Outrageous Love, by M. Gafni and K. Kincaid, are available online. See https://www.onemountainmanypaths.org/outrageous-love-books.

[168] "2.4 Billion without Adequate Sanitation. 600 Million without Safe Water. Can We Fix It by 2030?," IEG World Bank Group, 2018, https://ieg.worldbankgroup.org/blog/over-24-billion-without-adequate-sanitation-600-million-without-safe-water-how-do-we-bridge.

[169] "Global Slavery Index," Walk Free, 2021, https://www.walkfree.org/global-slavery-index/map/.

[170] See R. Segal, The Black Diaspora: Five Centuries of the Black Experience outside Africa (1995), 4. See also M. Meredith, The Fortunes of Africa (2014), 191.

in all of its forms, and you begin to get the picture. We live in a world of outrageous pain. Outrageous pain—whether personal, communal, or broader—is always sourced in a breakdown of relationships.

We are now waking up to the realization that **the personal and the evolutionary are inseparable**. The Universe is not just a place in which we live. The entire history of the Universe lives in us. Not only are we the highest expression of the evolutionary process, but we are also personally implicated in evolution's unfolding. The evolutionary impulse is throbbing in us, living through us, and depending upon us. The way we live our lives directly affects the very course of evolution. As such, the only response to outrageous pain is Outrageous Love. *Outrageous Love* is not just a phrase; it is a new way of living and relating. **Outrageous Love is the next step in the evolution of love.**

Outrageous Love is the interior quality of the evolutionary impulse awakening in us. It drives Reality to more complex and more stable relationships. It is the Force that allured quarks to bond, and which gave birth to atoms. Outrageous Love is the Force that drives the evolution of relationships all the way up the chain of life. Naturally then, Outrageous Love is at the core of our yearning for an evolution in relationship. It is the evolutionary impulse moving us into evolutionary relationships.

This is not surprising, because the core structure of Reality is Relationship. Science has shown relationships to be the essential structure of Reality. Emergence science, neuroscience, systems theory, quantum theory, attachment theory, to name just a few, have each in their own way shown us that Reality is Relationship.[171]

The core structure of Reality is not a thing or an object or a substance; it is a set of relationships. The deepening and transformation of those relationships is what we call *evolution*. It is therefore not by accident that our shared spiritual path in the world today is the path of relationships. Relationships are not an adjunct of our lives; they are essential to lives well lived. Outrageous Love, as we will see in this chapter, drives the evolution of relationships to their highest expression. Put differently, Outrageous Love is specifically involved in the emergence of a life well

---

171 See Chapter 1, "The Arc of Evolution," and Chapter 6, "Whole Mate," Entry 1.

lived. It is the next great revelation of science, psychology, and spirit.

The word *love* has grown tired. Even though it is one of our most cherished words, we have lost contact with its essential meaning. The evolution of relationships depends upon the evolution of love. We must start by evolving our relationship to the very *notion* of love. We can do this by building a clearer understanding of the concept of Outrageous Love. There is nothing offhand, saccharine, or clever in the motivations underlying our use of this term. Outrageous Love holds within it the unfathomable depth, power, and potency of Reality itself; it captures everything this book is about.

There is a better way to live and love. It is the way of Outrageous Love, which moves well beyond Mars and Venus. When you live with Outrageous Love, you live from within an evolutionary relationship, fully in touch with your sense of wholeness. This is what it means to move from role mate to soul mate to whole mate. Whole mate relationships are driven by Outrageous Love. Role mate and soul mate relationships, on the other hand, are driven by ordinary love. In their highest expression, soul mate relationships begin to touch a quality of Outrageous Love, but that does not become the core driver of relationships until whole mate has emerged.

Entry 3. Evolution of Love and Intimacy

Outrageous Love has been recognized by interior scientists from the East and West alike. For the ancient Greeks, Eros carried the spark of Outrageous Love, the drive toward ever-deeper relationship throughout the Cosmos. For the Hebrew wisdom masters, the word *Zohar* carried similar meaning.

The new sciences recognize Outrageous Love as the power of allurement, sometimes called *alluring intelligence*. It creates the set of relationships that hold the world together. At the level of galaxies, Outrageous Love is called *gravitational interaction*. Gravity draws the stars together and maintains the wholeness of galaxies. At the level of atoms, it has many names. One of them is *electromagnetic attraction*. At the level of molecules, the force of allurement is called *chemical bonding*. The molecules in our body are being held together moment-by-moment by this alluring force expressed as various forms of intramolecular and intermolecular bonds.[172] This very same force of allurement goes all the way back to the Big Bang.[173]

From Elementary Particles to Human Beings

Imagine, for example, the second after the Big Bang, when the most advanced units in existence were atomic particles such as protons, neutrons, and electrons. It was Outrageous Love that drove these units into union. It was Outrageous Love that drove these separate parts into newly emergent, larger wholes. Ordinary love, the strategy of the ego as it strives for comfort and some measure of belonging, simply does not have that power. Within minutes, separate protons and neutrons, or nucleons, found themselves in close proximity to each other and in a new relationship and *voilà*, the atomic core of a hydrogen isotope called *deuterium* or *heavy hydrogen* was formed.[174] From separate subatomic units, whole atomic nuclei were born.[175] Previously separate particles miraculously came together in relationships. This is an example of Outrageous Love, Reality's self-organizing drive toward deeper relationships.

Some 380,000 years later, helium and hydrogen found themselves in proximity to each other and *voilà*, helium hydride was formed. As these separate atoms came together in relationship, the very first manifestation of the next larger whole, molecules, was born. This early molecule was the next product of Outrageous Love.

Many billions of years later, an even more extraordinary evolutionary transformation took place on our planet. As alkaline hydrothermal vents released hot fluid into the surrounding acidic sea water, an electrochemical

---

172 There are four different forms of chemical bonding: ionic bond, covalent bond, metallic bond, and hydrogen bond.

173 There, it first appears as the strong nuclear force that allures quarks together to become protons and neutrons during the very first second after the Big Bang.

174 The very same process—parts forming new wholes—led to the creation of whole protons and neutrons out of previously separate parts that made up a quark gluon plasma. We skipped this step, which happened in the very first nanoseconds to the first second after the Big Bang, just to keep things simple.

175 However, it took the Universe another 380,000 years to cool off enough for these atomic nuclei to bond with electrons in order to form whole atoms.

gradient led to the spontaneous formation of molecules that served as the building blocks of proteins, RNA, and DNA. In this frothy, primordial soup, the first cell-like bubbles were formed. Some of these bubbles encapsulated self-replicating sets of molecules forming the very first protocells. Then, once these early protocells produced enough energy on their own, energy generated by their own interior intensifications of intimacy, they left the vents and began their life as the first bacteria and archaea, which are known as *the first two branches on the tree of life*.[176]

The evolutionary process that led separate molecules to join together as the first cells is dazzlingly complex and was driven by the force of Outrageous Love. A collection of disparate parts (molecules), managed to find their way into complex relationship, birthing the first instance of the next larger whole (cells). These single cells were bound by a cell membrane that started out as a bubble, formed in the perfect place at the perfect time. Without the inherent Force of Outrageous Love driving Reality toward higher and deeper levels of relationship, cells may have never come to exist. A single cell is a truly stunning example of Outrageous LoveIntelligence, LoveBeauty, and LoveDesire in action.

Outrageous LoveIntelligence does not stop with single cells, however. It is ceaselessly creative. Outrageous LoveIntelligence continues to move parts into deeper and higher relationship. This process, driven by the force of Outrageous Love toward greater complexity and deeper consciousness, continues on up the evolutionary spectrum until the emergence of human beings themselves.[177]

From Egocentric to Ethnocentric Love

Human beings have now emerged. Consciousness is in full bloom. The term *consciousness* has many meanings, but all of them refer to some form of interior depth. One expression of this interior depth is the

---

[176] M. Le Page and N. Lane, "How Life Evolved: 10 Steps to the First Cells," New Scientist, October 2009, https://www.newscientist.com/article/dn17987-how-life-evolved-10-steps-to-the-first-cells/.

[177] For more examples from the entire evolutionary spectrum, see the companion volume The Evolution of Love: From Quarks to Culture—the Rise of Evolutionary Relationships in Response to the Meta-Crisis.

extraordinary human capacity for highly sophisticated self-reflection. We don't just *do* things, we reflect, sometimes with great depth, poignancy, and profundity, about what we are doing.

This leads to a second expression of consciousness, a second deepening of inner experience: choice. Reflection is the beginning of the move from operating on automatic pilot to operating with choice. We step beyond the exclusive trajectory of instinct and begin to make conscious choices. We begin to choose, at least in some small way, our direction, our identity, and the nature of our relationships. It is a very gradual, incremental movement from instinct to conscious choice.

Having wider and deeper choice is just one expression of the evolution of consciousness. This evolution is demonstrated in the choices we make concerning our circle of love—our circle of intimacy. Who is included in our intimacy circle? This expression of the evolution of consciousness takes place throughout the history of humanity and in the life of every individual. This evolution of consciousness is driven by the same force of Outrageous Love that has operated, as we just saw, from the moment of the Big Bang itself.

Our circles of intimacy expand in tandem with our four-fold expansion of our identity—from egocentric to ethnocentric to worldcentric to cosmocentric.[178] Not all human beings have grown through the entire spectrum. Large sectors of humanity and many individuals get stuck for a time in a particular circle. However, despite these evolutionary hang-ups, the full evolution of love—the unfolding through all four circles—is possible both in society and for individuals. In fact, it is happening at the leading edge of consciousness and relationships at this very time.

Each of the four circles of intimacy is important. Each is necessary. Each has a shadow and light expression. The shadow of egocentric intimacy is the inherent limitation of an egocentric perspective, which is largely self-focused, somewhat inflexible, and not fully capable of honoring the needs, views, and ideas of others. For many people in the world today, egocentric intimacy is their primary form of intimacy. This is one primary aspect of what we have referred to as *ordinary love*. It is

---

178 See Chapter 1, "The Arc of Evolution," Entry 6.

real and even sacred. But because it is easily confused with the striving of the separate self for security, it is not *clarified*.

Identity, like all of evolution, is driven by Eros. For most people, it is entirely possible that an egocentric identity will expand to an ethnocentric identity. Along with that comes an ethnocentric form of intimacy, which extends to include people who are in your group or tribe as defined by family, nationality, race, sex, or religion. Ethnocentric intimacy is deeper and wider than egocentric intimacy. It seeks to protect and serve anyone whom we deem to be similar to ourselves. It is the source of loyalty to family that goes beyond the strategies of the separate self, seeking egocentric support.

Ethnocentric intimacy is also the root of our excitement over a sports team. Fifteen years ago, I was in Germany when the soccer World Cup was hosted by Germany. As a result of the Second World War, Germany has been largely denied the right to embrace an ethnocentric consciousness. This is not without reason, for the shadow expression of ethnocentric consciousness led to the Holocaust and other wartime atrocities. The World Cup I witnessed in Germany took place in 2006, some sixty years after the end of the war. These Germans had nothing to do with the evils of the war. There was palpable joy in the streets. They were loving the German team as well as their role as hosts for the other teams and visitors and, through that, loving Germany. It was a beautiful expression of ethnocentric intimacy, a crucial and fully legitimate expression of evolution's arrow.

From Egocentric Intimacy to Ethnocentric Intimacy: Jet Li's *Hero*

The movement to a higher level of relationship and identity is a key movement in the evolution of consciousness. At each next step in the expansion of intimacy, something entirely new is birthed in consciousness. That is, each new level is a completely new emergent. It is like putting on a new pair of glasses that reveal lines of connection and relationship that were invisible to you before.

The epic Jet Li movie *Hero* is about just such a moment. The hero is a hero not because of his almost mystical prowess in the martial arts. He is a hero because of a moment of transformation in which he evolves his consciousness. In this moment, he expands his circle of intimacy and thus participates in the evolution of love. Our nameless hero comes from a narrow, egocentric-based intimacy, in which his allegiance is to his local kingdom,[179] and he evolves to a more universal intimacy, which unites many kingdoms into a larger circle of intimacy. He does not fully reach worldcentric consciousness because, at that moment in history, worldcentric awareness had not yet emerged. Regardless, his expansion from identification with the local clan to an identification with the entire empire indeed constitutes an important move into a wider and deeper ethnocentric awareness.

In the scene in question, the assassin has succeeded in evading all of the king's defenses, and he is now alone with the king in the throne room. He has clearly attained his goal. He is within striking distance of the king. Nothing can stop him, except for an internal evolution of consciousness, which expands his circle of intimacy to include the emperor. The following dialogue is the heroic moment where this evolution of love takes place:

> **Moon:** Master Nameless, although I am just a humble servant, allow me to say a few words. I've been with my Master since I was eight. He taught me martial arts and how to be a decent person. Whatever my master does is for a good reason. The words he has given you carry a deep meaning. Master Nameless, please take his advice.
>
> **King of Qin:** What were the words that [Broken Sword] wrote?
>
> **Nameless:** "All under Heaven."
>
> **King of Qin:** All under Heaven . . .
>
> **Nameless:** Broken Sword said, "The people have suffered years of warfare. Only the King of Qin can stop the chaos by

---

179 See Chapter 2, "Role Mate," Entry 2.

uniting all under Heaven." He asked me to abandon the assassination for the greater good of all. He said, one person's suffering is nothing compared to the suffering of many. The rivalry of Zhao and Qin is trivial when compared to the greater cause.

King of Qin: The person who really understands me is my most feared enemy. Alone, I have endured so much criticism, so many attempts on my life. No one understands my intentions. Even my court officials see me as a tyrant. But I never imagined that Broken Sword, my archenemy, would truly understand and appreciate my real motives.

[The King pauses]

King of Qin: I would like to know how you mean to kill me without your sword?

Nameless: By capturing yours!

King of Qin: This sword has protected me through all my battles. Having found a true confidant in Broken Sword, if I die, I am content with my life. Let "All under Heaven" guide your decision.

[Army gathers outside palace]

King of Qin: It's just dawned on me! This scroll of Broken Sword's isn't about a sword technique, but about swordsmanship's ultimate ideal. Swordsmanship's first achievement is the unity of man and sword. Once this unity is attained, even a blade of grass can be a weapon. The second achievement is when the sword exists in one's heart. When absent from one's hand, one can strike an enemy at one hundred paces even with bare hands. Swordsmanship's ultimate achievement is the absence of the sword in both hand and heart. The swordsman is at peace with the rest of the world! He vows not to kill, and to bring peace to mankind.

[Nameless jumps in the air as if to stab the King]

Nameless: Your Majesty, your visions have convinced me that you are committed to the highest ideal of ultimate swordsmanship. Therefore, I cannot kill you. Remember those who gave their lives for the highest ideal: peace.

From Ethnocentric to Worldcentric Love: The Red Baron Story of World War I

At the leading edges of evolution, Eros continues its drive to expand our circles of love. From the enduring beauty of ethnocentric consciousness emerges an even higher unity, whereby our circle of love expands to include all human beings, regardless of race, sex, color, creed, or any other ethnocentric group distinction. With this expansion comes the move from ethnocentric identity and relationship to worldcentric identity and relationship.

At worldcentric consciousness, we extend our care, compassion, and regard not just to our tribe, nation, or religion, but also to every human being on the face of the planet. At this stage, we do not lose our special connection to ourselves, our families, or our partners, or to our larger tribe. But for the first time, our core identity expands to embrace the entire family of humanity.

A little-known 2008 movie, *The Red Baron*, chronicles Baron Manfred von Richthofen's evolution of love from ethnocentric to worldcentric consciousness. As always, the evolution of love is motivated by an evolution in identity and an evolution in relationship. As we have pointed out, the evolution of identity and relationships occurs together.

> Richthofen was born into the German aristocracy. In the movie, he is initially depicted as embodying a classic ethnocentric consciousness. He is identified with the German cause.

He is fighting in the early planes of the First World War. His form of battle is unique. It is a kind of hand-to-hand combat in the air. The face of the enemy is clearly visible. What makes it even more poignant is that his enemies were often friends before the war. They virtually all came from upper-class European families, and they often drank together at the universities and social events of prewar Europe. The basic theme of the movie is the gradual process by which Richthofen realizes that the limitations of ethnocentric consciousness render it absurd. As we see him pulling an enemy pilot out of a burning plane and dropping a wreath on the grave of another enemy pilot whom he knew, what we are being shown is his evolution to the next circle of love.

Later, during an aerial dogfight, Richthofen encounters Canadian Pilot Captain Brown again, who he had shot down earlier. Brown has escaped from a German POW camp after being nursed by Käte, Richthofen's love interest in the movie. Brown lands his damaged aircraft in no-man's-land, and Richthofen lands to make sure Brown is safe. In the process, Richthofen damages his aircraft. They share a drink, and hope they will not meet again until after the war is over. Brown tells Richthofen that Käte has feelings for him. When Richthofen asks how he can be sure, Brown retorts, "She kept bitching about you for weeks."

When Richthofen learns that his close friend, the Jewish pilot Friedrich Sternberg, has been shot down and killed, he makes no secret of his grief and refuses to leave his room. His enraged brother Lothar reminds him that "a leader cannot afford to mourn."

Shortly thereafter, Richthofen is wounded and is sent to be nursed by Käte. Their relationship deepens on account of the ordeal.

As a result of his many victories in the air, Richthofen gradually becomes a national icon of German prowess and pride. However, he begins to realize that he is being used as propaganda by Kaiser Wilhelm II and his generals. On the eve of the Spring Offensive in February 1918, Richthofen approaches General von Hindenburg and tells him that the war has become a no-win situation that should be ended as soon as possible. Hindenburg is outraged and orders him back to his squadron.

As the offensive begins, Richthofen's squadron sets out to clear every Allied plane and balloon out of a target area. As Käte tends to the wounded on the ground, she is horrified to learn that her beloved has returned to combat. She confronts him and demands to know why he has turned down the chance to remain safe. He states that he will not betray the soldiers in the field "by remaining the immortal god that Berlin wants me to be." He continues: "You are my greatest victory."

On the morning of April 21, 1918, after making love to Käte, Richthofen is awakened to the report of a British formation approaching the front. He has a brief talk with his pilots and tells one of them not to get involved in combat. As Richthofen climbs into his cockpit, he exchanges a sad smile with Käte. He later dies in battle.

Two weeks later, Käte crosses over Allied lines with Brown's assistance. She directly addresses Richthofen's grave: "I could not come sooner. It is not so easy to cross the lines into British territory. Finally, a friend of ours helped me. He asked me why it was important for me to come here. I told him I love you. Did I ever tell you?"

The camera pans to a funeral wreath left by the Royal Flying Corps, "To our friend and enemy, Manfred von Richthofen."

While many of the details of this story are fictional, the core trajectory of the movie is about the Red Baron's awakening from the illusion of ethnocentric consciousness. Awakening is gradual. He continues to fight the war. But he also realizes the absurdity of German superiority. Sadly, this realization was not internalized by German leadership at that time. Twenty-five years later, the same ethnocentric fervor fueled the Second World War. However, in the aftermath of that conflict, large swaths of humanity began to engage the same expansion, from ethnocentric to worldcentric consciousness, in their circles of intimacy.

From Worldcentric to Cosmocentric Love

The fourth and final step in the evolution of love's arrow is the transformation from worldcentric to cosmocentric identity. Cosmocentric love is love fully awakened in human beings at the leading edge. At this level, a profound relationship with all of Reality emerges. There is a felt sense of love, care, and concern for all of Reality and all beings.

Cosmocentric identity deepens and expands our circle of love to include the entire planet and all of its inhabitants. It recognizes that we live in a self-organizing Universe characterized by extreme beauty and dazzling complexity. It recognizes that the Universe has direction and inherent purpose and creativity. Cosmocentric love sees that the Universe is always evolving to wider and deeper love. It recognizes that this evolution is expressed in wider and deeper relationships, beginning with elementary particles, and extending all the way up through human beings. And it recognizes that human love expands further through the four circles of love described in the last few sections.

At each level in the expansion of love, evolution manifests as three transformations, which are distinct yet inseparable from each other.

- First, there is a **wider sense of identity**: *I am a member of a larger community.*

- Second, there is a **broader Field of Love** in relationship: *I embrace a wider circle of people.*

- Third, there is an **expanded depth of care and concern**, which expresses itself in action: *I am responsible for and in devotion to a wider circle of Reality.*

All of these are part of what we are calling alternately an *evolution of intimacy* or an *evolution of love.*

In these four circles of love—egocentric, ethnocentric, worldcentric, cosmocentric—each step is an Eros-driven expansion of our care and concern; each step is an important milestone in the evolution of love and relationship.

Entry 4. Love Is the Ultimate Truth at the Heart of Creation

There are five misunderstandings about the nature of love rooted in equating *Love* with *ordinary love*:

- It is commonly understood to be an experience *limited to human beings.*

- It is understood to be an *emotional experience.*

- It is virtually always thought to be the experience of a particular emotion—the emotion of *infatuation* or the feeling of falling in love, for example. Like every emotion, it *lasts for a short time* and then dissipates.

- It is thought to be an emotion that ought to be reserved for a *very small band of people*: family and perhaps one or two other friends.

- It is thought to be *blind*—something we dive into without thought, intention, or purpose.

Open any book on love and you will find the same answer to the question of *What is love?* Love is understood to be an emotional reaction to some form of outside stimulus, person, place, idea, or thing. **Ordinary love is a *reaction*.** It is a transitory feeling that arises in response to something outside of us. Unfortunately, this is what passes for love today. We think love is something that happens *to us*, particularly as an *emotion* happening to us. We've all had the experience of falling in love. It's as if we fall *out* of our normal power, self-control, and free will and *into* love.

This is precisely what the core essence of Love is *not*. While ordinary love is an emotion or a reaction, blind or otherwise, the True Nature of Love is Outrageous Love.

Outrageous Love is not a blind or reactive emotion. It is radically perceptive, precise, and intelligent. Outrageous Love is the Love that drives the entire process of Reality, all the way up and all the way down the evolutionary chain. Science refers to it by many names, the most powerful of which is *the self-organizing Universe*. It is Outrageous Love that animates self-organization in the Universe.

Consider an early-stage embryo. In a self-organizing process driven by Outrageous Love, what starts as a collection of identical cells differentiates and specializes, eventually becoming the cells for different organs. Outrageous Love as self-organization underlies the laws of physics, chemistry, and biology. It drives the ceaseless creativity of Cosmos from elementary particles all the way to human beings.

Outrageous Love is the inner quality of Reality itself. There is only One Heart and One Love. It was in reference to Outrageous Love that the Bengali mystic Tagore said,

Love is the only reality and it is not a mere sentiment.
It is the ultimate truth at the heart of creation.[180]

The ancient shamans would say to a person before a journey of awakening,

---

[180] The above is the most common translation of the quote by Rabindranath Tagore. Another translation from his Essay 4, Sadhana, 4.4, Realization in Love in The Complete Works of Rabindranath Tagore: All Short Stories, Poetry, Novels, Plays & Essays (2017): "For love is the ultimate meaning of everything around us. It is not a mere sentiment; it is truth; it is the joy that is at the root of all creation."

May you find your heart in this journey, and may you discover that your heart is One Heart.

Tagore and the shamans were referring to the same truth alluded to now by the leading edges of science.

To sum up, Outrageous Love is not mere human sentiment; it is the Heart of Existence itself, the force of Allurement that binds, animates, and evolves Cosmos.

Reality itself moves to make greater and greater levels of contact between ostensibly separate parts. Reality moves to create relationships. There is no ultimate separation. Newtonian physics spoke of discrete parts that were fundamentally disconnected from each other. That turned out to be a limited view of reality. All parts are in fact part of a larger field of interconnection. They are drawn to each other by the allurement of Outrageous Love. The interior force of cosmic attraction is what makes the entire Universe hang together.

The Christian mystic Dante talked about "the love that moves the sun and other stars."[181] The turn-of-the-century philosopher Alfred North Whitehead spoke of evolution as the *lure to creative emergence,*[182] and we refer to *the lure of becoming* or, as he is often paraphrased, as the *movement toward God* by the sometimes tender and sometimes fierce *persuasion of love.*

Tagore, Dante, the shamans, Whitehead, and the leading edges of evolutionary and complexity theory are all pointing to the truth of what we call *Outrageous Love.*

Outrageous Love is not a pallid strategy for ego security that so often masquerades as love. This ego-based love is ordinary love. Outrageous Love is the force of gravity, the irreducible allurement not yet fully explainable in terms of anything other than itself. Outrageous Love is what protons do to create stable relationships with electrons. Outrageous Love

---

181 The Divine Comedy, Volume 3: Paradiso, by Dante Alighieri, Canto XXXIII. translated by Henry Wadsworth Longfellow (1867). Original work published in 1320.

182 See Whitehead, Process and Reality: "A propositional feeling is a lure to creative emergence in the transcendent future." (263).

is what moves single-celled organisms to come together as multicellular organisms. It is the force that drives the emergence of all subsequent evolutionary stages.

Outrageous Love is not an *abstract* force of the Cosmos. When you awaken to it as a lived experience, you begin to access it as the evolutionary impulse living through you. The Outrageous Love of the evolutionary impulse becomes the core aliveness and motivating power of your life. When you awaken to it, the core quality of every aspect of your life begins to shift. **The evolutionary transformation from ordinary to Outrageous Love is the one change that changes everything.**

When we live from the Outrageous Love of the evolutionary impulse, we are capable of love in any and all situations. We are able to keep our hearts open in all circumstances, even at the most difficult times. We are able to live fully alive and radically empowered in every dimension of our lives. In other words, when we become capable of living from Outrageous Love, we have access to the Source from which all other forms of love emerge.

Every other iteration of love, however distorted its pseudo-eros expression may be, is the spark of a holy desire for recognition, connection, union, or embrace. Outrageous Love is the opposite of dissolution, deconstruction, and destruction.

Outrageous Love is not ordinary. It is epic and extraordinary. It is not reactive but responsive. It is what philosopher Charles Sanders Peirce referred to as *Evolutionary Love*.[183] Outrageous Love is the very impulse of evolution. It is the only Force that is more powerful than entropy. It is the Love that animates and drives the entire evolutionary process.

Entry 5. Ordinary Love and Outrageous Love

What is the difference between ordinary love and Outrageous Love?

Ordinary love is a strategy of the ego. It aims to keep us safe and secure, and to give us a core sense of belonging and self-esteem. Ordinary love has proven insufficient. It is not able to fulfill the deepest yearnings

---

183 See Charles S. Peirce, "Evolutionary Love," in The Monist (1893), 176-200.

of our hearts. The outrageous pain of depression, addiction, disease, brutality, and loneliness is ever-present in this world. While we seek to deaden its impact, the balm of ordinary love can only touch the surface. The only response to outrageous pain is Outrageous Love.

To be clear, there is absolutely nothing wrong with ordinary love. It is lovely and comforting. It is just not what love *is* at its very core. Therefore, ordinary love cannot take us home. It cannot deliver on all the promises made in the name of love. It cannot transform our relationships, and it cannot evolve love.

The difference between ordinary love and Outrageous Love is like the difference between a very large number and Infinity.

Eros and Pseudo-Eros

One way to think about the distinction between ordinary and Outrageous Love is through the polarity of Eros and *pseudo*-eros. Eros is the experience of radical aliveness, when one enters the inside of Reality, stepping into the clarified desire for ever-deeper contact and ever-greater wholeness. Eros is characterized by interiority, fullness of presence, clarified desire, and wholeness. Pseudo-eros is characterized by the lack of Eros. The failure of Eros that generates a sense of emptiness or void is the catalyst for pseudo-eros. Eros flows from fullness, pseudo-eros moves to cover up the emptiness, the hole.

One simple example would be great healthy, unimaginably delicious, nourishing food (Eros) versus junk food (pseudo-eros). Another example would be unimaginably great sex with the right person at the right time and in the right place (Eros) and bad sex you do not want to be having, with the wrong person, at the wrong time, and in the wrong place (almost always pseudo-eros).

Pseudo-eros does contain within it what the interior sciences often referred to as a *spark* of Eros. The spark, however, is trapped in the broken vessel of the pseudo, yearning to be liberated. And yet, in some profound way, pseudo-eros also participates in the Field of Eros—hence its attractiveness.

In a similar fashion, ordinary love very clearly participates in the Field of Eros. In other words, ordinary love *is* real love. But it all-too-often has a pseudo-eros character to it. All too often, it is motivated merely by convention or the desire for social appropriateness, status, or simply to cover up the hole of emptiness or loneliness. Those are not disqualifying motivations—quite the opposite. They are holy motivations. But those motivations often take us only to a narrow, egocentric love that splits us off from the Whole, focusing whatever attention and radiance it has on the narrowest band of intimacy, those necessary for our very limited personal surviving and thriving. All others are excluded from the circle of intimacy—from our felt care and concern. This mind set or heart posture is one of the two primary generator functions of suffering in general, and particularly of the catastrophic and existential risk that we face at this juncture in history.[184]

Having said that, it is entirely possible for a person to experience a beautiful and noble form of ordinary love—and not to exclude others intentionally but simply to be unaware of them. This person's ordinary love participates in some way in the Field of Outrageous Love. But their access to the larger Field of Outrageous Love and to wider circles of intimacy is blocked by their structure of consciousness, which may be egocentric, ethnocentric, or worldcentric.[185]

Eight Distinctions between Ordinary and Outrageous Love

Let us deepen the distinction between ordinary love and Outrageous Love. Here, with a very practical eye, we will look at seven interrelated distinctions between the two forms of love.

1. Fickle versus Steady

You feel ordinary love in good times. It is a pleasant and lovely feeling. You feel Outrageous Love even when you just lost your sweetheart or your job. Ordinary love is what you feel when you look in on your child

---

[184] We discuss this more fully in the companion volume The Evolution of Love: From Quarks to Culture—the Rise of Evolutionary Relationships in Response to the Meta-Crisis.

[185] See Entry 3 of this chapter.

sleeping. But when she is sick or throwing a tantrum for the third straight hour, ordinary love is usually insufficient to get you through it. When times are good, Outrageous Love is not merely pleasant; it is passion and pleasure awakening as your life. Outrageous Love is not lovely; it is the pulse of Love itself. Ordinary love is fickle; it comes and goes. Outrageous Love is as steady as the pulse of your own heart.

2. Scorecards versus the Secret of the Kiss

In ordinary love we keep a scorecard. The nature of our exchange is *tit for tat*. If there is a violation of the implicit *quid-pro-quo* exchange, we feel cheated. The ego is a brilliant accountant. Whether implicitly or explicitly, people keep an incredibly precise accounting of their exchanges. Ordinary love is always trying to get a great deal in both life and love. The nature of this deal is typically to give the least and get the most. In Outrageous Love, there is also an exchange, but this exchange emerges from a place of radical, mutual devotion. Each side is devoted to the other's emergence. The qualities of devotion and delight are naturally associated with Outrageous Love exchanges.

Outrageous Love Giving is a natural expression of Outrageous Love itself. It does not stem from externally imposed duty or obligation. In mysticism, one of the terms used for Outrageous Love is *the secret of the kiss*. The kiss is where giving and receiving merge into one. The giver and receiver blur in the Outrageous LoveIntelligence, LoveBeauty, and LoveDesire of evolutionary relationships. The giver and receiver are replaced by the ecstatic dance of mutual interpenetration.

3. Codependent Grasping versus Interdependent Devotion

Ordinary love may become codependent, while Outrageous Love is interdependent. In codependency, a partner *requires* their lover to form an ego identity, basically saying: *Without you, I don't exist*. In Outrageous Love, both partners have powerfully independent and autonomous identities, even though they are fully identified with each other. Partners in Outrageous Love are absolutely committed and absolutely free. When the Outrageous Lovers exchange rings, they say: *With this ring, I set you free*. This is an important quality of evolutionary relationships.

4. Comfort versus Pleasure

In ordinary love there is a direct relationship between comfort and love: the more you make me comfortable, the more I love you. With Outrageous Love, love is extended to and evoked by people who make you uncomfortable by challenging your expectations. We usually think that the opposite of pain is pleasure. This is the thinking of ordinary love. The Outrageous Lover knows that the opposite of pain is comfort, and that authentic pleasure always involves some degree of tension or pain.

Think about an experience of great pleasure. Did it not always involve some measure of pain? It may have been the pain of loss or the pain of finding your way into higher expressions of your love. Ordinary love seeks to avoid pain at all costs. Outrageous Love is not afraid of pain. It embraces your pain and your beloved's pain. Outrageous Love is simply the most authentically pleasurable feeling in the world, a Force that can truly transform your life, inside and out.

5. Disconnect versus Melting

Hold hands with ordinary love, and quite quickly your hands feel clammy. You want to move your hand far quicker than you actually do. Hold hands with Outrageous Love, and you melt into each other. Hold a crying baby who is not crying in order to fulfill ordinary needs. The baby is crying for seemingly no reason. Hold the baby with ordinary love. The baby will keep crying. Hold the baby with Outrageous Love; the baby will almost always melt tenderly into you, having found home once again.

6. Separate Self versus True Self, Unique Self, and Evolutionary Unique Self

The exchange of ordinary love happens between separate selves. Each separate self grasps for its own benefit. Anyone who is outside the boundary of my separate self is considered an *other*. Where there is other, there is fear, and fear fuels further grasping. The grasping is often hidden under the polite veneer of ordinary love.

The exchange of Outrageous Love happens between Unique Selves. Remember that Unique Selves are unique expressions of True Selves. True Self is the singular that has no plural. It is the realization that we all participate in the same LoveIntelligence, LoveBeauty, and LoveDesire, which is the seamless coat of the Universe. The unique features of that seamless coat are Unique Selves. When a Unique Self begins to live in a larger evolutionary context, Evolutionary Unique Self emerges.

Evolutionary Unique Selves encounter each other; they recognize each other in their full splendor, as another Unique Self. Each is fully free and is able to enter into authentic communion with one another. Each is fully devoted to the deepest emergence of their beloved. Each partner is in ecstatic service to the full unfolding of the other's essence.

Separate self virtually always seeks ordinary love. True Self, more deeply Unique Self, and even more deeply the Evolutionary Unique Self are lived by Outrageous Love. The movement from True Self to Unique Self to Evolutionary Unique Self may be accurately understood as an expression of the evolution of love.

7. Conventional versus Surprising

Ordinary love shows up in conventional or traditional ways. Specifically, it looks and feels the way that culture, family, and early psychological conditioning tells you it should look and feel. Outrageous Love may be surprising in the way it manifests. It may also look somewhat conventional on the outside. On the inside, however, it tastes and feels totally different. **Ordinary love is nice and polite. Outrageous Love is fierce and often impolite.**

Outrageous Love is sometimes dramatic and shocking and sometimes seemingly mundane in its manifestation. Mother Teresa famously said something along the lines of *Love is not great deeds, but small deeds done with great love.*[186] She was referring to Outrageous Love and where it makes its most important appearance—in ordinary life. The simple truth is that you need Outrageous Love to sustain your ordinary relationships. You cannot live a fulfilled life of aliveness, joy, and true success without

---

186 The way it is usually quoted is: "Not all of us can do great things. But we can do small things with great love." In Come Be My Light: The Private Writings of the Saint of Calcutta by Mother Teresa, edited and with commentary by Brian Kolodiejchuk (2007), it is quoted as "Don't look for big things, just do small things with great love ... the smaller the thing, the greater must be our love (34).

some measure of Outrageous Love.

8. Unconditional Love versus Outrageous Love

Many people ask if Outrageous Love is another word for unconditional love. It is not. Outrageous Love is not unconditional, at least not in the way that the phrase is typically used. Unconditional love is often sought in a strategy of the ego demanding its due without being willing to give. Unconditional love, which suggests that you should love me no matter what, is not Outrageous Love. The ego's demand for that form of unconditional love is simply another strategy of ordinary love.

Outrageous Love, on the other hand, is unconditional love deployed in an entirely different way. It emerges from Source. That means that it wells up from a place that is before and beyond the very idea of conditions. Outrageous Love is not dependent on cultural, social, or psychological conditions or conditioning. In Outrageous Love, essence meets essence and recognizes itself in delight. So, it *is* unconditional in the sense that it exists before and beyond all conditions. Or said slightly differently, Outrageous Love is an expression of the ultimate condition—Essence or Infinite Value or Divinity, whose very Nature is Outrageous Love.

Outrageous Love Is the Strongest Force in Cosmos

Outrageous Love has the strength to create new realities, values, and conditions for living and love. It delights in every moment. Outrageous LoveIntelligence, LoveBeauty, and LoveDesire are literally the strongest forces in Cosmos, holding everything together and organizing everything. The core method of Outrageous Love is to drive reality to ever higher and deeper forms of relationship. This method is simple, even though its productions are staggeringly beautiful and complex.

Love is not just a feeling between two separate selves. That would be ordinary love. Outrageous Love drives the self-organization of matter[187]

---

[187] The self-organizing properties of matter were demonstrated by Nobel Prize–winning chemist Ilya Prigogine. He showed that, long before there were human minds, chemicals could self-organize into complex patterns capable of coordination. There was no human intention or governing body. There was no genetic set of instructions driving them. Matter itself has self-organizing properties that guide these complex

and thus overcomes the power of entropy. Ordinary love is limited. Outrageous Love is the motivating Force driving and animating the entire Universe.

Your personal experience of Outrageous Love is evolution itself living through you. That is what it means to be lived as love. Outrageous LoveIntelligence, LoveBeauty, and LoveDesire are both the currency of connection between human beings and the essential LoveIntelligence, LoveBeauty, and LoveDesire driving the evolutionary process. An evolutionary relationship emerges when Outrageous Love wakes up from unconscious to Conscious Evolution. At that moment, relationship becomes not just the goal, but the natural evolutionary vehicle that serves the larger Whole.

This shift in context begins with a simple shift in alignment and intention. Each partner aligns with their Unique Self and the evolutionary impulse. They cease to align with the contraction of separate self. When beloveds intend that everything they do for each other is for the sake of evolution, an entirely new level of relationship emerges: evolutionary, or whole mate, relationship.

Outrageous Love Is Perception and Action

Ordinary love is a reaction and an emotion. A ball hits the wall and reacts by bouncing off of it. Very quickly, however, the energy of the reaction peters out, and the ball ceases its motion. An emotion is energy in motion, sourced in a reaction to outside stimuli. Because it is born of a reaction, the emotion comes to a rest. Ordinary love inevitably withers and dies. The feeling and the power that derive from ordinary love never last. That is simply the nature of something reactionary.

At its source, Outrageous Love is a perception and an action. For an evolutionary couple, their shared vision and activism are rooted in Outrageous Love. Outrageous Love is not a reactive emotion that eventually wears off. It is sourced in a deep capacity for perception—a

---

interactions, which create order from chaos. See, for example, *Order Out of Chaos: Man's New Dialogue with Nature* by I. Prigogine et al. (2017). The inherent quality of self-organization in Cosmos that Prigogine pointed toward is an expression of what we are calling Eros or Outrageous Love.

capacity of consciousness that deepens over time. The more we clarify our perception, the deeper our experience and emotion of love. Naturally, after years of clearly perceiving one another, our love will grow exponentially in both intensity and depth. Instead of love growing stale and eventually disappearing, which is the inevitable trajectory of ordinary love, Outrageous Love invites us to a path where love grows ever-more powerful, passionate, vital, and erotic in the fullness of time. Only Outrageous Love has the sustaining power to transform both our personal lives and our planet.

I remember sharing this particular distinction around the nature of love as perception in a dialogue I had with the Dalai Lama in his home in Dharamshala.[188] He was so excited. He kept saying, "Beautiful, beautiful!" He understood that this set of distinctions between what we now call *Outrageous Love* and *ordinary love* would forever change the entire game of love. Being science-friendly, he further realized, correctly, that this concept of Love is not fanciful conjecture, but instead emerges from an integration of the leading edges of mystical science and evolutionary theory.

Ordinary love is a reaction. It is a transitory feeling that arises in response to something outside of us. Love that arises in response to something external to us is not inherently bad. It can remind us of the Outrageous Love that we have forgotten. But it never lasts. When we experience Outrageous Love only on rare occasions, it simply makes the rest of life seem dull and drab. Only by awakening directly to the Outrageous Love that lies dormant in us can we access the full aliveness that gives our relationships power and meaning.

To live in purpose and in joy, liberated from aching anxiety, simply being in love is not enough. More than being *in* love, you have to *be* Love. Being *lived as* Love is a much more awake and evolved state than being *in* love. It is another key difference between ordinary love and Outrageous Love. It is the difference between soul mate and whole mate relationships.

Ordinary love is being *in love* induced by an external source.

---

[188] See the recording of this dialogue here: https://www.marcgafni.com/dialogues/dali-lama-dialogue/.

Outrageous Love is being *lived as Love*. Being lived as Love emerges from the Inside of the Inside of our core identity. When we become Love, we do not need to search for pleasing external stimuli. We are the evolutionary impulse, Love incarnate. Being lived as Love is the essential experience of Outrageous Love.

It is no surprise that the core distinction between ordinary love and Outrageous Love appears directly in the patterns of our heart rhythms. The heart has long been recognized as having its own intelligence, independent and prior to the rational mind. Science has now discovered that Outrageous Love and ordinary love literally produce different heart patterns.[189] The heart wave patterns of the security- and comfort-seeking strategies disguised as love, or what we have called *ordinary love*, are jagged, crooked, and incoherent. The heart wave patterns of Outrageous Love are sloping, beautiful, and coherent. Love that generates coherent heart patterns yields a series of immunological, neurochemical, hormonal, and psychological benefits that have been clearly measured and documented. Coherence is the defining feature of *being Love*, and incoherence, all too often, defines the experience of *being in love*.

All Love Is Sourced in the Great Love

Whenever you feel love, at whatever level of consciousness, you are actually feeling a force that stretches throughout the Universe and goes all the way back to the Big Bang. Regardless of whether you call it *Eros* or *self-organization through self-transcendence*, it is Outrageous Love. Simply put, it is the drive to ever higher levels of mutuality, recognition, union, and embrace that animates the entire evolutionary process. It reaches all the way down to subatomic particles and all the way up to an identity with All-That-Is, an identity with all of manifestation itself. It is one and the same Outrageous Love, one and the same Force of Allurement, one and the same drive to ever higher levels of unification. Because of this, you can let yourself feel Outrageous Love, right now.

Ordinary love is usually egocentric or ethnocentric. Outrageous Love

---

189 See, for example, R. McCraty and M. A. Zayas, "Cardiac Coherence, Self-Regulation, Autonomic Stability, and Psychosocial Well-Being," Frontiers in Psychology 5 (2014): 1090.

becomes possible once you move from ethnocentric to worldcentric consciousness: it starts to reveal itself with a felt sense of love and care for every human being on the planet.[190] Outrageous Love then reveals itself most fully at the cosmocentric level of consciousness. At the cosmocentric level, you come to realize that your heart is the One Heart that beats in the very Core[191] of the Cosmos itself. In the old world, this experience of your heart being the One Heart was the province of very few people. Ordinary people were for the most part limited to ordinary love. Today, however, this realization of Outrageous Love is becoming available to more and more people who are waking up as Outrageous Lovers.

We have identified separate self with ordinary love, and Unique Self and Evolutionary Unique Self with Outrageous Love. We have also just identified egocentric and ethnocentric consciousness with ordinary love, and worldcentric and cosmocentric consciousness with Outrageous Love. These are important and valid distinctions. But **at the deepest level, all expressions of love are fanned by the sparks of Outrageous Love.**

The original spark or impulse is always sourced in Outrageous Love. What typically happens, however, is that love at the level of separate self, just like love at the level of egocentric and ethnocentric consciousness, is utterly intertwined with the need to survive. Thus, at these levels, love all too often appears as ordinary love, the ego's strategy to meet its needs. But if we trace it back to its deepest source, it is always sourced in Outrageous Love.

Our personal experience of love is always a reflection of Outrageous Love. Whatever form love takes, it connects us to the Reality of Universal

---

190 There is also, however, a tragic reality where one has an actual realization of Outrageous Love as the Heart of Existence itself, and yet mediates that realization through an ethnocentric prism which excludes all but their tribe, religion, or nation. Tragically, strains of this position occur in many teachers, including my lineage teacher Mordechai Lainer of Izbica.

191 By that Core of the Cosmos, we, of course, don't mean a physical location. Time and space emerged together at the moment of the Big Bang, so every place in the Universe is literally the Center of the Universe. The One Heart that beats in the very Core of the Cosmos is an interior quality and not an exterior location.

Love. Our identification with the body and emotions can distort the pure expression and feeling of Love, but if we focus deeply on our feelings of love, we realize that the feeling itself will take us back to its Source. No matter how strange or codependent or wounded our individual experience of love might be, at its core it is the Great Love of the Cosmos.

Whenever you feel love, you are feeling the One and same Force operating throughout the entire Cosmos. This is not merely the human emotion of ordinary love. It is the primary Force reaching all the way back to the Big Bang and forward into the future indefinitely. In this moment, that Force is awakening in you as a desire for contact, recognition, and connection.

At the highest level of cosmocentric consciousness, you are aligned with the evolutionary impulse itself. You begin to incarnate consciously the very evolutionary impulse that drives all of Reality. Evolution awakens as you in person. Reality is having a *You* experience. Whenever you are identified with Outrageous Love, you are identified with the deepest, highest, and truest level of Unity or Oneness that you are capable of expressing at your own present level of consciousness. This Evolutionary Love evolves in you and through you. When you recognize this happening, you are directly participating in the evolution of love.

The move from soul mate to whole mate takes place precisely when you can no longer ignore the growing yearning to play a larger game than your own personal life and success. The impetus for this transformation of consciousness is rooted in the following two sentences:

I want to play a larger game.

I want to participate in the evolution of love.

We do not often clearly articulate these sentences, even to ourselves. But, at a certain point, smaller satisfactions no longer sate our hunger for aliveness. Personal fulfillment no longer fills us. It is too small a game. This is when the transition from soul mate relationship to evolutionary or whole mate relationship begins to unfold. It starts with a shift in identity. You move from egocentric or ethnocentric to worldcentric or even cosmocentric consciousness and intimacy. You evolve from separate self to Unique Self and maybe even Evolutionary Unique Self. When you are no longer moved by ordinary love, the emergence of evolutionary relationship is likely afoot.

Ordinary love does not allure you in the way it once did. You are drawn forth by a new and greater allurement. You are inexorably drawn to the radically alive and potent quality of Reality's inner Face beckoning you. You are drawn by the Face of Outrageous Love.

Entry 6. Taking Responsibility for Your Own Arousal

Reality Practice

It is your responsibility to know that you are loved in every moment. You are responsible for your own arousal. You are responsible for your own recognition of Outrageous Love. That is the essence of what we call *Reality practice*. The first step in Reality practice is *not* to learn how to love. Rather, it is to know that you *are* outrageously loved. It is only from this realization that you awaken as Outrageous Love. We usually think of spiritual practice or psychological work as developing our capacity to love. Of course, there is some validity to that. But it is Reality practice that changes everything.

The core of Reality practice is simply sanity. To be sane is to know Reality. To know Reality is to arouse your capacity to recognize and receive the love that's already raining down on you like a thundershower. Reality practice is about being open, not closed. In every moment, you are either open or closed. In every instant, the moment is either open or closed. When you open yourself, the moment opens. Reality practice is about opening ourselves, again and again, to the truth of Outrageous Love.

Reality practice is the source of our power. By opening ourselves in every moment, we are plugged in to the Infinite Power of Reality. Let's trace this power back to the Source. Just travel a mere ninety-three million miles and check out our Sun. It is 875,000 miles across and it burns at a brightness of about 3 x 10^{27} candelas (which is the brightness of 3 octillion candles). It is 27,000,000 degrees Fahrenheit at the center. Every second, it releases energy at a mass–energy conversion rate of 4.26 million metric tons and generates power equivalent to about 9.192×10^{10} megatons of TNT.[192]

Let's not stop there. Zoom out 434 light-year into space and take a look at the North Star, Polaris. It is a yellow supergiant star with about six times the mass of our Sun and shining with the luminosity of 1,260 Suns.

If you really want to blow your mind, zip out into space and head out 8,000 light-years into our Milky Way Galaxy and encounter the star Eta Carinae, which radiates about five million times more power than the Sun.[193] Or you could travel 13,000 light-years away to a remnant of a supernova that expands at speeds of four million miles per hour.[194]

Isn't this radically amazing? Isn't it insanely mind-bending? Sure, but it's actually minuscule in terms of power when compared to the formation of the Universe. Just a few years ago, NASA launched a space probe named WMAP to capture data about the cosmic background radiation left behind by the Big Bang. The images generated were astounding. They provided evidence of tiny temperature fluctuations that later became several hundred billion galaxies in the observable universe.[195]

That's all pretty impressive, but the unexpected surprise was the

---

192 F. Cain, "How Does the Sun Produce Energy?," Universe Today, https://phys.org/news/2015-12-sun-energy.html.

193 Hubblesite, "The Doomed Star Eta Carinae," https://hubblesite.org/contents/media/images/1996/23/430-Image.html.

194 ESA Hubble, "NASA's Great Observatories Provide a Detailed View of Kepler's Supernova Remnant," https://esahubble.org/images/opo0429a/.

195 As the universe is isotropic, meaning it is uniform in all orientations, the distance to the edge of the observable universe is roughly the same in every direction. That means that the observable universe is a spherical region centered around the observer. It also means that every location in the whole universe has its own observable universe, which may or may not overlap with the one centered on Earth. The observability of the universe is not limited by our technological ability to detect light but by the speed of light itself. That is why the actual size of the universe is unknown.

unthinkable, unfathomable, and absolutely incomparable power of the cosmic event that left behind this radiation. We are talking about the power of Eros—Outrageous Love, Evolutionary Love—that led the Cosmos to expand from a singular point of nothingness, by more than a trillion-fold in less than a trillionth of a trillionth of a second.[196] Now *that* is power. It is the power and passion of Reality. It is the power and passion of a Reality that knows your name, recognizes you, needs you, chooses you, and loves you. Knowing this Source of Power is what it means to take responsibility for your own arousal and to awaken to your Unique Self. This is what it means to engage in Reality practice. Let's bracket this thought for a moment. It is almost too big, and its implications too vast, to take in all at once.

From Power to Passion

Passion is an expression of the power and potency of the force of attraction. *Webster's Dictionary* uses words like *intense feeling, ardent affection, zeal,* and *fervor* to evoke the meaning of *passion*. It is the inner quality of Cosmos. It is Reality looking for you. Failing to understand this important point is the source of all breakdowns. At their core, all crimes are crimes of passion. Or more precisely, they are crimes of the lack of passion. They are crimes that come from losing connection to passion.

All acting out happens because of a loss of passion. It shows up when we do not take responsibility for our own arousal—when we do not feel the personal passion that Reality has for us. The opposite of this is precisely what it means to be a Unique Self. Imagine that someone worked for years on end saving money so that they could gift you with a precious piece of art that was potent, beautiful, and engineered with dazzling complexity and allure. Imagine as well that it was exactly the right present for you. You would know that the person who manifested that gift for you loved you madly. However, if the gift were generic, a one-size-fits-all kind of present, you might appreciate the gift, but would not feel personally loved in the same way. Feeling personally loved and needed is what it means to be a Unique Self. It's what it means to be

---

[196] NASA, "WMAP Produces New Results," National Aeronautics and Space Administration, https://map.gsfc.nasa.gov/news.

connected to the passion that Reality has for us.

Your Unique Self results from the dazzling complexity and unique wonder of trillions of your unique cells, all engaged in unique complementary relationships. You are a unique piece of art with a unique gift to give. It would take volumes to explicate the full depth of your beauty.

The point is, *you* are Reality's gift to you.

Every human being has eight core Eros needs:

The need for Eros itself.

The need to be intended.

The need to be recognized.

The need to be chosen.

The need to be love-adored.

The need to be desired.

The need to be needed.

The need to grow and transform.

All of these are bidirectional:

You need to incarnate Eros, which you share.

You need to intend.

You need to recognize.

You need to choose.

You need to love-adore.

You need to desire.

You need to need.

You need to cause growth and transformation.

In the worldview of ordinary love, held by most of the world and related to separate self consciousness, all of these needs are outsourced to one person (occasionally, one romantic beloved plus immediate family). That, however, is a tragic abandonment of one's own power and true nature.

Your uniqueness is an expression of your Eros, even as you have the capacity to gift Eros into the world through your very uniqueness.

> Your uniqueness tells you that you are intended.
> And through your uniqueness you intend uniquely.
>
> Your uniqueness tells you that are seen and recognized.
> And through your uniqueness you see and recognize uniquely.
>
> Your uniqueness tells you that you are chosen.
> And through your uniqueness you choose uniquely.
>
> Your uniqueness tells you that you are loved and adored.
> And through your uniqueness you love and adore uniquely.
>
> Your uniqueness tells you that you are needed.
> And through your uniqueness you need uniquely.
>
> Your uniqueness tells that you are desired.
> And through your uniqueness you desire uniquely.
>
> Finally, through your uniqueness you transform.
> And you cause transformation—uniquely.

When you are caught up in the busyness of daily life, you do not arouse yourself to the truth of the Universe's passion for you. When you fail to recognize this passion, your life begins to break down. You seek the experience of being intended, recognized, chosen, loved, needed, and desired from one person. The love of one person can indeed transmit to you the truth of Reality's choosing you, loving you, seeing you, and needing you. But one person cannot in himself or herself be the sum total of all that. If you make one person the sum total of being chosen, loved, recognized, and needed, you will be in agony when they withdraw their love. The outrageous pain that you feel from their withdrawal will be unbearable. Such pain will move you to act out, to commit crimes of passion, to withdraw into depression or addiction, and otherwise to lose connection with the full purpose and potency of your being.

We spend our whole lives waiting for that one person. We put it all on them. We look for them to heal us. We want their love to heal all of the trauma, all of the wounding, all of the pain. Everything hangs in the balance as we desperately wait for them to say, *I love you.* When we search endlessly for that one person, we actually miss the Universe whispering in our ears: *I love you.* To know this is to turn to Reality and say *Yes, I know, you love me.* That is what it means to take responsibility for your own arousal: it is to know that Reality loves you.

The Universe feels, and the Universe feels Love. That Love is the interior Face of the Cosmos. It addresses your Unique Self in every moment. And it says:

> *I love you. I love you madly. I love you absolutely. I love you ecstatically. Every place you fall, you fall into my hands. There is no place that I do not catch you. There is no moment when I am not holding you.*

When you awaken and realize that Reality loves you, you can begin to have a love relationship with another person, because you cease to put it all on them. You are held in the arms of Reality, so you can freely surrender to the embrace of another. That is what we mean when we say that we live in an Intimate Universe. We can feel the Infinite Power of the Universe because the inside of that Infinity of Power is the Infinity of Intimacy. Intimacy is the force of allurement and attraction that moves power to act.

What flows from all of this is the second expression of passion, which is a natural expression of Unique Self. The Universe says:

I recognize you, I choose you, and I need you.

Reality needs your service. Reality needs your passion. Your passion, which is the driver of your potency and power, is sourced in your Unique Self. Your Unique Self is the unique end of the electrical cord which plugs into the energy socket of All-That-Is. Your Unique Self is the precise portal to your potency and power. To live with full passion is possible only when you are living from and as your Unique Self.

When the Universe whispers *I love you*, if you listen more closely, you will also hear the words, *I need you*. There is nothing more enlivening than being needed. Not just needed in a small sense but needed by Reality in the ultimate sense. Reality needs the unique gift that is a function of your unique perspective and your unique quality of intimacy. This quality births your unique insight which itself fosters your unique gift. This gift engenders your unique capacity to respond to a unique need in your circle of intimacy and influence. That is precisely what it means to be a Unique Self, an irreducibly unique expression of the LoveIntelligence, LoveBeauty, and LoveDesire of All-That-Is acting in you, as you, and through you.

Finally, your uniqueness tells you that you are not small, but powerful beyond measure. Your uniqueness tells you that you are not extra, but vitally needed. Your uniqueness tells you that you are of ultimate significance. Your uniqueness tells you that you are the culmination of Reality's passion for creation. **Taking responsibility for your arousal to these truths of Love is what we call *Reality practice*.**

From *I Love You* to *You Love Me*

In the emergent context of Evolutionary Intimacy, everything changes. One of the key changes is that you do not wait to be aroused to love; you take responsibility for your own arousal.

When you don't take responsibility for your own arousal, relationships break down under a pressure they cannot possibly bear. If your beloved is the exclusive source of your knowing that you are loved, needed, recognized, and chosen, the love you share is sure to buckle.

This is why soul mate relationships often collapse. They do so under the weight of expectations that they cannot possibly meet. The love of your soul mate is a function of the Love that all of Reality has for you. But all too often, soul mate love replaces the Love of Reality. This is the tragic Achilles heel of soul mate relationships.

To become a whole mate is to arouse yourself to the larger Whole. You hear the Whole moving toward you. You hear the Whole holding your unique part. You feel the full power and passion of the Whole saying *I love you* in every moment. From that place, you are able to turn to your beloved as a whole mate. The love between you is absolutely unique, personal, and intimate. Your love story, however, is not separate from the Whole. Your love is not a tragic and desperate narcissism of two. Rather, your love story participates in the Universe, which is itself a Love Story.

The love you share is sourced in Outrageous Love, not ordinary love. Your love draws sustenance from the power and potency of the Outrageous Love that exists in the space between and around you. Your passion is infused with the passion of Reality seeking to love you open. You no longer cling to your partner, desperately awaiting the next *I love you*. Rather, you deeply know of their love. You take responsibility for your own arousal. You look at your partner, and you know that you are both part of the larger Whole that is showering Love on you in every second. You see your partner and say, *You love me*. What if you signed letters to your beloved with *You love me* instead of *I love you*? What if you signed letters to the Beloved with *You love me* instead of *I love you*?

Philosopher and paleontologist Pierre Teilhard de Chardin famously wrote,

> The day will come when, after harnessing the ether, the winds, the tides, gravitation, we shall harness for God the energies of love. And, on that day, for the second time in the history of the world,

man will have discovered fire. [197]

De Chardin was not talking about *I love you,* but about *you love me.* De Chardin was not talking about the dulling comfort of ordinary love designed by the ego to soothe our challenging lives. He was evoking the fierce and tender fire of Outrageous Love. Fire is not tepid or weak. Fire is outrageous. To master the capacity of Outrageous Love is to be on fire. It is to awaken a capacity in you for joy, aliveness, intimacy, and manifestation that is beyond your current imagination. It is to know that you love me.

From *Do You Love Me?* to *You Love Me*

Instead of asking your partner, *Do you love me?* turn to your partner and say, *You love me.* You might do this with a play of delight in your eyes. You might do this with gravitas and deadpan. You might say this with laughter, or you might say it with tears. *You love me* is a statement of trust and recognition of the depth of the bonds between you and your partner. This might be your role mate, soul mate, and whole mate partner. Naturally, what those words mean differs substantively based on whether we are engaged in a role mate, soul mate, or whole mate context.

At the level of role mate and soul mate, rooted in two separate selves relating, it is a stand for the trust and love that lives between the beloveds.

But at the level of whole mate, *You love me* means something different. At the level of whole mate, *You love me* refers not only to *your* beloved, but to *the* Beloved. There is a realization that we are held and loved by Reality. There is a realization that the Divine is not merely the Infinity of Power but the Infinity of Intimacy. That intimacy inheres in Reality and in self. You yearn for intimacy even if you have the power to gift intimacy to your beloved. You realize that the Divine is no less than the Second Person of Reality. The Name of God is the *Infinite Intimate* who not only inheres in you and as you but also knows and holds you—and madly loves your very unique existence.

---

[197] Pierre Teilhard de Chardin, in the essay "The Evolution of Chastity" in Toward the Future, 1936, XI, 86-87. With regard to the word ether, the editor notes that if Teilhard were writing today, he would say "space."

From the place of knowing that you are loved by the Personal Face of Reality, the Infinity of Intimacy, you become more trusting in your own inherent nature, which deserves to be loved. From that place, you turn to your partners and say: *You love me*. This knowing of the truth, *You love me*, requires something. All interior *gnosis*, any genuine attainment of inner knowing, happens through a process of transformation. To realize the truth of *You love me*, you need to *arouse* your own capacity to know that you are loved.

This happens in one or two ways. The first is breakthrough events; the second is constant practice.

The former might be the radical infatuation of falling in love, where you love and are loved. And this form of falling in love is not limited to romantic beloveds. As we have already seen, Outrageous Love is the quality of Reality itself moving in you, as you, and through you. Your capacity to fall in love, not romantically but outrageously, can become not the exception but the pattern of your life.

You might also access the knowing of being loved by Reality in a particular form of medicine journey (carefully guided and responsible), in which the realization of being loved by All-That-Is shines through.

The second way, however, without which the first way has no ultimate effect, is the way of constant practice. One core of practice is connecting the dots and collecting evidence. Not collecting evidence that you are unloved—the ordinary pastime of beloveds in both role mate and soul mate relationship. Instead, whole mates collect evidence that we are loved. Whole mate relationships, rooted in Unique Self and Evolutionary Unique Self and the Field of Outrageous Love, direct their attention to connecting the dots and collecting evidence of being loved.

Role mate and even soul mate separate selves collect their traumas as part of their default engagement with life. Whole mates, of course, also recognize and honor the need to transform trauma. But their core default context is the constant collection of evidence that we are actors, each with unique parts to play, in the Outrageous Love Story of Reality. We are actors in the tale of the Intimate Universe and the personal Outrageous Love Story of our most intimate lives. Deepening in the knowing of the Outrageous Love Story of Reality and our place in it is the constant practice of whole mates. That deepening may take place through the study of science. For example, molecular and cellular biology, genetics, and epigenetics remind us of the virtually unimaginable and dazzlingly complex LoveIntelligence, LoveBeauty, and LoveDesire that holds us and sustains us in literally every second of our lives.

Awaken as Outrageous Love

When we really get that the Universe is not a fact but an Outrageous Love Story, our relationships begin to change. We begin to realize that our love stories are a chapter in the larger Love Story of Reality. By awakening to Outrageous Love, we recognize that we are not a spectator of this Love Story. We recognize that each of us is an irreducibly unique actor in it. Evolution awakens as each of us and through each of us. We are all ultimately needed by All-That-Is. No one else can do it, whatever *it* is for each of us, other than each of us as Unique Selves. And *it* desperately needs to be done if we are to live in a world of Outrageous Love.

Once you get the storyline and realize that you are an actor, you need a script. The script is your Unique Self. To awaken as an Outrageous Lover is to awaken as the irreducibly unique incarnation of the LoveIntelligence, LoveBeauty, and LoveDesire of All-That-Is, living in you, as you, and through you—your Unique Self. You awaken within the overall operating system of Reality. The overall operating system comprises the interior laws of Outrageous Love that govern the Universe and explain how you interface with, align with, and incarnate those core Principles of Reality. Outrageous Love is fundamentally who and what you are at the leading edge of your own evolution.

The need for a new Love Story is urgent. We need an Outrageous Love Story that inspires and animates our lives. We need a politics of Outrageous Love. That must be based on a new evolutionary narrative: an Outrageous Love Story.

Once our realization of Outrageous Love unfolds, there is only one compelling invitation to which every human being must respond. It is an invitation dripping with Eros, pulsing with delight, and throbbing with ecstatic urgency. It is the invitation to awaken as Outrageous Love. It is the invitation to transform from an ego-based separate self, grasping at the straws of ordinary love, into an Outrageous Lover.

You might ask what that means practically. *What does an Outrageous Lover do?* The answer is clear: **an Outrageous Lover commits Outrageous Acts of Love**. Not satisfied? Perhaps you want to know which Outrageous Acts of Love an Outrageous Lover performs. After all, there is so much that needs to be done. How do we know what door to enter? How do you know what is yours to do? The answer is: **you commit the Outrageous Acts of Love that are a function of your Evolutionary Unique Self**.

This sense of being participatory in the Outrageous Love Story of Reality and committing Outrageous Acts of Love that are an expression of *your Unique Self* and *our Unique We* is the core of whole mate relationship.

Entry 7. The Birth of Evolutionary Intimacy

In a whole mate evolutionary relationship, Outrageous Love wakes up in you. It unfolds as you wake up to the realization, championed by systems science and interior wisdom, that you live in a larger field of LoveIntelligence, LoveBeauty, and LoveDesire. In this larger, unified Field, each being in the Universe, in different ways, depends on other beings in the Universe. Humans, for example, depend on tiny organisms in the Pacific Ocean along with photons from the Sun. From the exterior, this looks like interconnectivity, or the web of life. From the interior, this feels like Outrageous Love.[198]

Paradoxically, the sense of connection between all the parts depends on each part playing its unique role. Uniqueness is the currency of connection. To wake up as part of the Field of Outrageous Love is to wake up as a unique personal expression. It is to know that you are not separate from anything and are needed by everything. In the deepest

---

[198] Another word that is used in this context is homeostasis. This is the quality of the Universe as a Whole to maintain its integrity as a living system, its wholeness, even as all of the parts are constantly changing. There is a sense of a deeper intimacy within the web of life, which holds it all together, even though everything is always shifting. For example, even though everything changes in a body, including all of its cells, the wholeness of the person is maintained.

sense, it is to know that we live in an Intimate Universe. This is possibly the single most important piece of information derived from leading-edge evolutionary science.

In evolutionary relationships, you are able to realize this intimacy for the first time. You come to know that your unique quality of intimacy is part of a larger field of unique intimacies. Your unique quality of intimacy is the puzzle piece that connects you with the larger puzzle, which is the larger field of Intimacy. From this perspective, you understand that loneliness is overcome in a much more potent way than is possible at the level of separate self. Separate selves may feel recognized and received by sharing each other's experiences of wounding and joy. That is important and good. But in evolutionary relationships, as an Evolutionary Unique Self awakening as Outrageous Love, you realize that you truly do have a place in the world. You are held in your unique location within the intimate field of the larger Universe.

From that place, you are no longer dependent on your partner to meet all your intimate needs. Your relationship is an evolutionary relationship. Both partners source their experience of being loved in the larger Field of Outrageous Love. You are not lonely because you know you are being held by an Intimate Universe. Your ground of intimacy is in the larger Ground of Intimacy, which holds you together with all beings in their unique and gorgeous symphony of interconnectivity.

The Evolutionary Intimacy experienced between you and your partner is part of the larger pattern of the Intimate Universe. Loneliness simply melts away in the space of this expanded knowing. For the first time in history, this expanded knowing, which was once rooted only in the interior sciences, is now corroborated by the information made available by the exterior sciences. If we lived in a world surrounded by beings and objects, all of whom were separate from us and from each other, life would be lonely beyond imagination.

The realization that we live in an Intimate Universe derives from two realizations. First, no being is separate from us. We contain all previous levels of evolution within us, and we are connected with every other being on the planet. Second, no object is separate. The Universe is not dead, but a living, self-organizing Reality. It is constantly transforming, deepening, and growing. When you really understand the implications of what emergence science calls *the self-organizing Universe*, you realize that we live in a world populated entirely by subjects, not objects. That is the Intimate Universe that holds us and loves us. That is what we meant earlier when we said that the Universe feels, and the Universe feels Love. That is the information that informs evolutionary relationships.

In an evolutionary relationship, you and your partner no longer depend exclusively on each other for intimacy or for your liberation from loneliness. You are no longer loved only if your partner person loves you. You are now free to receive their love as a gift that you infinitely desire. You are also liberated from the contracted grasping that makes you choose the wrong partners for the wrong reasons. You are free from pathological desperation and can instead live into the wholeness of your desire. Your desire can pulse and throb and make you shudder at the core of your being, but it is not clutching, grasping, or deranged.

Imagine a moment when you felt totally needed. You were in the right place, at the right time, with just the skill and presence necessary to save the day. In that moment, did you feel lonely or disconnected? Very likely, you did not. You probably felt seen and at home. You felt connected and part of the larger Field. You felt intimate with Reality. That is the experience of Evolutionary Unique Self. It is what you and your partner can feel in an evolutionary relationship.

In an evolutionary relationship, you experience that there is something to be done and that it can be done by you and your partner together. You experience yourselves as an expression of Outrageous Love. You are evolution awakening as love in action through the gifts of your evolutionary relationship. The love between you is not ordinary, but outrageous. It is suffused with the Outrageous Love of your Evolutionary Unique Selves waking up as the evolutionary impulse. There is something unbelievably alluring and erotic about acting together in that way. It creates a level of attraction and passion that cannot be matched by anything at the prior levels of relationship.

Sometimes, it is easier to see a quality of consciousness in its shadow expression. One of the most iconic movies of the twentieth century, *Bonnie and Clyde*, is the glamorized story of two outlaws (who were actually much less glamorous in real life, but we'll stay with the movie version). Bonnie and Clyde are sexy and hot. That is one of the recurrent themes in the movie that Warren Beatty and Faye Dunaway brought to life beautifully. Why are they sexy and hot? Because they are doing hot things together.

In one scene, Clyde introduces himself and Bonnie. He says, "We rob banks," in just the right voice. He is sourcing their relationship in its purpose, in the audacity and daring of what they do together. If you read the analysis of what made the movie great, a big part of it is, to sum it up simply, that Bonnie and Clyde shared a powerful passion, because they had a shared purpose.

Bonnie and Clyde are a shadow version of Neo and Trinity from *The Matrix*. When Neo and Trinity show up for battle, clad in tight leather, they are hot. They pull out their weapons at precisely the same moment and begin a synchronized dance of fighting side-by-side. They never glance at each other. There is no face-to-face. The raw intimacy and intense passion of the scene is no less palpable than it would have been in an erotic sexual scene. They are not joining genes but joining genius. It is a fusion of Unique Self into a larger synergy of sensual purpose. Outrageous Love, as an expression of the evolutionary impulse, is activist at its core. It calls the evolutionary relationship into action. The action emerges from a shared vision. Shared vision and shared activism are at the heart of evolutionary relationships.

Entry 8. Unique Self and Outrageous Love

Unique Self and Outrageous Love are two Faces of the same Reality. They are Reality structures that literally refashion our identity. Once identity is transformed, the transformation of relationship naturally follows.

Unique Self and Outrageous Love are two Faces of the same realization that Reality is Relationship, and that the Universe is a Love Story in which you are the central actor. You can access Outrageous Love only through your Unique Self. And your Unique Self is the conduit through which you receive Outrageous Love. When you are identified with separate self, as role mate and often even as soul mate, love is another strategy of the ego. That's what we call *ordinary love*. At the level of whole mate, as Unique Self, you are able to access Outrageous Love.

We can think of Unique Self as the plug at the end of an electrical cable. Put the plug into the wall socket and you are plugged into the energy, the Eros, the juice of Reality. The underlying Eros of Reality is Outrageous Love.

But it is even deeper than that. Outrageous Love shows up through the portal or prism of **uniqueness**. Outrageous Love appears in you, as you, and through you as the irreducibly unique expression of LoveIntelligence, LoveBeauty, and LoveDesire. Outrageous Love is not only the Eros and energy of the evolutionary process, but also the energy of the evolutionary impulse disclosed in your own radically unique and personal love. An Outrageous Lover recognizes herself as an irreducibly unique expression of the Outrageous Love that is the Source and evolutionary Power of All-That-Is.

Allurement is not generic. Our attractions are entirely our own. Just like oxygen atoms, we have our own unique set of attractions. As we have seen, one of the core trajectories in the evolution of love is increasing uniqueness. Uniqueness of an entirely different order of beauty and depth emerges along with human beings. Each person reveals a field of unique allurement. That field of allurement is sourced in each individual's Unique Self.

This is what the poet Rumi was referring to when he wrote:

Let yourself be silently drawn
by the stronger pull of what you really love.[199]

These lines capture our unique allurements. Unique Self is the strange attractor of our destiny. Remember, *Reality needs your service* means that Reality needs you to pursue your unique set of fascinations and allurements.

Uniqueness is not only infinitely deeper in humans; it is also different

---

199 The Essential Rumi: A Poetry Anthology (2003), 51.

in another key respect. Human evolution moves from unconscious to conscious uniqueness. You cannot merely be born as your Unique Self. You are born with a Unique Self *potential*. But to claim that potential, you must awaken to your Unique Self over time.

Outrageous Love can only appear mediated through your uniqueness. One way to understand this is through the experience of intimacy. Outrageous Love creates radical intimacy. Ordinary love creates pseudo-intimacy—when you feel like you don't really know the other person. It is the feeling of intimacy co-arising with the sense that the other person is hiding. It is when the true contours of your partner's uniqueness are not visible. Or it is when they are wearing a mask that creates a false picture of their uniqueness. You access radical intimacy in a relationship only when you have an authentic sense of having received the other person's uniqueness. The more we receive the unique texture, contours, and shade of another's uniqueness, the more intimate we become.

In whole mate, evolutionary relationships, a new form of intimacy becomes possible, *Evolutionary Intimacy*. It emerges from knowing that you live in an Intimate Universe. In that Universe, your unique quality of intimacy is irreplaceable. And you are in the perfect place, and it is the perfect time, to give your unique gift of intimacy.

Evolutionary Intimacy is a quality lived by the Evolutionary Unique Selves who come together in evolutionary relationship. In such relationships, instead of the relationship being an island of intimacy in a sea of separation and disconnection, the relationship is completely intertwined and supported by an Intimate Universe. The whole mates are not extras in that Intimate Universe. Rather, the Universe intends, recognizes, chooses, desires, needs, and love-adores their Unique We and needs their unique expression of intimacy.

Uniqueness works in two directions. First, as we have seen, uniqueness is Reality speaking to you. It says, *I love you, I choose you, and I need you*. However, we also must choose, or step into, our uniqueness. The philosopher Nietzsche really got this when he wrote:[200]

---

[200] F. Nietzsche, Schopenhauer as Educator: Friedrich Nietzsche's Third Untimely Meditation, translated with notes by D. Pellerin (2014), 2-3.

Anyone who does not wish to be part of the masses need only stop making things easy for himself. Let him follow his conscience, which calls out to him: "Be yourself! All that you are now doing, thinking, desiring, all that is not you."

Every young soul hears this call by day and by night and shudders with excitement at the premonition of that degree of happiness which eternities have prepared for those who will give thought to their true liberation. There is no way to help any soul attain this happiness, however, so long as it remains shackled with the chains of opinion and fear. And how hopeless and meaningless life can become without such a liberation! There is no drearier, sorrier creature in nature than the man who has evaded his own genius and who squints now towards the right, now towards the left, now backwards, now in any direction whatever . . .

"None of that is really you," says the soul to itself. "No one can build you the bridge on which you, and only you, must cross the river of life. There may be countless trails and bridges and demi-gods who would gladly carry you across; but only at the price of pawning and forgoing yourself. There is one path in the world that none can walk but you. Where does it lead? Don't ask, walk."

There is a boldness and audacity required to walk your one path. But it is the only way of living that gives you a true experience of the joy of life. When you are in the aliveness and purpose of your Unique Self, you do not ask, Why am I alive? It is self-evident.

By following the call of your creative allurement, you help bind the Universe together. The wholeness of Reality depends on each Unique Self pursuing his or her unique passion and gifting Reality with his or her unique gift.

Entry 9. Love the Moment Open

Every moment is either open or closed. If the moment does not find its Unique Self, then it is closed. If the moment is living its unique quality, then it is open. There are no extra moments, just as there are no extra people. Of course, a moment is not conscious like a person, but the unique need that a person has the capacity to address also lives in a unique moment. One of the key insights of emergence science has to do with the unique quality of different times. Not all time is the same.

There are moments in evolutionary time that can give birth in ways that other moments cannot. Every moment of time has its own unique character and its own unique invitation. Hebrew foreshadows the future revelations of science in the very word used for *time*, *zeman*, which literally means both *time* and *invitation*. Time contains within it a unique invitation. We might even say that time has a Unique Self. Every moment of time has something that wants to be born through it. The midwife of that birth is always the Unique Self of a person.

When a person drops into her Unique Self, she has the ability to *love the moment open*. Ordinary love does not have that capacity. Only Outrageous Love can love the moment open. That is precisely what we mean when we say, together with Whitehead, that evolution is the *creative advance into novelty*. Newness is constantly being generated. When evolution operates unconsciously, it is the self-organizing drive of the Cosmos that creatively advances into novelty. The Outrageous Love which drives the evolutionary process loves the moment open. But when evolution awakens as your Unique Self, the moment can be loved open only by you.

The mandate of the Unique Self is to love the moment open. You do this through the Force of Outrageous Love that lives through your Unique Self. As we said, every moment is either open or closed. Also, every person is either open or closed. When you open your heart, you have the capacity to love the moment open. You might walk into an evening dinner where everyone is closed but through the radiance or clarity of your presence, everyone else is blown open. When the moment opens, it blows your heart open even wider. Imagine witnessing a moment of exceptional poignancy that blows your heart open. When a virtuous cycle is created between a person and time, each one loves the other one into deeper and more powerful openness.

PART THREE

EVOLUTIONARY RELATIONSHIPS AND UNIQUE SELF SYMPHONY

CHAPTER 10

EVOLUTIONARY RELATIONSHIPS: A NEW VISION EMERGING

Entry 1. Evolutionary Relationships Reloaded

We have considered the crisis in relationship based on the realization that we cannot solve a problem at the level of consciousness that created it. As such, we have called for an up-leveling in consciousness and a transformation of identity. We have laid out some new models and outlined how those shifts may look. Our exploration led us to a vision of a new level of relationship—whole mate or evolutionary relationship. The larger context for this relationship vision is that Reality is Relationship. This vision can be summarized simply: *the Universe is a Love Story*.

The two major dimensions of the new model of relationship, which we explored in Parts One and Two, are three levels of relationship (*role mate, soul mate,* and *whole mate*), and *Unique Gender*.[201] In Part Two, we also explored three key models that provide the foundation for a full download of evolutionary relationships:

- The four selves, with a particular emphasis on *Unique Self* and *Evolutionary Unique Self*.

- Living in an *evolutionary context*, in alignment with the evolutionary impulse, in an evolutionary relationship to life.

---

201 See Chapter 6 (Entry 9) and Chapter 7 (Entry 2).

- The core distinction between *Outrageous Love* and *ordinary love*.

Now we are ready to tie the ribbons together in an elegant overview of whole mate, evolutionary relationships. As we bring all of the ideas of this book together, the overarching aim is to facilitate the birth of whole mate relationships. Notice that we are engaging in a potent form of what philosopher Matt Ridley called *idea sex*.[202] What happens in idea sex is that new mental models come into relationship with each other. This is the movement of Outrageous Love laying down key aspects of a new structure of relationship.

As the ideas we present in this book come together to form a larger whole, a new emergent is born. A new level of identity and relationship takes shape. The core structure of both is a new expression of Reality, an entirely new type of human whom we are calling a whole mate. By becoming a New Human, a whole mate, you are able to manifest deeper forms of relationship that express levels of intimacy, passion, potency, and purpose that were unreachable at earlier levels.

Entry 2: Role Mate, Soul Mate, and Whole Mate in Evolutionary Context

As we have seen, role mate relationships are driven by the desire to survive and materially thrive. It is important to remind ourselves of an earlier insight: the fact that we seek to survive is not a given. It is mysterious and surprising. Every entity is driven to live. If there is a threat to life, it does everything possible to avoid the threat. However, there is no reason for this, except that the drive to survive and thrive is a potent expression of Evolutionary Eros. **This mysterious and magnificent desire to survive is the primary motivation of role mate relationships.**

---

[202] See works by Matt Ridley: "When Ideas Have Sex," TEDGlobal, July 2010; "When Ideas Have Sex," 2012, https://studiogreig.wordpress.com/2012/11/21/when-ideas-have-sex-article-by-matt-ridley/; "How Innovation Works" [Video], https://iai.tv/video/how-innovation-works-matt-ridley. Ridley's evolutionary view is also contained within his books The Rational Optimist: How Prosperity Evolves (2010), The Evolution of Everything: How New Ideas Emerge (2015), and How Innovation Works (2020).

On the human level, survival is the first expression of the evolutionary impulse. It does not require conscious choice; it is hardwired into us by the LoveIntelligence, LoveBeauty, and LoveDesire of Reality itself. *Functional aloneness*—the lack of a partner with whom to effectively fulfill one's role obligations, not *existential loneliness*, is a primary issue for role mates. For role mates, *the good life* includes a stable relationship, family, job, and community. Maslow's most primary needs for survival and belonging are met in role mate relationships. **To be the hero in role mate relationship was to fulfill your role effectively.** For a man, that meant to be a provider and protector. For a woman, that meant to be the homemaker and nurturer.

At their highest expression, role mate relationships tip into soul mate relationships. Role mates turn to face each other, and a love beyond roles is born. They move from shoulder-to-shoulder to face-to-face. They steal a moment away from looking at the shared horizon of survival and instead look into each other's eyes.

Soul mate relationships include the best of role mate relationships but embody a critical new dimension. **Soul mate relationships are motivated by personal fulfillment and the desire to be liberated from loneliness.** Soul mates are also committed to salving and occasionally even healing their early wounds and trauma.[203] Soul mates are focused on themselves, their partners, and the success of the relationship. They often focus on their children as an extension of themselves or their relationship. For soul mates, *the good life* includes depth, healing, and experiences of loving and being loved by their partners and their closest friends and family members. **To be a hero in a soul mate relationship means to communicate effectively, share interests, share intimacy, have regular sex, and gain personal fulfillment while living a reasonably meaningful life.**

In most soul mate relationships, two *separate selves* come together. They seek intimacy, comfort, and communication. Each partner's unique abilities are thought of as capacities of the separate self. The more evolved the relationship, the deeper the level of communication. It is in

---

203 See Supplementary Essay 2, Entries 2 and 3.

communication that fairness is created, intimacy is established, and some measure of loneliness is overcome. The quality of love in most soul mate relationships is *ordinary love*. Ordinary love can be a beautiful expression of two separate selves celebrating each other. It is simply limited in all of the ways we have explored. When we are devoted to our egos' desires to survive, thrive, and be fulfilled, love becomes a negotiation to get our role mate and soul mate needs met. Our soul mate needs are more poignant than our role mate needs, but they are still rooted in ordinary love. In such a context of love, very small versions of ourselves emerge, completely disconnected from the larger Whole.

At their highest expression, soul mate relationships tip towards whole mate relationships. The partners get a sense that, while each is a separate self, there is something luminous and infinitely special in that separate self.

In Unique Self Realization, you have a sense that you are not merely separate, that you are part of a larger Whole. You may not understand the science precisely, but you get the powerful truth that you are a part of the web of life. You are indivisible from that web. You are connected, inside and outside, by visible and invisible lines of connection. That is the experience of Unique Self. When you awaken to your Unique Self, you catch a glimpse of yourself as a unique feature of the seamless coat of the Universe. That does not mean that, when you step into your Unique Self, you lose your sense of being separate. Of course, you don't; to lose your sense of being separate would be psychotic. You are separate *plus*, not separate *minus*.

Another dimension of whole mate in contradistinction to soul mate is in the place from which the beloveds meet. In a soul mate relationship, the beloveds are generally meeting from the depths of their respective separate selves. Those separate selves experience their quality of spirit or their soul, their depth, their Beauty, their Goodness. Nonetheless they are conceiving of themselves as separate selves so they meet looking at each other as separate selves.

Looking deeply into each other's eyes, they see beyond the separate self and into the depths of soul of the other. But because the place that they are looking from—their basic location is separate self—at some point the relationship may well break down.

Whole mates are quite different. Whole mates first ascend into the Whole together. They ascend into the space, the location, the quality of the whole. And from that space of the Whole, they turn toward each other. But the movement begins by their entering the space of the whole. There are multiple doors to the whole. One of the doors is radical sexing. In the radical union, in the wholeness of certain modes of sexing, the beloveds enter into the Whole. They are not just separate selves engaging in superficial pleasure play or even psychological pleasure play. They are not just separate selves with soul, making love. No, there is a deeper mode of sexing in which the beloveds literally merge together into the whole, and then from within the whole they turn to each other. That's an entirely new quality of whole mate.

As we saw earlier, soul mate relationships without role mate dynamics aren't working.[204] Without some aspect of role mate, the relational center of soul mate does not hold. Fully egalitarian couples lack a compelling narrative to stay together when soul mate sharing is the only component of the relationship. As a result, they begin to lose potency and passion. Presence and poignancy are insufficient to sustain a relationship that lacks the power of purpose.

Soul mate relationships tip into whole mate relationships when soul mates begin to relate in devotion not only to each other but also to a third side.[205] Usually, the third side is for the sake of love or the sake of personal growth and transformation. Soul mates begin to stand not only face-to-face but also shoulder-to-shoulder as they look at a third side. When they look deeply into each other's eyes, they see a third side.

Whole mate relationships are evolutionary relationships. This transcends and includes the best features of soul mate relationship. It has poignancy and presence, while adding critical new components that change everything. The added dimensions up-level the consciousness of the relationship in a way that naturally addresses the crisis of soul mate relationships.

---

[204] Chapter 4, "Limitations of Soul Mate," Entries 9 and 10.

[205] Chapter 5, "From Soul Mate to Whole Mate," Entry 5.

Whole mate relationships emerge from a new level of consciousness. **Whole mate relationships are based on core values that exist beyond the relationship itself.** They are relationships between *Unique Selves*. Each partner stands for the full emergence and total fulfillment of the other's Unique Self. In whole mate relationships, being liberated from loneliness by sharing your fears, hopes, and dreams with your partner is simply not enough. Whole mates need something bigger.

Whole mates stand for the highest level of unique expression that their partners can achieve. Each partner is committed to the emergence of the other's unique voice. Each takes a stand for the other's Unique Self. Each partner falls in love with the other's Unique Self. Your whole mate partner falls in love with your vision and direction. There is an alignment that exists beyond the chemistry and the soul attraction of soul mate relationships. They fall in love with each other's dreams. They become the basis for each other fulfilling those dreams. Beyond even shared dreams, **whole mates have shared vision.**

Whole mates look deeply into each other's eyes like soul mates do, but they also look at a shared horizon. And, in some profound sense, the difference between the two ways of looking falls away in whole mate relationship. While looking at a shared horizon, you also see each other's eyes in whole mate relationship. When looking deeply into each other's eyes, you see your shared horizon. You stand shoulder-to-shoulder and face-to-face at the same time. The shared horizon is the larger Whole, which draws you to itself and to each other at the same time.

When you are with your whole mate, your own wholeness shows up. When you are with your whole mate, you fall in love with yourself. You want to be with that person because the highest and best version of you shows up when they are around. You love yourself more when they are around because you *see* yourself more. You become more whole. Part of the reason that they are able to see you is because they did not grow up with all of your wounds and trauma. They do not have the limiting beliefs you have about who you are and the capacities you possess. You are always going to hold a radically limited view of yourself in comparison to your whole mate. Your vision is always occluded by all the places in your life that you got hung up with.

Your whole mate sees those hang ups as well. But those hang-ups are not their focus. They see beyond your limitations into your most potent and powerful possibility. Your whole mate dreams bigger dreams for you than you ever dreamed possible. And when you are not yet ready to claim or reclaim your highest Unique Self dreams, your whole mate partner holds them for you.

In this sense, a whole mate relationship is a crucible for your Unique Self emergence. In your whole mate's arms, you can dive into the vision of the person you always wanted to be. With this man, you can be that woman. With this woman, you can be whole. With each other, you can each be exactly who you are. That is what your whole mate partner desperately wants for you more than anything else. And your radical desire for the full emergence of your whole mate allows you to give up the hidden strategies of emasculation and competition that almost always underlie even the most poignant soul mate relationships.

Your whole mate acts as the midwife at the birth of your Unique Self. They see the most goodness, truth, and beauty in you, and they call you to embody it. In a whole mate relationship, your partner holds the highest and most whole vision of who you are. You find yourself in the face of your partner. Your whole mate stands for the most epic and extraordinary vision of your life. Your whole mate takes a radical stand for your Unique Self and your unique life. In doing so, your whole mate is always sculpting the next evolution of you.

You are tender and sometimes fierce with each other. You are also endlessly kind, but there are no words that can't be spoken. You stand for each other's self-realization and highest transformation. Your passionate commitment to the whole beauty of each other's Unique Self is the guiding vision of your relationship. When you look into her eyes, you see not only infinite beauty, but infinite possibility. And her beauty and possibility are inextricably intertwined. You see infinite possibility in her, even as she evokes your infinite possibility.

In your whole mate's eyes, you overcome your fear of inadequacy. You see the highest vision of your potency and power. You receive permission to stop being small. In your whole mate's eyes, you see the fiercely loving demand that you step up and play your largest game.

Looking into your whole mate's eyes, you know with absolute clarity that you are a good child of the Universe.

In your whole mate's eyes, your Unique Self is born anew in every moment.

In your whole mate's eyes, you know that your uniqueness means that you are loved, you are chosen, and you are needed.

In your whole mate's eyes, you know that Reality needs your unique service.

In your whole mate's eyes, your own vision is widened, and you step into life lived in an evolutionary context.

In your whole mate's eyes, you awaken as the personal face of the evolutionary impulse beating your heart as the One Heart.

In your whole mate's eyes, you awaken as an Outrageous Lover, called to commit the Outrageous Acts of Love that are a natural function of your Evolutionary Unique Self.

In your whole mate's eyes, you see the invitation to follow your unique allurement.

Through your whole mate's eyes, you bind the Universe together in the way that only you can.

As your whole mate liberates you with these gifts, they give you the power to liberate them. This is the marriage of potency, power, and passion with poignancy and presence. It births whole mate, evolutionary relationship anew in every moment.

Entry 3. Confession of Greatness

The core of both soul mate and whole mate relationships is to confess yourself. The difference lies in what dimension of yourself you are confessing. **In soul mate relationship, you confess your vulnerability. In whole mate relationship, you confess your greatness.**

Your greatness is your Unique Self. Confession of greatness has a particular method. In confessing your greatness, you find the moments in your life when you totally rocked—when you were in your greatness. They might have been private or public moments. They might have been personal or professional moments. They could have been any or all of the above. They were moments when you felt at home in the world. You were showing up as your Unique Self, completely and without restraint. You were giving your unique gift, either through your presence or through your unique form of gifting.[206]

In a soul mate relationship, no matter how much love there is, you often have to dim yourself down. Your light is too bright to shine fully. Indeed, part of the way that you express your love is by subtly and often unconsciously dulling yourself, so that neither your brightness nor your sharp edges will hurt your partner's feelings. Sometimes, it gets so extreme that all you are left with is the smallest version of you meeting the smallest version of your partner. Even if it is not the smallest version of you, it is definitely a much smaller version of you than the radiant wholeness of your Unique Self.

In a soul mate relationship, you often learn methods of effective communication and nonviolent conflict resolution. You make sure to remove any sharp edges, so that you don't clash with your partner. But you also remove the catalysts for transformation. You do not have permission either to be your largest Self or to speak your most powerful truth.

In a whole mate relationship, you each give each other permission to be that largest, most whole Unique Self. Not only do you give *each other* permission; you also give *yourself* permission. And, going a step beyond the granting of permission, you also make demands of each other. Each of you makes the radical demand, of the other and of yourself, to show

---

206 See also Chapter 7, "Unique Self," Entry 11.

up as your most gorgeous Unique Selves.

Entry 4. Unique We

There is one more critical step. In a whole mate, evolutionary relationship, you don't just stand for each other's Unique Selves. You don't just realize that both of you are Unique Selves that are irreducibly unique expressions of the LoveIntelligence, LoveBeauty, and LoveDesire that is the initiating and animating Eros of All-That-Is, living in you, as you, and through you. You don't just stand for the fulfillment of the promise that is implicit in each of your Unique Selves: that you each have a unique perspective and incarnate a unique quality of intimacy.

As whole mates, you take one crucial step further:

In the most evolved form of evolutionary relationship, you and your partner form a Unique We. Unique Selves come together to birth a new whole, a Unique We, which is greater than the sum of its unique parts. Two whole mates form a new larger whole: $1 + 1 = 1$. This unique whole has a unique perspective that is wider and deeper than the perspective of its individual Unique Selves. Your Unique We incarnates a unique quality of intimacy that has a different taste than your individual qualities of intimacy. These birth the unique gifts of your Unique We, which address the unique needs in your shared unique circle of intimacy and influence that can be addressed by your Unique We alone. No one and no we—that ever was, is, or will be ever again—can address these unique needs the way that your *We* can.

The great meeting of Unique Selves and the formation of a Unique We that happens at the level of whole mate relationship is not just for the sake of the people in the relationship. It is for the sake of the Whole. In whole mate relationship, you begin to live in an evolutionary context and to develop an evolutionary relationship to life. Living in an evolutionary context begins by living with an awareness of the larger Whole. It deepens once you realize that the larger Whole is not just a *place* where you live—it is a *story* that lives in you.

All of evolution is a Story that has a beginning in time and unfolds chapter after chapter. The Cosmos, biosphere, and humans evolved through stage after stage of evolution through the first three Big Bangs. Consider that the fourth Big Bang occurs when evolution awakens to itself through us—when we become aware that evolution is a story.[207] The fourth Big Bang then evolves even further with the full realization of Unique Self. In the full expression of the fourth Big Bang, we first realize that no one is actually separate or substantively apart from the larger Whole. Everyone, and everything, is part of the great web of life. We then realize that evolution moves to higher and higher levels of uniqueness.

As a part of the four Big Bangs, you realize you are an irreducibly unique expression of the great web of life. The web is seamless, but not featureless, and you are its unique feature. You are a central actor in the story, with a unique life to live and gift to give that is needed, valued, and honored by All-That-Is. You realize that evolution is not only happening out there, but also in you, and you in it. You realize that the entire process of evolution animates your being. You realize that your DNA is coded with the memory of every evolutionary emergent that came before you. You are literally the elementary particles birthed at the Big Bang—atoms, cells, molecules, and every other evolutionary stage, all the way up through human beings. All of it is recorded, remembered, and coded in your DNA.

You realize that evolution is not just a Story. Evolution is a Story in which you are personally implicated. You begin to understand that the evolutionary impulse beats your heart and drives your life. You awaken to the potent insight of the new science: that you are personally implicated in the evolutionary process. That you are the personal face of the evolutionary impulse. Evolution awakens as your Unique Self. Reality needs your service. Reality needs the unique gifts that are yours to give and the unique life that is yours to live.

In evolutionary relationship, your Unique We awakens as the personal face of the evolutionary impulse. Your shared hearts incarnate the One Heart in a way that can happen only through your relationship. The evolutionary creativity of your Unique We is needed to take the next evolutionary step. Reality needs the service that emerges from your

---

207 See "The Four Big Bangs: A Meditation on the Reality of Evolution as You," Entry 12.

Unique We, which incarnates the evolutionary impulse.

It is this knowing that lights up your and your partner's personal and shared love and commitment to transformation. Together, you offer up your love and your transformation for the sake of the Whole, even as it is totally personal and intimate between you. You realize in accord with the principles of science that your transformation directly affects the Whole.

From that place, each whole mate brings love to truth and truth to love, so that each one evolves beyond the remnants of the self-centered state that has dominated consciousness since the childhood of humanity. You are always shoulder-to-shoulder and face-to-face at the same time. The contradiction between those two postures disappears.

When we wake up to the fact that we *are* evolution, we break the trance of waiting. We have always been waiting for someone else to do it for us. When we awaken to evolutionary relationship, we realize that we are the ones we have been waiting for. Being personally implicated in evolution means that our destinies are linked to the destiny of the Whole. That is what it means to be a whole mate. The evolutionary couple sees where their unique gifts and the gifts of their Unique We intersect with the needs of the larger Whole. This is exhilarating beyond measure for two reasons:

First, we realize that the game is not fixed. The world and culture are not fixed. We realize that the past does not determine the future. We finally recognize that the great slave driver of today is the limiting belief that yesterday determines tomorrow. We understand that the evolutionary impulse, pulsing as our evolutionary relationships, is potent and powerful. We see that the *creative advance into novelty* lives in our Unique We. Our relationships are rooted in this larger orientation. Our relationships serve our lives. We don't simply serve our relationships. Our lives become about getting into right relationship with others and the larger Whole.

Second, this shared commitment to being in right relationship to Reality creates a new form of intimacy that is simply not available at earlier levels of relationship. This new form of intimacy is what we have called *Evolutionary Intimacy*. When you and your beloved awaken as a Unique We, incarnating the evolutionary impulse, Evolutionary Intimacy is born between you. You are moved to join together, not merely by the striving of your separate selves, but by the ecstatic urgency of your Evolutionary Unique Selves. In the moment when this becomes your context for relating, everything changes. Your relationship itself becomes a Field for Conscious Evolution.

There is a deep yearning for this larger context for relationships. It is the quality of relatedness that so many of us long for but have not been able to name. Nothing that came before is excluded. But something undeniably new and thrilling is added. There is a highly charged erotic quality to a relationship that is organized around something larger than itself. It is the thrill of knowing that your Evolutionary Unique Self and your evolutionary relationship are absolutely needed and desired.

Entry 5. The Unique We Plugs Whole Mates into the Larger Field

Uniqueness is always the currency of connection. Remember the distinction between *separate* and *unique*.[208] Separation creates loneliness and alienation, regardless of whether we are speaking of disconnected particles, cells, or people. Separation causes decay and death. A cancer cell is so intoxicated by its own independent power that it disconnects or alienates from the larger Whole. The result is decay and death of the whole system.

Uniqueness, on the other hand, is the way that the key opens the lock, the puzzle piece fits into the puzzle, and the instrument contributes to the symphony. The very contour of uniqueness creates integration and wholeness. Uniqueness creates the pull and attraction between whole mates. Each comes bearing unique gifts, which when combined, comprise a Unique We. **Just as the currency of their individual uniqueness plugs them into each other, the currency of their Unique We plugs them into the larger Field of Life.**

The beauty of whole mate is even more than that. **In loving your unique whole mate partner, you are loving the Whole.** Radical jealousy

---

208 See Chapter 7, "Unique Self," Entry 5.

and tyrannical possessiveness are often shadow expressions of soul mate love. Intention for the Whole through madly loving each other is a natural expression of whole mate love.

I am radically committed to helping to heal the wounds of my whole mate. I do so through presence, radical kindness, and fierce loving. But my intention is not for her alone. While my devotion is intensely personal, it is beyond the personal. In the quivering tenderness of standing for the healing of her untransformed wounds, I am fully intending the honoring and healing of the wounded feminine everywhere. Because she is truly my whole mate, she receives my fierce commitment to her in precisely this way. She experiences it as being fully intimate in a very specific and personal sense, but she also experiences my commitment to her wholeness as our shared commitment to healing the Whole through her. Every word I just spoke about her healing, she could speak about mine.

Through healing your evolutionary whole mate, you are healing the Whole. That is precisely why you are not merely soul mates but whole mates. The move from soul mate to whole mate is often expressed not by a shift in action but by an up-leveling and evolution of intention. This was the quality of whole mate intention we saw in the story of wounding in the very beginning of our discussion of whole mate relationship.[209] It was the story of the master of Sans and his beloved. Because it is so relevant in this new context, we cite the end of the story once more.

> "Once I knew your name, however, I could not stop. I felt—I did not even know why—like I had to see you. The angels were furious and absolutely refused my request. I would not relent. I fasted, meditated, and prayed forty days and forty nights until finally they gave in. You were not even born yet."
>
> He continued: "They showed me a picture of you in your twentieth year, when we would marry. I cried out in pain. For the entire left side of your body was wounded. I could not bear it. I cried and cried and begged the angels to let me take

---

[209] See Chapter 5, "From Soul Mate to Whole Mate," Entry 4.

your wounding on myself. They would not hear of it. But I insisted, praying, and fasting for another forty days and forty nights. In the end, they relented, and at age twenty, I fell sick and received all of your wounds onto me.

"In us coming together," he explained, "know we will both be made whole again, and we will offer that wholeness up for the sake of the Wholeness of All-That-Is. For you are not only my *Basherte*, or soul mate, but you are my *Hashlamah*, or that which makes me whole. May it be thy will that through our love, we contribute to the Wholeness of everything.

"That," concluded the master, "is the special quality of relationship that birthed me into the world. All my wisdom, and all my power, is from that quality."

This is a story about working with wounds. In a profound and poignant sense, soul mate beloveds take on each other wounds. But this is not merely working with wounds for the sake of personal healing. In this evolutionary story, the personal and the Cosmic are One. Healing the wound of my beloved makes us both whole. But it is not just *our* wholeness that is at stake. By transforming our wounds into wholeness, we reweave the very fabric of the Whole. Our transformation is offered up in service of the Whole. We act for the sake of *a third side*,[210] and we do this in three ways: for the sake of love, for the sake of transformation, and for the sake of the Whole.

Entry 6. Evolutionary Relationships and Outrageous Love

When we know we are needed and desired by Reality, when we realize that the past does not determine the future, when we feel the power of participating in Evolutionary Love, it is then that we begin to awaken

---

210 See Chapter 6, "Whole Mate," Entry 14.

from ordinary love to Outrageous Love. When our relationships are called together by an expression of Outrageous Love, we enter a higher order of being entirely. Outrageous Love, as we have seen, is Evolutionary Love. It is the Love that moves the entire evolutionary process.

Outrageous Love is the combination of two evolutionary forces: emergence and synergy. Emergence refers to the ceaseless creativity of Cosmos, which is always birthing new levels of Reality. The synergy of Outrageous Love, allurement, and creativity is the driving force of the entire evolutionary process. To awaken as Outrageous Love is essential to what it means to be plugged in. You are not sourcing your love in your separate self, which, as wonderful as it may be, is simply limited. Rather, your love is sourced in the Infinite Power and Creativity that drives all of Reality to higher and deeper relationships. An evolutionary relationship is radical and alive because it is plugged into the evolutionary juice of Outrageous Love.

The essence of evolutionary relationships is beautifully captured in one of the classic movies of the early twenty-first century, *The Lord of the Rings*. Based on Tolkien's classic story, this movie speaks to elemental truths that people recognize, even if they are not able to articulate them fully.

As much as it is about anything else, *The Lord of the Rings* is a movie about relationships. In this mythic tale, only the *Fellowship of the Ring* can save the world. The Fellowship captures the natural expression of the core truth that Reality is Relationship. Let's look for a moment at a scene between the mortal king Aragorn and the immortal elf maiden Arwen. Their relationship is clearly rooted in what we call *Evolutionary Love*. The depth and detail of their epic love story is beyond the space we have in this book, but for our purposes here, the following scene is essential. Aragorn can choose to stay with Arwen, or he can leave her to lead his people. The king in this story, as in all ancient legends, is the archetype of the Unique Self.

Arwen: *Go to sleep.*

Aragorn: *I am asleep. This is a dream.*

Arwen: *Then it is a good dream. Sleep.*

Aragorn: *You told me once this day would come.*

Arwen: *This is not the end . . . it is the beginning. You must go with Frodo. That is your path.*

Aragorn: *My path is hidden from me.*

Arwen: *It is already laid before your feet. You cannot falter now.*

Aragorn: *Arwen—*

Arwen: *If you trust nothing else, trust this, trust us.*

In saying, "My path is hidden from me," Aragorn is implying that he does not know whether going with Frodo would be in alignment with his Unique Self. Perhaps he is to stay with Arwen. Perhaps he should choose their soul mate relationship over their evolutionary relationship. Arwen says, *No, you must meet your Unique Self.* "Your path is laid before your feet. You cannot falter now," she insists. "If you trust nothing else . . . trust us." In the movie, she gestures to their entwined bodies, and they kiss.

Trust us, in this context, means *Trust our love and the purpose of our relationship*, and follow your Unique Self. This is the place where soul mate and whole mate relationship intersect. Looking deeply into each other's eyes, they see the horizon of their evolutionary destiny. Each evokes the Unique Self of the other. And for a time, that means they must go separate ways. The movie ends, after the great battles have been won, with Aragorn's coronation. He thinks that, on her father's command, Arwen has sailed away to be with her people in the immortal lands. She has chosen otherwise. She returns from the land of the immortals to be with her king and to be his queen. Their meeting at his coronation is epic; their soul mate and evolutionary relationships merge into one. They are shoulder-to-shoulder and face-to-face in the same moment. They embrace the best of soul mate and integrate it with the essence of whole mate.

Entry 7. Falling in Love as Arousal from Above

We have seen that falling in love at the role mate and soul mate levels happens for reasons that are both overlapping and very different. There are two major drivers at play. One driver is dominant in role mate relationships, and the second driver is dominant in soul mate relationships.

The first driver, as we have seen, is often referred to as *chemistry*.[211] The beloveds are flooded by a cascade of hormones that all signal the same thing—that this is a good evolutionary match for survival and for producing children. She is a good child-bearer and homemaker, and he is a good provider and protector. This quality of love animates the need to survive and thrive in role mate relationships.

The second driver, central to soul mate relationships, is the desire to complete unfinished business with early caretakers.[212] A person is attracted to someone who matches the combined images of their early caretakers. That combined image, often referred to as the *imago*, may be strongly colored by either mother, father, or both. It might also be colored to various degrees by other powerful early caretakers. A person is then attracted to someone who resembles, or who is the opposite, of their *imago*. The person is either trying to close the gap and get closer to Mother or Father, or they are rejecting or rebelling against mother and father. In either case, the person is acting from the place of an unconscious reaction to the imago composite of these caretakers.

This unconscious pull toward another is one of the key ingredients that cause one to fall in love. This is the natural quality of falling in love that animates soul mate relationships, which are often focused on sharing and hopefully transforming our wounds. The fact that your partner embodies your early caretakers is often related to your wounding, making this the perfect recipe for soul mate relationship.

Much ink has been spilled on these two drivers in the literature of evolutionary science and imago psychology. Both drivers have some level of truth, but they are partial and do not articulate a third and more potent driver of our falling in love. This more potent quality is called *arousal*

---

[211] See Chapter 2, "Role Mate," Entry 4.

[212] See Chapter 3, "Soul Mate," Entry 9.

from above by the ancient teachers. What that alluring phrase points to is no less than Outrageous Love.

When you fall in love, for a period of time you see the full beauty of your partner. You see your partner with evolutionary eyes, and from the perspective of the evolutionary impulse. **Falling in love can gift you with a vision, even if it is short-lived, of your shared evolutionary destiny.** When falling in love, there is a felt experience of a momentary explosion of Outrageous Love stepping in and guiding your choice. It is the experience of making your choice from a place of expanded evolutionary consciousness. This choice invites you into the possibility of an evolutionary relationship, even if you do not fully understand all of its implications.

From this place of deeper understanding, you are brought into relationship, not merely by unconscious evolutionary forces seeking survival only. You are brought into relationship, not merely by unconscious forces of the psyche, which seek to complete the unfinished business of healing old wounds with your caretakers. Rather, in the experience of falling in love, there is also the fragrance of whole mate consciousness. You fall in love because you are called together by Outrageous Love seeking to incarnate the evolutionary impulse in your relationship.

Why? Because the potential Unique We is an irreducibly unique expression of the evolutionary impulse, with gifts to give that address the unique needs in your unique circle of intimacy and influence that can only be addressed by you. Because Outrageous Love has called you together, naturally the experience of love at this first stage is outrageous. It has a power, potency, and passion that are not reducible to psychological forces or blind evolutionary forces seeking survival for its own sake. Moreover, the notion of being guided only by the drivers of role mate and soul mate love does not match your own experience.

Your experience of falling in love is that you are being personally addressed by the Cosmos. You have a heightened sense of vitality and well-being. Your heart is open, and you feel almost invulnerable. You feel like there is nothing you cannot do together. This creates profound passion, which is often expressed as powerful emotion and potent sex. You trust each other to discover your destiny together. The reason this experience often fades is not because the chemicals wind down or the psyche becomes less attracted. Why should that be the case? The reason the experience of falling in love recedes is because you do not have a frame of reference that can hold and sustain the experience.

Neuroscience has shown us that, when you fall in love, the radical amazement and wonder of the experience suspend your ingrained brain patterns.[213] In essence, the circuits of ordinary love are overridden by the more powerful currency of Outrageous Love. If new, higher-order brain patterns replace the old patterns, then you can sustain the experience. These new patterns require a vision of evolutionary relationships. In this vision, not only are you brought together by Outrageous Love, but also your relationship itself becomes an expression of Outrageous Love. Together, as Unique We, you incarnate the evolutionary impulse. You are drawn together by a vision and purpose that are beyond your personal fulfillment. You live in an evolutionary relationship, which is allured to a higher purpose even as it is held by a deeper presence. Together, *in* your relationship and *through* your relationship, you awaken as Outrageous Love. Together, you participate directly and powerfully in the evolution of love.

Entry 8. From Sex to Supra-Sex: From Joining Genes to Joining Genius

Soul mate relationships are about being in love with your partner. All too often, that experience of being in love is also used as a cover to hide from the intense pain of loneliness. When you cross over to Evolutionary Unique Self, you are going way beyond being in love with your partner. **The experience of Evolutionary Unique Self is the experience of *being lived as Love*.** Whole mate, evolutionary relationships are relationships *lived together as Love*. This applies not only to your Unique Self but also to your Unique We.

This is the key to getting the joy and potency of whole mate or evolutionary relationships. We are *being lived together* as the evolutionary impulse. We are the impulse in action as us and through us. Our love

---

213 See N. Doidge, The Brain That Changes Itself: Stories of Personal Triumph from the Frontiers of Brain Science (2007).

impulse and the evolutionary impulse are no longer distinct. We join genius in an explosion not only of sex but also of *supra-sex*. Supra-sex is the erotic thrill of action for the sake of a larger purpose. It happens through the *joining of our genius*, which is the ethical and erotic core of evolutionary relationships. It involves a new form of sensual polarity that is not available through the impulse to *join genes*. Only the impulse to *join genius* produces this higher and hotter polarity.

As we have alluded to earlier,[214] at each level of relationship, we see a different form of sexuality:

> At the **role mate level**, sex is primarily focused on having children. This is called *procreative sex*.

> At the **soul mate level**, sex is about personal fulfillment. This is called *recreational sex*. It can be deep and intimate, and ideally it recreates the relationship anew each time.

> At the **whole mate level**, sex is deeply *co-creative* in its nature. Sexual polarity and attraction are natural erotic expressions of the co-creative vision and activism of evolutionary partners. Joining genius is arousing.

In soul mate relationships, the hope was that emotional arousal would spill over and foster sexual arousal. It did not. For a great many couples at least, we saw, in our study of egalitarian couples, that emotions were insufficient to foster passion.[215]

In whole mate relationships, emotional arousal is still essential. Remember that each level always transcends and includes the best of the prior level, so the whole mate relationship transcends and includes the best of soul mate relationship. But in evolutionary partnerships the emotional arousal is in the background. In the foreground is a powerful *vocational* arousal. You look over to your partner and see them not as

---

214 See Chapter 6, "Whole Mate," Entry 10.

215 See Chapter 4, "Limitations of Soul Mate," Entry 9.

fused with you but as a powerful other who is partnering with you to fulfill a shared purpose. A vocational arousal that honors the potency and power of your partner often spills into sensual arousal.

Entry 9. Eros in Evolutionary Relationships

Outrageous Love and Eros

Let's go back for a moment to a key sentence in our definition of Unique Self:

> *You are an irreducibly unique expression of the animating energy and Eros of Reality.*

What do we mean by *Eros*? It is that which captures a part of the flavor of Outrageous Love. Outrageous Love is the Eros of Life itself.

Over time, the term *Eros* has become so limited that it has lost much of its original intended meaning. Usually when we hear the word *erotic*, it evokes *only* the sexual. Although the sexual is a part of Eros, it is only a limited part. At its core, Eros is way beyond the merely sexual. It is presence, poetry, and passion. It is the sustaining Force that runs through and wombs the world. Eros is the underlying erotic, sensual, and loving Force that births us and knows our name. *Our name* is just another way of saying our *Unique Self*.

Eros is Outrageous Love, not ordinary love. Eros is not the casual, pallid, and sometimes anemic way we often talk of love. Eros is the Outrageous Love on the inside of things, where all is aflame. To live in Eros, to live erotically, is to live where everything is alive, intertextured, interwoven, and full of meaning. **Eros contains the qualities of both being and becoming:**

> **Being** is the experience of waking up in the morning full of utter joy for the arrival of the day. **Being** is weeping over the splendor of the sunset, the scent of the ocean, or the fragility of a newborn.

Becoming is the unique evolutionary creativity that emerges from Unique Self Realization.

The full pleasure of living, along with the joy of fullness and creativity, can only come when we re-eroticize our lives. That is what it means to awaken as Unique Self, to incarnate your unique Eros, to live as an Outrageous Lover. Eros, Unique Self, and Outrageous Love are three different Faces of the same authentic experience of Reality. Any relationship that seeks presence, poetry, and passion must be grounded in these three qualities.

The full Eros of being and becoming, experienced through the Evolutionary Unique Self, is the quality of evolutionary relationship. But here is the rub: **without accessing that level of aliveness and Eros, relationships simply do not work well.** That is what we mean when we say that role mate and soul mate are insufficient grounds for a truly successful relationship. At this moment in history, for a relationship to truly thrive, it needs the passion and purpose of Unique Selves standing for each other's most epic and extraordinary expression.

A thriving relationship needs each partner to be their Unique Self, and it needs them to create a Unique We. This Unique We has its own unique gifts that are needed by Reality. The partners' Unique We has an evolutionary relationship to life. The couple intends that their devotion, personal love, and transformational work serve not only their own fulfillment but the larger evolutionary context. This intention is not an extra in the leading edge of relationships today. Role mate and soul mate relationships are too limited to sustain such intentions. Without the larger context of Unique Self and Unique We, relationships quickly lose passion, power, and potency. Over time, without the purpose and vision of Unique Self and Unique We, the poignancy and presence of even soul mate relationships dissipate and eventually disappear.

Eros and Pseudo-Eros

What happens when we are unable to live in Eros born from unique purpose and passion? We become very frightened of emptiness. We are numb to the joy of living. We try to fill the void with the many forms of pseudo-eros. We fill it with anger, competition, fanaticism, and excessive consumption of all types and varieties. On a personal level, the result is often depression or an underlying deadness of spirit, which we often attempt to hide under the facade of success. On a global level, the result is terrible wars, as we fight to validate the superiority of our religions, to affirm our national pride, or to protect our economic power. At the same time, we rape the environment, forcing it to produce the glut of goods that we desperately require to provide us with more and more hits of pseudo-eros.

The Eros of purpose and passion inherent in Unique Self and Unique We is about feeling the fullness of being and becoming that is the opposite of emptiness. Every human being has encountered emptiness. Sadly, in our society, human beings are defined as consumers, not lovers. We buy, buy, buy, hoping the hawked elixirs might finally fill us, and yet, the emptiness lingers. This is the great paradox of emptiness. The path to Eros is filled with detours to pseudo-eros, but they are all dead ends.

Addiction is, at its root, the inability to stay in the emptiness. So, we rush to fill the emptiness with whatever gives us the quickest hit of pseudo-eros, which is always addictive. It has many disguises—sex, food, gossip, public acclaim, drugs, and work. We pretend that all of these are able to fill our emptiness, but they never satiate us.

Eros calls us to live the life of Outrageous Love in all aspects of our being. Outrageous Love calls us to feel the palpable unique Eros of a shared vision, which dissolves anger, anxiety, and the walls of separate self. Ordinary love shows itself as almost always plagued by various forms of pseudo-eros. On the other hand, **Outrageous Love *is* Eros!**

The invitation and the challenge of Spirit in our generation is to create a politics of Eros and a politics of Outrageous Love. We need politics that are awake to expressions of the Erotic Force of Connectivity and Outrageous Love. That can begin to happen only when relationships become evolutionary relationships. Such an emergence requires us to take responsibility for the unique erotic quality of our lives lived as our Unique Selves.

We need to, and we can, realign ourselves with the fountain of being.

We need to, and we can, connect to the vital currents of the energy of Eros coursing through our Universe.

We need to, and we can, realign with the evolutionary impulse of Outrageous Love.

We need to, and we can, decide to enter the flow.

From that place on the inside, we need to, and we can, transform our individual lives, our relationships, and ultimately our world.

The first step must always be the reclamation of Eros, of Outrageous Love! This is true because at their core all breakdowns in ethics are failures of Eros. When we are not filled with Eros, we seek every form of pseudo-eros to fill the emptiness. This is where the good becomes distorted, and contraction sets in. It is in this mode that evil and hatred are born. To reverse evil, aliveness must be reclaimed. By taking responsibility for our arousal to the full unique Eros of relationship and life, we can do just that!

Eros and Evolution of Desire

One Face of Eros is Desire. In its pathological form, our inability to sate our desires creates disease. In its potent form, however, desire is the source of our yearning, aliveness, and power. Our greatest yearnings are not merely grandiosity, as psychologists may have you believe. Rather, our greatest yearnings are the truest indicator of our essential nature. We do not long for that which is not ourselves. A fish does not yearn for dry land.

Pretty much everything we do is to get a particular feeling. When you have that feeling, the painful questions about *why you are here* and *whether your life is worthwhile* disappear. They do so, not because they are not important, but because the answer is so obvious that the question itself disappears. The feeling is of the radical aliveness of pulsating Eros. This is not merely sexual Eros, but the Eros of existence that is itself alive in and as you. When you feel that fullness living in you, the goodness, truth, and beauty of your own existence become self-evident. We desire a gorgeous new car, not for the efficient means of transportation, but because of the feeling of Eros it gives us. We desire a new level of relationship, a great home, an awesome job, not merely for themselves, but for the stunning feeling of aliveness that they might give us.

Our truest desire is for Desire itself. Buddha is popularly understood to have given desire a bad name. But in the original canon of Buddha's teaching, he is reported to have said, *Have few desires but have great ones.* Every new level of relationship expresses a greater desire. Each level of desire transcends and includes the previous level of desire:

Role mates desire to survive and materially thrive.

Soul mates desire to be liberated from loneliness and to be personally fulfilled.

Whole mates desire to align their desire with the desire of Reality by giving their unique gifts. Whole mates have clarified their desire beyond its surface expression. For a whole mate, fulfilling on his or her authentic desire is the North Star that guides their life. Whole mates incarnate the unique Desire of Reality that can be met only by their unique gifts.

Entry 10. Evolution of Dependency in Relationship

In role mate relationships, men and women need each other in the most basic ways. Men need women to create a family and a home. Women need men to be protectors and providers. Both partners need each other for sexuality. Both need each other to fulfill the roles that society and their own internalized sense of self need them to fulfill. Both need each other for love, that is ordinary love, mixed with a heavy dose of dependency needs. However, that love may sometimes deepen and grow into beautiful expressions of soul mate love. On rare occasions, role mates may even wake up and realize they are also whole mates, participating together in the evolution of love. But that is not usually the case—at least not yet.

In soul mate relationships, men and women need each other for personal fulfillment and validation. They need each other for depth, sharing their heroes' journey, and for passion and romance. Soul mate dependency features a different kind of need. Partners are no longer dependent on each other as role mates. Each has the capacity to make their own way in the world in terms of core survival and material thriving. From the perspective of survival drives at least, there is more consciousness and more possibility for choice. Soul mates still need each other, but their dependency rests in more emotional and personal reasons. In a word, they need each other for intimacy.

In soul mate relationships, women need men to be protectors and providers in a new way. Remember our earlier discussion of *line and circle qualities* in the context of Unique Gender.[216] In soul mate relationships, women might need men to help them find their circle qualities. Being engaged in the world of line energy all day at work, the woman might be dependent on the man to help her access her own circle quality, so that she does not become hardened into her line essence. In their turn, men rely on women for love, appreciation, and recognition.

Dependency remains, but it shifts from physical survival to emotional, spiritual, and psychological flourishing. When we needed each other to survive, the temptation to manipulate was overwhelming. The power of equal partnership was often not available in the old versions of the role mate level. Getting what you wanted through being coy, sexy, seductive, dominating, or controlling was a powerful temptation. When we needed each other to survive, we would often go to any lengths to ensure that aim.

Of course, it is very rare to have a soul mate relationship without any role mate dynamics. Even if you do not need your partner to survive literally, you may need them to provide a certain standard of living made affordable by two salaries. You may need them to help raise the kids, to make your career work, and for myriad other role mate capacities

---

216 See Chapter 6, "Whole Mate," Entry 9, and Chapter 7, "Unique Self," Entry 2.

or dimensions. Nonetheless, at level-two soul mate relationship, there is an emphasis on independence, and there is a deep discomfort with surrender. Indeed, the greatest sin at level two is codependency.

At level three, evolutionary or whole mate relationship, need and dependency reappear and are embraced in an entirely different way. Codependency gives way to a new form of *interdependency*. Men and women need each other as evolutionary partners. As whole mates, they stand for each other's Unique Self, for their shared Unique We, and for the larger Whole. They are able to say *I love you, I choose you*, and *I need you* in the same sentence without losing power. **Men and women need each other in order to live extraordinary lives.**

They need each other to show up as Unique Selves. They need each other to form a Unique We and to give their deepest gifts to each other and to their larger circles of intimacy, for the sake of the larger Whole. At level three, you realize that Reality needs the service of your Unique Self *and* your Unique We. You need each other to be the most extraordinary version of yourself that you can be.

At this level, both men and women are protectors and providers, nurturers and homemakers, and both partners realize that these roles do not serve merely themselves. They intend, as Unique Selves and as Unique We, to protect and provide, nurture and care for, the larger Whole. Even if their actions are entirely focused on their family and immediate circle of intimacy, their intention has shifted. They are no longer disconnected from the larger Whole. All of their service to each other is for the sake of the larger Whole.

Dependency comes back online in a potent and poignant way. Men and women voluntarily embrace the vulnerability of mutual surrender in evolutionary relationships. *I need you* becomes a declaration of love and power instead of an expression of weakness and fragility. Fragility and power, surrender and autonomy, are no longer opposites. They become part of a greater wholeness in evolutionary relationships.

Entry 11. Loneliness and Happiness

At level-one role mate relationship, the experience of loneliness is addressed in a significant way through the sense of mutually dependent, shared roles. The expectation of intimacy is not in play at this level. Fulfilling your role is primary. Your sense of being at home in the world is directly connected to meeting the obligations mandated by society.

At level-two soul mate relationship, liberation from loneliness through being received by your partner is radically central. This is in large part because the experience of loneliness has become far more central. Once survival needs are met, there is more space for introspection. Turning inside leads to a deeper awareness of loneliness, even while it generates a new level of soul mate romance and love.

At level-three whole mate relationship, you realize that looking deeply into your soul mate's eyes is insufficient to liberate you from loneliness. You are in need of a larger alignment with Reality itself. You awaken from loneliness by realizing that you are an irreducibly unique expression of the evolutionary impulse beating your heart. You realize that not only do you live in the Universe, but the Universe lives in you. Once your love evolves from ordinary to Outrageous Love, you are liberated from loneliness by performing the Outrageous Acts of Love that can be done by no one else but you.

The nature of happiness changes as well:

At level one, you are happy if you have fulfilled your role.

At level two, you are happy if you are loved. Happiness is both achieved and pursued directly.

At level three, as at level one, happiness is not directly achieved but is rather a byproduct of the achievement of another goal. At level three, unlike level one, the goal is living your Unique Self. Happiness is a natural result of being aligned with your Unique Self and your expression of the evolutionary impulse. **Happiness emerges indirectly through performing your Outrageous Acts of Love and giving your unique gifts.**

Entry 12. Evolution of Honor, Duty, and Obligation

Level-one role mate relationship is all about honor, duty, and obligation; and, just as dependency, they take a back seat in soul mate relationship.

Soul mates are all about choosing. Soul mates say things like, *We are committed to love*, but they do not like the notion that love might impose duties and obligation. The sense of being honor-bound is also absent from the traditional soul mate conversation.

However, at level-three whole mate relationship, honor, duty, and obligation come back online in a big way.

The difference between level one and level three comes down to *who* and *what* evokes a call to honor and duty. To whom is one obligated? At level three, the sense of duty is to the larger Whole. One is obligated to the larger Whole. One is honor-bound to be in integrity with the larger Whole. When making a decision, having personal integrity within your own narrow circle is no longer enough. When you awaken as Evolutionary Unique Self, you realize that your decisions require not just personal integrity but Evolutionary Integrity. When you evaluate the effect of your actions, you want to take into account, not just their effect on your immediate family and friendship circle, but also their effect on the longest future and on the widest possible circle that you can imagine.

In role mate relationships, people often stay in a relationship for the sake of the kids.

In soul mate relationships, the assumption that honor, duty, and obligation would keep you in a relationship for the sake of the kids was roundly challenged. Personal fulfillment was argued, by many soul mate writers, to be a higher value than staying with the kids. Many psychologists have argued that your kids not seeing you personally fulfilled was actually more detrimental to them than ending a relationship in divorce.

Each of these are valid points. The automatic assumption that you must always stay married for the kids was successfully challenged, just as **a whole new level of commitment to a larger vision and purpose came online at the next level of relationship**. The goal of personal fulfillment is no longer the sole arbiter of whether or not you will stay in relationship. At level three, a larger vision of the Whole more powerfully affects the trajectory of our relationships.

Entry 13. From Choice to Choicelessness

In level-one role mate relationship, men and women are chosen as appropriate for each other by the dictates of social norms. Your social role might include a spiritual or religious dimension, an ethnic dimension, or an educational or professional one. You are chosen to the precise extent that you fulfill your social role.

At level-two soul mate relationship, men and women choose each other based on *true love*. This personal choosing has the power to override society's choosing. This is the promise of *Romeo and Juliet*. Although it does not work out well for them in the end, their story points us in the right evolutionary direction. Of course, *true love* is often filtered through the role mate prism. Each of the prior roles impact the opening of the heart. Nonetheless, there is a dimension of choosing each other, a new emergence of choice, in soul mate relationship. This choice is not present in role mate relationship.

At level three, choice falls away again. There is a sense of a larger destiny having brought us together. This sense of a larger destiny is what we will call *choicelessness*. At level two, you may have a strong sense of your own independent choices that powerfully affect your life and destiny. This might be true about both negative and positive choices. At level three, however, you have a sense of being lived by larger Forces that guide what seem to be independent choices. This is not the same as level one, where your choices were determined by society's demands. Level three is *beyond* choice, not *before* it.

At the same time, the sense of being chosen no longer depends on each other or on fulfilling social roles. **Once each partner awakens to the powerful realization of Unique Self, the experience of uniqueness becomes the realization of being chosen by Reality.** All of Reality conspired to create the very precise conditions to manifest your irreducible uniqueness. At level three, there is a sense that you are chosen and that your destiny leaves you choiceless.

Knowing that we are chosen is essential to the human experience:

At level one, we fulfill the need to be chosen by meeting society's mandated roles.

At level two, we liberate ourselves in part from the dependency of society's choosing, just as a new form of choosing comes online—that of being selected by your soul mate. This creates great joy and an equal amount of pain because it creates enormous dependency on the emotional whims and caprices of people looking for ordinary love. When we are not chosen in love by the one we have chosen, we are often devastated. The need to be chosen is always present.

There is a great scene in the recent movie *Fifty Shades of Grey* that captures this beautifully:

Christian is polyamorous and into domination. He does not want a long-term romantic commitment. Anastasia, however, wants classic romance and commitment. She has, however, agreed to engage Christian on his own terms—no long-term commitment or classic romance.

At some point, love begins to grow between them. Before Christian is ready to transform, Anastasia asks how many other women have done this with him. He replies: *Fifteen*. And then, in a different scene, he says: *I never took anyone on a helicopter. Never had sex on my own bed. Never slept next to anyone. Ever. Only you.* What he says here satisfies, for that moment, her need to be chosen, to be the one.

The shadow of soul mate relationship lies in the fact that we often give our partner too much power over our experience of being chosen.
At level three, we are chosen by Reality itself. We awaken to the reality that we are each a unique expression of grandeur, outrageously

loved and supported by Reality in every moment. To be chosen means to be recognized in that uniqueness. It is not the grasping of the ego but the natural experience of Unique Self. The one who chooses me is also the one who needs me.

> At level one, I am needed by my immediate circle, partner, family, and clan to assure survival and thriving.

> At level two, I am needed primarily by my soul mate, and perhaps also my children, to recognize, love, and adore them.

> At level three, I realize that Reality needs my service.

Once you recognize that your unique gifts are needed in your unique circle of intimacy and influence for the sake of All-That-Is, you recognize that you are outrageously loved, chosen, and needed by All-That-Is. All of this directly relates to the experience of loneliness at all three levels of relationship.

CHAPTER 11

THE UNIVERSE: A LOVE STORY AND UNIQUE SELF SYMPHONY

The Universe is an Outrageous Love Story, and every Unique Self is a star of this story. Evolution is driven by self-organization at every level. At the human level, the guiding principle of self-organization is Evolutionary Unique Self, which leads to the emergence of Evolutionary We-Space and Unique Self Symphony.

Entry 1. Unique Self Is a Central Star of the Universe Story

Understanding the essence of Outrageous Love changes your perception of life and love. Traditionally, this understanding was available only to an elite few. Today, it is available to everyone. We are in an age where insight and realization are democratized and true wisdom is increasingly available and accessible. This does not mean that everyone knows what we are about to share, quite the opposite. But there are growing numbers of people at the leading edges of consciousness connecting the dots.

The fact that you are reading this book means that you are at the leading edge. You have the capacity of consciousness to connect the dots. As you connect the dots, you'll become increasingly clear that the Universe is a Story. And it is not an ordinary story; it is a love story. It is not a typical romantic love story; it is an Outrageous Love Story. The Universe has a plot. Its plot is Love. And you are a central actor in the Story. **You are a star in the Story of the Universe whose plot is Outrageous Love.**

Cosmology has revealed a potent truth: Reality has nearly an infinite number of centers. For example, from the perspective of mathematics and physics, each star in the galaxy is a center. The implications of what it means for the Universe to locate itself in a nearly infinite number of centers simultaneously are staggering.

The implications for our discussion are clear. Every Unique Self is a central star of the Universe Story. This means that *you* are at the center. **The whole Story, in some genuine sense, depends on you.** Your unique capacity for love is necessary for the success of the whole Story. That is precisely what it means to be a Unique Self. The Universe has cast you, uniquely, as a star. You are an irreducibly unique expression of the larger Field of the LoveIntelligence, LoveBeauty, and LoveDesire that animates all of Reality. That larger Field is not static. It moves and evolves. It is an Outrageous Love Story.

This is not a fanciful idea. It is not a spiritual conjecture or flaky New-Age assertion. It is the aggregate result of the best wisdom of leading-edge science. It honors the truths of premodern, modern, and postmodern wisdom traditions. **The Universe is not an unmoving fact, but an ever-evolving Story. It is not an ordinary story. It is a Love Story. It is not an ordinary love story. It is an Outrageous Love Story.**

We always see the world through the prism of our mental frameworks. We live inside of these frameworks, but they are invisible to us. If these frameworks are inaccurate, they distort Reality. But if our frameworks are accurate, we see Reality more clearly. When your framework is unconscious, you become its prisoner. When the framework is consciously chosen, based on the best information available, it can set you free. The framework becomes your friend and guide. If you want to change your life at its root, change your framework. If you want to up-level your life, up-level your framework—not arbitrarily, but in a very real sense. Access a more accurate framework that holds a more accurate and comprehensive view of Reality.

At the leading edges of science, information is being gathered that discloses, to the eyes not blurred by dogmatic materialism, that the

Universe is a Love Story. That is the most accurate framework, which accounts for the most information from the most dimensions of Reality.

When you see yourself and your relationships in this framework, your life's love stories forever change. You'll never go back to being the same person, and your love stories will never shrink back to their original proportions. Even if you forget what you read here, it will remain inside of you, alluring you to play a larger game.

Entry 2. Reality Is an Outrageous Love Story

As we have seen, the Universe is not just a fact; it is a Story. The storyline is not linear, but there is, over time, an unmistakable direction to the Story's movement. The self-organizing properties and inherent creativity of Reality move the Universe to ever-more profound complexity, structure, depth, and beauty. Galaxies are a step along the way in that movement. Science teaches us that Reality is always writing new chapters in the Universe Story, even as the mainstream of culture rejects the idea that the Whole might be real and have an intrinsic direction.

Before we knew about evolution, we thought the Universe was an eternal fact.[217] But evolution has now shown us that things are always changing. The Universe has direction. It is going somewhere. For those who thought, like the Buddha, that the world was at its core an unchanging eternity, the goal of spiritual practice was to step out of the ever-changing world and identify with eternity. That is why so many spiritual teachers who are shaped by Eastern traditions tell their students to *move beyond the story*. However, once you realize that the Universe *is* a Story, the nature of spiritual practice changes. The goal becomes more alluring. When you step out of your superficial story into your authentic, depth story, everything shifts.

---

[217] Pretty much everyone thought the world was unchanging. Aristotle, Buddha, and Albert Einstein were among those who thought the Universe was an eternal fact. The biblical prophets intuited (correctly, it turns out) that the world began in time. But once it began, according to the popular worldview of the Bible, it was unchanging. The biblical mystics, however, were evolutionary at their core and had a clear sense of evolutionary stages, even though they had no sense of biological evolution as revealed by science.

Understanding the Universe as a Story also rejects the postmodern dogma, which argues that the only grand narrative about Reality is that there is no story. Postmodern spokesperson Albert Camus' novel, *The Stranger*, opens with the lines, "Maman died today. Or maybe yesterday, I don't know."[218] Camus's point was that narrative does not matter.

We now realize that there is a narrative to Reality. It is not a dogmatic narrative owned by one nation or religion. It is the great Universe Story. The Story reveals precisely that there *is* a Story. Reality has direction. Its direction is honorable and can be trusted. Reality moves toward more complexity, more consciousness, more care, more compassion, more uniqueness, and more connectivity. Reality is a movement toward ever-higher levels of mutuality, recognition, union, and embrace.

The Universe is not just a Story. It is a very particular kind of Story—a Love Story. The old neo-Darwinian universe story about a tooth-and-claw world, in which brutal competition assured that only the fittest survived, was one of the most influential narratives of the twentieth century.

Notice that we called this a *neo*-Darwinian story. It was certainly not Darwin's story. Seminal evolutionary thinkers like our good friend David Loye and multiple other earlier thinkers[219] have shown conclusively that Darwin placed love front and center in his view of evolution.[220] For Darwin, the Universe was clearly a Love Story. Evolutionary science after Darwin has shown in far more conclusive terms than Darwin ever imagined that Reality is Relationship. Reality is drawn together by allurement and moves toward ever higher and deeper levels of cooperation, collaboration, and love.

When we say that the Universe is a Love Story, we are also saying that the Universe has *an interior*. That means something very simple: **interiors are real**. For example, when you fall in love, your levels of serotonin

---

218 A. Camus, The Stranger translated by Matthew Ward (2012).

219 This heterodox line of Evolutionary Love thought that more accurately represents Darwin may be traced back at least to Peter Kropotkin in his classic work, Mutual Aid: A Factor of Evolution.

220 See D. Loye, Darwin's Lost Theory of Love (2000).

and oxytocin increase. That does not mean that love *is* serotonin or oxytocin. You can take certain drugs that will induce an experience of ecstasy. That does not mean that ecstasy is not a real experience. Love is not reducible to neurotransmitters and hormones. Every exterior expression has an interior expression. Interiors and exteriors are part of a larger unified Field.

We have to be very careful to avoid any dogma that reduces all of Reality to exteriors. Such reductionism has little place any longer in serious, balanced thinking. The relationship between interiors and exteriors is a great philosophical issue. Love is both an interior felt experience and an exterior hormonal experience. The interior aspect of love is just as real, just as true as the exterior aspect. Put simply, interiors are real and love is real. That is part of what we mean when we say the Universe is not merely a matter of fact.

The Universe is a Love Story. It's not a clichéd, Hollywood, saccharine love story. It's not a love story without suffering, but it is a Love Story. The Universe is not an ordinary love story; it is an Outrageous Love Story. And all of us are central actors. The way this Love Story turns out is directly and absolutely dependent on our ability to awaken as Outrageous Love.

Entry 3. The Universe Feels, and the Universe Feels Love

Let's put the pieces together. All of Reality is a single event. We are not separate from any of the levels of Reality. Each of them lives in us. We are a product of each level of emergence that came before—subatomic particles, atoms, molecules, cells, and on up the spectrum. All of it lives in us as human beings.

The primary Force moving us is Eros or what we have called *Evolutionary Love* or *Outrageous Love*. That is why, if we do not have anyone or something to love, our lives become dull and empty. For some it is romantic love, for others the love of God or country, and for others the love of ideas or nature. It could also be love of creativity or power. Regardless, love is utterly central to our lives. It is surely not an accident of culture or consciousness that virtually all songs revolve around some theme related to love. Being in love is not merely a delight of life. Without love, life becomes outrageously painful.

We feel our aliveness through being allured by other beings, places, things, and ideas. The force of attraction operates at every level of Reality. As we have seen throughout this book, Reality is Relationship. Allurement is a quality of the Cosmos that brings everything together into relationships. Love is but another name for allurement.

When we really get this, we are almost blinded by the insight. When we fall in love with someone, at first blush, they are the beginning and the end of love. But, if we reflect a bit deeper, we realize that this is not the case. The person whom we love is not the totality of love, but rather the subject that inspires the feeling of love within us. The love itself is ever present. The person triggers or evokes our love, but they are not the source of love. That is why people fall in love more than once. It is why people love an intimate partner with one form of love and a son with another form of love. It is why, even if you lose your daughter or your partner, your ability to love endures. In fact, your grief is an expression of your love.

Consider the felt experience of being in love even more deeply and you realize that you are not the ultimate source of love, either. Rather, being in love puts you in touch with the quality of Love in the Universe. In those moments of love, you are feeling what is always already there. The invisible lines of Love-Connection become visible in the presence of your beloved.

Imagine that you feel enormous love for someone. You likely do not feel that you are the source of the love you experience. Rather, you feel impelled to extend to that person the love that naturally connects you—the love that lives in the space between you. In loving them, you are an expression of the love that exists beyond you. You likely do not feel that if you disappeared, they would no longer be loved. Rather, your allurement expresses the allurement that animates all of Reality.

When we talk about love in the human world, we speak of interior and exterior expressions of love. From the exterior, allurement appears as people moving toward each other. It may involve living together, talking to each other, supporting each other, or being intimate with each other in myriad ways. Love on the outside appears as an action. But that exterior expression of allurement is obviously not the whole story. Those exterior actions correspond with interior experiences. There is a clearly felt experience of allurement that goes by many names, including love.

Allurement, or love, has an exterior—expressed as movement and action. It also has an interior—expressed as feelings, emotions, or motivation. Interiors and exteriors are both real. Both are valid. Both can be understood empirically, that is, both can be accessed via direct sensory experience. Love, attraction, and allurement are all names for the same truth. Love describes its interior; attraction describes its exterior. Allurement combines them both. Because you cannot separate the interior from the exterior, we can use each of these words interchangeably.

When you really get a deep sense of this, the following sentences begin to make perfect sense. Not only do they make sense; they are self-evident.

The Universe feels. And the Universe feels love. Not ordinary love, but Outrageous Love—the Evolutionary Love that moves the Sun and other stars and holds us in every moment. In every single moment, whether you are aware of it or not, you are drenched in the Outrageous Love that animates the cosmos and is alive in and as All-That-Is. Every single corner of you is loved and accepted in that love. It is utterly nourishing, radically enlivening, and profoundly awakening. In this sense, love is not hard to find. Love is not difficult to achieve. Love is impossible to avoid.

Entry 4. Science Whispers in Your Ear: *You Are Evolution*

So, what do we know? We know that the Universe is a Love Story. It is an Outrageous Love Story.

Who are we? We are unique expressions of LoveIntelligence, LoveBeauty, and LoveDesire, arousing ourselves to the *gnosis* that Outrageous Love lives in us, as us, and through us uniquely.

Is that a mythic idea? Is that a New-Age idea? No, it is the best take that we have of Reality today, according to the interior and exterior sciences.

Who are you? You are an irreducibly unique expression of the LoveIntelligence, LoveBeauty, and LoveDesire that is the initiating and animating energy of All-That-Is, living in you, as you, and through you, and that never was, is, or will be again. You have a unique perspective that births your unique insight—your unique gift that creates your unique capacity to address a unique need in your circle of intimacy and influence. This need can be addressed by no one other than you. If you don't wake up as Outrageous Love, there is an important corner of the world that is UnLove.

Does that make you uncomfortable? To really get a handle on your true identity is sometimes too much, so the voice in you that is saying *It's too much* might get really loud now. But when you actually get the previous paragraph, you realize that evolution is awakening as you. The Universe is signed with your name. The next stage of evolution is not out there. It is in you.

Do you get the shift? We think evolution is a process happening out there. But it's not. It is actually happening right inside of you and me. Evolution is happening. We are evolution. Your mother is evolution. Your friends are evolution. Your boss is evolution. You are evolution. Evolution is love in action. It is Outrageous Love in action. You are Evolutionary Love in action. Evolution moves through your Outrageous Acts of Love. You are the evolutionary impulse awakening as you. That's so shocking. It is so far beyond imagination. It is so wild. It is so thrilling. It is so humbling. It is so demanding of radical integrity and responsibility. As we have seen, the Universe feels, and the Universe feels love. And you are a unique expression of that LoveIntelligence, LoveDesire, and LoveBeauty. You are a unique expression of Outrageous Love. And your Unique We is, too.

What does it mean to be unique? To be unique means that you are intended, recognized, chosen, desired, needed, and love-adored. You are the only person who exists at this particular place in this particular spacetime continuum. You have an irreducibly unique genome. You have an irreducibly unique immune system. You have a cellular signature that took 13.7 billion years to develop. You are made up of thirty trillion unique cells. All of this is the signature of Reality signed as you.

To realize your uniqueness is to realize that you are uniquely loved and uniquely seen. You are uniquely chosen and uniquely needed. To really get Unique Self is to get that the Universe is whispering three things in your ear. These are little love whispers, little love caresses. Little words, secret words, of the Intimate Lover that is the personal Face of the Universe and knows your name. The Universe is whispering in your ear:

I love you. I need you. I choose you.

But these Outrageous Love whispers are not addressed to you alone. They are addressed to you together with your whole mate. These whispers address not only Unique Self but also Unique We.

Entry 5. Outrageous Love Is Ceaseless Creativity and Allurement

Let's bring some of the key strands together. We have already seen that Outrageous Love is a core quality of Cosmos. Outrageous Love has two core dimensions, which are inseparable from each other.

The first dimension is a ceaseless creativity that drives Reality to deeper and higher levels of emergence. Emergence means more complexity, consciousness, creativity, connection, and care.

The second core dimension of Outrageous Love is what leading-edge cosmologists have referred to as *allurement*. Allurement is the quality of attraction that creates relationship. As we have seen, the drive to relationship is also an essential feature of Reality. Creativity and allurement drive the unfolding of the evolutionary process. With the emergence of humans, the process of creativity and allurement has moved from an unconscious to a conscious expression.

Think for a moment about the one hundred billion galaxies dancing through space. They are literally held together by Outrageous Love, or creative allurement. It is encoded within the laws of physics, mathematics, chemistry, and everything else. The intimacy that exists between the Sun and the Earth is the direct result of this scientifically verified quality of allurement. Without these forces, none of the relationships in our Universe could ever have been established.

The essential quality of Reality, the creative allurement, or Outrageous

Love, is the quality that draws what is separate into relationship. It is a profound and powerful energy that suffuses all of life at every level of Reality. It is allurement that draws clouds of hydrogen atoms into relationship to form a star. It is the mystery of allurement operating at the human level that allows two whole mates to come together in one evolutionary relationship. Because of allurement, 1 + 1 = 1. Two whole mates form one new larger whole.

The quality of Outrageous Love is the strongest force in the Universe. It literally defines the Cosmos on every level, regardless of whether we are talking about galaxies, stars, planets, subatomic particles, cells, plants, animals, mammals, or humans. There is a vast science on the core principles of allurement, which draw everything to something else into a specific form of relationship. Science tells us even more than that, however. Not only does Outrageous Love move everything into relationship, but it also moves everything toward higher and higher levels of relationship. At this moment in time, the leading-edge expression of the evolution of relationships is evolutionary relationships, whole mate relationships.

Entry 6. Outrageous Love and Outrageous Obligation

Now, let's bring a second idea online—the super sexy and alluring idea of *obligation*. When we talked about this in the Unique Self chapter (Chapter 7), we noted that the original Hebrew words *love* and *obligation* derive from the same root word. The love being referenced here is not ordinary love but Outrageous Love. When Outrageous Love awakens in you, there is a life for you to live—the sum total of your unique allurements that can be lived only by you. When Outrageous LoveIntelligence, LoveBeauty, and LoveDesire awakens in you, there are gifts to give, the sum total of your unique obligations that can be given only by you.

These are not imposed from without. They are not imposed by family, religion, or country. They are not even imposed by the Universe. The Universe does not live outside of you; the Universe awakens from within you. All of evolution is a single event that does not forget anything. All of Reality, from subatomic particles through all the stages of humanity, is remembered. It all literally awakens in you. Every level of evolution is encoded and physically present in your body. Evolution awakens uniquely as you, in person. Your obligation emerges from Outrageous LoveIntelligence, LoveBeauty, and LoveDesire giving its unique gifts as you. That is Outrageous Love awakening as you. That is the source of your aliveness and joy. Joy, as we have seen, is a byproduct of living from your Unique Self while being aligned with the evolutionary impulse and committing the Outrageous Acts of Love that are yours alone to commit.

From the perspective of separate self, obligation is imposed from the outside. Culture, society, and religion all impose obligations. Of course, they are imposed from without. When you live from your separate self, you are apart from everything else. Where else could obligation be imposed from, other than from without? As separate self, everything is outside of you except for that narrow band of reality that is your skin-encapsulated ego. Once you get that evolution is awakening as you in person, you come to understand on some very profound level that all of the Universe lives in your unique being. Obligation then becomes purely internal. It becomes not an imposition, but the delight of your life.

Earlier, we described the five components of Unique Self obligation:

(1) There is a need,

(2) it is a genuine need,

(3) you clearly recognize the need,

(4) you are capable of fulfilling the need, and

(5) you are not only capable, but *uniquely* capable of addressing the need.

The shocking realization of Unique Self is that there is no one who ever was, is, or will be who has the capacity to meet that need in the way that you can and will. The shocking Reality of Unique Self is that, if you do not awaken as an Outrageous Lover, there is a corner of the world that remains trapped in UnLove. Your unique obligation and joy are to bring love to that corner of the world.

Entry 7. Our Ability to Feel and Our Ability to Heal

Why are we not out in the world committing the Outrageous Acts of Love that are a natural expression of our Unique Selves? Why do couples not create evolutionary relationships committed to the Outrageous Acts of Love that emerge from their Unique We? Because we close our hearts. For most of us, it is hard to open our hearts, and it is even harder to live with them open over time. But it is only from the place of an open heart that one can commit irreducibly unique Outrageous Acts of Love.

It is only when you realize that your open heart is the very heart of the evolutionary impulse that you can awaken to the ecstatic urgency of your life and relationship. It is only when you live with an open heart that you can live with the realization that you are personally implicated in the evolutionary process. It is only when you awaken as an Outrageous Lover that you can begin to realize the enormity of what it means to know that Reality needs your service as an individual and as an evolutionary couple. It is only from the place of Outrageous Love that you begin to live the extraordinary Unique Self life that is the ground for an evolutionary relationship imbued with radical joy, purpose, and aliveness.

Why is it so hard to open our hearts into evolutionary relationship? One reason is that our hearts have been broken so many times. But it is not merely that our loyalties have been betrayed. Our hearts also have been broken in other ways. We are full of personal wounds and contractions. And at this moment in history, our hearts can be wounded much more broadly and easily. After all, we are connected to what is going on around the world in ways we have never been before. Our hearts can be wounded on a truly global scale by what we see on Facebook, Twitter, CNN, and beyond.

As a digitally interconnected humanity, we have the painful ability to know in great depth and graphic detail the horrific pain happening all over the world. Images of unbearable suffering penetrate our hearts, bodies, and minds daily. We experience ourselves as impotent. We seem unable to heal the suffering that surrounds us. For most of us, the only way to respond is to close our hearts. Not because we are bad, asleep, or narcissistic, but because the gap between our ability to feel and our ability to heal is simply too great to bear.

The problem is that you have only one heart. When your heart closes, your lifeforce begins to shut down. When you close your heart again and again in the face of suffering, something breaks in your inner core. In our generation, the level of suffering to which we are exposed is so vast, and the gap between the ability to feel and the ability to heal is so great that it triggers a deliberate and powerful closing of the heart. The direct result of this closing is a level of depression, anxiety, mental illness, addiction, and breakdown, the likes of which we have never seen before.

There is only One Heart and One Love. That is the nature of Reality. You can ignore Reality, but Reality does not change; it all lives within you. All of history and the entire Universe is coded in your genes. There is only One Heart and One Love—Outrageous Love. That One Heart lives in you as your own heart. When you close your heart, you lose access to the power of One Heart and One Love.

You cannot block access to your heart in response to suffering and then expect to retain access to it in your relationships. That simply does not work. If you close part of your heart to outrageous pain in one part of your life, you cut off access to Outrageous Love in every part of your life. We have never seen so much suffering and been so unable to heal it. The feeling of impotence in the face of overwhelming vital need is massively destructive to our hearts and psyches. This feeling corrodes our soul. The gap between our ability to feel and our ability to heal simply feels too big to risk allowing ourselves to be lived as Love. The Outrageous Lover reclaims her potency by closing the gap between her ability to feel and her capacity to heal by reopening her heart.

Entry 8. Unique Self and Unique We in Unique Self Symphony

There is only one way to heal the collective trauma of our generation: you answer the great questions of *Who are you?* and *Who are we?* You wake up to your true identity. You begin to play a larger game. You realize that you are not merely a skin-encapsulated ego, but an irreducibly unique expression of the LoveIntelligence, LoveBeauty, and LoveDesire that is the initiating and animating Eros of All-That-Is. A stunningly singular expression of the LoveIntelligence lives in you, as you, and through you in a way that never was, is, or will be ever again. You are a Unique Self. You are part of a Unique We. You have a life to live and a gift to give that perfectly co-responds to a unique need in the world of UnLove. This place of UnLove in the world can be addressed and healed only by you and your Unique We.

Perhaps you feel impotent because the pain of the world is so great. Because you felt impotent in the face of pain that is too much to bear, you closed your heart. However, at this stage in time, at this point in the Outrageous Love journey, your consciousness has evolved. You can now realize that you cannot heal the entire world as a separate self or as a part of a role mate or soul mate relationship that is just about you and your partner. And that is entirely OK. You are not called to heal all of Reality by yourself.

You can give your unique gifts. And your Unique We can give its unique gifts. When you and every other person and every other evolutionary couple give their unique gifts, a *Unique Self Symphony* is formed in which everyone is needed and no one is extra. It is out of tune and impotent if anyone, any relationship, or any instrument is missing. The power and potency of this symphony releases a virtually infinite wave of creativity and innovation that has the power to heal almost anything. Emerging from the meta mind of Unique Selves and Unique Wes, innovation and evolutionary creativity are collectively released into Reality. This is what will help us take the next evolutionary step.

You are not called to fix it all by yourself. You are called by your uniqueness. You are charged to action by your uniqueness. You are no longer alone. Once your Unique Self and Unique We are aroused within the chorus of all Unique Selves and Unique We-s, a new sound is heard. It is the sound of the Unique Self Symphony. You are needed *only*, and it is a big *only*, to play your Unique Self and Unique We instrument in the Unique Self Symphony. Cosmos produced only one you as a result of an unimaginable 13.7-billion-year string of synchronicities. It produced your Unique Self. And that makes possible your Unique We. As we have seen, Reality needs your Unique Self. Reality also needs your Unique We. That means, very simply, that the world needs the love that can come only from you and your Unique We.

To really understand the nature of Reality and your power as a Unique Self and Unique We in the large context of Reality's Unique Self Symphony, let's access for a moment the quality of symphony.

> Roger Nierenberg, a symphony orchestra conductor who also consults with businesses, did something like the following at an engagement with one of the largest management consulting firms in the world. As one thousand senior-level managers walked into a large room, they noticed that interspersed among their seats were seats set aside for the various sections of a symphony orchestra. Soon enough, the orchestra members came in and took their places. Then, Nierenberg, the stereotypical conductor, hair and all, strode into the room and proceeded to make a variety of points about running a team. He used orchestral principles to make the point.
>
> Using a Wagner overture, the conductor said: *Let's hear only the second violins and the triangle from measure X to measure Y.* This allowed the managers to hear how the triangle related to the overall piece without being drowned out by the whole orchestra. Next, he had the entire orchestra, minus the triangles, play the same passage. Then, finally, he had the entire orchestra, this time with the triangles, play the same passage. With the addition of the triangles, the already magnificent piece was sprinkled with musical fairy dust. The piece transformed from

gorgeous to transcendent.[221]

The point here is that your Unique Self and Unique Wes are not extras or mere adornment. They are essential to the sound of music. There are no extras in the Unique Self Symphony.

The emergence of a new whole that is more than the sum of its parts is a core feature of erotic synergy. This is true on all levels of Reality, including human relationships. As we have seen throughout this work, that erotic property of synergy plays out in our human world of relationships. On the human level, we are attracted to form relationships by the allurement of becoming more whole. We are allured by wholeness. That is the evolutionary dynamic at play in relationships.

Erotic synergy not only creates new wholes in the personal realm, but also creates new social wholes. Social synergy is but another form of Eros or intimacy. It is the impetus to bring together co-creators worldwide who are each at the forefront of innovation and transformation.

Barbara developed a method to catalyze the Eros of social synergy that she called the Wheel of Co-Creation. It focuses not on what is *broken* in the world but on what is *working*. It includes all the major sectors of society, from education to science to technology to spirituality and everything in between. In an exquisitely designed exercise, leaders locate themselves in different sectors of the wheel and proclaim their unique innovations. They are then invited to present what they might need from the other sectors in order to succeed. The isolation and fragmentation among society's different sectors is overcome in this exercise. A new form of intimacy, social synergy, is born. New possibilities emerge. New wholes are formed. Cultivating the contexts of allurement, the social incubators where these new wholes might be formed, is an essential evolutionary need.

---

[221] This is a made-up example based on Nierenberg's own experiences. See, for example, Roger Nierenberg, Maestro: A Surprising Story About Leading by Listening (2009). The book is a novel told by a narrator who is a leader in an organization and learning about the art of leadership through listening from a conductor. It is based on Nierenberg's own method of training organizations through watching him conduct, train, and lead his orchestra. See also "The Music Paradigm" (https://www.musicparadigm.com/).

Paradoxically, it is only through focusing on what is working best, and then creating new strategies of transformation through social synergies, that we can hope to heal what is broken. A reality that is not shattered and fragmented into isolated sectors is more whole, and therefore more erotically potent in its ability to transform and to heal.

Entry 9. Evolutionary Unique Self in the Self-Organizing Universe

One of the core structural principles in the formation of the Unique Self Symphony is the scientific principle of self-organization. The idea of *self-organization* is among the most important scientific ideas to emerge in our time.

Self-organization, or the self-actualizing Cosmos, is a basic principle of Reality that operates at all levels. The inherent, ceaseless creativity of the Cosmos moves Reality to higher and deeper levels of complexity, consciousness, and love. This process of evolutionary emergence is a function of self-organization. Self-organization is what allows slime molds to separate into individual cells and then come back together as a larger organism, without there being any command-and-control chain giving orders. It is also what organizes an ant colony or a beehive.

These are not isolated examples. This is the structure of Reality. A human embryo is formed when undifferentiated cells move to self-actualize as the organs and systems of the human body. Each set of cells is coded with an inherent intelligence that exceeds that of any supercomputer. We are held in every second by this LoveIntelligence, LoveBeauty, and LoveDesire—literally embraced by Reality in every single second. Reality *is* in every single second showering us in Eros from without and within. We *are* Eros, uniquely personified, even as we are held by and as the Infinity of Intimacy in every single second. But Reality is not only holding us in being. Reality is ceaselessly becoming. Becoming means that Reality is self-actualizing towards ever-deeper possibility in every moment. This process of becoming begins in the world of matter and moves through the world of life and then to the depth of the self-reflective human mind. This is the nature of the self-organizing Universe.[222]

The question is: What guides self-organization at the level of human culture? The answer is dramatic yet elegantly simple: **the guiding principle of self-organization in the human world is Evolutionary Unique Self.** As you will remember, Evolutionary Unique Self is simply the Unique Self being aware of the larger evolutionary context. The Unique Self that understands itself not only as the unique completion of the puzzle but also as capable of and responsible for evolving the entire puzzle is an Evolutionary Unique Self.

Your Evolutionary Unique Self has a unique perspective, which creates your unique insight. This manifests as your unique gifts, which give you the ability to respond to a unique need in your circle of intimacy and influence. When every Unique Self is roused to their unique creativity, an Evolutionary We-Space is formed. This We-Space is what we call *Unique Self Symphony*.

Stars self-organize. It is simply true, scientifically, that both ants and human beings self-organize. Humans, however, are uniquely aware that they are self-organizing. That is part of Conscious Evolution. Humans are evolution awakening from unconscious to Conscious Evolution, part of which is expressed as the movement from unconscious to conscious uniqueness. As we each realize that we are unique expressions of the LoveIntelligence, LoveBeauty, and LoveDesire acting through us, we become aware of our self-organizing tendency. And we self-organize through reaching to fulfill our uniqueness, both as Unique Selves and as Unique Wes. We self-organize at the macro level as unique communions of religions, countries, corporations, and at the more micro-local level, as every form of social, religious, political, economic, entrepreneurial,

---

[222] It is not a linear process of evolutionary progress. With every new potential comes new potential pathology. Rocks don't have cancer; horses do. And yet horses have infinitely more lifeforce and feeling and intelligence than rocks. Horses don't build hospitals; human beings do. And yet human beings also build gas chambers, which other human beings fail to destroy. And human beings often fail to realize their own True Nature or the nature of Reality. This is because they cannot quite muster the requisite power and passion to do the practice, the work, required to self-realize. The result is failed human frameworks of value, gaps between interior and exterior technologies, all of which together result in existential risk.

and professional communion.

Poets often come before scientists. The Persian poet Rumi did not know evolutionary science, but he did understand that we are all lead actors in a script that needs us each, as Walt Whitman reminded us, to *contribute a verse*. Your unique verse is one that can be spoken only by you.

The stars come up spinning

every night, bewildered in love.

They'd grow tired

with that revolving, if they weren't.

 They'd say,

"How long do we have to do this!" God picks up the reed-flute world and blows.

Each note is a need coming through one of us,

a passion, a longing-pain.

Remember the lips

where the wind-breath originated,

and let your note be clear.

Don't try to end it.

Be your note.

I'll show you how it's enough. Go up on the roof at night

in this city of the soul. Let everyone climb on their roofs

and sing their notes! Sing loud!

—Rumi[223]

All of this is part of the consciousness of whole mates in Unique Self Symphony with each other, forming a Unique We. Each one plays its own unique instrument in the larger Unique Self Symphony.

Entry 10. Evolutionary We-Space

Unique Self Symphony depends upon every person contributing his or her unique verse. It is built on the democratization of creativity. It emerges when every Unique Self awakens to the realization that we are all part of a self-organizing Universe. As this realization deepens, the self-evident truth of it presents itself in a thunderbolt of clarity.

The guiding principle of the self-organizing Universe is Evolutionary Unique Self. When billions of Unique Selves awaken to their evolutionary context and give their unique gifts, the Outrageous Love and infinite creativity of the Unique Self Symphony emerges. This marks the formation of an Evolutionary We-Space and the emergence of a higher global wisdom. In this space, each individual has irreducible rights and dignity and, at the same time, contributes to a larger collective intelligence.

Evolutionary Intimacy arises through the formation of the Evolutionary We-Space. This is where personal love, intimacy, and activism merge. Our hearts reopen. We close the gap between our ability to feel and our ability to heal. We are alive as Outrageous Love from our consciousness of our Evolutionary Unique Selves. This is the matrix of a politics of love—the most hopeful vision we have for the future of humanity. It is based on the democratization of greatness, or what we call the *democratization of enlightenment*.

The Evolutionary We-Space and Evolutionary Unique Self are

---

223 The Essential Rumi, 103 ("Being a Lover: The Sunrise Ruby—Each Note").

directly related in the emergence of collective consciousness. The Evolutionary We-Space emerges from the profound realization that uniqueness fosters connection, not separation. Uniqueness is like a puzzle piece. It is the currency of connection, not the source of separation. Separate selves cannot form Evolutionary We-Spaces because the ego competition is too great. True Selves cannot do so because there are no we-spaces when everything is one. Only Unique Selves can do so. Only Evolutionary We-Spaces formed by Evolutionary Unique Selves committing Outrageous Acts of Love have the capacity to address the urgent needs of civilization at this moment in time.

But it is even more than that. When human beings come together to incarnate as autonomous, yet intimate Unique Selves, something essential shifts in Reality. Such human beings come together as a community of Outrageous Lovers to form an Evolutionary We-Space. When this happens, great joy and transformation are liberated into the world. This is the creation of Evolutionary Intimacy.

The Evolutionary Unique Self understands that each person's unique expression of love is needed in the world and that such love can become visible only from each of us living our Unique Selves and participating in our Unique We. You can feel into the sensual joy and potency of Evolutionary Intimacy by participating as an Evolutionary Unique Self in the Evolutionary We-Space.

Awakening to your participation in the Unique Self Symphony is the way both to heal the personal pain of your life and to participate in the very transformation of Reality itself.

CHAPTER 12

EVOLUTIONARY HEROES

As we move to transcend and incorporate role mate and soul mate, we must also transcend the concept of *hero* that arose with and infused those levels of relationship. This is crucial for whole mates, because our vision of the hero is deeply entwined with our experience of attraction, partnership, and purpose in our relationships.

Entry 1. The New Hero of Whole Mate Relationships

As we have seen, the old notion of male hero—protector and provider—was based on him being the primary breadwinner. Since we are heading into a generation where men may not be the primary breadwinners in the majority of homes, at least in the Western world, the classic male hero is becoming outdated.

How does the new, evolutionary notion of hero look like? How will the man be a hero? Women are wanting to claim their own role as hero as well. How will they do it? How will men access classic manhood in all of its best senses, and how will women access classic womanhood in its best senses? What will be the new vision of the evolutionary masculine and evolutionary feminine?

In this chapter, we will focus on the new vision of the hero. Articulating this vision is essential in the context of the evolution of relationships, because one of the most important topics explored by evolutionary science is what has been called *sexual selection*.

Our friend Geoffrey Miller, one of the leading experts in his field, wrote a fantastic book, *The Mating Mind*.[224] He basically says that the vision of a man that women are attracted to determines the course of history. Men will change, adapt, and transform for the love of a woman. What women find potent and powerful in men will shape the values of society. If men become killers-as-heroes, whether in war or on Wall Street, it is because women most valued men in that role of protector and provider. Every time there has been a leap in consciousness from one level to the next, it has been because women were not satisfied with how things were. Leading-edge men transformed themselves, in order to meet the desires of women. Women, however, did not only want men who were success objects. Leading sexual selection studies showed that women chose men because of an entire host of qualities including being kind, funny, or musically gifted. Women also chose men for their creative intelligence. Traits for which women would select included unique gifts such as storytelling, poetry, art, music, dance, sports, and leadership.

As Miller aptly points out, the attempt by old-school evolutionary psychologists to explain all of these traits in terms of their being good for survival is simply wrong. Women chose men who were kind because they valued kindness. Women chose men who were funny because they valued humor. To be clear, women loved men who had an authentic version of these unique qualities. They are qualities that require cultivation, audacity, and sensitivity. They are sexy and alluring in and of themselves, independent of their survival value.

Clearly, not only do men transform themselves for women, but women also transform themselves for men. Strangely enough, however, it is not quite the same thing. To get the distinction clearly, you just have to notice one cultural phenomenon happening at the time this book is being written. Even though marriage and family are no longer mandated by social or religious expectation, and sex is widely available outside of marriage, men still, for the most part, clearly understand the value of a partner. Men want women not only for sex, but primarily for love, home,

---

[224] G. Miller, The Mating Mind: How Sexual Choice Shaped the Evolution of Human Nature (2001).

and family. Men are not saying: *Why do I need a woman?* But according to the research conducted by Liza Mundy, women are asking in droves: *Why do I need a man?* When we talk about the new vision of how men become heroes, we are talking about the answer to this question.

A vision of evolutionary relationships is the essential challenge at this moment in time, and this vision must articulate what it means to be a hero in today's world. How we answer that question will change history. **If a man does not have his own internal sense of heroism that he brings to his life and relationship, he will be radically unfulfilled.** If he is not a hero in his own story, he will not be attractive to his partner, nor will he feel potent in himself. We can extricate ourselves from this downward spiral only through a new vision of a hero.

The only compelling way to articulate this new vision is to envision a hero from a different level of consciousness. What would a hero look like who was not living from ordinary love, separate self, role mate, or soul mate consciousness? The new vision of a hero must be rooted in a new sense of identity. A new sense of identity will then birth a new form of relationship. Those are the core components of the new vision that we have explored in this book. Now, we just need to tie the last pieces together elegantly.

Here it is, in a few short sentences:

- Unique Self is the new hero.

- Evolutionary Unique Self is the new hero.

- Outrageous Lover is the new hero.

Each of these are key dimensions of the new identity of both men and women. As we have seen, they are the key building blocks in the emergence of evolutionary relationships.

He is an attractive hero because he is awake as a unique expression of the evolutionary impulse. He is a hero because he is an irreducibly unique expression of the LoveIntelligence, LoveBeauty, and LoveDesire of All-That-Is, living in him, as him, and through him. He is a hero because he is lived as Love. He is a hero because his unique perspective and unique quality of intimacy engender his unique gifts that address a corner of the world that will remain unloved without him. He is a hero because Reality needs his service.

But here is a big new leap: *so is she*. He has the capacity to make room for her as a hero as well. Together they awaken as Unique Selves who form a Unique We. Together, their Unique We incarnates the evolutionary impulse.

He is a hero not merely because he takes the garbage out or has developed good communication skills. He is a hero because his unique gifts are absolutely essential to address a set of authentic unique needs. She is a hero for the same reasons. They come together in an evolutionary relationship to serve, as heroes, a vision larger than the aims served by earlier levels of relationship.

Unique Self, whole mate relationships are passionate because they are potent not only in the bedroom. We are moved not only by our partners' passion but by their potency in the world. That is sometimes manifest in public, but it is even more deeply manifest in their evolutionary intention for every act they do to be for the sake of the larger Whole.

Moreover, our whole mate, Unique We relationships are potent in the depth of their evolutionary partnership. We realize that in partnering with them, our Unique Selves will be realized in ways that might be impossible without them. A Unique We will be born through our partnerships with Unique Selves, which gives its own great gifts. Our new heroes have these realizations about each other. These realizations are the invitation of the new hero. This is the heroic quality of Evolutionary Intimacy.

In soul mate relationship, it is essential to know one another's love languages.

In whole mate relationships, that is insufficient. The love language of whole mates is Outrageous Love. Being in love is essential but not sufficient. Whole mates must each respond to the Universe, which has chosen them to be lived as Love.

If we want a new vision of what it means to be a hero, there is really no alternative to being a Unique Self. It is only from the deeper awareness of Unique Self that we can live our full attractiveness. You always fall in love with a person who is doing *their thing*. That is the way that the Outrageous Love of the Universe moves them. Since uniqueness is the force of Outrageous Love being lived through a person, it naturally evokes Outrageous Love in us.

We will often fall in love with powerful characters in movies who are not rock stars, kings, karate masters, or sports stars. We fall in love with them because we are getting to know their Unique Selves. The moviegoer does not have the perspective of the people who take part in the character's actual story. The moviegoer has what we might call *God's perspective*, or *Reality's perspective*. The viewer knows an enormous amount of facts, inner motivations, and history that is not available to the story's participants. For example, if the hero stands falsely accused, the movie viewer is often aware of his innocence, while the other characters are not. We see how he heroically navigates life, and we fall in love with him because he is heroically living from his Unique Self.

Now let's add something to this. Imagine that you are watching a fantasy movie about a kid who has been identified by the king as having particular gifts that are needed to save the kingdom. Perhaps these gifts will never be made known in the public realm. They are known only to him, the king, his parents (perhaps), his girlfriend (for sure), and a very close circle of intimate friends. He has a choice of whether to choose the path of fame and riches or to respond to the king's—or more accurately his Unique Self's—calling and to live a life that, on the surface, seems more ordinary. Imagine now that we follow him through the exploits of his life. We see the nobility of his character. We witness his private deeds of heroism. We fall madly in love with him. We are not falling in love with his capacity as a protector or provider. We are not falling in love with him because he is a success object. We are falling in love with him because he is a Unique Self Hero. We are falling in love with him because he is the personal expression of the evolutionary impulse needed at this moment in time.

The Unique Self Hero expresses his most genuine impulses freely and without constraint. He does so in a way that he knows is loved, valued, and precisely what is needed from him at the moment.

We fall in love with him because he is loved by the king. We see him as the good king sees him. We fall in love with him because he is chosen. We fall in love with him because his Unique Self and unique gift are needed by All-That-Is. Reality needs his service, so how could we not cheer him on? His heroism depends on being able to transcend ordinary love and access the current of Outrageous Love that animates, drives, and holds together All-That-Is. When our movie character demonstrates the qualities of the Unique Self Hero, when he awakens as Outrageous Love, we fall in love with him.

All of this demonstrates clearly that we fall in love and are fiercely attracted to Unique Self Heroes. We are attracted to and allured by Outrageous Lovers. Conversely, a movie will often depict rock stars, kings, karate masters, or sports stars who are boorish and bullying. Even though they are powerful success objects, and even though they are successful as protectors and providers, we detest them. They lack character. They lack nobility, higher purpose, and Unique Self grace and grit.

Being a success object in the classic sense has stopped being sufficient as an attractive force. In Chapter 4 ("Limitations of Soul Mate"), we saw that many women still want the man to be the primary breadwinner. Most women are not looking for that job. However, it also turns out that, against popular belief, women can be attracted to and fall deeply in love with a man who is not the primary breadwinner.

Women who were interviewed by sociologist Liza Mundy groped vainly for words to articulate the quality of a man that makes him sexy and attractive, regardless of whether or not he is the primary breadwinner. Words like *drive*, *intellect*, *motivation*, and *aspiration* came up. It was not that those exact qualities were critical, but rather that the women wanted the kind of man who, at his core, would generate those qualities. Both the women and Mundy were inchoately but authentically trying to find some language for a felt sense that a man could be compelling and attractive even without fitting into the classical role mate molds. But *how*, they asked? Mundy and her interviewees could not quite come up with an answer despite their best efforts. This was because they were trying to solve a problem on the same level of consciousness that created it. What they were reaching for was the vision of the Unique Self Hero that we are articulating here. The Unique Self Hero awakens as Outrageous Love incarnating the personal face of the evolutionary impulse. The Unique Self Hero has drive, motivation, intellect, and aspiration—all of the qualities that they listed as important.

Entry 2. A Generation in Need of Heroes

In a powerful way, a whole mate is an evolutionary role mate. Remember that role mate relationship is about surviving and materially thriving. Survival is not merely instinctual, as we pointed out at the very beginning of this book. Survival is a clear purpose and direction built into Reality itself. Reality moves toward more and more life. That is what the mysterious drive to survive tells us about the direction of evolution.

Since Reality is Relationship, all levels of Reality move toward creating deeper forms of relationship. It is natural, then, that for the entire first stage of relationship history, the first two drives of Reality—relationship and survival—became almost inextricably linked. Reality moved toward more complex forms of relationship, and Reality moved toward survival. When core needs for survival and thriving needed to be met, relationship naturally served those needs. Other values served by relationships—love, contact, companionship—were present, but not front and center. Moreover, as long as we were focused on surviving and thriving, whatever that meant at different periods in history, focusing on satisfaction and personal fulfillment did not make it onto the relationship agenda.

The First Shock of Existence and the Emergence of Role Mate Relationships

An important milestone in the emergence of human consciousness, often referred to as *dawn man*, took place when early hunter-gatherers confronted the possibility of death. When human consciousness came face-to-face with death, it resulted in what cultural anthropologists called the *shock of existence*, and what we have called the *first shock of existence*.[225]

---

[225] The term shock of existence seems to have been coined by philosopher Robert Creegan in The Shock of Existence: A Philosophy of Freedom (1954). A colleague,

Their conclusions are best summarized by Ernest Becker's classic work, *The Denial of Death*.[226] Becker reminds us that, in some real sense, the entire project of culture is an attempt to come to grips with this first shock.

Death happened for early humans just as it does in the animal world, but it was not an existential issue that caused dread. And yet, for Becker and other anthropologists, death was a force that drove a complex cultural project, one that has gone through many distinct permutations across cultures. Death became the driving cultural force, as humans became more and more aware of his separation from nature. As the hunter-gatherer societies emerged, the first rituals around death and dying appeared on the cave walls of southern France. At that stage, man still had a rather undeveloped sense of time. The goal was to survive the immediate threat of the tiger, the flood, or the drought.

The realization of death was the first shock of existence. This first shock deepened when early farmers emerged as more distinct and aware separate selves. Their new sense of self engendered the first shock of existence. The ability to store food removed the immediate threat of death. That created space that allowed man the reflective time to deepen into his sense of self apart from nature's rhythms of life and death. *Dawn man* emerged from his enmeshment with his environment and became aware of time and his own mortality. The new awareness of time also brought about the specter of time running out. He was terrified by the realization of his own demise. Death grinned at the banquet.

Every great ancient literature memorializes this first shock of existence in its myths. In the West, it is the foundation story of the exile from Eden. Man eats off the tree of knowledge and knows death for the first time. The consciousness of death has entered his heart and now becomes the core driver of his reality. The desire to erect edifices of thought, heart, and body that stand as a bulwark against death is a major motivating

---

Mauk Pieper, an excellent thinker in his own right, attended my seminars themed around Your Unique Self in response to collective existential crises in Holland between 2009 and 2013. He published a book entitled Humanity's Second Shock and Your Unique Self (2014), for which I gladly wrote an afterword. Mauk coined the term second shock of existence, which we happily acknowledge.

226 E. Becker, The Denial of Death (1974).

force of cultural evolution. One of the key emergents in response to this first shock is role mate relationships. Role mates stood together against death. Once agriculture emerged, men assumed the protector-provider role, and women assumed the homemaker-nurturer role.

Role mate relationships dominated the human scene until very recently. It was only when some level of survival and thriving was assured, and the roles associated with those goals were no longer socially or religiously mandated, that soul mate relationship took center stage. We no longer needed role mate heroes in the way we once did. Children also stopped being a biological and cultural imperative, so the roles of homemaker and mother were no longer a necessity. Despite all this, role mate did not disappear entirely. Other ways to survive and thrive presented themselves.

In soul mate relationship, the man was no longer necessarily the primary breadwinner, and the woman was no longer necessarily the homemaker and mother. Relationships became an end in and of itself. Soul mate was a great evolutionary step forward, but it had some significant limitations. It still understood itself in the context of personal life and death—personal wounds and personal triumphs. But, as we have seen, any crisis in relationships becomes an evolutionary driver for the emergence of the next level. Next in line was whole mate or evolutionary relationships.

The Second Shock of Existence and the Emergence of Whole Mate, Evolutionary Relationships in Response to the Meta-Crisis[227]

The emergence of relationships that serve a higher evolutionary purpose comes online just in the nick of time. Just as we are intuiting the first faint glimmers of being able to virtually defeat personal death, a far more devastating death looms on the horizon. This is not the first, but the second shock of existence—the possible death of our species.

Accompanying the second shock is the realization that our contemporary vision of success has failed in two ways:

---

[227] We discuss this topic at a greater depth in the companion volume, The Evolution of Love: From Quarks to Culture—the Rise of Evolutionary Relationships in Response to the Meta-Crisis.

First, our runaway technological success has ignored its impact on the larger Whole.

Second, success is considered primarily an achievement of the individual, group of individuals, or the individual state.

This vision of success is rooted in the limited consciousness of the separate self. It is not understood in the context of the larger Whole. It is not understood in a global and evolutionary context. The result is that individual successes are producing a series of devastating externalities that are about to cause a system-wide failure, commonly referred to as *death*. Death is grinning once again at the banquet.

There is a global crisis of dangerously dwindling resources. Whether the sense of impending doom comes from growing awareness around ozone depletion, peak oil, climate change, or global terrorism, the result is the same. Our planet faces huge global threats. Those threats could easily result in the loss of billions of lives. Those who will be hit hardest are the most vulnerable and destitute among us. These same threats could also destroy nature. They could easily invoke a death sentence on all of humanity.

What does it mean to grow up in the shadow of death? Noah's flood is being predicted again, and life goes on as usual. Why? Because if we truly let the fear in, we would not know how to respond. The threat is too large. What are we, as individuals, to do? Virtually every major threat confronting us requires global action. We have the technical capacity to gradually, but effectively, offer a significant response to every crisis facing the world today. **What we lack is a shared narrative to bring us together.**

We need a narrative that guides us into a deeper relationship with the larger Whole.

We have no shared language of meaning to unite us.

We need a common vision and a shared horizon.

We need a normative narrative that allows us to create a *we-space* beyond the seemingly powerful veils of separation.

We need a new story.

If this story is to hold us together and inspire us toward tomorrow, it must be a love story—not an ordinary love story but an Outrageous Love Story. **It is only the lived realization—lived cognitively, emotionally, and bodily—that the Universe is an Outrageous Love Story that will enliven us and enact the next stages of evolutionary emergence.**

Without such a narrative, separation feels insurmountable, boundaries impermeable, and borders hostile. We need a flag of Outrageous Love values around which we can rally. We need both a larger sense of identity and a new context for relating. Reality is Relationship. Reality moves to affirm life, to survive. With a new threat to survival, relationships and survival once again need to be integrated. Every crisis is an evolutionary driver. Every challenge to survival has created a new form of relationship. Every crisis births a new form of relationship. Today is no exception.

Outrageous Acts of Love

The new context for relating is the new narrative of the Universe: A Love Story. The love story of our relationships is not separate from the larger context of the Whole. Our love story supports the Love Story of Life. As whole mates, our relationships support the larger Whole. But the Whole has become much larger than it was at earlier levels of relationship. The larger Whole has become the largest context. It includes all human beings, all sentient beings, and the planet itself.

Evolutionary whole mates do not give up any of the depth and beauty of soul mate relationships. Quite the opposite. Soul mate love itself has evolved from ordinary to Outrageous Love. We realize that the unique allurement between lover and beloved is not merely between the two of them. Rather, their unique allurement is all of Reality being fulfilled through them. In evolutionary relationships, lover and beloved awaken as Outrageous Love, feeling the evolutionary impulse beating in their hearts. There is no split between looking deeply into each other's eyes and looking at a shared horizon. There is no difference between the Outrageous Love exchanged between us and the Outrageous Love that animates and drives Reality.

We feel the Eros, energy, and passion of all of Reality moving through us. Our love is outrageous. It is Life itself, awake as us, seeking the next phase of its emergence. We awaken as the Evolutionary Love that moves the entire evolutionary process. We stand not as separate selves or ordinary lovers. We stand as Evolutionary Unique Selves coming together in the Unique We of evolutionary relationships. We are, together, an irreducibly unique expression of the LoveIntelligence, LoveBeauty, and LoveDesire that animates all of Reality. We have a unique gift to give that is needed not only by each other and by our children, but by All-That-Is.

That does not necessarily mean that our job is to start a social movement or to run for Congress. To be a Unique Self means that your unique perspective and your unique quality of intimacy has a unique gift to give that addresses a unique need in your unique circle of intimacy and influence. We awaken as Outrageous Love. We realize that *as* Outrageous Love we must act. We move to commit the Outrageous Acts of Love that are ours to commit. Which Outrageous Acts of Love are those? Those that are a function of our Unique Self or Unique We.

Our role, as individuals and as evolutionary couples, is not to do *everything*. It is to do that which is ours to do. But even before anything is done, there is a significant shift we can make. This shift evolves our context for relating. It marks the transformation from soul mate to whole mate relationship. It is a shift not in action, but in intention. We continue to do the same things, but with a different and deeper intention. We love each other, we work on personal transformation, we raise our kids, we give our gifts, not only for the sake of our local lives, but for the sake of the larger Whole. When we begin to act for the sake of the larger Whole, we become whole mates.

Entry 3. Whole Mates, Outrageous Love, and the Emergence of the Evolutionary Hero

Whole mates are the new heroes. The hero always feels outrageous pain and moves to respond heroically. In the classic hero's journey, however, it was almost always about his own pain. His own wounds or pain might have included those of his family, his clan, his nation, or his religion. The hero embarked on this journey in order to heal and transform. The hero's journey was a primary feature of soul mate relationships. Each partner had his or her own hero's journey. Each held space and witnessed the hero's journey of their partner. This was the essence of soul mate relationships.

All of this is true at the level of whole mate relationship as well. But evolutionary relationships add a crucial dimension. The pain the hero feels is larger. There is an evolution of tears. The whole mate evolves from an egocentric or ethnocentric context of relating to the worldcentric context of relating. In a worldcentric context, all human beings matter. The new hero evolves even further, to the cosmocentric context. He or she is connected to the pain of the larger Whole. He or she wants to act as a hero for the sake of the larger Whole.

The evolutionary hero wants to be part of something larger than herself. She wants to be part of a powerful response at this moment in history when we stand before a *tale of two futures*. One future is a world interconnected by bonds of empathy and love that encircle the planet. The second is a fragmented and splintered world of ethnocentric conflict, brutal violence, and horrible loss of life that results from all the ways we have failed to take care of each other or the planet.

Today, *normal* consciousness is insane. Normal consciousness says that we are all separate from each other and that we need to compete with each other for success and status. That is insane. *Insane* means that it is out of touch with Reality. Insanity is to go about business as usual, as if there is no existential threat to our survival as a planet. *Insanity* means to be OK with about two hundred million people being killed in wars and conflict in the twentieth century.[228] Sanity is to know Reality and to

---

[228] M. Leitenberg, Deaths in Wars and Conflicts in the 20th Century, 2006, https://cissm.umd.edu/sites/default/files/2019-08/deathswarsconflictsjune52006.

come into right relationship with Reality. To know Reality is to know the absolute, scientific knowledge that no one is truly separate from anyone else. It is to know that, because of this profound system interconnectivity, every action we take affects the Whole.

When we feel that our child is in danger, we have the energy and power to save her. That is the power of the mother. The father goes to war to protect his wife and children and the larger community in which they live. We feel the outrageous pain that might touch our people, and we move with fierce courage to protect them. That is the power of role mate relationships.

To be an Evolutionary Hero, then, is to feel the outrageous pain beyond your narrow circle of interest. It is to have the power to save not only *your* child but all the children of the world. If your child is sick, you stop business as usual. You investigate every possible option to save them. When you engage evolutionary consciousness, this becomes true not only for *your* child, but for all the children of the world. You access the warrior mojo of the hero, and you act in service to the people you love. When you evolve to a genuine worldcentric consciousness, you love personally even the people you do not know personally.

That does *not* mean, however, that you need to take on the mission to *save all the children of the world*. As we pointed out earlier, trying to reach for something so large without the alignment of your Unique Self shuts your heart rather than opens it. When the gap between our ability to feel the pain and our ability to heal the pain is too wide, we close our hearts.

As an Evolutionary Hero, you need to access your power to address the unique need in your unique circle of intimacy and influence that is beyond the needs of your own narrow circle. When you wake up as an Evolutionary Hero, you commit Outrageous Acts of Love that are not about serving your *self* in a small sense. They are about expanding your sense of *self* to include wider and wider circles of intimacy. When you begin to think in this larger evolutionary context, you begin to access Evolutionary Intimacy. Again, that does not mean you have to save everyone. It means two things. First, you have to do what is yours to do. You address the unique needs that your unique gifts can address. Second, you have to offer up all of your personal work for the sake of the healing of the Whole.

That is what it means to an Evolutionary Hero. You access the energy to lift a car not for *your* boy, but for *all* boys. You charge the barricades not for *your* girl, but for *all* girls.

When Evolutionary Heroes come together in relationship, you have evolutionary relationship. It does not nullify soul mate romance. It includes all of soul mate but adds the crucial new dimension of the hero. This is what it means to be a whole mate. Feeling the pain of the larger Whole is a joy because feeling it means you are connected to the larger Whole. If you are connected to the larger Whole, you can impact the larger Whole.

This is the longing that every unique being shares. We want to live outrageously. We want to play a larger game. **Our deepest yearning is always Reality's deepest need.** Reality needs you to play a larger game. It is when this yearning becomes democratized that greatness becomes democratized. It is only when greatness is democratized that the Unique Self Symphony activates. We can no longer respond only to our own narrow needs. Reality's need is your deed. But Reality needs not only your egocentric deed that takes care of your own survival and thriving. It needs not only the deeds of true love, commitment, and presence you offer to your soul mate. Reality also needs your unique deed that addresses the unique need in your unique circle of intimacy and influence for the sake of the larger Whole.

Evolution awakens as you in person. There is a precise lock and key match between your unique gifts and the unique needs of Reality. This is true not only for you, but for everyone. **Every Unique Self, giving their unique gifts in the larger context of a Unique Self Symphony, unleashes virtually infinite resources for the healing and transformation of every form of pain on the planet.** Every person commits their Outrageous Acts of Love for the sake of the larger Whole. Only Outrageous Love responds to outrageous pain.

You were born at precisely the right place and right time. You have the exact gifts that Reality needs. You are precisely what is necessary. Reality needs your gifts. Knowing that Reality is precisely designed to be healed by your unique gifts transforms bravado to authentic confidence. We live in a world of outrageous pain. The only response to outrageous pain is Outrageous Love.

Outrageous Love is a universal Field of pulsing kindness that you tap into and deploy with delight in your life. Its quality merges the affection of a grandmother and the erotic charge of a lover. Even though the erotic charge might never actually manifest sexually outside of your romantic relationship, it is both the context for transformation and the energy of transformation.

Let's face it. Outrageous Love is the only force that can change the planet. Outrageous Love enacts the Possibility of Possibility. The challenges that face us in this moment are truly global. The old world of merely local challenges is over. In order to meet these challenges, we must come together in a new way. **We need to evolve our consciousness to a point where we are capable of fostering an Evolutionary We-Space that can take concerted and effective global action.** Global threats need global solutions. Global solutions need the consciousness of a global community. The evolution of consciousness necessary to facilitate this mode of Evolutionary We-Space is no less than the evolution of love. The evolution of love happens when love awakens to its true nature. This is not an abstract or generalized process. Love awakens to its true nature in you. This happens when you awaken to the realization and practice of Outrageous Love. You transform from an ordinary lover to an Outrageous Lover.

CHAPTER 13

JOINING GENIUS: A CASE STUDY

Editor's note: In this book, like in many other writings on CosmoErotic Humanism, Marc Gafni and Barbara Marx Hubbard not only join voices, but speak from their *joined genius*. This book and its powerful vision of whole mate, or evolutionary, relationship emerges, in this very specific sense, from the relationship type it envisions for all of us—from the unique configuration of intimacy which could only exist in Barbara and Marc's Unique We. But in this very special chapter, Barbara and Marc speak in their individual voices to allow us a glimpse of how it actually happens: how Unique Selves come together and birth new ideas from the Evolutionary We-Space. The first part of the chapter is written by Barbara Marx Hubbard in March 2019, the second, by Marc Gafni. Originally, these stories of intellectual and visionary emergence were written as prefaces to the book, but it became clear later in the editorial process that they can only be fully heard and received after you have read the book and understood its core concepts.

Barbara's Story

Many years ago, following in the wake of Julian Huxley, Teilhard de Chardin, Buckminster Fuller, Hindu cosmologist Sri Aurobindo, and others, I wrote of a new worldview that has been arising since the Renaissance, and crystallized in the nineteenth century. I described this worldview as the culmination of all of human history, wrote a book with its name as a title, and dedicated my life to inseminating that meme into culture in every way I could.

It is the worldview of *Conscious Evolution*.[229]

I articulated this vision in terms that were something like this:

In the past, evolution was unconsciously operating by chance. We knew nothing about its operation. We were unconscious to evolution, and evolution seemed unconscious to itself. Today, for the first time in history, we are conscious of the evolutionary process. But even more powerfully, we understand that we are not separate from the process. We *are* evolution. The evolutionary impulse beats in our hearts. Evolution becomes self-reflective in our self-reflection. Evolution becomes conscious of itself in us, as us, and through us. Evolution awakens to itself in our consciousness. This is the movement that I have described as *the momentous leap from unconscious to Conscious Evolution.*

Conscious Evolution, with its focus on human activism, holds the promise of fulfilling the great aspirations of the past and heralds the advent of our next stage of evolution.

In the past, our glorious visions of the future—heaven, paradise, nirvana—were thought to happen after death. The newer thought is that we do not have to die to get there. We are not speaking of life after death in some mythical heaven but life more abundant in real time in history. We are speaking of the next stage of our social evolution, which will take place through the human awakening to Conscious Evolution.

In 1966, I had a particularly strong spiritual vision of Conscious Evolution. In a flash, I was catapulted into the future. I saw human

---

[229] B. Marx Hubbard, Conscious Evolution: Awakening the Power of Our Social Potential (2015, originally published in 1998).

knowledge and social systems meshing into a positive, empathetic force. What Christ and all the great beings came to Earth to reveal is, *we are one, we are whole, we are good, we are universal.* What we add to that perennial wisdom is that we are evolution becoming conscious of itself. This insight came with the message, *"Go tell the story, Barbara."*

We Need a Story Equal to Our Power

My first husband, Earl Hubbard, who first introduced me to this worldview, often said that when a culture has a story that everyone understands, it gives direction and meaning to that culture. When people no longer believe that story, the culture disintegrates. Or, as Marc Gafni often says, *when the story no longer meets the depth of our experience, and no longer weaves together in an integral fashion all the threads of our lives, then it can no longer guide our personal and collective evolution, and culture itself dangerously disintegrates.*

When I was a sixteen-year-old girl, my father brought me to meet President Eisenhower. I spoke to him of the bomb. I asked him what the meaning of our new power was. He said to me, "Young lady, I do not know." I understood at that moment that we had no story equal to our power. It was this conversation with the president that originally spurred the search that led me to the realization of Conscious Evolution as the New Story equal to our power. Since that conversation in the midfifties of the last century, our power has increased exponentially as has, in direct proportion, the need for the Story of Conscious Evolution.

The following is an extract from a letter that Marc Gafni, Zachary Stein, and I wrote as part of an invitation to the recent leadership conclave for the Center for World Philosophy and Religion.

> The evolution of culture and consciousness must include a new story of power. If we have the power of ancient gods, we must become the new gods. But by *new gods* we mean the New Human and the New Humanity who have realized our Divinity and are willing to take exponential responsibility for our exponential power.

We went on to say:

> Exponential power has already created exponential goods—the great dignities of modernity, from human rights to the goods of modern medicine to democracy, to name but a few. But our new power has also already created exponential suffering. These are not the dignities but the devastations of modernity. Often the goods themselves carry with them their own new pathologies. Such is the case with modern medicine. Such is also the case with the goods of exponential tech, including infotech, biotech, and nanotech, all of which create enormous promise and an equal amount of peril.

This is the polarity inherent in our new power. Let's look at one often overlooked set of facts. Our new power has exploded human life on the planet from half a billion to more than seven billion persons, which is itself a stunning expression of the innate goodness of our power. We have healed disease in ways that were unimaginable before the modern evolution of our new power.

But, as Marc Gafni so often points out to challenge the naive techno-optimists, at the same time, the number of people suffering on the planet from starvation and alienation in all of its distressing disguises is *objectively* higher than at any other time in history. When you move from half a billion to seven billion people, and two billion people are suffering intensely, you have objectively, at the very least, quadrupled the amount of suffering. This simple fact is regularly ignored by thinkers like Steven Pinker, Mathew Ridley, and the techno-optimists, who hold only the dignities of modernity while all too often shifting their gaze away from its disasters.

This is but one of myriad expressions of the catastrophic risk, and hence radical responsibility, inherent in our evolution into exponential power. But beyond even catastrophic risk, the exponential evolution of our power has also generated *existential* risk—risk to our very existence on the planet.

It is for these reasons that, as Marc and I wrote in that letter,

> The emergence of our exponential power must co-arise with the emergence of exponential love. It is only in such a manner that we will have the capacity—the power—to meet both catastrophic and existential risk. The evolution of our power, via exterior technologies, must be matched by an evolution of love, via interior technologies. The greatest interior technology is a new story. Story is the organizing power of evolution.

Or, as our dear friend, cultural critic, and philosopher of science Howard Bloom, Marc Gafni, and I said it recently on a podcast together, "It is the capacity to tell a new cultural story that has forever been the engine of cultural evolution." Only a story of exponential love will arouse us to exponential responsibility.

Power is not an evil or abusive force to avoid, as it is often presented. Rather, power is a quality of the Divine, whom we refer to as the *Infinity of Power*. It is in that sense that we often say: *absolute powerlessness corrupts absolutely*. We must love our power and invest it with the most potent force of all, the power of our love, exponential love.

New Meaning of Conscious Evolution

Before we met, Marc Gafni had already written profoundly and poetically about Evolutionary Spirituality and Conscious Evolution.[230] While our world views were both anchored in complexity theory and evolutionary science, he was only loosely familiar with Buckminster Fuller, Teilhard de Chardin, and Aurobindo, who had been my three primary sources of influence.

And yet, Marc reminded me more of Bucky Fuller than anyone else I had ever met. In a letter I wrote about him, I went as far as to say that he was the natural inheritor of Bucky's mantle. But that is not because Marc is a scientist. He is not. As more insightful people than myself have noted,

---

[230] See the two beautiful chapters on Conscious Evolution and Evolutionary Spirituality in Your Unique Self: The Radical Path to Personal Enlightenment, by M. Gafni (2012). See also his core construct of Evolutionary Unique Self in Chapter Four of the same work. The book you are holding in your hands contains Marc's most extensive writing on Evolutionary Unique Self.

Marc absorbs science into his very cells—but not based on the mathematics of cosmology but rather based on the memetic implications. And it was Howard Bloom who told me that Marc is a "brilliant and original philosophical reader of the hard sciences." It is in that very specific sense that he evokes Buckminster Fuller. While drawing on entirely different sources, he, like Bucky, naturally envisions and experiences Reality as an organismic Whole with axioms in both the interiors and exteriors that operate across the Whole in every domain.

Much of Marc Gafni's work revolves around Eros, evolution, and unique identity, as they impact our Universe Story and our narrative of identity. His work derives from a close reading of science as well as a combination of his own interior experience and a set of Hebrew lineage sources entirely different from the work that informed me. These were texts of what he refers to as *the interior sciences*, sourced in contemplative traditions including Kabbalah, the nondual Tantric Shaivism of India, and many other parallel sources.

Marc Gafni traced for me the emergence of Conscious Evolution from Hebrew mystic Isaac Luria's Renaissance Kabbalah, to the Christian Kabbalah of the same period, to Hegel, Fichte, and Schelling in Germany, who are commonly thought to be the founders of Evolutionary Spirituality. I was also intellectually stunned and wonderfully surprised to read a section on his website entitled *Evolutionary Kabbalah*, which he prepared in 2004, translating key Hebrew mystical Renaissance sources which were clearly telling—in marked contrast to the Eastern religions of eternal return—a proto-evolutionary story, at whose very center was the evolution of consciousness as the evolution of God. The apex of this virtually unknown tradition, which Marc has brought to life, included the twentieth-century evolutionary sage Abraham Kook, whose writings were sourced in what Marc and I call *evolutionary mysticism*.

Originally, I thought that the new Story of Conscious Evolution meant that we are moving from unconscious evolution by chance, through natural selection, to Conscious Evolution by choice. In this crucial view, which I dedicated my life to championing, the human being becomes the decisive active agent in charting the next stage of evolution. In this moment, when we have the power to destroy the world, we also awaken to our roles as Conscious Evolutionaries with the capacity to create heaven on Earth.

Our crisis is a birth. This has been true throughout the arc of evolution: **every crisis is an evolutionary driver**.

I stand fully with the seminal insight of Conscious Evolution, but my thinking about what it really means has significantly deepened and evolved. I now realize, based on in-depth research and shared exploration with my evolutionary thought partner Dr. Marc Gafni, that the articulation of unconscious evolution as a purely random process moved only by the mechanism of blind selection is *not* the most true, good, or beautiful story we can tell. In this vein, I want to amend my classic formulation, which describes the move from unconscious evolution to Conscious Evolution as the move from evolution by chance to evolution by choice.[231] Rather, I now understand, together with Marc, Conscious Evolution to refer to *our* awakening to evolution as being awake and alive in us. It is not that *evolution* is becoming conscious but that *we* are becoming conscious.

Marc and I discussed this important evolution of Conscious Evolution in a shared white paper on Conscious Evolution, written for the members of our activist think tank, The Center for Integral Wisdom,[232] and our Foundation for Conscious Evolution. Here is but a portion of that white paper, which I will cite at some length because of its relevance. We will expand these ideas in future work, but this section from our paper will be enough to convey this more evolved understanding of Conscious Evolution.

> While there is a methodology of evolution that includes a dimension of randomness, nonrandomness is built into the Heart of Cosmos. We speak not of a cosmic vending-machine

---

[231] Evolution was never unconscious, nor was it purely driven by chance. And yet, there is a new level of choice in what we call Conscious Evolution: the human being consciously choosing to participate in the evolution of the Whole through their own evolution.

[232] The Center for Integral Wisdom was renamed as Center for World Philosophy and Religion in 2023.

god who is outside the world, waving a wand and creating fixed structures, but of an evolutionary God, whose face is the innate inherent intelligence of the evolving Cosmos, which, in at least much of its significant expression, is nonrandom in the extreme. Here is but one of countless possible examples:

Millions of years ago, the force of evolution generated *mitosis* and *meiosis*[233]—the two forms of cellular reproduction that are the true evolutionary drivers of basic biological life forms. These are fundamental processes of life, which came into play long before there was a human neocortex anywhere on the horizon. The generator of mitosis and meiosis was clearly not merely blind chance—these processes are so dazzlingly precise and sophisticated that even our most powerful supercomputers exponentialized have not been able to generate them. Mitosis and meiosis, like the entire evolutionary process, disclose such levels of self-evident elegantly resplendent and complex symmetry and blinding beauty that one cannot but gasp with awe. Paraphrasing physicist David Bohm, mitosis and meiosis make no sense independently of the innate informational intelligence of evolution's implicate order.

The attempt of what Alfred North Whitehead in the early twentieth century and Rupert Sheldrake[234] in the early twenty-first century identified as the blind faith of dogmatic materialism to dismiss the inherent intelligence of Cosmos as mere chance defies both simple and statistical facts and has nothing to do with genuine science. It is not the result of investigation nor is it the fruit of the scientific method. This kind of dogmatic claim is no less fundamentalist dogma than that which is

---

[233] Mitosis is the process of cell division. All the different types of cells in a body can undergo mitosis. Meiosis is the process of producing eggs and sperm in sexual reproduction.

[234] See R. Sheldrake's important book critiquing the dogmatic materialism of science, The Science Delusion (2012).

asserted by the premodern religions in their most distressing modern disguises, including the fundamentalist claim of a non-evolutionary, de-facto intelligent design of reality from a god who is utterly transcendent to Cosmos.

Moreover, the denial of the self-evident *telos* of Cosmos driven by its own inherent evolutionary attractors flies in the face of Occam's Razor, as expressed in the Latin motto, *Simplex sigillum veri*—the simple is the seal of the true—inscribed in large letters in the physics auditorium of the University of Göttingen.[235] Science appropriately rebelled against the medieval god. It was and is a crucial battle for the sake of the Good, the True, and the Beautiful. Evolutionary mystic Abraham Kook beautifully described this holy rebellion of science against the corruption of truth in the premodern religions as "Heresy which is Faith."

But science itself now needs to evolve. We need to say to science, "The god you don't believe in doesn't exist. But beware, men and women of science, of becoming the new oppressor who downloads depression and malaise into the Heart of

---

[235] This is a paraphrase of Werner Heisenberg, who made similar points in much of his writing. See W. Heisenberg, Across the Frontiers (1974). On Heisenberg's understanding of the revelatory power of simplicity and beauty, see Physics and Beyond: Encounters and Conversations (1971). The German title of the book conveys more of its content, Der Teil und das Ganze = The Part and the Whole. This citation is from a conversation between Heisenberg and Einstein: "I [Heisenberg] believe, just like you [Einstein], that the simplicity of natural laws has an objective character, that it is not just the result of thought economy. If nature leads us to mathematical forms of great simplicity and beauty—by forms I am referring to coherent systems of hypotheses, axioms, etc.—to forms that no one has previously encountered, we cannot help thinking that they are 'true,' that they reveal a genuine feature of nature. [. . .] You may object that by speaking of simplicity and beauty I am introducing aesthetic criteria of truth, and I frankly admit that I am strongly attracted by the simplicity and beauty of mathematical schemes which nature presents us. You must have felt this too: the almost frightening simplicity and wholeness of the relationships which nature suddenly spreads out before us." [Thanks to our editor Kerstin Tuschik for this reference.]

Reality by claiming that Cosmos is driven by pure chance and ignoring the self-evident, inherent, creative, erotic intelligence that animates the self-actualizing Cosmos." As we have often discussed with philosopher of science Howard Bloom, Reality is not only moved by the causal push of the past. Cosmos is also drawn forward by the causal pull of the future.

There is a self-evident *telos* or direction, which is inherent to Reality. It is time for science to disambiguate the battle against fundamentalist religion from its own fundamentalist claim that rejects the obvious innate *telos* of Cosmos. Science brilliantly describes some of the ways that matter, energy, and life operate in Cosmos deploying its unique methods of measurement, which include mathematical abstractions and instrumentation. But only a nonscientific dogmatic materialism that is willing to fly in the face of incontrovertible evidence would suggest that Reality is not self-organizing to ever deeper and higher levels of dazzling depth, complexity, and consciousness. As the epic mathematician and philosopher of science Alfred North Whitehead continually reminds us, each new level of emergent evolution is clearly not only the result of prior causes but of the inherent evolutionary attractor toward tomorrow.[236]

That is precisely the notion of synergistic emergence that is the backbone of evolutionary science. Emergence is by definition inexplicable without a larger inherent self-organizing movement toward ever-deeper patterns of complexity, coherence, relationship, and elegant order. Each new whole is, at every level of Reality's emergence, greater than the sum of the previous parts. The very nature of evolutionary emergence is that yesterday contains insufficient ingredients in its prior parts to generate the wholeness of today.

---

[236] See for example the excellent series of essays by leading Whitehead scholar, David Ray Griffin, Religion and Scientific Naturalism: Overcoming the Conflicts (2000), especially Chapters One, Four, and Eight.

Reality is drawn forth by its own inherent *telos* or nature toward ever deeper and wider wholes. In that precise sense, the interior experience of every human life is both evidence and expression of the entire evolutionary process.

We human beings, like all of evolution, are defined not only by the memory of our past but by the memory of our future. Both materialist psychology and evolutionary science are just now, at their leading edges, beginning to correct their shared pivotal mistake, the notion that today is determined only by yesterday instead of being drawn toward transformation by the call of tomorrow.[237]

This, of course, does not mean that previous stages derive their value only as instrumental handmaidens to later stages. To borrow Holmes Rolston's distinction, plants and animals have not only instrumental value but intrinsic value.[238] It also does not suggest a kind of Pollyannaish notion of progress of the kind so often evinced by the likes of Peter Diamandis and the techno-optimists. Every new level of emergence brings in its wake new potential pathologies.

That is what we mean when we say that exponential tech creates potential exponential suffering and even extinction. Nuclear drones are more destructive than bows and arrows. And yet the inherent *telos* of evolution is clear. Reality moves from elementary particles to bacteria to Bach, from mud to Mozart, from matter to life to mind. Reality is drawn forward by a self-evident inherent *telos* of ever-increasing levels of wholeness. This is not merely the result of yesterday's

---

237 In psychology, see for example Homo Prospectus, by M. Seligman et al. (2016); in science, see for example, The Science Delusion, by R. Sheldrake (2012), especially Chapter Five.

238 See Environmental Ethics, by H. Rolston III (1989).

causation but the pull of the future.

But my meeting with Marc Gafni created an even more fundamental change in my understanding of evolution. I used to talk about evolutionary emergence, following Teilhard de Chardin, as moving to higher levels of complexity, freedom, and elegant order. When I met Marc, he spoke of the same evolutionary impulse, but he added an entirely new dimension, which included but transcended the way I described Reality in my book *Conscious Evolution*. Marc spoke and wrote of evolution moving toward *ever-deeper levels of intimacy*. In fact, the **progressive deepening of intimacies** is, in Marc Gafni's view, the primary trajectory of the evolutionary story.

Based on his extensive study of the biological sciences, a deep grounding in the interior sciences, and his own evolutionary mystical experience, he described evolution as being the *evolution of intimacy*. For Marc, in very specific and scientific ways, *evolution is the evolution of intimacy*, or what Marc has long referred to as the *evolution of love*. But for Marc, and now in our shared work, love is not merely a metaphor or simile. Love is not merely a mythopoetic form of expression. When I once asked Marc to sum up his life work in three words, he said the *ontologizing of love*, or said somewhat differently, *Love is Real*.

When Marc and I join the Reality of Love at the foundation of Cosmos with its self-evident *telos*, we breathe new life into what I have called before, and we now call together, *Teleros*, or the *Telerotic Universe*. In Marc's and my own shared nomenclature, *the CosmoErotic Universe is the Telerotic Universe; the Amorous Cosmos is the purposeful Cosmos.*[239]

---

[239] Before integrating this notion of the Intimate Universe, I had written of the brutality of evolutionary process. Certain responses, which took my writings out of context, understood my words to mean that the unconscious part of humanity that does not have the capacity to wake up to Conscious Evolution needs to be somehow purged in the process. My intention was not to imply that we humans ever had the right to participate in such a purging, but that it would be an inevitable by-product of the evolutionary process. I thought that would be self-evident to any feeling being, but in retrospect could have been made more explicit. Sometimes, the obvious needs to be said more explicitly. As I integrated Marc's understanding around the Intimate Universe, I was infused with an almost unbearable love for every human being, and I stand fully in our sacred obligation to protect in the most

Joining Genius

For the reasons I have shared and many more, the encounter with Marc Gafni felt like a rare meeting of two evolutionary mystics, both entrained at the same frequency of evolution's pulsation. We compared texts, personal histories, and mystical experiences and were able to generate a new whole greater than the sum of either of our parts. I have worked with Marc, in these latter years of my life, to *join genius*[240] and co-author books that would tell this true, good, and beautiful evolutionary story in as many ways as possible.

I realized that locating our new power in the New Story of Conscious Evolution was by itself not enough. Rather, the next step of Conscious Evolution needs to be contextualizing Conscious Evolution in the core memes that Marc is articulating through multiple terms, including *the Intimate Universe, the evolution of intimacy, Evolutionary Love* and *the evolution of love, the Universe: A Love Story, Outrageous Love,* and *Homo amor*.[241] Merging these memes with *Conscious Evolution*, based on the best information available today on the planet, is, as Marc often says, the urgent moral imperative of our time. This has been the animating ecstatic urgency and gravitas of my *joining genius* with Marc.

In many ways, these have been the happiest years of my life. I had never met someone whose evolutionary impulse was so resonant with my own. I was finally able to collaborate with another mystic thinker in the way that I had always hoped.

I have also never met anyone as kind or filled with integrity as Marc. I have witnessed him in the most joyous and the most painful moments and have never seen him ultimately close his heart or turn away from love,

---

appropriate ways, all of life.

[240] I created this term, joining genius, a long time ago, but it was only in my shared work with Marc Gafni that it really came to life for me, and my deepest heart's desire was fulfilled.

[241] I originally used to deploy the term Homo Universalis to refer to the emerging New Human. Marc deployed the term Homo amor. For a while we used—and still do—the term Homo Amor Universalis. But in the end, the clarity and simplicity of the term Homo amor, which includes the elements of Homo Universalis, has won my heart.

even when he chose to turn away from a specific form of relationship. In some sense, Marc's heart has been broken by life. He lives in the pain of immense personal and collective suffering. But through some grace, he transmutes the pain into love that seeks the next stages of not only personal but evolutionary emergence. I never ceased, in these years, to be dazzled by the joy and exuberance that characterizes his original brilliance.

As I wrote several years ago in a public letter,[242] I believe Marc to be a direct heir to my own teachers, de Chardin, Bucky Fuller, and Aurobindo. He has added crucial dimensions to the vision of *Conscious Evolution*, and I am sure that, through this thought, teaching, and convening, he will ultimately emerge as one of the most important evolutionary leaders of our time.

Finally, as I have written in several public communications,[243] after thousands of hours of in-depth research and conversation with Marc and many others, I am also proud to stand not only for his greatness but for the depth of his goodness and integrity.

I have asked Marc to take responsibility, if I should pass, for bringing our shared work into the world. This volume and its sister volume are just a first entrée to the series of volumes that Marc and I, together with Dr. Zachary Stein and others, intend to share in the next years. I cannot state clearly enough how important I believe this work to be. These volumes contain, from my perspective, the crucial next steps in Conscious Evolution.

---

242 See "Barbara Marx Hubbard about Marc Gafni," November 2015 (http://www.marcgafni.com/barbara-marx-hubbard-about-marc-gafni/).

243 See "Barbara Marx Hubbard Telling the Truth about Stephen Dinan's Smear Campaign against Marc Gafni" (video), http://www.whoismarcgafni.com/2016/08/barbara-marx-hubbard-tells-the-truth-about-marc-gafni-controversy/) and "Barbara Marx Hubbard Is Speaking Out for the Evolution of Public Culture" at (http://www.whoismarcgafni.com/2016/05/barbara-marx-hubbard-speaking-marc-gafni/.

Marc's Story

Loving Your Way to Enlightenment

Like so many of us, I have always been unreasonably moved by love in all of her outrageous forms. Love has ceaselessly exalted my heart, shattered my life, caused me unimaginable suffering, and gifted me with unspeakable, almost unimaginable joy. Love has evolved, clarified, and even purified its intentions in me over the years. For all of it, I am wildly grateful to love. And I know well, in my own life, the truth of the interior sciences: *there is nothing more whole than a broken heart.*

Since I was very young, all I have wanted to do is love everyone as deeply and intensely as possible. The notion of limiting love to one person, to one nation, to one idea, to one place feels unbearably painful, even as I happily know that love demands from me intense singular focus on the utter uniqueness and irreducible quality inherent in every encounter, be it fleeting or forever. It is the work of a lifetime, or many lifetimes, to clarify the nature of our LoveDesire, disambiguate love from grasping, and learn to truly live with an open heart.

My deepest heart's desire in life is to love and give as much as I can, as deeply as I can, as widely as I can, and as purely as I can. In the depth of true love, giving and receiving become one. Nothing else matters. Every day I seek to clarify my love, to evolve my love, and to purify my love. And I remain, as we all do, an imperfect and even flawed vessel for the light. That is the nature of Infinity disclosed in finitude.

I began my story with a mad love for sacred texts, particularly from the Hebrew and Aramaic lineages of Hebrew wisdom. It was in the subtle weavings of the ethical pietism of the *Talmud*, the mysticism of *Merkava*, the Eros of the *Zohar*, the heroic audacity of the writings of Luria and the Hasidic masters that made me feel at home in the world.

For years, I poured over sacred text as a form of intellectual mysticism—with the deliberate intention of erotic merger with the Divine. I was driven by a yearning to become a sacred text myself. All I wanted was to become Outrageous Love—a unique expression of Outrageous Love—myself. I wanted to *love my way to enlightenment*.

But I knew in my heart, mind, and body that this yearning was not original to my being. It was the core movement of *apotheosis*, the desire to realize our True Nature, the Possibility of Possibility that lives in the depth of all the sages, yogis, avatars, and saints in every era and in every part of the world. *Apotheosis* is the yearning to realize our literal participation in the LoveDesire, LoveIntelligence, and LoveBeauty of Divinity, and in doing so, come home to the fullness of our Original Identity, to live uniquely as Love itself. It is this unbearable longing that has rigorously allured me for my entire life.

It was, however, only later that I realized that this is not merely the province of the leading edge of spirit or thought. It is rather the deepest (albeit often unconscious) yearning of every human being. Every time we are on our knees, we are always on our knees to God. We are devastated by our alienation from our own Divine LoveIntelligence.

We want to honor and follow this yearning home on a collective level. The manifestation that would emerge from this collective coming home to our most authentic selves[244] is what I began to call, many years ago, *the democratization of enlightenment*. I began to realize that it is only such a democratization of enlightenment that can ground a new emergent order, a new cultural enlightenment of the kind and quality that is crucial for our very survival as a species.

It is true that we must not lose our devotion to the masters in every field. But it is equally true that we will not be saved by elites. Ultimately, every woman, man, and child must drink directly from the waters of Realization.[245] We are, each of us, the unique intimacies of the Divine Field of LoveDesire, who madly loves us, even as He/She/It lives, yearns, and loves *as* us.

---

[244] These authentic selves live below what Nobel laureate Daniel Kahneman called our fast thinking. See Thinking, Fast and Slow, by D. Kahneman (2011).

[245] The vision is ancient. See, for example, Jeremiah 31:34 ("No longer will they teach their neighbor, or say to one another, 'Know the LORD,' because they will all know me, from the least of them to the greatest," declares the LORD. "For I will forgive their wickedness and will remember their sins no more") or Habakkuk 2:14 ("For the earth will be filled with the knowledge of the glory of the Lord as the waters cover the sea"). But as is the case with most of the ancient realizations, we now live in the time when these great visions can be realized.

Unique Self Realization

In the late nineties, I began to write about what I originally called *Soul Prints* (in a book by that name), and later in the same book, I began to refer to it as *Unique Self*.[246] Realization of our irreducible uniqueness within the greater Field of Being and Becoming, not in the Myers-Briggs character-structure sense but as a unique expression of the seamless coat of the Universe, seemed to be utterly essential in taking us the next step. Sharing the good news of Unique Self became core to my calling.[247]

At the same time, in a second book, *The Mystery of Love*,[248] I began to realize that without a new vision of Eros, rooted in the evolutionary impulse itself, we would not be able to transform either ourselves or our planet. I understood then that all ethical breakdowns, personally and collectively, are ultimately rooted in a failure of Eros. **Eros, evolution, and Unique Self needed to be brought together in a memory of our future, a vision of the New Human and the New Humanity.**

Barbara met the evolutionary impulse and Conscious Evolution in the pages of Teilhard de Chardin, Sri Aurobindo, Julian Huxley,[249] and later in the thinking of Jonas Salk and others. I had never read any of them.

I met the evolutionary impulse and Conscious Evolution early in my intellectual development in the pages of my teachers Mordechai Lainer and Abraham Isaac Kook, their teacher Luria, and the masters of the *Zohar* and *Talmud* who preceded them.

At some point, I realized that I needed to move beyond my ethnocentric joy and commitment. I found philosophers—from Plato, Kant,

---

246 Gafni, Soul Prints.

247 Gafni, Your Unique Self. See also Chapter 7, "Unique Self."

248 Gafni, The Mystery of Love.

249 It was Julian Huxley who was one the first contemporary figures to voice the idea that, in the mind of modern humanity, evolution had become conscious of itself and that therefore the future of evolution is taking place through us, consciously. Huxley expressed this idea in many places and was echoed by many of his contemporaries, such as Teilhard de Chardin. One of the more interesting places the idea appears in print is in the essay "Transhumanism," by J. Huxley, in New Bottles for New Wine (1957), 13–18.

and Saussure to Sartre, Rorty, and many more. I devoured literature of all kinds. Kashmir Shaivism and the tantric strains of Buddhism allured me.

And then, at some later point, my focus moved from the *interior* sciences—as I have just described them in the preceding paragraphs—to the *exterior* sciences. Math, physics, molecular biology, and more seduced me with their wonder. Anthropology, emergence science, the implications of evolutionary microbiology, deconstruction, perennial philosophy, postmodernism, and Integral Theory, each beckoned at the door.

The years 2002 to 2003 were the beginning of a long, deep, wondrous and tumultuous, intellectual and spiritual friendship with Ken Wilber, which generated both great love as well as new chapters in Integral Theory (e.g., Unique Self) of which I was privileged to be the founding theorist. Our discussion on the Personal Quality of Divinity beyond the Impersonal— what I have called *the Infinity of Intimacy*, or *the Infinite Intimate*—helped catalyze other chapters (e.g., "Three Faces of God"). Ken and I also co-initiated what we referred to as *World Spirituality based on Integral Principles*; co-founded the Center for World Spirituality, which we later renamed together as the Center for Integral Wisdom, and it ultimately evolved into the Center for World Philosophy and Religion; and talked for many dozens of hours over almost two decades, birthing new chapters in the Future of Love and Integral Sexuality.

My own academic work, including the two volumes on Solomon's Wisdom, *Radical Kabbalah*,[250] which I originally called *Nondual Humanism*, was mediated through the prism of Integral Theory. In particular, the survey of structure stages of consciousness was pivotal in inserting a developmental lens at the heart of my work. *Wake Up* and *Grow Up* (the clarion calls of Trungpa Rinpoche, and later of both Ken and our colleague John Welwood)—and later *Show Up*, *Open Up*, and *Clean Up*—were reformulated in my writing and mediated through the prism of Unique Self.[251]

---

250 Gafni, Radical Kabbalah.

251 My beloved friend and co-parent, Mariana Caplan cites Trungpa Rinpoche's student, John Welwood, who reports that Om Mani Padme Hum Grow Up, which in effect means Wake Up and Grow Up, was a classical invocation of Trungpa Rinpoche (Om Mani Padme Hum means "Praise the Jewel in the Lotus" in Sanskrit); see Eyes Wide Open: Cultivating Discernment on the Spiritual Path by M. Caplan (2009). This

Waking up refers to contemplative stages of enlightened consciousness, where one realizes the Infinite and Eternal Ground of Being that imbues all of finitude. One has a direct experience that all evolutionary manifestation is literally in-formed by the Eternal. The direct knowing of this truth is what is referred to in multiple traditions as *waking up*.

Some lineage traditions emphasized the quality of the Infinite Personhood in Spirit, and others focused on the more Impersonal Quality, sometimes called the *Tao*. As I have explored in depth in Unique

---

phrase was a classical call to enlightenment, whose deeper hermeneutic is beyond the purview of this footnote. This phrase, Wake Up, Grow Up, was later echoed and published by Trungpa's student John Welwood, a close colleague and mentor of Mariana's and later my good friend for a number of pivotal conversations toward the end of his life (See the dialogue John Welwood and Marc Gafni: "The Phenomenology of Unique Self—In Dialogue with Buddhism: An Intimate Conversation, Thought Leader Dialogues" (https://tinyurl.com/welwood-gafni)). John deployed Wake Up to refer to enlightenment and Grow Up to refer to spiritual maturity, within a psychological context (see Toward a Psychology of Awakening by J. Welwood (2002), p. 6). In parallel to John but independently of him, these terms were deployed by Ken Wilber. Wilber (who, like Welwood, was a close associate to Trungpa and his circle) deployed Wake Up and Grow Up very differently from John. For Ken, Wake Up refers to classical enlightenment (states of consciousness) and Grow Up refers to levels of developmental (stages of consciousness). Three terms were later added. The first was Clean Up by Dustin Diperna to name Wilber's emphasis on shadow work. I used the term Lighten Up to describe this same dimension of shadow work. I also, in various iterations of the work, added the term Open Up to refer to the opening to the unique channel of amor, or Evolutionary Love, that flows through you. Show up was added independently first by Dustin and later by myself. I deployed it to refer to a new chapter in Integral Theory that I developed identifying the consciousness of Unique Self (later to become Unique Self Theory). The sense of it is to Show Up as the unique incarnation of the LoveIntelligence that lives as you (i.e., simply to Show Up as your Unique Self). Ultimately, Unique Self Theory, and now CosmoErotic Humanism, deploys all five terms to refer to the multiple expressions of the Eros of Unique Self. CosmoErotic Humanism understands classical enlightenment as the realization of the Unique Self Expression of your True Self Consciousness (a unique expression of the One Field of Consciousness) and shadow as Unique Shadow, a distortion of your unlived Unique Self. Grow Up as well moves toward Unique Self as a core quality of the highest levels of development. Thus, in Unique Self Theory, all of the core terms, Wake Up, Grow Up, Show Up, Clean Up, and Open Up refer to different dimensions of Unique Self (see World Spirituality Essentials by M. Gafni (https://tinyurl.com/world-spirituality-essay)). One of my projects, in collaboration with Zachary Stein, is to publish a complete essay on World Spirituality in our upcoming volume, Homo Amor Essays. For now, however, see https://worldphilosophyandreligion.org/world-religion/.

Self Theory, these are two sides of the One that we have direct access to in our own experience. We access the Intimate Personal Quality of Cosmos, even as we access the surging Impersonal Lifeforce that pulses through everything. Being radically informed and enlivened by the lived Reality of both dimensions is the full experience of waking up.

Growing up refers to evolving through developmental stages of consciousness. At each stage, there is a new set of values, a new sense of identity, a new set of needs, and a new sense of purpose and community. These levels of developmental consciousness were famously mapped by Jean Gebser, and later by Clare Graves, to name but two of literally dozens of theorists that have drawn overlapping maps of developmental levels.

The great traditions had an inkling that your social or economic matrix as well as your character are prisms through which your contemplative experience of enlightenment is filtered. For example, one text in the interior sciences of Hebrew wisdom argues that one's *vision of the Divine Chariot*[252] (that is, *waking up*) is directly changed by one's cultural/social context, particularly whether one dwelled in a city or village.[253]

The point of this passage is that enlightenment is not a given. It is filtered through our cognitive frameworks. But this realization was esoteric and underdeveloped. This understanding has been deepened by the leading edges of contemporary interior sciences into the crucial realization that waking up is mediated through the prism of growing up. The core insight of waking up and growing up is that your waking-up experience (your state) is mediated through the prism of your level (or stage) of consciousness (growing up).

This is a crucial realization. Let's say, for example, that you are at a tribal level of consciousness—a stage which was dominant historically in the premodern period but continued into modernity and is reemerging in the currents of retribalization around the world. At this tribal *level of consciousness*—which might be called your *level* or *stage of growing*

---

[252] A core feature of the mystical experience, called Ma'aseh Merkava, the Story of the Chariot, in Hebrew mysticism, sourced in the mystical visions of the prophets Ezekiel and Isaiah.

[253] Talmud, Tractate Chagiga.

up, you experience a contemplative *state of consciousness*—what we will refer to as a *state of waking up*. At a tribal stage of consciousness, you will experience your state of waking up as God speaking to only your people who are chosen, or you might experience the enlightened quality of Infinite Consciousness as living uniquely in your people and your land. If you further evolve your level of consciousness (growing up) to worldcentric consciousness, the exact same contemplative experience (waking up) will be experienced by you as Divine Cosmic Force, Personal and Impersonal Cosmic, that suffuses, embraces, or addresses every human being and every nation. Thus one's state experience of waking up is interpreted through one's level of growing up.

After many years of research and study, I understood that it is in Unique Self Realization that *wake up* and *grow up* meet and merge. For it is only in the higher stages of development—what are often referred to as the *second tier* of developmental levels—that Unique Self clarifies as one's natural life compass.

For example, Don Beck, a close student of developmental master Clare Graves, contacted me excitedly after reading the Unique Self book,[254] saying, this book is *the Bible of Yellow*, yellow being the color that, in the Spiral Dynamics system that Don Beck teaches,[255] had been symbolically assigned to the first level of the second tier of developmental consciousness[256] (growing up). That first level is defined by the person being able to locate their own authority and creativity not in their separate-self personality but rather in their Unique Self, their irreducibly

---

254 Gafni, Your Unique Self.

255 Graves didn't use colors, but certain letter combinations, for the levels of Spiral Dynamics. It was his students Chris Cowan and Don Beck who attached colors to his system.

256 The co-arising of Unique Self and one's developmental center of gravity is what we have called (with Zachary Stein) Unique Voice. For a deeper discussion, see Gafni, Your Unique Self, 441-442 and 448-452; K. Wilber and M. Gafni: "Unique Self Dialogues" (audio podcast episodes, https://tinyurl.com/wilber-gafni-us); 2011 Special Scholarly Issue on Unique Self of the Journal of Integral Theory and Practice, 6 no.1, ed. by M. Gafni [as guest editor]; Susanne Cook-Greuter & Marc Gafni: "Unique Self & Development" [audio podcast episode, Part 1: https://tinyurl.com/Gafni-Cook-Greuter-US1 & Part 2: https://tinyurl.com/Gafni-Cook-Greuter-US2).

unique expression of the Field of Consciousness.

At the same time, Unique Self (as opposed to an earlier stage, separate self) is the unique expression of your *True Self*, which is the state of contemplative or meditative consciousness that is often referred to as *enlightenment*.[257] Waking up and growing up, states and levels of consciousness, merge in Unique Self.[258]

At the center of everything was always love—what I came to call *Outrageous Love*, or *Evolutionary Love*. By *Outrageous* or *Evolutionary Love*, I mean Love, or Eros, as a First Principle and First Value of Cosmos—the Love that is not a mere social construction or fiction but rather the eternal and evolving Heart of Existence itself.

Unique Self means that we are each unique configurations of that Evolutionary Love.

I realized that the Universe, at its core, only makes sense as a Love Story.

And our personal lives only make intellectual, spiritual, and scientific sense if we understand that our love stories are not merely the personal drama of our lives, but rather our love stories are chapters and verses in the Universe: A Love Story. Our personal evolution is chapter and verse in

---

[257] Enlightenment, as the term is generally used in mysticism, is generally not a permanent feature but, more often than not, a state of consciousness (that is, a passing temporary state). But in the interior sciences—for example in Sufism—a more stable enlightenment is also described. This is based on what Integral Theory refers to as state-stages, which is when the passing states stabilize or can be accessed more or less at will.

[258] My dear friend, with whom I co-founded the think tank, Ken Wilber, in his later work The Religion of Tomorrow, writes that it is only the Self at the final level of third tier, or what he calls the white (or clear) light level (p. 240), or what Aurobindo called the supermind, that can be called Unique Self—or Unique Suchness. We could say that in second tier, you can know that you are a Unique Self, you get it intellectually, you may even have had peak experiences of waking up on all state-stages (gross, subtle, causal, nondual), or you may even have some kind of stable realization of these, in the sense of personal enlightenment. But at third tier, these dimensions become permanent features of your structure states of consciousness. You have a permanent awareness of awareness, and you can, in Ken's terms, first, see gross wholes, then, feel subtle wholes, then, witness causal wholes, and finally, be nondual wholes. So, in that sense, it is only at that highest level where you can finally be your Unique Nondual Self.

Evolution: The Love Story of the Universe. Our personal transformation participates in, and is even cause for, the transformation of the Whole.

Even evil can only be approached and recognized, and therefore healed, if we understand that the Universe yearns for ever-increasing levels of love, recognition, union, and embrace. It is only in that context that we can even articulate the depth of our cry against both suffering and evil. The mystery of suffering and evil can only be approached at all if we understand that we live in an Intimate Universe, and evil is a failure of intimacy. Without this understanding of the Intimate Universe, there is no mystery of suffering, there is only the pedestrian banality of suffering. And that is existentially intolerable, which is exactly how we know it is not true.

Gradually, the outlines of what I came to call *the Universe: A Love Story*, or *the Intimate Universe*, began to become apparent, and a new species, a New Human and a New Humanity, which I, together with Barbara and Dr. Zachary (Zak) Stein, termed *Homo amor*,[259] began to disclose itself. All of the work of the last decades began to self-organize as a new school of thought, which we have called *CosmoErotic Humanism*.

The Evolution of Conscious Evolution

CosmoErotic Humanism, as we are describing it here and in other writings, is the next step after *Conscious Evolution*. My dear evolutionary partner and co-author, Barbara Marx Hubbard, has been called *the mother of Conscious Evolution*. In our collaboration, she shared so much that was of value and wonder, and we were also able to evolve together the presentation of Conscious Evolution.

In the old presentation, as Barbara articulated it over the years, unconscious evolution meant two things:

1. Until now, evolution has been unaware of itself.

---

[259] I originally suggested the term Homo amor, Barbara had deployed the term Homo Universalis. But they meant very different things. Homo Universalis was connected with a kind of techno-optimism, which I did not fully share with Barbara, while Homo amor was related to the realization of that the CosmoErotic Universe lives in us personally. We are personally implicated in the Whole, the Whole is Eros, and as Homo amor we are omniconsiderate for the sake of the Whole in response to the meta-crisis.

2. Until now, evolution has been a chance process, or what Barbara called *evolution by chance*.

These two points reverse themselves in Conscious Evolution:

1. Evolution has only now become conscious of itself through human awareness of evolutionary processes.

2. We can now move from what Barbara called *evolution by chance* to *evolution by choice*.

This early understanding is important, inspiring in certain ways, and true, but, as Barbara and I understood together in many conversations, only partial. We must evolve our understanding of Conscious Evolution. In our new understanding, we do not mean by *Conscious Evolution* that evolution becomes conscious of itself for the first time through us, for five reasons:

First, evolution, from the beginning, possesses its own intrinsic consciousness. In other words, evolution is inherently—at some level of depth—intelligent or conscious.[260]

Second, the consciousness that inheres in evolution is evolving. The evolution of consciousness inherent in the evolutionary process has evolved through stages, from matter to life to mind, and through all of each of their substages (e.g., within matter, the evolution from elementary particles to atoms to molecules). As Reality dances into becoming, from matter, to life, to the depth of self-reflective mind, and through all the sublevels of each, consciousness clearly evolves. That does not mean that evolution is a linear movement of ever-more consciousness in all regards, in which the earlier is always lower and the latter always higher.[261]

---

[260] See M. Gafni et al., Three Universe Stories: Beyond Scientism and Creationism: CosmoErotic Humanism (https://worldphilosophyandreligion.org/three-universe-stories-beyond-creationism-and-scientism-cosmoerotic-humanism/).

[261] In Hebrew wisdom texts, for example, thinkers and evolutionary mystics point to the dialectic between what is called Yeridat Hadorot, the descent of the generations, as history moves away from the original revelations of Sinai (1200 BCE),

According to a vast literature of various forms of empirical observation, for example, bacteria, anthills, and beehives seem to have depths of super-organism consciousness that human beings have not yet cultivated. Indeed, the simple exercise of epistemic humility[262] reminds us that we do not have interior access to the quality of consciousness of any dimension of Reality other than our own. At the same time, there are dimensions of consciousness that most definitely seem to evolve in some genuine fashion. For example, there would seem to be a clear evolution of potentials for goodness, truth, and beauty. To the best of our knowledge, there are no hospitals caring for the vulnerable in the wild, nor is there a general felt sense of kindness, care, or sacrifice for the sake of a stranger who is not of one's kind.[263]

Moreover, in the worlds of matter and life, there do not seem to be creations of art, drama, music, literature, or the like, as we know them in the human world of value, including the classic triad of goodness, truth, and beauty. There also does not seem to be a process that transmits and evolves truth through bodies of knowledge, like science or moral philosophy. It is, therefore, fair to say that, although evolution possesses innate consciousness at the cellular and even, perhaps, the molecular level, there is also an evolution of consciousness.

Third, in the evolutionary process, eventually, human beings emerge, who are more evolved or advanced expressions of consciousness than anything before. As such, they have the capacity to become aware of the entire evolutionary process.

---

and the evolutionary movement of ever-clearer discernments of Reality in both its interiors and exteriors. Historians David Graeber and David Wengrow, writing in their opus The Dawn of Everything, similarly complexify the simple linear view of evolutionary emergence.

262 On epistemic humility see: M. Gafni et al. Three Universe Stories: Beyond Scientism and Creationism: CosmoErotic Humanism (https://worldphilosophyandreligion.org/three-universe-stories-beyond-creationism-and-scientism-cosmo-erotic-humanism/).

263 The cute videos of animals nursing babies of another species are exactly so adorable because they are clearly exceptional, and we don't know the mechanism behind that phenomenon. And yet, they point to the continuity even within the discontinuity of this sort of behavior.

Fourth, as part of that process, human beings have become self-aware to the extent that they consciously realize that they are part of the process. The human being at the leading edge of consciousness self-identifies as evolution. In other words, the human being can speak the identity statement *I am evolution*, and more particularly *I am an irreducibly unique expression of evolutionary intelligence, desire, and intimacy.*

Fifth, all these qualities together have generated the *Anthropocene*, a world in which human choice has virtually infinite impact on the course of evolution. And the human being is consciously aware of the power of choice. This is clearly a new level of Conscious Evolution that is just coming alive in this period of human history. In that sense, it is accurate to say that evolution is becoming aware of itself in what may be a qualitatively different way than ever before.[264] It is the emergence *not* of Conscious Evolution itself, but of a dramatically new stage of Conscious Evolution, in which human choice can either create a more beautiful future than we have ever known—or destroy the future.

This next iteration of Conscious Evolution is infinitely more hopeful (and accurate) than the old view of Conscious Evolution. In the old view, human consciousness was alone in the Cosmos, alienated from the evolutionary process, which was said to be unconscious. In the more evolved view of Conscious Evolution, human consciousness is rather the next stage of emergence in a fundamentally Conscious Universe.

Thus, human consciousness can align with, and be supported by, the inherent consciousness of Cosmos. The human becomes not the inventor of the Good, the True, and the Beautiful, disassociated from the larger Field of Cosmos, but rather the evolutionary expression of the next stage of Value unfolding in, as, and through human consciousness. This is the realization that we are participatory in Cosmos and not alienated from Cosmos. Conscious Evolution in human form is a momentous leap but not a dissociative leap—the next stage of unfolding

---

[264] Of course, as pointed out earlier, we do not have absolute clarity on this claim, because we do not know the interior consciousness of, let's say, cells at an earlier stage. It is true that cells do not seem to be writing poetry, but they are rewriting their own genetic code when in crisis, and the quality of consciousness required for that is unclear to us as we have no direct access to it.

in the Conscious Universe.

Responding to the Second Shock of Existence

All of my work in one form or another has been focused exclusively on one point: the healing and transformation of suffering through telling a new validated Story of Value rooted in First Principles and First Values that transcends a particular religious orientation and can serve as a shared basis for a common grammar of value.[265]

At some point, however, my work shifted from personal existential to collective existential. I realized, somewhere around 2009 or 2010, as a number of us did, that the level of risk we faced in the world—the potential death of humanity—was the *second shock of existence*. The *first shock* was the realization of personal death at the dawn of history. This realization generated the momentous revelations of spirit that we call the great religious and spiritual traditions. But I gradually understood, together with close colleagues at the leading edge, that we are facing the second shock of existence—not the personal death of the individual human but the potential death of humanity. I realized that only a new vision of identity and a new Universe Story could respond to the second shock of existence.

Then, around 2012, right before Barbara and I met, something happened. I was about to share a teaching on Skype to a group of some fifty students in Europe, but I could not find any words. The intense pain of the previous years welled up and choked my heart and chest. As the wave of pain rolled through, I went silent. The students thought it was a silence of presence, but in truth, it was a silence of absence. I had nothing left to say. I thought to myself in the apparent emptiness of that silence: *This is the end. I must stop teaching. I cannot find the Shekhinah,*

---

[265] Until 2006, I did this work in the context of rereading Hebrew and Aramaic lineage texts and attempting to discern their import both to the Jewish and global community with the intention of fostering a language that could bridge the false divide between the ostensibly secular and sacred. In 2008, due to a tragedy in my life, my orientation shifted to evolving the source code of consciousness and culture in the form of the articulation of a universal grammar of value for the global community. I remain, however, fiercely honoring the sages and practices of my original lineage even if that honor lacks vessels to hold its intention.

She, the Goddess, inside of my heart anymore.

Then, somehow in the very long silence—I am not sure how—I began to talk. The words truly did not come from me. The following sentence spilled out:

We live in a world of outrageous pain. The only response to outrageous pain is Outrageous Love.

And the entire teaching of Outrageous Love, mixed with the next level of the Eros and Unique Self teachings, poured out of my shattered but ecstatic heart. When it was over, my dear friend Sally Kempton, who had been in the other room writing, said to me:

Something happened today. I took notes on the teaching for
you, so you would have it. It is important.

And she very kindly gave me the notes because I remembered none of it.

I turned my attention to Eros, the evolution of love, the evolution of intimacy, the tenets of intimacy, and the laws of Outrageous Love—looking at all of them from a deeply structural perspective, enlisting the gamut of exterior and interior sciences. Just like the great traditions emerged in response to the first shock of existence, the second shock of existence generated in myself, Barbara, and our colleagues known and unknown around the world, a new Universe Story. The volume you hold in your hands is but one the first expressions of the larger current of the new Universe Story of *Homo amor* and CosmoErotic Humanism. The first volume of CosmoErotic Humanism was published in early 2024. It is called *First Principles and First Values: Forty-Two Propositions on CosmoErotic Humanism, the Meta-Crisis, and the World to Come,* by David J. Temple. David J. Temple is a pseudonym created for enabling ongoing collaborative authorship at the Center for World Philosophy and Religion, a leading international think tank whose mission is to address existential risk by articulating a shared universal Story of Value for global intimacy and global coordination. The Center focuses its work on a world philosophy, CosmoErotic Humanism, as the ground for a global vision of value, economics, politics, and spiritual coherence. The two primary authors behind David J. Temple are myself and Zak Stein. For different projects specific writers will be named as part of the collaboration. In *The First Principles and First Values*, we are joined by Ken Wilber. Barbara is of course deeply integrated in the voice and heart of David J Temple.

Now, with true joy, love, and honor, I turn to my meeting with Barbara.

Joining Genius

Let's go back a bit. It was somewhere in the midst of all of this, in 2013, that I met Barbara. The first meeting was special but never would have unfolded further due to the intensity of each of our commitments and the natural inertia of our very different lives. Then, in early 2015, our close mutual friend Daniel Schmachtenberger persuaded us both to spend several days together with him at Barbara's home, recording an early course, which, after many conversations, we called *Becoming a Future Human*.[266] The meeting turned out to be pivotal on many levels.

In Barbara I met someone who shared a profoundly similar resonance. As she often phrased it, the evolutionary impulse—at least in part—resonated in the same frequency inside of us. We were both passionately committed, with very great Evolutionary Love merged with a sense of sober yet ecstatic urgency, to weaving together a new story of humanity in direct response to the looming existential risks of our age.

There was great creative joy between me, Barbara, and Daniel Schmachtenberger in our respective dyads. It was Daniel, however, who envisioned the next step of collaborative love and depth between himself, me, and Barbara. One day he called me and Barbara and enrolled us, with all of his wonderful certainty, in meeting for five days at Barbara's house and recording a course together, which would, he thought, bring our respective work into alignment and new synergy. Daniel was and is

---

[266] "Becoming a Future Human: Changing the Source Code of Reality: A Gift and a Call to Play Your Full Role in the Birth of a New Humanity" (2018), Center for World Philosophy and Religion Courses (https://cosmoerotichumanism.shop/avada_portfolio/becoming-a-future-human-changing-the-source-code-of-humanity/).

a beloved close friend, unique collaborator, and brother, so how could I say *no*? And he had grown up in some sense in Barbara's house, and she loved him dearly, so how could she say *no*?

Daniel was convinced that the synergizing of three sets of memes would be world historical in its impact. First, the memes of CosmoErotic Humanism,[267] which I was articulating and which I had shared with Daniel in hundreds of hours of deep-dive conversations. Second, Daniel's own deep work on the meta-crisis, the hard problem of consciousness, and the new structure of world civilization needed to respond to this moment in time. That was a topic that was also at the center of my work with Zachary Stein, before we met Daniel, and we had published a key article on it in 2011 that was called "Responding to the Second Shock of Existence," and much else. Third, Barbara had spent decades championing and deepening Conscious Evolution and what she called the Wheel of Co-Creation as an expression of Conscious Evolution, a response to what she already saw as the impending meta-crisis and named as such in innumerable presentations spanning many decades.

Emerging from this time with Daniel at her home was a special creative relationship that flowered between Barbara and me in the last five years of her life. It was not a romantic relationship but rather what I called a *whole mate relationship* and Barbara called *joining genius to co-create*.

Barbara and I were personally delighted and moved by the historic invitation to model what it might mean to *join genius to co-create*. For all those five years, Barbara and I communicated, quite literally, some three to four times a day—pretty much every day. Much goodness, truth, and

---

267 My work at the time was (and still is) together with my student and today full partner and collaborator Dr. Zachary Stein, the co-president at the Center, and my dear friend and brother Ken Wilber, the co-founder of the Center, and the key leaders and thinkers gathered around the think tank. Part of the context for the work at the time was the twenty-five or so biannual mystery school and wisdom schools, the two Integral Spiritual Experience events I had initiated, convened, and invested with new chapters of Integral Theory, together with Ken Wilber, Diane Hamilton, and Sally Kempton, as well the Success 3.0 Summit, which I initiated and convened together with John P. Mackey and Kate Maloney, and last but far from least, the Outrageous Love Project with my beloved Dr. Kristina Kincaid. All of these persons and many more were part of the fabric of the Center, and all of them received Barbara with enormous love, honor, and delight.

beauty flowed from our conversations. Our years of shared creativity and joining genius were creative, beautiful, and painful—often excruciatingly so. The potency of the joining was threatening. Barbara, in her audacity and courage and utter disregard for *process and politics*, had generated some political maelstroms that took root in the usual fertile grounds of human weakness. Through all of it—much of which was painful and devastating—we kept close daily contact and never stopped studying, practicing, laughing, drinking wine, and creatively agonizing for a better world. Barbara and I truly became what we call in this book *whole mates*. We recognized each other in our respective depth and greatness as well as in the pain of our respective lives. My beloved romantic and evolutionary partner Dr. Kristina Kincaid and Barbara also loved and honored each other with enormous grace and beauty.

Barbara and I had joined genius to co-create. We started a weekly online community that we called Evolutionary Church, later renamed as One Mountain, Many Paths. We articulated what we called the Wheel of Co-Creation 2.0, gave a course on what we called The Five Keys, where we sought to integrate CosmoErotic Humanism and Conscious Evolution,[268] studied texts, and engaged in profound spiritual practice together every week, literally until several days right before Barbara died.

Barbara was sharp as a whip, her mind and heart acute and alive, with almost indefatigable energy till right before she passed. I talked to Barbara in the hospital on Friday night, and she was strong and resonant. Her doctor said she would be fine. When I called the next morning, her doctor said there had been an incident in the early morning hours. I asked him to hold the phone to her ear, and I said good morning, and she called out with all of her wonder and beauty, *Maaaaaarc*, after which she lost consciousness and passed three days later. I was honored to be at her bedside for those three days.

Barbara's favorite set of distinctions in CosmoErotic Humanism was the whole mate teaching we present in this book, which, as I have noted, paralleled Barbara teaching of moving beyond joining genes to

---

268 The Five Keys and the Wheel of Co-Creation are the subjects of their own forthcoming volume based on the course transcripts and other original writings that we did together.

joining genius.

It was a time of wild and sacred creativity, *two mad geniuses* in Barbara's depiction, *joining genius to co-create*. We were in love with life, with co-creation, feeling the full pain of the world and the call to tell a new Story, joined in the first stages of writing what came to be called *Great Library of CosmoErotic Humanism*.

I would not say that Barbara's spirit never wavered. That would indicate not spiritual greatness but narcissistic obliviousness. It is more accurate to say that, whenever Barbara's spirit did waver, she went—often in shared conversation and meditation, or in her own process of journal writing, walking, and good afternoon wine—to find ever-new inner resources, courage, and audacity. She literally renewed herself, and sometimes me with her, day after day. I am proud of how we walked together in these years. Barbara, in her own self-description, *did not get older but newer every day*.

During these years, we brought together two sets of memes:

The first set of memes was not originated but championed and clarified by Barbara over many years. This set of memes was around Conscious Evolution, joining genius, *Teleros*, and what Barbara called *Homo Universalis*, which incarnated the positive dimension of the new technologies in the vision of the New Human. I think it would be accurate to say that Barbara is more responsible than any other human being for inseminating the crucial meme of Conscious Evolution into culture and consciousness. She was not only a wonderfully bright and alive thinker. She was also, and perhaps even more importantly, the greatest evolutionary storyteller of our time.

The second set of memes, which I articulated, revolved around the themes I described as central to CosmoErotic Humanism, including the move from *Homo sapiens* to *Homo amor*, the Intimate Universe, or what I also have referred to over the years with great delight as the *Amorous Cosmos*, the *CosmoErotic Universe*, the *Universe: A Love Story*, or *Evolution: The Love Story of the Universe*, as well as the *future of relationships* with the movement from *role mate* to *soul mate* to *whole mate*, this last being the primary topic of this volume, to which I will turn in a moment.

Together with our colleague Dr. Zachary Stein, I named the New

Human and New Humanity *Homo amor*, as a direct refutation of the reductionist and even nihilistic image of *Homo sapiens* and *Homo deus* suggested by our colleague Yuval Harari.[269] Finally, in a meeting with Barbara, Zachary, and Dr. Kristina Kincaid, I called the meta-theory that emerges from *Homo amor* and all of its corollary distinctions *CosmoErotic Humanism*.

Before Barbara passed, I promised her to bring our shared work into the world, in order to participate, with so many others, in the critical evolution of consciousness, which is the evolution of love, that is so desperately needed at this moment. Indeed, we memorialized, in a legal document, the titles and names of the books to which we were committed. Our intention in these books, together with our close colleague Zachary Stein, is to download these distinctions and *Dharma* into culture through the Great Library of CosmoErotic Humanism.

A Word on Power

Finally, one more word on *power* is perhaps in order. One of the key topics that we discussed time and again between ourselves was the issue of power—and particularly the level of existential risk created by exponential power. Barbara has already alluded to these conversations. I will just add a cultural context, which perhaps conveys the utter centrality of the issue of power.

Think for a moment of the epic *Star Wars* Saga. *Star Wars* is, of course, a primary artifact of a contemporary cultural evolution narrative. It tells of a Universe, in which the *Empire*, and later the *First Order*, ultimately succeeded by the *Final Order*, harness and deploy exponential power. It begins in the form of the *Death Star*, a battle station equipped with the capacity to destroy an entire planet with a single blast (Episode IV), and climaxes in an entire fleet where every single starship is equipped with this same level of technology of planet-destroying power (Episode IX).

Indeed, the name of the first planet destroyer, the *Death Star*, aptly captures the nature of existential risk. And the Death Star can cause both the first form of existential risk, extinction events, as well as a second

---

[269] See works by Y. N. Harari: Sapiens: A Brief History of Humankind (2015) and Homo Deus: A Brief History of Tomorrow (2018).

form of existential risk, the destruction of the character of a species through technocratic control, in which freedom, nobility, and love are all but extinguished.

And it is not by accident that the key method to combat the Death Star is the telling of a better Universe Story that is equal to the realization of the depth of inherent power that the Universe makes available, through different channels, to every species. The Jedi, for example, reject the story of power told by the Sith, and instead, articulate a deeper and more accurate vision of the Universe rooted in a more good, true, and beautiful story of power.

But in many ways, the Jedi's story was incomplete. For example, it left out the dignity of desire. The only image intended to convey sexual desire, in all of the *Star Wars* episodes, is Princess Leia being forced to dress as a sex object for the sake of the ultimate caricature of degraded desire, Jabba the Hutt. There is no other narrative of desire in the Jedi order. It is not insignificant that the Jedi could not marry or fall in love. In multiple ways, the Jedi split off the fullness of Eros, rather than integrate its dark side. Indeed, Palpatine uses Anakin Skywalker's intense LoveDesire for Padme to *seduce him to the dark side*.

But for all of its weaknesses, some of which we will correct in this and other writings, the epic got something very right. Culture is transformed by the telling of a better story. The story of the Force is, at its core, a love story. For the Force is no less than the Force of Eros, which binds all things together, which lives in each of us and is the deepest plotline of Reality.

The Universe Story in *Star Wars* was naturally imperfect, but the reason the saga attracted such intense devotion for over fifty years was because we know that we need a new story. And that the new story must be a Love Story, not a pallid love story, limited to ego selves, but an Outrageous Love Story—the ontology of Love—that is the Heart of Existence itself. It must be a Love Story, because that is the true and mysterious Nature of Reality, as it lives in us and the greater Whole.

EPILOGUE

THERE ARE NO EXTERNALITIES IN THE COSMOEROTIC UNIVERSE

The evolution of relationships is an expression of the evolution of Eros, or what we might call *the evolution of intimacy*. The drive not only to join genes but to join hearts and ultimately to join genius is the trajectory of the evolution of Eros in human relationships. Role mate is about joining genes, soul mate is about joining hearts, and whole mate is about joining genius. At each level, intimacy evolves and a new whole is created.

Reality is Eros.

We live in an Intimate Universe.

These are two ways of saying the same thing. But since there are no true synonyms, each field of language, each phrase, gives us greater access to the vision and felt sense of Reality. A third way of saying the same thing is that *there exists a meta-meme, which includes all other memes*. The meta-meme is a larger whole, incorporating many sub-memes into its whole-world vision.

Evolution means that the Universe is not a fact but a Story. The Universe is not an ordinary love story but an Outrageous Love Story. By *Outrageous Love* we mean Eros.

Ordinary love is when persons living non-erotic lives believe they are separate from All-That-Is. They love each other in order to gain advantages of security and comfort. This is a legitimate form of love. Ordinary love, however, is highly limited in its pleasure, potency, and sustainability.

Outrageous Love is the Eros that animates and drives all Reality, all the way up and all the way down the chain of being. The Universe is an Outrageous Love Story. When Outrageous Love awakens at the human level, when we awaken to our true identity as Outrageous Lovers, the pleasure, potency, and sustaining power of the love relationship are virtually infinite.

That the Universe is a Love Story is not a metaphor. It is a fact. It is the best explanation of Reality, culling all the information we have from all quadrants of knowledge at this moment in history. *The Universe is a Love Story* is the most accurate worldview available to us at this moment in time. Generating new realities from within this erotic worldview will alleviate more suffering and effect more healing than any other single social movement or scientific technology. The realization of this worldview is the core of the return to Eros,[270] which is so urgently needed and yearned for at this pivotal moment in the arc of time. The realization that the Universe is a Love Story births a new form of Eros and intimacy.

The Love Story of the Universe is not chaste. We live in a sexual Universe, sexing all the way up and all the way down. Said differently, Reality is allurement all the way up and all the way down.

From the microcosm of subatomic particles to the macrocosm of celestial attraction between planets, the Universe is making love. Between the micro and the macro is the plant world, where the birds and the bees are symbolic of the great pollination dance.[271] From fish to early animals, then mammals, and into the human realm, erotic allurement defines and guides Reality. We live in a CosmoErotic Universe. The Universe is driven by Evolutionary Eros—the desire for contact, in order to form ever-deeper and ever-greater wholes. The point is not just that everything is *connected*. It is that everything is *allured* to everything else.

---

[270] See also M. Gafni and K. Kincaid, A Return to Eros: The Radical Experience of Being Fully Alive (2017).

[271] See, for example, Michael Pollan's wonderful work The Botany of Desire (2001).

Everything is moved, driven, and passionately drawn to make contact. The interconnected Universe could be a static given, but it is not. It is a dynamic CosmoErotic Reality.

The realization that this is the nature of Reality awakens us to the possibility of Evolutionary Intimacy. On the outside, this is the enlightened realization that everything is interconnected, and everything affects everything else. Systems theory, chaos theory, and complexity theory all address the radical interconnectivity of all things. This is a scientific realization at a depth that was not even vaguely approximated in any previous generation. Yet that is only the exterior expression of Reality. **The interior of interconnectivity is intimacy.** For this reason, the great Buddhist teacher Master Dōgen defined enlightenment as *intimacy with all things*.[272] A Universe of mutually interdependent, co-arising beings is an Intimate Universe. Enlightenment is but the realization of the True Erotic Nature of Reality. Enlightenment, Eros, and intimacy all turn out to mean the same thing. Eros means that no one is left out of the circle, that no one is grasping for pseudo-eros by pushing someone else outside. Enlightenment means that nothing and no one is left outside.

It is not at all inaccurate to say that Eros is simply another word for enlightenment. Enlightenment is not some esoteric Eastern meditative practice; it is sanity. Sanity is simply knowing the True Nature of Reality—allurement to form the highest possible wholes.

Reality is intimate. We live in an erotic, Intimate Universe. Therefore,

---

[272] The great thirteenth-century Japanese Zen master Dōgen Zenji refers to this state of mind succinctly and beautifully: "One who studies Buddha's Way studies self. One who studies self forgets self. One who forgets self is enlightened by all phenomena. One who is enlightened by all phenomena lets body and mind be cast away (身心脱落), in self and others." Our friend and colleague Zen Buddhist teacher Soryu suggested the following translation of the Dōgen passage:
To study the Buddha's path is to study the self.
To study the self is to forget the self.
To forget the self is to be confirmed by all things.
To be confirmed by all things is to drop the body and mind of self and others.
We are translating confirmed by all things as intimacy with all things and identifying the forgetting the self as being a term for enlightenment, hence our statement in CosmoErotic Humanism that we attribute to Dōgen: "Enlightenment is intimacy with all things."

we can fairly say that *enlightenment means there are no externalities*. There is nothing we can simply commodify, claiming its value is purely its ability to serve as a means to someone else's end. Whales are not simply whale oil, and humans are not merely disposable soldiers in the games of pseudo-eros played by corrupt elites. Everything, and everyone, is in the circle. Nothing and no one is outside the circle. Nothing and no one is unloved. We need to love our way to enlightenment. That is not a sweet, spiritual idea but simply what it means to return to Eros and align with the True Erotic Nature of Reality.

Anything less than this erotic experience may well destroy our planet. We abuse each other personally. Nations mass-murder other nations. We rape the environment and allow nine million people to die of hunger or related diseases every year.[273]

The simple and essential cause is a lack of Eros. We desperately need to feel that we are on the inside, but we don't. So, we settle for pseudo-eros. We pretend we are on the inside by placing others on the outside. We do not feel embraced in the Real Eros of Love, so we grasp for the pseudo-eros of fear, war, and obsessive consumption.

We have only two choices:

Eros or death.

Love or die.

Let's choose to be Outrageous Lovers living the erotic life.

The great Kabbalist Isaac Luria, writing in sixteenth-century Safed, taught that all evil is a failure of love and Eros. I can hurt you only if I feel that you are not connected to me. Would the hand stab the foot to take revenge?

For Luria, love, in its very essence, is the erotic *re-ligaring* with all of being. It always starts, however, not with all of being, but with a friend

---

[273] The World Counts, "Around 9 Million People Die Every Year of Hunger and Hunger-Related Diseases," accessed January 2024, https://www.theworldcounts.com/challenges/hunger-and-obesity/how-many-people-die-from-hunger-each-year.

whom you already know:

> The master Moshe Leib of Sassov said he never knew what it meant to be a lover until he learned it from a drunkard. It happened that the master was in a tavern and overheard a dialogue between two men deep in their drink. One was professing how much he loved the other, but the other argued that it was not so.
>
> "Ivan," Igor cried, "believe me when I tell you, I love you more dearly than anything in the world."
>
> "Not so, Igor," Ivan replied. "You don't really love me at all."
>
> Igor gulped down a glass of vodka. The tears streamed down his face. "I swear, Ivan, I love you with all my heart." He wept.
>
> Ivan shook his head. "Igor, if you really do love me, tell me why I am not satisfied in my life. If you really loved me, you would know what I desire."
>
> With this, Igor was silent. This time Ivan was the one who cried.

Four Faces of Eros, which we study in our book *A Return to Eros*,[274] show themselves in this tale: **wholeness, yearning, interiority, and presence**. If you really love me, then we are deeply connected. If you are truly not **whole** without me, then you will hear the deepest **desires** of my soul because their melodies resonate in your soul as well. You learn to hear my soul's music by being fully **present** in our encounters. Moreover, you are radically empathetic to my needs. Radical empathy comes when the fullness of **presence** engenders a great **yearning** to move beyond the alienation that separates us. There is a sense of devotion between

---

[274] Gafni and Kincaid, A Return to Eros.

us. Devotion is an intimate sister of **yearning**. The **yearning** to move beyond the loneliness of the separate self is what propels us to shatter the ego boundaries that alienate us and enter the **inside** of another's story. Then we are each other's erotic lovers.

SUPPLEMENTARY ESSAYS

Essay 1. Four Core Principles of Soul Mate Relationship

The physical sciences reveal the exterior principles of the cosmos. The interior sciences reveal the principles that govern its interior face. We saw that the Universe is not merely a fact, but a Story. At each level of evolving relationship, the eternal principles of evolution show up in a new and deeper way. Just as a scientist evolves technology by knowing the exterior principles, you evolve love by knowing the interior First Principles and First Values.[275]

In this essay, we will discuss four of these Principles that govern soul mate relationships (and deepen even further in whole mate relationships):

(1) Each soul mate holds a piece of their partner's story that is the soul mate's sacred obligation to return to their beloved.

(2) Intimate Communion requires contact in the present.

(3) Labels obstruct contact.

(4) The power of not knowing.

---

[275] For a key discussion of what I have called, together with my student, friend, partner and interlocutor Zachary Stein, see: First Principles & First Values: Forty-Two Propositions on CosmoErotic Humanism, the Meta-Crisis, and the World to Come by David J. Temple (2024). The four soul mate distinctions that we articulate in this essay are expressions of core First Principles and First Values of Reality.

We also suggest several soul mate practices to integrate these Principles into your life.

Principle One. Soul Mates Hold Pieces of Each Other's Stories

You each hold a piece of the other's story. In every soul mate relationship, partners hold a piece of each other's stories, a piece of who we are. These stories must be returned for each to feel complete. Your soul mate is the person who can return to you a significant piece of your story that you have either lost or never found. Conversely, you should return to your soul mate the missing and magnificent pieces of his or her story. This unique dynamic of returning to your beloved missing pieces of their story is an expression of the unique quality of soul mate relationship. Partners discover what these missing pieces might be, and they commit to helping each other piece their stories back together.

The following story illustrates the power of helping someone to reclaim elements of their story.

> The Baal Shem Tov, Master of the Good Name, was on his deathbed. His students gathered around him, and to each, the master revealed his particular calling in the world. To one, commerce; to the other, healing; to a third, the ministry. To his student Gabriel the master said, "You will be my storyteller. Your job will be to travel far and wide, from town to town, from village to village, telling the stories and wonders you have seen in my company."
>
> Gabriel hoped the Baal Shem was pointing to someone else, because the last thing he wanted to be was an itinerant storyteller. But what could he do? He had been called.
>
> He asked the Baal Shem, "Will this be my role for the rest of my days? How will I know if and when my task is done?"

"You will know," the Baal Shem told him. "You will know."

After the death of the master, Gabriel dutifully began to wander the countryside, relating the stories and wonders of the Baal Shem. Some years went by, and Gabriel longed for home. One day he heard that in Italy, in Siena, there was a wealthy man who paid fifty rubles for every new Baal Shem story he heard. Fifty rubles was a lot of money, and Gabriel had a lot of stories. After all, he was the storyteller of the Baal Shem. "This," he said to himself, "must have been the Baal Shem's intent. I will become instantly a wealthy man and will be able to devote the rest of my life to my family and my studies."

Gabriel traveled to Siena. Word spread quickly that the Baal Shem's storyteller had come to town, and the next day, Friday evening, the entire town gathered in the home of the wealthy patron, eagerly anticipating a rich repast of tales.

Gabriel rose to speak. He opened his mouth. Silence. Not a word came out. His face went white. He concentrated. Still silence. Three or four slow minutes inched by. Finally, Gabriel stammered, "I'm so sorry, but I can't remember a story, not even one."

The patron was gracious. "You're surely tired from your travel," he said. "Rest. Tomorrow you'll be refreshed and at the afternoon meal you will tell us your tales."

The next day the people gathered for lunch. Again, Gabriel opened his mouth and stopped, unable to remember a single story. It happened again at the evening meal—the same silence as before. The Sun set upon his silence and the patron, looking unusually sad, gave Gabriel a few rubles and sent him on his way.

Gabriel was devastated, crying bitterly. "What is a storyteller who has forgotten his stories?" he asked himself.

Just as he reached the outskirts of the city, he noticed a house with its shutters all closed up. It provoked a flash of memory, a story he'd forgotten. A story he'd never told. It was the only one he could remember. Quickly, he turned around, raced back to the house of the patron, and burst through the door, rushing past the servants to enter the study. Much to his surprise, he found the man slumped over his desk, racked with sobs. But Gabriel had no time for questions or explanations. He had to tell the tale. "Quick," Gabriel said. "I remember a story, a story I've never told. Let me tell it to you before it too recedes." The patron opened his mouth to respond, but Gabriel had already launched into his tale.

"It was on a Wednesday morning that the Baal Shem called me. He said, 'Hitch up the wagon. I want you and you alone to accompany me.' And we traveled what seemed like a great distance in the shortest time. We arrived in the Jewish quarter of a town I did not recognize. All the houses were shuttered up. In the midst of the houses was a square and in the square people were gathering to hear the address by the priest upon a high pulpit.

"The Baal Shem asked me to knock on the door of one of the houses adjoining the square. We knocked and a voice from inside said, 'Get away from here. Don't you know? The priest is about to rile people up to commit a massacre. Any Jew found outside is fair game for the slaughter.' 'You have nothing to fear from me,' responded my master. 'Open the door.' His was a voice you could not disobey. The door opened; the Baal Shem turned to me and said, 'Cross the square and tell the priest that I would like to talk to him.' 'Are you sure?' I asked timidly. 'They'll kill me before I even take a few steps.' 'Go now,' said the Baal Shem.

"I crossed the square, and the people parted before me like the splitting of the Red Sea. And I said to the priest, 'The Baal Shem Tov would like to speak to you.' You can imagine my surprise when his face paled and he began to tremble. He did not want to respond to my call, that was clear, but somehow, I don't know why, he came with me. We crossed the square together, and he disappeared into the back room of the house with the Baal Shem. They were in there for thirteen hours. Afterward, the priest came out, tears streaming down his face, and he was heard from no more. That's all I remember."

Gabriel stood there like an emptied pocket, his story told.

The patron had become very quiet. He sat staring at the storyteller with an almost desperate look in his eyes. He got up, took Gabriel by the shoulders, and with his face inches away from Gabriel's, he shook him. "Don't you recognize me?" he asked. "Recognize me!"

Slowly, a flicker of recognition illuminated Gabriel's face. "Why, why—you're the priest! How could it be? You're the priest!"

"I am the priest. Yes. I am the priest," the man replied, as if for the first time reconciling himself to that fact. He loosened his grip on Gabriel's shoulders, and as he spoke, his features began to relax.

"Let me tell you my story. I was raised in a Jewish home, a precocious child with great aspirations. But as you know, there is not much a Jew can do to advance in the world. I wanted to get out of my hamlet and rise, to become something in the world. I thought, why don't I join the most successful enterprise around—the church? So I did. And what better way to join than to become a priest? I converted and threw myself into the priestly task. As the years passed, I did so well, I rose so high, that I was considered to be a bishop. There remained, however, some faint suspicion in the church that perhaps I had not fully left my former life as a Jew.

"And, dear storyteller, I so much wanted to be a bishop that I decided to foment riots against the Jews of my town to prove to the church that I was loyal. And just as I was about to give my inflammatory speech, rousing the villagers to riot, you came to me, saying the Baal Shem wanted to see me. I had never heard of him, but there was something in your voice I could not ignore. I felt pulled. I had to go with you.

"The Baal Shem spoke to me for some thirteen hours. He spoke of my soul, my past, my calling. 'Return,' he said, 'Return to yourself.' And that is what I did. I committed myself to fully returning to my roots and to making amends for the enormous suffering I had caused. Before I left the house, though, I asked the Baal Shem, 'How will I know that my return has been accepted on high, that I have been forgiven?' He answered, 'You will know your return has been received when you hear someone telling your story, and both you and the teller realize the tale belongs to you.'"

It is only when you recognize and embrace your story that you come home. And we each have pieces of each other's story. By telling this story, Gabriel completed a piece of the priest's story that only he could complete. In so doing, the priest finally came to know that he was forgiven. Without Gabriel that would never have come to pass.

We complete each other's story in innumerable ways. Some are explicit, as in this story, and others are more implicit, as when your passion for learning rekindles an old love of learning that your partner once had. Without an important aspect of the other's story, our story remains incomplete.

This story is about names. One of the primary characters is Israel

Baal Shem—literally translated as the Master of the Name. In this context, *name* means something like *story*. He is the master of his story. That does not mean he is perfect, but it does mean that he is fully living inside of his own story. And that is very great mastery. He is master in that he is fully living his story and responding to his call. From this place he can guide others to recover the print of their own souls—in other words, their stories.

This is precisely his role in our story.

It is a story about stories. Gabriel is a storyteller not entirely pleased with his calling. He would rather be someplace else. He has not embraced his story, so he must wander the world, searching, trying to tell the story right. The erstwhile priest is also a man who had fled from his story. He was driven to foment a massacre of the Jews in his town. Why? Because they remind him that he is not in his story. Because a person living in a story not his own can be driven to the darkest places in order to maintain the disguise. He needs to prove he is a character in his foreign tale by changing his costume, accent, and religion. He can only push his way into his inauthentic story by nullifying his previous story in the most dramatic way possible. His intended murder of his former community is really a form of suicide. How many small murders have you committed in order to maintain your disguise in a story that is not your own? Usually, the people you wind up hurting the most are the people closest to you, for it is they who remind you of your impostor status.

This is a story about returning to your story. Both of the major characters in this tale can only be redeemed if they find their way back to their own stories.

I once heard that there are four signs of getting old:

1. When you sink your teeth into steak and they stay there.

2. When your back goes out more often than you do.

3. When the old lady you are walking across the street turns out to be your wife.

4. When you get to the top rung of the ladder you've been climbing and find it is leaning against the wrong wall.

Up until number four we are in comedy. Number four is tragedy. No matter what your age, the only legitimate fear in your life should be that maybe you're living the wrong story, leaning your ladder against the wrong wall. To succeed in a story not your own is failure.

This is one of the many reasons that we cannot judge another person's failure or success unless we are intimately connected to their story. Even then, we don't really know enough to judge. A bishop is a beautiful thing to be if *that* is your story. If it is not your story, if you are doing it for all the wrong reasons, then the church should be the first to say: *You must return to your story.* Being a teacher in your hometown with stable family life and a sustaining community is beautiful—unless the narrative arc of your life calls you to be a wandering storyteller.

The meeting between the priest and the storyteller, each disconnected from his own story, becomes the model of a new, enormously exciting part of the Unique Self dharma—intimate encounter between soul stories.

The priest provokes the storyteller to remember a story he had forgotten.

What is the significance of the forgotten story?

Gabriel's forgetting has two functions. First, it shows how Gabriel is disconnected from his story. He is a storyteller who has forgotten his stories. He can only recover his stories, the entirety of his calling, by remembering the piece of his story that he has lost. This is the story he had forgotten about his master's stranger meeting with the bishop. He must then return this story to the bishop. In receiving his lost story from Gabriel, the bishop returns to Gabriel his vocation of a storyteller. This is an intimate encounter between soul stories.

Principle One is what we have called elsewhere *the fourth law of Unique Self Encounter*:[276] every person you meet in a significant meeting possesses a piece of your story. Some people may have a sentence, others

---

276 See Chapter Twenty-One: Evolutionary Intimacy—The Seven Laws of Unique Self Encounters in Your Unique Self: The Radical Path to Personal Enlightenment by M. Gafni (2012).

a missing word, while still others may hold a paragraph or even a whole chapter. Significant meetings involve soul story encounters.

The ultimate soul story encounter may well be with your significant other in life. The person you choose should be the person who can return to you a significant piece of your story that you have lost or never found. Conversely, you hold and need to return the missing and magnificent pieces of their story. The soul story encounter is a committed, dynamic process of discovering just what these missing pieces might be and puzzling them back together.

An intimate encounter between soul stories is in no sense limited to romantic partners. Your sphere of colleagues, friends, family, neighbors, employers, and employees all may have pieces of your story, and you theirs. Nor are soul story encounters limited to long-term connections within your fixed orbit. Often a person who is a meteor or comet in your life may have an enormously significant gift for your story. You may be riding an elevator with a person you have never met and will never meet again. It might be a coincidence or a profound invitation to your story. Responding to this story invitation doesn't mean you need to talk about your relationship with your mother or about your innermost secrets. However, it is highly likely that, somewhere in your casual conversations, there will be important messages for each of you. Similarly, the person who returns your lost wallet may have more to return than your credit cards.

There is an entirely different way that our partners hold a piece of our story, which begins to show up dramatically in soul mate relationship and deepens in whole mate. This is the realization that there is a *part of me that only appears when you are around*. This is a self-evidently true but shocking realization. There are many faces to self that is us. And our self, as we have noted earlier, is a unique configuration of Eros and intimacy.[277]

This means that the Self is a unique configuration of many different parts—physical, spiritual, cultural, psychological, and existential—that

---

[277] We have alluded to your unique configuration of intimacy and Eros numerous times in Chapters 6, 7 and 8. See also our forthcoming six-volume set, The Universe: A Love Story—First Meditations on CosmoErotic Humanism in Response to the Meta-Crisis, by M. Gafni et al.

are configured in the Unique Self of a human being. To be a Unique Self is to be an irreducibly unique configuration, an irreducibly unique pattern of Eros and intimacy. As such, it makes precise sense that we become someone new through deep interaction with another human being who is themselves a unique configuration of Eros and intimacy. In the depth of our encounter our very identity changes. New dimensions of Self appear that are evoked by the unique configuration of intimacy evoked by the Unique Self Encounter. Said simply, when I love you, I spread myself open to receive you inside of me. When that happens, I become different, new, emergent. I am, in some true sense, reborn into a new identity. Our partners hold a piece of who we are. Only they can bring out that very same piece in us.

> **Soul Mate Practice.** Bring to mind a close relationship—your partner, someone at work, or a close friend. Spend some time reflecting on the nature of this relationship. See if you can identify two or three gifts or unique capacities or qualities of presence that the other person possesses that bring out, evoke, or support something truly special in you. Then, create a meeting with that person, and share with them about how they help to complete your story. Share your appreciation and consider tenderly inquiring how you help to complete their story.

Principle Two. Intimate Communion Requires Contact in the Present

Radical Presence

Intimate communion requires contact in the present. Soul mate relationships require partners to have authentic contact with each other. Without contact, intimate communion cannot take place. The only place your story is ever unfolding is right now. Yesterday's and tomorrow's stories help shape your identity today, but it is in the present moment that we experience our stories fully and directly. A true soul mate encounter is impossible if you think you are here today when you are actually in some bygone yesterday. Intimate communion and contact can be made only in the timeless unfolding of now. Put differently, presence is possible only in the present.

When you think that you are talking to your soul mate, but you are really completing an unfinished conversation with your mother, you cannot make authentic contact. The unique quality of any given moment in time supports the expression and manifestation of a unique intimacy that can manifest only in that precise moment. To experience that intimacy, you must be fully present in the interaction.

*Inter*action is the opposite of *re*action. Reaction comes from an unconscious replay, rehash, or reliving of moments long dead. You cannot live a past moment. There can be no spontaneous, present-inspired action during an unconscious reenactment. This is precisely what psychology calls *transference*, or the unconscious *transferring* of the energy and agenda of a past encounter onto a present encounter. When you are reacting, you are transferring your reactions from an old situation to the present situation even though they do not apply. In order to show up for intimate communion in the present, you must first leave the constantly replayed past.

One of the ways to make contact in the present is through radical presence. Radical presence is obscured when we confuse old stories with what is happening in the present. When we lose ourselves in the past in this way, we enter a type of trance. Eye-gazing will often evoke a de-trancing, which snaps one or both parties out of their old stories and into the present. Through this practice you can come to transcend (*trance-end*) old patterning. This does not mean you leave the past behind. Rather it means you are breaking out of the trance that causes you to confuse the past with the present.

Soul Mate Practice. Sit or stand facing your soul mate in a quiet, comfortable setting. Place your left hand gently on your partner's chest, over their heart. Place your right hand over your partner's hand on your chest. Focus your gaze into your partner's left eye. Slowly synchronize your breathing and hold your gaze, gently and in full acceptance of everything that is arising within and between you. Continue for just a few minutes at the start and build up from there. This practice can be a bit awkward at first. You may want to giggle or look away. Whatever arises, embrace it as a gorgeous expression of present-moment aliveness and return to your partner's gaze.

Invitations of Time

The intimate communion of soul mate encounters requires authentic contact. Authentic contact requires you to be present in this moment. Every moment has its own revelation. In order to sense and receive the unique intimacy invitation of every moment of time, we need to become sensitized to the rhythms of time itself. Developing that sensitivity is one of the primary goals of soul mate relationship.

We unfold in time. One of Carl Jung's great contributions was an affirmation of the enormous excitement that awaits us in middle age: If you are truly living, then time is unfolding before you. You are not farther from youth—you are closer to wisdom. We can comprehend tomorrow what we are not yet prepared to comprehend today. Each day brings its own revelation. Each day brings us closer to ourselves.

Indeed, the very word for *time* in Hebrew, *zeman*, is layered with a second meaning: *invitation*. The idea is elegant and simple: *Time is an invitation*. You can experience a month as one day that happens thirty times or as thirty days, each of which builds on the one that preceded. Too often, we miss the invitation of time, but we can learn to respond to it. We can be aware of a moment when we are making a memory; we can create a conscious practice around it that lets us accept that invitation.

Two decades ago, I was sitting with a close friend in Cafit, my Jerusalem writing café. We were working together—collating and doing some light editing on a book I had written. I was called to the phone, which afforded me an outsider's view of our table. It was piled high with books, making it look much more like a library cubicle than a café table. My friend was passionately crossing something out on the text in front of her, and I had been sitting across from her writing a moment before. My imagination raced forward some forty years. I saw myself, old—much closer to the end than the beginning—sitting and recalling those days way back when we worked on that very first book. We had no idea of what the future held. We believed in our wisdom, our passion, our God. Life was a magical place. Probably a minute later, but what seemed like much longer, I snapped out of my reverie. I looked at the table, the books, and my friend, and felt overwhelmed by the joy of being able to step into that memory and live it now.

> **Soul Mate Practice.** Try to sense the special moments in your life right as you are creating the memories. Step out of the moment, go forward in time, and visualize yourself as an old man or woman remembering the scene. Stay there for a moment. Then step out of your visualization and walk into your memory, which is now part of your present.

Collecting Your Days

Abraham was old—and came with his days.[278] This is a wonderful phrase from an ancient text that describes the mythical historical patriarch Abraham in his old age. All the myth masters are troubled by this phrase. What could it mean? One wisdom text suggests that every single day brings a radically new intimacy, specific to it alone.

I never quite understood this idea until an encounter I had with a famous Israeli avant-garde writer, Pinchas Sadeh. He was known for the intensity of his prose, the depth of his intimacies, and his startling insight

---

278 Genesis 25:5. In most translations this is translated as full of years. For example, in the New International Version it says: "Then Abraham breathed his last and died at a good old age, an old man and full of years; and he was gathered to his people." In other translations it is translated as something along the lines of being satisfied with life. For example, in the New American Standard Bible: "Abraham breathed his last and died at a good old age, an old man and satisfied with life; and he was gathered to his people." Two more examples: "And Abraham became ill and died in a good old age; he was old and satisfied with his days and was gathered to his people" (Aramaic Bible in Plain English) and "And Abraam failing died in a good old age, an old man and full of days, and was added to his people" (Brenton Septuagint Translation). All translations from Bible Hub, https://biblehub.com/genesis/25-8.htm.

into the everyday. I went to visit Sadeh in Jerusalem when he was an old man dying of cancer. He was in a particularly nostalgic mood that night, and he spun story after story of his life. I sat there, wrapped in the wonder of his memories. As I was leaving, I thanked him for sharing with me from the wealth of his days. His smile turned serious as he looked into my eyes and replied:

> When I was young, like you, I read Goethe but did not understand him. You see, Goethe had written that he was able to collect from his life fourteen days of intimacy.
>
> How could it be, I asked myself, that Goethe—who was so successful in his own lifetime, whose wife was so beautiful, whose fame so widespread, who was surrounded by friends—how could it be that he was able to collect only fourteen days of true intimacy? Was he so unappreciative, so insensitive and senile, that he could not remember more?
>
> Now, at the end of my life, I finally understand Goethe. But I more than understand, I am amazed by the man! That he was able to collect so many days of joy! I have tried to collect my days and have come up with a meager handful. Pieces and fragments of communion come to me, snatches, like the stories you heard tonight. But I am not sure what was real and what was fantasy, imagination, or dream. Very few days of intimacy remain entire and whole in my memories. The ones that do sit like gems in my hand. But they are so few. Imagine the wealth of fourteen full days of present joy!

The days that you are able to take with you are what we call *days of communion*. These are days when you felt fully present, when you responded with full presence to your beloved, or when you fully lived the intimate contours of your story. That Abraham was able to *take his days with him* meant that he was able to collect his days. His intimacy unfolded daily, becoming richer, more colorful, and textured all the time. It also meant that Abraham's days built on each other—each one giving birth to the next in a way that made aging a great joy. **If you can understand your life as the process of unfolding your intimate self, then the passage of time can bring great joy to you as well.**

Jung wrote that many of his middle-aged patients suffered not from any clinical condition, but "from the senselessness and emptiness of their lives." "It seems to me, however," continued Jung, "that this can well be described as the general neurosis of our time."[279] In another passage he was even more emphatic: "Among all my patients in the second half of life—that is to say, over thirty-five—there has not been one whose problem in the last resort was not that of finding a religious outlook on life."[280] This problem, he said, had nothing to do with organized religion as we know it. Rather, in the language of our book, the problem is that we all seek the affirmation that, as human beings, we each have a unique quality of intimacy—a special story possessing infinite value, meaning, and dignity. It is that quality of Self we must be aware of to create the intimate communion of soul mate relationship.

> **Soul Mate Practice.** Try to gather fourteen days from the last year. Describe as much of each of those days as you can. Remember the feelings they engendered, along with the intimacies and the joys, the pleasures and the pains, the lessons learned. You may find that this is not an easy task. Yet to take our days with us is an art of the highest form.

---

279 Modern Man in Search of a Soul by C. G. Jung (2011), p. 58.

280 Jung, p. 196. Jung then continues: "It is safe to say that every one of them fell ill because he had lost that which the living religions of every age have given to their followers, and none of them has been really healed who did not regain his religious outlook. This of course has nothing whatever to do with a particular creed or membership of a church" (196-197).

There Are No Extra Moments

> *From the day the world was manifest until the end of all generations, there is no day which is equal to another . . . and no two moments which are not distinct . . . and no two people equal to each other . . . for if [everyone were not unique], what need would there be for each one?*
>
> —Wisdom Master Menachem Mendel of Vitebsk[281]

We are used to thinking that we must turn to ancient eternal wisdom for our guidance. There is of course some truth in this. But the deeper view of evolutionary time is the knowing that every moment births new intimacies.

This means that even the wisdom of ancient sacred texts evolves in every new moment of time. The deepest masters of ancient wisdom knew this, and they wanted their words to be read and reread and interpreted anew in the light of every day's uniquely intimate invitation. *The Zohar*, literally *The Book of Illumination*, reads, "These changes are taking place at each and every moment, and in accordance with these changes . . . the sayings of the book of the Zohar are changing, and all are the words of the living truth."[282]

To receive the fullness of the present moment is to receive the unique intimacy of that time. In ancient myth, the symbol of the power of the now is *manna*. *Manna* is the bread that was said to fall from heaven every morning during the forty-year period that the Hebrews wandered the desert. Although the bread fell from the heavens every day, one was only allowed to collect enough for oneself and one's family for that day alone. If someone tried to collect enough for tomorrow as well, the manna went bad. The manna archetype is critical for us. **If we make ourselves fully available to the intimacy of the now, it will give us the nourishment we need.**

---

[281] Menahem Mendel of Vitebsk. Peri Haaretz, Vayeishev 3 (See https://www.sefaria.org/Peri_HaAretz). On the theology of Menahem Mendel, see also the writings of Moshe Hallamish.

[282] Zohar Hai, vol. 1, 3a.

Always the Very First Time

The power of the now lies behind the mystical secret of re-creation. This is a doctrine that Islamic and Christian mystics have embraced for at least two thousand years. A central question of the doctrine, also known as the *doctrine of continuous creation*,[283] is: *Did God create the world in one act that took place in a specific moment of time? Or is creation a constant reality, the world being recreated anew every second?* My unspoken internal question as I sat in theological seminary was, *Who cares?*

One day, thinking about this, while in analytic meditation, it became perfectly clear why we care. The issue at stake was not theology, but intimacy. Intimacy comes from the realization of evolutionary science that every moment is fundamentally new. Philosopher Alfred North Whitehead called this moment-to-moment newness the *creative advance into novelty*, and it is the essential nature of Reality. Reality is always birthing a new emergent that holds a deeper and more profoundly intimate consciousness than what came before. We see this in the move from quarks to atoms, to molecules, to cells, to multicellular life, to plants, to animals, to mammals, to humans, and to increasingly evolved expressions of humanity.

The progressive intensification of intimacy is a radical notion of emergence foreshadowed in the ancient doctrine of *continuous creation*. Reality is an evolutionary artist constantly creating the Universe again and again, more and more beautifully, with more and more goodness and more and more truth, every day. In the language of the mystics, Source makes love, inseminating the world anew each moment. Every moment in time is a new existence that never was and never will be again.

This understanding animates the Eros of soul mate relationships. Each relationship is a living organism, which was, and is, a constant co-creation of the beloveds. Since every moment is new, the relationship is new in every moment. Originality becomes the affirmation of the constant emotional intercourse.

A Tibetan Buddhist master, Milarepa, composed some of the most

---

[283] See, for example, E. Salim and S. A. Malik, "Creatio Continua and Quantum Randomness," in K. J. Clark and J. Koperski (eds). Abrahamic Reflections on Randomness and Providence (2022).

beautiful spiritual prose known to man entirely in the moment. There was no preparation. His writings were completely spontaneous.

My son's awesome mother, Mariana Caplan, is among other things a great teacher of intimate writing. She teaches writing as a ritual, where the practice involves remaining open to the unique revelation of the moment, allowing it to flow through you onto paper.

One of the ancient Hebrew words for time is *paam*. It also means *arousal*. There is a unique arousal in every moment. Every moment has a new truth. For this reason, Buddhist masters could work weeks on an exquisite sand mandala, and a moment after it is completed, destroy it. The mandala belonged only to the moment in which it came into being. For any other moment, it was already *passé*.

This erotic understanding of continuous creation moved the soul mate masters of Islamic mysticism to oppose adamantly the idea of a one-shot creation. It would have created a love-starved, de-eroticized world. How could we have survived in a world where we don't hear the constant whisper of *I love you*? As we feel personally addressed anew in every moment and invited and seduced anew into intimate communion, we find ourselves in the experience of a soul mate relationship.

Love Is Only in the Now

To go against what is, in any given moment, is to lose touch with the force of Evolutionary Love in the Cosmos. All failures in love are failures of realization. All failure in love is a form of mental illness, which is defined in this context as the loss of recognition of the True Nature of Reality. It involves a loss of correct identity when we are convinced that we are our names or that others are theirs—*Rosa Parks* or *Barack Obama*, for example.

Or in a subtler expression of the same phenomenon of *misidentification*, you think you are no more than a skin-encapsulated ego. You have lost touch with the perception of love, in which your True Identity *is* a uniquely intimate expression of Big Heart and Big Mind—what physicist Roger Penrose called *Reality*.[284] Mental illness stems from losing touch

---

[284] See, for example, R. Pengrove, The Road to Reality: A Complete Guide to the Laws of the Universe (2004).

with the unique quality of the infinitely intimate communion that is present in the moment. At its core, mental illness is a breakdown of Unique Self and unique communion. Or said differently, mental illness is a failure of intimacy, with self or with other.

The mystery of love saves us from our skin-encapsulated egos and returns us to full presence. By doing so, it reconnects us with the healing power of the moment. When we fully live in the present moment, we become powerful. We gain complete presence and confidence. The infinity experienced in that time enriches us beyond measure. Indeed, it is priceless.

Intimate communion requires contact in the unique intimacy of the present moment. A familiar ancient text makes this incredibly real in all of our lives:

> *Therefore shall a man leave his father and his mother and be intimate with his wife and they shall be one flesh.*[285]

The text refers not just to the natural transition from parents' home to marriage. It talks of the necessity of leaving the original family circle of mother and father in order to create intimacy. That is an unbelievably powerful statement. You cannot create true intimacy without leaving your parents behind in a psychological sense. If you do not leave them behind, you marry them. You marry someone similar to or opposite from your parents in order to complete your unfinished business with them. Through that person, who is similar to Dad, you seek to receive the love you didn't get from Dad. Or through that person, who is opposite of Mom, you seek to run away from Mom. In either case, you are in a relationship not with your partner but with your parents.

Let's reframe that idea in terms of the unique intimacy of the present moment in time. You think you are in the present relating to your partner. Really, you are in the past, arguing or pleading with a parent. In this situation, the energy and wisdom you need for intimate presence with your partner is not available. That energy is available only in the

---

[285] Genesis 2:24.

present moment. (Incidentally, it has in it everything you require for your healing.) But you are not present. You are stuck in a conversation of the past. Soul mate relationship requires full presence in the present.

The Pain Trance

The inability to remain present is the source of much suffering.

Take the story of Clare, an alcoholic.[286] In order to heal, together with her therapist or guide, Clare must consider what prompts her drinking. Since Clare does not go on destructive binges all the time, we know that she is capable of being sober. So, we need to look at what mechanism triggers her drinking. What we have discovered over time is that drinking and other addictions are almost always caused by a radical challenge to our self-worth. But here is the key. These are *not* challenges to our self-worth that happen in the present moment. We always have the resources to deal with all challenges in the present moment when we are indeed present. Instead, addictions come from instances in the present that throw us back into the past where we may have been badly hurt.

The story of Jonathan provides a good example. Jonathan is up for review at work and the boss says to him, "I think you have potential, but you are still really sloppy in your execution. Go to work on that, and you have a great future here." On hearing that, Jonathan slips into a depression. It causes him to respond destructively. He gets angry at his boss and denies the critique, or he gets home so depressed that he picks a vociferous argument with his partner about nothing. Or he calls up an old romantic partner for dinner and inappropriately sleeps with her to fill the emptiness revealed by his boss's critique. Or, like Clare, he starts a binge of excessive drinking, which, in the end, causes him to lose the job he has held so dear.

To say the least, all of these responses do not add joy to Jonathan's life. Indeed, they wreak havoc on his world. Why then wouldn't he control himself? He's not perfect, but he usually has a decent amount of self-control. What happened here? He slipped into a trance that took

---

[286] Clare and (later in this section) Jonathan are made-up names for typical clients, whose stories we tell here.

him out of the present moment and threw him into the past.

His father used to hit him when his room wasn't clean. Dad was fastidious, and Jonathan wasn't. Dad would go into a rage and call him a worthless, filthy slob. He remembers that phrase; it is indelibly imprinted on his soul. Like all of us, he craved the blessing of the father, but he did not get it. When his boss critiqued him as *sloppy*, all Jonathan could hear was *worthless, filthy slob*. He couldn't even hear his boss's great praise and promise of a future.

Jonathan might not have actually heard his father's exact words. He might not have even consciously associated his boss's critique with his father's actions, and he might not have even accessed the memory of those words. Yet whenever something or someone presses that button, he regresses to those early childhood moments and responds just as he did then. In early childhood incidents, we respond with a shut-down trance. We bring that response into adulthood.

As is so often the case, Emily Dickinson, that wonderfully sensitive observer of inner space, captures the subtle dynamic of this trance.

> *There is a pain—so utter—*
> *It swallows substance up—*
> *Then covers the Abyss with Trance—*
> *So Memory can step*
> *Around—across—opon* [sic] *it*
> *As One within a Swoon—*
> *Goes safely—where an open eye—*
> *Would drop Him—Bone by Bone*[287]

Dickinson understands that there are times when only trance can block out the pain. The trance saves us from the abyss. In childhood, the trance is protective and therefore loving. But in adulthood, using the trance from childhood can be damaging.

---

287 The Poems of Emily Dickinson: Reading Edition, ed. by R. W. Franklin (1999). The poem was not published during Dickinson's lifetime. The original version, with Dickinson's typical dashes, was restored by scholar Thomas H. Johnson for his 1955 edition of The Poems of Emily Dickinson.

Jonathan's response to his boss is an invocation of his childhood *pain trance*. His response may be anger, closed-down emotions, and distance, or a terrible emptiness, which brings depression on its heels. Jonathan does not understand this emptiness and therefore lacks the resources to walk through it, so he covers it up with compulsive addictive behavior. We will refer to this as a *pain trance*.

What provokes a pain trance is virtually always the meeting with something or someone that triggers our emptiness. We are suddenly and unconsciously thrown back to that early place where we first encountered the emptiness and the lack.

Our sense of goodness in early childhood depends on our caretakers serving as a conduit for the Universe's loving embrace. When those love vessels are constricted, our soul feels attacked. We withdraw into ourselves for protection. This prevents the pain of the emptiness from drowning us. Meeting with emptiness in the present often evokes this old challenge to our self-worth. We withdraw into whatever our unique trance patterns are and look for a way to navigate the emptiness without being swallowed up.

In childhood, such an event is always interpersonal—a reaction to another person outside of ourselves. In adulthood, the same mechanism is triggered, but this time it kicks in autonomously, or without it being a protective strategy against a real person. Anything that sets off our emptiness barometer returns us to the place of original trauma. We react, automatically and unconsciously, as we did then.

We all have trances, in which we leave the present moment and enter another time or dimension. One common example of a regular trance is daydreaming. You drift into a midafternoon reverie and come out calmed and refreshed—or exhausted and distressed. Another example is what psychological literature calls *spontaneous age regression*, which is exactly what happened to Jonathan in our example. In a therapeutic setting, a trained professional can also lead one out of the present moment and into childhood. As you can imagine, that can be quite lovely and even necessary for the healing process; it can also be horrible and damaging if not done with the appropriate care.

Smell, taste, sight, and food can invoke trances, too. Consider the famous eating of the madeleine in Marcel Proust's novel *In Search of Lost Time*. The mere tasting of a pastry moves the book's narrator to the magical *Remembrance of Things Past*.[288] For me, bananas in my Cheerios somehow transport me to the more magical moments of childhood. A scent that your mother or grandmother used to wear, or scenes from a movie that evoke long-past moments of joy or peace provide other examples of trances. Each of these types of experiences moves you out of the present and into a wonderful reverie in the past. We lovingly refer to these as *trips down memory lane*.

We take trips *up* memory lane, as well. Waiting for your beloved to return, you fast-forward through time and imagine how making love will be on the first night of her return. After ten minutes of being lost in that future, you return to the present—satisfied and refreshed. Or, while decorating your baby's room during your pregnancy, you imagine what it will be like when the child sleeps there, bathes there, and giggles there. Although you did not necessarily choose these trances, they are a welcome part of your life. They are welcomed because they are conscious trances—ones that you know you are in.

What are most unwelcome are pain trances, such as Jonathan's and Clare's. They take them out of the present and into the painful past without their even knowing it. Both Clare and Jonathan lack the presence to deal with the challenges facing them in the now. Because they are not aware of their pain trance, they also lack the presence to heal the painful past.

Staying in the Present

The brilliant psychologist Milton Erickson clearly describes the *deep trance phenomenon*.[289] He notes that one of the most important identi-

---

[288] The first six volumes of the original seven volumes by Marcel Proust, À la recherche du temps perdu, were first translated into English by the Scotsman C. K. Scott Moncrieff under the title Remembrance of Things Past, a phrase taken from Shakespeare's Sonnet 30.

[289] See The Collected Works of Milton H. Erickson, MD: Volume 1: The Nature of Therapeutic Hypnosis (1989) and Beginner's Guide to Quantum Psychology, by S. Wolinsky. The entire following section draws directly on Wolinsky's excellent

fying characteristics of a trance is the distortion of time. This is called *pseudo-orientation in time*. Virtually every negative trance involves spontaneous age regression. All such trances trigger a narrowing of focus. This is precisely what happens, for example, in most phobias or anxiety attacks. Our focus shrinks to the extent that the rest of the world feels completely cut off. We narrow our focus to a specific image, word, or sensation that effectively blocks out all other words, images, or emotions. In Jonathan's story, the word *sloppy* became the involuntary mantra of his trance. What happens then is simple and tragic: *we forget our larger Selves*. Psychology calls it *amnesia* or *negative hallucination*. We don't see options or resources that are right in front of us. We become virtually paralyzed and cannot change our course of action.

Remember, a trance is usually a return to the childlike reaction that we employed to protect ourselves from trauma long ago. Any event that is too painful for the child to integrate is met by a childhood trance. Let's say, for example, that your mother was verbally abusive. No matter your actions, she screamed at you in a frightening way. Your protective trance response comprised two internal movements. First, you watched your mother very carefully, even without knowing you were doing so. Second, you anticipated her moods and tried to be out of the way when the volcano erupted in the future.

Later in life, this will manifest itself as slippages into pain trances. As an adult, when you get into an argument with your partner, you spontaneously and unconsciously regress back to childhood. Like your mom, you get terribly abusive. You raise issues and use them to bash your spouse in an outburst rather than communicating and solving your problems effectively. After the outburst, you feel ashamed, but it is too late—the damage is done.

Consider that our outbursts—whether abusive, charged by dramatic emotion, or otherwise triggered by events of the past—have been a primary cause of our inability to create lasting intimate relationships with

---

work. See also Trances People Live, by S. Wolinsky and M. O. Ryan (1991); Quantum Consciousness: The Guide to Experiencing Quantum Psychology, by S. Wolinsky and C. Wilson (1993); as well as the three-volume work The Way of the Human: The Quantum Psychology Notebooks (1999).

soul mates. At the root of this challenge is your inability to stay in the present. In the present, you have all the resources you need to heal and for intimate communion. De-trancing opens the door for full presence with your beloved.

As the adage goes, 95 percent of life is showing up. But how do you stay in the present? Said differently, how do you de-trance? The trance is a lapse in consciousness. True transformation in relationship is about moving past the blanked-out time when you stopped being present and you disconnected. Intimate communion begins with a return to yourself.

There's a wonderful story from the Hindu *Upanishads* that speaks to this idea of de-trancing and returning to one's self.

> Ten men are walking through the woods. They come to a raging river that they must cross. The current being very strong, they are afraid that, if they do not interlock arms, some of them might be washed away. They know well the wisdom that Benjamin Franklin later expressed as: *Either we all hang together, or we'll all hang separately.*
>
> Well, they hang together and seem to cross safely. Just to be sure, though, one of them says, "Let me count everyone to make sure all ten of us are here." He counts: one, two, three, four, five, six, seven, eight, nine. Only nine. Someone else says, "Wait, you must be mistaken." He turns to the group and counts slowly from left to right: one, two, three, four, five, six, seven, eight, nine Only nine? Very strange! Who is missing?
>
> Every single person counts, and they all come up with only nine. Duly confused, they are relieved to meet a sage traveling in the countryside. After sharing their perplexity, they are relieved and astonished by his gentle smile and words: "You are the tenth one," he says to each one.

Of course! What each has forgotten is to count himself. When you are in a trance, you have lost your most important ally: *yourself.*

Staying in the Symptoms

Psychologists noticed that when clients told the story of the symptom, the trance was reinduced.[290] If they could help their clients short-circuit the trance during the telling of the story, they could teach the client how to short-circuit the trance when it kicked in at other times. The key is to pay attention and notice when trance symptoms kick in. The critical assumption is that the trance induces the negative behavior. Short-circuit the trance, and nine times out of ten, you can short-circuit the destructive behavior.

> Take a young woman who comes to therapy with the real problem of not being able to have an orgasm. She knows that she was molested by her stepfather at age nine. One could engage in a long and complex process of *working through* the abuse. Or the trained therapist or guide could say something like, "Jill, when you are having sex, at the moment that you go numb or freeze up or space out, get a picture of that moment and describe it for me."

> While recreating her symptom trance, Jill might answer slowly, "My shoulders are tight . . . my jaw is tight . . . my stomach is tight . . . I'm holding my breath . . . I'm thinking to myself, *Don't touch me, don't come near me, don't hurt me.*"

> "All right, Jill," the therapist continues, "what I'd like you to do is to merge with the picture . . . continue to hold your muscles tightly while you breathe and look at me." This is the pivotal point. "Stay with your trance symptoms, but don't disappear. Stay here with me." Just keeping the eyes open and looking into the eyes of the therapist keeps the client in the present, rather than disappearing in the inner movie, or the trance of the past.

---

[290] Ibid.

A trance is almost always marked or induced in part by a shift in normal breathing. In the ancient Hebrew, the word for *breath*, *neshima*, comes from the word for *soul*: *neshama*. From an evolutionary perspective, respiration represents the emergence of what we call *life*. The ancient texts foreshadow evolutionary science with the powerful phrase, "The Infinity of Intimacy breathed into man the breath of life."[291] This *breath of life* is the flow of intimacy in the Universe. When one cuts off this loving flow, he or she is cutting off the breath of life. This is reflected in a tightening in the chest or other shifts in breathing. When one moves through trance symptoms and reconnects with the loving breath of the Universe, the trance is short-circuited.

Remember the soul mate wisdom text we cited earlier, "Therefore shall a man leave his father and his mother and be intimate with his wife and they shall be one flesh." We interpret this to mean: *Therefore shall a man leave his father and mother and create intimate communion with his partner*. **There are two steps:**

Step one. "He shall leave his father and his mother." He[292] needs to de-trance. Those meetings with emptiness, which cause spontaneous age regression, need to be short-circuited. You need to move beyond old conversations with Father and Mother. Father and Mother here are, of course, only symbols of the formative relationships of our early years.

Step two. "And he shall create intimate communion with his partner." Having become de-tranced, he can now create intimacy with his partner. He now has the ability to receive the present moment fully. Eros is now a possibility.

---

291 By the phrase the Infinity of Intimacy we intend to convey the interior sense of Divinity that suffuses the writing of the Zohar, from which this text is drawn. I first articulated this phrase in other writings of CosmoErotic Humanism, particularly in Your Unique Self: The Radical Path to Personal Enlightenment by M. Gafni (2012).

292 Obviously, while the ancient texts speak of men, these steps are exactly the same for women.

Unfinished Business

Intimacy between soul mates happens only if we actively tend to unfinished business from the past. Of course, it doesn't have to be connected to a parent. It could be connected to an internal conversation or, as is so often the case, to unresolved prior relationships. Whenever I meet with a soul mate couple before their marriage, I tell them this unfinished business story:

> One morning, Master Israel told his disciples that they were going on a journey. There was a wedding of a great man that they had to attend that afternoon. They eagerly climbed into the wagon and as usual, Lexi, the wagon driver, sat facing the Master, his back to the horses, letting the horses go as they must. It was a magical journey, the kind the mystics call *the jumping of the path*. Somehow the air became thin, and it seemed like the wagon was light and transparent, floating on air. There was no noise, no people, no animals, no places. They all seemed to dissolve into the All. After traveling thus for an instant, or an eternity, the wagon seemed to slowly set itself down.
>
> They found themselves in a great city, standing before a fantastic wedding hall. A host of people stood outside, talking excitedly to each other. After inquiring as to the cause of the commotion, they were told that a great man was to have married an hour before. However, as they reached the wedding canopy, his young bride, who was strong and healthy, had collapsed and died. Somehow understanding it all already, Master Israel pushed through the crowd and went straight to the groom.
>
> "Dear Sir, I am sorry about this grievous news. But if I may assist you, then perhaps, we could turn grief to celebration."
>
> The man looked at Master Israel. Though a stranger to him, what had he to lose?

The Master instructed: "Have a grave dug immediately and have your wife placed there. Yet, let no earth be thrown upon her and let her remain dressed in her wedding gown." "You also," he said to the groom, "come to the gravesite dressed in wedding clothes and stand by the graveside awaiting my instructions."

All was done as was requested. The Master went to sit by the graveside and looked intently at the face of the departed. Slowly, his face went white, and all could see that the spirit had left his body and gone to some other place. After what seemed like an interminable time, the Master opened his eyes. The people noted that a warm glow of red had returned to the bride's cheeks. "Lift her up," said Master Israel. They did, and she opened her eyes, looking around, still a bit dazed.

The Master turned to the groom and said, "Take her immediately to the wedding canopy and let the ceremony take place. Mazel tov. Congratulations."

The groom of course insisted that the Master stay and perform the wedding ceremony. As soon as the Master began the wedding blessing, the bride cried out, "That's him! That's him!" "Be silent!" the Master rebuked her. He finished the ceremony, and before anyone could protest, he was gone.

At the wedding feast, the bride herself stood to tell the story.

"My husband, as you all know, was married many years ago to my aunt. She had brought me to attend to the house during the time that she was sick. When her end grew near, she called my husband and extracted a promise from him. Knowing that I was in charge of the affairs of the house, she naturally thought that her husband and I would grow close and ultimately want to marry. The thought was too painful for her, so she made us both swear that we would never marry each other. It was her deathbed request. We both swore. For years, although the connection between us was strong, we avoided each other, until we could no longer, and knew that we must marry.

"But as I was being led to the wedding canopy, my aunt came back and demanded my life for the violation of our oath. I pleaded that we had done all we could and could do no more. A tribunal was set up in heaven, and after much argument a voice issued the decree, 'Judgment is with the living and the dead must let them go. Let the marriage take place.' It was at that moment I awoke and felt myself being lifted from the grave and I stood up again among you. When the Master recited the blessing, I recognized his voice. It was his voice that issued the decree in heaven."

This is a story about unfinished business. Whenever we take the next step in life's journey, old promises, commitments, and relationships return to demand their due. Sometimes we need to honor promises made and broken in our past. Other times, we need to wisely let them go, understanding that they were made in a different time and in a different place. Unfinished business comes in many guises—parents, old visions of self, former loves, unfulfilled dreams. It is only by seeking closure with those parts of our lives that we are able to live fully in the infinite power of the present moment.

Mind Trance and Mindfulness

There is another type of trance that prevents soul mates from entering intimate communion in the present moment. We refer to it as the *mind trance*. The mind trance is the ordinary state in which most of us live our lives. We operate with a dull, throbbing pain that wears incessantly on our souls. Most of the time it is a low hum of *dis-ease* that persists in the invisible background noise of our lives. In order to avoid it, our minds take over, and we think about everything in the world except for the present moment—in which this incessant drone of discomfort whirrs on. Much like an air conditioner, we usually notice it only when we turn it off.

Our minds spend an enormous amount of time avoiding the present. We think about everything that happened yesterday, usually dwelling on what did not go right and replaying it a thousand times. Or we dwell in the future, imagining all the things that might go wrong. There is a famous saying, the source of which is unknown, that gets often (mis)attributed to Mark Twain: "I've had a lot of worries in my life, most of which never happened."[293] If you watch your mind for just a moment or two, you will see that there is a constant low-level mind chatter. Your mind darts like a monkey from thought to thought, moving in and out of past and future, rarely settling anywhere for more than the shortest time.

To heal the mind trance, we invoke a counter-trance often referred to as *mindfulness*. Through mindfulness, we free ourselves from our unconscious, everyday trance and reconnect to the expansive state of alignment with the world's flow. All great achievements in science, theater, sports, or music come from a place of radical concentration, which frees a person from the trap of mind and lets them move effortlessly in the world flow.

> **Soul Mate Practice**. To practice mindfulness, find a great poem. Read it out loud by yourself. Observe as your mind wanders. Don't judge yourself for losing yourself in thoughts. Just return to the poem as you notice your mind straying.

When I started this practice, it would often take me nine or ten tries to focus all the way through the poem. Our minds like to wander off in a thousand directions—anything to avoid staying in the present. There is a constant low-level hum, a kind of incessant internal dialogue of *dis-ease* in our minds. This constant chatter, sometimes called *monkey mind*, is the pattern of the mind that makes us strangers to ourselves because we are never home. Here is the paradox: the only way to turn off the

---

[293] There is another version of it, which we also couldn't source: "I've lived through some terrible things in my life, some of which actually happened."

low-level hum and to heal past pain is to *be* home. By staying deeply in the now, you plug into the healing energy of Reality's LoveIntelligence, LoveBeauty, and LoveDesire.

When we escape the monkey mind, we let the mind enlarge to its full natural expanse. While this might be called *mindfulness* in some circles, in clinical work it is called *therapeutic trance*. The guide invokes a trance in order to break the superficial identification with one's monkey mind. This allows for a merging with the Infinite Healing Power of the Universe that is accessible to all who are in the now. (This is, of course, completely different from de-trancing work.)

The goal of both the psychological and mindfulness approaches is to break the trance. In meditation, we do so by narrowing our focus even more, in order to reenter the present, which naturally expands us to our innately infinite proportions, ending the mind trance. In the psychological approach, the goal is to short-circuit the trigger that initiates the pain trance, preventing us from spontaneously regressing to an earlier age and earlier trauma. Mind trances and pain trances obscure the natural fact that we are part of the great web of Reality. When this happens, the Infinite Healing Resources of the Universe are blocked. The door to these nurturing riches is the portal of the now, which is also the portal to soul mate relationship.

Principle Three. Labels Obstruct Contact

Intimate communion requires contact, and labels obstruct contact. *Name-calling* is always off the table in soul mate encounters. No matter what happens, name-calling or labeling is destructive of intimate communion. If it happens, a sincere apology and a retraction of the label must take place immediately. If it doesn't, intimate communion will profoundly erode.

> When Janis was a student of dance therapy at New York University, she did her internship on Bellevue Hospital's locked psychiatric ward. After she held her first session, which was quite successful, she hurried to leave the ward to get to

class. She went up to the guard and asked to be let out. He looked at her with a slightly surprised smile and asked, "What do you mean? I'm not going to let you out!"

Janis was a little bewildered by his answer but tried to explain. "I'm a student at NYU and have to get to class. Can you please let me out?"

He laughed at her again incredulously. "Yeah, right! And I'm at Harvard. I can't let you out!"

Janis suddenly realized she was stuck in a locked ward, and that anything she said would not be believed. Her pleas would be thrown right back at her. She was locked in the guard's conception of her as a patient! She tried to reason with the guard for a few more minutes, but to no avail. She felt anxious, trapped, everything she said to the guard just plunging her deeper into trouble.

Finally, she decided to turn back and look for her supervisor, the doctor in charge. When she found him and told him what had happened, he looked at her, suppressing a smile, and asked, "But Janis, why were you asking a patient to let you out?"

As the story illustrates, labeling is all around us. We all do it, and most of the time we are not aware of it. This is not to say that labels aren't also helpful. Third-person descriptions, definitions, and categorizations help us navigate complex situations and interactions. Labeling is a natural biopsychological tendency.

Labels come in two general types or flavors: descriptive and evaluative. While both have the power to obstruct authentic contact, labels that evaluate are particularly destructive. Let's look briefly at each type. Descriptive labels are simple. They describe some state of affairs as it appears: big or small, Asian or African, Christian or Buddhist, for example. Evaluative labels are more complex. They act as vehicles for implicit or explicit judgments: smart or stupid, beautiful or ugly, moody or expressive.

Each type of labeling serves similar functions. Each helps us reduce and deal with complexity and confusion. Each aims to make the unknown known. Each makes something frightening into something familiar. Evaluative labels, however, go one step further: they judge the thing or person being labeled. These judgments create distance, which is the opposite of intimate, authentic contact. When you label an encountered object or subject, you become shut down to the possibility of change, blind to what you have not seen, or cannot see, and distanced from intimate engagement.

While problematic, labeling is also entirely normal. We have been doing it since birth. We affix labels to objects, others, and ourselves. And others affix labels to us. Sometimes those labels are meant simply to describe (descriptive), and sometimes they are meant to judge (evaluative). The judgments made by evaluative labels can be negative or positive; some are meant to hurt us; others are meant to clarify or praise.

An often-mentioned ethical guideline in the western world's best-selling book of all time, the Bible, is *Deal kindly with the stranger*.[294] A stranger is anyone whose uniqueness is blocked from view by a label. As much as labels disclose and divulge, they also obscure and obfuscate and therefore stand against intimate communion and contact. This is true in two ways: First, we often label compulsively to feel a sense of control and comfort in a situation, using labels that are often sloppy, inaccurate, or just plain false. A false label yields false conclusions, which often lead to wrong and destructive action. Second, labels grab our attention and block accurate perception. When we cannot see what's real, we cannot make contact, even with that which is right in front of us. False or limiting labels often end the conversation. They blind us to other possibilities. They prevent us from seeing more deeply. They prevent a more profound and nuanced understanding of any given person. And this is most powerfully

---

[294] See, for example, Leviticus 19:34 (English Standard Version): "You shall treat the stranger who sojourns with you as the native among you, and you shall love him as yourself, for you were strangers in the land of Egypt: I am the LORD your God."

true for evaluative labels, which should be used only with very careful discernment for specific purposes of accurate diagnosis, which leads to providing care in limited professional contexts. But the rule of thumb in relationships is: *labels often lie*. For a soul mate relationship, the demand is to never let labels transform the other into a stranger.

Soul Mate Practice. The key to stopping the destructive power of labeling lies in the ability to recognize when you are in fact labeling. The following simple practice aims to help you build that skill.

Start by recognizing that you, like practically every other human being, label all the time, and that most of that labeling activity is automatic and difficult to spot. Then, as you go about your day, bring awareness to your inner voice, your inner labeler.

You'll notice that you are labeling everything—other people, things you read, things you hear, and so on. When you spot yourself labeling something, for example, "He is ignorant," "She is lazy," or even "This is a hopeless situation," ask yourself a simple question: *Is my label descriptive or evaluative?* If it is descriptive, follow up with the question: *Is this label needed?* If it doesn't help to communicate something important, let it go. If it is evaluative, ask yourself the following: *Why am I being judgmental? Is it bringing me closer to something, or pushing something further away?* Either way, evaluative labels obstruct contact.

When you notice an evaluative label, stop labeling. It's as simple as that. Then, if you have actively labeled another person (versus a thing), take the next step in the practice. Let that person know that you labeled them. Ask them what impact it has had on them and make amends. Then, attempt to communicate to them how you are feeling in a way that does not rely on labels. Repeat this practice daily and, over time, you'll notice that you won't label so frequently or so blindly anymore.

Principle Four. The Power of Not Knowing

You never know. The goal of intimate communion is to receive your beloved fully and openly with deep understanding and empathy. If labeling obstructs such authentic contact, actively holding a space of not knowing works to promote it. When are we simply unable to meet each other in the present, are we to give up, or is there a path of receiving that can create potent intimacy, even when we cannot fully grasp the full essence of our beloved? Is there a way to receive what seems at times so unreceivable? Is there a way to liberate our partners from the loneliness of being unseen?

This quandary inspires one of the more subtle ideas of St. Thomas Aquinas, the medieval writer who did so much to define Christianity. Although his formal concern was what he called *our connection with God*, his ideas have important implications for human-to-human intimate communion. Whether or not you are a person of spirit is of no matter right now. Just follow the inner logic of the next paragraph, and it will give us a gorgeous distinction of soul mate encounters, which you will be able to deploy in your relationship.

Our task, assumes St. Thomas Aquinas, is in some sense to receive God. As the Platonic philosopher Plotinus once said, *God is the lonely one*.[295] You don't have to read the Bible, or any religious document for that matter, to realize that God has a serious communication problem. God's Essence, his Divine Unique Self, remains unshared with most of humanity.

---

295 See, for example, J. B. Soloveitchik, "The Lonely Man of Faith," in Tradition: A Journal of Orthodox Jewish Thought 7, no. 2 (1965): 5–67: "In my 'desolate, howling solitude' I experience a growing awareness that, to paraphrase Plotinus' apothegm about prayer, this service to which I, a lonely and solitary individual, am committed is wanted and gracefully accepted by God in His transcendental loneliness and numinous solitude" (p. 7). The "desolate, howling solitude" here refers to Deuteronomy 32:10 (see, for example, in the New International Version: "In a desert land he found him, in a barren and howling waste. He shielded him and cared for him; he guarded him as the apple of his eye").

So, mystics ask, how can we liberate God from Divine Loneliness? *But, asks Aquinas, if the very Essence of God is his unknowability, how can we create intimate communion with God?* After all, to be intimate is to know. How can they both write that the human being is enjoined to know God and at the same time write that God is unknowable?

Aquinas and Maimonides proposed an ingenious solution, which we might refer to as *the affirmation of not knowing*. That is, we recognize God by acknowledging that we do not know him. In the words of a character created by French writer Edmond Jabès, "I know you, Lord, in the measure that I do not know you."[296]

For years I thought that the affirmation of not knowing was a classic example of irrelevant medieval sophistry. Then, a seemingly casual incident profoundly changed my heart and mind.

> On a rare stormy day in Jerusalem, I made my way to the small neighborhood grocer to pick up essentials for some bad-weather hibernation. My mood was about as foul as the gust of smoke that greeted me at the door. The source of the noxious fumes, I soon found out, was a middle-aged man, loitering in my corner store! Shirt open to midchest, large gold necklace blaring, he stood there smoking his postbreakfast cigar. Fanning and coughing my way through his smoke, I mumbled to the grocer my consternation at the torrential rains that had soaked me through and through.
>
> The man with the gold necklace turned and looked at me with the gentlest look you could possibly imagine. In an instant, all of his features appeared handsome and majestic. The gold necklace seemed regal, the smoke sweet as incense. "Don't you know?" he said. "It's raining today because a holy man has passed to the next world."

---

[296] Edmond Jabès, "The Book of Questions," in Paul Auster, Collected Prose: Autobiographical Writings, True Stories, Critical Essays, Prefaces and Collaborations with Artists (2011).

I felt like some gate had swung open inside of me. Something in my heart went soft. I just wanted to reach out and hug him for being so beautiful. It was an epiphany moment, pure and simple. Only later, when I got home and read the paper, did I see that one of Jerusalem's great saints had, in fact, died that morning.

If I said that I thought the man with the cigar and the gold necklace was an angel, I would be taking the easy way out. Indeed, he was not an angel, but a man of flesh and blood. And I had totally misjudged him. I thought him to be a boor—coarse and crass, involved only in his immediate needs. However, the shining beauty and Zenlike understanding on his face, as he told me that a holy man had died, let me know how superficial my vision had been. I had assumed I knew him, and yet I had not truly known or received him at all. In that moment, the words "You never know, you never know, you never know," flashed through my mind.[297]

We can never be certain of the nature of the person standing before us. And we are entirely certain that we are rarely fully seen for who we are. That is precisely what Aquinas meant when he said that God was lonely. Loneliness is the experience of being invisible. Loneliness means that I cannot share my *soul print*,[298] the unique contours of who I am, with another person. In one sense, we can never *fully* know or understand our partners. All too often, we label, categorize, dismiss, or otherwise put our beloveds in a box. Beloveds in boxes are doomed to be lonely.

The only core response to loneliness, which then becomes the first fragrance of intimacy, is the humility to acknowledge that we do not know. We must answer the call to honor the mystery of our beloved. But it is not a painful humility. Rather it is a devotional humility in relation to the beloved. She or he remains ultimately unknowable, just like the

---

[297] The words are a refrain from modern mystical master and singer Shlomo Carlebach. He would sing them as a refrain in teaching and concerts.

[298] See Gafni, Soul Prints.

Divine. We must honor the mystery and gently remember, "You never know, you never know, you never know."

Soul Mate Practice. Over the next week, pay particular attention to every time that you feel someone is judging you. They can be judging actively and openly, or it can be implicit. Do your best to suspend any overt emotional reactions or defensive responses. Then, in your mind, identify three things that you know to be true about yourself, which, if they were known by the other person, would very likely change their judgment. By identifying these three truths, notice how your tendency to be defensive decreases. **Repeat this process as many times as possible, and you'll notice that you are getting more deeply in touch with the power of not knowing.**

Now, here's the tricky part: you'll need to bring balance to the equation by engaging in the same practice whenever *you* make a judgment. Any time you catch yourself judging what someone says or what they are doing, bring to mind three things about the other person, which, if true, would render your judgments inappropriate or otherwise wrong. It doesn't matter if what you bring to mind is actually true. The point is that *you don't know*, and they very well might be true. Again, repeat this process each time you find yourself making a judgment about someone else. **Over time, you'll recognize that just as people don't know every aspect of you, you don't know every aspect of them. The true power of the practice of not knowing emanates from this balance.**

Finally, it is critical to realize that this is not ultimately tragic. Rather, mystery and revelation, *gnosis* and ignorance, the hidden and the revealed are themselves First Principles and First Values embedded in the very structure of Cosmos.

The distinctions and practices discussed in this supplementary essay have a dual effect on soul mate relationships. First, they deepen soul mate encounters by harnessing some of the core strengths of soul mate consciousness. Second, they act against many of the limitations that have come to characterize soul mate relationships. Yet ultimately, the limitations of soul mate can only be resolved by the next step in evolution of relationships: whole mate or evolutionary relationships.

Essay 2. Wounds in Role Mate, Soul Mate, and Whole Mate Relationships

Role mates, soul mates, and whole mates relate to their personal wounds in very different ways. They also have different expectations for how their partners ought to relate to their wounds.

Identity and relationship are a virtuous cycle. The nature of your identity directly and profoundly affects your relationship, as well as the degree of your identification with your own wounds. Moreover, it affects how you expect your partner to hold your wounds.

Neither level one nor level two gets this entirely right. Understanding the full range of crucial responses to wounds is indispensable to the whole mate relationship consciousness. These responses are captured in eight principles described in this essay; each applies primarily to one of the three levels.

Dealing with wounds is a critical topic, both in the spiritual world and in the psychotherapeutic world. Both worlds have important contributions to make, and both make a series of mistakes. We want to integrate the insights of both, while correcting for their shortfalls. From that place, we hope to offer a more potent, good, true, and beautiful vision of how we can engage our wounds.

Principle One. Get Over It

Principle one captures the primary approach to wounds in role mate relationships: *get over it*. This stems from the fact that, at level one, we are engaged in the very important business of meeting our core survival needs. In the context of survival, there is no room to get stuck in wounds. From the role mate perspective, excessive engagement with wounds is narcissistic and indulgent. *Stop it. Get over it. We need to attend to more important matters.* When a fire is burning, we do not engage the fireman in therapeutic conversations about how he feels about the fire.

To give just one example of this consciousness: When immigrants come to a new country, their focus is often on survival and thriving. Their wounds are deep and real, born out of the transition to a new country and uprooting from the old country. But in the first phase, which may last several years or a generation, the focus is on ensuring that core needs are satisfied. Typically, it is only the children of successful immigrants who have the space to explore wounds. In this scenario, the parents' partnership is characterized by role mate dynamics, while the children have more freedom to seek and engage in soul mate relationships.

Principle Two. Honor, Engage, and Work to Transform Wounds

The second principle is crucial for the soul mate level of consciousness. Once the needs for survival and thriving have been met, the relationship to wounds evolves. Here, individuals recognize and honor the realness of their wounds. They don't engage in emotional bypass because they have been too busy meeting core needs. They don't engage in denial. Wounds and pain are not dismissed. They are not trivialized. Soul mate partners engage their personal histories. They engage and transform the trauma of the past, so it does not drive their present or prevent their presence. You cannot create authentic intimacy in the present when the past poisons your ability to show up and be truly vulnerable with your partner.

At the core of principle two is the notion that the past is *living*. As such, you have to engage it. Bypass is neither possible nor preferred. You have to honor the past, care for the wounds, recognize them, and work with them. This is at the core of level-two soul mate relationships.

Of course, even at level two, you have to be wary of retelling the story again and again and again. You want to transform yesterday, not get mired or stuck in it. You want to avoid recursive loops of narcissistic indulgence. There is a danger here that requires sensitive attention. In soul mate relationships, partners are often identified with their separate selves. From this place, there is an attraction to wounds. When you live in limited, separate-self-consciousness, the indulgence of past wounds is necessary and becomes seductive, because your feeling of aliveness often comes from your sense of being wounded.

Principle Three. Don't Cry More Than It Hurts

Principle three is an extension of principle two. It is similarly crucial in guiding soul mate relationships. It is about accuracy and precision: be accurate and precise when talking about your wounds, regardless of whether you are talking to yourself or to someone else. One of the best definitions of sanity is *appropriate proportionality*—suggesting that we should take things in their right proportion. One of the most painful symptoms of many psychological disorders is the wrong weighting of events.

> There's a beautiful story, told in the Hebrew mystical tradition, about Master Naftali of Rophsitz. It's a story about a king who has a son. The son is crying. He just can't stop crying. He's devastated. He's in grief, overcome by depression. He's been checked for a formal psychiatric disorder, which might cause nonstop tears. None of them match his state. But he can't stop crying. The king tries every therapeutic approach possible. None of them are effective.
>
> After several years of failed treatments, a wise, bent-over woman comes to the court. She asks the king for permission to meet with his son for fifteen minutes.

The king is at his wit's end. He doesn't know who this woman is. He posts guards at the door to make sure that it's safe. She goes in and sits with him for about fourteen minutes, at the end of which she leans over and whispers several words in his ear. She then walks out. She says, "My work is done," and leaves. An hour goes by, and the king's son begins to cry a little bit less. Two hours go by, and the crying abates a bit more, and within several hours, the king's son has stopped crying altogether.

The king is amazed and sends his guards to bring the old woman, who is now some distance from the town, back to the court. When she returns, he thanks her profusely and offers her a rich reward. "Tell me," he says, "please just tell me one thing, if you would: What did you do?"

She answers quietly but directly, "I sat with him in his pain."

The king is silent for a moment and nods slowly, understanding. "But what did you say to him at the end? Was it an incantation, a spell? What magic did you use?"

She responds, "I did not use magic of the kind of which you speak, Your Majesty. I spoke to him only six simple words: 'Don't cry more than it hurts.'"

The message of this story is powerful and important for all of us. We need to fully recognize, honor, and engage all of our trauma and all of our wounds. In the sweepstakes for childhood wounding, we each have fairly strong entries of different kinds. We have firsthand knowledge about wounds and trauma. We know that, after engaging in all the best ways that we can, there comes a moment where we need to move on—where we should not get stuck.

The key is to avoid the very powerful temptation to create your identity through the story of your wounding. *Don't cry more than it hurts.*

Don't let hurt be a fig leaf for a thousand ways of acting out. Beware of unconsciously moving from the victim to the perpetrator role, which is often what happens when you overidentify as a victim. Don't allow the hurt to become a free pass for attack, dehumanization, and demonization in various forms. *Don't cry more than it hurts.* Don't let your experience of being hurt justify inflicting hurt that is often many times more devastating than what you suffered.

But here is the most insidious part of the *crying more than it hurts* trap. When you do so, you tend to root your very identity in your victimhood. Even as our hearts and hands are open to support every victim and to dry every tear, to be a victim is to be powerless. You are particularly prone to this form of impotence when you are not rooted in the deeper identity of your Unique Self. You get trapped in your powerless state. **Your identity is your power. When you derive your identity from being a victim, your power comes from being powerless. Impotence is the price of your perfect and perpetual innocence.** And, at the very same time, our heart and hands are open to support every victim and to dry every tear.

Principle Four. Experience Your Wounds in an Evolutionary Unique Self Context

The last five principles are relevant to the whole mate level of relationship. When you are in a larger context, wounds tend to matter less. When you start to engage in a relationship from a place of whole mate consciousness, your wounds simply do not hurt as much. You are playing a larger game. The obsessive replaying of your victim story ceases to be attractive. It is just not that interesting. It is not sexy. It is actually quite boring.

You are now playing in a much bigger Field. You are living in a larger context. From that larger context, you are able to hold the right proportion in relation to your wounds. You are liberated from the credo of hypersensitive, narcissistic *I am wounded, therefore I am*. No! Rather, you feel:

> I am an Evolutionary Unique Self; therefore I am. I am an Outrageous Lover, therefore I am. I have a unique expression

of LoveIntelligence, LoveBeauty, and LoveDesire to live and share in the Cosmos; therefore I am. From that place, I am going to do all the work on my wounds that is necessary, but that's not who I am. I am not an addict. I may have an addiction to work with. I am not a wounded being; I am a Unique Self. I have wounds, but I engage from the bigger context of my Evolutionary Unique Self.

Let's just feel this for a moment from another perspective. There is a beautiful and clear psychological insight in Abraham Maslow's hierarchy of needs, which describes how, at different stages of consciousness, human beings have different needs.[299] At the early stages, wounds play a large role. Maslow's first five levels of needs are survival, safety, belonging, self-esteem, and self-actualization. These are the levels that most relationships play out on. At these levels, the consciousness of the person is often that of separate self. The love at play is what we have called *ordinary love*.[300] Wounds are front and center in relationships that take place at these five developmental stages.

The needs of these five stages are legitimate and important, particularly for the separate self. Maslow was insightful when called these five levels *deficiency needs*. You feel empty and want to be full. The drive to survive, be safe, belong, and feel self-esteem is driven by a sense of lack or emptiness. But later in his career, Maslow realized that there was one more level of needs that came from an entirely different order of consciousness. He called these *self-transcendence needs*.

At this level of needs, the human being feels an essential need to play a larger game. Maslow recognized this is as a core yearning of the human heart. He wisely pointed out that it is not a deficiency need. Rather, it is a need that comes from an intuition of our greatness. It comes from the

---

299 See, for example, Abraham H. Maslow, "Critique of Self-Actualization Theory," in Edward Hoffman (ed.) Future Visions: The Unpublished Papers of Abraham Maslow (1996), 26–32. See also Maslow, "The Farther Reaches of Human Nature," Journal of Transpersonal Psychology 1, no. 1 (1969): 1–9 and Maslow, The Farther Reaches of Human Nature (1971).

300 Chapter 9, "Outrageous Love."

feeling that our identity is much larger than we might have imagined.[301]

After the lack-driven (or wound-driven) needs have been met, we turn to our larger identity. This is the identity of the Outrageous Lover. It is the sense of being a Unique Self in a larger evolutionary context. It is the profound knowing that I cannot be an extra on the set. It is the inchoate recognition that my life matters, that I can play a larger game, that I can participate uniquely in the evolution of love. At this level of consciousness, wounds are simply not central. Your larger identity is so filled with Eros and aliveness that the need to form an identity rooted in victimhood simply falls away. When the obsession with wounds falls away, the real questions emerge: *What does the Universe want through me? What does Reality need from me?* Huge energy is released when we are no longer carrying around wounds and resentments.

Principle Five. Stay Open through the Pain

Evolution beyond an exclusive identification with the separate self, whether through mindfulness or Reality practice, profoundly transforms your relationship to your wounds. This transformation is essential to any person who wants to live a decent life. In our hypersensitive, slightly narcissistic cultural context, there has been an almost obsessive emphasis on personal hurt. That is not entirely surprising. When the ego is the center of gravity of your personal identity, you will experience hurt as a terrible insult to your very existence.

Obsession with Personal Hurt Activates the Ritual of Rejection

Your hurt activates the *ritual of rejection* along with degenerative patterns of recrimination. The ego will tend to take hurt and turn it into an insult, which offends your existence. To compensate, you set into motion the ritual of rejection. It goes something like this:

1. You experience the pain of hurt and/or rejection.

---

[301] Maslow called that growth needs.

2. As a result, you feel small and insignificant—and it even puts you in touch with your nonexistence.

3. To feel less small, you lash out and inflict hurt. By hurting the other, you experience power, which makes you feel like you exist again.

In order to assert your power, you seek to hurt the one who, as you feel, has hurt you. By damaging the one who hurt you, your ego is sated. You have proven to your hypersensitive, empty self, and to whoever the spectators might be, that you exist. Unfortunately, you have done this in the most degraded way, by inflicting hurt.

In our contemporary victim culture, saying *I was hurt* is all too often a justification for the most insidiously motivated malice. *Being hurt* has become an idol that forgives all sin. It is only through stepping up into your larger identity as Evolutionary Unique Self that you learn the freedom of staying open as Outrageous Love through the hurt. You practice staying open as Outrageous Love through the pain. You turn the egoic insults of the small self into the wounds of love of the Unique Self. When you expand the context of your consciousness and widen your circle of caring and concern, the obsession with your wounds will begin to dissipate and ultimately disappear as you begin to realize your own liberation.

Let me tell you a story I first read in a Buddhist text some decades back.

> There was a woman—Kiso Gotami may have been her name—who was so broken, to whom life had dealt such a harsh hand, that she simply was unable to get up in the morning. So, she went to the Buddha and asked what she could do. She had come to the end. Life was just too painful. The Buddha said to her, "If you bring me a mustard seed from a house that knows no sorrow, then all will be well with you." She thought, "This will be very simple." Life was hard for her, but so many of her neighbors led such easy, happy lives.

She knocked on the door of her neighbor's house, the couple with the wonderful relationship and seven smiling children. She told them, "The Buddha has told me to bring a mustard seed from a house that knows no sorrow, and all will be well with me. I know you have such a joyous house! Might you please spare me a mustard seed?"

They looked at her almost angrily and said, "You have no idea what is going on in our house. You don't know about . . ." And they began to tell her of the tragedies they had suffered—tales of secret woe and hidden sorrow, the likes of which she had never heard. (We think we know so well what is going on in someone else's reality.) She heard their story and decided to stay and offer comfort. A good while later, she left and went to the next house. She was sure this house was a house of joy with no sorrow. She asked again for a mustard seed. The response again was, "Why did you come to us? You think we're a house with no sorrow?" They began to tell her their story of sadness and woe.

What could she do? Again, she was so moved, she wanted to comfort them. She stayed with the second family for a period of time, comforting, soothing, and trying to cheer them.

She went to a third house and again met the same story of sorrow. Her compassion was aroused once again. She stayed with them and comforted them as well. And so it continued from house to house. She was comforted as she gave comfort. Her ego fell away as she entered the unique calling of her life and realized her liberation.

When you add an alignment with the evolutionary impulse itself to this teaching of compassion, the obsession with wounds begins to take on a sense of the ridiculous. To make contact as a whole mate in an evolutionary relationship, you must know how to avoid the ritual of rejection that so often arises from the ego's contraction. To know how to inhibit the ritual of rejection, you need to know how its dynamics work. When you feel hurt, your small-self contracts. Unless you make an effort to counter the ego's inertia, you fall out of your alignment with the evolutionary impulse. You fall out of Outrageous Love. You fall into ordinary love or even into explicit UnLove. Evolutionary relationships ask that you fall into Outrageous Love again and again. You refuse to be limited by ordinary love. At their core, evolutionary relationships demand that you always free yourself again and again from the coiled contraction of your limited identity as separate self.

In order to enter a whole mate evolutionary relationship, you must resist the downward pull of ordinary love. You must identify as part of the larger Field of Outrageous Love. This is the Source of your authentic power. This will allow you to receive hurt inflicted by others as a wound of love, and not as an insult. You wear your hurt as a battle scar in your struggle for love. You bear it with pride and dignity. You are freed from the compulsive need to inflict pain on the one who hurt you in order to prove you exist. You know you exist because you are aligned with the evolutionary impulse—you are identified with the larger Whole beyond your particular part.

Live as Outrageous Love

The transcending of the limited identity of separate self into Unique Self Realization is animated by the quality of Outrageous Love. Outrageous Love motivates and manifests the spontaneous action of care and compassion. Self-contraction has the quality of fear. Fear motivates and manifests the reactive rituals of egotism. To live and act as Outrageous Love means to keep your heart open through the pain of heartache and hurt. To live and act as fear means to allow the pain to close your heart.

You can practice Outrageous Love by practicing opening your heart even when you feel hurt. Rather than turning away, closing down, and striking out, you keep your heart open. This will help you act skillfully instead of reacting clumsily in these situations.

When you practice opening as Outrageous Love in the face of the hurt, the power of the past weakens. Old wounds are in the past. If you open your heart in the present, time after time, the power of the past recedes.

You will probably always feel the pain when you meet your only beloved with ordinary love. Although you are speaking words of love, you can feel your heart closed underneath the words. But you do not need to resign yourself to the closure, which deadens your heart and your lifeforce. You can continually practice Outrageous Love rather than closing down into ordinary love. You can feel your heart's movement toward closure and choose to inhibit the closure. From a place of Outrageous Love, you can choose to change the way you react.

You are not *only* a victim of your past. You are also pulled by your future. When you stop ignoring or overdramatizing past events, you also stop unconsciously using past trauma to avoid giving the depth of Outrageous Love that is yours to give in the present moment.

The pain of the past may have come to you through another. Your present reaction is yours. *You* are doing it. You must assume responsibility for your own complex of reactivity. Reactive emotion and reenactment do not need to be a fact of your nature. You can take your armor off. You can unguard your heart and trust yourself to live and love from an intense, armor-less vulnerability. This is the safest place from which to live.

For some people, especially those with fortunate childhood circumstances, opening through hurt is not so hard. For others, it may be the work of a lifetime. For all of us, it is perhaps the most important work we can do for our own love and freedom, and the love and freedom of the others in our lives.

To be weak in love is to identify exclusively with your separate self, which is always already insulted and empty with craving. To love outrageously is to know that we are all lost and found in the same Reality together. To love outrageously is to stay open in gratitude and joy even as you know that love breaks your heart.

Ordinary love is a strategy of the separate self. It is insufficient to *stand against* outrageous pain. The only response to outrageous pain is Outrageous Love—the Infinity of Intimacy that is the interior Face of the Cosmos holding you in every second.

Outrageous Love is the Evolutionary Love that animates every moment of existence. It is the Love that is not hard to find; it is the Love that is impossible to avoid. It is the Love that is showering you in every second. Realize that there are one hundred billion neurons[302] in your brain at this moment, working for you, holding you in every second. There are trillions of cells in your body, uniquely operating and caressing you in every moment. You have about sixty-two thousand miles of nerve pathways feeling you in every instant.[303] Dazzlingly complex, Outrageous LoveIntelligence, LoveBeauty, and LoveDesire expressed in molecular and cellular interactions that outstrip the most advanced supercomputers are cradling you in this very second. When you wake up to this scientific reality, you realize that you are part of this larger Field of Outrageous LoveIntelligence that holds you right now.

You begin to realize that the entire Evolutionary Story is love in action pulsing through your body as you read these words. As you read, you are being held. The most elegant sophisticated systems of biology, chemistry, and physics are holding you right now in the embrace of their Outrageous LoveIntelligence, LoveBeauty, and LoveDesire focused directly on you uniquely.

Out of the depth of this realization, you begin to be lived as love.

To be lived as love, you've got to be willing to open your heart through the pain again, and again, and again. You must practice opening as love, even when you feel hurt. When you practice opening as love, the power of the past weakens. Old wounds that need to be engaged are real, but they are actually in the past. You will always feel the pain, but you won't feel the closure. Even when you feel the self-contraction, you are able to choose your response to the hurt.

In one of the great moments of biblical myth, Jacob sees Rachel, the love of his life, for the first time standing by the well. It is the original story of love at first sight. When you see another truly, your seeing plunges you

---

302 See, for example, S. Herculano-Houzel, "The Human Brain in Numbers: A Linearly Scaled-Up Primate Brain," Frontiers in Human Neuroscience 3, no. 31 (2009), https://doi.org/10.3389/neuro.09.031.2009.

303 See, for example, The Nervous System, compiled by Howie Baum, University of Cincinnati (https://pdf4pro.com/amp/view/the-nervous-system-university-of-cincinnati-69596c.html): the nervous system "is so vast and complex that, an estimate is that all the individual nerves from one body, joined end to end, could reach around the world two and a half times."

into love. In their first meeting, the story goes, Jacob kissed Rachel; he then raised his voice and cried. *Why the crying?* asks the master, Torah scholar Rashi, commenting on the text. *Because he saw he would not be buried with her.*[304]

To love is to know that you will feel the pain of separation. This is the paradox of love: love is suffering, yet to live and not to love outrageously is madness. We do not liberate ourselves from the suffering of love by detaching ourselves from Love itself. Liberation in the path of Outrageous Love is to suffer the mortal circumstances of your love so completely that you are moved beyond yourself.

We live in a world of outrageous pain. The only response to outrageous pain is Outrageous Love. You are moved beyond your small self to your True Self and then to your Unique Self, where you realize that you and your beloved will always meet again. Only then can you love fully from your unguarded heart.

Principle Six. Bring Your Wounds to the Mother

Bring your wounds to rest in the Mother. All of Rumi's work is about this. When you really get Sufism, or the erotic realization of Hebrew wisdom, you see that it is about bearing the agonizing pain and bringing it to the Mother and offering it up. This is a huge topic—beyond what is possible to engage with in this book. For now, we just want to offer you an image to hold this principle.

You are carrying a suitcase to the train station. It is heavy. You have just gotten on the train. But you keep holding the suitcase in your hand. It is getting heavier by the moment. But it does not occur to you that you might put it down. You do not quite realize that you are now on the train. You are not walking by yourself any longer. The conductor says, "You can put your suitcase down now. The train will hold both you and everything you carry." That is what it means to know that you and everything you carry is held in the arms of the Mother. That is what it means to know that you live in an Intimate Universe.

---

304 See The Torah: With Rashi's Commentary, edited by Herczeg (1995, 1999).

Principle Seven. Hurt Is a State

You choose the framework of interpretation that directly impacts how you experience your hurt. Hurt is *a state*. All states, whether they be altered, mystical, or ecstatic, are temporary. States overtake you and shift your consciousness. However, you invariably return to your natural state of consciousness. At that point, without even being aware that you are doing it, you begin to interpret your state experience. All states are subject to interpretation through many different prisms—cultural, social, psychological, emotional, and developmental. For example, states are interpreted through the prism of the stage of consciousness in which the person experiencing the state usually locates.

A *stage*, unlike a state, is not passing and temporary. Rather, it is a stable and irreversible level of consciousness. States do not yield any information by themselves; they are always interpreted through the prism of stages. It is for this reason that so many aphorisms suggest that a person's true level of consciousness and interior psychological self is revealed when they are drunk. Some people get very kind and open when drunk, and others seem to get very mean and cruel. Some reveal their open heart, and others reveal their racism.

Mystical states, too, are interpreted through the prism of stages of consciousness. Let's say you have a genuine mystical experience.

If you are at an **egocentric level of moral development**, you may interpret your experience as unique to you. If you are obsessively egocentric in a narcissistic way, you may think that you are the only enlightened being on the planet.

The same experience, interpreted at an **ethnocentric level of consciousness**, may suggest that your people and no other are the chosen people of God.

If you are at a **worldcentric level**, you will be more likely to interpret your experience as a call that obligates you to engage in healing and transformation on a global scale.

If you are at a **cosmocentric level of consciousness**, then the level of depth and wisdom with which you approach the global activism sparked by your mystical state will be of a fundamentally deeper quality. Cosmocentric implies an expansive and integral embrace of all systems and forms of knowing available to you. At this level, you are more likely to engage the situation with an integrated mind, body, and heart, and a whole system understanding of the evolutionary possibilities available to meet the moment. Your wisdom merges profound reverence for the past, penetrating insight into the present, and a humble boldness toward the future. **Your state, in this case a mystical state, is always interpreted through your level of consciousness.**

Hurt is also a state, and it is interpreted in the same manner. This is a huge insight. Hurt is not an objective reality that gives you license for cruelty under the cover of *I was hurt*. Hurt is interpreted through your level of consciousness. As you evolve, your relationship to your wounds naturally shifts. More than any other single barometer, what you do with your hurt reveals to you and others your genuine level of consciousness. When you feel hurt, the masks of piety and the guises of liberation from ego are stripped away, and your naked heart is revealed to yourself and those with eyes to see.

Once you approach your hurt from this wider context, you can begin to appreciate the next exercise. If we learn to live wide open, even as we are hurt by love, then the Divine wakes up to its own True Nature. To be firm in your knowing of Love, even when you are desperate, and to be strong in your heart of forgiveness, even when you are betrayed, is what it means to be an Outrageous Lover.

Opening as Love to the Pain: An Outrageous Love Whole Mate Practice

Next, we'll invite you, tenderly and fiercely, to engage in a short exercise about your wounds. For this exercise, we suggest that you not bring to mind a huge, old trauma, but instead locate an ordinary, everyday trauma. Find a manageable hurt, in which you feel closed, and we'll see if we can help you to love it open through the pain. The way to do it is very simple.

Start by finding a trusted other; your partner or a close friend is ideal. Then, describe this moment of hurt to your partner. Describe what happened and how the pain felt. The goal here is to get back in touch with the feeling of hurt, but not to wallow in it. Then, when you are finished, say the following to your partner while looking into their eyes: "I am opening as love to the pain." Then, your partner, who has remained silent until this point, replies: "I honor your opening as love to the pain." OK? That's the whole exercise. It is really powerful. As you say, "I am opening as love to the pain," you should actually be able to feel your heart opening. Importantly, this is not a one-time event. Repeat this practice with another past trauma, until you feel yourself stepping into love.

As simple as this practice may seem, it is actually a core spiritual practice, one which I consider to be one of my most central practices. I work hard to keep opening my heart again and again, and again, and again. I refuse to become bitter, refuse to get lost in anger, and refuse to close. Whatever life is throwing at me, at least until now, the Divine has given me the grace to keep opening my heart. Because of this practice, each hurt becomes not an insult, but a wound of love. When your heart breaks, it cracks open. The irreducibly unique Outrageous Lover, which lives in you, as you, and through you, is able to speak your love into the world, unlike any other being that ever was, is, or will be. When this Love comes online, you begin to feel your aliveness, which is God's Aliveness living in you. When Outrageous Love comes online, something happens, something really important shifts. It is the root of all transformation, and it is only through this type of practice that relationships become an evolutionary crucible of Outrageous Love.

Principle Eight. Never Bypass Authentic Wounding

Even when you awaken as Outrageous Love, and even when you are living in an evolutionary context as your Evolutionary Unique Self, personal wounds must always be honored. This is especially true when we are talking about someone else who needs us to help them honor and hold their wounding. To use the passion of living your Unique Self as a deflector shield against feeling and responding to the legitimate wounds and needs of your beloved is never OK. When you fail to hold the dignity of personal wounds, you may begin to engage in manipulation or possibly even psychological abuse. When you begin to see yourself as aligned with the evolutionary impulse, you must always keep hold of the intimate details of that which is intensely personal.

The authentic wounds of your beloved and of others can never be bypassed. For me, it was always the Hasidic master Levi Isaac of Berdichev, who radically reminded me of the primacy of the personal, even when in the throes of evolutionary ecstasy. We told this story earlier in the book, but it is really relevant here and is well worth repeating.

> Levi Isaac was leading the prayers at the close of *Yom Kippur* services. *Yom Kippur* is a day of fasting and the holiest day in the Hebrew calendar. The twilight hours at the end of the fast are filled with potency. During that time, mystical *Kabbalah* says, the enlightened prayer leader may enter the source code of Reality and effect a *tikkun*, or a momentous leap in the evolution of consciousness for the sake of all sentient beings throughout time, past, present, and future.

> This is precisely what Levi Isaac was doing on that particular *Yom Kippur*. Night had already fallen, and the fast should have been officially over. However, the ecstasy of Levi Isaac was still rippling through the upper worlds. Everyone present held their breath in awe. All of Reality was pulsating with him and through him toward an ecstatic, evolutionary crescendo. Just as a great breakthrough was about to happen, Levi Isaac spotted an old man who was thirsty. The fast had been very long, and the old man was in desperate need of a drink. In the midst of his ecstasy, Levi Isaac brought the whole evolutionary process to a halt. He immediately ended the fast and personally brought the old man a drink of water.

Levi Isaac, recognizing an authentic personal need, an important personal wound, if you will, was moved to address it despite the ecstasy, importance, and grandeur of what was unfolding in that very moment. Authentic personal needs or wounds should never be bypassed.

If you are living within the narrow identity of your ego, and you have suffered betrayal or abuse, it is likely that the pain of these wounds will take up an enormous amount of your psychic and emotional energy. However, if you have evolved beyond exclusive identification with separate self to a lived identity with your Unique Self, your relationship with your wounds will dramatically shift. Your Unique Self lives and breathes in alignment with a larger evolutionary framework. It seeks to contribute your unique gifts for the sake of the larger Whole, even when the larger Whole is best served by bringing a glass of water to someone in need.

In such a large context, the evolutionary perspective of Unique Self naturally puts your wounds in perspective. This means that you will be much more likely to see your wounds from a cosmocentric perspective. When you identify yourself as a unique expression of the Divine, responsible for co-creating the next evolutionary leap toward greater love, inclusion, and embrace, you situate your wounds in a wider, fuller context. From this place, your somewhat natural tendency toward personal obsession with petty insults and minor hurts is exposed. The narcissism that those insults and wounds may evoke is defused and released.

By holding your realization of Outrageous Love more deeply, you understand that you are not merely part of the Whole, in the sense of being a cog in a machine or a link in a process. Rather, you recognize that your part is the Whole itself. Your part (that is to say, *you*) has infinite value, dignity, and worth. The pain of your part (that is, *your* pain) is the pain of All-That-Is. The Love and Compassion that *is* the Reality of All-That-Is feels your pain. You and Reality meet in an empathetic embrace within the depth of your wounding, for which Reality weeps. That is what it means to be a unique quality of intimacy living in an Intimate Universe.

Reality is not only the Infinity of Divine Power; Reality is also the Infinity of Pain for the wounds of every finite being. And the Infinity of Pain implies the Infinity of Intimacy. This is the great paradox of your wounds. The abuse you suffered matters infinitely. And from the context of your larger Evolutionary Unique Self, you can forgive and move on, while being held all the while in the sweetness of Evolutionary Intimacy and the promise of the unique gifts that are yours to manifest and give in this lifetime.

Essay 3. Unique Gender

We have seen that the emergence of whole mate relationship requires the emergence of new answers to the question, *Who am I?* We have engaged with these answers in our exploration of Unique Self and Outrageous Love. Another essential quality of identity, which has been mostly implicit throughout this book, is *Unique Gender*. It is the major topic of a forthcoming book, *Beyond He and She*.[305]

In the philosophy of Unique Gender, we have woven together four strands of wisdom to bring a new fabric of revelation to Reality. Two of them have already been introduced:

- The new understanding of identity that we call *Unique Self*, which has been explored in depth in Chapter 7 and beyond.

- The notion of lines and circles constituting the core structure of all units of Reality, introduced in Chapter 6 (Entry 9); we discuss it in somewhat more detail in this essay.

This essay focuses mainly on the other two strands of wisdom:

- The concept of *Hieros Gamos*, the Divine Marriage. In ancient wisdom, this took place between the Divine Principles of the Cosmos, incarnate as God and Goddess.

- The transgender movement's critique of the traditional understanding of gender.

---

[305] See also A Return to Eros: The Radical Experience of Being Fully Alive. by M. Gafni and K. Kincaid (2017), Chapter 17.

Entry 1. Lines, Circles, and Living the Erotic Life

One of the core principles of the interior sciences is known formally by the name *Hieros Gamos* (literally *the Divine Marriage*). This is but another name for the realization of the interior sciences that we have unpacked in this book: *Reality is Eros*. It means that at every level of existence, the God and Goddess—which the hard physical sciences might well understand as the initiating and receptive Forces of Reality, which we traditionally have called *male* and *female*—are constantly conjoined, making love, and constantly giving birth to new, higher, and deeper orders of existence.

In the great traditions, these two forces used to be called *masculine* and *feminine*, but we can no longer exclusively identify them with men or women. Borrowing a term from the Renaissance-era interior scientist Isaac Luria, we prefer to call them *lines* and *circles*. Lines and circles are the core structure of Reality from the beginning—prior to the arising, much later in history, of engendered forms. They include such dual distinctions as allurement and autonomy, attraction and independence, reception and thrusting, perhaps centrifugal and centripetal, fusion and fission, directional and cyclical—all primary qualities of the Cosmos.[306] In Luria's evocative image, *every moment of reality, on all levels and in all worlds, is born from the* [unique] *interpenetration of lines and circles that takes place in that moment*.[307]

As I have discussed in depth with science writer Howard Bloom, these qualities are present from the first nanoseconds of the Big Bang, even as they evolve all the way up the evolutionary chain. Line and circle qualities appear all the way down and all the way up the evolutionary chain in different forms—including of course at the human level. In our own lives, these complementary but opposite forces—lines and circles—are expressed through the prism of the Unique Self. Eros is a unique

---

306 Interestingly, in physics, one branch of string theory is now being brought together with loop quantum gravity. These two theories are still widely considered incompatible by their practitioners. Now some practitioners are bringing them together. String theory postulates that matter, at its deepest level, is made up of one-dimensional fiberlike strings (lines), while loop quantum gravity postulates that spacetime is made up of finite loops (circles) with nodes connecting them.

307 See Gafni, The Mystery of Love endnote to p. 187 (on p. 345).

event, happening uniquely in every human being. Understanding that truth is essential if we are to return to Eros. You cannot live an erotic life generically. You must incarnate the unique Eros that is the texture and invitation of your life.

In the ancient mystical world, the core properties of existence were thought to be masculine and feminine. Men incarnated the masculine principles, and women incarnated the feminine principles. Our friend and colleague John Gray captured this vision in his book *Men Are from Mars, Women Are from Venus*. This book is a profoundly insightful exploration of how the qualities of masculine and feminine show up in men and women. Books like *The Female Brain* and *The Male Brain*, both by neuropsychiatrist Louann Brizendine, provide powerful scientific structures that validate in significant ways the core intuitions of John's work.

But today we are at a new crossroads. We are at a place where men and women are no longer able to locate themselves fully in their identity as either men or women. Indeed, they probably never were. Books like Niobe Way's *Deep Secrets: Boys' Friendship and the Crisis of Connection* explode any superficial categories that easily stereotype the masculine and the feminine. Key research around autism and its treatment is one of the many areas where understanding masculine/feminine distinctions seems to be a prerequisite for effective treatment.[308]

So, on the one hand, *Boys are boys, and girls are girls* clearly means something important. But it does not necessarily mean what the stereotypes of boys and girls indicate. For example, as Niobe Way points out, it does not mean that boys are less emotional than girls. Rather, masculine and feminine emotions are often triggered in different ways and play out in different ways. But these distinctions, while partially grounded in physiology and hormones, are equally grounded in culture and its social constructions. It is not easy to disambiguate what is the hard wiring of nature and what are the new codes of nurture.

This quandary destroys self-love because it undermines identity and causes a profound alienation from self, which is the root of all breakdown

---

[308] See the important work of Professor Simon Baron-Cohen and Dr. Meng-Chuan Lai from the Autism Research Centre at the University of Cambridge.

and suffering. The contradictory cultural truth is that, in this contemporary moment, a rejection of the Venus/Mars distinction alienates men and women from important truths of their nature, even as the embrace of the classic Mars/Venus distinctions does the same.

We need to move from contradiction to paradox. We need to move beyond Mars and Venus to evolutionary relationships. That is not only because, at a deeper level, feminine and masculine exist in every person, as recognized by the great wisdom traditions of spirit and the later wisdom traditions of psychology. John Gray argues that men and women are called on to balance their masculine and feminine qualities, with the understanding that men are primarily masculine with some feminine and women are primarily feminine with some masculine. There is obviously great truth in that realization.

Balance, however, is not quite the issue. We now understand, based on the leading-edge research, that there is not merely a male and a female brain, but something much closer to an intersex brain. That does not mean an androgynous brain. Line and circle qualities expressed as masculine and feminine orientations are clearly an orienting dimension of Cosmos as culture. But it is not the only orientation. **We are awakening to a new realization that every person is a unique synergy of line and circle qualities.** We are realizing that, while classic gender distinctions are the beginning of the conversation, they are not the end of the conversation.

We have termed this new emerging understanding *Unique Gender*. This is not simply the right *balance* of masculine and feminine in a person. It is rather an entirely new emergent. To bring this evolutionary emergent forward, which is to participate in the evolution of love, we need new language. This is because, as the interior scientists of Hebrew wisdom and others remind us, language creates reality. The terms *Unique Gender* and *lines* and *circles* are important first steps.

Lines and circles are qualities of Reality that live in every person, in every situation, and in every dynamic.[309] You might say that lines

---

[309] Luria already made this claim, but he was still stuck in a cultural reality, in which classical line qualities were largely masculine, and classical circle qualities were largely feminine. Reality and love have evolved, however.

and circles appear as the dynamic erotic contact that connects different people, ideas, particles, and forces of nature. The Eros of lines and circles takes place not only between things and people but within each thing and each person.

Unique Self is the unique calibration of lines and circles that live in every person. This is part of what manifests a person's unique quality of intimacy, unique perspective, unique gifts, and unique insights—the unique constellation of Eros that manifests within each person. Lines and circles merge and calibrate uniquely in each individual. That merging/calibrating is Unique Gender. The implication that *Reality is erotic* takes place uniquely within every person. Every Unique Self has a Unique Gender. Lines and circles uniquely interweave in every uniquely gendered being.

Entry 2. Between the Literature of Difference and the Literature of Androgyny

I spent about a year reviewing dozens of books and academic and popular work representing two contemporary schools of thought on the differences between men and women. One is what we might call the *literature of difference*, the other is the *literature of androgyny*. Both are deeply flawed; they claim to be the whole story, when in fact they are true but partial.

In the literature of difference and the literature of androgyny, only a small number of writers are really looking at empirical evidence. These authors state their position, but also recognize the complexities of the empirical evidence and acknowledge at least some veracity in the opposing position. However, most of the literature is dogmatic on both sides of the aisle. The androgyny position seeks to dismiss or radically downplay any real intrinsic difference between men and women. The difference position points only to those differences, and radically downplays the counterevidence. Both groups cherry-pick facts and are politically motivated. They both set up the counter-position as a straw man instead of recognizing its partial truth.

In the literature that erases the differences, there is a clear agenda, which is well beyond classical equal rights and opportunity for men and women. There is a desire to undermine difference itself. There is a sense in which difference itself is regarded as a tool of domination and must be overthrown. Of course, this position itself is partially true. Racial distinctions, gender distinctions, distinctions between human beings and animals, and many more, have been deployed in horrific ways as tools of domination. But the literature of androgyny views *distinction itself* as debased. At the same time, the literature of differences is often hijacked by various forms of regressive fundamentalism, to subtly roll the clock back and deny women full participation and dignity in all sectors of society.

What emerges from a more careful reading of the literature, however, is a rejection of both the absolute distinctions position and the androgyny position. Instead, something else entirely emerges: Unique Gender. Unique Gender affirms the core distinctions between men and women that are outlined in books like *The Male Brain* and *The Female Brain* by Louann Brizendine, which support the Mars/Venus distinctions generally articulated by our dear friend John Gray in his classic popular work *Men Are from Mars, Women Are from Venus*. But that is only the starting point of the conversation. It is clear as well that books like *The Myth of Venus and Mars*, by Oxford professor Deborah Cameron,[310] offer important critiques of the intrinsic difference position and point toward crucial dimensions of gender that are socially constructed (a position that Gray often acknowledges as well).

Here is what emerges from an integration of both literatures into a deeper story of value and identity. First, the reality is that male and female brains' distinctions are real, and the androgyny position does not ultimately hold water. However, there is a second key factor in the conversation, which needs to be considered: *neuroplasticity*. What it means, in essence, is that brains evolve. And without question, cultural evolution and context affect the evolution of the brain. While we may begin with male or female brains, the way we engage the world socially, politically, and economically evolves our brain, and what emerges is, to use Daphne Joel's term, an *Intersex* brain.[311] In writing a draft of a yet

---

310, D. Cameron, The Myth of Mars and Venus: Do Men and Women Really Speak Different Languages? (2008).

311 D. Joel, "Male or Female? Brains Are Intersex."

unpublished work, *Beyond He and She*, some eight years ago, I spoke to Daphne Joel and shared with her the core realizations of Unique Gender, which are deeply supported by her research.

The basic realization is as follows. There are strong intrinsic differences between men and women. They are real. Drawing from the interior sciences, this is what I have called *lines and circles*. There are line and circle qualities of Reality, which exist before gender. They are structural to Reality itself. Men tend to default toward the line qualities, and women tend to default toward the circle qualities. This needs to be honored and appreciated.

However, every human has *both* line and circle qualities. And this is also reflected anatomically, as Daphne Joel and many others point out. How those qualities *interact* with each other is a function of every irreducibly unique intrinsic nature, as well as of culture and education. Both those sets of factors come together to form the Unique Gender. Unique Gender is not a leveling of differences. It recognizes and honors the manifestation of Reality, which expresses itself anatomically, in hormonal, physical and neurological terms, as line and circle differences between men and women.

But Unique Gender also recognizes the intrinsically unique and uniquely evolving interinclusion of lines and circles in every human being, as a function of Unique Self. Unique Self is a unique emergent, a source-code evolution in our narrative of identity: a unique quality of intimacy and presence, a unique configuration of Eros, which has its own unique polarity, its unique quality of attraction and allurement, Unique Gender. Each of us is Unique Gender and is shaped by the unique allurements of that Unique Gender. We are all He and She by default. We are also Unique Gender, even as we are shaped by the evolution of our Unique Gender.

Entry 3. Why We Need Mars and Venus Today

As a result of the dogmatic move to level all differences between men and women, difference came to be seen as a tool of oppression, and weak androgyny became the new norm. Strong expressions of Mars or Venus were replaced by attempts to cycle more neutrally between both poles.

This wound up being a disaster for soul mate relationships. The new soul mate expectations—passion, mutual understanding, and intimacy—depended on good communication, but communication was not working. It failed because if men and women were fundamentally the same, then there were no differences that needed to be considered in our attempts to understand and communicate with each other.

In soul mate relationships, this dogmatic leveling of differences leads *Venus* to say:

> If you are just like me, why don't you react as I would? When I go to my girlfriend with a problem, she listens and empathizes. When I come to you with a problem, you cut me off, tell me it is not really a problem, and then propose a list of solutions. I feel invalidated, unheard, and degraded. I am trying to connect to you, and you are disconnecting from me. You do not seem to get how I feel. All you ever do is tell me that I am making a big deal about my feelings. Don't you get it? My feelings **are** a big deal!

Meanwhile, *Mars* says:

> I have done everything I can to make you happy. In fact, making you happy is what I want to do more than almost anything else in the world. But all you do is complain and nag. You're always telling me how to improve, you do not trust my direction, and you rarely appreciate me. I want to be your hero and protector, and you make me feel like a failure. I look to you to know that I am doing well by my commitments, but I am only reminded of my inadequacy and impotence.

Are Mars and Venus more alike than they are different? Both Mars and Venus desire deeper connection, but otherwise, the differences are striking and obvious. Difference, importantly, isn't inherently bad. Biologically speaking, differences abound. Women incarnate a strong cellular sense of Venus energy. Women grow life in their own bodies, give birth, and nurse. They are flooded with the bonding hormone of oxytocin at key moments. Men, meanwhile, incarnate a strong cellular sense of Mars. Men have more upper-body strength and are flooded by the forward-moving, problem-solving hormone of testosterone at key moments. Knowing the key differences between Mars and Venus energies is essential to learning how to communicate productively in soul mate relationships. Communication is essential to fulfilling soul mate expectations and living together in right relationship. Right relationship means more love, more fulfillment, more delight, more goodness, and more integrity.

Without the soul mate translation dictionaries, women reasoned that men should respond to them just as their girlfriends did, but they did not. Men reasoned similarly: if men and women are the same, then women should respond to them the same way that their guy friends did, but they did not. Women were led to assume that men were insensitive hairy women; they were misbehaving on purpose, because they were obtuse and more than slightly brutish.

The assumption that men were misbehaving on purpose went hand in hand with a disturbing trend to demonize men. This trend showed up in many strains of the literature that has come to be called *victim feminism*. In this literature, men (or *the male nature*) is strongly attacked and even demonized.

About a decade ago, I was going to write an intellectual history of feminism. Even though I identify with many of its key tenets, I felt challenged by some of the ways it viewed men. To prepare for the book, I read about fifty of the most popular mainstream feminist books. There was one thing that shocked me. I collected reference after angry reference where men were almost casually equated with Nazis. The work of Andrew Dworkin and others of that ilk has found its way into the mainstream of women's studies, where masculinity itself is inherently problematized with Holocaust references in multiple forms abounding. This tendency was noticed by a number of feminist scholars, including Katie Roiphe, Camille Paglia, and Christina Hoffsommers. I thought to myself, *What would happen if a man, in a book on women, compared any feminine trait to Nazism? He would be shot on the spot.*

This is what first opened my eyes to this virulent strain of male bashing. These texts are often insightful and even wise, but men are routinely labeled as predators, women are defined as survivors of men, and any conflict is relabeled as abuse. Assertions like *All men are potential rapists* abound, and distorted statistics like *One in every four women is sexually abused* are common. This literature was written by many of the original leading feminist activists. These very same activists, literally the same people, often went on to found or teach in women's studies departments all over the United States. These same ideas were then taught by them and their students in gender studies curricula.

All of this produced a societal meme in which men as a class of people were routinely demonized. Normal relational conflict can be massively intensified when you take a normal misunderstanding as evidence of your partner's badness. When your partner is a man, and culture bombards you with images that seriously or even laughingly demonize men, something starts to corrode in your psyche. Instead of holding the beauty and nobility of men, as we hold the beauty and nobility of women, a more degraded image begins to crystalize in your mind. This cannot help but undermine love in your relationship.[312]

It is critical to understand that the feminine is not an expression of the light, while the masculine is an expression of darkness and shadow. Rather, both masculine and feminine possess both light and virtue as well as darkness and shadow. Indeed, there is both a masculine and a feminine shadow.

Entry 4. Does the Feminine Have Shadow? Between Hurt and What We Do with Our Hurt

Do some women have the right, from their perspective, to be angry or hurt in their relationships? Of course. But there is a far cry between being hurt at the way a relationship unfolds and filing false complaints or

---

[312] It has the same effect as degrading images of women, such as bimbo, dumb blondes, greedy, gold digging, and the like. All of these images, which appeared in different forms for the last two thousand years, are appearing again in the popular culture of reality shows and the internet.

making false claims, which can ruin a person's life, lifework, and family. The latter must be named for what is: an explosion of feminine shadow. It should not be coddled or justified. It must be confronted and condemned in precisely the same way that we relate to masculine shadow.

Here a critical point needs to be drawn clearly about the confused portrayal of the masculine and feminine in so much alternative spiritual literature. All too often, New-Age spiritual literature and certain strains of what has been referred to as *victim feminism* collude in their unconditional positive view of women and negative view of men.

The feminine is viewed as good, kind, and nurturing; and the masculine is inevitably portrayed as aggressive, narcissistic, base, and depraved. In these accounts, men have shadow and women have light. Men come together in lynch mobs, and groups of women are assumed to be always telling the truth. Of course, the truth of the matter is far different. Both men and women have great light and potentially great shadow. In each group, shadow is triggered by a threat to what each group sees as most essential to its identity.

The masculine, by most accounts, is known to be more concerned with linear progress, status, and power. Threaten the masculine's power and status, and you will get an explosion of masculine shadow. Masculine vulnerability is connected to the unique form of masculine insatiability—which is for sex and sexual variety. This expresses itself as well in the masculine inability, at times, to create appropriate sexual discipline and boundaries.

The feminine, by most accounts, is more concerned with circular progress, which is expressed in connection, interdependence, and relationship. Feminine status and identity are connected to relationship to others, while masculine status and relationship is connected to power over others. For this reason, if you threaten the feminine at the place of relational intimacy, feminine shadow explodes. It is to this truism that Shakespeare referred when he said, "Hell knows no fury like a woman scorned." Such fury, when expressed in action, produces feminine shadow that is every bit as evil as masculine shadow.

The feminine clusterfuck, where a group of women gets angry and moves to take down a man whom they feel has hurt them relationally, is the feminine equivalent of the masculine lynch mob. The distortion of a relationship, after the fact, through a public name-rape, is a shadow expression no more justifiable than all forms of masculine shadow.

In much of victim-feminist literature, feminine shadow is justified with affirmations of feminine rage. The anger of women against what is termed *patriarchal oppression* is viewed as a sufficient response to all of the shadow expression of the feminine. Crimes and abuses range from domestic violence against male partners, which, as feminist writer Cathy Young reminds us, is shockingly high,[313] to false complaints that destroy lives. These are common expressions of feminine shadow. The latter forms of feminine abuse are chronicled in detail by several contemporary writers, including recent books by Laura Kipnis,[314] Daphne Patai,[315] Cathy Young,[316] Christina Hoff Sommers,[317] Alan Dershowitz,[318] Warren

---

313 See, for example, the opinion piece by Cathy Young, "There Are Also Battered Men" from The New York Times, 2006. See also "Johnny Depp and the Other Side of Domestic Violence: Men Can Be Victims. Women Can Be Abusers. Welcome to Equality," by Cathy Young, 2020, in Arc Digital on Medium.com.

314 See, for example, Ecstasy Unlimited: On Sex, Capital, Gender, and Aesthetics (1993), Bound and Gagged: Pornography and the Politics of Fantasy in America (1996), Against Love: A Polemic (2003), The Female Thing: Dirt, Sex, Envy, Vulnerability (2006), Men: Notes from an Ongoing Investigation (2014), Unwanted Advances: Sexual Paranoia Comes to Campus (2017).

315 For example, The Orwell Mystique: A Study in Male Ideology (1984), Brazilian Women Speak: Contemporary Life Stories (1988), Professing Feminism: Cautionary Tales from the Strange World of Women's Studies (with Noretta Koertge, 1994), Heterophobia: Sexual Harassment and the Future of Feminism (1998), What Price Utopia? Essays on Ideological Policing, Feminism, and Academic Affairs (2008).

316 Growing Up In Moscow: Memories of a Soviet Girlhood (1989). Ceasefire!: Why Women and Men Must Join Forces to Achieve True Equality (1999).

317 For example, Vice & Virtue in Everyday Life: Introductory Readings in Ethics (1984), Who Stole Feminism?: How Women Have Betrayed Women (2000 and 2013). The War Against Boys (2005).

318 Guilt by Accusation: The Challenge of Proving Innocence in the Age of #MeToo (2019).

Farrell,[319] Ken Wilber,[320] and Charles Sykes.[321] Each of these writers cites cases in which women, or groups of women, made false complaints of sexual harassment or worse against men. In virtually every case, the knee-jerk liberal establishments supported the women. Interests standing behind the complaints of the women remained all invisible, and blatant lies stood as truth, sometimes for many years, until someone had the courage to step up and speak.

We must get over the myth that women and groups of women do not lie; they do. Feminine shadow is just as real as masculine shadow and cannot be excused by feminine rage any more than masculine shadow can be excused by masculine anger. The essential premise of any system of ethics and justice is that, while we have compassion for legitimate rage, that does not excuse the commission of crimes. One cannot justify committing an evil act against another simply because one was hurt or is enraged. Jean Gebser[322] and other developmental theorists[323] remind us that the level of consciousness that justified evil based on anger or hurt is tribal, magical in nature, and regressive. Such thought forms appear today in preschoolers and Mafia families and in the fundamentalist strains of religious extremism that produce global terrorism.

All of this gives lie to the old canard that a woman would not make a complaint of sexual harassment if it were not true. This is a dangerous myth, because it produces injustice and unwarranted human suffering and tragedy when it is believed. Forty years ago, when there was no

---

[319] The Myth of Male Power: Why Men Are the Disposable Sex (2001), Women Can't Hear What Men Don't Say: Destroying Myths, Creating Love (2001), Why Men Earn More: The Startling Truth Behind the Pay Gap and What Women Can Do About It (2015).

[320] See, for example, Sex, Ecology, Spirituality: The Spirit of Evolution (1995 and 2001).

[321] See, for example, A Nation of Victims: The Decay of the American Character (1992).

[322] The Ever-Present Origin, by J. Gebser, authorized translation by Noel Barstad with Algis Mickunas (1985, 1991).

[323] For a list of developmental theories see, for example, Integral Psychology: Consciousness, Spirit, Psychology, Therapy by K. Wilber (2000),

sexual harassment law, and the burden of proof was on the feminine, unjustly, women were less likely to make false complaints. This situation has been appropriately rectified with the passage of an extensive body of sexual harassment law.

However, as has been pointed out by many, *power corrupts*. Feminist writer Gloria Jean Watkins, better known by her pen name Bell Hooks has already noted that, whenever women have had power, they have made false complaints against men of sexual abuse in various forms. As she writes, just ask any black person who grew up in the old South if white women did not make false complaints of sexual harassment against black men.[324] Their complaints often literally cost the men their lives—lynched by the *righteous* mobs of white men looking for a powerless victim upon whom to vent their rage.

Today, the new form of white women making false complaints against innocent (black) men is women who hide behind the victim chic of feminine powerlessness and male brutality. They file their false complaints knowing full well that they suffer no significant risk, that they will be embraced by the community as feminist heroines, and that the complaint itself has the power to destroy the career and even the life of the man they are attacking.

Entry 5. From Transgender to Unique Gender

The transgender movement's critique of the way our culture understands gender poses a critical challenge to our most basic sense of identity. Transgender consciousness says: *My identity is deeper than man or woman or even masculine and feminine. Those are boxes that actually obfuscate and often distort my true identity.*

When all of the old identities based on religion, nationality, and race had fallen away, gender remained identity's last safe haven. At least we still had some sense of who we are. You are either a man or a woman, and that was at least a point of origin for the all-important identity conversation.

---

324 See Teaching Community: A Pedagogy of Hope by Bell Hooks (2003), Chapter 12, "Passionate Pedagogy."

Along came the transgender movement, and it powerfully challenged this one remaining bastion of identity. The transgender movement's questions intuited a much more profound sense of personal identity underneath the old gender structure of man/woman, masculine/feminine.

Tragically, however, the transgender movement did not offer any deeper sense of identity. It was all questions, with an almost dogmatic anathema towards answers. But the collapse of identity is catastrophic both for a person and for a culture's sanity. Identity is erotic. When identity is lost, then the person, or culture, is de-eroticized. A de-eroticized person or culture is dead and thus prone to any and all forms of regressive pseudo-life that seek to replace or cover up lost forms of Eros that had their source in the old identities.

With the incisive questions of the transgender movement, the last remaining bastion of identity was swept away. This has resulted in myriad forms of breakdown—sexually, personally, and culturally. The transgender movement is the latest expression of the classic postmodern movement—a brilliant deconstruction with no reconstruction.

The evolution of love and the emergence of whole mate relationships may be appropriately seen as part of a larger reconstructive project. This honors the questions, but then, by integrating all of the leading-edge streams of wisdom available at this moment in time, we point not to dogmatic answers but toward a new vision of meaning, the vision of Unique Gender, which emerged from the ancient enlightenment teachings in a new form.

Paradoxically, the transgender movement's challenge to identity is the same challenge posed by all of the great schools of enlightenment. The great question of enlightenment inquiry practice is: *Who are you?* The point of the question is to get underneath all of the culturally constructed contexts that are in the way of your most authentic identity. You are not merely boy or girl. You are not merely Christian or Jewish. You are not simply British or French. You are *essence*, a unique essence. You are a Unique Self. Unique Self is an identity that is underneath gender and all the other superficial structures of self. But Unique Self does not ignore gender. Rather, it says that the core qualities of gender—what we call *lines* and *circles*—are qualities of the Cosmos.

And these Cosmic Qualities show up uniquely, in unique integration, texture, and calibration—in you, as you, and through you. You are your Unique Gender. This is not to be confused with the need to have balance between your masculine and feminine sides. While that is certainly true, Unique Gender is not saying that. The philosophy of Unique Gender says that you are a radically new and unique emergent—a unique integration of line and circle qualities in a way that never was, is, or ever will be again. It is not so much that your masculine and feminine are balanced. It is rather that you are something else, something new and precious, which is far deeper than masculine and feminine. It does not leave masculine and feminine behind but transcends and includes them.

Who are you? You are your Unique Self. What is that? It is the unique expression of your Eros. Your Eros is your unique *Hieros Gamos*. In the ancient world, this took place only in the realm of the Divine. In the philosophy of Unique Gender, we bring it not only to Earth but also to a democratized vision of *Hieros Gamos*. Every single human is a Unique Self, who is a unique integration of the Cosmic Qualities of lines and circles.

At the leading edge of neuroscience, researchers like Daphna Joel have moved beyond the vision of the male and female brain. Joel writes of what she calls *the intersex brain*.[325] The intersex brain is not a concept: it is an anatomical and cellular reality. Every human brain is a unique integration of what we are calling *line and circle properties*. Said differently, every human brain is a unique expression of the Eros of the Cosmos.

The brain structure is but the exterior expression of an interior reality. Every human being is heart, brain, mind, and body in a unique *Hieros Gamos*—a unique incarnation of the perpetual Eros of the Cosmos, the unique Eros that yearns to occur in every person. It is only by living your unique Eros, in your own interior self, that you can live your erotic life.

Naturally, your Unique Gender will directly affect your sexuality. Attraction is no longer aroused only between male and female or even between masculine and feminine. Attraction is between Unique Genders—that is, between Unique Selves. That opens entirely new worlds.

---

325 Gender Mosaic: Beyond the Myth of the Male and Female Brain by D. Joel and L. Vikhanski (2019).

For many of us, Venus and Mars do not express our identities. It is the failure of gender to meet the unique experience of our own identities that, at least in part, gave rise to the transgender phenomenon, which argues for ultimate fluidity in gender identification. But that also does not match our experience. The transgender movement is asking all the right questions, but the answer is *not* to kill the very category of gender. That is rooted, *in part,* in the deeper structure of Cosmos—lines and circles. We need to go from the transgender dogma, which denies any kind of orienting gender, to something new and emergent in the evolution of gender. This is core to the evolution of relationships, which is the evolution of intimacy—and the evolution of love.

CONCLUSION

BIRTHING A NEW HUMAN

by Barbara Marx Hubbard

Evolution is relationships. Evolution is longing and desire. It longs for more life, more love, more joining. This is a 13.7-billion-year trend! You and I originated in the first flaring forth billions of years ago, coded with the capacity to form energy, matter, and life—and now us, going around the next turn on the spiral. The only difference is that now we are conscious that this is happening. We are alive at the most critical moment in our entire planetary evolution, where we can either destroy our own life support systems or consciously evolve our world into a positive future that has never been possible before.

At this precise moment of human history, a new form of relationship is entering our lives. We call it *whole mates*. We are evolving from role mates to soul mates to whole mates. This is an evolutionary breakthrough that forms the basis of the new civilization now emerging.

Role mates are the traditional man/woman relationship, which evolved to care for the survival of children, family, and life for the past 250,000 years. It is still the primary form of relationship around the world. Around the 1970s, another form of relationship entered the mainstream: soul mates. This beautiful next phase of relationship is based on a deep one-on-one commitment for personal fulfillment, healing of wounds, sharing our stories, and overcoming loneliness. The depth of allurement in a soul mate relationship becomes so central and potent that, for many, it actually becomes the meaning of life.

While role mates are still primary, soul mates are growing beyond the confines of role mates, as described by John Gray in *Men Are from Mars, Women Are from Venus*. This book sold over fifty million copies. It is still helping countless people to learn to communicate better, to separate impact from intent, and to love one another with greater freedom and compassion. However, as described in this book, something surprising and disappointing is happening among soul mates. We are going beyond Mars and Venus. It turns out that soul mates, even if sexually attracted to one another, lose a subtle yet powerful sexual drive. Equality between men and women tends to diminish sexuality. Focusing as two co-equals for the purpose of self-fulfillment alone does not, in many cases, fulfill the creative potential of either. People reach out for more life and more love through divorce, polyamorous relationships, free sexuality, single parenting, living together without marriage, etc.

Something new, wonderful, exciting, and sexy—as well as supra-sexy—is happening in response to this evolutionary crisis. Marc Gafni was the first to call it whole mate, or evolutionary, relationship.

It is part of a new Story of Value that I am telling together with my evolutionary whole mate, Marc Gafni, joined by Zachary Stein, my old friend Daniel Schmachtenberger, who has been like a son to me, my old friend Ken Wilber, Sally Kempton, Kristina Kincaid, Lori Galperin, Kerstin Tuschik, Kate Maloney, Peter Fiekowsky, Claire Molinard, Chahat Corten, Kathy Brownback, Paul Bennett, Carol Herndon, Tom Goddard, Terry Nelson, Warren Farrell, John Gray, John Mackey, and many others, who have joined us at different stages of the journey. We call this new Story of Value *CosmoErotic Humanism*. Whole mate relationship is a key part of the new Story.

I am fully aligned with Marc's assertion that only a new Story of Value—with a new vision of relationship we call *whole mate*—responds to the meta-crisis that, at its core, is about a breakdown in our relationship to the Whole. In a whole mate relationship, you are attracted to one another for a shared purpose. By joining together for something greater than yourself, your own evolutionary passion is aroused; you become more creative. The impulse of evolution within you, joined with your lover, turns you both on toward more meaning, passionate love, and a sense of a vocation of destiny, a profound life purpose entering your life.

As we evolve toward whole mate, we attempt to include yet transcend the best of role mate and soul mate.

What is the essence of becoming a whole mate?

People are attracted to each other to *join genius* through creativity and shared life purpose, to produce not a new baby, but a new work. And in the process, you begin to feel you are evolving into a new kind of human, one who is fulfilling the deepest passion to create through loving one another's creativity.

As a whole mate, you become *vocationally aroused*. Your partner loves what you give, as you love what your partner gives to you. Each of you is turned on to your own creativity.

You get excited *supra-sexually*. *Supra-sex* is a new word to describe the passion to *join genius*. It offers the thrill of two people's hidden potential, being aroused by each other in communion for the fulfillment of each. This shared fulfillment arouses further creativity, intimacy, and evolutionary intelligence.

Supra-sex expands the erotic into the *telerotic*. You become a *telerotic* human. This means you are fusing the high purpose of both of your lives (*telos*) with juicy love (Eros) of one another. You are loving one another the *whole way*, nothing left out. It feels as though the very impulse of evolution within you is connecting with the impulse of evolution within your partner. You feel like you are being activated internally, inside yourself, with creative purpose, not just of yourselves, but also of the deeper patterns of evolution in you becoming self-aware. In other words, you are activating the Spirit of Evolution, the Process of Creation Itself, when you come together to co-create. Instead of focusing, as soul mates do, just on one another, as whole mates you face outward together, to bring many others in to co-create with you.

For women over fifty, becoming *telerotic* is almost as though a new species were being born. After fifty, a woman has no more eggs. You *become* the egg. In whole mate loving, you accelerate your untapped creative potential by joining together. You become a *feminine co-creator*. That means you are giving birth to the creativity within you, supported by your partner, who is doing the same through you. This is fulfilling! This is the deepest heart's desire. This is the next phase of attraction through relationship.

It seems that nature itself is calling us toward supra-sexual co-creation rather than massive procreation. Precisely during the overpopulation crisis on planet Earth, when we must have fewer children to survive, the sexual drive that attracts us to have more babies is evolving into the supra-sexual drive to evolve ourselves and our work in the world.

Once, at a World Future Society Meeting, I spoke about a new energy that was being discovered on Earth—not another source of fuel, but a new energy arising in women, turning us on to become supra-sexual co-creators, seeking to join genius with men.

How do we become whole mates? What are the processes required? Here are a few elements:

You are encouraged to say *Yes!* to your own untapped creative potential. You become a strange attractor by saying *Yes!* to what attracts you to create.

You feel *newer* every day, not older or younger. You *are* becoming newer when you say *Yes!* to your creativity, joining in love with someone else's untapped creativity. Joining genius with your beloved creates newness, just as joining genes begins to create a new child when the sperm hits the egg.

In this passionate way, nature is creating more love, more life, more creativity. In the great multibillion-year trend from atom to cell to animal to human to us, now we are going around the next turn on the spiral of evolution together.

As whole mates, you begin to feel the billions of years of evolutionary impulse in your body-mind. You awaken to an irresistible longing to be more of your Unique Self, to become an *evolutionary woman* or an *evolutionary man*, one imbued with the actual driving intelligence of evolution itself toward more love, freedom, and conscious co-creativity.

As you become a whole mate, you are joining in love with your partner. In some sense, you are evolving not only your personal existence but also the quality of life itself. As sexuality was a great evolutionary leap (from single cells dividing to reproduce to eukaryotic cells reproducing sexually, and then to multicellular life), so supra-sexuality, too, catalyzes a jump to a more vital and creative human. In the words of Sri Aurobindo, the great Indian sage of evolution, when you overcome the illusion of separation within yourself, you are able to download the *supramental genius* of evolution itself.

The entire 13.7-billion-year trajectory of evolution is awakening in you as your unique passion, purpose, and power joined with your whole mate. Each of you becomes more than you could possibly be alone. As nature gave us sexual passion to join genes to have babies, she is now awakening in us the passion to join genius to give birth to the creativity we are born to express in the world, as we help our partner give birth to his or her own creativity.

This whole mate passion is vital now since we already have a growing population in a polluted world. One more doubling of the population would destroy all life on Earth. Within women, the drive to have more children is shifting to the longing to give birth to one's own potential through co-creative love. The evolutionary woman is imbued with the passion to co-create rather than massively *procreate*. She longs for self-evolution rather than self-replication.

She does not seek equality with men in a dysfunctional world, but rather partnership with men and women to help *evolve* the world. She is a new kind of lover on this Earth, in love with giving birth to a new culture, a society equal to human greatness and goodness. Just so, evolutionary men seek to activate their own unique creativity and to join it with their beloved whole mate. If it is true that men do what women want, then women wanting supra-sexual co-creation is going to evolve the world! It will also evolve sexuality. Sexuality when joined with supra-sexuality becomes evolutionary sexuality, sacred and passionate for the new purpose of birthing the New Human and the new world.

You discover that by joining genius with your lover, you are giving birth to your greater Self. You are becoming what we call a *New Human*. You feel the New Human arising as you join genius as a whole mate in supra-sexual co-creativity with your erotic nature turned on at full force.

This book helps you discover new ways to activate your whole life—spiritually, sexually, and socially. For example, at age eighty-seven I am finding that I am not age specific. As my co-creative partner is turned on in his own way to release the greater power of his genius, his eloquent understanding of evolution, his profound ability to reach and communicate worldwide, so am I. I literally feel newer every day because I *am* newer! The world is newer, and so are we.

What is our purpose, in this book and beyond?

It is to call forth and support whole mate relationships as they are emerging everywhere. It is to form greater community and support among the growing evolutionary family. It is to discover and deepen together the next phase of love, both for ourselves and for the larger world.

We are working together with a growing team to catalyze a Planetary Awakening in Love through Unique Self Symphonies. This is a time when all of us who are attracted to express our Unique Selves, our full potential selves, are allured to each other to express our gifts to the world through Unique Self Symphonies. A Unique Self Symphony is a process newly designed to realize and synergize our collective goodness, beauty, and greatness as an evolving species of humankind.

Ultimately, we realize that we are becoming collectively a new species. Many of us are already experiencing a deepening sense of *evolutionary spirituality*, feeling the growing power of the evolutionary impulse arising within us. We are already aroused by expanding vocations; our supra-sexual attraction to join with each other is already igniting our creativity. We are discovering innovations that work in every field and function.

The internet, if encoded with Eros and value, could become a kind of planetary nervous system, rapidly connecting our hearts and minds within the wider Fields of Consciousness and Meaning. If the internet is encoded with the recognition that we live inside a Field of Value and Eros that is the very nature of Reality itself, it could then become a compelling technology to connect and co-create the very Field, functions, and culture of the world. Indeed, all the genius of high technology in artificial intelligence, genetics, robotics, nanotechnology, quantum computing, space travel, and more are giving us the radical powers of our ancient mythological gods.

But we need a Story of Value rooted in First Principles and First Values that is equal to our power. We can create new worlds. We can blow up this world.

As we develop whole mate relationships, as we join genius to create supra-sexually, we are already evolving beyond the state of *Homo sapiens* to *Homo amor*—which is the new name that Marc and I are suggesting as the description of the New Human and the New Humanity that is now emerging. As Marc says,

Homo amor is the initiating LoveIntelligence, LoveBeauty, and LoveDesire of all of Reality, in person, alive and pulsing—in you, as you, and through you, most personal, most intimate with your closest beloved and yet at the same time passionately omniconsiderate for the sake of the Whole.

All our new capacities are already connecting and tending to self-organize into a new whole system far greater than the sum of our separated parts. Nature has been creating such new whole systems out of separate capacities for billions of years, as species gain ever-greater consciousness and freedom through more complex and loving order. From single cells to multicells, to animals, to early humans, to *Homo sapiens* and now to us—*Homo amor*—we are evolving.

This is the nature of Reality. This is the intention of creation: to evolve beings ever-more capable of expressing *Evolutionary Love* or *Outrageous Love*—terms that Marc has invoked, and I am fully aligned with—which drive the process of evolution from the origin of creation to us.

We are incarnating the impulse of evolution itself as whole beings, as co-creators, as universal humans. Many new names are arising to describe this evolutionary shift occurring within us. As we gain an evolutionary perspective, we see that we are already becoming a new species. We already have new powers to heal the Earth, free ourselves from deficiencies, and explore the vast regions of inner and outer space. In the deepest sense, whole mates are coming together in love at this crossroads of evolution to give birth to a New Human and a New Humanity within us, and in the world.

Barbara Marx Hubbard
March 2017
Loveland, Colorado

TABLES

Table A: Role Mate, Soul Mate, and Whole Mate

	ROLE MATE	SOUL MATE	WHOLE MATE
Self	Separate self	Separate self	True Self, Unique Self, Evolutionary Unique Self, and participation in the Unique Self Symphony
Level of Consciousness/ Intimacy/ Identity	Egocentric Ethnocentric	Ethnocentric Worldcentric	Worldcentric Cosmocentric
Core Value	Survival and thriving	Personal fulfillment	Service to the Whole
Relationship to the Field of Value	As separate self, role mate does not necessarily experience oneself as part of the Field of Value	As separate self, soul mate does not necessarily experience oneself as part of the Field of Value	Experiences oneself as inside and participatory in the Field of Value
Falling in Love	Social, religious, cultural fit Exchange of value	Chemistry between the beloveds Imago theory Looking deeply into each other's eyes	Third side Looking at a shared horizon

	ROLE MATE	SOUL MATE	WHOLE MATE
Quality of Love	Ordinary love experienced as a human sentiment or a social construct even if a beautiful and moving social construct	Ordinary love experienced as a human sentiment or a social construct even if a beautiful and moving social construct	Outrageous Love, Evolutionary Love, or the Eros of Cosmos as the intrinsic Reality of the Cosmos, not mere human sentiment but the Heart of Existence itself
Characteristics	Dependency: I need you Protectiveness Achievement	Independence: I choose you Intimacy/ Communication Presence	Interdependency: I choose to need you Evolutionary partnership Guided by larger narrative/ Telerotic
Shadow	Power plays Manipulation Narcissism of one	Leveling of differences Loss of passion Narcissism of two	Individual self and personal intimacy are lost in the desire to liberate or heal the Whole
Principles	Protect Sacrifice Duty Honor Obligation	Poignancy Presence Communication Transcend Loneliness Heal Wounding	Shared Horizon Transformation Evolution Purpose Vision
Goals	Personal survival Thriving of self & family Fulfill obligations	A good relationship (A good life has a good relationship in it.)—Liberation from loneliness Heal wounding Love each other	A good life (The relationship serves the shared vision of a good life—for the Whole of Life.) Transform the Whole Be lived as Love
Question	"What is in it for me?"	"What am I getting in exchange for what I have given?"	"What am I willing to give up in mad love and devotion to the larger Whole?"

Table B: The Four Selves: Separate Self, True Self, Unique Self, and Evolutionary Unique Self

	SEPARATE SELF	TRUE SELF	UNIQUE SELF	EVOLUTIONARY UNIQUE SELF
Emergence	Emerges from the prepersonal, around the age of three Persists throughout life	Begins with awakening to a larger context, to the larger Field of Wholeness Often results from an awakening experience, a crisis, or pivotal life events	Includes and transcends True Self Includes a fundamental location in and as the Field of Wholeness Begins with awakening to the notion that one is both a unique part and indivisible from the larger Whole—a unique incarnation of the Whole	Includes and transcends Unique Self and True Self Emerges when one awakens to the evolutionary impulse living uniquely in and through one's own Self
Identity	Ego-based Identity revolves around survival needs	Transcends the exclusive identification with the ego Individual self-sense still operates but is known as part of larger Field of Wholeness	Self-sense is that of a unique expression of the Whole with a unique perspective, unique gifts, and unique obligations Unique obligation is a natural expression of the unique configuration of Eros and intimacy that is the Unique Self fostering unique gifts that are needed by the Whole Ego points toward Unique Self, but Unique Self is, at least in part, liberated from the perpetual grasping of the ego	Identity is the Unique Self living fully and freely in an evolutionary context Unique obligation is not only to foster the unique gifts that are needed by the Whole, but also the unique gifts that are needed for the evolution of the Whole. Another unique obligation of Evolutionary Unique Selves is to come together as Unique Wes and give the unique gifts that emerge from these Wes.

	SEPARATE SELF	TRUE SELF	UNIQUE SELF	EVOLUTIONARY UNIQUE SELF
Importance of Individual	The individual is important as an individual. Its perspective is limited to that directly around him or her.	The individual is important because he or she is also the Whole. There is no distinction between the individual and the Whole. Its perspective is limited to the Whole because it is no longer important as an individual.	The individual is important as an individual because he or she offers a completely unique perspective and expression to the Whole. The Whole needs the uniqueness of the individual.	The individual is a unique expression needed by the Whole. The individual devotes his or her uniqueness not only to the Whole, but to the evolution of the Whole.
Goals	Develop personality and capacities Seek personal healing Move from victim to self-responsibility	Move beyond the personal story Transcend personality to identity with one's essence Generate appreciation for personality and use it as an ally	To confess one's greatness To live one's greatness To live into the future and not from the past To give one's unique gifts and fulfill one's unique obligations	To consciously participate in the process of evolution To devote relationships to the transformation of the Whole To express goodness, truth, and beauty in feelings and behavior

	SEPARATE SELF	TRUE SELF	UNIQUE SELF	EVOLUTIONARY UNIQUE SELF
Place in the Puzzle	Individual puzzle piece with distinct boundaries Embraces puzzle piece-ness Longs to know the whole puzzle Told the puzzle does not exist	Not a puzzle piece but the puzzle itself (the Wholeness itself) Separation and distinction disappear into the Whole	The individual is a distinct puzzle piece Its unique shape and perspective completes a part of the larger puzzle that no other piece can	The individual is a distinct puzzle piece Its unique shape and perspective not only complete but evolve a part of the larger puzzle that no other piece can
Gifts	Healthy separate self facilitates development, healing, and growth Sets up the individual to recognize True and Unique Self	All beings included in one's circle of compassion and concern Intimately aware of the connection with the larger Whole	Knows that Unique Self is valued and needed by Reality Contributes uniqueness to the Whole Has unique gifts and makes unique contributions to relationship	Contributes uniqueness to the evolution of the Whole Experiences joy of being an expression of evolution in action Recognizes and accepts that Evolutionary Unique Self is needed to evolve consciousness and complexity

	SEPARATE SELF	TRUE SELF	UNIQUE SELF	EVOLUTIONARY UNIQUE SELF
Shadow	Isolation, lonely, limited identity Appears to be the whole picture Does not experience self as inside or participatory in the Field of Value Can only access ordinary love, not Outrageous Love Alienated from the Whole—both from interior wholeness and from the larger exterior context of the Whole	Beauty of the individual is lost or disregarded Sense of uniqueness, importance, and relevance often disappears into the Whole	Unique Shadow—not discussed in this book On Unique Shadow, see Gafni, Marc. *Your Unique Self: The Radical Path to Personal Enlightenment*, with Introduction and Afterword by Ken Wilber, Integral Publishers, 2012, Chapter 4, Station 6, and Chapters 17-19.	Unique Shadow—not discussed in this book On Unique Shadow, see Gafni, Marc. *Your Unique Self: The Radical Path to Personal Enlightenment*, with Introduction and Afterword by Ken Wilber, Integral Publishers, 2012, Chapter 4, Station 6, and Chapters 17-19. Shadow of impersonal identification with the evolutionary impulse in which the individual is lost [often comes to the fore in Marxist or Fascist forms as well as in various forms of evolutionary humanism]
Levels of Relationship	Role mate: Role is the primary source of self Soul mate: Identifies as part of a couple Whole mate: Entices separate self into True Self and Unique Self	Entices role mate into soul and whole mate Gateway to Unique Self once whole mate emerges	May characterize the leading edge of soul mate relationships (often unconscious) Is the basis of whole mate relationships	Primary sense of self in evolutionary relationships Recognized by some but not all whole mates Unique Self Symphony

	SEPARATE SELF	TRUE SELF	UNIQUE SELF	EVOLUTIONARY UNIQUE SELF
Questions	1. How can I make myself a better person? 2. What actions can I take to bring more happiness into my life? 3. What actions can I take to bring my body, mind, and soul into better health? 4. What actions can I take to make my life more stable and secure? 5. What actions can I take to heal my personal wounds? 6. What can I do to make my life more beautiful, happy, and fulfilling? 7. How can I improve my romantic, platonic, and familial relationships and make them happier, healthier, and more fulfilling?	1. What do I need to liberate myself from to realize my True Nature? 2. What attracts my attention that I need to let go of in order to focus my attention on the nature of Self? 3. In what ways do I most want to serve my communities and the world? 4. Who is suffering and how can I help? 5. How can I get out of my own way to help the Whole? 6. What parts of my personality seem to keep me from connecting with others or contributing to my communities?	1. What do I most love about myself and my unique personhood? 2. What do I most love to do? 3. What are my unique gifts that the world needs? 4. What personal growth and development can I engage in to become more self-expressed as a distinct expression of the Whole? 5. What do I seem to be most allured to in this world? 6. What kind things do other people say about me that feel most right and true? 7. What is my unique essence? Or what makes me who I am? 8. Who do I say I am for myself, my communities, and the world?	1. How does my unique essence distinctly evolve to the Whole? 2. What actions can I take personally, professionally, or as a part of my communities that would evolve the Whole? 3. What actions of mine and my relationships can I devote to the evolution of the Whole?

BIBLIOGRAPHY

Books and Essays

Alighieri, Dante. *The Divine Comedy, Volume 3: Paradiso*, Canto XXXIII. translated by Henry Wadsworth Longfellow, 1867, University Press: Welch, Bigelow, & Co., Cambridge.

Banks, Ralph Richard. *Is Marriage for White People? How the African American Marriage Decline Affects Everyone.* New York: Dutton, 2011.

Barks, Coleman. Rumi, Jalal Al-Din. *The Essential Rumi—reissue: A Poetry Anthology.* HarperCollins. Kindle Edition, 2003.

Barks, Coleman. Rumi, Jalal Al-Din. *The Soul of Rumi, A New Collection of Ecstatic Poems*, Harper One, 2010. (HarperCollins. Kindle Edition.)

Becker, Ernest. *The Denial of Death* (1974, MacMillan).

Blake, William (1757–1827). "Proverbs of Hell" from *The Marriage of Heaven and Hell*. 1790–1793.

Bohm, David. *Wholeness and the Implicate Order* (Routledge Classics). Taylor and Francis. Kindle Edition.

Bolen, Jean Shinoda. *Goddesses in Everywoman: Powerful Archetypes in Women's Lives*, Harper Paperbacks, 2014.

Brizendine, Louann. *The Female Brain*, Expand. Random House, 2006.

Brizendine, Louann. *The Male Brain*. Expand. Random House, 2010.

Cain, Fraser. "How Does the Sun Produce Energy?" *Universe Today*. https://phys.org/news/2015-12-sun-energy.html. Retrieved January 2024.

Cameron, Deborah. *The Myth of Mars and Venus: Do Men and Women Really Speak Different Languages?* Oxford University Press, 2008.

Camus, Albert. *The Stranger* (Vintage International, 2012). Translated by Matthew Ward. Knopf Doubleday Publishing Group. Kindle Edition.

Caplan, Mariana. *Eyes Wide Open: Cultivating Discernment on the Spiritual Path.* Sounds True, 2009.

Chang, Jiin-Ju, Joachim Fisch, and Fritz-Albert Popp (Editors). *Biophotons*, Springer Science+Business Media Dordrecht, 1998.

Cohen, Andrew. *Autobiography of an Awakening*, Enlightenment Media (1992).

Cohen, Andrew. *Evolutionary Enlightenment: A New Path to Spiritual Awakening*, Select Books (2011).

Cordovero, R. Moshe. *Pardes Rimonim* (Orchard of Pomegranates).

de Chardin, Pierre Teilhard. *Toward the Future*, 1936.

Dershowitz, Alan. 2019: *Guilt by Accusation: The Challenge of Proving Innocence in the Age of #MeToo.*

Dickens, C. *David Copperfield* London, England; Bradbury & Evans (1850).

Doidge, Norman. *The Brain That Changes Itself: Stories of Personal Triumph from the Frontiers of Brain Science*, Penguin Life; Reprint edition (December 18, 2007).

Edin, Kathryn, and Maria Kefalas. *Promises I Can Keep: Why Poor Women Put Motherhood Before Marriage* (Berkeley and Los Angeles: University of California Press, 2005).

Erickson, Milton H. *The Collected Works of Milton H. Erickson, MD: Volume 1: The Nature of Therapeutic Hypnosis* (edited by E. L. Rossi et al.). Irvington Publishers, New York, 1989.

Farrell, Warren. *The Liberated Man: Beyond Masculinity: Freeing Men and Their Relationships with Women*. Random House, 1974.

Farrell, Warren. *The Myth of Male Power: Why Men Are the Disposable Sex*. New York: Berkley Books (2001).

Farrell, Warren. *Why Men Are the Way They Are: The Male-Female Dynamic*. McGraw-Hill (1986).

Farrell, Warren. *Why Men Earn More: The Startling Truth Behind the Pay Gap and What Women Can Do About It*. New York: American Management Association (2005).

Farrell, Warren. *Women Can't Hear What Men Don't Say: Destroying Myths, Creating Love*. Sydney: Finch Publishing (2001).

Farrell, Warren, and John Gray. *The Boy Crisis: Why Our Boys Are Struggling and What We Can Do About It*. Dallas, TX: BenBella Books (2018).

Fine, Lawrence. *Physician of the Soul, Healer of the Cosmos: Isaac Luria and His Kabbalistic Fellowship*, Stanford University Press; 1st edition (2003).

Franklin, R. W., ed. *The Poems of Emily Dickinson: Reading Edition*. Cambridge, MA: The Belknap Press, 1999. The poem "There is a pain—so utter" was not published during Dickinson's lifetime. The original version, with Dickinson's typical dashes, was restored by scholar Thomas H. Johnson for his 1955 edition of *The Poems of Emily Dickinson*.

Gafni, Marc. "The Evolutionary Emergent of Unique Self: A New Chapter in Integral Theory." *JITP* 6, no. 1: 1–36.

Gafni, Marc. *The Mystery of Love*. Atria, 2003.

Gafni, Marc. *Radical Kabbalah*. Integral Publishers, 2012.

Gafni, Marc. *Self in Integral Evolutionary Mysticism: Two Models and Why They Matter*, 2014.

Gafni, Marc. *Soul Prints: Your Path to Fulfillment*. Fireside, 2002.

Gafni, Marc. *Your Unique Self: The Radical Path to Personal Enlightenment*, with introduction and afterword by Ken Wilber. Integral Publishers, 2012.

Gafni, Marc, Barbara Marx Hubbard, and Zachary Stein. *The Evolution of Love: From Quarks to Culture—the Rise of Evolutionary Relationships in Response to the Meta-Crisis* (2025).

Gafni, Marc, Barbara Marx Hubbard, and Zachary Stein. *The Universe: A Love Story—First Meditations on CosmoErotic Humanism in Response to the Meta Crisis*. Volumes 1–6. World Philosophy & Religion Press (forthcoming).

Gafni, Marc, and Kristina Kincaid. *A Return to Eros: The Radical Experience of Being Fully Alive*. BenBella Books Inc, 2017.

Gafni, Marc, and Zachary Stein. "Reimagining Humanity's Identity: Responding to the Second Shock of Existence." *World Futures Review* 7, no. 2–3 (2015): 269–278.

Gafni, Marc, and Zachary Stein. *Toward a Politics of Evolutionary Love* (forthcoming).

Gebser, Jean. *The Ever-Present Origin*, authorized translation by Noel Barstad with Algis Mickunas (Athens: Ohio University Press, 1985, 1991).

Graeber, David, and David Wengrow. *Dawn of Everything: A New History of Humanity*. Farrar, Straus and Giroux, 2021.

Gray, John. *Mars and Venus in the Bedroom: A Guide to Lasting Romance and Passion*.

HarperAudio, 2016.

Gray, John. *Mars and Venus on a Date: A Guide to Navigating the 5 Stages of Dating to Create a Loving and Lasting Relationship.* HarperCollins, 2009.

Gray, John. *Mars and Venus Starting Over: A Practical Guide for Finding Love Again After a Painful Breakup, Divorce, or the Loss of a Loved One.* HarperCollins, 1998.

Gray, John. *Men Are from Mars, Women Are from Venus: A Practical Guide for Improving Communication and Getting What You Want in Your Relationships.* HarperCollins, New York, 1992.

Griffin, David Ray. *Religion and Scientific Naturalism: Overcoming the Conflicts*, 2000, SUNY Press.

Haisch, Bernard. *The Purpose-Guided Universe: Believing in Einstein, Darwin and God*, New Page Books, 2012.

Harari, Yuval N. *Homo Deus: A Brief History of Tomorrow.* Harper Perennial, New York, 2018.

Harari, Yuval N. *Sapiens: A Brief History of Humankind.* Vintage Books, London, 2015.

Heisenberg, Werner. *Across the Frontiers*, 1974, Harper & Row.

Heisenberg, Werner. *Physics and Beyond: Encounters and Conversations*, 1971, Harper & Row. (The German title of the book is: *Der Teil und das Ganze = The Part and the Whole.*)

Herculano-Houzel, Suzana. "The Human Brain in Numbers: A Linearly Scaled-Up Primate Brain. *Frontiers in Human Neuroscience* 3, no 31 (2009): https://doi.org/10.3389/neuro.09.031.2009.

Herczeg, ed., *The Torah: With Rashi's Commentary* (New York, 1995, 1999).

Hesse, Hermann. *Demian. The Story of a Youth.* Originally published by Harper & Row/NY in 1925. New translation by Damion Searls: Hermann Hesse: *Demian: The Story of Emil Sinclair's Youth.* Penguin Publishing Group; New Translation edition (July 2013). Original German edition: Hermann Hesse, *Demian. Die Geschichte von Emil Sinclairs Jugend.*

Hoff Sommers, Christina. *Freedom Feminism: Its Surprising History and Why It Matters Today.* Washington, DC: AEI Press, 2013.

Hoff Sommers, Christina. *Right and Wrong: Basic Readings in Ethics.* San Diego: Harcourt Brace Jovanovich, 1986. Co-edited with Robert J. Fogelin.

Hoff Sommers, Christina. *The Science on Women in Science.* Washington, DC: AEI Press, 2009.

Hoff Sommers, Christina. *The War Against Boys.* New York: Simon & Schuster, 2000.

Hoff Sommers, Christina. *Who Stole Feminism?: How Women Have Betrayed Women.* New York: Simon & Schuster, 1994.

Hoff Sommers, Christina. *Vice & Virtue in Everyday Life: Introductory Readings in Ethics.* San Diego: Harcourt Brace Jovanovich, 1984.

Hoff Sommers, Christina, and Sally Satel. *One Nation Under Therapy.* New York: St. Martin's Press, 2005.

Hooks, Bell. *Teaching Community: A Pedagogy of Hope.* Routledge, 2003.

Hudis, Peter and Anderson, Kevin B., eds., *The Rosa Luxemburg Reader* (New York: Monthly Review Press, 2004).

Jabès, Edmond. *The Book of Questions*, in Paul Auster, *Collected Prose: Autobiographical Writings, True Stories, Critical Essays, Prefaces and Collaborations with Artists*, Faber and Faber Ltd, 2011.

Joel, D. "Male or Female? Brains Are Intersex." *Frontiers in Integrative Neuroscience* 5 (2011): 57. https://doi.org/10.3389/fnint.2011.00057.

Joel, Daphna, and Luba Vikhanski. *Gender Mosaic: Beyond the Myth of the Male and*

Female Brain, Little, Brown Spark (2019).

Jung, C. G. *Modern Man in Search of a Soul* (Routledge Classics). Taylor and Francis. Kindle Edition.

Kauffman, Stuart A. *Reinventing the Sacred: A New View of Science, Reason, and Religion*. Basic Books. Kindle Edition.

Kempton, Sally. *Awakening Shakti: The Transformative Power of the Goddesses of Yoga*. Sounds True, 2013.

Kipnis, Laura. *Against Love: A Polemic* (New York: Pantheon Books, 2003).

Kipnis, Laura. *Bound and Gagged: Pornography and the Politics of Fantasy in America* (New York: Grove Press, 1996).

Kipnis, Laura. *Ecstasy Unlimited: On Sex, Capital, Gender, and Aesthetics* (Minneapolis, Minn.: University of Minnesota Press, 1993).

Kipnis, Laura. *The Female Thing: Dirt, Sex, Envy, Vulnerability* (New York: Pantheon Books, 2006).

Kipnis, Laura. *How to Become a Scandal: Adventures in Bad Behavior* (New York: Metropolitan Books, 2010).

Kipnis, Laura. *Love in the Time of Contagion: A Diagnosis* (New York: Pantheon Books, 2022).

Kipnis, Laura. *Men: Notes from an Ongoing Investigation* (New York: Metropolitan Books, 2014).

Kipnis, Laura. *Unwanted Advances: Sexual Paranoia Comes to Campus* (New York: HarperCollins, 2017).

Koestler, Arthur. *The Ghost in the Machine* (1967). Publisher: Hutchinson (UK) and Macmillan (US).

Kropotkin, Peter. *Mutual Aid: A Factor of Evolution*. McClure Phillips & Co, 1902.

Laszlo, Ervin. *The Self-Actualizing Cosmos: The Akasha Revolution in Science and Human Consciousness*, Inner Traditions International (2014).

Le Page, Michael, and Nick Lane. "How Life Evolved: 10 Steps to the First Cells." *New Scientist*, October 2009. https://www.newscientist.com/article/dn17987-how-life-evolved-10-steps-to-the-first-cells/—retrieved January 2024.

Leitenberg, Milton. "Deaths in Wars and Conflicts in the 20th Century." *Cornell University Peace Studies Program Occasional Paper #29*, 3rd edition, 2006. See https://cissm.umd.edu/sites/default/files/2019-08/deathswarsconflicts-june52006.pdf. Retrieved January 2024.

Lipton, Bruce. *The Honeymoon Effect: The Science of Creating Heaven on Earth*, Hay House Inc.; Reprint edition (April 1, 2014).

Lovejoy Paul E. "The Impact of the Atlantic Slave Trade on Africa: A Review of the Literature." *Journal of African History* 30 (1989).

Loye, David. *Darwin's Lost Theory of Love*. iUniverse (2000).

Loye, David. *Darwin's Second Revolution*. Benjamin Franklin Press, 2010.

Loye, David *Rediscovering Darwin: The Rest of Darwin's Theory and Why We Need It Today*. Riane Eisler. Kindle Edition, 2018.

Luria, Isaac. *Eitz Hayim*.

Luria, Isaac. *Sod Iggulim Ve-yosher*. Jerusalem 1964.

Mahler, M. S. "On Child Psychosis and Schizophrenia: Autistic and Symbiotic Infantile Psychoses." *The Psychoanalytic Study of the Child* 7 (1952): 286–305.

Mahler, M. S. "On Human Symbiosis and the Vicissitudes of Individuation." *J Am Psychoanal Assoc*. 15, no. 4 (October 1967):740-63. doi: 10.1177/000306516701500401. PMID: 4170516.

Mahler, Margaret. *Psychological Birth of the Human Infant Symbiosis and Individuation*. Basic Books; Illustrated edition (July 13, 2000).

Hubbard, Barbara Marx. *Conscious Evolution: Awakening the Power of Our Social Potential*, revised edition, New

World Library, 2015.

Maslow, Abraham H. "Critique of Self-Actualization Theory." In Hoffman, Edward (ed.). *Future Visions: The Unpublished Papers of Abraham Maslow.* Thousand Oaks, CA: Sage, 1996.

Maslow, Abraham H. "The Farther Reaches of Human Nature," *Journal of Transpersonal Psychology* 1, no. 1 (1969).

Maslow, Abraham H. *The Farther Reaches of Human Nature.* New York: Viking Press, 1971.

Maslow, Abraham H. *Toward a Psychology of Being.* Princeton, NJ: Van Nostrand, 1962.

Matt, Daniel C., Nathan Wolski, and Joel Hecker. *The Zohar: Pritzker Edition* (12 vols.) Stanford: Stanford University Press, 2004–2017.

McCraty, R., and M. A. Zayas. "Cardiac Coherence, Self-Regulation, Autonomic Stability, and Psychosocial Well-Being." *Frontiers in Psychology* 5 (2014): 1090. https://doi.org/10.3389/fpsyg.2014.01090.

Mendel, Menahem. *Peri Haaretz.* https://www.sefaria.org/Peri_HaAretz.

Meredith, Martin (2014). *The Fortunes of Africa.* New York: PublicAffairs. p. 191.

Meyer Levin. *The Golden Mountain* [1932], p. 71, at sacred-texts.com: https://sacred-texts.com/jud/gm/gm10.htm.

Miller, Geoffrey. *The Mating Mind: How Sexual Choice Shaped the Evolution of Human Nature* (2001, Anchor).

Mother Teresa, edited and with commentary by Brian Kolodiejchuk. *Come Be My Light: The Private Writings of the Saint of Calcutta* (Doubleday Religion, Hardcover, 2007).

Mundy, Liza. *The Richer Sex: How the New Majority of Female Breadwinners Is Transforming Sex, Love, and Family.* Simon & Schuster, 2012.

Nierenberg, Roger. *Maestro: A Surprising Story About Leading by Listening.* Portfolio. 2009. See also, "The Music Paradigm," https://www.musicparadigm.com/.

Nietzsche, Friedrich. *Schopenhauer as Educator: Friedrich Nietzsche's Third Untimely Meditation.* Translated with Notes by Daniel Pellerin. CreateSpace Independent Publishing Platform (November 25, 2014). German original: *Unzeitgemäße Betrachtungen.*

Patai, Daphne. *Brazilian Women Speak: Contemporary Life Stories* (Rutgers University Press, 1988; 1993).

Patai, Daphne. *Heterophobia: Sexual Harassment and the Future of Feminism* (Rowman & Littlefield Publishers, 1998).

Patai, Daphne. *Historia Oral, Feminismo e Politica* (São Paulo: Letra e Voz, 2010).

Patai, Daphne. *Myth and Ideology in Contemporary Brazilian Literature* (Associated University Presses, 1983).

Patai, Daphne. *Professing Feminism: Cautionary Tales from the Strange World of Women's Studies* (written with Noretta Koertge; Basic Books, 1994).

Patai, Daphne. *Professing Feminism: Education and Indoctrination in Women's Studies* (with N. Koertge; new and expanded edition; Lexington Books, 2003).

Patai, Daphne. *The Orwell Mystique: A Study in Male Ideology* (University of Massachusetts Press, 1984).

Patai, Daphne. *Rediscovering Forgotten Radicals: British Women Writers 1889-1939* (co-edited with Angela Ingram; University of North Carolina Press, 1993).

Patai, Daphne. *Theory's Empire: An Anthology of Dissent* (co-edited with Will H. Corral; Columbia University Press, 2005).

Patai, Daphne. *What Price Utopia? Essays on Ideological Policing, Feminism, and Academic Affairs* (Rowman and Littlefield, 2008).

Patai, Daphne. *Women's Words: The Feminist Practice of Oral History* (co-edited with Sherna Berger Gluck; Routledge, 1991).

Pollan, Michael. *The Botany of Desire.* Random House, 2001.

Peirce, Charles S. "Evolutionary Love." *The Monist* (1893): 176–200.

Penrose, Roger. *The Road to Reality: A Complete Guide to the Laws of the Universe.* 2004. Publisher: Jonathan Cape. Parent Company: Penguin Random House.

Popp, Fritz-Albert. "About the Coherence of Biophotons." Published in: *Macroscopic Quantum Coherence, Proceedings of an International Conference on the Boston University*, edited by Boston University and MIT, Editors: E. Sassaroli, Y. Srivastava, J. Swain, and A. Widom. World Scientific 1999.

Prigogine, Ilya, Isabelle Stengers, and Alvin Toffler. *Order Out of Chaos: Man's New Dialogue with Nature.* London: Verso, 2017.

Proust, Marcel. *À la recherche du temps perdu*, first translated into English by the Scotsman C. K. Scott Moncrieff under the title *Remembrance of Things Past*, a phrase taken from Shakespeare's Sonnet 30.

Ridley, Matt. *How Innovation Works* (Fourth Estate, 2020).

Ridley, Matt. "How Innovation Works" [Video]. https://iai.tv/video/how-innovation-works-matt-ridley. August 8, 2022.

Ridley, Matt. *The Rational Optimist: How Prosperity Evolves* (Harper, 2010). *The Evolution of Everything: How New Ideas Emerge* (Harper, 2015).

Ridley, Matt. "When Ideas Have Sex." TED Global. July 2010.

Ridley, Matt. "When Ideas Have Sex." 2012. https://studiogreig.wordpress.com/2012/11/21/when-ideas-have-sex-article-by-matt-ridley/

Rochon, Thomas R. *Culture Moves: Ideas, Activism, and Changing Values.* Princeton University Press, 2018.

Rolston III, Holmes. *Environmental Ethics.* Temple University Press, 1989.

Rosin, Hanna. *The End of Men: And the Rise of Women.* Penguin, 2013.

Salim, E., and S. A. Malik. *Creatio Continua* and Quantum Randomness. In: Clark, K.J., Koperski, J. (eds) *Abrahamic Reflections on Randomness and Providence.* Palgrave Macmillan, Cham. 2022. https://doi.org/10.1007/978-3-030-75797-7_12.

Schneider, Sara. *Kabbalistic Writings on the Nature of the Masculine and Feminine.*

Segal, Ronald. *The Black Diaspora: Five Centuries of the Black Experience Outside Africa.* New York: Farrar, Straus and Giroux, 1995.

Seligman, M., et al. *Homo Prospectus.* Oxford University Press, 2016.

Sheldrake, Rupert. *The Science Delusion: Feeling the Spirit of Enquiry*, 2012, First Edition, Coronet.

Soloveitchik, Joseph B. "The Lonely Man of Faith." *Tradition: A Journal of Orthodox Jewish Thought* 7, no. 2 (1965): 5–67. http://www.jstor.org/stable/23256062.

Sontag, Susan. *As Consciousness is Harnessed to Flesh: Journals and Notebooks, 1964-1980.* Farrar, Straus and Giroux; 1st edition (April 10, 2012).

Swimme, Brian, and Thomas Berry. *The Universe Story: From the Primordial Flaring Forth to the Ecozoic Era–A Celebration of the Unfolding of the Cosmos.* San Francisco: Harper, 1992.

Sykes, Charles J. *A Nation of Victims: The Decay of the American Character.* New York: St. Martin's Press, 1992.

Tagore, Rabindranath. Another translation from his Essay 4. Sadhana, 4.4. Realization in Love in *The Complete Works of Rabindranath Tagore: All Short Stories, Poetry, Novels, Plays & Essays,*

General Press, February 2017.

Temple, David J. *First Principles and First Values: Forty-Two Propositions on CosmoErotic Humanism, the Meta-Crisis, and the World to Come*, World Philosophy & Religion Press, Dandy Lion Publishing Group, 2024.

Temple, David J. *First Principles and First Values: Towards an Evolving Perennialism—Introducing the Anthro-Ontological Method* (forthcoming).

Thomas, Dylan. *The Poems of Dylan Thomas*, published by *New Directions*.

Ury, William L., *The Third Side: Why We Fight and How We Can Stop*, Penguin Publishing Group; updated edition (2000).

Way, Niobe. *Deep Secrets: Boys' Friendship and the Crisis of Connection*. Harvard University Press, 2011.

Welwood, John. *Toward a Psychology of Awakening*. Shambhala, 2002.

Whitehead, Alfred North. *Process and Reality. An Essay in Cosmology*. Gifford Lectures Delivered in the University of Edinburgh During the Session 1927–1928, 1929, Macmillan, New York, Cambridge University Press, Cambridge UK.

Whitman, Walt. "O Me, O Life!" from *Leaves of Grass* (1892).

Wilber, Ken. *Integral Psychology: Consciousness, Spirit, Psychology, Therapy*, 2000,

Wilber, Ken. *The Religion of Tomorrow: A Vision For The Future of the Great Traditions*, 2017.

Wilber, Ken. *Sex, Ecology, Spirituality: The Spirit of Evolution*, 1st ed. 1995, 2nd rev. ed. 2001.

Wilber, Ken. *Trump and a Post-Truth World*, 2017.

Wilcox, W. Bradford, ed. "When Marriage Disappears: The Retreat from Marriage in Middle America." *The National Marriage Project at the University of Virginia and the Center for Marriage and Families at the Institute for American Values*, December 2010. http://stateofourunions.org/2010/when-marriage-disappears.php.

Wilson, David Sloan. *Does Altruism Exist? Culture, Genes, and the Welfare of Others*. Yale University and Templeton Press, 2015.

Wolinsky, Stephen. *Beginner's Guide to Quantum Psychology*. Quantum Institute Inc; First Edition (US) First Printing (2000).

Wolinsky, Stephen. *The Way of the Human: The Quantum Psychology Notebooks*. Volumes 1-3. Quantum Institute, Inc. 1999.

Wolinsky, Stephen, and Colin Wilson. *Quantum Consciousness: The Guide to Experiencing Quantum Psychology* 1993.

Wolinsky, Stephen, and Margaret O. Ryan. *Trances People Live* (1991).

Yosef, R. Gikatilla's *Sha'are Orah* (Gates of Light).

Young, Cathy. *Ceasefire!: Why Women and Men Must Join Forces to Achieve True Equality* (1999).

Young, Cathy. *Growing Up In Moscow: Memories of a Soviet Girlhood* (1989).

Articles

"Atomic Education Urged by Einstein: Scientist in Plea for $200,000 to Promote New Type of Essential Thinking." The New York Times. May 25, 1946.

Baum, Howie. "The Nervous System." University of Cincinnati. https://pdf4pro.com/amp/view/the-nervous-system-university-of-cincinnati-69596c.html.

The Center for American Progress. "Breadwinning Mothers Continue To Be the U.S. Norm." 2019. https://www.americanprogress.org/article/breadwinning-mothers-continue-u-s-norm/.

"Einstein's Misquote on the Illusion of Feeling Separate from the Whole." Thy Mind, O Human. Accessed January 2024. https://www.thymindoman.com/einsteins-misquote-on-the-illusion-of-feeling-separate-from-the-whole/.

ESA Hubble. "NASA's Great Observatories Provide a Detailed View of Kepler's Supernova Remnant." Accessed January 2024. https://esahubble.org/images/opo0429a/.

Gottlieb, Lori. "Does a More Equal Marriage Mean Less Sex?" *The New York Times Magazine*. February 2014.

Hubblesite. "The Doomed Star Eta Carinae." Accessed January 2024. https://hubblesite.org/contents/media/images/1996/23/430-Image.html.

IEG World Bank Group. "2.4 Billion without Adequate Sanitation. 600 Million without Safe Water. Can We Fix It by 2030?" 2018. Accessed January 2024. https://ieg.worldbankgroup.org/blog/over-24-billion-without-adequate-sanitation-600-million-without-safe-water-how-do-we-bridge.

Jabr, Ferris. "How Does a Caterpillar Turn into a Butterfly?" *Scientific American*. August 10, 2012. https://www.scientificamerican.com/article/caterpillar-butterfly-metamorphosis-explainer/.

Kornrich, Sabino, Julie Brines, and Katrina Leupp. "Egalitarianism, Housework, and Sexual Frequency in Marriage. *American Sociological Review* 78, no. 1 2012): 26–50. DOI: 10.1177/0003122412472340.

NASA. "WMAP Produces New Results." National Aeronautics and Space Administration. Accessed January 2024. https://map.gsfc.nasa.gov/news.

Pew Research Center. "In a Growing Share of U.S. Marriages, Husbands and Wives Earn About the Same." April 2023. https://www.pewresearch.org/social-trends/2023/04/13/in-a-growing-share-of-u-s-marriages-husbands-and-wives-earn-about-the-same/.

Walk Free. "Global Slavery Index." 2021. https://www.walkfree.org/global-slavery-index/map/.

The World Counts. "Around 9 Million People Die Every Year of Hunger and Hunger-Related Diseases." Accessed January 2024. https://www.theworldcounts.com/challenges/hunger-and-obesity/how-many-people-die-from-hunger-each-year

World Hunger. "World Child Hunger Facts." Accessed January 2024. https://www.worldhunger.org/world-child-hunger-facts/.

Young, Cathy. "Johnny Depp and the Other Side of Domestic Violence: Men Can Be Victims. Women Can Be Abusers. Welcome to Equality." Medium.com. 2020.

Young, Cathy. "There Are Also Battered Men." *The New York Times*. 2006.

Bible, Talmud, Zohar, and Quran Passages

Deuteronomy 32:10.
Genesis 2:24.
Genesis 25:5.
Leviticus 19:34.
Song of Songs, 3:10.
Song of Songs, 1:4.
Talmud, Sanhedrin, 37a.
Quran, 5:32.
Zohar Hai, vol. 1, 3a.

ABOUT THE AUTHORS

DR. MARC GAFNI

Dr. Marc Gafni is a visionary world philosopher and futurist, one of the leading formulators of world spirituality and religion of our time, and a beloved teacher and public intellectual.

He holds his doctorate in philosophy from Oxford University, as well as Orthodox rabbinic ordination. He co-founded the activist think tank now called the Center for World Philosophy and Religion, where he serves as the co-president with Dr. Zachary Stein. He also served with Barbara Marx Hubbard as co-president of the Foundation for Conscious Evolution, which he consented to lead at Barbara's request after her passing.

He is known for his "source code teachings"—including Unique Self theory and the Five Selves, the Amorous Cosmos, a Politics of Evolutionary Love, a Return to Eros, and Digital Intimacy—and has more than twenty books to his name, including the award-winning *Your Unique Self*, *A Return to Eros*, and three volumes of *Radical Kabbalah*.

He teaches on the cutting edge of philosophy in the West, helping to evolve a new "dharma" or meta-theory of Integral meaning that is helping to re-shape key pivoting points in global consciousness and culture, with the aim of participating in the articulation of what Dr. Gafni together with Dr. Stein and colleagues are calling CosmoErotic Humanism.

At the core of CosmoErotic Humanism is what Dr. Gafni and Dr. Stein are calling First Principles and First Values, Anthro-Ontology, and a Universal Grammar of Value. This is the ground of a new shared universe story and a new narrative of identity for the new human and the new humanity. This is what they are calling the emergence from *Homo sapiens* to *Homo Amor*. This shared story rooted in First Principles and First Values can then serve as the matrix for a global ethos for a global civilization.

Together with Dr. Stein and Ken Wilber, Dr. Gafni is writing a series of seminal books under the collective pseudonym of David J. Temple, which intend to evolve the source code of consciousness and culture in response to the meta-crisis. The first of those books is *First Principles and First Values: Forty-Two Propositions on Cosmo-erotic Humanism, the Meta-Crisis, and the World to Come.*

BARBARA MARX HUBBARD

Barbara Marx Hubbard (born Barbara Marx; December 22, 1929–April 10, 2019) was an American futurist, author, and public speaker. She is credited with the Wheel of Co-Creation and together with Dr. Gafni, the Wheel of Co-Creation 2.0, as well as the concepts of the Synergy Engine and the "birthing" of humanity.

As co-founder and president of the Foundation for Conscious Evolution and the chair, for the last five years of her life, of the Center for World Philosophy and Religion, she posited that humanity was on the threshold of a quantum leap if newly emergent scientific, social, and spiritual capacities were integrated to address global crises.

She was the author of seven books on social and planetary evolution. In conjunction with the Shift Network, she co-produced the worldwide "Birth 2012" multimedia event. She was also the subject of a biography by author Neale Donald Walsch, *The Mother of Invention: The Legacy of Barbara Marx Hubbard, and the Future of "YOU"*. Deepak Chopra called her "the voice for conscious evolution."

In 1984, she was symbolically nominated for the vice presidency of the United States. She also co-chaired a number of Soviet-American Citizen Summits, introducing a new concept called SYNCON, to foster synergistic convergence with opposing groups. In addition, she co-founded the World Future Society and the Association for Global New Thought.

INDEX

Note: Page numbers in **bold** indicate tables in the text, and references following "n" refer notes.

A
accelerating returns, rate of, 38
acts of service, 84
addiction, 92, 345, 402, 425, 510
adjustment to reality, 129–31
affirmation:
　cards, 197
　of feminine rage, 559
　formal, 306
　of goodness of Reality, 284
　of not knowing, 527
　originality as emotional intercourse, 507
　quality of intimacy, 505
　words of, 84
Alighieri, Dante, 343n181
allurement, 40, 66, 204, 243, 343, 371, 418–19
　alluring intelligence, 330
　Outrageous Love as, 421–22
　in soul mate relationship, 565
　toward relationship, 26–27
androgyny, 3, 552–54
ani-Ayin-ani, 260
ani, 260. *See also* Separate Self
Anthropocene, 252, 476
antithesis, 139
apotheosis, 466
arousal/arousing, 32, 419, 508. *See also* responsibility for own arousal
　emotional, 399
　erotic, 177
　falling in love, 396–97
　responsibility for own, 356–67
　sensual, 400
　sexual, 399
　vocational, 81, 399–400
　whole mate, 180
Atman, 274
atomic particles, 331
Auel, Jean, 56
Aurobindo (Sri), 451, 455, 467
authentic wounding, 545–47
awakening of evolution, 316–17
Ayin, 260, 274

B
Baal Shem Tov, 235, 492–96
Bank, Ralph Richard, 123
Baum, Howie, 541n303
Beck, Don, 471, 471n255
Becker, Ernest, 442
Beckwith, Michael, 262
"become better", definition of, 282
Becoming a Future Human, 479
becoming of Reality, 27, 246, 275–77, 278, 288
　Eros and, 29, 401, 402
　evolution, 457, 476
　faces of, 282
　Field of, 275
　lure of, 343
　newer, 568–71
　process of, 429–30
　unique configuration of, 233
　unique presence of, 232
　and Unique Self, 223, 233, 286, 299
　as universal species, 202
　urge to emerge, 285–86
　of women, 567
being of Reality, 27, 246, 275–77, 288
　Eros and, 29, 401, 402
　evolution, 286
　higher order of, 149

primordial Ground of, 160
resting in Ground of, 259
unique presence of, 232
and Unique Self, 223, 233, 299
urge to emerge, 285–86
The Bell Jar (Plath), 103
Bennett, Paul, 566
beyond-Mars-and-Venus relationship, 88. *See also* whole mate relationship
consciousness, 181
evolutionary relationships into Reality, 117–18, 122
role mate relationship, 45–46, 78–82
model, 108–9, 139
soul mate relationship, 65–66, 161
steps on path to, 130
vision of polarity and passion, 9
whole mate relationship, 96, 122, 161, 167, 229
wholeness, 118
Beyond *Romeo and Juliet* story, 137–40
Big Bang(s), 160, 257, 311–18, 389. *See also* lines and circles
awakening of evolution, 316–17
cosmological evolution, 25, 26, 39, 148, 284–85
Eternity before, 159–60
evolutionary chain, 254–55
evolutionary impulse, 311–14, 315
Evolutionary Unique Self, 317
evolution of humanity, 315–16
life creation, 314–15
Outrageous Love, 317–18
primordial *Yes* of, 257
Reality from, 145, 159
binding energy, 37n24
bio-logic dynamic of love, 54
bio-logic matches, 53
biophoton:
coherent field of, 235
coherent frequencies of, 235
emission, 234
black women, 123–24
Blake, William, 160
Bloom, Howard, 455–56, 460, 549
bodhisattva, 299–300
Bohm, David, 248–49, 458
Bonnie and Clyde (movie), 369–70

brokenheartedness, 237
brokenness:
self-recognition of, 245
soul mate relationship, 178
whole mate relationship, 178
Brownback, Kathy, 566
Buddhist texts, 259–60n148
busyness, 225, 276–77, 361
butterfly effect, 191, 312

C

calligraphy, 241
Camus, Albert, 416
cancer cells, qualities of, 248
Caplan, Mariana, 468n251, 508
Carlebach, Shlomo, 528n297
ceaseless creativity, 315
of Cosmos, 146, 289, 289n157, 342, 394, 429
Outrageous Love as, 421–22
of Reality, 32, 274
Center for Integral Wisdom. *See* Center for World Philosophy and Religion
Center for World Philosophy and Religion, 453, 457n232, 468, 478
Chapman, Gary, 83–84
Chariots of Fire (movie), 276
charity, 250–51, 256
chemical bonding, 330, 331n172
chemistry, 86, 396
children, idolatry of, 100–103
choicelessness, relationship from choice to, 409–11
choose-a-partner-to-survive relational structure, 111
Christianity, 243, 526
circle of intimacy, 30, 333, 334–35
cosmocentric, 30
egocentric, 30, 48
ethnocentric, 30
unique, 232, 233, 286, 294, 388, 397, 411, 420, 430, 446, 448–49
worldcentric, 30
circles. *See* lines and circles
The Clan of the Cave Bear (Auel), 56–57
classic intimacy, 114
classic role mate relationships, 62
co-breadwinners, 5n5

codependency, 347, 406
Cohen, Andrew, 275n151, 282n154
coherence, 353, 479
  of biophotons, 234
  islands of, 148
comfort, 325, 486
  and dignity, 95
  pain, 284
  vs. pleasure, 348
commitment, 83–86, 96, 128, 449, 467, 520
  against conflict manifests as harmony, 194
  to living extraordinary life, 196
  long-term, 132
  sole commitment, 161
  for whole mates, 181
common ground, 136–37
common-sense sacred axioms of value, 203
communication, 13, 94, 99, 179, 187
  egalitarian relationships, 8
  methods within living organism, 234
  relationship from commitment to, 83–86
  role mate dependency, 111
  skills, 25
  soul mate relationship, 65, 66, 381–82, 556
  women expectations from partners, 6, 82, 89
complexity, 290
  need of deeds, 249
  science, 294
  self-organizing movement toward, 460
  of Universe, 27–28
compromise, 196
  willingness to, 193
confession of greatness, 245–46, 387–88
Conscious Evolution, 39–41, 81, 294, 391, 462n239, 467. *See also* evolution, arc of
  and evolutionary relationships, 291–93
  evolution of, 473–76
  giving unique gift, 233, 298
  in human form, 476
  memes of, 482

new meaning of, 455–62
new Story, 453, 455–56, 463
Outrageous Love, 351
self-organizing, 430
spiritual vision of, 452–53
Wheel of Co-Creation as, 480
and whole mate relationship, 319
Conscious Evolution: Awakening the Power of Our Social Potential (Hubbard), 216n128
consciousness, 28, 36, 143, 162, 332–33
  cosmocentric level of, 543–44
  ethnocentric level of, 543
  evolution of, 333, 474
  normal, 214, 216
  optical delusion of, 213
  second deepening of inner experience, 333
  worldcentric level of, 543
conscious uniqueness, 317
  from unconscious to, 295–97, 372
continuous creation, doctrine of, 507
Coontz, Stephanie, 113
Core of the Cosmos, 354n191
Corten, Chahat, 566
cosmic accident and Unique Self, 242–43
Cosmic qualities of lines and circles, 563
Cosmic Scroll, letter in, 240–42
cosmocentric circle of intimacy, 30
cosmocentric level of consciousness, 543–44
cosmocentric love, from world centric to, 340–41
CosmoErotic Humanism, 225–27, 327, 473, 566
  Barbara's story, 451–64
  Marc's story, 465–84
cosmological evolution, 25, 26, 39, 148, 284–85
Cosmos, 315, 460
  ceaseless creativity of, 146, 289, 289n157, 342, 394, 429
  mystery of, 159–60
  Outrageous Love as strongest force in, 350–51
  self-actualizing, 289, 293–95, 429
  telos of, 459, 460

covalent bond, 331n172
Cowan, Chris, 471n255
Creegan, Robert, 441n225
cultural evolution, 553
    consciousness of death, 442–43
    of love, 316
    stages of, 315

D

Dalai Lama, 261–67, 352
Damon, Matt, 220, 286–87
Darwin, Charles, 7, 23
David Copperfield (Dickens), 240–41
dawn man, 441, 442
dealmaking, 147, 192–93
death/dying, 47, 444
    Charity saves from death, 256
    consciousness of, 442–43
    potential death of humanity, 477
    realization of, 442
    scenes in movies, 181, 184, 186–87
    whole mate *vs*. soul mate relationship, 181–87
Death Star, 483–84
decay, 25n16, 391
de Chardin, Pierre Teilhard, 363–64, 451, 455, 462, 467, 467n249
deepening of wholeness, 290
deep trance phenomenon, 513–14
deficiency needs, 535
democracy, 163
democratization:
    of enlightenment, 432, 466
    of greatness, 286–88
The Denial of Death (Becker), 442
dependency, 408
    dynamics of, 45, 46, 55, 57
    evolution in relationship, 404–6
    imbalances in power between men and women, 57
    mutual, 4, 48, 56, 62
    relationship of role mates, 81, 94, 111
    value of, 228
Dershowitz, Alan, 559
The Descent of Man (Darwin), 23
descriptive labels, 523
desire, 93, 285, 396
    Eros and evolution of, 403–4
    for life, 21
    of Reality, 229, 404
    sex-object, 134
    sexual, 94, 162
    success-object, 134
    for survival, 21, 22, 36, 46
    of Universe, 297
deuterium, 331
devotion, 13, 146, 195, 200, 280, 347, 490
    interdependent, 347
    personal, 392
Diamandis, Peter, 461
Dickens, Charles, 240–41
Dickinson, Emily, 511
divorce, 14, 100, 110, 124
Dunbar number, 47
Dunbar tribe, role mate love in, 48
duty, 12, 47, 67
    value of, 228
    evolution of, 408–9
    role mate relationship, 46–48
Dworkin, Andrew, 556

E

ecstatic urgency, 172, 275–77, 280, 285, 391, 424
Edin, Kathryn, 125
egalitarian couples, 94, 111, 141, 161, 383, 399
"Egalitarianism, Housework, and Sexual Frequency in Marriage," 112
egalitarian marriage, passion in, 110
    equality a panacea for sexuality, 110–11
    key results from, 118
    polarity, passion, and power, 113–14
    sex tonight, 111–13
    Zeitgeist stories, 115–17
egalitarian relationships, 8–9, 112, 117, 118
ego, 239–40, 347
    ego-based love, 343
    evolution beyond, 214
    Uniqueness at ego level, 296
egocentric circle of intimacy, 30, 48
egocentric intimacy, 30, 333
    to ethnocentric intimacy, 334–37
egocentric level of moral development, 543
egocentric love, 48, 316, 346

to ethnocentric love, 332–34
Einstein, Albert, 14, 213, 314
electromagnetic attraction, 26–27, 31, 330
electromagnetic charge, 177
embodiment, 199
emergents/emergence, 33–34, 199, 285
emotional arousal, 399
emotional kindred spirits, 113
The End of Men: And the Rise of Women (Rosin), 104–5, 127
enlightenment, 215, 216, 307, 472, 487
  democratization of, 432
  individual, 307
  loving your way to, 465–66
  personal, 276
Erickson, Milton, 513
Eros, 23, 29–31, 45, 199, 204–6, 261, 345–46
  in Evolutionary Relationships, 400
  and evolution of desire, 403–4
  four faces of, 489
  needs for, 359–60
  Outrageous Love and, 400–401
  power of, 358
  and Pseudo-Eros, 401–3
  of soul mate relationships, 507
  on steroids, 274
  uniqueness and, 360–61
erotic arousal, 177
erotic life, 549–52
erotic synergy, 428
Eternity before Big Bang, 159–60
Eternity/eternity, 37, 159–60, 415, 518
ethnocentric intimacy, 30, 334
  from egocentric intimacy to, 334–37
ethnocentric level of consciousness, 543
ethnocentric love:
  from egocentric love to, 332–34
  to worldcentric love, 337–40
Ethos/ethos, 23, 204–6
evaluative labels, 524
evolution, 286, 290–91, 457n231, 565
  by chance, 474
  by choice, 474
  cosmological, 25, 26, 39, 148, 284–85
  of dependency in relationship, 404–6
  beyond ego, 214
  of humanity, 315–16
  of intimacy, 16, 485
  of love, 16, 161–62, 316, 325–27, 330–44, 419–21
  of relationships, 485
evolution, arc of, 37–39. *See also* Conscious Evolution
  allurement toward relationship, 26–27
  emergents, 33–34
  intimacy and Eros, 29–31
  life and love, 21–22
  LoveBeauty, 31–32
  LoveDesire of Reality, 31–32
  LoveIntelligence, 31–32
  protozoa, 34–36
  Reality, 24–26
  survival of the fittest, 22–24
  trajectories of evolution, 27–29
  transformation relationship, 36–37
evolutionary chain, 254–55
evolutionary consciousness. *See* whole mate consciousness
evolutionary crisis, 117
Evolutionary Heroes, emergence of, 447–50
evolutionary imperative, 289
evolutionary impulse, 274–75, 278, 288–91
  Big Bang and, 311–14, 315
  of CosmoErotic Universe, 289
  creative, 315
  sexual expression of, 279
  Unique We and, 397, 398
  Universe Story and, 314
Evolutionary Intimacy, 372, 390. *See also* intimacy/Intimacy
  birth of, 367–70
  from *do you love me?* to *you love me*, 364–66
  from *I love you* to *you love me*, 362–64
evolutionary Kabbalah, 291n160, 456
Evolutionary Love, 344, 394, 417, 472
Evolutionary Love (Peirce), 23, 53
evolutionary man, 568
evolutionary partner, 200
  searching for, 165–67
evolutionary relationships, 14–15, 36, 96, 168, 273, 318. *See also* whole mate

relationship(s)
between being and becoming, 275–77
Big Bangs, 311–18
from choice to choicelessness, 409–11
confession of greatness, 387–88
conscious evolution and, 291–93
democratization of greatness, 286–88
direct access to four selves, 309–11, **320–24**
Eros in, 400–404
evolutionary context for relating, 297–99
evolutionary impulse, 288–91
Evolutionary Unique Self and, 273–75, 318–19
evolution of dependency in relationship, 404–6
evolution of honor, duty, and obligation, 408–9
falling in love as arousal from above, 396–98
loneliness and happiness, 407
love story, 225–27
and Outrageous Love, 393–95
reloaded, 379–80
role mate, soul mate, and whole mate in evolutionary context, 380–87
second shock of existence and emergence of, 443–45
self-actualizing Cosmos, 293–95
sex to supra-sex, 398–400
from unconscious to conscious uniqueness, 295–97
unique gifts and unique obligations, 299–309
Unique We, 388–91
Unique We plugs whole mates into larger field, 391–93
unrelenting positivity of Yes!, 283–85
vision of, 437
evolutionary spirituality, 455, 456, 570
evolutionary story, 16, 39–40, 291–92, 463, 541
Evolutionary Unique Self, 273–75, 294, **320–24**, 413, 437, **576–80**
direct access to, 311
and evolutionary relationships, 318–19
experience of, 317, 398

inner experience of, 277–83
love and, 348–49
obligation at level of, 300–301
in self-organizing Universe, 429–32
wounds in, 534–36
Evolutionary We-Space, 432–33
evolutionary woman, 568
evolution awakening, 316–17
conscious evolution, 291–93
evolutionary relationships, 291–93
self-actualizing Cosmos, 293–95
from unconscious to conscious uniqueness, 295–97
evolution of humanity, 315–16
existential loneliness, 381
existential risk, 454
exponential power, 454
exterior sciences, 468
Eye:
of Consciousness, 259
of Contemplation, 259
of Heart, 259
of Mind, 258–59
of Senses, 258–59
of Spirit, 259
of Value, 259

F

falling in love, 167
in role mate relationships, 53–54
as soul mates, 86–88
familial intimacy, 47n28
Family Circle, 2
Farrell, Warren, 82, 559–60, 566
Fiddler on the Roof play, 76, 187
Fiekowsky, Peter, 566
field/Field, 222–23, 273–74
of Becoming, 275–76
of Being, 275–76
Field of Becoming, 275
finding field exercise, 225
quantum field, 273
of Value, 15n9
whole mates into larger field, 391–93
zero-point, 146, 273
Fifty Shades of Grey (movie), 410
fight-or-flight response, 21
first shock of existence, 441

Fisher, Helen, 121, 135
Fivefold Principles of Authentic Obligation, 301
The Five Love Languages (Chapman), 83
Four Weddings and a Funeral (movie), 73–75
Franklin, Benjamin, 515
Fuller, Buckminster, 451, 455, 456
functional aloneness, 381

G
Gafni, Marc, 451, 566
 evolution of conscious evolution, 473–76
 joining genius, 479–83
 loving the way to enlightenment, 465–66
 responding to second shock of existence, 477–79
 Unique Self Realization, 467–73
 word on power, 483–84
galaxies, 284
Galperin, Lori, 566
Gasca, Jessica, 119–20
Gebser, Jean, 470, 560
Geist, 274
Getting the Love You Want (Hendrix), 83
Gibran, Khalil, 147, 153, 155
Goddard, Tom, 566
Gottlieb, Lori, 112–13
Graeber, David, 47
Grant, Hugh, 73
Graves, Clare, 471
gravitational interaction, 330
Gray, John, 81, 83, 85, 566, 566
great flaring forth. *See* Big Bang(s)
Great Flaring Forth, 160
Great Library of CosmoErotic Humanism, 482, 483
greatness:
 confession of, 387–88
 democratization of, 286–88
Griffin, David Ray, 460n236
Ground of Being, 260, 274, 277, 469
 Infinite and Eternal, 469
 primordial, 160
 resting in, 259
 Value as, 15n9

growing up, 470–71
Gyatso, Tenzin, 263–64

H
Hafiz (Persian poet), 146–47, 149, 245
Haisch, Bernard, 288
Hamilton, Diane, 480n267
happiness, 95, 104, 407
Harari, Yuval N., 483
harmony, 194, 223, 225, 293
heart commitment, 84
heavy hydrogen nuclei, 25
Hebrew mysticism, 241
Hebrew wisdom, 205–6, 260, 291n160, 300, 465
Hegel, Georg Wilhelm Friedrich, 308
Heisenberg, Werner, 459n235
Henderson, Darren, 125
Hendricks, Gay, 81
Hendrix, Harville, 83, 87
Herndon, Carol, 566
hero/heroism, 3, 7–8, 228, 435
 Evolutionary Heroes, 447–50
 first language of, 46–48
 generation in need of, 441–46
 Hero movie, 334
 in *The Matrix* movie, 173–74
 need of new language for, 131–33
 new hero of whole mate relationships, 435–41
 Unique Self Hero, 439–41
 value of, 228
Hesse, Herman, 236
Hieros Gamos, 548, 549, 563
Hoff Sommers, Christina, 556, 559
holon as basic unit of reality, 247–48
Holy Grail of soul mate relationships, 100
homeostasis, 367n198
Homo amor, 143, 200–201, 463n241, 473, 571
Homo imaginus, 143, 202
Homo sapiens. *See* human beings
Homo Universalis, 463n241, 473n259, 482
honor, 7, 67
 evolution of, 408–9
 role mate, 46–48

value of, 228
hooks, bell, 561n324
Hubbard, Barbara Marx, 451–53
   joining genius, 463–64
   need story equal to power, 453–55
   new meaning of conscious evolution, 455–62
Hubbard, B. Marx, 216n128
human beings, 28–29, 143, 200–201
   elementary particles to, 331–32
   frequency of light, 235
   represents evolution of love, 316
humanity, evolution of, 315–16
Hunt, Helen LaKelly, 87
hurt, 543–44
Huxley, Julian, 451, 467
hydrogen bond, 331n172

I

I choose you, saying, 372, 406
identity:
   creation through wounding, 533–34
   of Outrageous Lover, 486, 536
   and purpose, 136
   quality of, 548
   and relationship, 530
   transformation of, 7, 13–14, 218–20, 225, 273–74, 275, 277, 318, 379
   up-leveling of, 273
idolatry of children, 100–103
I love you, saying, 77, 187, 406, 508
   in communication, 13
   limitations of, 89–93
   tends to *I need you*, 252–54
   and uniqueness, 372
   in whole mate level, 256, 361–62
   to *you love me*, 362–64
imaginal cells, 164
imaginal discs, 163–64
imago, 87–88, 396
Imago Theory of relationships (Hunt), 87–88
immune system, 164, 231
impact, 86
incoherence, 353
individual holons, 247–48
Industrial Revolution, 4, 315
I need you, 362, 372, 406
I love you tends to, 252–54
   in soul mate relationship, 254
   and vulnerability, 255
infatuation, 167, 200, 341
Infinite/Infinity, 248–49
   of Intimacy, 235, 248, 256, 362, 364–65, 429, 468, 517, 517n291, 540, 547
   Intimate, 234, 256, 364, 468
   of Power, 362, 364, 455
   Reality, 248
injustice, 14, 560
innovation, 34, 277, 278, 281–83, 426, 428
insane/insanity, 213, 216, 228, 244, 287, 447
Integral Theory, 468
Integrity/integrity, 7, 57, 116, 117, 146, 172, 212, 246, 367n198, 464
   Evolutionary Integrity, 293, 306, 307, 408
   personal, 408
   radical, 420
intention, 86, 190–91
interaction, 501
   gravitational, 330
interconnectivity, 27, 247, 290, 448
   of all Reality, 247
   and Intimacy, 146
   radical, 487
interdependency, 406
interdependent devotion, love and, 348
interior sciences, 32, 216, 259, 456, 462, 465, 491
   eastern, 260
   Greek and Hindu, 8n7
   of Hebrew wisdom, 205–6, 300
   Hieros Gamos, 548, 563
   Reality in, 160, 235
   spark of Eros, 345
intersex brain, 175, 563
intimacy/Intimacy, 6, 28–31, 290, 362. *See also* Evolutionary Intimacy
   with all things, 487
   cosmocentric circle of, 30
   egalitarian relationships, 8
   evolution of love and, 330–44
   four circles of, 333

progressive deepening of, 462
progressive intensification of, 507
role mate dependency, 111
soul mate relationship, 65, 66, 68–71, 381–82
whole mate relationship, 380
women expectations from partners, 6, 82, 89
intimate communion:
  collecting your days, 503–5
  goal of, 526
  invitations of time, 502–3
  love at present, 508–10
  mind trance and mindfulness, 520–22
  no extra moments, 506
  pain trance, 510–13
  radical presence, 500–502
  requiring contact in present, 500
  staying in present, 513–15
  staying in symptoms, 516–17
  unfinished business, 518–20
Intimate Universe, 462n239
Invergordon, Adele, 220–25
ionic bond, 331n172
Isaac, Levi, 102–3, 308–9, 546
islands of coherence, 148
Is Marriage for White People? (Bank), 123

J

Jabès, Edmond, 527
Jabr, Ferris, 164
Jagger, Mick, 168
Joel, Daphna, 563
Jogiches, Leo, 296
joining genius, 463n240, 463–64, 479–83
  joining genes to, 34, 162, 398–400, 481–82
joy:
  compass of, 97
  radical, 256–58, 424
Jung, Carl, 502, 505n279
Junuh, Rannulph, 220–25, 273, 286

K

Kabbalah, 307
Kafka, Franz, 244
Kauffman, Stuart, 289, 289n157

kavanot, 306
Kefalas, Maria, 125
Kempton, Sally, 478, 480n267, 566
Kent, Clark, 7, 116
killer reflex, 6
Kincaid, Kristina, 480n267, 481, 483, 566
Kipnis, Laura, 559
Koestler, Arthur, 247
Kolodiejchuk, Brian, 349n186
Kook, Abraham Isaac, 456, 459, 467
Kropotkin, Peter, 416n219

L

labeling, 522–24
labels obstruct contact, 522–26
Lainer, Mordechai, 354n190, 467
Lane, Lois, 7, 116
Laszlo, Ervin, 289
The Legend of Bagger Vance (movie), 220
Lelouch, Claude, 243
Lennon, John, 325
LeShem Yichud, 294, 306
level-one role mate relationship, 408
level-three whole mate relationships, 189
level-two relationships, 195–96
Levi Isaac of Berdichev, 102, 308
The Liberated Man and Why Men Are the Way They Are (Farrell), 82
Liddell, Eric, 276
life creation, 314–15
Li, Jet, 334
Lincoln, Abraham, 328
lines and circles, 3, 117, 548, 549, 551. *See also* Big Bang(s)
  Eros of, 552
  and *LeShem Yichud*, 294, 306
  as masculine and feminine (men and women), 219n129, 554
  qualities, 174–76, 219–20, 405, 549, 551, 554, 563
  Unique Gender, 554
  Unique Gender of Trinity, 176
  Unique Self, 552, 562–64
Lipton, Bruce, 21
loneliness, 14, 67–68, 70, 407, 528
The Lord of the Rings (movie), 394
love, 1–2, 17–19, 21–22, 24–25, 235, 325,

330, 350, 417, 419
   all failure in, 508
   bio-logic dynamic of, 54
   calling to serve, 146–48
   circles of, 341
   evolution of, 16, 161–62, 316, 325–27, 330–44, 419–21
   falling in love as arousal, 396–98
   journey, 73
   languages, 77, 84–85, 438
   ontologizing of, 462
   at present, 508–10
   questions about, 326
   reflex, 6
   sourced in great love, 353–56
   stations of, 98–100
LoveBeauty, 31–32, 34, 39, 161–62, 221, 223, 231, 274, 301, 414
LoveDesire of Reality, 31–32, 34, 39, 161, 221, 223, 231, 274, 301, 414
LoveIntelligence, 31–32, 34, 39, 161–62, 221, 223, 231, 274, 301, 414
Love Story (movie), 71–73, 98–99, 119, 169–70, 177, 179, 181, 184
Loye, David, 23, 416
Luria, Isaac, 241, 306, 308–9, 456
Luxemburg, Rosa, 296

M
Maat, 274
MacDowell, Andie, 73
Mackey, John P., 480n267, 566
Mahler, Margaret, 212
Maloney, Kate, 480n267, 566
Manna, 506
marriage, 10, 57, 62, 83
   egalitarian, 110–11, 113
   middle-class, 119–26
   therapy, 115
Mars-and-Venus communication techniques, 161
Mars-and-Venus relationships, 18, 184
Mars, men as, 2–4. *See also* beyond-Venus-and-Mars relationship
   characteristics, 2–4, 85–86
   qualities, 10, 174
   role mate, 45–46
   soul mate, 78–82

The Martian (movie), 286–87
Maslow, Abraham H., 9, 535
Maslow's hierarchy of needs, 49, 535
The Mating Mind (Miller), 436
The Matrix (movie), 169–70, 173, 177, 181–82, 215
meiosis, 458
Men Are from Mars, Women Are from Venus (Gray), 81–83, 85–86, 99, 566
men/masculine, 3
   vulnerability, 558
   communication consciousness, 83
   desire for survival, 36, 46
   differences with women, 554–57
   evolution from role mate to soul mate, 82
   evolution of love, 18
   evolution of relationships, 18
   power imbalance, 57
   relationship in western culture, 55
mental illness, 508–9
meta-crisis, 443–45
metallic bond, 331n172
meta-meme, 485
middle-class marriage, 119–26
Milarepa (Tibetan Buddhist master), 507
Miller, Geoffrey, 435
mindfulness, 520–22
mind trance, 520–22
misidentification, 508
mitosis, 458
Mitzvah, 302–5
molecules, 247–48
Molinard, Claire, 566
Moshe Leib of Sassov, 489
Mundy, Liza, 106, 119–20, 437
music, 326
mutuality of value, 31
The Mystery of Love (Gafni), 467

N
name-calling, 522
narcissism, 95–98, 297, 363, 547
neglect, 14
Nelson, Terry, 566
neuroscience, 325, 329, 398
newness, 28, 34, 143–44, 201, 374

new Story, 445, 482, 484
  Conscious Evolution as, 453, 455–56, 463
  CosmoErotic Humanism, 225, 566
  of humanity, 479
  of sexing, 280
  of Value, 226n133, 297, 566
Nierenberg, Roger, 427, 428n221
Nietzsche, Friedrich, 372
Nondual Humanism. See *Radical Kabbalah*
normal consciousness, 214, 216, 447

O

obligation, 67, 300, 422
  dynamics of, 45, 46–48, 55
  evolution of, 408–9
  role mate, 46–48
  value of, 228
observable universe, 357, 357n195
old-deal relationships, 12, 36
Oliver, Mary, 3
ontogeny, 46–47
optical delusion of consciousness, 213–14
ordinary love, 325, 331, 333–34, 342, 382, 486–87, 535, 540
  ego-based love, 343
  vs. Outrageous Love, 344–56
originality as emotional intercourse, 507
Outrageous Acts of Love, 424–25, 445–46
Outrageous Love, 317–18, 325, 342, 344, 417, 450, 472, 486
  as ceaseless creativity and allurement, 421–22
  distinctions between ordinary love and, 346–50
  and emergence of Evolutionary Heroes, 447–50
  and Eros, 400–401
  evolutionary relationships and, 393–95
  evolution of love and intimacy, 330–44
  live as, 539–42
  love sourced in great love, 353–56
  moment exposing, 374–75
  ordinary love and, 344

perception and action, 351–53
response to outrageous pain, 327–30
as strongest force in Cosmos, 350–51
taking responsibility for own arousal, 356–67
Unique Self and, 370–73
whole mate practice, 544–45
Outrageous LoveIntelligence, 332, 347, 350, 351, 541
Outrageous Lover, 328, 347–48, 354, 366–67, 371, 386, 424, 440, 544–45
  community, 433
  identity of, 486, 536
  ordinary lover to, 450
Outrageous Love Story, 413–14
  Reality as, 415–17
outrageous pain, 327–29, 345, 361, 447–49, 478, 542
oxygen crisis, 33–34

P

Paglia, Camille, 556
pain:
  comfort, 284
  outrageous, 327–30, 345, 361, 447–49, 478, 542
  of separation, 542
  staying open through, 536
  trance, 510–13
passion, 9, 113–14, 180, 358
  Outrageous Love, 397
  and polarity, 93–94, 118, 142
  and potency, 362
  whole mate relationship, 258, 380
Patai, Daphne, 559
patriarchal oppression, 559
Peirce, Charles Sanders, 23, 344
The Peloponnesian War (Thucydides), 92
Penrose, Roger, 508
personal enlightenment, 276
personal fulfillment, 67–68, 146, 187–88, 408–9
personal love, 146, 371, 401, 432
personal transformation, 146, 446, 472–73
pheromones, 293, 294
phylogeny, 46–47
physical touch, 84

Pieper, Mauk, 442n225
Pinker, Steven, 454
Plath, Sylvia, 103
pleasure, 143
   fleeting, 9
   of living, 401
   love and, 348
   superficial, 37, 383
Plotinus (Platonic philosopher), 526
poignancy and presence, 93, 113–14, 118, 133, 141, 188
   of evolutionary relationship, 228
   lead to potency and passion, 179
   merge with potency and purpose, 181
   in soul mate relationships, 161–62, 383, 401
polarity, 113–14, 117, 484
   passion and, 93–94, 118, 142
   sensual, 399
   sexual, 399
   unique, 176–77, 554
Pollan, Michael, 486n270
Popp, Fritz-Albert, 234
potency:
   of choice, 248
   emergence from realization of Unique Self, 258
   of Evolutionary Intimacy, 433
   of joining, 481
   Outrageous Love, 397
   passion and, 362
   of role mate relationships, 162
   shared love, 363
   of symphony, 426
   Unique Self, 362
   vocational arousal,, 81, 399–400
   in whole mate relationship, 258, 380, 385
power, 113–14, 455
   of not knowing, 526–30
   Outrageous Love, 397
   passion and, 362
   shared love, 363
   Unique Self, 362
   whole mate relationship, 258, 385
   word on, 483–84
presence. *See* poignancy and presence
Prigogine, Ilya, 32n19, 350n187

primordial cosmology, 27
primordial Ground of Being, 160
procreation, 279–80, 568
procreative sex, 399
profoundly different, meaning of, 142
progressive intensification of intimacy, 507
prokaryotes, 33
proportionality, appropriate, 532
The Proposal (movie), 116
protector-provider role, 109–10
protozoa, 34–36
Proust, Marcel, 513n288
pseudo-Eros, 345–46, 401–3
pseudo-orientation in time, 514
purpose:
   of Cosmos, 318
   and direction, 288
   identity and, 136
   life, 101, 143
   of role mate relationships, 162
   shared, 98, 142, 169, 172, 181, 193, 199–200, 202, 228, 231, 370, 400
   value of, 228
   whole mate relationship, 380
purpose-guided Universe, 288

Q

quality time, 84
quantum field, 273

R

radical joy of being needed, 256–58
Radical Kabbalah (Gafni), 468
radically similar, meaning of, 142
Reality is Relationship, 15–17, 27, 31, 40, 159, 196, 216, 247, 252, 370, 379, 394, 445
   core structure, 329
   deeper forms of relationship, 441
   and evolutionary science, 251, 416
Reality/reality, 24–26, 30, 145, 159–60, 196, 232, 290, 291, 429
   adjustment to, 129–31
   affirmation of goodness of, 284
   from Big Bang, 145, 159
   ceaseless creativity of, 32, 274
   core structure of, 329

of evolution, 311–18
in interior sciences, 160, 235
as Outrageous Love Story, 415–17
practice, 356–58
telos of, 24, 460, 461
and Unique Self Realization, 223
realization of Buddha Nature, 259
real love, 325, 345
recreation, 280
recreational sex, 399
The Red Baron (movie), 337
reflection, 333
Reinventing the Sacred: A New View of Science, Reason, and Religion (Kauffman), 289n157
relationship, 1, 10, 22. *See specific relationship*
  crisis, 173–74
  dynamic of passionate love, 128
  evolution of, 485
  evolution of dependency in, 404–6
  revolution, 1–2
residual strong force, 31
responsibility for own arousal, 356–67
  awaken as Outrageous Love, 366–67
  from *Do you love me?* to *You love me*, 364–66
  from *I love you* to *You love me*, 362–64
  from power to passion, 358–62
  Reality Practice, 356–58
resting in Ground of Being, 259
A Return to Eros (Gafni and Kincaid), 489
revelations of uniqueness, 258–61
Richer Sex: How the New Majority of Female Breadwinners Is Transforming Sex, Love, and The Family (Mundy), 106
Richthofen, Baron Manfred von, 337–39
Ridley, Mathew, 380n202, 454
ritual of rejection, 536–39
Rocky (movie), 252–53
Roiphe, Katie, 556
role mate relationship(s), 12, 17, 45, **63**, **156–57**, **207–8**, 330, 441, 485, 565–66, **573–75**. *See also* soul mate relationship(s); whole mate relationship(s)

The Clan of the Cave Bear, 56–57
duty, honor, and obligation, 46–48
end of, 54–56
essence of, 45–46
in evolutionary context, 380–87
evolution responds to crisis, 61–62
falling in love in, 53–54
first shock of existence and emergence of, 441–43
gifts and shadows of, 48–52
Mars and Venus, 45–46
to soul mate relationship, 57–61
value in, 203–4
wounds in, 530–47
Rolston, Holmes, 461
Rosin, Hanna, 104–6, 125–27
Rumi, 371

S

sacred autobiographies, 228, 232, 236, 241
Salk, Jonas, 144, 467
sanity, 213–14, 228, 356, 447–48, 487, 532, 562
Schmachtenberger, Daniel, 479, 566
scorecards, love and, 347
second shock of existence, 477–79
secret of the kiss, love and, 347
Segal, Erich, 71
self-actualizing Cosmos, 289, 293–95, 429, 460
self-actualizing people, 97
self-discovery, 73
self-love, 23, 256, 296, 550
self-organization, 32n19, 284, 294, 429
self-organizing Universe, 342
  Evolutionary Unique Self in, 429–32
self-transcendence needs, 535
self/Self/selves, 1, 3, 211. *See also specific self*
  Separate Self. *See* Separate Self
  True Self. *See* True Self
sensual arousal, 400
sensual polarity, 399
Separate Self, 211–14, 218, 260, **268–71**, **320–24**, **576–80**. *See also* True Self
  direct access to, 309
  language and transmission at level of,

297
  love and, 348–49
  Uniqueness at, 296
separation, 98–99, 217
  effects, 391
  illusion of, 259, 260
  pain of, 542
sex/sexual/sexuality, 93, 178–79, 279, 285, 568, 569
  equality a panacea for, 110–11
  negative, 279, 281
  neutral, 279, 281
  positive, 279–81
  revolution, 1
  selection, 7, 82n37, 435
  sex-sacred view, 280
  Sex Erotic, 278–81
  to supra-sex, 398–400
sexual arousal, 399
sexual desire, 484
  of women, 94, 162
sexual polarity, 399
shadows of role mate relationships, 48–52
shared horizon, 75, 159, 167–69, 171, 200, 204, 384
shared purpose, 98, 142, 169, 172, 181, 193, 199–200, 202, 228, 231, 370, 400
shared values, 194
  discovery in whole mate relationship, 197–99
Sheldrake, Rupert, 458
shock of existence, 441
silence of absence, 179
silence of presence, 179
single-celled life, 33–34
single cell, 25, 332
singularity, 284, 312–14
Slate (online platform), 106n50
social holons, 247–48
soft animal, 3
Song of Solomon. See *Song of Songs*
Song of Songs, 204–5
soul mate expectations, 555
soul-mate marriage, 125
soul mate relationship(s), 12, 17, 65, 125, 147, **156–57**, **207–8**, 244, 261n149, 277–78, 330, 485, 565, **573–75**. See also role mate relationship(s); whole mate relationship(s)
  commitment to communication, 83–86
  context for relating in, 187–90
  end of men, 103–7
  in evolutionary context, 380–87
  falling in love as, 86–88
  four core principles of, 491
  Four Weddings and a Funeral, 73–75
  holding each other's stories, 492–500
  idolatry of children, 100–3
  I Love You limitations, 89–93
  intimacy, 68–71
  intimate communion requiring contact in present, 500–22
  invitations of time practice, 503
  labels obstruct contact, 522–26
  level of consciousness, 65
  limitations of, 89
  Love Story, 71–73
  mantra, 76–78
  middle-class marriage, 119–26
  narcissism, 95–98
  new yearnings, new expectations, 78–82
  passion, 93–94
  passion in egalitarian marriage, 110–18
  personal fulfillment and loneliness, 67–68
  power of not knowing, 526–30
  radical presence practice, 501–2
  relationships, 65–66
  Beyond Romeo and Juliet, 137–40
  search of solutions, 126–33
  soul mates holding each other's stories, 492–500
  three stations of love, 98–100
  value in, 203–4
  Venus and Mars, 78–82
  work without role mate, 107–10
  wounds in, 530–47
  yearnings, 133–37
soul mate to whole mate transformation:
  calling to serve love, 146–48
  dawning of evolutionary consciousness, 141–45

holes into wholeness, 149–52
third side of love, 152–55
to whole, 148–49
Soul Prints (Gafni), 467
spark of Eros, 345
spiral, 15, 86, 437, 565, 568
spontaneous age regression, 512, 514, 517
star, 24
startle, 106
starvation, 14, 213, 454
Star Wars (movie), 483–84
Stein, Zachary, 453, 464, 480, 480n267, 482, 566
Sternberg, Friedrich, 338
Stevenson, Betsey, 113
The Stranger (Camus), 416
strong force, 31
strong nuclear attraction, 26
submission, 98
Sunyata, 274
superexponential Eros, 274
supra-sex, 567
sex to, 398–400
survival, 21–23, 381, 441
desire for, 21, 22, 36, 46
of the fittest, 22–24
sweetness, 99
of evolution, 260
of Evolutionary Intimacy, 547
Sykes, Charles, 560
synergistic emergence, 118, 460
synthesis, 139
Synthesis Dialogues III, 261
systems theory, 148, 191, 294, 329, 487

T
Tagore, Rabindranath, 342n180, 342–43
Tao, 206, 469
Teleros, 202, 462, 482
telerotic human, 567
Telerotic Universe, 462
telos, 21, 199, 202, 288, 567
of Cosmos, 459, 460
of Reality, 24, 460, 461
of role mate relationship, 45
of Universe, 288
Temple, David J., 478–79
Teresa, Mother, 349

therapeutic trance, 522
Theron, Charlize, 220
thesis, 139
third side:
love as, 152–55
of relationships, 172, 178, 191–94, 196
Thomas, Dylan, 278, 291n159
Thucydides, 92
Tikkun, 294, 307, 308
time:
invitations of, 502–3
pseudo-orientation in, 514
Toute Une Vie (And Now My Love) (movie), 243
Toward a Psychology of Being (Maslow), 97
trajectories of evolution, 27–29
trance, 515, 517
deep trance phenomenon, 513–14
eye-gazing, 501
mind, 520–22
pain, 510–13
therapeutic, 522
transference, 501
transformation, 117, 136, 277, 282–83
of identity, 7, 13–14, 218–19, 225, 273–74, 275, 277, 318, 379
relationship as, 36–37
from soul mate to whole mate, 211
of Whole, 146, 149, 152, 200
transgender:
consciousness, 561
movement, 561–62
to Unique Gender, 561–64
triumphalism, fragrance of, 107
true authentic swing, 220–25
true love, 91, 152, 409, 449, 465
True Self, 214–16, 259, **268–71, 320–24, 576–80**. See also Separate Self
awaken to, 273–74
direct access to, 310
love and, 348–49
The Truman Show (movie), 242–43
Tuschik, Kerstin, 566
Tzadik, 300

U
unconditional love 350

unconscious to conscious uniqueness, 295–97
unique fixing, 251, 294
unique frequency of light, 234–35
Unique Gender, 3, 174–77, 218–20, 379.
   See also lines and circles; Unique Self
   Hieros Gamos, 549–52
   hurt in women relationship, 557–61
   literature of androgyny, 552–54
   literature of difference, 552–54
   Mars-and-Venus relationship, 554–57
   strands of wisdom, 548
   from transgender to, 561–64
   wholeness, 118, 219–20
unique gifts, 232, 436, 547, 552
   expressions, 299
   and Unique Obligation, 299–302, 423
   in Unique Self relationships, 235
   in Unique Selves, 235, 242, 286, 299
   of Unique We, 388, 401, 426
unique need, 232–34, 286
   of All-That-Is, 298
   as Evolutionary Hero, 448
   unique gifts and, 302, 362, 449
   of Unique We, 358, 438
Uniqueness/uniqueness, 27–28, 217, 231–32, 290, 367, 371, 372, 391, 433
   at ego level, 296
   at level of separate self, 296
   at level of Unique Self, 295
   and Outrageous Love, 439
   revelations of, 258–61
   from unconscious to conscious, 295–97
unique obligations, 299
   answering call of Reality, 299
   to give Unique Gift, 299–302
   living *Mitzvah*, 302–5
   for sake of whole, 306–9
unique polarity, 118, 174–77, 554
Unique Self, 14, 211, 216–17n128, 216–18, **268–71**, **320–24**, 437, 438, 472, **576–80**
   confession of greatness, 245–46
   cosmic accident, 242–43
   direct access to, 310–11
   holon as basic unit of reality, 247–48
   identity transformations, 218–20
   I love you, I need you concept, 252–54
   letter in Cosmic Scroll, 240–42
   love and, 348–49
   memory of future, 244–45
   new context for relating, 225–29
   obligation, components of, 423
   and Outrageous Love, 370–73
   radical joy of being needed, 256–58
   relationships, 227
   revelations of uniqueness, 258–61
   role in evolutionary process, 318
   sacred autobiographies, 236
   true authentic swing, 220–25
   unique frequency of light, 234–35
   unique need, 232–34
   uniqueness, 231–32
   in Unique Self Symphony, 426–29
   in Universe Story, 413–15
   whole in part, 248–49
   whole mate, 261–67
   whole mate needs, 254–56
   whole needs the part, 249–52
   yearning, 229–31
Unique Self, 216n128
Unique Self Hero, 439–41
Unique Self Realization, 176, 224, 228, 229, 294, 382, 467–68
   becoming from, 401
   experience of, 258
   growing up, 470–71
   Homo amor, 473
   new Story of Value, 226n133, 297, 566
   Reality and, 223
   Story of Value, 226n133, 297, 566
   and unique need, 233
   Unique Self, 472–73
   waking up, 469–70
Unique Self Symphony, 216–17n128, 426–29, 430, 570
Unique We, 159, 235, 258, 263, 319, 388–91, 432, 446, 451
   Conscious Evolution through, 293
   evolutionary impulse and, 397, 398
   Outrageous Acts of Love, 367
   Unique Self and, 401–2, 406, 433, 438
   in Unique Self Symphony, 426–29
   whole mates, 372

whole mates into larger field, 391–93
Universe, 16–17, 26, 298, 329, 413
    direction from nature of Reality, 16
    evolution of love, 419–21
    love and, 361
    observability of, 357n195
    telos of, 288
    Universe Feels, and Universe Feels Love, 417–19
Universe Story, 26, 416, 477, 478, 484
    animating Eros of, 40
    evolutionary impulse, 314
    evolutionary relationships, 225–26
    human beings and, 32
    neo-Darwinian, 416
    Unique Self and, 413–15
UnLove, 86, 153, 327, 420, 424, 426, 539
up-leveling:
    in consciousness and a transformation of identity, 379
    of identity, 273
    intention, 190–91
Ury, Bill, 191–92

V

value, 159
    common-sense sacred axioms of, 203
    Eye of, 259
    Field of, 15n9
    mutuality of, 31
    new Story of, 226n133, 297, 566
    in role mate, soul mate, and whole mate relationships, 203–4
    shared, 194, 197–99
Vance, Bagger, 273, 286
Venus, women as. *See also* beyond-Venus-and-Mars relationship
    characteristics, 2–4, 85–86
    qualities, 7, 10, 174
    role mate relationship, 45–46
    soul mate relationship, 78–82
victim feminism, 556, 558
vocational arousal, 81, 399–400

W

waking up, 469–70
Welwood, John, 468, 468–69n251
Wengrow, David, 47

What question, 227n134
Where question, 227n134
Whitehead, Alfred North, 28, 33, 343
Whitman, Walt, 431
whole-part harmony, 248–49
whole mate consciousness, 141–45, 306
whole mate relationship(s), 12, 36, 96, 159, **207–8**, 273, 318, 485, 565–66, **573–75**. *See also* role mate relationship(s); soul mate relationship(s)
    context for relating, 187–90
    crisis, 173–74
    dying, 181–87
    and emergence of Evolutionary Heroes, 447–50
    emergents, 162–65
    Eros and Ethos, 204–6
    and Evolutionary Unique Self, 277–78, 311
    evolution/movement of, 46–47
    evolution of love, 161–62
    in larger whole, 170–73, 177
    love the world through loving each other, 199–202
    in *The Matrix* movie, 169–70
    mystery of, 159–60
    needs Unique Self, 254–56, 261–67
    new hero of, 435–41
    relationships in evolutionary context, 380–87
    searching for evolutionary partner, 165–67
    second shock of existence and emergence of, 443–45
    in service, 194–97
    shared horizon, 167–68
    shared value discovery in, 197–99
    soul mate *vs.*, 177–81, 285
    third side, 191–94
    Unique Gender and Unique Polarity, 174–77
    Unique We plugs whole mates into larger field, 391–93
    up-leveling of intention, 190–91
    value in, 203–4
    wounds in, 530–47
wholeness, 118, 219, 278
    deepening of, 290

sake of, 306–9
transforming holes into, 149–52
whole needs the part, 249–52
Who question, 227n134
Why question, 227n134
Wilberforce, William, 328
Wilber, Ken, 468, 479, 480n267, 560, 566
Wilcox, Brad, 124
Wilhelm II, Kaiser, 339
Wilson, David Sloan, 22–23
Wolinsky, S., 513n289
women/feminine/feminism, 3. *See also* Venus, women as
   becoming of telerotic, 567
   in classic role mate relationships, 62
   co-creator, 567
   communication consciousness, 83
   depth of intimacy and communication, 6
   desire for love, 81–82
   desire for survival, 36, 46
   differences between men and, 554–57
   and egalitarian relationship, 8–9
   evolution from role mate to soul mate, 82
   evolution of love, 18
   evolution of relationships, 18
   expectations from partners, 6, 82, 89
   explosion of shadow, 557–61
   female mate-choice, 125
   feminine hero articulation, 8
   during ovulation, 54n31
   against patriarchal oppression, 559
   power imbalance, 57
   relationship in western culture, 55
   sense of autonomy and power, 82
   sense of choice, 5–6
   sexual desire of, 94, 162
   in U. S. workforce, 4–5
   victim feminism, 556, 558
words of affirmation, 84
worldcentric circle of intimacy, 30
worldcentric level of consciousness, 543
worldcentric love:
   to cosmocentric love, 340–41
   from ethnocentric love to, 337–40
World Spirituality based on Integral Principles, 468
wounding/wounds, 151, 368
   authentic, 545–47
   childhood, 533
   creating identity through, 533–34
   dealing with, 530
   soul mate relationship, 71, 178–79, 263
   tenderness of, 178
   whole mate relationship, 178, 392–93
woundology, 179

Y

yearning, 78–82, 229–31, 403, 466, 489
   apotheosis, 466
   for beyond-Mars-and-Venus relationship, 167
   deeper/deepest, 133–34, 161, 166, 344–45, 449
   for evolution of love, 325–27
   to move beyond loneliness, 490
   to play larger game, 93, 96, 355
Yeridat Hadorot, 474n261
Yom Kippur services, 308, 546
Young, Cathy, 559

Z

Zeitgeist, stories from, 115–17
Zenji, Dōgen, 487n272
zero-point field, 146, 273
The Zohar, The Book of Illumination, 98, 330, 465, 467, 506, 517n291

www.ingramcontent.com/pod-product-compliance
Lightning Source LLC
Chambersburg PA
CBHW020629230426
43665CB00008B/96